What They Said
in 1993

What They Said

In 1993

The Yearbook Of World Opinion

Compiled and Edited by

ALAN F. PATER

and

JASON R. PATER

MONITOR BOOK COMPANY

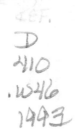

TWENTY-FIFTH ANNUAL EDITION

Printed in the United States of America

Library of Congress catalogue card number: 74-111080

ISBN number: 0-917734-26-2

To

The Newsmakers of the World . . .

May they never be at a loss for words

Table of Contents

PART THREE: GENERAL

Preface to the First Edition (1969)

Words can be powerful or subtle, humorous or maddening. They can be vigorous or feeble, lucid or obscure, inspiring or despairing, wise or foolish, hopeful or pessimistic . . . they can be fearful or confident, timid or articulate, persuasive or perverse, honest or deceitful. As tools at a speaker's command, words can be used to reason, argue, discuss, cajole, plead, debate, declaim, threaten, infuriate, or appease; they can harangue, flourish, recite, preach, discourse, stab to the quick, or gently sermonize.

When casually spoken by a stage or film star, words can go beyond the press-agentry and make-up facade and reveal the inner man or woman. When purposefully uttered in the considered phrasing of a head of state, words can determine the destiny of millions of people, resolve peace or war, or chart · the course of a nation on whose direction the fate of the entire world may depend.

Until now, the *copia verborum* of well-known and renowned public figures—the doctors and diplomats, the governors and generals, the potentates and presidents, the entertainers and educators, the bishops and baseball players, the jurists and journalists, the authors and attorneys, the congressmen and chairmen-of-the-board—whether enunciated in speeches, lectures, interviews, radio and television addresses, news conferences, forums, symposiums, town meetings, committee hearings, random remarks to the press, or delivered on the floors of the United States Senate and House of Representatives or in the parliaments and palaces of the world—have been dutifully reported in the media, then filed away and, for the most part, forgotten.

The editors of *WHAT THEY SAID* believe that consigning such a wealth of thoughts, ideas, doctrines, opinions and philosophies to interment in the morgues and archives of the Fourth Estate is lamentable and unnecessary. Yet the media, in all their forms, are constantly engulfing us in a profusion of endless and increasingly voluminous news reports. One is easily disposed to disregard or forget the stimulating discussion of critical issues embodied in so many of the utterances of those who make the news and, in their respective fields, shape the events throughout the world. The conclusion is therefore a natural and compelling one: the educator, the public official, the business executive, the statesman, the philosopher—everyone who has a stake in the complex, often confusing trends of our times—should have material of this kind readily available.

These, then, are the circumstances under which *WHAT THEY SAID* was conceived. It is the culmination of a year of listening to the people in the public eye; a year of scrutinizing, monitoring, reviewing, judging, deciding—a year during which the editors resurrected from almost certain oblivion those quintessential elements of the year's *spoken* opinion which, in their judgment, demanded preservation in book form.

WHAT THEY SAID is a pioneer in its field. Its *raison d'etre* is the firm conviction that presenting, each year, the highlights of vital and interesting views from the lips of prominent people on virtually every aspect of contemporary civilization fulfills the need to give the *spoken* word the permanence and lasting value of the *written* word. For, if it is true that a picture is worth 10,000 words, it is equally true that a verbal conclusion, an apt quote or a candid comment by a person of fame or influence can have more significance and can provide more understanding than an entire page of summary in a standard work of reference.

The editors of *WHAT THEY SAID* did not, however, design their book for researchers and scholars alone. One of the failings of the conventional reference work is that it is blandly written and referred to primarily for facts and figures, lacking inherent "interest value." *WHAT THEY SAID*, on the other hand, was planned for sheer enjoyment and pleasure, for searching glimpses into the lives and thoughts of the world's celebrities, as well as for serious study, intellectual reflection and the philosophical contemplation of our multifaceted life and mores. Furthermore, those pressed for time, yet anxious to know what the newsmakers have been saying, will welcome the short excerpts which will make for quick, intermittent reading—and rereading. And, of course, the topical classifications, the speakers' index, the subject index, the place and date information—documented and authenticated and easily located—will supply a rich fund of hitherto not readily obtainable reference and statistical material.

Finally, the reader will find that the editors have eschewed trite comments and cliches, tedious and boring. The selected quotations, each standing on its own, are pertinent, significant, stimulating—above all, relevant to today's world, expressed in the speakers' own words. And they will, the editors feel, be even more relevant tomorrow. They will be re-examined and reflected upon in the future by men and women eager to learn from the past. The prophecies, the promises, the "golden dreams," the boastings and rantings, the bluster, the bravado, the pleadings and representations of those whose voices echo in these pages (and in those to come) should provide a rare and unique history lesson. The positions held by these luminaries, in their respective callings, are such that what they say today may profoundly affect the future as well as the present, and so will be of lasting importance and meaning.

ALAN F. PATER
JASON R. PATER

Beverly Hills, California

Editorial Treatment

ORGANIZATION OF MATERIAL

Special attention has been given to the arrangement of the book—from the major divisions down to the individual categories and speakers—the objective being a logical progression of related material, as follows:

(A) The categories are arranged alphabetically within each of three major sections:

Part One:	"National Affairs"
Part Two:	"International"
Part Three:	"General"

In this manner, the reader can quickly locate quotations pertaining to particular fields of interest (see also *Indexing*). It should be noted that some quotations contain a number of thoughts or ideas—sometimes on different subjects—while some are vague as to exact subject matter and thus do not fit clearly into a specific topic classification. In such cases, the judgment of the Editors has determined the most appropriate category.

(B) Within each category the speakers are in alphabetical order by surname, following alphabetization practices used in the speaker's country of origin.

(C) Where there are two or more quotations by one speaker within the same category, they appear chronologically by date spoken or date of source.

SPEAKER IDENTIFICATION

(A) The occupation, profession, rank, position or title of the speaker is given as it was *at the time the statement was made* (except when the speaker's relevant identification is in the past, in which case he is shown as "former"). Thus, due to possible changes in status during the year, a speaker may be shown with different identifications in various parts of the book, or even within the same category.

(B) In the case of a speaker who holds more than one position simultaneously, the judgment of the Editors has determined the most appropriate identification to use with a specific quotation.

(C) The nationality of a speaker is given when it will help in identifying the speaker or when it is relevant to the quotation.

THE QUOTATIONS

The quoted material selected for inclusion in this book is shown as it appeared in the source, except as follows:

(A) *Ellipses* have been inserted wherever the Editors have deleted extraneous words or overly long passages within the quoted material used. In no way has the meaning or intention of the quotations been altered. *Ellipses* are also used where they appeared in the source.

(B) *Punctuation and spelling* have been altered by the Editors where they were obviously incorrect in the source, or to make the quotations more intelligible, or to conform to the general style used throughout this book. Again, meaning and intention of the quotations have not been changed.

(C) *Brackets* ([ ]) indicate material inserted by the Editors or by the source to either correct obvious errors or to explain or clarify what the speaker is saying. In some instances, bracketed material may replace quoted material for sake of clarity.

(D) *Italics* either appeared in the original source or were added by the Editors where emphasis is clearly desirable.

Except for the above instances, the quoted material used has been printed verbatim, as reported by the source (even if the speaker made factual errors or was awkward in his choice of words).

Special care has been exercised to make certain that each quotation stands on its own and is not taken "out of context." The Editors, however, cannot be responsible for errors made by the original source, i.e., incorrect reporting, mis-quotations, or errors in interpretation.

DOCUMENTATION AND SOURCES

Documentation (circumstance, place, date) of each quotation is provided as fully as could be obtained, and the sources are furnished for all quotations. In some instances, no documentation details were available; in those cases, only the source is given. Following are the sequence and style used for this information:

Circumstance of quotation, place, date/Name of source, date:section (if applicable), page number.

Example: *Before the Senate, Washington, Dec. 4/The Washington Post, 12-5:(A)13.*

The above example indicates that the quotation was delivered before the Senate in Washington on December 4. It was taken for *WHAT THEY SAID* from *The Washington Post*, issue of December 5, section A, page 13. (When a newspaper publishes more than one edition on the same date, it should be noted that page numbers may vary from edition to edition.)

(A) When the source is a television or radio broadcast, the name of the network or local station is indicated, along with the date of the broadcast (obviously, page and section information does not apply).

(B) An asterisk (*) before the (/) in the documentation indicates that the quoted material was written rather than spoken. Although the basic policy of *WHAT THEY SAID* is to use only *spoken* statements, there are occasions when written statements are considered by the Editors to be important enough to be included. These occasions are rare and usually involve Presidential messages and statements released to the press and other such documents attributed to persons in high government office.

INDEXING

(A) The *Index to Speakers* is keyed to the page number. (For alphabetization practices, see *Organization of Material*, paragraph B.)

(B) The *Index to Subjects* is keyed to both the page number and the quotation number on the page (thus, 210:3 indicates quotation number 3 on page 210); the quotation number appears at the right corner of each quotation.

(C) To locate quotations on a particular subject, regardless of the speaker, turn to the appropriate category (see *Table of Contents*) or use the detailed *Index to Subjects*.

(D) To locate all quotations by a particular speaker, regardless of subject, use the *Index to Speakers*.

(E) To locate quotations by a particular speaker on a particular subject, turn to the appropriate category and then to that person's quotations within the category.

(F) The reader will find that the basic categorization format of *WHAT THEY SAID* is itself a useful subject index, inasmuch as related quotations are grouped together by their respective categories. All aspects of journalism, for example, are relevant to each other; thus, the section *Journalism* embraces all phases of the news media. Similarly, quotations pertaining to the U.S. President, Congress, etc., are in the section *Government*.

MISCELLANEOUS

(A) Except where otherwise indicated or obviously to the contrary, all universities, organizations and business firms mentioned in this book are in the United States; similarly, references made to "national," "Federal," "this country," "the nation," etc., refer to the United States.

(B) In most cases, organizations whose names end with "of the United States" are Federal government agencies.

SELECTION OF CATEGORIES

The selected categories reflect, in the Editors' opinion, the most widely discussed public-interest subjects, those which readily fall into the over-all sphere of "current events." They represent topics continuously covered by the mass media because of their inherent importance to the changing world scene. Most of the categories are permanent; they appear in each annual edition of *WHAT THEY SAID*. However, because of the transient character of some subjects, there may be categories which appear one year and may not be repeated the next.

SELECTION OF SPEAKERS

The following persons are always considered eligible for inclusion in *WHAT THEY SAID*: top-level officials of all branches of national, state and local governments (both U.S. and foreign), including all United States Senators and Representatives; top-echelon military officers; college and university presidents, chancellors and professors; chairmen and presidents of major corporations; heads of national public-oriented organizations and associations; national and internationally known diplomats; recognized celebrities from the entertainment and literary spheres and the arts generally; sports figures of national stature; commentators on the world scene who are recognized as such and who command the attention of the mass media.

The determination of what and who are "major" and "recognized" must, necessarily, be made by the Editors of *WHAT THEY SAID* based on objective personal judgment.

Also, some persons, while not generally recognized as prominent or newsworthy, may have nevertheless attracted an unusual amount of attention in connection with an important issue or event. These people, too, are considered for inclusion, depending upon the specific circumstance.

SELECTION OF QUOTATIONS

The quotations selected for inclusion in *WHAT THEY SAID* obviously represent a decided minority of the seemingly endless volume of quoted material appearing in the media each year. The process of selecting is scrupulously objective insofar as the partisan views of the Editors are concerned (see *About Fairness*, below). However, it is clear that the Editors must decide which quotations *per se* are suitable for inclusion, and in doing so look for comments that are aptly stated, offer insight into the subject being discussed, or into the speaker, and provide—for today as well as for future reference—a thought which readers will find useful for understanding the issues and the personalities that make up a year on this planet.

ABOUT FAIRNESS

The Editors of *WHAT THEY SAID* understand the necessity of being impartial when compiling a book of this kind. As a result, there has been no bias in the selection of the quotations, the choice of speakers or the manner of editing. Relevance of the statements and the status of the speakers are the exclusive criteria for inclusion, without any regard whatsoever to the personal beliefs and views of the Editors. Furthermore, every effort has been made to include a multiplicity of opinions and ideas from a wide cross-section of speakers on each topic. Nevertheless, should there appear to be, on some controversial issues, a majority of material favoring one point of view over another, it is simply the result of there having been more of those views expressed during the year, reported by the media and objectively considered suitable by the Editors of *WHAT THEY SAID* (see *Selection of Quotations*, above). Also, since persons in politics and government account for a large percentage of the speakers in *WHAT THEY SAID*, there may exist a heavier weight of opinion favoring the philosophy of those in office at the time, whether in the United States Congress, the Administration, or in foreign capitals. This is natural and to be expected and should not be construed as a reflection of agreement or disagreement with that philosophy on the part of the Editors of *WHAT THEY SAID*.

Abbreviations

The following are abbreviations used by the speakers in this volume. Rather than defining them each time they appear in the quotations, this list will facilitate reading and avoid unnecessary repetition.

ABC:	American Broadcasting Companies
ACLU:	American Civil Liberties Union
AIDS:	acquired immune deficiency syndrome
AMA:	American Medical Association
ANC:	African National Congress
APEC:	Asia-Pacific Economic Cooperation forum
ATM:	automatic teller machine
BATF:	Bureau of Alcohol, Tobacco and Firearms
BTU:	British thermal unit
CAA:	Creative Artists Agency
CBS:	Columbia Broadcasting System (CBS, Inc.)
CEO:	chief executive officer
CF:	cistic fibrosis
CIS:	Commonwealth of Independent States
CNN:	Cable News Network
D.A.:	district attorney
D.C.:	District of Columbia
DEA:	Drug Enforcement Administration
DNC:	Democratic National Committee
EC:	European Community
EEOC:	Equal Employment Opportunity Commission
EPA:	Environmental Protection Agency
FAA:	Federal Aviation Administration
FBI:	Federal Bureau of Investigation
FDA:	Food and Drug Administration
F.D.R.:	Franklin Delano Roosevelt
GATT:	General Agreement on Tariffs and Trade
GDP:	gross domestic product
GE:	General Electric Company
GM:	General Motors Corporation
GNP:	gross national product

GSA:	General Services Administration
G-7:	Group of 7 industrial countries
HHS:	Department of Health and Human Services
HIV:	human immunodeficiency virus (AIDS virus)
HUD:	Department of Housing and Urban Development
IBM:	International Business Machines Corporation
IDF:	Israeli Defense Forces
IOC:	International Olympic Committee
IPO:	initial public (stock) offering
IRA:	Irish Republican Army
KKK:	Ku Klux Klan
MBA:	Master of Business Administration
MFN:	most favored nation (trade status)
MIA:	missing in action
NAACP:	National Association for the Advancement of Colored People
NACC:	North Atlantic Cooperation Council
NAFTA:	North American Free Trade Agreement
NASA:	National Aeronatics and Space Administration
NATO:	North Atlantic Treaty Organization
NBA:	National Basketball Association
NBC:	National Broadcasting Company
NCAA:	National Collegiate Athletic Association
NEA:	National Education Association
NEA:	National Endowment for the Arts
NFL:	National Football League
NHL:	National Hockey League
NIH:	National Institutes of Health
NRA:	National Rifle Association
NSC:	National Security Council
OAS:	Organization of American States
OPEC:	Organization of Petroleum Exporting Countries
PAC:	political action committee
PBS:	Public Broadcasting Service
PC:	personal computer
P&G:	Procter & Gamble Company
PGA:	Professional Golfer's Association
PLO:	Palestine Liberation Organization
RAD:	Royal Academy of Dancing
ROTC:	Reserve Officers' Training Corps
RTC:	Resolution Trust Corporation

SDI:	Strategic Defense Initiative
SEC:	Securities and Exchange Commission
SOC:	State of Cambodia
START:	strategic arms reduction talks
TV:	television
UN:	United Nations
UNITA:	National Union for the Total Independence of Angola
U.S.:	United States
U.S.A.:	United States of America
U.S.S.R.:	Union of Soviet Socialist Republics
VAT:	value-added tax
VCR:	video cassette recorder
WIC:	Women, Infants and Children nutrition program

Party affiliation of United States Senators, Representatives, Governors and state legislators:
> D: Democratic
> I: Independent
> R: Republican

The Quote of the Year

Whether we see it or not, our daily lives are touched everywhere by the flows of commerce that cross national borders as inextricably as the weather. Capital clearly has become global. Some $3-trillion of capital race around the world every day. And when a firm wants to build a new factory, it can turn to financial markets, now open 24 hours a day, from London to Tokyo, from New York to Singapore. Products have clearly become more global. Now if you buy an American car, it may be an American car built with some parts from Taiwan, designed by Germans, sold with British-made advertisements, or a combination of others in a different mix. Services have become global. The accounting firm that keeps the books for a small business in Wichita may also be helping new entrepreneurs in Warsaw. And the same fast-food restaurant that your family goes to—or at least that I go to—also may well be serving families from Manila to Moscow and managing its business globally with information, technologies and satellites. And most important of all, information has become global and has become king of the global economy. In earlier history, wealth was measured in land, in gold, in oil, in machines. Today, the principal measure of our wealth is information: its quality, its quantity and the speed with which we acquire it and adapt to it . . . The truth of our age is this, and must be this: Open and competitive commerce will enrich us as a nation. It spurs us to innovate. It forces us to compete. It connects us with our customers. It promotes global growth without which no rich country can hope to grow wealthy. It enables our producers, who are themselves consumers of services and raw materials, to prosper. And so I say to you, in the face of all the pressures to do the reverse, we must compete, not retreat.

—BILL CLINTON
President of the United States
At American University
Washington, D.C., February 26.

PART ONE

National Affairs

Presidential Inaugural Address

Delivered by Bill Clinton, President of the United States, at the Capitol, Washington, D.C., January 20, 1993.

My fellow citizens, today we celebrate the mystery of American renewal. This ceremony is held in the depth of winter, but by the words we speak and the faces we show the world, we force the spring. A spring reborn in the world's oldest democracy that brings forth the vision and courage to reinvent America.

When our Founders boldly declared America's independence to the world and our purposes to the Almighty, they knew that America to endure would have to change. Not change for change sake but change to preserve America's ideals—life, liberty, the pursuit of happiness. Though we march to the music of our time, our mission is timeless. Each generation of Americans must define what it means to be an American.

On behalf of our nation, I salute my predecessor, President Bush, for his half-century of service to America.

And I thank the millions of men and women whose steadfastness and sacrifice triumphed over depression, fascism and communism. Today, a generation raised in the shadows of the cold war assumes new responsibilities in a world warmed by the sunshine of freedom but threatened still by ancient hatreds and new plagues.

Raised in unrivaled prosperity, we inherit an economy that is still the world's strongest but is weakened by business failures, stagnant wages, increasing inequality and deep divisions among our own people.

World Perspective

When George Washington first took the oath I have just sworn to uphold, news traveled slowly across the land by horseback and across the ocean by boat. Now the sights and sounds of this ceremony are broadcast instantaneously to billions around the world. Communications and commerce are global, investment is mobile, technology is almost magical, and ambition for a better life is now universal. We earn our livelihood in America today in peaceful competition with people all across the earth. Profound and powerful forces are shaking and remaking our world. And the urgent question of our time is whether we can make change our friend and not our enemy.

This new world has already enriched the lives of millions of Americans who are able to compete and win in it. But when most people are working harder for less, when others cannot work at all, when the cost of health care devastates families and threatens to bankrupt our enterprises great and small, when the fear of crime robs law-abiding citizens of their freedom, and when millions of poor children cannot even imagine the lives we are calling them to lead, we have not made change our friend. We know we have to face hard truths and take strong steps, but we have not done so. Instead, we have drifted, and that drifting has eroded our resources, fractured our economy and shaken our confidence.

Change

Though our challenges are fearsome, so are our strengths. Americans have ever been a restless, questing, hopeful people, and we must bring to our task today the vision and will of those who came before us. From our Revolution to the Civil War, to the Great Depression, to the civil rights movement, our people have always mustered the determination to construct from these crises the pillars of our history.

Thomas Jefferson believed that to preserve the very foundations of our nation we would need dramatic change from time to time. Well, my fellow Americans, this is our time. Let us embrace it.

Our democracy must be not only the envy of the world but the engine of our own renewal. There is nothing wrong with America that cannot be cured by what is right with America. And so today we pledge an end to the era of deadlock and drift, and a new season of American renewal has begun.

American Renewal

To renew America we must be bold. We must do what no generation has had to do before. We must invest more in our own people—in their jobs and in their future—and at the same time cut our massive debt. And we must do so in a world in which we must compete for every opportunity. It will not be easy. It will require sacrifice. But it can be done and done fairly. Not choosing sacrifice for its own sake, but for our own sake. We must provide for our nation the way a family provides for its children.

Our Founders saw themselves in the light of posterity. We can do no less. Anyone who has ever watched a child's eyes wander into sleep knows what posterity is. Posterity is the world to come. The world for whom we hold our ideals, from whom we have borrowed our planet and to whom we bear sacred responsibility. We must do what America does best: offer more opportunity to all and demand more responsibility from all.

Government's Role

It is time to break the bad habit of expecting something for nothing from our Government or from each other. Let us all take more responsibility not only for ourselves and our families but for our communities and our country.

To renew America we must revitalize our democracy. This beautiful capital, like every capital since the dawn of civilization, is often a place of intrigue and calculation. Powerful people maneuver for position and worry endlessly about who is in and who is out, who is up and who is down, forgetting those people whose toil and sweat sends us here and pays our way.

Americans deserve better, and in this city today there are people who want to do better. And so I say to all of you here, let us resolve to reform our politics so that power and privilege no longer shout down the voice of the people. Let us put aside personal advantage so that we can feel the pain and see the promise of America. Let us resolve to make our Government a place for what Franklin Roosevelt called bold, persistent experimentation, a Government for our tomorrows, not our yesterdays. Let us give this capital back to the people to whom it belongs.

Foreign Challenges

To renew America, we must meet challenges abroad as well as at home. There is no longer a clear division between what is foreign and what is domestic. The world economy, the world environment, the world AIDS crisis, the world arms race—they affect us all.

Today, as an old order passes, the new world is more free but less stable. Communism's collapse has called forth old animosities and new dangers. Clearly, America must continue to lead the world we did so much to make.

While America rebuilds at home, we will not shrink from the challenges nor fail to seize the opportunities of this new world. Together with our friends and allies we will work to shape change lest it engulf us. When our vital interests are challenged or the will and conscience of the international community is defied, we will act, with peaceful diplomacy whenever possible, with force when necessary.

The brave Americans serving our nation today in the Persian Gulf and Somalia, and wherever else they stand, are testament to our resolve.

But our greatest strength is the power of our ideas, which are still new in many lands. Across the world we see them embraced and we rejoice. Our hopes, our hearts, our hands are with those on every continent who are building democracy and freedom. Their cause is America's cause.

America's People

The American people have summoned the change we celebrate today. You have raised your voices in an unmistakable chorus, you have cast your votes in historic numbers, and you have changed the face of Congress, the Presidency and the political process itself. Yes, you, my fellow Americans, have forced the spring.

Now we must do the work the season demands. To that work I now turn with all the authority of my office. I ask the Congress to join with me. But no President, no Congress, no government can undertake this mission alone. My fellow Americans, you, too, must play your part in our renewal.

I challenge a new generation of young Americans to a season of service; to act on your idealism by helping troubled children, keeping company with those in need, reconnecting our torn communities. There is so much to be done. Enough, indeed, for millions of others who are still young in spirit to give of themselves in service, too.

In serving, we recognize a simple but powerful truth: We need each other and we must care for one another. Today, we do more than celebrate America, we rededicate ourselves to the very idea of America: An idea born in revolution and renewed through two centuries of challenge; an idea tempered by the knowledge that but for fate we, the fortunate and the unfortunate, might have been each other; an idea ennobled by the faith that our nation can summon from its myriad diversity the deepest measure of unity; an idea infused with the conviction that America's long, heroic journey must go forever upward.

And so, my fellow Americans, as we stand at the edge of the 21st century, let us begin anew with energy and hope, with faith and discipline. And let us work until our work is done. The Scripture says, "And let us not be weary in well-doing, for in due season we shall reap if we faint not."

From this joyful mountaintop of celebration we hear a call to service in the valley. We have heard the trumpets, we have changed the guard. And now each in our own way, and with God's help, we must answer the call.

Thank you, and God bless you all.

The State of the Union Address

Delivered by Bill Clinton, President of the United States, at the Capitol, Washington, D.C., February 17, 1993.

Mr. President, Mr. Speaker:

When Presidents speak to the Congress and the nation from this podium, they typically comment on the full range of challenges and oportunities that face us. But these are not ordinary times. For all the many tasks that require our attention, one calls on us to focus, unite and act. Together, we must make our economy thrive once again.

It has been too long—at least three decades—since a President has challenged Americans to join him on our great national journey, not merely to consume the bounty of today but to invest for a much greater one tomorrow.

Nations, like individuals, must ultimately decide how they wish to conduct themselves—how they wish to be thought of by those with whom they live, and, later, how they wish to be judged by history. Like every man and woman, they must decide whether they are prepared to rise to the occasions history presents them.

We have always been a people of youthful energy and daring spirit. And at this historic moment, as Communism has fallen, as freedom is spreading around the world, as a global economy is taking shape before our eyes, Americans have called for change—and now it is up to those of us in this room to deliver.

Our nation needs a new direction. Tonight, I present to you our comprehensive plan to set our nation on that new course.

I believe we will find our new direction in the basic values that brought us here: opportunity, individual responsibility, community, work, family and faith. We need to break the old habits of both political parties in Washington. We must say that there can be no more something for nothing, and we are all in this together.

Economic Problems

The conditions which brought us to this point are well known: Two decades of low productivity and stagnant wages; persistent unemployment and underemployment; years of huge Government deficits and declining investment in our future; exploding health care costs, and lack of coverage; legions of poor children; educational and job training opportunities inadequate to the demands of a high wage, high growth economy. For too long we drifted without a strong sense of purpose, responsibility or community, and our political system too often was paralyzed by special interest groups, partisan bickering and the sheer complexity of our problems.

I know we can do better, because ours remains the greatest nation on earth, the world's strongest economy and the world's only military superpower. If we have the vision, the will and the heart to make the changes we must, we will enter the 21st century with possibilities our parents could not even have imagined, having secured the American dream for ourselves and future generations.

I well remember, 12 years ago Ronald Reagan stood at this podium and told the American people that if our debt were stacked in dollar bills, the stack would reach 67 miles into space. Today, that stack would reach 267 miles.

I tell you this not to assign blame for this problem. There is plenty of blame to go around—in both branches of the Government and both parties. The time for blame has come to an end. I came here to accept responsibility; I want you to accept responsibility for the future of this country, and if we do it right, I don't care who gets the credit for it.

Our plan has four fundamental components:

Four Components

First, it reverses our economic decline by jump-starting the economy in the short term and investing in our people, their jobs and their incomes in the long term.

Second, it changes the rhetoric of the past into the actions of the present, by honoring work and families in every part of our lives.

Third, it substantially reduces the Federal deficit, honestly and credibly.

Finally, it earns the trust of the American people by paying for these plans first with cuts in Government waste and inefficiency—cuts, not gimmicks, in Government spending—and by fairness, for a change, in the way the burden is borne.

Tonight, I want to talk about what government can do, because I believe our government must do more for the hard-working people who pay its way. But let me say first: government cannot do this alone. The private sector is the engine of economic growth in America. And every one of us can be an engine of change in our own lives. We've got to give people more opportunity, but we must also demand more responsibility in return.

Job Creation

Our immediate priority is to create jobs, now. Some say we're in a recovery. Well, we all hope so. But we're simply not creating jobs. And there is no recovery worth its salt that does not begin with new jobs.

To create jobs and guarantee a strong recovery, I call on Congress to enact an immediate jobs package of over $30 billion. We will put people to work right now and create half a million jobs: jobs that will rebuild our highways and airports, renovate housing, bring new life to our rural towns and spread hope and opportunity among our nation's youth with almost 700,000 jobs for them this summer alone. And I invite America's business leaders to join us in this effort, so that together we can create a million summer jobs in cities and poor rural areas for our young people.

The Long Term

Second, our plan looks beyond today's business cycle, because our aspirations extend into the next century. The heart of our plan deals with the long term. It has an investment program

designed to increase public and private investment in areas critical to our economic future. And it has a deficit reduction program that will increase savings available for private sector invesment, lower interest rates, decrease the percentage of the Federal budget claimed by interest payments, and decrease the risk of financial market disruptions that could adversely affect the economy.

Spending, Investment and Business

In order to accomplish public investment and deficit reduction, Government spending is being cut and taxes are being increased. Our spending cuts were carefully thought through to try to minimize any economic impact, to capture the peace dividend for investment purposes and to switch the balance in the budget from consumption to investment. The tax increases and spending cuts were both designed to assure that the cost of this historic program to face and deal with our problems is borne by those who could most readily afford that cost.

Our plan is designed to improve the health of American business through lower interest rates, improved infrastructure, better trained workers, and a stronger middle class. Because small businesses generate most of our nation's jobs, our plan includes the boldest targeted incentives for small business in history. We propose a permanent investment tax credit for small business, and new rewards for entrepreneurs who take risks. We will give small business access to the brilliant technologies of our time and to the credit they need to prosper and flourish.

With a new network of community development banks, and one billion dollars to make the dream of enterprise zones real, we will begin to bring new hope and new jobs to storefronts and factories from South Boston to South Texas to South-Central Los Angeles.

Our plan invests in our roads, bridges, transit facilities; in high-speed railways and high-tech information systems; and in the most ambitious environmental clean-up of our time.

Foreign Trade

On the edge of the new century, economic growth depends as never before on opening up new markets overseas. And so we will insist on fair trade rules in international markets.

A part of our national economic strategy must be to expand trade on fair terms, including successful completion of the latest round of world trade talks. A North American Free Trade Agreement with appropriate safeguards for workers and the environment. At the same time, we need an aggressive attempt to create the hi-tech jobs of the future; special attention to troubled industries like aerospace and airlines, and special assistance to displaced workers like those in our defense industry.

I pledge that business, government and labor will work together in a partnership to strengthen America for a change.

Health Care

But all of our efforts to strengthen the economy will fail unless we take bold steps to reform our health care system. America's businesses will never be strong; America's families will never be secure; and America's government will never be solvent until we tackle our health care crisis.

The rising costs and the lack of care are endangering both our economy and our lives. Reducing health care costs will liberate hundreds of billions of dollars for investment and growth and new jobs. Over the long run, reforming health care is essential to reducing our deficit and expanding investment.

Later this spring, I will deliver to Congress a comprehensive plan for health care reform that will finally get costs under control. We will provide security to all our families, so that no one will be denied the coverage they need. We will root out fraud and outrageous charges, and make sure that paperwork no longer chokes you or your doctor. And we will maintain American stan-dards—the highest quality medical care in the world and the choices we demand and deserve. The American people expect us to deal with health care. And we must deal with it now.

Perhaps the most fundamental change our new direction offers is its focus on the future and the investments we seek in our children.

Each day we delay carries a dear cost. Half our two-year-olds don't receive immunizations against deadly diseases. Our plan will provide them for every eligible child. And we'll save ten dollars for every one we'll spend by eliminating preventable childhood diseases.

The Women, Infants and Children nutrition program will be expanded so that every expec-tant mother who needs our help receives it.

Education

Head Start—a program that prepares children for school—is a success story. It saves money, but today it reaches only one-third of all eligible children. Under our plan, we will cover every eligible child. Investing in Head Start and WIC is not only the right thing, it's the smart thing. For every dollar we invest today, we save three tomorrow.

America must ask more of our students, our teachers and our schools. And we must give them the resources they need to meet high standards.

We will bring together business and schools to establish new apprenticeships, and give young people the skills they need today to find produc-tive jobs tomorrow.

Lifelong learning will benefit workers through-out their careers. We must create a new unified worker training system, so that workers receive training regardless of why they lost their jobs.

Our national service program will make college loans available to all Americans, and challenge them to give something back to their country—as teachers, police officers, community service workers. This will be an historic change on a scale with the creation of the Land Grant Colleges and the G.I. Bill. A hundred years from now, historians who owe their education to our plan for national service will salute your vision.

We belive in jobs, we belive in learning, and we believe in rewarding work. We believe in restor-ing the values that make America special.

There is dignity in all work, and there must be dignity for all workers. To those who heal our sick, care for our children, and do our most tiring and difficult jobs, our new direction makes this solemn commitment:

By expanding the Earned Income Tax Credit, we will make history: We will help reward work for millions of working poor Americans. Our new direction aims to realize a principle as powerful

29

as it is simple: If you work full time, you should not be poor.

Welfare and Families

Later this year, we will offer a plan to end welfare as we know it. No one wants to change the welfare system as much as those who are trapped by the welfare system.

We will offer people on welfare the education, training, child care and health care they need to get back on their feet. Then, after two years, they must get back to work—in private business if possible; in public service, if necessary. It's time to end welfare as a way of life.

Our next great goal is to strengthen American families.

We'll ask fathers and mothers to take more responsibility for their children. And we'll crack down on deadbeat parents who won't pay their child support.

We want to protect our families against violent crime which terrorizes our people and tears apart our communities. We must pass a tough crime bill. We need to put 100,000 more police on the street, provide boot camps for first-time non-violent offenders, and put hardened criminals behind bars. We have a duty to keep guns out of the hands of criminals. If you pass the Brady Bill, I'll sign it.

Political and Government Reform

To make government work for middle-class taxpayers and not the special interests, we must reform our political system.

I'm asking Congress to enact real campaign finance reform. Let's reduce the power of special interests and increase the participation of the people. We should end the tax deduction for special interest lobbying and use the money to help clean up the political system. And we should quickly enact legislation to force lobbyists to dislcose their activities.

But to revolutionize government we have to insure that it lives within its means. And that starts at the top—with the White House. In the last few weeks, I have cut the White House staff by twenty-five percent, saving ten million dollars.

I ordered administrative cuts in the budgets of agencies and departments, I cut the federal bureaucracy by 100,000 positions, for combined savings of nine billion dollars. It's time for government to be as frugal as any household in America. That's why I congratulate the Congress for taking similar steps to cut its costs today. Together, we can show the American people that we have heard their call for change.

But we can go further. Tonight, I call for an across-the-board freeze in federal government salaries for one year. Thereafter, federal salaries will rise at a rate lower than the rate of inflation.

We must reinvent government to make it work again. We'll push innovative education reform to improve learning, not just spend more money. We'll use the Superfund to clean up pollution, not just increase lawyers' incomes. We'll use federal banking regulators, not just to protect the security and safety of our financial institutions, but to break the credit crunch. And we'll change the whole focus of our poverty programs from entitlement to empowerment.

The Deficit

For years, there has been a lot of talk about the deficit, but very few credible efforts to deal with it. This plan does. Our plan tackles the budget deficit—seriously and over the long term. We will put in place one of the biggest deficit reductions and the biggest change of federal priorities in our history at the same time.

We are not cutting the deficit because the experts tell us to do so. We are cutting the deficit so that your family can afford a college education for your children. We are cutting the deficit so that your children will someday be able to buy a home of their own. We are cutting the deficit so that your company can invest in retraining its workers and retooling its factories. We are cutting the deficit so that government can make the investments that help us become stronger and smarter and safer.

If we do not act now, we will not recognize this country ten years from now. Ten years from now, the deficit will have grown to 635 billion dollars a year; the national debt will be almost 80 percent of our gross domestic product. Paying the interest on that debt will be the costliest government program of all, and we will continue to be the world's largest debtor, depending on foreign funds for a large part of our nation's investments.

Our budget will, by 1997, cut 140 billion dollars from the deficit—one of the greatest real spending cuts by an American president. We are making more than 150 difficult, painful reductions which will cut federal spending by 246 billion dollars. We are eliminating programs that are no longer needed, such as nuclear power research and development. We are slashing subsidies and cancelling wasteful projects. Many of these programs were justified in their time. But if we're going to start new plans, we must eliminate old ones. Government has been good at building programs; now we must show that we can limit them.

National Defense

As we restructure American military forces to meet the new threats of the post-Cold War world, we can responsibly reduce our defense budget. But let no one be in any doubt: The men and women who serve under the American flag will be the best trained, best equipped, best prepared fighting force in the world, so long as I am President.

Backed by a leaner and more effective national defense and a stronger economy, our nation will be prepared to lead a world challenged by ethnic conflict, the proliferation of weapons of mass destruction, the global democratic revolution, and the health of our environment.

Taxes

Our economic plan is ambitious, but it is necessary for the continued greatness of our country. And it will be paid for fairly—by cutting government, by asking the most of those who benefitted most in the past—by asking more Americans to contribute today so that all Americans can do better tomorrow.

For the wealthiest—those earning more than 180,000 dollars per year, I ask you to raise the top rate for federal income taxes from 31 percent to 36 percent. Our plan recommends a ten percent surtax on incomes over 250,000 dollars a year. And we will close the loopholes that let

some get away without paying any tax at all.

For businesses with taxable incomes over ten million dollars, we will raise the corporate tax rate to 36 percent. And we will cut the deduction for business entertainment.

Our plan attacks tax subsidies that reward companies that ship jobs overseas. And we will ensure that, through effective tax enforcement, foreign corporations who make money in America pay the taxes they owe to America.

Middle-class Americans should know: You're not going alone any more; you're not going first; and you're no longer going to pay more and get less. Ninety-eight point eight percent of America's families will have no increase in their income tax rates. Only the wealthiest one point two percent will see their rates rise.

Medicare and Social Security

Let me be clear: There will be no new cuts in benefits from Medicare for beneficiaries. There will be cuts in payments to providers: doctors, hospitals, and labs, as a way of controlling health care costs. These cuts are only a stop-gap until we reform the whole health care system. Let me repeat that, because it matters to me, as I know it matters to you: This plan will not make new cuts in Medicare benefits for any beneficiary.

The only change we are making in Social Security is to ask those older Americans with higher incomes, who do not rely solely on Social Security to get by, to contribute more. This change will not affect eighty percent of Social Security recipients. If you do not pay taxes on Social Security now, you will not pay taxes on Social Security under this plan.

Our plan includes a tax on energy as the best way to provide us with new revenue to lower the deficit and invest in our people. Moreover, unlike other taxes, this one reduces pollution, increases energy efficiency, and eases our dependence on oil from unstable regions of the world.

Taken together, these measures will cost an American family earning 40 thousand dollars a year less than 17 dollars a month. And because of other programs we will propose, families earning less than 30,000 dollars a year will pay virtually no additional tax at all. Because of our publicly stated determination to reduce the deficit, interest rates have fallen since the election. That means that, for the middle class, the increases in energy costs will be more than offset by lower interest costs for mortgages, consumer loans and credit cards. This is a wise investment for you and for your country.

Change

I ask all Americans to consider the cost of not changing, of not choosing a new direction. Unless we have the courage to start building our future and stop borrowing from it, we are condemning ourselves to years of stagnation, interrupted only by recession; to slow growth in jobs, no growth in incomes, and more debt and disappointment.

Worse yet—unless we change, unless we reduce the deficit, increase investment, and raise productivity so we can generate jobs—we will condemn our children and our children's children to a lesser life and a diminished destiny.

Tonight, the American people know we must change. But they are also likely to ask whether we have the fortitude to make those changes happen.

They know that, as soon as we leave this chamber, the special interests will be out in force, trying to stop the changes we seek. The forces of conventional wisdom will offer a thousand reasons why it can't be done. And our people will be watching and wondering to see if it's going to be business as usual again.

So we must scale the walls of their skepticism, not with our words, but by our deeds. After so many years of gridlock and indecision, after so many hopeful beginnings and so few promising results, Americans will be harsh in their judgments of us if we fail to seize this moment.

This economic plan cannot please everybody. If this package is picked apart, there will be something that will anger each of us. But, if it is taken as a whole, it will help all of us.

Resist the temptation to focus only on a spending cut you don't like or some investment not made. And nobody likes tax increases. But let's face facts: For 20 years incomes have stalled. For years, debt has exploded. We can no longer afford to deny reality. We must play the hand we were dealt.

The test of our program cannot simply be: What's in it for me? The question must be: What's in it for us?

If we work hard—and work together—if we rededicate ourselves to strengthening families, creating jobs, rewarding work, and reinventing government, we can lift America's fortunes once again.

Tonight I ask everyone in this chamber—and every American—to look into their hearts, spark their hopes, and fire their imaginations. There is so much good, so much possibility, so much excitement in our nation. If we act boldly, as leaders should, our legacy will be one of progress and prosperity.

This, then, is America's new direction. Let us summon the courage to seize the day.

Thank you very much. Good night. And may God bless America.

The American Scene

William J. Bennett
Former Secretary of Education
of the United States

1

My [Republican] Party likes to say, "It's the pocketbook issues." And the Democrats say, "It's the economy, stupid." But I believe the most important issues before us as a country are *cultural* issues . . . In America, things are not so good. Crime is way up. Child abuse is way up. Illegitimacy is way up. More than 65 percent of black children in this country are born out of wedlock. Family dissolution is up. Perhaps even more important, there are more and more children in this country who never live in a real family. They don't know what a father is . . . What we see is social breakdown, which is caused in part by moral breakdown. I identified the moral education of the young as the single most important task we have—in all generations, but emphatically now.

Interview/
Christianity Today, 9-13:31,32.

Robert H. Bork
Former Judge,
United States Court of Appeals
for the District of Columbia;
Former nominee for Associate Justice,
Supreme Court of the United States

2

"Political correctness," I think, is something that is widespread in this society, and it's part of a mood of radical egalitarianism which has taken hold. Of course, equality does not occur for all people without coercion. And I'm afraid that's what we're seeing. We're seeing it in affirmative action and quotas in the universities. And we're seeing it in the speech codes, which are judging speech not by what it objectively means, but by how somebody perceives it, over which the speaker has no control. And I think, this kind of leveling in speech and of rejection of the achievement principle for quotas isn't going to work. This kind of thing, I think leads to hostility, a loss

of civility and a rejection of the achievement principle upon which this society is really based.

Broadcast debate,
University of Pennsylvania/
"Firing Line," PBS-TV, 12-13.

James Bredar
United States Public Defender
for the District of Maryland

3

As we face our generation's social problems, we must be mindful of the real dangers for all of us in allowing the balance of power to shift too far to the government's side. In theory, in America any person of any race can live his life within the law, minding his own business, and the government will leave him or her alone. Our Constitution essentially guarantees this. Now we are seeing an erosion of this theory—it's not as true as it used to be. Do we really want to give up our way of life in exchange for, at best, incremental progress in attacking our current social problems?

At his investiture, Feb. 5/
The Washington Post, 3-5:(A)20.

Bill Clinton
President-elect
of the United States

4

A lot of the problems of America are problems of the spirit as well as physical. I believe they can only be solved when people are dealing with each other one on one, and when we reconnect and we reach across the lines that divide us.

At Georgetown University, Jan. 18/
USA Today, 1-19:(A)3.

5

An astonishing number of average American citizens say, "Don't be afraid to ask us to sacrifice. Just make it fair. If you give me marching orders, give them to everybody else, too." One guy said exactly that. He said, "Give

(BILL CLINTON)

me marching orders; just make sure you give them to everybody else, so we're all walking."

Interview, Little Rock, Ark./
Newsweek, 1-25:37.

Bill Clinton
President of the United States

1

Thomas Jefferson believed that to preserve the very foundations of our nation, we would need dramatic change from time to time. Well, my fellow Americans, this is our time. Let us embrace it. Our democracy must be not only the envy of the world but the engine of our own renewal. There is nothing wrong with America that cannot be cured by what is right with America.

Inaugural address,
Washington, D.C., Jan. 20/
The New York Times, 1-21:(A)10.

2

[On his proposed national-service plan]: There are some among us who do not believe that young Americans will answer a call to action, who believe that our people now measure their success merely in the accumulation of material things. They believe this call to service will go unanswered. But I believe they are dead wrong . . . The American dream will be kept alive if you will answer the call to service.

At Rutgers University, March 1/
USA Today, 3-2:(A)4.

3

I think [Thomas Jefferson] would be delighted by the range of personal choices and freedom of speech that the American people enjoy today, even to say things that he would find offensive, for he understood the clear meaning of the First Amendment. But I think he would be appalled at the lack of self-respect and self-control and respect for others which manifests itself in the kind of mindless violence to which this city and others have been subject for the last several

years, and appalled at the millions of young people who will never know the full measure of their freedom because they have been raised without order, without love, without family, without even the basic safety which people need to be able almost to take for granted in order to be citizens of a real democracy. In short, I think Thomas Jefferson would tell us that this is one of those times when we need to change.

At ceremony marking 250th anniversary
of Thomas Jefferson's birth,
Washington, D.C., April 13/
The Washington Post, 4-14:(A)20.

4

[On this year's Summer of Service program, a precurser to his projected national-service program, in which the government arranged for young people to take part in social and public-works programs around the country]: Don't you find that you see the world in a different way once you do this? I mean, you know what the problems are, but you also have a sense that you can solve them and make a difference . . . I don't believe [that in 10 years] it will not be 10,000 kids a year or 50,000 or 100,000 [taking part in the program]. I think that the program will become so popular and will so capture the imagination of the country that, in effect, anybody who wants to be a part of it to help defray their college costs [the program will pay participants toward their college tuition] or just because they want to serve will be able to do it.

To participants in
Summer of Service program,
University of Maryland, College Park,
Aug. 31/Los Angeles Times, 9-1:(A)25.

5

Unless we can be secure in our work and families, unless we can be secure on our streets, unless we can be secure in our health care, I'm not sure the American people will ever be able to recover the personal optimism and courage to open up to the rest of the world.

Before Democratic National Committee,
Washington, D.C., Oct. 8/
The Washington Post, 10-9:(A)6.

Mario M. Cuomo
Governor of New York (D)

1

I know we [Americans] always believe in rugged individualism. And that's a good thing: making it on your own merits. But do we also believe in family, that rugged individualists should come together once in a while as brothers and sisters and share benefits and burdens for the good of everybody?

> *At National Baptist Convention,*
> *New York, N.Y., Sept. 10/*
> *The New York Times,*
> *9-11:11.*

Ruth Bader Ginsburg
Judge,
United States Court of Appeals
for the District of Columbia;
Associate Justice-designate,
Supreme Court of the United States

2

This country is great because of its accommodation of diversity. I mean, the first thing that I noticed when I came back to the United States from a prolonged stay in Sweden, and after I was so accustomed to looking at people whose complexion was the same, and I took my first ride on a New York subway and I thought, "What a wonderful country we live in—people who are so different in so many ways and yet we, for the most part, get along with each other." The richness of the diversity of this country is a treasure and it's a constant challenge, too, to remain tolerant.

> *At Senate Judiciary Committee hearing*
> *on her nomination, Washington, D.C., July 22/*
> *The Washington Post, 7-23:(A)18.*

Arthur Helton
Director, Refugee Project,
Lawyers Committee
for Human Rights

3

[On the wave of illegal immigration to the U.S. and what the government might do about it]: We might see accelerated exclusion hearings as well as automatic and prolonged detention, the theory

being if you mistreat these individuals you will send a signal to others not to come. [But] we should be sure we do not extinguish the opportunity for genuine refugees to receive asylum. We should work toward a system that balances immigration control and the human rights of refugees.

> *The New York Times, 6-8:(B)15.*

Rosemary Jencks
Senior analyst,
Center for Immigration Studies

4

[On the increasing anti-immigration sentiment in the U.S.]: When U.S. citizens watch immigrants crowd public education, health care and welfare rolls, and compete for public services and jobs, it really gets them talking about their government's priorities.

> *The Christian Science Monitor, 7-27:2.*

John Paul II
Pope

5

[On violence in the U.S.]: The violence is tragic for a country like the United States, the most advanced country in the world. What is [the] reason for this demoralization, this violence? It is a civilization, no? And for this civilization someone is responsible. Who is responsible for this degradation of the young people? . . . The orientation, the climate of the communications media are against the civilization, against progress. We cannot be astonished of having such a result.

> *To reporters, enroute to Kingston, Jamaica,*
> *Aug. 9/Los Angeles Times, 8-10:(A)7.*

Edward M. Kennedy
United States Senator,
D-Massachusetts

6

[Supporting President Clinton's national-service program proposal]: National and community service is one of the best investments that we can make for the generations to come. It is what the effort to "reinvent America" is all about, because

(EDWARD M. KENNEDY)

it is the most significant step we have taken so far to return to our roots—to revitalize the sense of community that has always been the hallmark of America at its best.

Aug. 3/Los Angeles Times, 8-4:(A)13.

John le Carre
British author

1

[On Washington, D.C.]: This city? Extraordinary! To me, as a Brit, the sense of power is amazing. The sense that decisions have consequences, which they don't seem to in Britain, is very strong and beguiling. I can always understand why the Brits come and colonize American newspapers, American media, or try to, because this is the real thing. It's played with live ammunition here.

Interview, Washington, D.C./
The New York Times, 7-9:(B)9.

Jurgen Moltmann
Professor of theology,
University of Tubingen (Germany)

2

America is a success-oriented society only when viewed from the outside. Behind this exterior is anxiety and fear—the fear that one won't make it; the fear that we are nothing and have to make something out of ourselves.

Interview/Christianity Today, 1-11:33.

Daniel Patrick Moynihan
United States Senator,
D-New York

3

The decline in our social institutions is really without equivalent. Most importantly, and absolutely essential, is the decline of the family—the small platoons without which a society cannot function. In 1943, the illegitimacy rate in New York City was 3 percent. Last year, it was 45 percent.

Before Association for a Better New York/
USA Today, 9-10:(A)13.

Ralph Nader
Lawyer; Consumer advocate

4

When the powers that be . . . in any society control too much power and too much wealth, and indeed control wealth that is owned by ourselves, like worker pension funds, then what happens is that the deterioration expands and before you know it, people are fighting people over ethnic differences, racial differences, because they are trying to grab a piece of the shrinking pie . . . We tend to forget what caused all this. I mean, this country should be prosperous, there should be no poverty, no homeless families. There should be a decent amount of income security. Can anyone say there shouldn't be? Why are we having this problem? Too much power and too much wealth in too few hands. One percent of the people in this country control over 35 percent of the wealth . . . The top 10 percent control as much as the remaining 90 percent. So it's important for us not to get so embroiled in the cussedness of daily life . . . and begin coolly analyzing why these things occur.

At University of Redlands (Calif.),
Sept. 21/Los Angeles Times, 9-24:(B)2.

Ronald Reagan
Former President of the United States

5

In America, every day is a new beginning, and every sunset is merely the latest milestone for a voyage that never ends. For this is the land that has never become, but is always in the act of becoming. Emerson was right: America is the land of tomorrow. Our work is not yet done. A great cause remains, because the task of peacemaker is never complete. Although we've certainly fought our share of battles, my fondest hope is that our nation's days will continue to be great, not on the battlefield, but in the science labs, and the operating rooms, performing-arts halls, and wherever empires of the mind can be assembled, and that we will collectively make our contribution to the age-old battle for individual freedom and with the belief that America's best days are yet to come.

Accepting the Presidential Medal of Freedom,
Washington, D.C., Jan. 13/
The Washington Post, 1-15:(A)22.

Richard Slotkin
Director of American studies,
Wesleyan University

1

[On the renewed interest in the U.S. in America's Old West]: As a nation, we are reassessing some very basic questions about race, gender, class, family, what the role of government should be in our lives, where we think we're going as a society. At such a moment of crisis, any culture goes back to its traditions, its myths. It takes them all out of storage and dusts them off and looks them over again. And, hopefully, it rewrites them.

Los Angeles Times,
5-5:(A)1.

Civil Rights • Women's Rights

Elijah Anderson
Professor of sociology,
University of Pennsylvania

1

Some black people have begun to see the condition of poor blacks as part of a plan by white people to commit black genocide. That plan involves AIDS, gentrification, high unemployment, crack [cocaine], even the Korean grocer down the street. When people sense that nothing but contempt is coming from white society, they have no problem giving contempt back.

Interview/
Mother Jones, March-April:6.

Ronald H. Brown
Secretary of Commerce
of the United States

2

[On the riots by blacks and other minorities in Los Angeles last year]: This is not about the 29th of April, 1992. This is about August, 1965 [when riots also erupted in the Watts area of Los Angeles]. This just didn't "happen." There was no response or an inadequate response 30 years ago. Until we start taking a long-term, non-crisis-oriented point of view, we are not going to be effective with these problems. We've got to have a Federal government that doesn't just parachute in and run out. That is the usual response. You either get chased out or run out because you give up. The attitude of this [Clinton] Administration is we can make a difference, we can help and we intend to.

Interview, Washington, D.C./
Los Angeles Times, 4-15:(A)19.

Jimmy Carter
Former President
of the United States

3

Basic rights of women have long been ignored or inadequately addressed in this country and throughout the world . . . In the U.S., some progress has been made, but the issue still has not been raised to a high enough level. This specifically includes equality of employment opportunities, pay for work done, and some residual feeling that women are not competent or qualified to provide professional services.

USA Today, 6-14:(A)13.

Benjamin F. Chavis, Jr.
Executive director,
National Association for the
Advancement of Colored People

4

Legitimate, non-violent protest is absolutely necessary. If we, in the civil-rights movement, do not create the constructive, non-violent forums and strategies for people to legitimately vent their justified anger, then people will engage in self-destructive, violent alternatives . . . Legitimate protest can help instill a modicum of calm. Protest is therapeutic. Marching and demonstrating, people are venting their anger.

Interview, Los Angeles, Calif./
Los Angeles Times, 4-18:(M)3.

5

No one is born a racist, so I disagree with these people who think prejudice is something biological. It's not. It's sociological. Racial stereotypes, racial prejudice are engendered or conditioned as part of the social conditioning. All the programs that just focus on young people are not going to change society because young people get their values from adults.

Interview/USA Today, 4-22:(A)11.

6

I think [black] history is important. Very often in the African-American community we become ahistorical. When we become ahistorical, we become apolitical. Much of the disillusionment or the hopelessness among young African-Americans today is derived from the ahistorical

(BENJAMIN F. CHAVIS, JR.)

consciousness. I'm not blaming young people. If young African-Americans don't know the value of the history of our struggle for justice in this country, it's because we as adults have not transmitted that history effectively.

Interview/Newsweek, 6-14:69.

1

I think there are many more voices [and diversity in the black community] in 1993 than we had in 1963, and the question is, is there a uniting theme among these voices. I would suggest that that uniting theme focuses around economic justice. In other words, racial justice and racial equality are seen now in the context of achieving . . . economic power.

The Washington Post, 8-28:(A)1.

Henry G. Cisneros
Secretary of Housing
and Urban Development
of the United States

2

Race is at the core of the problems which confront America's urban areas . . . I know this is a difficult subject and that people tire of hearing of the role of race. [But] it is so clear, the effect that it has in America's urban settings, that I think we have to deal with it.

Interview/
The New York Times, 7-8:(A)8.

Roberta Clarke
Professor of marketing,
Boston (Mass.) University

3

[The recent increase in advertising aimed at racial harmony represents] a growing recognition of minorities—and of the increasing power they have in this country. Sure, you can be cynical and say that marketers are only doing this to make money. But if we can get companies to even act as if they respect these ideals, that may be the most we can expect from them. One thing is for sure: Marketers can't sweep minorities under the rug anymore.

Los Angeles Times, 1-19:(D)6.

Bill Clinton
President-elect
of the United States

4

One of the great regrets of my life is that even though I was a Southerner who passionately believed in everything [the slain civil-rights leader] Martin Luther King did, I never got to meet him. Even though he came to my state [Arkansas] many times and his life ended in Memphis on the border of my state, I never got to meet him. [King was] the most eloquent voice for freedom and justice in my lifetime.

At Howard University,
Jan. 18/Los Angeles Times, 1-19:(A)7.

Bill Clinton
President of the United States

5

[Announcing a lifting of the ban on abortion counseling at Federally funded family-planning clinics]: This dangerous restriction censors the medical information and advice that health-care professionals can give their patients. As a result of today's action [lifting the ban], every woman will be able to receive medical advice and referrals that will not be censored or distorted by ideological arguments that should not be a part of medicine.

Washington, D.C., Jan. 22/
The New York Times, 1-23:7.

6

[On his decision not to take part in a gay-rights march in Washington]: I meant no snub [to homosexuals]. But Presidents don't participate in marches. [The decision] has nothing to do with my commitment on the fundamental issue of being anti-discrimination. I have, I believe it's clear, taken a stronger position against discrimination than any of my predecessors. And it is a position that I believe in deeply, one that I took publicly before there was any organized political support for me in the gay community.

News conference,
Washington, D.C.,
April 16/Los Angeles Times,
4-17:(A)2.

39

(BILL CLINTON)

1

[On his nomination of Lani Guinier to head the Justice Department's Civil Rights Division, which has caused controversy because of her unorthodox civil-rights writings]: I want to re-affirm two positive things about her. One is everyone can see she is a first-rate civil-rights lawyer, and no real civil-rights lawyer has ever held that position before, someone who's made a career of it. Secondly, I think any reasonable reading of her writings would lead someone to conclude that a lot of the attacks [on her] cannot be supported by a fair reading of the writings. And that's not to say that I agree with everything in the writings; I don't. But I think that a lot of what has been said [about her] is not accurate.

At photo opportunity, Washington, D.C.,
June 2/The New York Times, 6-5:8.

2

[Announcing his withdrawal of the nomination of Lani Guinier to head the Civil Rights Division of the Justice Department because of contro-versy over her views]: At the time of the nomina-tion, I had not read her writings. In retrospect, I wish I had. Today, as a matter of fairness to her, I read some of them again in good detail. They clearly lend themselves to interpretations that do not represent the views that I expressed on civil rights during my [election] campaign, and views that I hold very dearly, even though there is much in them with which I agree . . . The problem is that this battle [on her nomination] will be waged based on her academic writings. And I cannot fight a battle that I know is divisive, that is an uphill battle, that is distracting to the country, if I do not believe in the ground of the battle . . . It is not the fear of defeat [in the Senate confirmation hearings] that has prompted this decision. It is the certainty that the battle would be carried on a ground I could not defend. I would gladly fight [for] this nomination to the last moment if nobody wanted to vote for her—nobody—if it were on the grounds that I could defend. This has nothing to do with the political center. This has to do with *my* center.

News conference, Washington, D.C.,
June 3/The New York Times, 6-5:8;
Los Angeles Times, 6-4:(A)1, 33.

3

Our Founders pledged their lives, their for-tunes and their sacred honor to a common cause. We fought a Civil War to preserve that unity. Every battle to expand civil rights has been to deepen and strengthen that unity, our ability to "go up together." After 200 years, we find ourselves a nation of 150 different racial and ethnic groups, confronting the challenges of a new era, still committed to the American promise of opportunity and the idea that we must seek the future together.

At University of North Carolina,
Chapel Hill, Oct. 12/
The Washington Post,
10-13:(A)20.

Hillary Rodham Clinton
Wife of President
of the United States
Bill Clinton

4

I feel excited, I guess, that there are so many options for women, and they're leading lives now that are filled with possibility. All over the world, not just in our country . . . I had a long talk with a number of Korean women, and it was very much along the same lines. To me, it's thrilling to see this happening worldwide . . . So many women are facing the same kind of decisions about how to balance family and work, and how to make use of education, to playing a role that is meaningful.

Interview, July 11/
The Washington Post, 7-12:(B)4.

Sharon Collins
Sociologist,
University of Illinois,
Chicago

5

Think of how much a black person has to sell of himself to try to get race not to matter . . . You have to ignore the insults. You have to ignore the natural loyalties. You have to ignore your past. In a sense, you have to just about deny yourself.

Newsweek, 11-15:62.

Charles Colson
Columnist;
Former Special Counsel
to the President
of the United States
(Richard M. Nixon)

1

For a long time I've written that the [anti-] abortion fight will not be won in the Supreme Court or Congress. It will be won in the hearts and minds of people. We're going to have to find a way to convince people about the dignity and sacredness of human life.

Christianity Today, 1-11:38.

Harlon Dalton
Professor,
Yale University Law School

2

[Criticizing President Clinton's withdrawal of his nomination of Lani Guinier for head of the Justice Department's Civil Rights Division because of her controversial writings]: What she was trying to do was to expand the universe of possible remedies [in the civil-rights area], and it's galling we ended up with this non-debate about it. Her Senate [confirmation] hearings would have been a conversation about what democracy looks like in a multi-cultural society in the 1990s, and I think that's a conversation we need to have. Instead, the Senate and the President ran away from it.

The New York Times, 6-5:9.

Darwin Davis
Senior vice president,
Equitable Life Assurance Society

3

[Saying even financially successful blacks today feel they are not treated as full human beings by white society]: There's an air of frustration [among young black managers in business] that's just as high now as it was 30 years ago . . . They have an even worse problem [than I did] because they've got MBAs from Harvard. They did all the things that you're supposed to do . . . and *things* are supposed to happen.

Newsweek, 11-15:57.

John deCecco
Editor,
"Journal of Homosexuality"

4

What I think the gay community has to do is to break down the notion that men and women are opposite and emphasize the continuity between the sexes. What will keep the [positive] change [in public attitude toward homosexuals] alive is the continued erosion of roles. Once we redefine what it means to be one gender or the other, there will be more latitude for both men and women to express behavior and feelings that are not stereotypically associated with their gender.

The Washington Post, 4-26:(A)11.

Morris Dees
President,
Southern Poverty Law Center

5

[On the increase in hate crimes by blacks against whites]: I think, over all, blacks are much more tolerant of whites than whites are of blacks. But not long ago, it was extremely rare to find cases that even hinted of blacks attacking whites in hate-crime-type situations. Now that's changed. I'm not a sociologist. But I think there's a rising sense of frustration among blacks that the promises of the civil-rights movement are not coming to pass, and that filters down to the street.

The New York Times, 12-13:(A)7.

Elizabeth Hanford Dole
President, American Red Cross;
Former Secretary of Labor
of the United States

6

There's been a tidal wave of qualified women coming into the workforce over the span of my career. For those qualified women in middle-management positions, it's a matter of giving them the rotational assignments, making sure they're in the developmental programs, the training programs and the reward structures that are the indicia of upward mobility . . . A lot of women have been in the pipeline, learning and gaining experience. I think we're going to see a lot of women going into top positions in the coming years, and we'll keep trying to smash the glass ceiling so they can move right up.

Interview, Washington, D.C./
The Christian Science Monitor, 8-17:14.

Marian Wright Edelman
President,
Children's Defense Fund

1

Not since slavery have we suffered the [black] family breakdown we see today. Never before has America or the black community permitted children to rely on guns and gangs rather than parents, neighbors and community institutions for their protection and love.

The Christian Science Monitor, 3-29:3.

Louis Farrakhan
Spiritual leader,
Nation of Islam
in the United States

2

The basis for getting along is [for blacks] to stop begging white folks to do for you what you can do for yourself. Racism is an attitude built over a long period of teaching by whites that we [blacks] are inferior—and by actions on our part that absolutely are inferior. We can help make white Americans and the institutions much more humane by busting up the mind of white supremacy by first attacking the mind of black inferiority.

Interview/Newsweek, 6-28:31.

Abraham Foxman
National director,
Anti-Defamation League
of B'nai B'rith

3

We did a recent survey, and we found the younger generation, under 30, were more inclined to racist views than baby boomers. One reason I think the baby boomers are less bigoted, less racist, is that when they grew up, they . . . experienced the visuals of the hoses directed at

men, women, children, attack dogs set upon blacks . . . That is missing from our current generation. We've legislated much closer to the promise of America, but we're a long way off from changing men's hearts.

USA Today, 8-27:(A)9.

Barney Frank
United States Representative,
D-Massachusetts

4

[On today's mass homosexual-rights march in Washington]: The major impact of demonstrations like these is on the participants. This march will have a significant impact in getting people to organize themselves, to be activated to act politically. A lot of members of Congress are going to hear from them instead of being guided by abstract opinion polls.

Washington, D.C., April 25/
The New York Times, 4-26:(A)1.

Ruth Bader Ginsburg
Judge,
United States Court of Appeals
for the District of Columbia;
Associate Justice-designate,
Supreme Court
of the United States

5

[Recalling when she was arguing a women's rights case before the U.S. Supreme Court]: Race discrimination was immediately perceived as evil, odious and intolerable. But the response I got when I talked about sex-based discrimination was, "What are you talking about? Women are treated ever so much better than men." I was talking to an audience that thought . . . I was somehow critical about the way they treated their wives, about the way they treated their daughters. Their notion was [that] women were spared the messy, dirty, real world, and they were kept in this clean, bright home. And so [I] was trying to educate the judges that [this] . . . was limiting the opportunities, the aspirations of our daughters.

At Senate Judiciary Committee hearing
on her nomination,
July/Vogue, October:473.

(RUTH BADER GINSBURG)

1

[Supporting a woman's right to have an abortion, but saying the father should not have equal rights in deciding whether or not an abortion should take place]: It's her body, her life. Men are not similarly situated. They don't bear the children. It is essential to a woman's equality with man that she be the decision-maker, that her choice be controlling. If you impose restraints and disadvantage her, you are disadvantaging her because of her sex.

At Senate Judiciary Committee hearing
on her nomination, Washington, D.C.,
July 21/ Los Angeles times, 7-22:(A)1.

2

I think rank discrimination against anyone is against the tradition of the United States and is to be deplored. Rank discrimination is not part of our nation's culture. Tolerance is . . . This country is great because of accommodation of diversity.

At Senate Judiciary Committee hearing
on her nomination, Washington, D.C.,
July 22/The New York Times, 7-23:(A)8.

3

I remain an advocate of the Equal Rights Amendment [for women], I will tell you, for this reason: because I have a daughter and a granddaughter, and I would like the legislature of this country and of all the states to stand up and say, "We know what that history was in the 19th century, and we want to make a clarion call that women and men are equal before the law, just as every modern human-rights document in the world does since 1970." I'd like to see that statement made just that way in the United States Constitution.

At Senate Judiciary Committee hearing
on her nomination, Washington, D.C./
The Christian Science Monitor, 8-17:19.

W. Wilson Goode
Former Mayor
of Philadelphia (Pa.)

4

In my eight years as Mayor, the people I saw most at risk were African-American men. Seven out of 10 African-American men between the ages of 17 and 44 are at risk—at risk of homelessness, AIDS, of dying violently in the street, of going to prison, of unemployment, of drugs, of illiteracy, of abuse in foster homes and in their own homes. One out of 20 black boys born in America today will be killed before he reaches his 21st birthday. If we're going to change this statistic over the next 10 years, we have to intervene now in the lives of young African-American boys in the inner city. In 1940, 9 out of 10 black families had a black man as head of the household. In 1970, it was 6 out of 10. In 1992, it's 3.5 out of 10. This should not surprise us if 7 out of 10 African-American males are at risk. So I want to work to bring back a complete black family. If we support family values, surely we're talking about working to bring these families back together so they can have a wholesome life.

Interview/
Christianity Today, 4-5:24.

5

It is difficult from a Christian perspective to support the abortion-rights people. I believe that conception is a gift from God. As a Christian, I don't believe anyone has the right to interfere with this process. On a public-policy level, however, does the government have the right to step in and tell individuals what they must do with their own bodies? I would state categorically that, as a Christian, I could not take a life, regardless of what point in the pregnancy the abortion takes place. I feel free to tell anyone my Christian views. But I have a difficulty saying that non-believers must agree with my perspective.

Interview/
Christianity Today, 4-5:25.

Linda S. Greene
Professor,
University of Wisconsin
Law School

6

I think that racism has changed its character. I think that racism still exists but its character is different. I think we have two types of racism

(LINDA S. GREENE)

going on, or at least two. In one type, we see the explicit racist remark or the explicit racial decision, sometimes because of an inadvertent slip. Other times, we have a veiled racism, not necessarily the product of a person's specific intent, but an unconscious comfort which we have with the status quo. What we need to do is not to focus on calling each other racist or sexist, but instead to try to understand how historical racism has affected our lives and consciousness, and not make charges but try to understand how we all—white, black, men and women—have been affected by our past.

Broadcast debate,
University of Pennsylvania/
"Firing Line," PBS-TV, 12-13.

Anthony Griffin
Lawyer;
General counsel,
Texas state office,
National Association
for the Advancement
of Colored People

1

[On the seeming paradox of his currently representing a Ku Klux Klansman in court]: Lord knows, don't hear me say I'm an apologist for the Klan. I can't stand them. I wish they didn't exist. But it's very easy to give the First Amendment to groups we like and make us feel good. It's very difficult to apply those principles to people who . . . anger us, that we want to shut up. And that's the beauty of the First Amendment. The First Amendment is not to protect me from you but us from the government. If you create a rule of law to have Klan lists obtained, you create a law that also comes back and gets you. If you're corralling them, if you're telling them they can't meet, you're also telling me to shut up, telling me to sit down, telling me for whatever reasons, you don't like me and you can go after me.

Interview,
Galveston, Texas/
The Washington Post,
9-29:(A)3.

Lani Guinier
Professor of Law,
University of Pennsylvania;
Former Assistant Attorney
General-designate,
Civil Rights Division,
Department of Justice
of the United States

2

[On President Clinton's withdrawal of her nomination for head of the Civil Rights Division because of controversy over her written views on racism]: I think that the President and many others have misinterpreted my writings. I think I represent an important and mainstream tradition that this Administration is also committed to. That is vigorous enforcement of the civil-rights laws as passed by Congress . . . I hope that [by the withdrawal of the nomination] we are not witnessing the dawning of a new intellectual orthodoxy in which thoughtful people can no longer debate provocative ideas without denying the country their talents as public servants.

News conference,
Washington, D.C., June 4/
Los Angeles Times, 6-5:(A)1,14.

3

[On President Clinton's withdrawal, under pressure, of her nomination to head the Civil Rights Division of the Justice Department]: I endured the personal humiliation of being vilified as a madwoman with strange hair . . . a strange name and strange ideas—ideas like democracy, freedom and fairness that mean all people must be equally represented in our political process. But lest any of you feel sorry for me, according to press reports the President still loves me. He just won't give me a job.

At NAACP convention,
Indianapolis, Ind.,
July 13/The New York Times, 7-14:(A)7.

Patricia Ireland
President,
National Organization for Women

4

[Saying President Clinton should appoint a woman as the next U.S. Attorney General]: He

(PATRICIA IRELAND)

should be politically savvy enough to know that appointing a woman as Attorney General is important. I think if he doesn't, it will hasten the end of his honeymoon with women voters who put him in office . . . The days are long past when a President can say with a straight face that there are not enough qualified women for the job.

Jan. 22/Los Angeles Times, 1-23:(A)14.

Jesse L. Jackson
Civil-rights leader

1

[Criticizing President Clinton's decision to drop his nomination of Lani Guinier for head of the Justice Department's Civil Rights Division because of controversy over her views]: If President Clinton and Senate Democrats had stood by Lani as [former] President [George] Bush and the Republicans stood by Clarence Thomas [when he was nominated and confirmed for the Supreme Court despite controversy], she would be confirmed. It was unfair [to drop her before her confirmation hearing]. She was never able to face her accusers or the public.

June 3/USA Today, 6-4:(A)1.

2

[President Clinton] spent his [election] campaign [last year] distancing himself from me. Now that he's President, he's trying to dismiss me. He's trying to prop up other black leaders. It's not working. Look at the polls; walk the streets. The other guys don't have the juice. It's only me.

Time, 12-13:40.

3

[On the proliferation of black-on-black crime]: There is nothing more painful to me at this stage in my life than to walk down the street and hear footsteps and start thinking about robbery—then look around and see somebody white and feel relieved.

Speech, Chicago, Ill./
Newsweek, 12-13:17.

4

I want [the Clinton Administration] to listen to its own covenant. [As yet in the Administration,] there's no Assistant Attorney General for civil rights. There's no Chair of [the EEOC], right? There's no youth policy. There's no urban policy. There are no community-development banks. And these are part of the covenant.

Interview/
U.S. News & World Report, 12-27:82.

Douglas Johnson
Legislative director,
National Right to Life Committee

5

[Opposing any government health-care reform program that includes benefits for abortion]: We would strongly oppose any mandate on the part of the Federal government that compelled employers, health-care providers and citizens to collaborate in abortion on demand. We would hope that the pro-abortion movement wouldn't try to hijack the national health plan.

April 13/Los Angeles Times, 4-14:(A)11.

John Lewis
United States Representative,
D-Georgia

6

The NAACP is much more at home signing agreements with banks and restaurant chains and utilities than it is looking out for the rights of individual black Americans. I think there's a role for the NAACP, especially in the Clinton Administration, but they need to come up with some new programs, not just the old rhetoric.

The New York Times, 3-31:(A)7.

7

Since [the civil-rights march of] 1963, I think we have witnessed—at least in the southern parts of America—what I like to call a non-violent revolution. We live in a different country . . . Thirty years ago, there was a tremendous amount of fear among black people. Black people could not participate in the democratic process; they couldn't register to vote. You still had lines for

(JOHN LEWIS)

white men and colored men, white women and colored women, white waiting and colored waiting. Those signs are gone, and they will not return.

The Christian Science Monitor, 8-27:2.

Roger Mahony
Roman Catholic Archbishop
of Los Angeles, Calif.;
Chairman, Committee for
Pro-Life Activities,
National Conference
of Catholic Bishops

1

[Criticizing President Clinton's orders that rescind restrictions on abortion counseling at clinics, use of fetal tissue in research and U.S. funding of international family-planning programs that include abortion counseling]: Surely you cannot reduce abortion by promoting abortion as just another method of birth control. You cannot reduce abortion by fueling a market for the tiny dead bodies of unborn children. You cannot reduce abortion by exporting abortion to the poor in the Third World.

Jan. 22/The New York Times, 1-23:7.

Vernon Masayesva
Chairman, Hopi Indian tribe

2

What bothers me is the attitude problem Arizonans seem to be having [about Indians]. As long as Hopis stay up on their Mesa, making their cute little kachina dolls, we're okay. The minute we become serious opinion-makers, decision-makers via the political process, we become a threat. And I see racism happening right here in Arizona, and we all ought to be ashamed.

The New York Times, 2-13:6.

Donald McHenry
Former United States
Ambassador/Permanent Representative
to the United Nations

3

I am not one of those who look upon [affirmative action] as a stigma. I personally don't

because I figure I [as a black] have done my work. I've tried to prepare myself, and all I'm asking for is a fair shot. So, if affirmative action gives me a fair shot, fine.

Newsweek, 11-15:63.

Cynthia McKinney
United States Representative,
D-Georgia

4

The agenda for civil rights never stops. In fact, in the 11th Congressional District [in Georgia], where we have black people who are [still] denied their right to vote, we have elections that have turned on blacks who have been turned away from the polls. No, I can't say that the civil-rights era is over.

Interview/
The Christian Science Monitor, 3-8:10.

Herbert Morris
Provost, University of California,
Los Angeles

5

[On the racial tension at many universities]: There is a sense of people generally on tenterhooks and extraordinarily sensitive to anything that could be seen as an affront. On issues of race, ethnicity and gender . . . all that has to happen is a gnat lands on the shoulder, and they shoot from the hip.

The Washington Post, 5-15:(A)1.

Carol Moseley-Braun
United States Senator,
D-Illinois

6

[Arguing against the Senate renewing the patent for the insignia of the United Daughters of the Confederacy because it includes the Confederate flag]: This vote is about race. It is about racial symbols, the racial past, and the single most painful episode in American history. It is absolutely unacceptable to me and to millions of Americans, black or white, that we would put the imprimatur of the United States Senate on a symbol of this kind of idea.

Before the Senate, Washington, D.C./
Newsweek, 8-2:30.

Torie Osborne
Executive director,
National Gay and Lesbian
Task Force

1

[President Clinton's election] victory put us [homosexuals] in the sunlight. Suddenly, the world is listening, and suddenly, we have a chance to tell our story and make our case to the American people. This decade really will be the "Gay '90s."

The Christian Science Monitor,
4-22:3.

William Raspberry
Political columnist

2

[We blacks have] spent a generation essentially telling [black children] that nothing good can happen for them because of racism. We thought we were saying it to the racists . . . to the political leadership . . . to people we could put a guilt trip on [so] they would come and help us. But whoever we were saying it to, our children heard it, and it's frightening to me to listen to some of them talk now about the futility of trying.

Interview/
The Christian Science Monitor,
1-15:10.

Shannon Reeves
Director,
Western regional office,
National Association
for the Advancement
of Colored People

3

The NAACP needs a younger perspective and more acute solutions. We've got to bridge the generation gap in black America. We can't wait for young people to come to us. We have to go out and get them . . . We have to catch people when they're young. We need a more active presence at the nation's 117 historically black colleges. Those are your future Mayors, Governors, CEOs. You have to grind into them the relevance of the NAACP in changing times.

Los Angeles Times, 4-8:(E)1,2.

Janet Reno
Attorney General
of the United States

4

[On anti-abortion protestors who block or otherwise interfere with an abortion clinic's services]: I want to look at the laws on the books now to see if there is any remedy that we might undertake in response. Just as there should be a Federal remedy for racial discrimination and for gender discrimination, I think in this instance somehow or another there has got to be a Federal response to interference through physical conduct which restrains access to a woman's right to choose.

To reporters, Washington, D.C.,
March 12/
The New York Times, 3-13:8.

William Schneider
Analyst,
American Enterprise Institute

5

[On the recent march for homosexual rights in Washington]: Marches give a sense of solidarity, of becoming a force. It happened for blacks. It was next for women. Now it's happened among gay Americans. Politicians don't just look at the numbers of votes an issue can generate. They look at intensity. And a march shows intensity, the ability to show you're an organized force and that if you go against them, you're in trouble. Congress already knew that about the religious right. Now this shows it's on the gay side as well.

The New York Times 4-27:(A)8.

Shelby Steele
Professor of English,
San Jose (Calif.)
State University

6

Two-thirds of black Americans are not in the underclass. If you look at blacks who are in the upper class or working class, the first thing that most of them have done is left situations where their children have to dodge bullets, where the schools are bad, where there are drug dealers on every corner, where there is no family life, where

47

(SHELBY STEELE)

most families are single-parent, where everyone is on welfare. Obviously, this is not a place to get ahead in life, period . . . When you cast people utterly as victims, you destroy their sense of self-determination. You make them passive; you make them waiters instead of actors.

Interview/
Mother Jones, Jan.-Feb.:6.

George Stephanopoulos
Director of Communications
for President
of the United States
Bill Clinton

1

[On President Clinton's desire to end the ban on Federal funding for abortions]: For 16 years, you've had the Federal government flat-out prohibiting states from spending the money to pay for abortions, whether or not they're medically necessary, whether or not they result from a case of incest, whether or not they threaten the life of the mother. The President feels that goes too far.

March 30/
Los Angeles Times,
3-31:(A)1.

Dorothy Thomas
Director,
Women's Rights Project,
Human Rights Watch

2

For years in many countries, the tendency of women participating in movements for political change was to accept the premise that they'd work for revolution first and change in the status of women later. Then they woke up and found that their agendas had not been taken up by the movements they supported, and they stopped depending on men in power. So in the late 1980s and 1990s, they began to organize politically and put themselves in power for the purpose of effecting the kind of change they want.

Los Angeles Times,
6-29:(H)5.

Cruz Torres
Sociologist,
University of Denver (Colo.)

3

In many areas of the isolated West, minorities don't pose a threat. But as social mobility increases for all ethnic groups, some people will suddenly find themselves competing for limited resources. It's just a gut reaction, but I think you find that as resources become scarce, prejudice is apt to increase. We're very generous when there's enough to go around.

Los Angeles Times, 4-8:(A)23.

Diana Chapman Walsh
President-designate,
Wellesley (Mass.) College

4

If women are taken very seriously across all aspects of life from sports to the classroom to governance of the community; if half of the tenured faculty are women and play very important roles in running the institution at the highest levels of management; if the rest of academia were to look like that—then I'd say maybe Wellesley's job [as a women's college] is done. But we are so far from that point that I don't see a day in the foreseeable future when a [women-only] Wellesley College won't be needed.

Interview,
Wellesley, Mass./
The Christian Science Monitor, 8-12:14.

Wellington E. Webb
Mayor of Denver, Colo.

5

I've always fought for the rights of others. If, as Americans, any group is denied opportunity because of some difference, whether it's religious, origin, marital status, skin color, ethnicity or even sexual orientation, we have an obligation as Americans to protect the rights of all Americans. Because if you deny one, you never can determine when the next one will want to deny your rights. So for me, it's either we fight for the rights of everybody or we don't fight for anybody.

Interview, Denver, Colo./
Ebony, December:32.

Cornel West
*Professor of religion and director
of Afro-American studies program,
Princeton University*

1

Integration was meant to be a two-way street. There was going to be learning on a variety of sides. Instead, it became watered down and degenerated into a notion of cheap assimilation, which meant black folks did all the work and had to fit into the larger society . . . We have large segments of the black community who have no interest whatsoever in fitting in that way. And it's having tremendously negative consequences on us. You think of young people now who associate going to the library with being white. That's one of the more pernicious consequences of a narrow conception of assimilation. And it's something that has to be combated.

Interview/USA Today, 6-22:(A)11.

Commerce • Industry • Finance

Toshi Amino
Executive vice president,
Honda of America

1

[On his Japanese auto firm's running its own manufacturing plants in the U.S.]: I don't think we can say we are a perfectly 100 percent American company. To be honest, I don't know what the definition of an American company is.
The Christian Science Monitor,
3-24:10.

William A. Anders
Chairman,
General Dynamics Corporation

2

[On his stepping down as chairman after being hired two years ago to help improve the company's fortunes]: I was asked to turn this company around and we did just that by lowering costs, improving the job prospects of those employees who remain and getting greater value for our shareholders. Frankly, if more CEOs were willing to do that and work themselves out of a job, we'd all be better off.
March 18/
The Washington Post, 3-19:(A)1.

Edwin Artzt
Chairman,
Procter & Gamble Company

3

[On his company's plan to eliminate 13,000 jobs]: I went around and talked to CEOs of other companies that had gone through this or more severe things like this. They all said pretty much the same thing, which is: It does come as a shock to the organization, but when it's over, there's a great sense of heightened security that replaces the anxiety and concern that existed before the whole thing happened. One of the components of P&G's culture has always been a sense of security about the future success of the company. That sense of security has been jolted . . .

by the recognition that we were getting too fat as a company. People were getting anxious about that.
Interview, Cincinnati, Ohio/
USA Today, 7-16:(B)2.

Erskine Bowles
Administrator,
Small Business Administration
of the United States

4

[The Clinton Administration wants to] get rid of the unnecessary paperwork and bureaucratic regulations that inhibit the growth and productivity of small business. Government regulations have a disproportionately adverse effect on small companies. The President wants to attack this issue head-on, and I am absolutely committed to doing that.
Before House Small Business Committee,
Washington, D.C., June/
Nation's Business, December:67.

Ronald H. Brown
Secretary of Commerce
of the United States

5

In an age in which change is the only constant, competitive success now requires constant, sustained innovation. That means for governments and businesses and workers, we must constantly be reinterpreting and reinventing how we work.
At Conference on the Future
of the American Workplace,
Chicago, Ill., July 26/
The Washington Post, 7-27:(D)1.

6

We are formulating a national economic strategy that means a new relationship between business and government. It means a government that understands clearly that it is the private sector that creates economic growth and jobs.

(RONALD H. BROWN)

There are times and places where the government needs to get out of the way. There are times and places where we need to be better partners. There is a clear understanding in the business community that they need a different kind of relationship with government, and that's going to help make us successful in this effort.

Interview/
USA Today, 9-28:(A)11.

Bill Clinton
President of the United States

1

[Saying he wants to ease government regulations that stifle banks' enthusiasm for making loans to businesses]: [We want] to try to make it possible for banks to loan money to businesses again, to try to release the energies for the old-fashioned character small-business loans, to try to reduce the fear that a lot of banks have that if they make sensible loans, the government will come down on them.

Before U.S. Chamber of Commerce,
Washington, D.C., Feb. 23/
The Washington Post, 2-24:(A)4.

2

Whether we see it or not, our daily lives are touched everywhere by the flows of commerce that cross national borders as inextricably as the weather. Capital clearly has become global. Some $3-trillion of capital race around the world every day. And when a firm wants to build a new factory, it can turn to financial markets, now open 24 hours a day, from London to Tokyo, from New York to Singapore. Products have clearly become more global. Now if you buy an American car, it may be an American car built with some parts from Taiwan, designed by Germans, sold with British-made advertisements, or a combination of others in a different mix. Services have become global. The accounting firm that keeps the books for a small business in Wichita may also be helping new entrepreneurs in Warsaw. And the same fast-food restaurant that your family goes to—or at least that I go to—also

may well be serving families from Manila to Moscow and managing its business globally with information, technologies and satellites. And most important of all, information has become global and has become king of the global economy. In earlier history, wealth was measured in land, in gold, in oil, in machines. Today, the principal measure of our wealth is information: its quality, its quantity and the speed with which we acquire it and adapt to it . . . The truth of our age is this, and must be this: Open and competitive commerce will enrich us as a nation. It spurs us to innovate. It forces us to compete. It connects us with our customers. It promotes global growth without which no rich country can hope to grow wealthy. It enables our producers, who are themselves consumers of services and raw materials, to prosper. And so I say to you, in the face of all the pressures to do the reverse, we must compete, not retreat.

At American University, Feb. 26/
The Washington Post, 2-27:(A)8.

William H. Donaldson
Chairman,
New York Stock Exchange

3

Cash payment for order flow [in which stock buy and sell orders are handled off the floor of the major exchanges] is a practice that should be outlawed. There is money being paid to an intermediary, not to the customer. That is the practice I think is outrageous. The practice must be banned.

Before House Telecommunications
and Finance Subcommittee,
Washington, D.C., April 14/
The Washington Post, 4-15:(D)11.

Terry Everett
United States Representative-elect,
R-Alabama

4

Small-business folks are hollering about [government] regulations, and I think . . . we need to make the Congress live under the same sort of regulations we make small business live under . . . Pass a law that would require that before anyone could serve in the House or Senate they either operate a small business or work for commission for a couple of years. If we had that simple law, I could guarantee you wouldn't find some of the silly rules and regulations and actions by the Congress that actually halt jobs.

Interview/Nation's Business,
January:24.

Patrick R. Fallon
Chairman,
Fallon McElligott, advertising

1

[On advertising agencies that, like his in Minneapolis, are not New York-based]: Imagination doesn't have any geographical limitations, and basically what we sell is disciplined imagination. Some clients feel that they have to have a New York agency, but there are fewer, and most of them are wrong.

Interview/
The New York Times, 1-18:(C)6.

Bill Gates
Chairman,
Microsoft Corporation

2

I think business is very simple. Profit. Loss. Take the sales, subtract the costs, you get this big positive number. The math is quite straightforward.

U.S. News & World Report,
2-15:72.

Louis V. Gerstner
Chairman, International
Business Machines Corporation

3

[On his becoming chairman of IBM at a time when the company is in economic difficulties]: I started 100-odd days ago with a company with $60-billion in sales that was losing billions of dollars. Spending a lot of time right now thinking about what parts of the computer business we should be in is not the best thing I could be doing

with my time . . . I want to deal with what's here. IBM is the largest hardware company, the largest software company and the largest information company in the world. It seems to me that if you're Number 1 in the market and you're not making money, the first priority is to fix what you've got before thinking about another portfolio of businesses.

Interview, Armonk, N.Y./
Newsweek, 8-9:42.

Sandra Gherzi
Management consultant

4

The best managers are learning that they need others' contributions—and that to get them, they need to share their sense of context; share information, not withhold it to maintain control. They also have to be willing to admit their fallibility, which builds—if not consensus—then at least an atmosphere in which team members feel taken seriously, understood . . . Most women, unlike most men, aren't comfortable turning business negotiations into confrontations where there are clear winners and losers. That's to their credit. These little competitions inhibit the free expression of ideas among colleagues, ideas companies need if they are going to survive.

Lear's, January:20.

Alan Greenspan
Chairman,
Federal Reserve Board

5

[Saying there have been too many government regulations on banking in the last several years]: Each new proposed piece of detailed banking legislation has to be evaluated in advance to determine what the impacts are likely to be on the health, vigor and competitiveness of the banking system. [Too many laws have] resulted in a drum-beat [of requirements]. Such micro-management has a chilling effect on bank lending attitudes, imparting a high degree of management uncertainty while the implementing rules are developed, debated and adopted.

Before House Small Business Committee,
Washington, D.C., March 25/
The New York Times, 3-26:(C)2.

Steven C. Gunderson
United States Representative,
R-Wisconsin

1

[Saying the Republican Party should support more of a government role in business]: We're trying to relive [former Presidents Ronald] Reagan and [George] Bush [and their *laissez-faire* policies] and the public is worried about how to survive in a fast-moving, high-tech world. Government must be a partner with business in preparing the workforce for the 21st century . . . Business leaders are in favor of this and, more and more, they are saying that Republicans are into government self-denial. If we lost [the support of] business, we are losing a very important part of our base.

At Republican conference,
Princeton, N.J., Feb. 26/
Los Angeles Times, 2-27:(A)17.

Lawrence A. Hunter
Former chief economist,
United States
Chamber of Commerce

2

[Criticizing Clinton Administration proposals for government to get more involved with private industry]: They entice entire industries—like Silicon Valley, like the auto industry—to say, "Cut a deal with the government and you'll get these goodies." There's no evidence that the market needs the government's help. But there's a lot of evidence that every time the government tries, it makes things worse.

Los Angeles Times,
2-24:(D)2.

3

[On President Clinton's recruitment of the business community to support his economic policies]: He wants to co-opt business to be a party to his enterprise. This is a new collectivism. It looks very much like the corporate state. Some call it fascism.

Interview/
The Washington Post,
3-1:(A)17.

Joe Knollenberg
United States Representative-elect,
R-Michigan

4

I feel very strongly about small business. It's the area of growth in this country. Government has to realize that people don't go into business unless they've got a chance of succeeding, and so [because of government over-regulation] many of them don't. We're making it too tough . . . It's the small businesses that are going to pay the way. And to allow them the freedom to expand, to stimulate growth, to bring people on the payrolls, they're going to need a little help.

Interview/
Nation's Business, January:26.

Richard L. Lesher
President,
United States
Chamber of Commerce

5

[On the Chamber's relations with the Clinton Administration]: The relationship we've built with those folks is quite good. We didn't agree with [former President George] Bush on a lot of things, and we don't agree with Clinton on a lot of things. In fact, I don't agree with my wife on many things. But you have to have a decent working relationship to get things done.

Interview,
Washington, D.C., April 13/
The New York Times, 4-14:(A)9.

6

[On President Clinton's efforts to relax government regulations on bank loans to encourage lending to small businesses]: The Administration's character-loan proposal should make it easier [to obtain a loan] for firms that have established a long or successful relationship with a banker. The Administration has gotten at the key elements that have thwarted many small-business loans in the recent past . . . Existing banking laws and regulations have made it more advantageous for banks to invest in securities than provide business loans. This is one way to finance the [Federal] deficit, but it certainly

(RICHARD L. LESHER)

doesn't encourage economic growth and small-business job creation.

Nation's Business, June:43.

Arthur Levitt, Jr.
Chairman,
Securities and Exchange Commission
of the United States

1

[On the ability of the SEC to watch over the burgeoning mutual-fund business]: [There is] a serious shortfall in the Commission's resources to oversee one of the fastest-growing and most important segments of the financial-services industry . . . If nothing is done to add to our ranks, the task the staff faces may become too great to provide any real measure of . . . investor protection.

Before Senate Securities Subcommittee,
Washington, D.C., Nov. 10/
The Washington Post, 11-11:(A)10.

Eugene A. Ludwig
Comptroller of the Currency
of the United States

2

[Saying banks should be given more rights to expand the types of financial services they can offer]: Lending is inherently risky, and bank lending is getting riskier as higher-quality credits increasingly move out of the banking system. If we leave banks without other safe lines of business, we are sowing the seeds of disaster—guaranteeing that the industry will become steadily less safe and sound, and that we will pay the price tomorrow.

At conference sponsored by
Merrill Lynch & Company,
New York, N.Y., Sept., 13/
The Washington Post, 9-14:(A)22.

Robert H. Malott
Chairman, executive committee,
FMC Corporation

3

In trying to run a company, I will tell you it is very, very helpful for me to pay [an executive] a

fair salary and to have annual performance expectations and targets against which I'm willing to pay extra cash compensation in the short term. For parts of your company or for individuals, you can create specific targets of expectation and emphasis that you want to make. It might be working capital one year. It might be market penetration in another part of the company in another year. There are all kinds of things that I think can be accomplished in the short term, and you want to have some incentive tied to that.

Interview/
The Wall Street Journal,
4-21:(R)12.

Bernard Marcus
Chairman,
Home Depot, Inc.

4

[On how he runs his business]: We get nervous when we are satisfied. Then we're dead in the water . . . It's not an ability to communicate how many things you do right, but how quickly you fix the things that are wrong that matter. In this company, it is vogue to listen, vogue to criticize, vogue to improve . . . Like anything else in the world today, if you are not competitive, you are not going to make it. If you are a dinosaur, your time eventually comes.

Interview, Atlanta, Ga./
The Washington Post,
3-29:(Washington Business)13,14.

John Markese
President,
American Association
of Individual Investors

5

[Warning against the average individual getting involved in buying initial public stock offerings, which are currently very popular]: The lesson for small investors is crystal clear: The average Joe or Jane should stay as far away from IPOs as possible.

Time, 11-8:62.

Edward J. Markey
United States Representative,
D-Massachusetts

1

[Criticizing what he sees as too-high execu-tive pay]: Too many of these executives seem to be getting something for nothing. Where are the boards of directors when we need them? . . . There is a delinkage between executive pay and corporate performance. One is heading up and one is heading down.

At House Telecommunications and
Finance Subcommittee hearing,
Washington, D.C., April 21/
The Washington Post, 4-22:(A)26.

2

[On government regulation of the securities industry]: The challenge before us is how best to factor in market developments and technological changes in a way which gives us a new mix while not abandoning old values. During the 1980s, I believe that we went through a period when the deregulatory agenda of the [Ronald] Reagan Administration sent an unfortunate signal to Wall Street that the securities cop had been disarmed.

Before Government Finance
Officers Association, January/
Los Angeles Times, 8-1:(D)3.

3

Mutual funds are a lot like the Philadelphia *Phillies* [baseball team]: great organization, great starting pitching, superb hitting—but they need to address a few shortcomings in order to be perfect.

Time, 11-8:58.

Howard M. Metzenbaum
United States Senator,
D-Ohio

4

[On the current wave of big mergers in the communications field]: Before any of these mergers is allowed to go forward, there's one overriding question that we must answer for the American consumer; that is, will this un-precedented convergence of telecommunications giants create a swarm of cost-cutting entre-preneurs or a handful of price-gouging monopo-lists? [It must be considered whether this] could lead to an industry dominated by a handful of telecommunications conglomerates that have powerful incentives to co-exist instead of compete.

At Senate Judiciary Committee hearing,
Washington, D.C., Oct. 27/
USA Today, 10-28:(B)2.

Ira M. Millstein
Founder,
Institutional Investor Project,
Columbia University

5

For years, we have been studying [corporate] boards and managers. Now it is time for the shareholders and [shareholder] institutions to be studied. We know little or nothing about how these major investor types exercise their share-holding responsibilities. To whom are these financial institutions accountable? Who is watching the watchers? Anyone?

At conference sponsored by
Columbia University's
Institutional Investor Project,
New York, N.Y./
The New York Times,
5-10:(C)4.

Paul Minus
President,
Council for Ethics
in Economics

6

[On the growth in the number of companies hit by internal fraud]: Some of the major traditional sources of values in our culture—our religious and educational institutions and the family—are in trouble and simply do not have the kind of value-forming influence that they once did. We cannot expect such movements to happen with-out fallout like an increase in fraud.

The Christian Science Monitor,
8-20:9.

Kabun Muto
Foreign Minister of Japan

1

Americans are marvelous workers . . . To see the American workers [in Japanese-owned automobile plants in the U.S.] was really impressive. I was greatly moved to see how much the American workers want to make high-efficiency, high-quality products. Even more than the Japanese employees you'd see at a plant in Japan, the Americans working in a Toyota or Honda plant in America have a way of working that is just splendid . . . [But] even with these marvelous American workers, if good management is lacking, things won't come out well. Management is key. Wouldn't it be a good thing if Americans would adopt what is called Japanese-style management—to produce good products at the best price to please consumers?

News conference,
Tokyo, Japan, April 7/
The Washington Post, 4-8:(A)37.

Anthony O'Reilly
Chief executive,
H. J. Heinz Company

2

[On competition with name brands by private store-label products]: The whole notion that brand-name products have lost their price leverage has taken root in the investment community. I don't think you'll see consumer branded stocks regain popularity for the next eight to 12 months, but I don't think this is a trend for the entire '90s. I think we will be able to raise prices on [name-brand] products, but just not as high as in the '80s. Longer term, the companies like us—General Mills, Kellogg, Ralston Purina—we'll be back . . . [But] the easy days for building great national brands are over. It's extremely difficult and expensive.

Interview/USA Today, 7-13:(B)8.

Donald S. Perkins
Member of the board
of directors of several
major corporations

3

[Criticizing the idea of giving a greater role to outside directors at U.S. corporations]: The mistake you are making is using the word "independent" without using the word "experienced." There is nothing worse than naive independent directors. There is nothing worse than an inexperienced director.

At conference of Council
of Institutional Investors,
Washington, D.C., March 25/
The Washington Post, 3-26:(D)3.

Roland Rust
Professor of marketing,
Vanderbilt University

4

[Sixty years from now, in 2053,] mass-media advertising will be history. As we approach the era of market segments of one individual, advertisers will supply information only to consumers who request it. They may even be willing to pay for it.

Interview/
U.S. News & World Report,
10-25:73.

William Sahlman
Professor of
business administration,
Harvard Business School

5

They say the difference between a good investor and a bad investor is how quickly they panic, because all of us have been involved in companies that say: If you give us a million dollars, we're going to create a $100-million business, and we'll never need another nickel of capital. And then about six months into it they say: We're going to need another $3-million. And the question is: Do people panic or not? Do they anticipate that call? And one of the problems with unprofessional angels is that they don't anticipate that call. They get upset, they panic, and it's very hard to raise money under the circumstances in which people haven't imagined that you're going to need more money than you said you were going to need.

Interview/
The Wall Street Journal,
10-15:(R)22.

William A. Schreyer
Chairman,
Merrill Lynch & Company

1

Here's one change you're going to discover as you go out in the world as an accountant, a marketing expert, a business professional. You're going to say, "Trust me. I know what I'm doing." Unfortunately, you're going to discover that basic trust is a very precious commodity these days. People have been burned . . . by what's seen as widespread decay in personal responsibility and accountability. So a big part of your job will be winning and holding their trust, and there's only one way to do that: through the personal example of integrity you set every day, in your dealings with customers, fellow workers, government regulators and fellow citizens. That's just a long way of saying "take the high road"— because over the long term it's the only road that takes you where you need to go.

At Smeal College of Business commencement,
University of Pennsylvania/
The Christian Science Monitor,
6-15:16.

Charles Schwab
Chairman,
Charles Schwab & Company,
securities broker

2

It's probably extremely good for the economy long term to have more people investing [in the stock market]. Many of the new people are certainly informed enough that they know they should be long-term investors and are not going into this for a quick 30-day move. They're 40 years old and have 20 years ahead of them to hold investments. They know long-term investing in equities is simply the way to get your highest return.

Interview/
USA Today, 7-16:(B)3.

Peter Schweizer
Author of book
on industrial espionage

3

[On industrial spying among friendly countries]: In the new world order, yesterday's political allies are today's economic competitors. Business secrets have become more vital than military secrets. And counting machine tools is now more important than tracking the number of battle tanks.

Time, 2-22:60.

Virginia Stafford
Official,
American Bankers Association

4

Consumers must shop around for the best [banking] services. [And] there are ways to avoid [bank] fees altogether if you shop around . . . Banking is a business. Banks don't operate in a vacuum. We cannot set prices without regard to consumer demand, or customers will go elsewhere.

The Christian Science Monitor,
12-7:11.

Laurence A. Tisch
Chairman, CBS, Inc.

5

Even in well-run companies, chief executives' [pay] is too high. You're getting to this problem of what's right . . . There is a certain obscenity in some of the greed taking place in corporate America.

Before House Telecommunications
and Finance Subcommittee,
Washington, D.C., April 21/
The Washington Post, 4-22:(A)26.

Nicholas Vonortas
Economist,
Center for International
Science and Technology Policy,
George Washington University

6

In Japan there is cutthroat competition between big firms. But they also talk; that is a very good trick they have discovered.

U.S. News & World Report,
5-3:67.

Ralph Whitworth
President,
United Shareholders Association

1

When you're talking about executive compensation, you're talking about these executives' own personal wealth. That's the single issue on which they have the greatest conflict of interest. Regardless of how conscientious someone is, there's something pulling you in a very distinct direction when you're talking about your own pay. We have to have safeguards to make sure that [company] decisions are made in the most objective way possible, and that the right interests are considered—and [those are] the shareholders' interests . . . We hope [executives] do get rich, by the way. We want them to be multi-millionaires. But they've got to make that money right alongside the shareholders in the form of either stock options or some plan that's linked to the stock price. All you have to do is look at the original prospectus of the company and that's what the company was formed for. It says right there: "Please give us your money. We'll make you rich." The only way the shareholders can get rich is by appreciation in the stock price or by dividends. And so that's the only way the top officers of the company should be able to get rich. Then you've got the interests aligned.

Interview/
Wall Street Journal,
4-21:(R)10,12.

Crime • Law Enforcement

Joseph R. Biden, Jr.
United States Senator,
D-Delaware

1

[On rape]: The American legal system has always treated cases of assault on our streets as serious crime, but violence that primarily targets women has too often been dismissed without response. When the victim knows the perpetrator, there is a tendency in our system to consider the crime a product of a private relationship, not a matter of public injustice.

May 27/
The Washington Post, 5-28:(A)20.

Paul Billings
Clinical geneticist,
Stanford University

2

We know what causes violence in our society: poverty, discrimination, the failure of our educational system. It's not the genes [in human beings] that cause violence in our society. It's our social system.

Los Angeles Times,
12-30:(A)14.

G. Robert Blakey
Professor,
University of Notre Dame
Law School;
Former Federal prosecutor

3

[On the FBI and BATF assault on a religious cult compound in Waco, Texas, which resulted in the death of many cultists and children in the compound]: I think they [the government] haven't made the public case for the necessity to do what they did. The question is, could we have done anything differently. And the answer is I would have exhausted all the alternatives, and one was simply waiting [the cultists] out.

The New York Times,
4-21:(A)11.

Thomas Blomberg
Professor of criminology,
Florida State University

4

Why is it that people are carrying weapons? Why are people able to pull the trigger and shoot someone in the face and walk away? We do have people in this society who have nothing to lose.

USA Today, 12-29:(A)2.

Robert C. Bonner
Administrator,
Drug Enforcement Administration
of the United States

5

[On judges who criticize the use of the courts to prosecute drug offenders because they say it is ineffective]: No matter how well intended, unfortunately no one judge in no one courtroom is in a very good position to judge the overall effectiveness of drug prosecutions. [Such prosecutions play] a critical role in the DEA's global strategy to incapacitate major trafficking organizations. While cocaine is far more available than any of us would like to see it be, it is less readily available in New York and other major urban areas than it was five years ago.

April 16/
The New York Times, 4-17:7.

David G. Boyd
Director,
science and technology team,
National Institute of Justice
of the United States

6

[On developing technological methods of helping fight crime]: Most cops really would like to find better ways to do things. The real tragedy is our police officers today have basically the same options Wyatt Earp had, and it's ridiculous. They can talk a subject into cooperating. They can beat him into submission. They can shoot him. You'd think, after a century of major

59

(DAVID G. BOYD)

advances in technology, we could offer more choices than that.

The Washington Post, 11-8:(A)19.

Tom Bradley
Mayor of Los Angeles, Calif.

1

[On the possibility of racial violence following the pending verdicts in the trial of Los Angeles police officers accused in the beating of black suspect Rodney King]: In this hour, and over the next days, I know in my heart that the overwhelming majority of our residents will accept whatever happens [in the trial] with calmness and reason, regardless of their personal feelings. To them I say: Keep the peace, because without it there can be no justice. To them I pledge: I will do everything in my power to maintain public order . . . To those who may be itching for an excuse to harm our neighborhoods [as occurred in riots after last year's trial in which the officers were acquitted], I have this warning: You will not get away with it, so don't even try.

Broadcast address to the city,
April 16/Los Angeles Times, 4-17:(A)1.

James S. Brady
Former Press Secretary
to the President
of the United States
(Ronald Reagan)

2

[On the just-signed Brady Bill legislation which mandates a nationwide waiting period for the purchase of handguns]: [This legislation will bring] the end of unchecked madness and the commencement of a heartfelt crusade for a safer and saner country. [Twelve years ago,] my life was changed forever by a disturbed young man with a gun [who shot Brady in an attempt to kill then-President Reagan. Too many young people] believe that a gun is the answer to their problems. I can tell them about the pain and the frustration. I hope they will listen.

At signing of Brady Bill
by President Clinton,
Washington, D.C., Nov. 30/
The Washington Post, 12-1:(A)8.

Lee Brown
Director, White House Office
of National Drug Control Policy;
Former Commissioner of Police
of New York, N.Y.

3

The police have not always been there to serve the black community, and that's changing. What we've seen happen right now is more enlightened police leadership. Many policemen are involved with increasing the ethnic composition of police departments. The goal should be an ethnic representation that approximates the ethnic population of the city. That's not the case now, but that's something that should be the goal for policing.

Interview/
USA Today, 7-26:(A)9.

Emanuel Cleaver
Mayor of Kansas City, Mo.

4

I don't think any local government can solve the problem of the proliferation of guns, firearms. I think it has to be done by Congress. And I don't think Congress will do it until it hears an outburst of irrepressible outrage from the public.

Interview/
USA Today, 12-29:(A)7.

Mario M. Cuomo
Governor of New York (D)

5

You must, of course, have tough laws and strict law enforcement. That is the first obligation of government—to keep you safe at this moment against this potential criminal. But at the same time, you must deal with the basic causes [of crime and violence], which are a loss of family values, a loss of sense of responsibility, deterioration of our whole sense of what's moral and what's right coming at our kids 6½ hours a day on the television, and the loss of opportunity—the inability to give the kids in my old neighborhood the sense that, hey, you go to school and you can wind up Governor, too.

Interview/
USA Today, 12-29:(A)7.

Bill Clinton
President of the United States

1

[The U.S.] can't be so fixated on our desire to preserve the rights of ordinary Americans to legitimately own handguns and rifles . . . that we are unable to think about the reality [of gun violence in the country]. I hope the leadership of the National Rifle Association will go back to doing what it did when I was a boy [promoting hunting and safety instead of fighting gun-control proposals] . . . [It is] an error [for the NRA] to oppose every attempt to bring some safety and some rationality into the way we handle some of the serious criminal problems we have . . . I don't believe that everybody in America needs to be able to buy a semiautomatic or an automatic weapon, built only for the purpose of killing people, in order to protect the right of Americans to hunt and practice marksmanship and to be secure.

To reporters,
Piscataway, N.J., March 1/
The Washington Post, 3-2:(A)9.

2

[On the FBI and BATF assault on a religious cult compound in Waco, Texas, which resulted in the death of many cultists and children in the compound]: We did everything we could to avoid the loss of life. They [the cultists] made the decision to immolate themselves, and I regret it terribly, and I feel awful about the children. But in the end, the last comment I had from [Attorney General] Janet Reno is when I talked to her on Sunday. I said, "Now, I want you to tell me once more why you believe—not why *they* [the FBI] believe—why *you* believe we should move now rather than wait some more." And she said it's because of the children. They have evidence that those children are still being abused, and that they're in increasingly unsafe conditions, and that they don't think it will get any easier with time, with the passage of time.

April 20/
The New York Times, 4-21:(A)1.

3

Throughout my lifetime, homicide never made the top 10 until 1989. And yet now, homicide is the second-leading cause of death among Americans aged 15 to 25, and more of our teenage boys die from gunshots now than any other cause . . . Neither those who love to hunt nor those who love to shoot weapons in contests nor the framers of the Constitution, when they wrote the Second Amendment, ever envisioned a time when children on our streets would illegally be in possession of weapons designed to kill other people and have more weapons than the people who are supposed to be the policemen. And we'd better stop it if we want to recover our country. [It is time] to get the guns out of the hands of the kids and give our law-enforcement officers a fighting chance to keep the streets safe.

St. Petersburg, Fla., Sept. 24/
The New York Times, 9-25:6.

4

[Supporting the Brady Bill gun-control legislation]: I come from a state [Arkansas] where half the folks have a hunting and fishing license. I can still remember the first day when I was a little boy out in the country putting the can on top of a fence post and shooting a .22 at it. I can still remember the first time I pulled a trigger on a .410 shotgun because I was too little to hold a 12-gauge. This is part of the culture of a big part of America. But we have taken this important part of the life of millions of Americans and turned it into an instrument of maintaining madness. It is crazy. Would I let anybody change that life in America? Not on your life. [But] has that got anything to do with the Brady Bill or assault weapons or whether the police have to go out on the street confronting teenagers who are better armed than they are? Of course not.

At signing of the Brady Bill,
Washington, D.C., Nov. 30/
The New York Times, 12-1:(A)14.

5

This [violent-crime] thing has gotten so serious that we should consider a lot of things that we haven't in the past. The most important thing is there has been a sea change in public attitude. I am convinced that most Americans now understand how profoundly important these crime and

(BILL CLINTON)

violence issues are and how it's time to face them.

To reporters,
Washington, D.C., Dec. 8/
USA Today, 12-9:(A)4.

Charles Colson
Columnist;
Chairman, Prison Fellowship

1

I have seen the dreadful cost of [the prison] system in the faces of thousands of human beings trapped in it. When I was a prisoner, I watched men spend their days lying on their bunks doing nothing, staring into the emptiness—bodies atrophying, souls corroding. Prison talk centered on how they would get even with those who had wronged them or with society in general. I have never been in a place so filled with anger, bitterness, despair, dejection. It is no wonder to me that, after being released, between 66 and 74 percent commit new crimes within four years; the wonder is that the 25 percent do not. The prison experience is brutal, dehumanizing, counterproductive. Of course, prisons do serve one very important function. They separate dangerous offenders from the rest of society. And I should add that the failure of the system is not due to correctional officials. I've been greatly impressed with the high quality of people who serve in corrections—some of the most dedicated public servants I've known . . . We came to believe that prisons are capable of rehabilitating criminals. But rehabilitation proved to be a costly myth. I don't know anyone in corrections today who honestly believes that prisons have a redemptive purpose. Nevertheless, the myth lives on.

At National Press Club,
Washington, D.C., March 11/
Christianity Today, 8-16:30.

John Conyers, Jr.
United States Representative,
D-Michigan

2

[Criticizing proposals to increase by 47 the number of crimes subject to the death penalty]: If you can show me how adding 50 more death-penalty provisions is going to deter one person, then I am for it. Why not 100 more? How about I reach your 100 and I bid 110, and someone else that's tougher on crime is for 150? So what? The one thing that's been proved in my 30 years in this business is that you can't deter people by guaranteeing them that they will go to jail or be executed.

Time, 8-23:25.

Gary Cordner
Authority on policing

3

[Future] technology will help police solve crimes they can't solve today. With a sample of air, for example, an officer might be able to determine who was in a particular room. The nature of crime may also change dramatically as we move to an international, cashless society.

Interview/
U.S. News & World Report,
10-25:74.

Michael A. Corriero
Acting Justice,
State Supreme Court
of New York

4

My job is to protect the public. But how do I do that best? By putting a 14-year-old in jail for one to three to satisfy the D.A.? So then the kid comes out at 17 and now he can't get a job with a felony conviction. Have we really protected society?

The New York Times, 5-25:(A)14.

Richard M. Daley
Mayor of Chicago, Ill.

5

[On his plan to put barriers and cul-de-sacs on streets in high-crime areas]: When you have those types of streets [open-ended where you can go for as many as 30 blocks without encountering a barrier], there's where you have drive-by shootings, there's where you have the rapists. So we're going to cul-de-sac the city . . . When you

(RICHARD M. DALEY)

cul-de-sac, you don't get the burglars driving by. You don't get the armed robberies. People know who is on the street. And then, on the weekends, people can use the street, so it's not a thoroughfare. People can go out there. Kids can play.

Interview, January/
The Washington Post, 2-10:(A)3.

Alfonse M. D'Amato
United States Senator,
R-New York

1

[Advocating Federal jurisdiction in prosecuting gun-related crimes]: It's time for the Federal government to step in and say to the criminals: "Use a gun to commit a crime and we will lock you up and throw away the key. Murder someone with a gun, and you will pay with your life." Now, that's real gun control.

The Washington Post, 11-10:(A)22.

Butler Derrick
United States Representative,
D-South Carolina

2

[Supporting a five-day waiting period for the purchase of handguns]: The waiting period will save lives by providing a cooling-off period that will prevent handgun sales during the heat of passion. [That delay would be] about the same time many of us wait on our dry cleaning.

The Washington Post, 11-11:(A)16.

Robert J. Dole
United States Senator,
R-Kansas

3

[Criticizing U.S. Surgeon General Joycelyn Elders's suggestion that a study be made to determine if now-illegal drugs should be legalized in order to reduce the crime rate]: Americans must be wondering if the Surgeon General is hazardous to our health. I am relieved that the President [Clinton] has disassociated himself from Dr. Elders's remarks, but [I] remain concerned

with this Administration's commitment to fighting drugs.

Dec. 7/
The New York Times, 12-8:(A)11.

Robert F. Drinan
Professor of law,
Georgetown University;
Former United States Representative,
D-Massachusetts

4

There's a streak of violence among us [Americans] that is deep. It's there, like the Rocky Mountains. No other civilized nation is like us.

USA Today, 12-29:(A)2.

Harold Dutton
United States Representative,
D-Texas

5

In Texas, we have this idea that you can mess with my wife and my dog, but don't mess with my pickup or my rifle. The thought is that you can't ever have too many guns, that the more guns you have the safer you will be. I think the reverse is true.

USA Today, 3-8:(A)3.

Marian Wright Edelman
President,
Children's Defense Fund

6

[On youthful violent criminals]: You've got to have law enforcement. People cannot go around killing people. You also have to have gun control—but that's not the long-term answer. There are no prisons that can hold the despair and the hopelessness that is all around us. We've got to talk about prevention . . . productive alternatives . . . jobs, decent education, rebuilding communities . . . decent role models . . . These 13-year-olds are children. What are you solving [if you send] them off to prison, which is just another breeding ground for more crime . . . Give me more jobs rather than more prison cells, and we'll begin to deal with that 13-year-old.

Interview, Washington, D.C./
Los Angeles Times, 11-21:(M)3.

Joycelyn Elders
Surgeon General
of the United States

1

I really feel very strongly that handguns [are] a public-health issue. When you look at the number of young people who die each year from handguns, it's probably more than from anything else. So it *has* to become a public-health issue.

Interview/
The Christian Science Monitor,
11-9:(A)5.

2

I do feel that we would markedly reduce our crime rate if [now-illegal] drugs were legalized. But I don't know all of the ramifications of this. I do feel that we need to do some studies. And some of the countries that have legalized drugs and made it legal, they certainly have shown that there has been a reduction in their crime rate, and there has been no increase in their drug-use rate.

Before National Press Club,
Washington, D.C., Dec. 7/
The New York Times, 12-8:(A)11.

Amitai Etzioni
Sociologist,
George Washington University

3

[On the increase in violent crime in once-safe neighborhoods]: People are worried more. They're worried sick. There is a new level of fright, one that is both overdone and realistic at the same time.

Time, 8-23:29.

Jim Florio
Governor of New Jersey (D)

4

There's got to be some nationalizing of some of the things states are experimenting with [in law enforcement]—for example, when the President [Clinton] very commendably stated there's a need for a national prohibition on assault weapons. When you deal with it on a state-by-

state basis, ultimately you have a hodgepodge, and then you have opportunities for people to circumvent the law.

Interview/
USA Today, 12-29:(A)7.

Louis J. Freeh
Director-designate,
Federal Bureau of Investigation

5

Crime prevention is like health prevention. If we don't innoculate children against diseases, we have epidemics that take a terrible toll. Prevention is one of the most valuable tools in the anti-crime arsenal, and we must use it to help reduce the pandemic of crime that now exists . . . As an FBI agent and prosecutor, I have seen first-hand the terrible poverty and hopelessness in our major urban areas. As a high-school student, I spent a summer working in a health-care and literacy program in a rural area where the grinding poverty was just as bad as in our cities. Such conditions are intolerable, and if we do not attack the root causes of crime and save our children, conditions will be even worse 10 years from now, and we will again have lost much of a new generation.

At Senate Judiciary Committee
hearing on his nomination,
Washington, D.C., July 29/
Los Angeles Times, 7-30:(A)15.

6

We need more [FBI] agents who speak foreign languages and understand other countries and cultures. We need more agents who can operate effectively in this country . . . especially in urban areas . . . We need diversity because without it the FBI cannot function to its maximum potential.

At Senate Judiciary Committee
hearing on his nomination,
Washington, D.C., July 29/
The Washington Post, 7-30:(A)4.

7

[Urging Italians to root out the Mafia organized-crime groups]: No more should the Mafia hang as

(LOUIS J. FREEH)

a millstone around the neck of freedom. Turn them out from the towns and churches where they can be exposed to the light of the law which will sear and destroy them . . . You [in the Mafia] are not men of honor but cowardly assassins of children, thieves who move in the night and greedy merchants of drugs, terrorists and bullies. We do not fear you. We do not respect you. We challenge you and will hunt you down to bring you to justice.

To church crowd,
Palermo, Italy, Dec. 12/
The New York Times, 12-13:(A)3.

Stephen Gale
Authority on terrorism,
University of Pennsylvania

1

[On the recent bombing of the World Trade Center in New York]: The question is: Who's really behind all of it? This [incident] seems to be treated as if it involved a lone group of terrorists who had something against the U.S. and its policy in the Middle East . . . I really don't believe this is just a group of crazies operating all on their own. Terrorism is rarely an act of individual groups that have no interaction with one another.

The Christian Science Monitor,
4-2:7.

Stuart M. Gerson
Acting Attorney General
of the United States

2

[Saying the Second Amendment to the Constitution does not provide for unrestricted, no-waiting-period ownership of handguns]: The framers [of the Constitution] tied an uninfringeable right to bear arms to the protection of the security of the country by a "well-regulated militia." They did so at a time when there was no standing army or organized reserve and where the "militia" was composed of every able-bodied man, each of whom was expected to arm himself for the common defense in war.

Feb. 22/
Los Angeles Times, 2-23:(A)10.

John Goldkamp
Professor of criminal justice,
Temple University

3

[On the idea of offering treatment instead of prison to some drug offenders]: This brings criminal-justice goals and drug-treatment goals together . . . The drug-treatment outcomes look very good . . . The public-safety outcomes look very good. The criminal-justice perspective and drug-treatment perspective are having to learn to come together and link up. It's a real uneasy marriage, but it's the theme in criminal justice today.

Los Angeles Times, 5-17:(A)19.

Thomas P. Griesa
Chief Judge,
United States District Court
for the Southern District
of New York

4

I believe the enforcement of the anti-narcotics laws serves a very important purpose. Even though it is far from successful in any ideal sense, it is society's way of doing the best it can to combat this deadly plague of a criminal nature. Beyond any statistical or tangible results, there is a moral value in having society take a stand against this.

April 16/
The New York Times,
4-17:7.

Susan Hendricks
Deputy director of litigation,
New York Legal Aid Society

5

People who live in communities that have close exposure to the police have always been somewhat distrustful of the police. But with expanded media coverage and video tape, police conduct is now more a part of what the [general] public knows.

The New York Times,
2-15:(A)8.

Cameron Hopkins·
Editor-in-chief,
Firearms Marketing Group

1

1993 was a banner year for the gun industry, especially for handguns and self-defense shotguns. The Rodney King beating [which was followed later by street riots in Los Angeles] and Hurricane Andrew really awakened a lot of Americans to the fact that in catastrophic times, the police won't be there to protect you.

Time, 12-20:22.

Henry J. Hyde
United States Representative,
R-Illinois

2

[On gun control]: The real gulf between points of view is geographic, not necessarily political. If you're from a rural area or the far West, your gun takes on an almost theological significance.

USA Today, 12-29:(A)2.

Jesse L. Jackson
Civil-rights leader

3

We lose more lives annually to the crime of blacks killing blacks than the sum total of lynching in the entire history of the country . . . If there had been as many blacks killed by whites, or whites killed by blacks, there'd be riots. But since it's blacks on blacks, there's a cultural concession to the killing.

USA Today,
10-28:(A)2.

Rob Jones
President,
Virginia Education Association

4

Violence is a societal problem which comes to school. Our increasingly violent schools are reflective of an increasingly violent society.

News conference,
Washington, D.C., Jan. 14/
The New York Times,
1-15:(A)8.

Frank Jordan
Mayor of San Francisco, Calif.

5

[On gun control]: Law enforcement is frustrated because they are being overpowered by the firepower [in the hands of criminals] on the streets. Police officers see this and say, "Where is this all going to end?" . . . We're not going to say guns are going to be outlawed, but there has to be some realistic balances. Guns should be licensed and registered just like your vehicles. If we can get that, it would be a major, major accomplishment.

Interview/
USA Today, 12-29:(A)7.

Nicholas deB. Katzenbach
Former Attorney General
of the United States

6

[On criticism of new Attorney General Janet Reno's ordering an FBI assault on a Waco, Texas, cult compound which resulted in the deaths of many cultists and children]: When you're new in office, you put more confidence in the judgment of the people who have been there a long time. [But] you have to learn to discount that. I don't really blame Janet Reno for taking that advice [to assault the compound]. I believe that if she had been in office for two years, she would not have done what she did. She would have asked a lot more questions.

Interview/
The New York Times, 10-26:(A)10.

Mark Kleiman
Associate professor
of public policy,
Kennedy School of Government,
Harvard University

7

The [coming] effort to control drug abuse is not a [Persian Gulf war] Desert Storm. It is what [the late President John] Kennedy called "a long, twilight struggle." It calls for patience rather than enthusiasm, endurance rather than animation, stamina rather than speed.

The Christian Science Monitor,
5-3:3.

(MARK KLEIMAN)

1

[On Surgeon General Joycelyn Elders's suggestion that legalizing now-illegal drugs might be an acceptable way to reduce crime]: Legalization is not an issue anyone wants to discuss seriously, because then you confront Americans with their own drug habits, notably alcohol and tobacco . . . Which drug is causing the most damage now [in terms of health, monetary costs to society and impact on families]? The first one has to be alcohol, and what makes people think legalization [of alcohol] has been an answer?

The Christian Science Monitor,
12-13:8.

Stephen Klineberg
Sociologist, Rice University

2

There's an absolutely solid, growing sense that we've got to do something about all those guns [in circulation]. Most Americans are against taking away the rights of individuals to own a gun. But what they're increasingly demanding is rational control over guns.

Time, 12-20:20.

David B. Kopel
Analyst, Cato Institute

3

[On the proposed Brady Bill's provision of a waiting period before purchase of a handgun is permitted]: There has never been a study which has found any statistically noticeable reduction in gun crime associated with a waiting period. Can anyone seriously believe that people who sell cocaine by the pound will not know where to obtain an illegal handgun? That a waiting period on guns will succeed where a complete prohibition on drugs has failed?

The New York Times, 11-23:(A)15.

David B. Kopel
Scholar,
Independence Institute

4

The nation was born in violent revolution. You can't say from our history that violence is always wrong.

USA Today, 12-29:(A)2.

Wayne LaPierre
Executive vice president,
National Rife Association

5

[Criticizing a proposed Federal law to ban the sale of more than one handgun a month to an individual]: It's another cheap political stunt from politicians too weak to attack criminals, but brave when it comes to attacking honest people. One gun a month won't work. Washington [D.C.] already has no guns a month and it has streets like butcher shops.

Jan. 14/
The New York Times, 1-15:(A)8.

6

[Criticizing a recent poll that showed a majority of Americans in favor of stricter gun-control laws]: You can get anything you want out of a poll. The questions were geared to get pro-gun-control results. If you asked, "Will more gun control reduce violent crime?" or "Do Americans have a Constitutional right to own a gun?" you'd get much different results.

USA Today, 3-17:(A)1.

7

People talk about a groundswell [against the NRA's opposition to gun-control laws]. Where is it? The last time I looked, a law in Virginia and a law in New Jersey isn't a groundswell . . . You've got a couple of Democratic [Party] consultants like [James] Carville telling other Democratic consultants to go after guns. We'll see who's right about that [in the elections] next fall. Despite what some of these professional consultants want to tell their candidates, the districts back home haven't changed. Seventy million people own guns, half the households have firearms and 20 million people buy hunting licenses. I'll take that base any day.

The Washington Post, 10-18:(A)8,9.

8

The whole debate over gun control is a public fraud in terms of doing anything in the world that affects violent criminals. What's missing from

(WAYNE LAPIERRE)

this whole debate is what we all know works: confronting violent criminals and taking them off the street. That's what politicians don't have the will to do, but that's what the American public is demanding.

Time, 12-20:26.

John Major
Prime Minister
of the United Kingdom

1

[On the arrest of two 10-year-olds for the murder of a 2-year-old in Britain]: I feel strongly that society needs to condemn a little more and "understand" a little less.

Newsweek, 3-8:17.

James Marquart
Professor of criminal justice,
Sam Houston State University

2

When people are besieged with new reports of crime every day, the perception grows that, by golly, maybe the cops are ineffective. It reinforces the perception of the criminal-justice system not working, and the next thing you know, people are mobilizing to protect themselves.

Time, 8-23:32.

Marc Mauer
Assistant director,
The Sentencing Project,
Washington, D.C.

3

We are in the midst of a vicious cycle. We have high crime rates, and the response of the politicians is to build more prisons. The more money we put into prisons means less money into programs that might prevent crime in the first place. But they think, if we build a few more prisons, we can start to make a dent in crime . . . If we look at countries with lower crime rates, such as Western Europe or Scandinavian countries, they don't achieve lower rates by having greater numbers of people in prison. What they have is a

decent standard of living for most people, and a safety net for them above the poverty line.

The Christian Science Monitor,
11-19:4.

Gerald W. McEntee
President,
American Federation of State,
County and Municipal Employees

4

[Criticizing the conditions under which prison guards and other prison employees work]: In the rush to bring public light to the condition of inmates and invest them with rights, a grave injustice has been done the thousands of men and women who, every day of their working lives, are often as much a prisoner as those who have been incarcerated.

Los Angeles Times, 5-27:(A)5.

Thomas R. Morris
President,
Emory and Henry College

5

The NRA is seeing the middle ground on gun control shift away from it. People are conceding that there are legitimate restrictions that can be put on gun rights. Ten years ago, [Virginia state] Assembly members wouldn't dare cross the NRA . . . Now they [the NRA] can no longer draw a line in the sand and know that the legislature won't cross it.

The Washington Post, 2-26:(A)8.

Carol Moseley-Braun
United States Senator,
D-Illinois

6

Responsible gun owners should address the carnage that is going on in our communities. For the NRA to continue to whipsaw well-meaning people into protecting untenable positions [against gun-control legislation] out of fear that the Constitution is going to be messed with is wrong. The call and the challenge now is to take the issue of gun control to the mainstream, to show the American people that responsible gun control is

(CAROL MOSELEY-BRAUN)

not inconsistent with the Second Amendment.
Interview, Washington, D.C./
Los Angeles Times, 10-31:(M)3.

Daniel Patrick Moynihan
United States Senator,
D-New York

1

It seems there is always a certain amount of crime in a society. You need to know what is deviant in order to know what is not. But when you get too much, you can always start to say that's not really so bad. Pretty soon, you are getting used to behavior that's not good for you at all.
Before Association for a Better New York/
USA Today, 9-10:(A)13.

Jeffrey Muchnick
Legislative director,
Coalition to Stop Gun Violence

2

The public is finally fed up with Congress listening to the NRA. You *can* vote for gun control and survive [in Congress]. The public, in fact, will reward you if you do.
Newsweek, 12-6:20.

Patrick V. Murphy
Former Commissioner of Police
of New York, N.Y.

3

[On the increase in corrupt police officers]: The drug money is so enormous, it's affecting local, state and Federal law enforcement. Even the FBI—and that's the last straw.
USA Today, 9-30:(A)2.

Dee Dee Myers
Press Secretary to
President of the United States
Bill Clinton

4

[President Clinton believes] that the crime issue threatens the rest of his domestic agenda,

that if we don't do something about crime it threatens health-care reform, job creation and economic growth, welfare reform and a number of the other items that he believes are important. So certainly, crime is at the forefront of his domestic agenda, but it works in conjunction with many of the other issues that he feels very strongly about, and he's going to certainly be talking about it and working with members of Congress, working with the local Mayors and police chiefs and people around the country to try to do something about not only crime but the decaying social structure that is some of the underpinning causes of crime.
Washington, D.C., Dec. 9/
The New York Times, 12-10:(A)12.

Don Nickles
United States Senator,
R-Oklahoma

5

[Criticizing Surgeon General Joycelyn Elders's suggestion that legalizing now-illegal drugs should be looked into as a way to bring down the crime rate]: I think it's outrageous for the nation's top health official to talk about legalizing drugs. What kind of message does that send to parents, teachers and law-enforcement officers who have spent a lifetime teaching young people that drugs can kill them, ruin their minds and ruin their futures.
Dec. 7/
The Washington Post, 12-8:(A)3.

Ruben Ortega
Chief of Police
of Salt Lake City, Utah

6

The frustrations of citizens and police have reached a point of no confidence in a system that repeatedly puts dangerous felons back on the street.
Time, 12-20:24.

Edward Peeples
Sociologist,
Virginia Commonwealth University

7

It used to be beer or a cigarette or sex that kids would use to mark their entry into manhood.

(EDWARD PEEPLES)

Now they've got to tote a piece [a gun]. Our culture is developing new ways of being a man.

USA Today, 12-29:(A)2.

Colin L. Powell
General, United States Army;
Chairman, Joint Chiefs of Staff

1

I've been very outspoken on drugs. I tell lots of stories about how we deal with drugs in the military through testing and through a zero-tolerance attitude, which we can do in the military. I'm not sure you can do it in a school system somewhere in one of our big cities. We have the advantage of military law and regulation, and we throw you out. But you can't throw them out of a big city.

Interview, Washington, D.C./
U.S. News & World Report,
9-20:51.

Marc Racicot
Governor of Montana (R)

2

[On gun-control laws]: Individual rights such as . . . the right to bear arms have a hallowed and almost sanctified history that is pretty deeply ingrained in Americans. So you have to be able to establish a sound and persuasive case to talk about any alteration of them. A lot of the questions we try to legislate ultimately can only be settled in the hearts of people—a free people recognizing their own individual responsibilities.

Interview/
USA Today, 12-29:(A)7.

Myrna Raeder
Chairman,
criminal justice committee
on Federal rules of procedure
and evidence,
American Bar Association

3

[On a jury's convicting two and acquitting two Los Angeles police officers in the Federal trial involving the police beating of black suspect Rodney King]: By weighing each count on its merit in a complex case like this, the jury showed our legal system can deal with big issues with subtlety and fairness under great pressure . . . The case sends a signal to police everywhere that are not being sensitive to their relationships with the minority community. It bodes strongly for sweeping changes both in training and policy of police forces across the country.

The Christian Science Monitor,
4-19:3.

Adrian Raine
Psychologist,
University of Southern California

4

It is irrefutably the case that biologic and genetic factors play a role [in violent criminal behavior]. That is beyond scientific question. If we ignore that over the next few decades, then we will never ever rid society [of violence].

Los Angeles Times, 12-20:(A)14.

William H. Rehnquist
Chief Justice
of the United States

5

The law by itself is not going to solve the problems of drugs and violence. [These are] questions of public policy which must be decided not by lawyers, judges or other experts, but by the popularly elected branches of government.

Speech, June/
The New York Times,
7-8:(A)13.

Albert Reiss
Sociologist,
Yale University

6

There are lots of things that we don't know [about the causes of violence]. What is it that accounts for the fact that we [the U.S.] have more interpersonal violence [than other nations], and that it is disproportionately among blacks? That's a puzzle. And why is it that women have so much less homicide, but suicide ranks higher?

(ALBERT REISS)

If you think we know the answers to all those questions, then there is no reason to do research.

Los Angeles Times, 12-20:(A)14.

Janet Reno
Attorney General-designate
of the United States

1

[As State Attorney in Dade County, Florida,] I have watched people at my office who we have prosecuted . . . We have gotten the death penalty, and to find those people still in prison without that penalty carried out after 10 and 13 and 15 years makes a mockery of the justice system and makes a mockery of what we try to do. It makes no sense.

At Senate Judiciary Committee
hearing on her nomination,
Washington, D.C., March 9/
The Washington Post, 3-10:(A)3.

Janet Reno
Attorney General
of the United States

2

Bad people are few and far between. [While hard-core criminals must be] put away for as long as we can ever get them put away, there are other people that have gone over to the realm of the bad that we can pull back. Most of those juvenile delinquents that are causing so many of the crime problems that we see basically want to be self-respecting people who can participate and contribute and be constructive in their communities. But they kept taking the wrong road, they kept being beat down. It's the police officers who are bringing them back.

At Police Foundation conference,
Washington, D.C., April 8/
Los Angeles Times, 4-9:(A)31.

3

[Saying she favors help for drug offenders rather than mandatory minimum prison sentences]: [There should be] alternative sanctions that work like a carrot-and-stick approach, a program that says, look, you need job training and placement because, if you come back out into the community, you're not going to have the resources or ability to cope. This nation has got to make sure that every person in America who wants drug treatment, who's asking for it, who's on a waiting list, gets it.

Before National Summit
on U.S. Drug Policy,
Washington, D.C., May 7/
The Washington Post, 5-8:(A)4.

4

What we're faced with in America now is that the dangerous offenders are getting out because other offenders are in [prison] on minimum mandatories [sentences] for non-violent offenses. What we all have to do is use our prison cells to house the truly dangerous offenders, the major traffickers, the major distributors [of drugs]. In other words, we need to have a punishment that fits the crime. We've got to have alternative sentences. We've got to explore preventative programs.

Interview,
Washington, D.C., July 2/
Time, 7-12:24.

5

I've never heard of comprehensive programs that provided a balance between punishment and [crime] prevention. I think one of the keys to any crime-prevention program that's got to be developed is to focus on punishment—to let people know that there is a sanction and a punishment for hurting others. Juveniles as well as adults need to know they're going to be punished for their violent acts. What has too often happened in the past is that people have threatened punishment but have failed to carry it out. It's imperative in any initiative that is undertaken that punishment be real and that there be truth in sentencing, and that the truly dangerous offenders—the recidivists and the career criminals—be put away and kept away.

Interview, Washington, D.C.,/
Los Angeles Times, 7-4:(M)3.

(JANET RENO)

1

We cannot respond [to violent crime] with demagogic promises to build more jails and put all the criminals away. We must never forget the awesome power of the Federal government. And we must harness that power to make sure that innocent people are not charged or even tainted by our actions, and that the guilty are convicted according to principles of strict due process and fair play, and with adherence to our Constitution.

Vogue, August:263.

2

More than 140 Federal agencies are responsible for enforcing 4,100 Federal criminal laws. Most Federal crimes involve violations of several laws and fall under the jurisdiction of several agencies. A drug case may involve violations of financial, firearms, immigration and customs law, as well as drug statutes. Unfortunately, too many cooks spoil the broth. Agencies squabble over turf, fail to cooperate or delay matters while attempting to agree on common policies. The first step in consolidating law-enforcement efforts will be major structural changes to integrate drug-enforcement efforts of the DEA and the FBI. This will create savings in administrative and support functions such as laboratories, legal services, training facilities and administration. Most important, the Federal government will get a much more powerful weapon in its fight against crime.

At U.S. Department of Justice,
Washington, D.C., Sept. 9/
The Washington Post, 9-10:(A)24.

3

I think it's important to understand . . . that there is no one single answer to the problem of violence. There is no one simple answer; there is no one inexpensive answer. It has got to be looked at in terms of a comprehensive effort, and it's clear to me that we've got to have enough prisons to house the truly dangerous people for the length of time the judges are sentencing them, both in state and Federal courts. We've got to have boot camps for youngsters who commit violent crimes, that give them an opportunity to know that there is no excuse for putting a gun up beside somebody's head and hurting them—not poverty, not broken homes, nothing excuses hurting people—and that there's going to be punishment . . . It's also clear . . . that the time has come to focus on a comprehensive prevention effort. First, we've got to make sure that our parents are old enough, wise enough and financially able enough to take care of their children and that they are taught parenting skills that enable them to be responsible parents and that they have the time to be with their children to be responsible parents.

Before Senate Commerce, Science
and Transportation Committee,
Washington, D.C., Oct. 20/
The Washington Post, 10-21:(A)30.

4

I think it should be at least as hard to get a license to possess a gun as it is to drive an automobile. I don't think somebody should have a gun unless they can demonstrate that they know how to safely and lawfully use it, that they're capable of safely and lawfully using it, and that they're willing to safely and lawfully use it.

News conference,
Washington, D.C., Dec. 9/
The New York Times, 12-10:(A)12.

Frank Reynolds
Presiding Judge,
Juvenile Court
of Philadelphia, Pa.

5

One thing is certain now about Juvenile Court. When a child comes through here, he will be dealt with. When I say he will be "dealt with," that doesn't necessarily mean we're going to lock him up. It means that we are going to find out exactly what his problems are, what are the issues that led him to commit a crime in the first place. We're not just going to see him and send him away. I believe you have to take that approach because, if you ignore children at the outset of their young criminal lives, you're going to have to send them over to adult court when they get to be 15 or 16.

Interview/
Los Angeles Times, 8-25:(A)18.

Ann Richards
Governor of Texas (D)
1

It is time to recognize that these assault-type weapons are not something that fits into the good old Texas view of gun ownership. I'm a gun owner myself; I grew up hunting . . . But these assault weapons aren't for anything but killing people.

USA Today, 3-8:(A)3.

Stanton E. Samenow
Psychologist;
Authority on criminal behavior
2

[On the trend of treating violent youths as adults in court]: I'd say 14 or 16, 13 or 12, these kids know right from wrong. But at the time they're committing an act, they're able to shut off such considerations to do what they want to do. That's the chilling thing. Kids develop conscience in the Oedipal years. That's 3 to 5 years of age.

The New York Times, 12-3:(B)9.

Barbara Shaw
Executive director,
Illinois Council for the
Prevention of Violence
3

Women are being encouraged to buy guns to protect themselves. That's the hardest argument to deal with because the fear can be very real. The gun can create an aura of control. But in reality, that isn't the case.

Time, 12-20:24.

Dewey R. Stokes
President,
Fraternal Order of Police
4

[On the proposed Brady Bill's provision of a waiting period before purchase of a handgun is permitted]: The legislation will not by itself solve the problem of handgun violence. What it will do, however, is give the law-enforcement community a very valuable and effective tool to deter the purchase of a handgun by someone who is not qualified to possess one.

Before Congressional subcommittee,
Washington, D.C./
The New York Times, 11-23:(A)15.

Keith Stroup
Executive director,
National Criminal Defense Lawyers
5

[On U.S. Attorney General Janet Reno's questioning the desirability of long mandatory minimum prison sentences for low-level drug offenders]: [This] is the most promising development I've heard about in the new [Clinton] Administration. [Until recently,] I was not aware of anyone in Congress who was willing to even propose the elimination of minimum mandatories. But having the Attorney General question the wisdom of such sentences is terribly important. Individual members of Congress who may want to do the right thing are now not going to worry about being labeled soft on crime.

May 3/
The Washington Post, 5-4:(A)9.

Leonard Supenski
Colonel,
Baltimore County (Md.)
Police Department
6

The reality that bothers me is there is no self-control, no self-policing, in the gun industry. The premise seems to be that if they've got the right to do something, then that's the right thing to do.

The Atlantic, January:50.

Robert W. Sweet
Judge,
United States District Court
for the Southern District
of New York
7

The present policy of trying to prohibit [illegal] drugs through the use of criminal law is a mistake. It's a policy that's not working. It's not cut-

(ROBERT W. SWEET)

ting down drug use. The best way to do this is through education and treatment.

The New York Times, 4-17:7.

Fred Thomas
Chief of Police
of Washington, D.C.

1

[Washington, D.C.,] is not the murder capital of the world. Don't believe it. The media need to get the facts straight . . . The media has a responsibility to report the news and they have the right to do that. But when you coin a phrase that the city is the murder capital . . . that portrays to the world that this is the worst place in the world and that you stand a chance of being killed if you come here . . . That is certainly not the case.

At his swearing-in ceremony
and in interview,
Washington, D.C., Jan. 8/
The Washington Post, 1-9:(B)1.

2

Law enforcement tends to be a really closed society. We're kind of myopic in our view of everything. We think if you don't wear a uniform, you don't know anything, you can't do anything. That's absolutely nonsense. The whole world operates, and only a few people have uniforms on. We need to admit that we don't know everything.

Interview/
The Washington Post, 2-15:(A)12.

Robert Turner
Associate director,
Center for National Security Law,
University of Virginia

3

[On the recent terrorist bombing of New York's World Trade Center]: I think it's important to send the message that the people who did it will not benefit from the experience. This could have been the worst terrorist incident in modern history . . . and if people believe the U.S. is a

sitting duck for terrorism, and can't do anything about it or is unwilling to use its resources to deal effectively with it, then I don't think this would be the end of it.

The Christian Science Monitor,
3-15:3.

Adam Walinsky
Lawyer;
Social activist

4

[Supporting a proposal that college students pay back government loans by serving four years on a local "police corps" following graduation]: The police corps starts from the premise that we have a national crisis of violence and disorder [that] is getting dramatically worse with every passing year. The corps is an attempt to mobilize the talents and energies which we have always depended on at times of national crises. Always before when we've had a war or a challenge to the very existence of the country, we've engaged the best talents of our most committed young people . . . It was only after the unprecedented wave of violence that washed over the cities in the late '70s that I realized that a collapse of urban order and civic order was directly connected to a tremendous shortfall in the strength of the police . . . Is the alternative to go on locking car doors every time you drive to your mother's house? Is the alternative, as so many people are doing, spending . . . thousands of dollars on home entertainment centers because people don't like the discomfort of going out at night? Is the alternative continuing to turn on the local news to watch a constant blood bath? All of these things are completely unacceptable. This is a great country, but it's one that was founded on courage and self-respect—not on hiding in holes, figuring out new ways to lock up your house and alarm your car.

Interview, New York, N.Y./
Los Angeles Times, 1-26:(A)5.

Samuel Walker
Professor of criminal justice,
University of Nebraska,
Omaha

5

Civilian review of police conduct [through civilian-review boards] was an idea that had died

(SAMUEL WALKER)

and gone to heaven in the 1960s. But it was reborn in the '70s, and it really caught on in the mid-'80s . . . Everyone's been so busy just getting civilian review off the ground that no one's really studied the process. But now we're entering a second phase in which people will examine what works and why.

The Christian Science Monitor,
11-22:14.

Eddie N. Williams
President,
Joint Center for Political
and Economic Studies

1

One of the most staggering statistics I have read recently indicated that, between 1985 and 1990, the number of young black men killed by firearms almost doubled. And in 1990 alone, more black males between the ages of 15 and 35 died of gunshot wounds than were killed in the entire Vietnam war! And most of them were killed by other black males. I realize that older folks also kill, but nowhere is the data more shocking than in the black community. The facts speak for themselves. When 30 to 40 percent of elementary schoolchildren in Boston, Chicago and D.C. report that they have personally witnessed a shooting or a stabbing, it is time to act. As a society, we must end what is literally an urban arms race and a devastating cycle of violence. We must stop the killing now.

At annual dinner of Joint Center
for Political and Economic Studies,
March 30/
The Washington Post, 4-6:(A)20.

James Q. Wilson
Professor of management
and public policy,
University of California,
Los Angeles

2

The most significant thing in the last half-century has been the dramatic expansion in personal freedom and personal mobility, individual

rights, the reorienting of culture around individuals. We obviously value that. But like all human gains, it has been purchased at a price. Most people faced with greater freedom from family, law, village, clan, have used it for good purposes—artistic expression, economic entrepreneurship, self-expression—but a small fraction of people have used it for bad purposes. So just as we have had an artistic and economic explosion, we have had a crime explosion. I think the two are indissolubly entwined. When that prosperity puts cars, drugs and guns into the hands of even relatively poor 18-year-olds, young people can do a great deal more damage today than they could in the 1940s or 1950s.

Interview/
Time, 8-23:31.

Pete Wilson
Governor of California (R)

3

Gun control is likely to generate a great deal of heated political rhetoric [in 1994]. We have to make sure, though, that it doesn't overshadow the really obvious fact that most of the damage done with guns is done by criminals, and that so-called gun control is not a panacea for stopping violent crime. You've got to be sure that you are targeting your effort where it is likely to produce the greatest protection for the law-abiding innocent citizens.

Interview/
USA Today, 12-29:(A)7.

Marvin Wolfgang
Criminologist,
University of Pennsylvania

4

[On youths who commit violent crimes]: A child of 14 does have a sense of right and wrong similar to an adult's . . . [but] he's in a subculture in which violence is expected, tolerated and in some cases required. The 25-year-old may be in the same situation but has been exposed to more environmental chances of disrupting that connection.

The New York Times, 12-3:(B)9.

75

Defense • The Military

Les Aspin
Secretary of Defense-designate
of the United States

1

The current situation in Congress [on defense] right now is not a split between hawks and doves, between liberals and conservatives, between Democrats and Republicans. It's between those people that have military bases and facilities in their districts and those that don't . . . If you don't have any impact at home on that, you're likely to want to [cut defense spending] very quickly and get a big chunk of money and spend it somewhere else. [But] . . . with people who have military bases, they're saying: "Whoa, time out, not so fast [in cutting spending and closing bases], you're talking about jobs here."

At Senate Armed Services Committee
hearing on his nomination,
Washington, D.C., Jan. 7/
Los Angeles Times, 1-8: (A)13.

Les Aspin
Secretary of Defense
of the United States

2

[On his decision to allow women to fly military combat missions and his proposals to permit women to take part in a wider range of combat roles]: The steps we are taking today are historic. The results of all this will be that the services will be able to call upon a much larger pool of talent to perform the vital tasks that our military forces must perform . . . Right now, we're not able to do that.

News conference, April 28/
The Washington Post, 4-29:(A)1.

3

[Announcing the end of the "Star Wars" space defense program]: These changes are possible because of the end of a battle that had raged in Washington for over a decade over the best way to avoid nuclear war. Like many Washington battles, that wasn't decided on the merits. It just went on so long that circumstances changed the terms of the debate. The fate of "Star Wars" was sealed by the collapse of the Soviet Union.

News conference,
Washington, D.C., May 13/
Los Angeles Times, 5-14:(A)1.

4

We can't hang a "closed for remodeling" sign on the door [of the armed forces] while we complete the resizing and reshaping of our forces in the post-Cold War, post-Soviet world. Our forces have to be ready to fight every day.

News conference,
Washington, D.C., May 19/
The New York Times, 5-20:(A)8.

5

[On the recent controversy between President Clinton and the military on the issue of homosexuals in the armed forces]: In a very interesting way, working out this whole thing has helped bring about a better relationship between Bill Clinton and at least the senior uniformed military. If you work something out together, it sometimes creates a certain amount of togetherness. I think that's what happened. [It] created a bond.

Interview/Newsweek, 8-2:4.

6

The United States must field military forces that can fight and win two major regional conflicts, and nearly simultaneously. If our forces are fighting in one major regional conflict, we don't want a second potential aggressor to be tempted to launch an attack somewhere else in the world because he believes the United States can't respond to an attack on an ally or friend. We can and we will.

Before International Institute
for Strategic Studies,
Brussels, Belgium, Sept. 12/
Los Angeles Times, 9-13:(A)4.

(LES ASPIN)

1

[On new Pentagon don't ask-don't tell rules permitting homosexuals in the military only if they keep a low profile about their orientation]: I would not say that the policy that we are implementing here today is the policy that will be forever. Attitudes on this issue have changed a lot in the [last] four or five years. Presumably, that change has not stopped. And if changes occur, I would anticipate that further changes might occur in the military.

News conference,
Washington, D.C., Dec. 22/
The New York Times, 12-23:(A)11.

Norman R. Augustine
Chairman,
Martin Marietta Corporation

2

The acquisition process [at the Pentagon] is broken, has been broken and probably will stay broken. The problem is everybody's in charge of everything, and no one's in charge of anything. I don't think there's a person alive today who can fix the system.

U.S. News & World Report,
9-13:52.

3

We must ensure that our defense industrial base remains capable of supplying the hardware that will be needed by our nation's fighting forces in the future. This is a complicated task in the era of the "come as you are war," when geopolitical circumstances literally shift overnight but defense industrial bases are rebuilt only over decades. One result of rapidly declining U.S. military procurement is an extraordinary degree of excess capacity. This ultimately will be resolved in one of two ways: through consolidation of healthy defense firms, or eventual bankruptcy. Consequently, the trend toward consolidation must accelerate . . . Pentagon officials are today arguing—correctly, I believe—for a defense industry with far fewer, more solvent and more efficient participants. One misconception about defense firms is that they operate within the free-

enterprise system. In fact, they are in a *monopsony* market, where companies bid for the business of one buyer, the government, which has overwhelming power to control the market . . . It is time to reshape our antitrust laws as they apply to firms engaged in national security . . . [We should introduce] reforms that encourage consolidation of our defense industry and the preservation of this most critical national asset.

Before antitrust section,
American Bar Association/
Los Angeles Times, 9-28:(B)7.

Haley Barbour
Chairman,
Republican National Committee

4

Certainly, the end of the Cold War should allow us to have a strong national-security apparatus for less money. We need to do that [reduce defense spending], but we need to be very careful that we don't do like we did in the inter-war years. We are still the one superpower in the world, and it's in our interest and the interest of world peace if we continue to be the one superpower.

Interview/
USA Today, 3-3:(A)13.

Carolyn Becraft
Authority on women
in the military,
Women's Research
and Education Institute

5

[On the Navy's proposal to allow women to serve on previously men-only combat ships]: The Navy desperately needs to do something positive for women. The news for women in the past two years [involving sexual harassment by male Naval officers] has been so bad. This is something that [the Navy] could have done long ago, but they should be given credit for having taken at least an interim step here. But it should be seen as an interim step to opening more opportunities.

Los Angeles Times,
4-2:(A)4.

77

Jesse Brown
Secretary of Veterans Affairs
of the United States

1

[Saying he is not taking a public position on whether the ban on homosexuals in the military should be lifted]: I am the Secretary of Veterans Affairs. It is my duty to ensure that any person who receives an honorable discharge, regardless of their sexual orientation, receives all the benefits to which he or she is entitled . . . The only thing I'm saying is that whole question has to do with people who are serving in the military. I deal with people once they are discharged from the military, so it does not matter to me if a person is gay or straight. If they have an honorable discharge, I'm going to make sure they get everything they are entitled to.

At National Press Club,
Washington, D.C., May 13/
The Washington Post, 5-14:(A)29.

George Bush
President of the United States

2

Military force is never a tool to be used lightly, or universally. In some circumstances it may be essential. In others, counter-productive. I know that many people would like to find some formula, some easy formula to apply, to tell us with precision when and where to intervene with force . . . But in every case involving the use of force, it will be essential to have a clear and achievable mission, a realistic plan for accomplishing the mission, and criteria no less realistic for withdrawing U.S. forces once the mission is complete. Only if we keep these principles in mind will the potential sacrifice be one that can be explained and justified.

At U.S. Military Academy,
West Point, N.Y., Jan. 5/
The New York Times, 1-6:(A)5.

Dick Cheney
Secretary of Defense
of the United States

3

Becoming Secretary of Defense forces you, if not to adopt a pessimistic view of the world, at least to always be aware of—or thinking about—how things can go wrong . . . If there's anybody in government who ought to be thinking about worst-case scenarios, it's the person who sits in this job. You always have to be conscious in this job of the 30,000 nuclear warheads that are still stockpiled inside the Russian Republic and some of the other [former Soviet] republics. It is a sobering responsibility.

Interview,
Washington, D.C., Jan. 4/
Los Angeles Times, 1-5:(A)14.

4

The thing that Les [Aspin, the new Secretary of Defense in the forthcoming Clinton Administration] will have to guard against is the enormous temptation of all those guys on [Capitol] Hill who will want to cut [defense spending] in a way that is not based on any consideration of maintaining our military capability but really is based on considerations that should not be part of the equation.

Interview,
Washington, D.C., Jan. 4/
Los Angeles Times, 1-5:(A)14.

Bill Clinton
President-elect
of the United States

5

[On the use of military force internationally]: I think it's justified when our vital interests or our commitments are at stake, when there is a clear military objective and when we feel that we can achieve that objective within a reasonable amount of time at an acceptable cost.

Interview, Little Rock, Ark./
U.S. News & World Report,
1-25:42.

Bill Clinton
President of the United States

6

The issue is not whether there should be homosexuals in the military. Everyone concedes that there are. The issue is whether men and

(BILL CLINTON)

women who can and have served with real distinction should be excluded from military service solely on the basis of their status [as homosexuals]. And I believe they should not. The principle on which I base this position is this: I believe that American citizens who want to serve their country should be able to do so unless their conduct disqualifies them from doing so. Military life is fundamentally different from civilian society. It necessarily has a different and stricter code of conduct, even a different code of justice. Nonetheless, individuals who are prepared to accept all necessary restrictions on their behavior, many of which would be intolerable in civilian society, should be able to serve their country honorably and well.

News conference,
Washington, D.C., Jan. 29/
The New York Times, 1-30:6.

1

[The military services] stand as one of modern history's great successes. Every color, every background, every region in our society is represented . . . It's constantly adapted to change, and always rising to the challenge of change.

Aboard U.S.S. Theodore Roosevelt,
March 12/
Los Angeles Times, 3-13:(A)20.

2

[On his cutbacks in military spending]: This isn't downsizing for its own sake. This is rightsizing for security . . . As long as I am your President, you and the other men and women in uniform will continue to be the best trained, the best prepared, the best equipped fighting force in the world. There is no single decision I take more seriously than those involving the use of force.

Aboard U.S.S. Theodore Roosevelt,
March 12/
The New York Times, 3-13:7.

3

[On cutbacks in defense spending]: I'm not taking another look at the cuts at this time. Let me remind you that basically I think we have still presented a responsible defense budget. But what I am doing is trying to make sure that we can fulfill the missions that we have to fulfill based on any projected developments within the confines of that budget as it's staged over the next five years. And we'll be able to constantly review that. Obviously these budgets are passed every year for five years in the future. And I expect, to whatever extent the world is uncertain, we'll have to be more vigilant in reviewing what our commitments are.

News conference,
Washington, D.C., March 23/
The New York Times, 3-24:(A)6.

4

[On homosexuals in the military]: If you can discriminate against people in terms of whether they get into the service or not, based on not what they are but what they say they are, then I would think you could make appropriate distinctions on duty assignments once they're in. The courts have historically given quite wide berths to the military to make judgments of that kind in terms of duty assignments.

News conference,
Washington, D.C., March 23/
The New York Times, 3-24:(A)6.

5

There are and always have been homosexuals in the military. The question is whether they should be kicked out, not because of what they do but because of who they are. My view is, people should be judged on their conduct. I have not called for any change in the Uniform Code of Conduct. I simply believe if people work hard, play by the rules and serve, they ought to be able to serve. That does not imply that the rest of the society agrees with the lifestyle, but you just accept as a fact that there are in every country, and always have been, homosexuals who are capable of honoring their country, laying down their lives for their country, and serving. And they should be judged based on their behavior, not their lifestyle . . . Most Americans believe if you don't ask and you don't say and you're not forced to confront it, [homosexuals] should be able to serve. Most Americans believe that the gay lifestyle should not be promoted by the military or anybody else in this country. The issue is a narrow one: Should you be able to acknowledge, if asked, that you are homosexual? And if you don't do anything wrong, should you be booted from the military? We are trying to work this out so that our country does not . . . appear to be endorsing a gay lifestyle, but we accept people as people and give them a chance to serve if they play by the rules. I think that is the tough issue for us. And I think we're very close to resolving it.

Broadcast "town hall" meeting,
Washington, D.C./
"CBS Morning News," CBS-TV, 5-27.

1

[On protests against his Memorial Day visit to the Vietnam Veterans Memorial because of his having evaded the draft and his anti-war protests during U.S. involvement in the Vietnam war]: To all of you who are shouting, I have heard you. I ask you now to hear me. I have heard you. Some have suggested that it is wrong for me to be here with you today because I did not agree a quarter of a century ago with the decision made to send the young men and women to battle in Vietnam. Well, so much the better. Here we are celebrating America today. Just as war is freedom's cost, disagreement is freedom's privilege, and we honor it here today. But I ask all of you to remember the words that have been said here today, and I ask you at this monument can any American be out of place? And can any Commander-in-Chief be in any other place but here on this day? I think not.

At Memorial Day ceremony
at Vietnam Veterans Memorial,
Washington, D.C., May 31/
The Washington Post, 6-1:(A)6.

2

[Calling for the Federal government to allocate $5-billion for communities adversely affected by the current cutbacks and closings of military

bases]: In the past, base closings forced communities to cope with a jarring economic upheaval without tools or resources. For communities from coast to coast affected by base closings, the Federal government will now work aggressively to help these patriotic citizens, cities and towns prosper.

Washington, D.C., July 2/
The Washington Post, 7-3:(A)5.

3

[On his new policy of "don't ask, don't tell, don't pursue" for allowing homosexuals to serve in the military]: It is not a perfect solution. It is not identical with some of my own goals [of lifting the ban entirely on homosexuals]. And it certainly will not please everyone—perhaps not anyone—and clearly not those who hold the most adamant opinions on either side of this issue . . . [But] those who want the ban to be lifted completely on both status and conduct must understand that such action would have faced certain and decisive reversal by the Congress.

At Fort McNair,
Washington, D.C., July 19/
USA Today, 7-20:(A)2.

4

[On suggestions that he has showed weakness by backing away from his prior commitment to allow homosexuals to openly serve in the military]: I am the first President who ever took on this issue. It may be a sign of madness, sir, but it is not a sign of weakness.

Interview,
Washington, D.C., July 20/
The Washington Post, 7-21:(A)12.

5

One of our most urgent priorities must be attacking the proliferation of weapons of mass destruction, whether they are nuclear, chemical or biological, and the ballistic missiles that can rain them down on populations hundreds of miles away. We will pursue new steps to control the materials for nuclear weapons. Growing stockpiles of plutonium and highly enriched uranium

(BILL CLINTON)

are raising the danger of nuclear terrorism for all nations. We will press for an international agreement that would ban production of these materials for weapons forever.

At United Nations,
New York, Sept. 27/
The Christian Science Monitor,
9-29:19.

1

As we reduce our nuclear stockpiles, the United States has also begun negotiations toward a comprehensive [worldwide] ban on nuclear testing. This summer I declared that to facilitate these negotiations, our nation would suspend our testing if all other nuclear states would do the same. Today, in the face of disturbing signs [from China], I renew my call on the nuclear states to abide by that moratorium as we negotiate to stop nuclear testing for all time.

At United Nations,
New York, Sept. 27/
The New York Times, 9-28:(A)4.

2

[On revelations that Bobby Ray Inman, nominated to be Secretary of Defense, failed to pay Social Security taxes for a housekeeper who worked for him]: Obviously, I can't say that I agree with the way Admiral Inman handled that. I think people should just pay. But the fact is that what he did and how he did it was pretty much the same as some other people who had been nominated. I just don't think it was disqualifying because I thought he was exceptionally well-qualified to do this job.

Interview,
Washington, D.C., Dec. 22/
The New York Times, 12-23:(A)11.

Dan Coats
United States Senator,
R-Indiana

3

[On the possibility that President Clinton will eliminate the ban on homosexuals serving in the

armed forces]: I am convinced that if President Clinton reverses current policy regarding gays in the military, he will find a temporary victory that is very much like a defeat. President Clinton will find a military that is demoralized. He will find a Congress that resents his high-handed tactics, and he will find an American public disturbed that their Commander-in-Chief is governed by the political promises of the past and not the military needs of the moment.

Jan. 26/
Los Angeles Times, 1-27:(A)10.

James Courter
Chairman,
Federal Base Closure
and Realignment Commission

4

[Criticizing the military's lack of coordination and less-than-desirable cooperation in the latest round of base closings recommended by his Commission]: There was no knowledgeable, strong, experienced leadership in the Pentagon. There's nobody there to restrain the military leadership from doing what they think is best for their own service . . . There was no cross-service analysis. They'll never get together until they're forced to. Never. Never. They'll start a war first.

Interview,
Washington, D.C., July 2/
The Washington Post, 7-3:(A)5.

John Dalrymple
Admiral,
United States Navy (Ret.);
Executive director,
Navy League
of the United States

5

[Arguing against lifting the ban on homosexuals in the military, citing recent cases of homosexual rape in the Navy]: What this shows is that homosexuals cannot be expected to remain celibate while on active duty in the military. Faced with the threat of court-martial or being expelled from the service, homosexuals still do this. With legalization, I believe there would be even more cases like this.

The New York Times, 6-4:(A)8.

Ronald V. Dellums
United States Representative,
D-California

1

The military budget is not a jobs bill. The military budget ought to represent our definition of national security based on a rational assessment of threats and what we perceive to be our appropriate role in the world. Seventy percent of that budget—$200-billion—was directed to fighting a [potential] protracted war in Europe with the Warsaw Pact, a threat that no longer exists. But as you start coming down, the impact is a human impact, because there are people in communities adversely affected and economically dislocated, and that's real.

Interview, Washington, D.C./
Los Angeles Times, 4-11:(M)3.

Diane Carlson Evans
Former United States Army nurse;
Founder, Vietnam Women's
Memorial Project

2

There are still so many veterans in pain—particularly Vietnam veterans. Time does not heal all wounds for all people. The rejection, the scorn, the stigma and America's stereotype of us being losers, killers and crybabies still exists . . . It's a sorry state of affairs and a national tragedy . . . Must we bear this cross of Vietnam alone on the streets, or until we die?

USA Today, 5-28:(A)2.

J. James Exon
United States Senator,
D-Nebraska

3

[On the current search for a new Chairman of the Joint Chiefs of Staff to replace Colin Powell, who will be retiring soon]: I don't believe anybody's been elevated to Chairman unless they had some significant political skills, and there certainly are politics played inside the armed forces. When you talk about somebody who's demonstrated he can bring people together for a common cause, that person could be accurately described as a politician. And the military's senior leadership is full of such people.

Los Angeles Times, 5-28:(A)13.

Barney Frank
United States Representative,
D-Massachusetts

4

[Saying he supports a compromise in the controversy over whether to lift the ban on homosexuals in the military]: If Congress now chooses between a complete and total removal of the ban and a statutory enforcement of the ban, I am not optimistic that the side I would like to see [lifting the ban] would win; and that, I think, is reality . . . [Under a compromise,] on base and on duty and in uniform . . . gays and lesbians will make the sacrifice, unlike anybody else, of not talking about it. On the other hand, off base, off duty, on their own time, they will be allowed without fear of any penalty or punishment to express their individuality and personality . . . If we don't compromise, we lose. If the choice is between 0 percent and 100 percent, we get zero, and that can't be in anyone's interest on our side. The question is, what can you salvage out of this? A total repeal is impossible.

To reporters and in interview,
May 18/
Los Angeles Times, 5-19:(A)20.

Don Fuqua
President,
Aerospace Industries Association

5

[On calls for defense manufacturers to convert to consumer products as the military cuts back]: It's difficult for our industry to convert. We can build a better commercial airplane, a more fuel-efficient airplane. But we can't make pies and cakes. That market is filled.

The New York Times, 3-12:(A)9.

Barry M. Goldwater
Former United States Senator,
R-Arizona

6

[Arguing against banning homosexuals from the military]: You don't need to be "straight" to fight and die for your country. You just need to shoot straight.

Newsweek, 12-20:52.

Clarence A. Mark Hill
Rear Admiral (Ret.) and
former Chief of Personnel,
United States Navy

1

[Criticizing the Clinton Administration's moves to allow women to take part more directly in military combat missions]: The bottom line is, there's no way women can improve combat readiness, but they sure as hell can degrade it. There is no privacy on board a combat ship and there never will be. If you have a disaster like a fire, there won't be any time for, "Pardon me, ma'am, may I come in?"

The Washington Post, 4-29:(A)8.

Bobby Ray Inman
Secretary of Defense-designate
of the United States

2

[Addressing President Clinton]: Mr. President, as you know, I had to reach a level of comfort that we could work together, that I would be very comfortable in your role as the Commander-in-Chief while I was Secretary of Defense. And I have found that level of comfort.

Accepting the nomination
for Defense Secretary,
Washington, D.C., Dec. 16/
The New York Times, 12-18:7.

Frank B. Kelso
Admiral and Chief of Operations,
United States Navy

3

[On the Navy scandal involving sexual harassment by male officers of female officers at 1991's meeting of the Tailhook Association]: We cannot undo the past, but we sure can influence the future, and we are. We have emerged from this experience a better, more effective, stronger institution . . . we are . . . committed to providing all our people a workplace free from harassment. We haven't solved the problem completely—it takes a long time to change attitudes. But we understand the problem, and we have moved out to fix it.

News conference,
Washington, D.C., April 23/
Los Angeles Times, 4-24:(A)16.

Edward M. Kennedy
United States Senator,
D-Massachusetts

4

[Supporting lifting the ban on homosexuals in the military]: It's time for the armed forces to stop discriminating against anyone because of who they are and what they do in their private life. Condoning prejudice is an appalling means to [military] unit cohesion. Whatever name discrimination takes, it ought to be exposed and rooted out.

At Senate Armed Services Committee hearing,
Washington, D.C., March 31/
The New York Times, 4-1:(A)7.

Joseph P. Kennedy II
United States Representative,
D-Massachusetts

5

[On U.S. Vietnam veterans]: These are men and women who were willing to fight and die . . . But after the war ended, we did not stick out our hand and say, "Welcome home" . . . What they found was a grate on the street to ward off the cold nights, a needle for their arms to escape reality, and a bottle to deal with the memories of a war that they were asked to fight and then told to forget.

USA Today, 5-28:(A)2.

Harold Klepak
Canadian military historian

6

Peace-keeping is no job for soldiers, but soldiers are the only ones who can do it.

The Washington Post, 4-27:(A)12.

Lawrence J. Korb
Former Assistant Secretary
for Manpower,
Department of Defense
of the United States

7

[Saying lifting the ban on homosexuals in the military would not present a long-lasting problem]: I find no convincing evidence that changing

(LAWRENCE J. KORB)

the current policy would undermine unit cohesion any more than the other social changes that society has asked the armed forces to make over the past 50 years . . . Since our armed forces are composed of people with different backgrounds and values, its leaders have had and will continue to have to adjust to this diversity in building cohesion.

Before Senate Armed Services Committee,
Washington, D.C., March 31/
The New York Times, 4-1:(A)1.

William P. Lawrence
Vice Admiral,
United States Navy (Ret.);
President,
Association of Naval Aviation

1

[On Clinton Administration moves to allow women to take part more directly in military combat missions]: There are certainly elements within the Navy that are going to be against it. [But] I've talked to a lot of senior active-duty flag officers and I have found very few of those that do not feel that this is the time to do this. [Women] have already proved they can do this.

The Washington Post, 4-29:(A)8.

Trent Lott
United States Senator,
R-Mississippi

2

[On President Clinton's stated desire to lift the ban on homosexuals in the military]: If the President would come to the Senate Armed Services Committee and work out an arrangement where . . . people would not be asked their sexual preference when admitted to the military, provided they keep their confidence and just do their job, I think we could work out that kind of arrangement. But if the President insists on an arrangement where homosexuals come out and announce their preference . . . I think it's going to be a big mistake.

USA Today, 5-13:(A)13.

Richard G. Lugar
United States Senator,
R-Indiana

3

[Saying President Clinton's plans to convert defense industries to civilian use won't always work]: A plant that produces submarines can't produce anything else. You just can't convert it to building refrigerators. Sometimes the best thing to do is padlock it and level it.

U.S. News & World Report,
3-22:26.

Carl E. Mundy, Jr.
General and Commandant,
United States Marine Corps

4

Although my words on another occasion have given the impression that I believe that some Marines, because of their color, are not as capable as others . . . those were not the thoughts in my mind, nor are they or have they ever been the thoughts of my heart . . . [The Marine Corps is made up of people from] the broad, strong ethnic fabric that is our nation, [and in the future,] that fabric will broaden and strengthen in every category to make our corps even stronger. [That is] a commitment of this Commandant, a personal commitment of this Marine.

At ceremony marking the 218th
anniversary of the Marine Corps,
Washington, D.C., Nov. 10/
The Washington Post, 11-11:(A)34.

Ralph Neas
Executive director,
Leadership Conference
on Civil Rights

5

[Supporting lifting the ban on homosexuals in the military]:This is a fundamental civil-rights issue. The ban is based on fear, prejudice and stereotypes. It is eerily, disturbingly reminiscent of the efforts to keep blacks [out of the ranks 45 years ago].

March 29/
Los Angeles Times, 3-30:(A)14.

Sam Nunn
United States Senator,
D-Georgia

1

[Arguing against lifting the ban on homosexuals in the military]: If there is one thing I've learned on military matters in my 20 years of serving in the United States Senate and working with the military virtually every day, it is that our armed forces function well if we respect and support their basic requirements for cohesion and effectiveness. Resolving this conflict between individual rights and the basic needs of our military is always difficult, but our nation has had an effective military because we have achieved an acceptable balance over the years. This balance must be maintained . . . In the discussions over the past week on how to resolve the current issue, I emphasized over and over again that I believed it was essential to maintain the current Department of Defense policy that excludes homosexuals from the military.

News conference,
Washington, D.C., Jan. 29/
The New York Times, 1-30:6.

2

I am astounded when I hear people talk as if the defense budget has not been cut. Unfortunately, there continue to be those who seem to believe that the defense budget can bear all of the [government's] budget cuts, and that we can get the [Federal] deficit under control if only [we] would cut the "Cold War" defense budget . . . The Defense Department seems to be the only part of the Federal government that has carried its fair share.

Before the Senate,
Washington, March 5/
The Washington Post, 3-6:(A)7.

Kate O'Beirne
Vice president,
Heritage Foundation

3

[Arguing against the Clinton Administration's moves to allow women to take part more directly in military combat missions]: If women are now

expected to kill and be killed . . . we can't pretend it won't have a very broad impact on the general society. The feminists would have achieved their gender-blind nirvana.

April 28/
The Washington Post, 4-29:(A)6.

Fred Peck
Colonel,
United States Marine Corps

4

[Saying he is against lifting the ban on homosexuals in the military]: My son Scott is a homosexual. And I don't think there's any place for him in the military . . . If he were to walk into a recruiter's office, it would be a recruiter's dream come true. He's 6-foot-1, blue-eyed, blond hair, great student . . . But if he were to go and seriously consider joining the military, I would have to, number one, personally counsel against it, and number two, actively fight against it, because my son is a homosexual.

Before Senate Armed Services Committee,
Washington, D.C., May 11/
The Washington Post, 5-12:(A)1.

Ross Perot
Industrialist;
1992 independent
Presidential candidate

5

[Saying President Clinton should pursue the issue of American MIAs from the Vietnam war of the 1970s]: There is little downside risk [in doing nothing]. There is tremendous upside potential, I think, particularly for President Clinton. I'm not saying he would do it for that reason. I think and I hope he would do it for the right reason. It would show the American people a lot of courage and a lot of commitment to the men and women who wear the uniform, and that would be a tremendous plus, I think, in terms of support in an area [the military] where his support is weak.

Interview/Newsweek, 4-26:42.

6

What breaks my heart is, from privates to generals and admirals, my phone rings off the

(ROSS PEROT)

wall all day and every day. Not only on this issue [of homosexuals in the military] but on the issue of sagging morale in the military. The military is being treated like trash by the White House, or is perceived to be by them.

USA Today, 10-11:(A)2.

Colin L. Powell
General, United States Army;
Chairman, Joint Chiefs of Staff

1

I care about strategy. I care about [the military] force structure. I care about doctrine. I care about all the papers that come out of think tanks telling me what to do. But the thing that really counts when the strategy changes or turns out not to have been right, what really does count is the quality of the force. You've got to see our force as a human living organism and treat it as such.

Before Professional Services Council/
The New York Times, 2-6:1.

2

[On the possibility that the ban on homosexuals in the military will be lifted by President Clinton]: We [in the armed forces] took on racism. We took on drugs. We took on scandals such as Tailhook. We found answers to them which made us stronger and more relevant to the society around us. We will do the very same, my friends, with the difficult issue of homosexuals in the military. The President has given us clear direction to solve the issue. I believe we are near a decision to do so.

At Harvard University commencement,
June 10/USA Today, 6-11:(A)9.

3

[On the downsizing of the military]: I think it's essential that as we bring the force down, we have a clear understanding of what we will not be able to do. And if those risks are acceptable, then we ought to go ahead and save money and bring the force down. It's a very difficult judgment to make.

News conference/
The Washington Post, 6-17:(A)17.

4

[On President Clinton's compromise plan of "don't ask, don't tell, don't pursue" on the question of allowing homosexuals in the military]: I think we have come up with a solution that we can all live with, that protects the force, that protects the privacy rights of all of those serving in the force and yet moves in the direction of those who wanted to have a more liberal policy with respect to homosexuals serving in the military. It is a policy that I believe all the Joint Chiefs of Staff can fully, fully support and . . . be able to implement.

July 19/
Los Angeles Times, 7-20:(A)14.

5

[Saying the military should not go too far in eliminating duplication and competition among the services]: We're not a church picnic group. I want an American Marine infantryman to believe there is no infantryman better on the face of the Earth. And I want an Army . . . infantryman to be sure that that Marine is wrong because he's better than he is. That kind of competition serves our interests well.

At National Press Club,
Washington, D.C., Sept. 28/
The Washington Post, 9-29:(A)16.

6

Reluctance to use military force is an American military tradition. Since war is ultimately a political act, not a military act, give political tools the opportunity to work first.

At National Press Club,
Washington, D.C., Sept. 28/
The Washington Post, 9-29:(A)16.

Stephen A. Saltzburg
Professor of law,
George Washington University

7

[On the controversy over whether to lift the ban on homosexuals in the military]: Military personnel are tradition-bound, much as lawyers

(STEPHEN A. SALTZBURG)

are precedent-bound. Thus, the notion that members of the military services may prefer the ban, even by a large margin, does not mean that the ban must remain. It is my belief, my opinion, that whatever [is decided] on these issues can be made to work.

Before Senate Armed Services Committee,
Washington, D.C., March 29/
The New York Times, 3-30:(A)13.

Jim Sasser
United States Senator,
D-Tennessee

1

[Arguing against continued development of the SDI space defense system]: For the past few years, some of us in Congress have waged what often seems like an uphill fight to cut funding for large parts of the SDI program and to limit deployments. But I think each year a few more recognize the folly of this spending and recognize that the threat is not there to justify it . . . Now we have a Defense Secretary [Les Aspin] and President [Bill Clinton] who seem to recognize we cannot fund every exotic weapons program that comes along. Maybe this year [SDI will be stopped].

Los Angeles Times, 3-22:(A)4.

David A. Schleuter
Professor of law,
St. Mary's University

2

[On the controversy over whether to lift the ban on homosexuals in the military]: Discipline is an indispensable ingredient in the military establishment. The persons best able to assess the risks to discipline [of lifting the ban] are the individuals who must deal with that issue on a daily basis [military commanders].

Before Senate Armed Services Committee,
Washington, D.C., March 29/
The New York Times,
3-30:(A)13.

H. Norman Schwarzkopf
General,
United States Army (Ret.)

3

[Saying the ban against homosexuals in the military should not be lifted]: The military establishment is not fragile, but in my mind [the lifting of the ban] would be seriously overloading their plate. [Officers] will faithfully try and execute the orders of their civilian leaders, but their hearts simply won't be in it. To me, they would be just like many of the Iraqi troops who sat in the deserts of Kuwait [when he commanded the U.S.-led coalition against Iraq in 1991's Persian Gulf war], forced to execute orders they didn't believe in. [If the ban is lifted,] I think in fact we will wind up with a second-class armed force for quite some time in the future. Are we really ready to . . . risk a possible decrease in our nation's ability to defend itself? . . . Whether you like it or not, in my years of military service, I've experienced the fact that the introduction of an open homosexual into a small unit immediately polarizes that unit and destroys the very bonding that is so important for the unit's survival in time of war.

Before Senate Armed Services Committee,
Washington, D.C., May 11/
Los Angeles Times, 5-12:(A)1,15.

4

I think all of us who served [in the U.S.-Vietnam war of the 1960s and '70s] and came back home felt a sense of betrayal. We didn't start the war. We were simply doing what our country asked us to do. I ran into several occasions where [Americans] looked with disgust upon the fact that I was wearing a uniform based upon my service in Vietnam, accusing me of all sorts of horrendous things I had never done. There was somehow a blame that was being placed on me simply because I was doing what I'd been taught to do all my life—and that's serve my country and go to their call when they ask me to.

Interview/
Los Angeles Times, 6-30:(F)6.

George P. Shultz
Former Secretary of State
of the United States

1

[Saying former President Ronald Reagan may have gotten the idea for the SDI space defense system while visiting the North American Air Defense Center in Colorado during the 1980 Presidential campaign]: Reagan asked a General what would happen if a Soviet SS-20 [missile] hit the base. The General said, "It would blow us away." Reagan then asked, "What can we do about it?" The General said, "Not a thing." The future President concluded that was a hell of a state of affairs.

At conference on the end of the Cold War,
Princeton University, Feb. 26/
The Washington Post, 2-27:(A)17.

David M. Smith
Spokesman,
Campaign for Military Service

2

[Criticizing those who are against lifting the ban on homosexuals in the military and who use the argument that unit cohesion will suffer if the ban is lifted]: That whole unit-cohesion line is based on the fact that [opponents of lifting the ban] think homophobia is stronger in the U.S. military than is military leadership. [They] feel that homophobia is so entrenched it cannot be uprooted by basic leadership. And we're saying racism also was entrenched in the U.S. military at one time, but it is currently being rooted out of the U.S. military with no problem.

Los Angeles Times, 3-29:(A)25.

Gene Sperling
Deputy Adviser to President
of the United States Bill Clinton
for Economic Policy

3

[On Clinton Administration plans for defense conversion, the shifting of defense industries and employees from military to civilian work]: The most compelling reason for defense conversion is the disgrace when someone trained as a scientist has to give up that profession. Our goal is not to do defense conversion as a government jobs program, but to do investments in civilian technologies . . . That will help economic growth, and to the extent it helps defense conversion and injured communities, it will be a double winner.

The New York Times, 4-26:(A)7.

Tom Stoddard
Coordinator,
Campaign for Military Service

4

[Arguing against a possible "don't ask, don't tell"-type of compromise on allowing homosexuals in the military]: It's not compatible with [President Clinton's] commitment [to lift the ban on homosexuals in the military]. It's not "don't ask, don't tell." It's simply, "Don't be." It's incompatible with the President's commitment to end discrimination based on status.

The Washington Post, 6-24:(A)7.

Gordon R. Sullivan
General and Chief of Staff,
United States Army

5

There is this propensity to take the [military] services apart after a war. This has almost always resulted in unreadiness, and we paid the price in blood. That vision animates me, inside the institution, and it gives me strength when I speak outside the institution. It gives me a focus. Outside the institution I'm able to tell people that the defense of the Unite States of America is a shared responsibility. We in uniform have a role to play, you [civilians] have a role to play, and so do our elected officials. I think the Chairman of the Joint Chiefs of Staff and the other chiefs have been successful in articulating that. Now inside the institution that's the focus I've been able to provide. It really began with [former Army Chief of Staff, General Carl] Vuono. We made a basic decision that we could cut forces to maintain readiness and said whatever we keep, we'll keep trained and ready. Essentially, that says to the Army that we're not going to retain structure simply for the sake of retaining it, that as the

(GORDON R. SULLIVAN)

budget goes down, structure will come down in a balanced and managed way. That's always been an issue in the Army. In 1960, when I went to the 2nd Division, it was a training center for individual recruits. I don't want that to happen again. What I keep, I will keep trained and ready to fight. To do whatever it's asked to do.

Interview/
American Heritage, December:53.

1

What kind of officer are we trying to create? You can find a metaphor in jazz. We're trying to create Dave Brubeck. What makes Brubeck great is that he was trained and educated as a classical musician, but he's also a highly skilled [jazz] improvisationist. He often does not respond exactly the same, but the theme remains constant. In the same way, we're trying to create officers like [U.S. General] John Shalikashvili, who commanded the Kurdish-relief effort on the Iraqi border with Turkey after the [1991 Persian] Gulf war. We're trying to create people who can improvise within a theme, people you can tell, as we told Shali-kashvili: "Go to southern Turkey, northern Iraq. Resettle the Kurds." This officer has to know how to conduct peacekeeping, peacemaking, resettlement operations, diplomacy, humani-tarian aid. How do you create an officer like that? How do you create a [General and Joint Chiefs Chairman] Colin Powell? It is critical for us to maintain a viable, capable, credible educa-tional system in the Army, because this is truly where we grow our future leaders.

Interview/
American Heritage, December:56.

Bernard Trainor
Lieutenant General,
United States Marine Corps (Ret.);
Director,
national-security program,
Kennedy School of Government,
Harvard University

2

The minute you use military power, the enemy will be able to see the limits and capabilities of that power. You're in your best posture the day before you're going to strike, because they don't know what you're going to do.

U.S. News & World Report,
5-10:50.

Caspar W. Weinberger
Former Secretary of Defense
of the United States

3

[Criticizing allegations that the military faked a successful test of the Strategic Defense Initiative anti-missile system in the 1980s]: The test was scientifically based, did succeed and was accurately reported to the Congress and the American public. [But] once these fairy tales [about fakery] are out, they are picked up as gospel truth by editorial writers, and never corrected.

Time, 8-30:27.

Boris N. Yeltsin
President of Russia

4

[On the just-signed U.S.-Russia START II arms-reduction treaty]: Today the Presidents of the two great powers, the United States and Russia, have signed a treaty on further radical cuts in strategic offensive arms of Russia and the United States . . . In its scale and impor-tance, the treaty goes further than all other treaties ever signed in the field of disarma-ment . . . It is not every century that history gives us an opportunity to witness and partici-pate in an event that is so significant in scale and consequences. The treaty signed today represents a major step toward fulfilling man-kind's centuries-old dream of disarmament.

News conference,
Moscow, Russia, Jan. 3/
The New York Times,
1-4:(A)6,1.

89

The Economy • Labor

Rex Adams
Vice president,
Mobil Corporation

1

[The U.S. economy is] still over-stored, over-banked and over-governed. We're still a country of excess capacity. There is going to be job growth, but there will still be fewer manufacturing jobs and fewer secure jobs. People are only going to start hiring in significant numbers when they feel they have a possibility of making some money.

Time, 2-1:53.

Roger Altman
Deputy Secretary
of the Treasury-designate
of the United States

2

As a nation, we have been consuming too much and investing too little. We need to move away from that and toward higher levels of investment. I do think that one form or another of a new tax on consumption is necessary.

At Senate Finance Committee
hearing on his nomination,
Washington, D.C., Jan. 13/
Los Angeles Times, 1-14:(A)20.

Roger Altman
Deputy Secretary
of the Treasury
of the United States

3

The country—and Washington, too—is so used to fiscal irresponsibility that there's a shock aspect to the idea that we're actually going to rein in the nation's finances. And it's really not easy to persuade people that we should do it, that it's important to do it. A lot of people think of [Federal] deficit reduction in the abstract: "We ought to reduce the deficit because an economic textbook would tell you to do so." It's difficult but absolutely necessary

to explain to people what it means to them in their own lives. Particularly for so many Americans who are experiencing stagnating incomes or falling incomes. After all, median family income is flat over many years now. It's critical, but not easy, to explain to people that the [Federal] deficit is the biggest reason why it's harder for them to make ends meet—to buy a home, send their kids to college, renovate the home or whatever.

Interview,
Washington, D.C., Feb. 17/
Los Angeles Times, 2-21:(M)3.

Robert Andrews
United States Representative,
D-New Jersey

4

Washington is the only city in the world where it's considered courageous to raise someone's gas bill [by raising gas taxes]. The truth is that it's courageous to tell people you're *not* going to subsidize their sewer system anymore or pay for their daughter's education. That's courageous.

Time, 8-16:23.

Lars Anell
Swedish Ambassador
to the European Community

5

It is clear that a successful conclusion of the [GATT Uruguay] round would give—both for psychological and economic reasons—a much needed boost to the world economy. In fact, it is one of the few decisions governments can take without economic risks in order to stimulate the world economy, since fiscal expansion is ruled out because of levels of debts and public deficits already being too high.

The Christian Science Monitor,
1-22:7.

Richard K. Armey
United States Representative,
R-Texas

1

My Democratic colleagues want to use fiscal policy to aggravate the economic situation. Then they want to say to the Fed, essentially, "You guys have to pull our car out of [the] ditch." [But] there's no way that monetary policy can undo the harmful effects of bad fiscal policy.

The New York Times, 5-13:(C)2.

2

This debate [about President Clinton's economic plan] defines the difference between Republicans and Democrats. Democrats believe prosperity comes from bigger government. Republicans know it comes from ordinary people acting on behalf of themselves and their families.

Before the House,
Washington, D.C., Aug. 5/
The New York Times, 8-6:(A)1.

David A. Aschauer
Professor of economics,
Bates College

3

[On President Clinton's economic plan, which includes increases in spending]: We can expect a payoff on these investment projects, maybe in four to six years. But a four-to-six year time horizon poses a serious political problem—it's not conducive for voters to re-elect this Administration.

The New York Times, 2-15:(C)1.

Steven Axilrod
Chairman,
Nikko Securities International

4

[On economic growth and inflation]: Right now, spending on goods and services in the industrial world as a whole is very moderate because of recessions in Europe and Japan. Toward the end of this year or early in 1994,

those recessions will end, growth will pick up, and worldwide spending will be greater . . . [Inflation] is largely a supply-and-demand issue. There'll be more demand for goods, therefore more opportunity for producers to raise prices. In addition, there'll be more demand for labor as U.S. exports improve. That will make it harder to hold down wage increases. Higher prices and higher labor costs equal inflation.

Interview/USA Today, 3-24:(B)5.

Jim Bacchus
United States Representative,
D-Florida

5

[Supporting the proposed NAFTA, even though he admits certain low-wage U.S. jobs may be lost to imports from Mexico]: We cannot cling to the past. We can't save both the high-wage and the low-wage jobs. If we have to choose, then we have to choose the high-wage jobs and prepare more of our people to hold those jobs. Otherwise, their standard of living will continue to decline.

The Christian Science Monitor,
11-17:4.

Haley Barbour
Chairman,
Republican National Committee

6

Right now [President Clinton's] economic plan so starkly shows the differences between Republican thinking and Democratic thinking that [it] overwhelms any other issue . . . He wants to impose $360-billion of the new taxes on this economy in the name of stimulating the economy. There's not an economist from left to right who says that a big tax increase will create jobs . . . Now he says, "Quit carping and give your [Republican] alternative." Well, we've given our alternative: Cut out his new spending to reduce the [Federal] deficit. He doesn't want our participation. He thinks he's going to jam this down the country's throat because he's got Democratic majorities in the House and Senate . . . The reason Clinton keeps hollering

(HALEY BARBOUR)

for the Republicans to throw out a detailed alternative before he has even presented a budget is he wants another rabbit out there for the dogs to chase because he knows anything that will take the spotlight off the details of his plan is good for his plan. We want this decided in the sunshine.

Interview/USA Today, 3-3:(A)13.

Richard Belous
Chief economist,
National Planning Association

1

[On the growing trend toward the use of temporary, part-time workers]: If there was a national fear index, it would be directly related to the growth of contingent work.

Time, 3-29:44.

William J. Bennett
Former Secretary of Education
of the United States

2

Right now the [Republican] Party is unified in opposition to [Democratic President] Clinton's economic plan and its philosophical assumption of more government, not less. The Clinton economic program will be to us [Republicans] domestically what Communism was in foreign affairs: a unifying force.

The Christian Science Monitor,
5-4:4.

Lloyd N. Bentsen
Secretary of the Treasury-designate
of the United States

3

There's no question but that the President-elect [Clinton] has a commitment to cut the [Federal] deficit and do it in a major way. Time is running out. We don't have a lot of wiggle room left before these things have to be faced up to.

At Senate Finance Committee
hearing on his confirmation,
Washington, D.C., Jan. 12/
Los Angeles Times, 1-13:(A)1.

Lloyd N. Bentsen
Secretary of the Treasury
of the United States

4

If the [Clinton Administration's proposed energy] tax is to effectively promote energy conservation, it must be borne by the ultimate consumers [the people]. The Administration is continuing to explore methods of assuring that the tax is, in fact, passed through to those who use the energy.

Statement, April 1*/Los Angeles Times, 4-2:(A)1.

5

Organized labor and others have some sincere concerns that NAFTA may cost jobs here in America. The point here is that jobs can go south to Mexico now, or the Far East, or anywhere. That's the effect of global competition, not NAFTA . . . For those who are affected by NAFTA, we have job-training programs. We want everyone to benefit from NAFTA and the prosperity it's going to bring . . . I know about the illegal immigration problem [of Mexicans entering the U.S.]. NAFTA is going to help raise living standards in Mexico, which will reduce the economic incentive to cross the border illegally and put demands on our public services. And a higher standard of living in Mexico means they will be buying more U.S. goods and creating more jobs here.

Before Los Angeles (Calif.)
World Affairs Council, Aug. 17/
Los Angeles Times, 8-20:(B)2.

David Berenson
Director of national tax policy,
Ernst & Young, accounting

6

[Criticizing Clinton Administration proposals to increase the corporate tax]: The idea [of lowering corporate taxes] was to take taxation out of business decision-making, to make taxation as simple and fair as possible, so that business could focus on economics in their decisions. If you ratchet up corporate taxes, that means more business decisions will be based on taxes, and not on efficiency and what's best for the economy.

The New York Times, 2-15:(C)3.

(DAVID BERENSON)

1

[There is] much greater focus on deficit reduction [by the Federal government] than you would have expected last year. But I would not give credit for that to either side of the aisle. I think it has been forced on them by the middle class and that squeaky little guy from Texas [industrialist Ross Perot].

Los Angeles Times, 6-25:(A)26.

C. Fred Bergsten
Director, Institute
for International Economics

2

Nobody in America knew that we were going to exit the VCR industry or the color-television industry, but we did. The U.S. government is very poorly positioned to judge these developments intelligently.

U.S. News & World Report,
2-1:47.

Richard Berman
Executive director,
Employment Policies Institute

3

Every time there is a mandate in labor costs [such as a raise in the minimum wage] that exceeds productivity, companies try to find more ways to convert service to self-service, or to convert work performed by people to work performed by machines. President Clinton wants people to leave welfare and take an entry-level job, but a policy of raising the minimum wage would encourage phasing out of these jobs.

Los Angeles Times, 1-30:(A)12.

James J. Blanchard
Former Governor
of Michigan (D)

4

My caution to President Clinton last week was, people may say that they want him to deal with the [Federal] deficit, they'll say they will sacrifice as long as everybody else has to. But when he does it, they'll say, "I didn't think you meant *me*." I think the President will have a much more difficult time selling deficit reduction and public sacrifice than he realizes. There is no political future in administering pain to people.

Interview/
Los Angeles Times, 2-16:(A)14.

David E. Bonier
United States Representative,
D-Michigan

5

[Arguing against the proposed NAFTA, and referring to an earlier pro-NAFTA gathering by President Clinton on the White House lawn]: My question is, how many products that used to be made in America have we lost to Mexico the past 10 years because our manufacturing plants have moved down there? I bet that number would more than fill the White House lawn.

News conference,
Washington, D.C., Oct. 20/
The Washington Post, 10-21:(A)16.

6

[Arguing against the proposed NAFTA]: Our future is tied to the people of Mexico, but we need an agreement that will raise their wages up, not drive ours down to theirs. NAFTA is a policy of the past, an extension of colonialism and [an] extension of selling our workers short.

The Washington Post, 10-30:(A)4.

7

[Criticizing the proposed NAFTA and the economists who support it]: There are a lot of people in this country who believe our workers are paid too much, a lot of economists. They view their [own] work as very special; but for someone who has to struggle at a factory, who sweats, the dignity and respect for those people is not very high.

The Washington Post,
11-8:(A)11.

David L. Boren
United States Senator,
D-Oklahoma

1

[Expressing reservations about President Clinton's economic proposals]: A lot of us here in the moderate wing of the [Democratic] Party don't want to vote out a $16-billion spending bill by itself before we have a chance to get the [Federal budget] deficit down. It's like saying to a child, "Eat your dessert first and then your spinach." The spinach doesn't get eaten.

Interview,
Washington, D.C., Feb. 18/
The Washington Post, 3-24:(B)1,4.

2

[Criticizing President Clinton's proposed Federal budget plan]: I think that if this President were to get his wish of passing this budget right now, exactly as it is, it would be the surest formula for the destruction of the Democratic Party and any chance he has for re-election that I have ever seen.

Interview,
Washington, D.C., May 21/
The Washington Post, 5-22:(A)7.

Michael J. Boskin
Professor of economics,
Stanford University;
Former Chairman,
Council of Economic Advisers
to the President
of the United States
(George Bush)

3

[Criticizing the Congress-White House compromise bill on President Clinton's economic plan]: These claims [that] this bill will produce 8 million jobs are really ludicrous. They stem from the baseline assumptions of the private forecasters that the private economy will create even more jobs than that over the next four years, and the Clinton plan will reduce that a little bit. If the bill comes through about as predicted, it will slow the economy about 1 percent per year for the next several years, costing . . . several hundred thousand jobs.

USA Today, 8-2:(A)5.

Lawrence Bossidy
Chairman, Allied-Signal, Inc.

4

[On criticism of NAFTA]: If this [criticism] continues, the nation will have made a mistake and, in my mind, a tragic mistake. There are 283 economists, including 12 Nobel laureates, and all of them have said that NAFTA will create U.S. jobs. So at the end of the day, we're going to win that argument and it's the linchpin argument . . . NAFTA would create the biggest market in the world. We're talking about a $6.5-trillion economy of 370 million people [in the U.S., Mexico and Canada]. Mexico, with its 70 million consumers, is already our third-largest trading partner, taking some $40.6-billion worth of exports. NAFTA could create more than 200,000 jobs—new, higher-paying U.S. jobs—and help preserve 700,000 existing jobs related to exports to Mexico.

Interview/USA Today, 9-13:(B)7.

Bill Bradley
United States Senator,
D-New Jersey

5

[On President Clinton's economic plan, which is to be voted upon by the Senate]: This package is not the vote of a lifetime, but it is an important first step—the biggest in the last decade—to reduce the increase in the [Federal] deficit. Remember, that's all this package does, reduce the increase in the deficit. It's a sad but true comment on our predicament and on the disastrous economic stewardship of the last 12 years. If we do nothing, the debt will go from $4-trillion to $5.4-trillion in five years. With this package, it will go from $4-trillion to $4.9-trillion. It's sobering to think that just 12 years ago the debt was $900-billion . . . If you are for [Federal budget] deficit reduction, you will vote for this bill. The time for making excuses and passing the buck is over. If you vote

(BILL BRADLEY)

against this package, you must either lay out a specific alternative plan to cut the deficit by $500-billion or be revealed as someone who doesn't care about the burden we're loading on our children's backs. Without specific alternatives with equivalent deficit reduction, opponents of this package are simply playing the old politicians' game, which is to deliver exclusively good news, never to level with constituents and, above all, to appear to be all things to all people.

Before the Senate, Washington, D.C./
The New York Times, 8-7:29.

1

[On the tax-the-wealthy aspect of President Clinton's economic plan]: Because you've done well and earned money doesn't mean that you are guilty of something. It means you worked hard and beat the competition—and were rewarded for it. To say that you got unjust gains in the 1980s, and now we're taking them back, is really shortsighted.

Interview/
The Wall Street Journal,
8-17:(A)14.

2

To pass NAFTA is to take the challenge [of a changing world economy] head on. I cannot help but see NAFTA as the test case of whether we hold on and lose or transform and win. To pass NAFTA will improve the chances for more jobs in America and a stronger economy to deal with the real threats to American jobs coming from Europe, Japan and China.

Before Center for National Policy,
Washington, D.C., Oct. 7/
The Washington Post, 10-8:(A)8.

William Brandon, Jr.
President,
American Bankers Association

3

[Supporting the Federal government's easing of regulations so that banks can lend to small

businesses more readily]: It will instantly allow bankers to make vitally needed loans to creditworthy small businesses that have had trouble meeting the government's magic formulas. This will spur economic growth and job creation while costing the government nothing.

The Christian Science Monitor,
4-14:4.

John B. Breaux
United States Senator,
D-Louisiana

4

[On President Clinton's proposed energy tax]: The problem many people have with it is political. I think the original idea was most people wouldn't know what a BTU tax was, so you could get it passed. Everybody knows what a gas tax is; you can see it. But when people start realizing that a BTU tax is a gas tax, and when they realize that they are going to see it on their utility bill every month, and when they realize they are going to see it in everything they buy, I would suggest that it's not the best way to go.

Los Angeles Times, 5-27:(A)24.

5

[Saying having a good economic plan is more important than meeting the specific goal of reducing the Federal deficit by the $500-billion amount being stated by President Clinton]: The $500-billion was not kicked out by some magical computer that said: "You've got to have this to have a strong economy." That's a number that was arrived at several months ago, and I think, [considering] the economy and the status of it, that a proposal that has less taxes and less spending cuts may be the right thing.

To reporters, July 13/
Los Angeles Times, 7-15:(A)12.

Ronald H. Brown
Secretary of Commerce
of the United States

6

[Saying government should work with industry to help U.S. businesses become more

(RONALD H. BROWN)

competitive]: For a long time in America, there has been a big debate about whether we ought to have any kind of national economic policy. I think it's time for that debate to end. This is no longer about philosophy or ideology or about partnership. It's about results, and it's about doing what is best for the economic growth and economic future of our country.

Before U.S. Chamber of Commerce,
Washington, D.C., April 15/
The Washington Post, 4-16:(A)1.

1

[Supporting NAFTA]: The bottom line is U.S. exports equal U.S. jobs. If you look at our economic performance over the past several years, one of the only bright spots has been exports. We accept the premise that for every billion-dollar increase in exports, you create 20,000 new jobs for the American people. Therefore, we think that's pretty important to focus on.

Interview/USA Today, 9-28:(A)11.

Pat Buchanan
Political columnist;
1992 candidate for the
Republican Presidential
nomination

2

NAFTA is a fraud. It is not a free-trade treaty at all, but an insider's deal among the transnational elites of three countries [the U.S., Canada and Mexico] . . . Six months in office and [President] Bill Clinton [who supports NAFTA] is sending our money to Russia and our jobs to Mexico. The American President has got to start looking out for his own country first.

News conference, Aug. 26/
USA Today, 8-27:(A)4.

Gary Burtless
Senior fellow,
Brookings Institution

3

[On President Clinton's summer-jobs plan for young people]: If it's like summer-jobs pro-

grams in the past, it's like baby-sitting to reduce the risk of urban conflagration. You're giving a lot of teenagers walking-around money.

The Washington Post, 3-13:(C)1.

Robert C. Byrd
United States Senator,
D-West Virginia

4

[Criticizing Democrats who express reservations about President Clinton's economic stimulus program]: I'm concerned some of our Democrats may be saying things and presenting certain courses of action that in reality rule out the President's options. There are just too many cooks dabbling in the brew.

Interview/
The Washington Post, 4-8:(A)8.

William H. Bywater
President, International Union
of Electronic Workers

5

[Arguing against the proposed NAFTA]: Our jobs at first went to the Far East, and now they are going to Mexico. You tell the workers [to] wait 20 or 30 years and it will be better. That is not practical, it's bull, it's crazy.

The Washington Post, 11-8:(A)11.

6

[On politicians who voted for NAFTA, which he was against]: I am not going to agree to let bygones be bygones as far as NAFTA is concerned. I am not giving a dime to any candidate who voted for NAFTA, and am going to redouble efforts for those who actually supported us. I am not going to forget NAFTA. I am not looking to shake hands with anyone and say, "Let's kiss and make up."

Interview/
The New York Times, 12-11:9.

Jimmy Carter
Former President
of the United States

7

[Criticizing industrialist and former Presidential candidate Ross Perot for his opposition

(JIMMY CARTER)

to NAFTA]: Unfortunately in our country now, we have a demagogue who has unlimited financial resources and who is extremely careless with the truth, who is preying on the fears and the uncertainties of the American public. And this must be met, because this powerful voice can be pervasive, even within the Congress of the United States, unless it's met by people of courage who vote and act and persuade in the best interest of our country.

At signing ceremony for NAFTA
supplemental agreements,
Washington, D.C., Sept. 14/
Los Angeles Times, 9-15:(A)13.

James A. Carville
Senior strategist
for President Bill Clinton's
1992 election campaign

1

Everyone has been sucked into believing that what the country's economic future is about is cutting the [Federal] deficit. And it isn't. It is about fundamentally changing the economy to create jobs, to retrain Americans for future jobs and change the direction of the economy. Bill Clinton did not get elected to cut the deficit. He got elected to change the economy for the better.

May 27/
The Washington Post, 5-28:(A)11.

Linda Chavez
Fellow, Manhattan Institute;
Director, Center for the
New American Community

2

[Civil-rights activist] Roger Wilkins and fellow liberals love to point to the loss of manufacturing jobs in the 1970s and 1980s, but fail to mention that employment grew by 19 percent in the 1980s, and that 21.5 million jobs were created from December, 1982 to June, 1990. While employment and labor-force participation rates were declining for blacks during that period, other low-skilled employees were

entering the job market, most notably Latin immigrants. Recent studies of Mexican immigrants and blacks in Chicago suggest that black men are far more hostile than Mexican men about performing low-paying jobs, are less willing to be flexible in accepting assignments outside their normal responsibilities, and are less willing to work as hard for the same low wages. The history of discrimination against blacks may make them more resentful of accepting low-paid work, while the extreme poverty that many Mexican men experience before coming to the U.S. may make them more willing to do so. Nonetheless, the behavior itself has important consequences in the relative employability of members of each group.

Interview/
Mother Jones, March-April:5.

Benjamin F. Chavis, Jr.
Executive director,
National Association for the
Advancement of Colored People

3

Congress debated the [summer] jobs package [for young people] as if it's part of some political football. Where's the human dynamics of this situation? I need to talk to the President [Clinton], because I think the President is giving in too soon, when he could be mobilizing public opinion [to favor the jobs plan]. You cannot go to an urban center where this is not a major issue . . . Having 500,000 jobs this summer could make a critical difference. It could be the difference between whether or not we have a long hot or a long cool summer. Particularly this year.

Interview/
USA Today, 4-22:(A)11.

Dick Cheney
Former Secretary of Defense
of the United States;
Former United States
Representative, R-Wyoming

4

Whatever happened to the "new Democrat"? I look at [President Clinton's economic] package and it looks to me that it's the same kind of package that Jimmy Carter, Walter Mondale and Michael Dukakis would have written.

At Conservative Political Action
Conference, Washington, D.C./
The Christian Science Monitor,
2-22:2.

Warren Christopher
Secretary of State
of the United States

1

[On the forthcoming G-7 summit in Tokyo]: What is new is the American President [Clinton] going to a summit acting from a position of strength because the United States has put its economic house in order. Now, for the first time, an American President will face his G-7 counterparts with a strong and credible economic hand to play.

The Washington Post, 7-5:(A)14.

Lawrence W. Clarkson
Vice president for planning
and international development,
Boeing Company

2

President Clinton visited [Boeing] and promised that he was going to work hard to help keep aerospace jobs in America. Well, if he does not renew China's [most-favored-nation trade] status or places unacceptable conditions on it, he will be doing the exact opposite of what he promised. We will lose orders and people will lose jobs.

The New York Times, 5-7:(C)2.

Bill Clinton
President-elect
of the United States

3

You've got to understand what most voters brought to [the 1992 Presidential] election, at least most people who voted for me. They brought a keen awareness that while most of them were worse off [economically] than they were 10 years ago, there had been a big divergence in income in America. Inequality had got worse, and all the tax breaks had gone to the people who were doing better anyway. This is a much more unequal country than it was 10 years ago.

Interview, Little Rock, Ark./
Time, 1-4:35.

4

[On newly revised estimates that push the projected U.S. deficit up beyond what was thought before]: We can now see the full magnitude of the debt we [his Administration] will inherit and the challenge that we must confront. The unsettling revelation—however camouflaged—is that the projected deficit for 1997 has grown by $60-billion, and that, if left unchecked, it could soar above $400-billion near the end of the decade. This sounds the final warning bell. This endless pattern of rising deficits must stop.

Little Rock, Ark., Jan. 6/
The New York Times, 1-7:(A)10.

5

[Saying he is no longer considering a middle-class tax cut as a priority, as he did during 1992's Presidential campaign]: I think the American people voted for me because they supported the big things we were running on. From New Hampshire forward, for reasons that absolutely mystified me, the press thought the most important issue in the race was the middle-class tax cut. I never did meet any voter who thought that.

News conference,
Little Rock, Ark., Jan. 14/
The New York Times, 1-15:(A)10.

6

Here in America we cannot sustain an active engagement abroad without a sound economy at home. And yet we cannot prosper at home unless we are engaged abroad. We will, there-

(BILL CLINTON)

fore, seek economic strength at home through increased productivity, even as we seek to ensure that global commerce is rooted in principles of openness, fairness and reciprocity.

To diplomats,
Georgetown University, Jan. 18/
The New York Times, 1-19:(A)8.

Bill Clinton
President of the United States

1

[Addressing middle-class America]: To those of you who gave the most in the 1980s, I had hoped to invest in your future by creating jobs, expanding education, reforming health care, and reducing the debt without asking more of you [in taxes]. I've worked harder than I've ever worked in my life to meet that goal. But I can't—because the [Federal budget] deficit has increased so much, beyond my earlier estimates and beyond even the worst official government estimates from last year . . . But I can assure you of this: You're not going alone anymore, you're not going first, and you're no longer going to pay more and get less. Seventy percent of the new taxes I'll propose—70 percent—will be paid by those who make more than $100,000 a year.

Broadcast address to the nation,
Washington, D.C., Feb. 15/
USA Today, 2-16:(A)11.

2

Our economic plan is ambitious, but it is necessary for the continued greatness of our country. And it will be paid for fairly—by cutting government, by asking the most of those who benefited the most in the past. [I am] asking more Americans to contribute today so that all Americans can do better tomorrow. The test of our program cannot simply be: What's in it for me? The question must be: What's in it for us? . . . This economic plan cannot please everybody. If this package is picked apart, there will be something that will anger each of us. But, if it is taken as a whole, it will help all of

us. Resist the temptation to focus only on a spending cut you don't like or some investment not made.

Before joint session of U.S. Congress,
Washington, D.C., Feb. 17/
The New York Times, 2-18:(A)1,11.

3

[On his economic plan]: I have already heard some people on the other side of the aisle say, "He should have cut more government spending." I say: "Show me where, and be specific—not hot air. Show me where."

At rally, St. Louis, Mo., Feb. 18/
The New York Times, 2-19:(A)1.

4

We're angry when we see jobs and factories moving overseas or across the borders or depressing wages here at home when we think there is nothing we can do about it. We worry about our own prosperity being so dependent on events and forces beyond our shores. Could it be that the world's most powerful nation has also given up a significant measure of its sovereignty in the quest to lift the fortunes of people throughout the world? It is ironic and even painful that the global village we have worked so hard to create has done so much to be the source of higher unemployment and lower wages for some of our people. But that is no wonder. For years our leaders have failed to take the steps that would harness the global economy to the benefit of all of our people: steps such as investing in our people and their skills, enforcing our trade laws, helping communities hurt by change; in short, putting the American people first, without withdrawing from the world and people beyond our borders.

At American University, Feb. 26/
The New York Times, 2-27:4.

5

The argument I was trying to make to the Boeing [aircraft-manufacturing] workers last week is that the adversity they have suffered in the market is through no fault of their own. That

(BILL CLINTON)

is, they have not failed by being unproductive or lazy or asking for too much. But that Europe was able to penetrate this market because of [their] Airbus [goverment-subsidy] policy. And the blame I placed was on our government for not responding, not Europe's for trying to get it. That was their right.

News conference,
Washington, D.C., March 9/
The New York Times, 3-10:(A)4.

1

[On criticism of his proposals that the Federal government spend money to build public swimming pools and other recreational facilities]: The Senate's got a swimming pool, doesn't it? And it was built with taxpayers' money and somebody had a job building it . . . If you put people to work in a city or a suburb or a small town building a city park that gives people—kids—the chance to have recreational opportunities in the summertime and you create jobs doing it, is that a waste of money?

To reporters,
Washington, D.C., April 7/
Los Angeles Times, 4-8:(A)19.

2

[On Senate Republicans' opposition to his economic stimulus plan]: Let's strip all this rhetoric away. This is about whether you want to reduce the unemployment rate in America by another half a percentage point for a very modest amount. And they [Republicans] don't—for whatever reason, they don't. They want more people to stay out of work.

Washington, D.C., April 12/
The Washington Post, 4-13:(A)7.

3

[On Republicans who oppose his economic stimulus plan because they say it will increase the Federal deficit]: This is the crowd that had the government for 12 years. They took the

deficit from $1-trillion to $4-trillion. Have they no shame? How can they say this? Sometimes, I think the secret of success in this town is being able to say the most amazing things with a straight face.

Before Builders and Construction
Trades Union,
Washington, D.C., April 19/
Los Angeles Times, 4-20:(A)6.

4

We have abandoned trickle-down economics. We have abandoned the policies that brought the debt of this country from one trillion to 4 trillion dollars in only a decade. The [Clinton] budget plan which passed the Congress, which will reduce the deficit and increase investment has led to a 20-year low in mortgage rates, dramatically lower interest rates. There are probably people in this room who have refinanced their home mortgages in the last three months or so and who have had access to cheaper credit. That's going to put tens of billions of dollars coursing throughout this economy in ways that are very, very good for the country. And so we are moving in the right direction, economically.

News conference,
Washington, D.C., April 23/
The New York Times, 4-24:5.

5

[On charges that he has reneged on a middle-class tax cut, which he promised in his Presidential campaign last year]: I've got four years. Give me four years to deliver on the middle-class tax cut.

Broadcast question-and-answer program,
San Diego, Calif., May 17/
Los Angeles Times, 5-18:(A)1.

6

[Asking for Congressional passage of his economic plan]: We could all argue until the cows come home about whether every last decision has been perfectly right; but it is perfectly clear that if you don't do both [cut spend-

(BILL CLINTON)

ing and raise taxes], you can't get where we're going. This is a difficult time for the Congress, a difficult time for the country. The worst thing we can do is walk away and do nothing and continue the perilous paralysis of the last few years. So I implore you to shoulder this, think of our kids and grandkids, and let's move this country forward in a bipartisan and open manner.

At White House ceremony,
Washington, D.C., May 25/
Los Angeles Times, 5-6:(A)23.

1

There's a global recession. Two-thirds of our jobs in the late '80s came from exports, and it's hard to generate jobs from exports when many European countries have actually negative growth and when Japan has no growth. That's why this . . . [upcoming G-7] meeting is so important, trying to get some growth back into the global economy that will get the export portion of our job growth going again. It's very hard for the United States alone to grow jobs without help from other nations.

To reporters, Washington, D.C., June 30/
Los Angeles Times, 7-1:(A)11.

2

The global economy is here to stay. We can't wish it away. We can't hide from it, and no political leader can promise to protect you from it. We simply have to compete, not retreat, and we have to do it while maintaining our position of world leadership.

Before National Education Association,
San Francisco, Calif., July 5/
The New York Times, 7-6:(A)6.

3

[Saying his economic plan will cost the average working family only $1 a week more in taxes]: You cannot make me believe, once you get out there and tell the truth to the people in any district represented in this room, that the average middle-class family with income above

$30,000 a year and below the income-tax threshold [of $115,000 a year] wouldn't pay a buck a week to get this [Federal budget] deficit down. I think they would.

To Congressional Democrats,
Washington, D.C., July 20/
Los Angeles Times, 7-21:(A)11.

4

[On his economic plan now before Congress]: Economists and business leaders alike warn us that growth will falter if we don't take dramatic steps to tame this [Federal budget] deficit, and soon. With so much at stake it would be irresponsible not to take decisive action. With this plan in place, the economy will grow and more than eight million new jobs will be created in the next four years. Without it, we put the economy and our standard of living at further risk. If we take this important first step now, over the long run we will see deficits go down and jobs go up.

Broadcast address to the nation,
Washington, D.C., Aug. 3/
The New York Times, 8-4:(A)10.

5

[On his economic plan]: The result will be very close to the $500-billion in [Federal] deficit reduction. It's going to [be] a big step forward in tax fairness because of the fact that over 70 percent of the tax burden will now be paid by people with incomes above $200,000, the 1.2 percent of the population that got a majority of the economic gains of the '80s. The working poor will be lifted out of poverty for the first time because of the [earned income tax credit increase]. That will be the most dramatic social reform probably in a couple of decades for this country, which is a stunning thing.

Interview, Washington, D.C./
U.S. News & World Report,
8-9:32.

6

[On his proposed program to provide young people with on-the-job training for their future

(BILL CLINTON)

careers]: If we are going to prosper in the world toward which we are heading, we have to reach out to every one of our young people who wants a job and don't have the training to get it. We don't have a person to waste. And believe you me, when we waste them, the rest of us pay. We pay in unemployment. We pay in welfare. We pay in jail costs. We pay in drug use.

To students and other residents,
Georgetown, Del., Sept. 3/
Los Angeles Times, 9-4:(A)23.

1

[Supporting NAFTA]: By raising the incomes of Mexicans, which this will do, they'll be able to buy more of our products and there will be much less pressure on them to come to this country in the form of illegal immigration. I think this will be a very stabilizing, economically healthy agreement.

Aug. 19/
The New York Times, 8-23:(C)1.

2

[On his plan to ease controls on foreign sales of U.S. high-tech equipment]: Everywhere I went [during last year's election campaign] where there were people who were trying to create the American economy of the future, someone would take me aside and talk about the problems of the export-control laws, which may have been needed in a former period when the technology was different and certainly the politics of the Cold War were different, but were clearly undermining our ability to be competitive today.

Sept. 29/
Los Angeles Times, 9-30:(A)15.

3

[Advocating passage of NAFTA]: What would we do in America if we turn away from this and [Mexican leaders] make this sort of arrangement with Japan or with Europe? And they make the investment there, and then we have to deal with their products coming through the back door from Mexico? What will happen to our job base? I'm telling you, everything people worried about in the 1980s will get worse if this thing is voted down and will get better if it's voted up.

Washington, D.C., Oct. 20/
Los Angeles Times, 10-21:(A)31.

4

[Seeking to allay fears by some U.S. workers that their jobs might be moved to Mexico if NAFTA passes]: I was the Governor of the state [Arkansas] that lost plants to Mexico. I used to go stand at plants on the last day they were open and shake hands with people when they walked off the job for the last time. I want you to understand this very clearly from somebody who's lived through this: This [NAFTA] agreement will make that less likely, not more likely.

Nov. 4/USA Today, 11-5:(A)7.

5

[Supporting the proposed NAFTA]: No one has shown how a wealthy country can grow wealthier and create more jobs unless there is a global economic growth through trade. There is simply no evidence that you can do it any other way.

To meeting of business leaders,
Washington, D.C., Nov. 9/
The Washington Post, 11-10:(A)7.

6

All wealthy nations are having difficulty creating jobs and raising incomes, even when there is economic growth. Why is that? Because workers in advanced countries must become ever more productive to deal with competition from low-wage countries on the one hand and high-skilled, high-tech countries on the other. Being more productive simply means that fewer and fewer people can produce more and more goods. And in an environment like that, if you want to increase jobs and raise incomes, the only way to do it is find more customers for each country's

(BILL CLINTON)

products. There is no alternative. We must compete, not retreat.

At Asia-Pacific Economic
Cooperation conference,
Seattle, Wash., Nov. 19/
The New York Times, 11-20:5.

John Conyers, Jr.
United States Representative,
D-Michigan

1

There's no question that uncontrolled entitlement spending is the single greatest problem with respect to deficit spending. But that reflects past failures to implement meaningful health-care reform and cost controls, and not the absence of some arbitrary entitlement cap.

The Washington Post, 5-18:(A)10.

E. Gerald Corrigan
President,
Federal Reserve Bank
of New York

2

Even today, with the outlook for inflation seeming to be so benign, we must remain vigilant and we must staunchly resist those voices who would suggest that a "little more" inflation may not be all that bad, especially if it brings a lot more growth. Above all, we must vigorously resist any suggestion that a "little more" inflation is something we can live with because we can fine-tune policy and somehow "cap" the inflation rate at some moderately higher, but stable, rate. I say to you in point-blank terms that such an approach will not work; when it does not work, I can absolutely guarantee that there will be no witch doctor nor any magic medicine that will be capable of reversing that "little more" inflation without incurring substantial costs in terms of higher unemployment and lost output.

Before New York State Bankers
Association, Jan. 27/
The Wall Street Journal,
2-26:(A)14.

Christopher Cox
United States Representative,
R-California

3

[On the Congressional debate about President Clinton's budget plan]: Listening to this debate, it has occurred to me that the American people might wonder who is telling the truth here. One side [those supporting Clinton's plan] says, "We are raising taxes but we are cutting spending." The other side [opposed to the Clinton plan] says, "You are not cutting spending, you are raising spending and raising taxes, and it is the same old tax-and-spend." I am going to put my money where my mouth is. I will write out a check from my own personal funds payable to Bill Clinton and the Democratic National Committee, $100,000, if spending next year [under Clinton's budget] is less than this year. I will resign my seat in Congress and I will write 100 times, "I apologize to the Democrats; they were telling the truth. They really did cut spending."

Before the Senate,
Washington, D.C., March 17/
The Wall Street Journal,
3-25:(A)14.

Alfonse M. D'Amato
United States Senator,
D-New York

4

[Criticizing President Clinton's economic plan]: Let me tell you what this budget is going to do: $32.5-billion—that's what it's going to take out of my state. And that's going to be 650,000 jobs in the next five years. Abracadabra, alakazam, presto. Gone. Chefs, waiters, cooks, bartenders. And what about the construction industry? Electricians, carpenters, plumbers, alakazam, presto, gone. Smoke and mirrors. Gone. $32.5-billion from New York. Let me tell you about senior citizens. Senior citizens in New York are going to pay in terms of their increase on Social Security an average of $957 more. And by the way, 60 percent of that comes from families that have an income of between $40,000 and $75,000. They are not rich. They are not the super wealthy. They are working people. Is there any reason why the American people are going to be fooled? No. Once again they see us [in government] playing our tricks.

Before the Senate, Washington, D.C./
The New York Times, 8-7:29.

John C. Danforth
United States Senator,
R-Missouri

1

We want to . . . encourage the [Clinton] Administration to think about broad-based consumption taxes and to let them know that there are people here who would be willing to work with them. We are the only industrialized country in the world without some form of national consumption tax, and we believe that the time has come to move in this direction.

News conference,
Washington, D.C., Jan. 25/
Los Angeles Times, 1-26:(D)1.

2

If government is going to get its hands on [industrial] research, if government is going to provide a kind of industrial policy, picking winners and losers—who's good in high tech, who's not so good, who's good in research, who's not so good—there is enormous potential for transforming what seems like a good idea into political pork. Is this going to be another grab bag for political reward?

At Senate hearing on the nomination
of Ronald H. Brown for Commerce Secretary,
Washington, D.C./
The Washington Post, 2-15:(A)25.

Bob Dederick
Chief economist,
Northern Trust Company,
Chicago, Ill.

3

This is not a full-blown rousing [economic] recovery; there is just enough increase to ward

off the wolves. The Clinton Administration will not be doing handstands with these economic numbers.

The Christian Science Monitor,
4-1:8.

Robert J. Dole
United States Senator,
R-Kansas

4

Before President Clinton demands that the farmer, the nurse, the factory worker, the shop keeper, the truck driver, or our senior citizens send one more dime to Washington [in increased taxes], they should demand of President Clinton, and those of us in Congress, that every outdated program, every bloated agency, and every item in the Federal budget takes the hit it deserves. Because without real spending cuts and an across-the-board sacrifice, the American people will be short-changed again by a government that refuses to change.

Broadcast address to the nation,
Washington, D.C., Feb. 15/
Los Angeles Times, 2-16:(A)14.

5

Despite the best efforts of the White House to make more government spending look like a good idea, the American people aren't buying it. The American people are hoping the Democrats will finally get the message—it's time to cut up Uncle Sam's credit card once and for all.

Washington, D.C., April 20/
The Washington Post, 4-21:(A)4.

6

[Criticizing President Clinton's economic plan]: The President says the tax increases will only punish upper-income Americans, as if that was something to celebrate. Well, he's wrong. Under his plan, millions of you who might think you were a member of the middle class will be paying more in taxes. [If the plan is approved by Congress,] more than 800,000 small businesses, over 5 million senior citizens and millions of

(ROBERT J. DOLE)

others will soon be sending more hard-earned dollars to Washington.

Broadcast address to the nation,
Washington, D.C., Aug. 3/
Los Angeles Times, 8-4:(A)10.

1

[Criticizing the retroactive provision of the tax increases contained in President Clinton's economic plan and the promises of government spending cuts in the future]: This President will go down in history as the only President who raised taxes before he took office and cut spending after he left office.

Before the Senate,
Washington, D.C., Aug. 6/
The New York Times, 8-7:1.

2

[Supporting NAFTA]: I come from a small state in the Midwest . . . and I've gone around my state meeting with small-businessmen and small-businesswomen and agricultural groups, and I would say that about 90 percent of these people support the North American Free Trade Agreement. Why? Because it's in our interest, that's why. It's also in Mexico's interest; it's also in Canada's interest . . . [And] Mexico is just the first of the Central and the South American countries. Other countries are waiting in line to see how this works and see whether or not [the U.S.] Congress will pass a North American Free Trade Agreement: Chile, Venezuela, Argentina. And what do they want? They want to trade with the United States. And when they trade with the United States, that creates jobs in the United States.

News conference, Oct. 13/
The Washington Post, 10-14:(A)30.

Pete V. Domenici
United States Senator,
R-New Mexico

3

[President Clinton's economic] package sounds like a very, very big tax increase with a few frills around the edges at this point. A little economic stimulus—you know, a gnat on a camel—and a huge tax package.

Feb. 16/
The Washington Post, 2-17:(A)7.

Samuel Doria Medina
Minister of Planning
and Coordination of Bolivia

4

We know that the free market is the only way to go. But trickle-down systems will never reach people who are entirely outside the market economy. There's no magic about it. The invisible hand of the market can't touch people who can't read or write who don't have roads or basic health services and who can't produce, much less buy . . . Just like the trade barriers which stop companies and countries from entering markets, there are economic and social barriers which prevent people from entering markets in their own country. Our policy is to break these down.

July 18/
The New York Times, 7-19:(A)5.

Rudi Dornbusch
Economist,
Massachusetts Institute
of Technology

5

Economists think they have a God-given right to powerful positions in government. But the typical economist has not spent much time researching the important issues that are facing [President-elect] Clinton—what to do about the inner cities, how to make American corporations Number 1 again, what to do about education, what to do about job training.

Los Angeles Times, 1-8:(A)21.

William C. Dunkelberg
Chief economist,
National Federation
of Independent Business

6

[In the small-business community,] there is a crisis in confidence about the [Clinton]

Administration, and employers continue to express their reluctance to invest in the future or to hire new people. Businesses aren't borrowing because the economic policies coming out of Washington are anti-growth.

The Christian Science Monitor,
11-8:14.

Lawrence S. Eagleburger
Secretary of State
of the United States

1

The [incoming Clinton] Administration, quite rightly, I think, has identified the domestic economy as the first thing that must be dealt with. I don't envy those from the [Clinton] Administration who, in the face of that correct analysis, must tell the Congress they need an additional $2-billion to deal with aid to Eastern Europe or what was the Soviet Union.

Before Council on Foreign Relations,
Jan. 7/
Los Angeles Times, 1-9:(A)4.

Robert Eaton
Chairman Chrysler Corporation

2

[On President Clinton's economic plan]: It's a tough package. But one look at the [Federal budget] deficit that is strangling this country, and you know that toughness is what's needed.

USA Today, 2-19:(A)11.

Steve Einhorn
Partner, Goldman Sachs,
investments

3

[On why President Clinton's economic plans may have a negative effect on the stock market]: First, Clinton is clearly going to rely more on higher taxes and less on lower government spending as the way to cut the Federal budget deficit. And then his proposals will go to Congress, where spending cuts tend to get lost. Second, and even more problematic, he is

going to increase the corporate tax rate to 36 percent. While that has been known for a while, news stories in the past week suggest that the rate could go higher in order to fund the Administration's plans for universal health insurance. Higher taxes will deter earnings growth. Third, there will be a sizable increase in energy taxes and taxes on upper-income people. That will slow consumer spending and corporate profit growth. Fourth, Clinton seems increasingly willing to consider price controls on the health-care sector of the economy. In our opinion, price controls do not work and will tend to make health care more expensive . . . Fifth, there has been a spate of disturbing rhetoric from the Administration that seems to vilify business. If vilification of the corporate sector is part and parcel of the Administration's policy, I would be worried.

The Washington Post, 2-18:(B)10.

Robert Eisner
Professor,
Northwestern University;
Former president,
American Economic Association

4

[On the national debt]: We're spending our children's money? That's utter nonsense. The money your children will spend hasn't even been printed. [Federal Reserve Chairman Alan] Greenspan and his successors will provide all the money they need.

The Christian Science Monitor,
3-16:11.

Stuart E. Eizenstat
United States Ambassador
to the European Community

5

[On the recent GATT trade agreement]: Not only is this the most important trade agreement by light years, but it is one of the most impressive international agreements of any kind ever reached. It will profoundly change the way societies are organized and the way they do business.

Dec. 15/
Los Angeles Times, 12-16:(A)16.

Stephen Elmont
Vice president,
National Restaurant Association
1

[Saying President Clinton's proposal to reduce the tax deductibility of business meals from 80 percent to 50 percent will hurt restaurants]: Why do politicians want to hurt the industry that contributes 5 percent to the GNP? This industry puts money in their coffers . . . I can understand how it [deductibility of business lunches] might not play well in Peoria. From middle America's viewpoint, it is perceived as a luxury . . . But people do it because it is what they have to do to earn a living . . . There isn't anybody I know that looks forward to a business meal: It's work.
The Christian Science Monitor,
4-16:8.

Amitai Etzioni
Sociologist,
George Washington University
2

[The Federal budget deficit is] 90 percent a moral issue and 10 percent economics. It's eating your heritage and depriving your children. If that's not a moral issue, what is?
Interview, Boston, Mass./
The Christian Science Monitor,
4-19:13.

Jack Faris
President,
National Federation
of Independent Businesses
3

[Criticizing the Clinton Admistration's proposed energy tax]: If the goal is to nip an economic recovery in the bud, there is no better way to do it than to impose an energy tax. The BTU tax will set off a mad rush by businesses to find ways to avoid getting burned. This is the worst of all possible ideas at the worst of all possible times.
May 25/
Los Angeles Times, 5-26:(A)23.

Martin Feldstein
Economist,
Harvard University;
Former Chairman,
Council of Economic Advisers
to the President
of the United States
(Ronald Reagan)
4

[On President Clinton's use of the word "investments" to describe his spending programs]: Clinton has decided that investment is a good word. But it is hard to think of anything in the [Federal] budget that couldn't be construed as an investment. Defense is an investment in the national security. Medicaid is investing in the health of the poor. The term becomes meaningless.
Los Angeles Times, 3-28:(D)7.

Bob Filner
United States Representative,
D-California
5

[Criticizing the proposed NAFTA]: This agreement, negotiated by former [U.S.] President [George] Bush, is a "trickle-down" treaty. It is designed to benefit big corporations and exploit our resources, both human and environmental. It is free trade for big business. We want fair trade for working Americans.
The Christian Science Monitor,
5-19:1.

Thomas S. Foley
United States Representative,
D-Washington;
Speaker of the House
6

[On Republican opposition to President Clinton's economic plan]: I think if I have a fundamental belief as a Democrat vis-a-vis the Republicans, it's that they have an instinctive, visceral desire to protect higher-income Americans from [contributing] a fair share of public finance and support. And they're at it again. The only group in the country. Every other group is being asked to do something [to help

(THOMAS S. FOLEY)

the economy]—farmers, workers, people who are Social Security recipients, people who receive government programs, students. Go down the list. The one group that the Republican Party doesn't want to have any participation in deficit reduction are people who earn over $200,000 a year.

Interview,
Washington, D.C., June 24/
The Christian Science Monitor,
6-25:1.

1

[On the proposed NAFTA]: It is not a perfect agreement. But this is, for the moment, an opportunity to expand our trade, to reach out beyond our borders . . . to seize the future. Is it good for America or not? I believe passionately it is good for America.

Before the House,
Washington, Nov. 17/
Los Angeles Times, 11-18:(A)1.

Malcolm S. Forbes, Jr.
President and editor-in-chief,
"Forbes" magazine

2

[On President Clinton's proposal to increase taxes on the rich]: If you want the economy to move ahead, you reward success, you don't punish it. Clinton's tax package comes out at a time when the economy is ready and raring to boom. We could have a boom that would leave Japan and Germany in the dust. He's slowing the pace of progress.

USA Today, 2-19:(A)11.

Gerald R. Ford
Former President
of the United States

3

[Calling for passage of NAFTA]: If you defeat NAFTA, you have to share the responsibility for increased immigration [from Mexico] to the United States, where they [Mexicans] want

jobs that are presently held by Americans. It's cold-blooded and practical, and members of the House and Senate ought to understand that.

At President Clinton's signing
of supplemental agreements to NAFTA,
Washington, D.C., Sept. 14/
The New York Times, 9-15:(A)12.

Robert P. Forrestal
President,
Federal Reserve Bank
of Atlanta, Ga.

4

[Saying the Federal Reserve should remember that economic growth, not just keeping inflation down, is important when formulating its policies]: I believe the Fed, like other policy institutions that act on behalf of society, must keep public preferences in mind when pursuing social goals.

Before Senate Banking Committee,
Washington, D.C., March 10/
The New York Times, 3-11:(C)6.

Gail Fosler
Chief economist,
The Conference Board

5

There is a realization among business people that they want [a U.S. President] who is engaged in the activities of the economy. We reached the limits of *laissez-faire* economics after the first term of the [Ronald] Reagan Administration. The ideology of allowing business to compete totally without government support is so in contrast with what businesses are encountering in the global marketplace that it creates a demand for a President who is engaged in making the U.S. economy the world's most competitive.

Interview/The New York Times, 3-1:(C)12.

Douglas A. Fraser
Former president,
United Automobile Workers
of America

6

[On his non-support of the proposed NAFTA, even though he thinks in the long run it would

(DOUGLAS A. FRASER)

be good for U.S. jobs]: When I see the depth of emotion and fear [about NAFTA] in labor's rank-and-file—a fear that it will cost them their jobs—it's hard to ignore it. I have never seen union members as fearful of a single issue . . . So it's not a question of whether I can or can't get into an argument with today's labor leadership. I don't care about that. It's a question of my not being willing to walk away from the rank-and-file who feel so strongly.

Interview/
Los Angeles Times, 11-14:(M)5.

Mitchell Fromstein
Chairman, Manpower, Inc.
(employment agency
for temporary workers)

1

[On the proliferation of temporary and part-time jobs]: The U.S. is going from just-in-time manufacturing to just-in-time employment. The employer tells us, "I want them [employees] delivered exactly when I want them, as many as I need; and when I don't need them, I don't want them here." Can I get people to work under these circumstances? Yes. We're the ATMs of the job market . . . We are not exploiting people. We are not setting the fees. The market is. We are matching people with demands. What would our workers be doing without us? Unemployment lines? Welfare? Suicide?

Time, 3-29:44,46.

Richard A. Gephardt
United States Representative,
D-Missouri

2

A high-wage, high-skill economy is what we want. This is not saying the government leads economic success. Wealth is created, jobs are created in the private sector, not in the government. But [government has] a vital role to play in aiding . . . what needs to happen in the private sector.

To reporters, Washington, D.C./
The Christian Science Monitor, 2-25:8.

3

[On President Clinton's economic program]: There's a clear perception in the country that this is it—there's only one game in town. This is the program, and if [the Congress] can't get behind this, then we really are just a bunch of individual entrepreneurs here.

Interview/USA Today, 3-5:(A)6.

4

Trade policy is the inescapable link to the world economy. If we do everything else right but we fail to have a trade policy that fights for the rights of our farmers, workers and businesses, then we will fall short of the goal of a high standard of living. At best, we will tread water. At worst—which is what's happening to us today—we will have decline or a furious effort just to hold the line.

Before Economic Strategy Institute,
Washington, D.C., May 11/
Los Angeles Times, 5-12:(A)14.

5

[Saying he does not intend to vote for NAFTA]: We are losing good-paying jobs and that will continue with or without NAFTA. The much greater threat is to our wages and our standard of living. And on this important point, there can be no doubt that NAFTA, as drafted, will only increase the downward pressure . . . A high and rising standard of living, and a long-term policy of ensuring better jobs at better wages, won't be achieved under this agreement. On the contrary, I think the agreement will undermine this goal.

At National Press Club,
Washington, D.C., Sept. 21/
Los Angeles Times, 9-22:(A)17.

Sam M. Gibbons
United States Representative,
D-Florida

6

[On the possibility of an energy tax in President Clinton's economic plan]: As soon as [such a tax is] introduced, there will be interest

(SAM M. GIBBONS)

groups jumping all over the proposal. It will be like another industry springing up in Washington. You won't be able to find a seat in the restaurants here, the city will be so jammed with people looking for exceptions and loopholes. You wait and see. You'll wind up with one paragraph of legislation levying the tax, and 40 pages on all the exemptions.

Time, 2-15:25.

Newt Gingrich
United States Representative,
R-Georgia

1

It's easy to write serious [Federal] budgets. It's just hard to pass them.

U.S. News & World Report,
2-15:36.

2

[Moderate Democrats who are against President Clinton's proposed energy tax are] responding to people back home who are calling them and saying: "Don't raise the tax on energy; don't raise the tax on driving to work; don't raise the tax on heating and air conditioning; don't raise the tax on agriculture." This is a grass-roots, back-home effort by real people.

May 25/
Los Angeles Times,
5-27:(A)24.

Roberto C. Goizueta
Chairman,
Coca-Cola Company

3

[Supporting President Clinton's economic plan]: It behooves everybody, businessmen and average individuals alike, to really make this work. If [the President] succeeds, we all succeed. If he fails, we all fail.

Interview/
The New York Times,
3-1:(A)1.

Jane Goodman
Director of communications,
Association of (airline)
Flight Attendants

4

[On labor strikes]: Nobody strikes without a great deal of forethought and a great deal of angst . . . The right to strike is crucial to keeping a level playing field. It's still the only way to get attention [of an uncooperative management].

The Christian Science Monitor,
11-24:3.

Al Gore
Vice President
of the United States

5

[On the possibility of trade wars as governments give subsidies to businesses]: We're not proposing anything that violates our trade agreements, and we are in favor of expanding world trade. But we're determined to rectify some of the imbalances in the world trading system. Immediately after World War II, it was sensible for our nation to accept inequitable arrangements as one of several ways to encourage the more rapid growth of economies in the rest of the world, because that was good for us. Well, now our trading partners are in many cases quite healthy and eating us [alive] in a number of areas.

Interview/
U.S. News & World Report,
3-8:30.

6

[Supporting the proposed NAFTA]: We [in the U.S.] make the best tires in the world, but we have a hard time selling them in Mexico because they have a 20 percent tax collected at the border on all of the tires that we try to sell . . . [If NAFTA passes, U.S. companies] will make more tires [for sale in Mexico]. And remember this: I mean, people think, "Well, they [Mexico] don't buy tires." Mexico bought 750,000 new cars last year. The Big Three [U.S. auto companies] sold them only 1,000 because they have the same barriers against our cars.

(AL GORE)

Those barriers will be eliminated by NAFTA. We'll sell 60,000, not 1,000, in the first year after NAFTA. Every one of those cars has four new tires and one spare. We'll create more jobs with NAFTA.

Broadcast interview,
Washington, D.C./
"Larry King Live," CNN-TV, 11-9.

1

[On a new bargaining relationship being established by the Clinton Administration between the Federal government and its employee labor unions]: [The challenge will be to] redefine success. In the past, both public and private sectors often measured success in size—bigger budgets and bigger staffs. We must measure success in terms of services provided to customers [the public] . . . We must abandon the idea that when management and labor sit down together, there has to be a winner and a loser.

The Washington Post, 11-22:(A)19.

Porter Goss
United States Representative,
R-Florida

2

[Supporting the proposed NAFTA]: A yes vote [by Congress] says to the world that America is alive and well and a champion of free enterprise. It says to our neighbors in this hemisphere that we can be trusted to negotiate faithfully and fairly. And it says to Americans—in business, on the farm, to workers and professionals and their families at home—that we can compete and win. Bring on the world—we're ready.

Before the House,
Washington, D.C./Time, 11-29:18.

Phil Gramm
United States Senator,
R-Texas

3

[On President Clinton's revised economic package]: The President has given us a new

proposal which glazes the ham but does not cut the fat. If these programs are important, let's pay for them. If they're not important, let's don't raise the deficit to fund more spending. We already have $300-billion worth of deficit spending. If that's an [economic] stimulus, why haven't we reached economic heaven?

Los Angeles, Calif./
Los Angeles Times, 4-17:(A)8.

4

[Criticizing President Clinton's economic plan]: I oppose this bill because you cannot create more investment by taxing investors. You cannot create more savings by taxing savers. You cannot create more jobs by taxing the job-creators. Hundreds of thousands of Americans will lose their jobs because of this bill. [President] Clinton will be one of those Americans, but he will *deserve* to lose his job.

Before the Senate,
Washington, D.C., June 23/
The New York Times, 6-24:(A)8.

5

I believe the [House-Senate compromise on President Clinton's economic plan] is going to pass . . . because the Democrats have convinced members of Congress that they ought to put Bill Clinton and his survival in front of the well-being of the country.

Los Angeles Times, 8-4:(A)11.

Eric Greenberg
Director of management studies,
American Management Association

6

[Criticizing the trend of U.S. companies to downsize by firing large numbers of employees]: A great many companies are asking the wrong question. They are asking, What is the irreducible core that we need to turn on the lights in the morning and lock up the doors at night and still continue to do business? The right question is, How can we change the way we do business so that the people we have are better able to contribute to organizational success? What companies have been doing is firing their customers and undercutting any hope of a consumer-driven [economic] recovery. People who lose their jobs are not spending their money and not driving the industrial machine.

Time, 11-22:36.

Stanley B. Greenberg
Chief public-opinion analyst
for President of the United States
Bill Clinton

1

[On President Clinton's reneging on campaign promises to cut taxes on the middle class]: Voters never believed in the middle-class tax cut, because they have never seen anyone get a tax cut. They always believed their taxes would go up whether Bill Clinton became President or George Bush was President. They voted for Bill Clinton because they believed he was going to submit a program to change the direction of the country, to improve the economy and to create jobs. They will be mad as hell if their taxes go up and there's no genuine commitment to change. But if there is, they will be willing to contribute. It is critical [that the rich be seen as bearing the brunt of a tax increase]. This says to voters that this is a President who is not a captive of the wealthiest people but who is, instead, responsive to the middle class. That is a critical issue. Since they are not going to see the results of economic growth for a long time, it is critical that you send them a very big signal about whose interests are being advanced.

The New York Times, 2-18:(A)11.

Alan Greenspan
Chairman,
Federal Reserve Board

2

[On President Clinton's economic plan]: It is a serious proposal . . . a detailed program-by-program set of recommendations, as distinct from general goals. It is not vague. But, I think,

having not yet looked at the extreme details, this is a credible endeavor. Whether it succeeds or fails will depend substantially on the Congress.

Before Senate Banking,
Housing and Urban Affairs Committee,
Washington, D.C., Feb. 19/
Los Angeles Times, 2-20:(A)1.

3

If one is looking at the probability of a sustained reduction in the [Federal] deficit, the probability is higher if it is done from the expenditure side than from the tax side.

Before House Budget Committee,
Washington, D.C., Feb. 24/
The New York Times, 2-25:(C)2.

4

Ultimately, the defense [spending] cutbacks will benefit the U.S. economy by freeing up resources to augment the nation's stock of physical and human capital. However, in the short run, lower defense spending depresses economic activity—as is obvious here in Southern California.

Before Independent Bankers Association
of America, San Diego, Calif., March 13/
The New York Times, 3-15:(C)4.

5

I do not like taxation. I think it's an inhibition to the [economic] system. But I like [Federal budget] deficits less, because I think they are a far more corrosive force.

Before Senate Finance Committee,
Washington, D.C., March 24/
The New York Times, 3-25:(C)4.

David Hale
Chief economist,
Kemper Financial Services

6

[Criticizing President Clinton's economic plan]: When future historians are asked to explain why the U.S. economy performed so poorly during the early and mid-1990s, [high on their list will be] the failure of the Clinton Administration to propose a bolder fiscal policy.

The Christian Science Monitor,
7-29:8.

Lee H. Hamilton
United States Representative,
D-Indiana

1

The Federal Reserve . . . is an enormously powerful institution, but it does not conform to the normal standards of government account-ability. Power without accountability simply does not fit into the American system of democracy.

The Christian Science Monitor, 10-14:3.

Stephen Hess
Senior fellow,
Brookings Institution

2

[Saying it is now Congress, more than the President, that is trying to cut government spend-ing the most]: It was supposed to be the other way around. It was Congress that was the big spenders . . . Yet it is the much-maligned Legisla-tive Branch that is pulling and tugging [President Clinton] toward a sensible debt-reduction pack-age. Very encouraging.

The Christian Science Monitor, 3-11:4.

David Hill
International jobs consultant;
Former chief information
systems officer,
General Motors Corporation

3

[On the fluid nature of much of today's and tomorrow's job market]: In the future, loyalty and devotion are going to be not to a Hughes [Aircraft Co.] or Boeing or even an industry, but to a particular profession or skill. It takes a high level of education to succeed in such a free-flowing environment. We are going to be moving from job to job in the same way that migrant workers used to move from crop to crop.

Time, 3-29:44.

Carla A. Hills
Former United States Trade
Representative

4

[Saying President Clinton's ideas on trade policy have been inconsistent]: The business community world-wide hates uncertainty; our trading partners loathe uncertainty and frequently miscalculate when the signals are not clear . . . You don't want our own business community going down paths that are cul-de-sacs.

The New York Times, 3-30:(C)9.

William Hoglund
Executive vice president,
General Motors Corporation

5

The so-called [economic] recovery is the slowest that man has ever seen, and it hasn't resulted in any more employment. [President Clinton's economic] program merely adds another note of uncertainty. So the consumer doesn't feel that anything is happening at all.

Time, 4-26:22.

Steny H. Hoyer
United States Representative,
D-Maryland

6

[Saying he supports the proposed NAFTA]: In weighing my decision, I have carefully con-sidered the position of my friends in organized labor [which is against NAFTA], as well as those of the President [Clinton] and his Administra-tion. Clearly, the labor community feels pas-sionately about this issue . . . However, the global economy is a reality that we can't make go away.

Nov. 9/
The Washington Post, 11-10:(A)6.

Lacy Hunt
Chief economist,
CM&M, securities broker

7

[On President Clinton's economic plan]: [This budget] will shove the economy into recession by the end of 1994. We've had significant tax increases under Eisenhower in the 1950s, Johnson in the 1960s and Bush in 1990. And within 18 months of all those tax increases, the economy slumped into recession. Now we have the biggest tax increase in history at a time when the economy is already fragile.

Time, 8-16:27.

John Irving
Lawyer;
Former General Counsel,
National Labor Relations Board

1

[Arguing against proposed legislation that would prohibit companies from hiring permanent replacements for striking workers]: There are many, many [companies] that . . . simply can't afford to [endure a long strike]; they must continue to operate, or their competitors will be all too happy to permanently take their customers . . . [If] they need to hire permanent replacements . . . they should have that right. Otherwise, the [striking] union just sits out there [on the picket line], and employees dictate when they're going to come back. Employers permanently replace their workers only as a last resort. No employer in his right mind wants to get rid of his skilled workers and have to train a bunch of "green" people.

Nation's Business, June:57.

Sharpe James
Mayor of Newark, N.J.

2

[Criticizing the Senate's rejection of President Clinton's economic stimulus plan]: The misery index is still there, the feeling of despair and hopelessness . . . When we hoped there would be thousands of jobs in the cities and people would see that we care, there was a show of force in the Senate to bring the President to his knees. That stimulus package was a right beginning for a new President to get off on the right foot by saying, "We do care." Instead, it's an embarrassment to the nation. It's rotten partisan politics at its worst.

The Washington Post, 5-26:(A)6.

James Jontz
Director,
Citizens Trade Campaign;
Former United States Representative,
D-Indiana

3

[Criticizing President Clinton's support for the proposed NAFTA]: Activists endured [former Presidents] George Bush and Ronald Reagan for 12 years; they worked hard to elect Clinton to change policy. To people at home, NAFTA is more of the same trickle-down economics, putting corporations ahead of people. NAFTA embodies what people have been fighting against. Clinton says this is a new policy. [But] people at home see Clinton lined up with the business lobbyists. They are mad. They are saying, "This is why we elected Bill Clinton?"

The Washington Post, 11-8:(A)10.

Mickey Kantor
United States Trade
Representative

4

[Supporting NAFTA]: If the NAFTA goes down [to defeat in the U.S.], we'll lose 400,000 jobs related to exports in Mexico. Can we afford to lose 400,000 jobs? I don't think so. Is that in the best interests of the U.S. workers? No, it's not. What really angers me is these critics don't have enough confidence in American workers and businesses to believe we can compete. I don't agree with them. I think we can compete with anyone in the world as long as we lower these tariff barriers and have fair rules. And if they don't believe that, they don't believe in American workers.

Interview/USA Today, 5-27:(A)15.

5

[Supporting the proposed NAFTA, which the U.S. labor movement is against]: The global economy is going to continue to grow whether we like it or not. The only question is whether we take advantage of it. Labor is living intellectually in a world that doesn't exist anymore.

U.S. News & World Report,
11-29:28.

Marcy Kaptur
United States Representative,
D-Ohio

6

[Criticizing President Clinton's alleged deal-making and pork-barrel promises used to obtain

(MARCY KAPTUR)

votes for NAFTA, which was just approved by the House]: [It won] strictly because of the buyouts. It had absolutely nothing to do with the debate. It had absolutely nothing to do with the merits of the issue. People are talking about ambassadorships, judgeships, etc. It's not what Bill Clinton campaigned on. Last November [during the Presidential election] he campaigned on change. This is business as usual . . . He's a candidate of Wall Street, not Main Street.

Interview, Nov. 17/
Los Angeles Times, 11-8:(A)20.

John R. Kasich
United States Representative,
R-Ohio

1

In the first year, [President Clinton proposes] $36-billion in new taxes, and $2-billion in [spending] cuts. The taxes come now, and they come forever; and the spending cuts come "tomorrow" . . . It isn't my job to roll over for "tax-and-spend" [Democrats]. The public hasn't read this [Clinton] plan. It's my job to show them that the government can function without this tax-and-spend philosophy.

Interview/
The Christian Science Monitor,
2-25:4.

2

[On the Republican alternative to President Clinton's economic plan]: To just sit back and criticize Clinton without a manageable, credible alternative [would be] a dreadful mistake. We didn't come here to be potted plants.

At House Budget Committee hearing,
Washington, D.C./
The Washington Post, 3-17:(A)21.

David Keating
Executive vice president,
National Taxpayers Union

3

[Arguing against a value-added tax for the U.S.]: Politicians and bureaucrats won't be able to help themselves [control their greed] if they get a VAT. If their European colleagues are any indication of what would happen here, we'd start with a VAT at 5% or so, and before long it would be 15% or 20% as they look for more and more revenue to spend. We do not want this.

USA Today, 4-19:(B)6.

Jack Kemp
Former Secretary of Housing
and Urban Development
of the United States;
Former United States Representative,
R-New York

4

It's been demonstrably and empirically proven that . . . raising tax rates on the productive sector of the economy does not raise but lowers [tax] revenues, does not bring down but increases the [Federal budget] deficit, does not create jobs but loses jobs.

Feb. 26/
The Christian Science Monitor,
3-1:2.

5

I believe the old Republican Party saw the goal of American economic policy not as liberals do—as the construction of a safety net under which people should not be allowed to fall—but as the construction of a ladder of opportunity upon which people can climb. Yes, we need a safety net, but it should be a trampoline, not a trap. And right now it's a trap. I think Mr. [Abraham] Lincoln would be turning over in his grave if he could know that his Party is debating whether there should be a safety net or a ladder. We need both.

Interview/American Heritage, October:55.

Edward M. Kennedy
United States Senator,
D-Massachusetts

6

[Arguing for an increase in the minimum wage]: For 70 percent of American workers, the [Presidents Ronald] Reagan-[George]Bush years saw a steady erosion in their real wages, and the trend has been particularly destructive for low-

(EDWARD M. KENNEDY)

wage workers. No one who works full time in America should have to live in poverty.

The New York Times, 6-3:(A)9.

Bob Kerrey
United States Senator,
D-Nebraska

1

The mood of the country is to cut [government] expenditures. The [Congressional] leadership tells us we'll have a chance to cut when the appropriations bills come up for a vote. We all know what's going to happen on the appropriations bills—nothing, a few nicks, that's all . . . They just voted $94-million this week for a courthouse I didn't even ask for, in Omaha.

Interview, Washington, D.C./
The New York Times, 7-30:(A)10.

Lane Kirkland
President, American Federation
of Labor-Congress
of Industrial Organizations

2

[Saying organized labor is willing to go along with higher taxes if they are distributed fairly throughout society]: We believe that if we want programs from our government, we ought to be willing to pay for them in a fair and equitable way. Our members are prepared to pay their fair share.

Bal Harbour, Fla., Feb. 15/
The Washington Post, 2-16:(A)9.

3

[On labor unions' opposition to President Clinton's support for NAFTA]: By and large, his agenda is our agenda, and we are and will be his most reliable troops. But we do have one major difference of opinion. Among the poison pills left behind by [former President] George Bush is a lethal one called NAFTA. Regrettably, President [Clinton] has concluded that he has no choice but to pursue it and we are of a deeply-held contrary opinion.

At AFL-CIO convention,
San Francisco, Calif., Oct. 4/
The Washington Post, 10-5:(A)13.

4

The labor movement is not weak. I was around when we were being widely condemned, when anti-union laws, like the Taft-Hartley Act, were being adopted. We had few friends in Congress in those days. But no such law has passed in the past 20 years, because labor has a strong political organization. We have had friendly majorities in the House and Senate for decades—even when we had no friend in the White House. Now we have a friend there, too [President Bill Clinton].

Interview, San Francisco, Calif./
Los Angeles Times, 11-7:(M)3.

5

There is absolutely no reason why working in a service trade should be low-wage. Mining is now a high-tech/high-wage job, but it was not at the beginning. They were pick-and-shovel jobs. The only reason mining and others like that aren't still low wages is because unions organized and negotiated higher wages. Good jobs don't come out of the goodness of the hearts of the owners. High-wage/high-tech jobs were a consequence of increased productivity, due to workers' skills and technological achievements. Higher wages came from unionization, and that is possible in most service jobs.

Interview, San Francisco, Calif./
Los Angeles Times, 11-7:(M)3.

6

[Criticizing NAFTA, which was just passed by the House]: Amid all the planes, trains and bridges and all the protections for citrus, sugar and wheat [which the Clinton Administration put into NAFTA to get Congressional votes], there was not one word about the rights of workers on both sides of the [U.S.-Mexican] border to obtain decent wages and safe working conditions or to defend themselves from gross exploitation.

News conference, Nov. 18/
The New York Times, 11-19:(A)11.

Marvin Kosters
Director of economic policy studies,
American Enterprise Institute

7

There is much talk that this is a jobless [economic] recovery, but that is not the real story.

(MARVIN KOSTERS)

The real story is that the job growth in this recovery has turned out to be more or less commensurate with the job growth in previous recoveries, when you take into account that [economic] output has been less than in those previous recoveries.

The New York Times,
7-17:1.

Laurence Kolikoff
Economist,
Boston (Mass.) University

1

Any sustainable [economic] policy has to stabilize the future tax rate. The real constraint on fiscal policy is that you can't take more than 100 percent of future income. Rising taxes on future generations—not the debt *per se*—show us that we're in a mess.

The New York Times,
1-14:(C)2.

William Kristol
Republican Party strategist;
Former Chief of Staff
to former Vice President
of the United States
Dan Quayle

2

[On President Clinton's economic proposals]: What is striking is that there is this class-warfare rhetoric, but what is creepy is how cynical it is. He doesn't really believe in this rhetoric. He has a Cabinet full of lawyer millionaires. The classic appeal against the rich is on behalf of the poor or the working class. Clinton's attack on the rich is allegedly on behalf of the middle class, and the political strategy underlying that is to build a Democratic coalition, ranging from the poor through the middle class, with a common interest in big government.

The New York Times, 2-18:(A)10.

3

[President] Clinton has a real problem [with his tax proposals]. Just as inside-the-Beltway

wisdom underestimated how damaging [former President George] Bush's breaking of the no-new-taxes pledge would be, people here underestimate the risk to Clinton of walking away from [his] middle-class tax cut [promise] and walking into a tax increase.

Washington, D.C./
The Christian Science Monitor,
3-4:3.

4

The Clinton [Administration] budget is like a giant pasture full of sacred cows, cheerfully mooing and contently munching at the Federal taxpayers' expense.

USA Today, 5-21:(A)11.

Thomas Kuhn
President,
Edison Electric Institute

5

The best way to increase [tax] revenues is to encourage the expansion of business activity. Energy taxes do the opposite.

Time, 2-15:26.

Anthony Lake
Assistant to President
of the United States Bill Clinton
for National Security Affairs

6

Unless the major-market democracies can act together . . . the fierce competition of the new global economy, coupled with the end of our common purpose from the Cold War, could drive us into prolonged stagnation or even economic disaster.

At Johns Hopkins School
of Advanced International Studies,
Sept. 21/
The Washington Post, 9-22:(A)16.

Joseph Lastelic
Spokesman,
American Petroleum Institute

7

[Raising] the gas tax to reduce the [Federal] deficit is unfair. It is regressive. It hurts those

(JOSEPH LASTELIC)

in areas where they have to drive long distances . . . We do not believe the Federal debt should be paid based on how many miles you drive . . . [Of the 5-cent gas-tax increase in 1990,] 2.5 cents went for roads and infrastructure, and 2.5 cents for deficit reduction. Well, they didn't reduce the deficit. They just spent the money.

The Christian Science Monitor,
1-14:4.

Jim Leach
United States Representative,
R-Iowa

1

The 1990s could be a good decade economically. In all but a few areas, the United States is leading its competitors. Our inflation is down. Spending for defense is being reduced worldwide. The negatives are the [Federal] budget deficit and the social dichotomies of largely inner-city pockets of drug, educational and social caste systems. Otherwise there is no reason the U.S. economy should not flourish.

The Christian Science Monitor,
2-24:18.

Charles Lewis
Executive director,
Center for Public Integrity

2

Free trade is like apple pie—who doesn't like it? But when decision-making is distorted by money and citizens' groups are excluded, it makes for sour apples and indigestion.

USA Today, 11-19:(A)13.

Nelson Litterst
Lobbyist,
National Federation
of Independent Business

3

We believe a minimum-wage increase will have a devastating effect just when jobs are starting to come back. Coupled with the [Clinton Administration's proposed] tax package and employer mandates on health care, this would be a final straw for small business.

The New York Times, 6-3:(A)9.

Trent Lott
United States Senator,
R-Mississippi

4

There are only three ways to get out of the [Federal budget] deficit problem. [First,] you encourage growth to get out of it. [Second,] you cut spending. [Third,] you raise taxes. I prefer one and two, and only three when these other two have been totally explored and exploited.

The Christian Science Monitor,
2-19:1.

Glenn Loury
Professor of economics,
Boston (Mass.) University

5

There are still jobs in the cities. Pretty much anybody can get a job driving a cab. Why is it that in a city like Washington, D.C., a lot of the cab drivers are foreigners? Part of it is that these immigrants may be hungrier, more disciplined and more willing to try. I know that's a politically incorrect thing to say. In terms of creating jobs, it is not fair to say the American economy has failed. It would be good if we could create high-wage manufacturing jobs for people who have no specialized skills. More power to [President] Clinton if he can do it.

Interview/
Mother Jones, March-April:6.

Ray Marcy
Chief executive,
Interim Services, Inc.
(employment agency
for temporary workers)

6

[On his company's supplying temporary workers for manufacturing industries]: Many manufacturers are taking a worst-case approach [to hiring]. Companies have surges in orders so

(RAY MARCY)

they need help, but they don't want to hire. And with unemployment at 6.5 to 7 percent, it gives us a pool of talented people whom we can recruit inexpensively for our clients.

The New York Times, 7-6:(A)1.

Pierre Mauroy
President,
Socialist International;
Former Prime Minister
of France

1

We [socialists] never accepted state-controlled economic planning; that was for the Communists. But neither did we accept market economies; that was capitalism. So now we are looking for a third course, but we have not found it. The market, which is seen as a panacea by the liberal and conservative parties, has become an indispensable tool. But the market brings with it a terrible contradiction. It allows competition and permits growth, but it also permits unemployment, and that is the cloud hanging over us now. The right is not going to be able to solve the unemployment problem, either. We are going to recover our equilibrium only if our ways of life change, if we reduce and redistribute our working hours . . . If socialists are able to reconcile the market economy, with its ability to feed competition, with the ability to provide work for the majority, then I am sure there will be happy days ahead for socialism, and we will see a comeback. For the moment, we do not have a solution—only the intuitive notion that society must change its ways of organizing its work time.

Interview/
World Press Review, August:17.

Paul McCulley
Chief economist,
Union Bank of Switzerland

2

[Saying tax increases on the wealthy and new government spending might not negatively affect consumer spending]: People ignore the fact that higher taxes on the affluent are more likely to

come out of saving than consumption. And more government outlays tend to put money in the hands of people who spend all of their incomes, and more.

The New York Times, 3-2:(C)4.

Bob McIntyre
Director,
Citizens for Tax Justice

3

[On President Clinton's new tax proposals]: [We support] the overall gist of the Clinton program. We're very concerned, however, that new tax loopholes in the plan throw overboard many of the fundamental principles of the 1986 Tax Reform Act. Most notably, while the top personal income-tax rate—including the 10 percent surtax on taxable income above $250,000—goes up to almost 40 percent, the top capital-gains tax rate stays at 28 percent. For high-income people, that's the equivalent of a 30 percent capital-gains exclusion—exactly what [former] President George Bush futilely called for every year he was in office. Not only will this undermine tax fairness, but it will also send investment capital chasing tax shelters rather than what's best for the economy. A far better option would be a slightly lower top rate that applies to all income, including capital gains.

The Washington Post, 2-26:(A)21.

Howard M. Metzenbaum
United States Senator,
D-Ohio

4

[Arguing against the proposed NAFTA free-trade agreement, saying it will result in U.S. jobs going to low-wage Mexico]: It will take jobs from Connecticut; it'll take jobs from Rhode Island. And they're going down to Mexico. Let's face it—there's a reality about this situation that cannot be denied.

The Washington Post, 3-18:(C)15.

Kweisi Mfume
United States Representative,
D-Maryland

5

[On President Clinton's economic plan]: This deficit-reduction plan . . . will offer a major step

119

(KWEISI MFUME)

forward in terms of getting people back to work and helping this country to achieve fairness toward all of its citizens, particularly as it relates to helping families . . . Is it all that we [in the Congressional Black Caucus] want? No. Will we continue to fight for more? Yes. Are there other venues and opportunities down the road? Indeed, there are . . . We would remind this Administration and . . . the [Democratic] Party that as long as we are here, we will continue to be as insistent as we are that people who have been left out of the process . . . be taken care of and looked after and, perhaps more importantly, thought of first as we go about deliberating and making decisions in a legislative way in this Congress.

News conference, Aug. 3/
USA Today, 8-4:(A)9.

Robert H. Michel
Unites States Representative,
R-Illinois

1

[Former] President [George] Bush handed over to [President Clinton] an economy that is growing, not shrinking, a rate of worker productivity that is rising, not falling. As a matter of fact, the past 12 years of Republican leadership have built a strong foundation for progress. We agree with the President that we have to put more people to work, but remember: 80 percent to 85 percent of the new jobs in this country are created by small business. So the climate for starting and expanding businesses must be enhanced with tax incentives and deregulation, rather than imposing higher taxes and more government mandates.

Broadcast rebuttal to President Clinton's
address on the Administration's economic plan,
Washington, D.C., Feb. 17/
The New York Times, 2-18:(A)11.

2

When you hear a Democrat call for taxes, do not ask for whom the tax rises; it will rise for *you.*
Broadcase rebuttal to President Clinton's
address on the Administration's economic plan,
Washington, D.C., Feb. 17/
The New York Times, 2-18:(A)11.

3

[Criticizing President Clinton's proposed economic plan]: [In 1992,] candidate Clinton promised middle-income Americans a tax cut. President Clinton now wants to thrust upon middle-income Americans an enormous tax increase. Let's face it: The Clinton White House is out of touch. It's out of synch. It's out of ideas. It's out of excuses. And it's out of control.

Before the House,
Washington, D.C., May 27/
The New York Times, 5-28:(A)8.

Lawrence Minard
Managing editor,
"Forbes" magazine

4

It's ironic that now that we're [the U.S.] in the most efficient position we've been in globally in years, there's protectionist talk coming out of Washington. Rather than worry about protecting the economy, we ought to be using our competitiveness and slaying foreign markets.
USA Today, 3-31:(B)2.

George J. Mitchell
United States Senator,
D-Maine

5

[Criticizing Republicans for being against President Clinton's economic plan]: When my Republican colleagues come here and say there should be no [new] taxes, their intent—their clear purpose—is to protect those who earn more than $200,000 a year [and to] shift the burden onto the poor and the middle class.

Before the Senate,
Washington, D.C., June 23/
The New York Times, 6-24:(A)8.

6

[On whether the American people will accept President Clinton's economic plan]: In a democratic society, particularly one that is as large and diverse as ours, can any great national enterprise other than war serve to unify the people in a way that will permit sacrifice? . . . The reality

(GEORGE J. MITCHELL)

today is that we have a very large and important national problem and it requires a united, national effort. And it's a question whether or not people can be summoned in that circumstance. I think they can. I think people will respond [positively to the plan] when they fully understand the implications and the substance and the direction of the policies.

To reporters/
The Christian Science Monitor,
7-13:19.

Carol Moseley-Braun
United States Senator,
D-Illinois

1

[On her support for NAFTA]: I believe we have to focus on the job-creating strategies that will boost our economy and put our people back to work in good-paying jobs. I believe that getting rid of trade barriers has historically done nothing but increase trade. And as you increase trade, you increase jobs.

Interview,
Washington, D.C./
Los Angeles Times, 10-31:(M)3.

Daniel Patrick Moynihan
United States Senator,
D-New York

2

[On the forthcoming Clinton Administration]: Our problem is that an Administration that legitimately campaigned promising an activist Administration now must face the fact of the [Federal] budget deficit. Those two things have to be worked out. And it won't be satisfactory to anybody . . . There is a basic fact, which is the deficit, which affects anything you try to do. The first question you ask is, "Can we afford it [a particular expenditure]?" And usually the answer is no.

The Washington Post, 1-5:(A)6.

3

[On President Clinton's economic program which is being modified by Congress]: There's

[now] a measured understanding [by Clinton] of "don't promise too much or someone will ask you to deliver." The bill that was sent up to us was too many things. It was a bill to cut the deficit and raise the level of social spending. It was one-third deficit reduction, one-third uplift and one-third business as usual. It makes for what the psychologists call cognitive dissonance. You turn white mice crazy.

Los Angeles Times, 6-29:(A)12.

Kevin Murphy
Economist,
University of Chicago

4

The economy recovering doesn't mean a recovery for all workers. That's been one of the major lessons of the last decade, and I expect it to continue. We economists tend to focus on the national numbers, but when it gets down to individuals, the national numbers are only a small part of the picture. What's going on in an industry, a region or your educational group is what matters for the individual.

The New York Times,
10-30:1.

Sam Nunn
United States Senator,
D-Georgia

5

Both parties pretend that we can get our fiscal house back in order with little or no sacrifice by the vast middle class, even though we all know that most revenues come from the middle class and most expenditures of our Federal government go to the middle class. We don't like to say that, but we're not doing a favor to the middle class if we do not tell the American people those facts . . . Until the President [Clinton] and the realists in Congress come together across party lines, the game of "Let's Pretend" will continue, the huge [Federal budget] deficits will continue and our economic problems will continue. The losers will continue to be the American people, particularly the middle class that Washington spends so much time talking about protecting.

Before the Senate, Washington, D.C./
The New York Times, 8-7:29.

Paul Osterman
Economist,
Massachusetts Institute
of Technology

1

[On President Clinton's summer-jobs plan for young people]: I think from everything we know about summer-jobs programs . . . they're a fine idea and they keep kids out of trouble, but it's not in any sense a long-term solution. What they're accomplishing is keeping kids out of trouble and that's not inconsequential.

The Washington Post, 3-13:(C)6.

Bob Packwood
United States Senator,
R-Oregon

2

[Criticizing President Clinton's economic proposal, which includes a plan to designate tax dollars specifically for reducing the budget deficit]: The pressure to take the money we're raising in this bill in taxes, which the President says is to reduce the deficit—the pressure to take that money and spend it on education, environment, highways, defense—will be inexorable. Maybe Republicans are on the wrong side of this issue. Maybe the public wants this money spent and is willing to pay taxes for it. But we're willing to take that gamble [and vote against the bill].

Before the Senate,
Washington, D.C., June 23/
The New York Times, 6-24:(A)8.

Leon E. Panetta
Director, Federal Office
of Management and Budget

3

[On President Clinton's economic plan]: If there are those [in Congress] that think it can be done differently, then let's hear the specifics. Don't give me balanced-budget amendments. Don't give me some kind of gimmick. Talk to me about specifics and we'll listen. But if you're just going to give me your regular speech that you give at the Rotary Club, forget it.

Feb. 18/
Los Angeles Times, 2-19:(A)21.

4

[President Clinton] intends to make a fight for his investments [government spending programs] . . . He believes very strongly in those investments. Having said that, I think he recognizes [that] the Administration faces a tough battle. One option is to try to push for all of the investments within the [budget] caps, by making some significant savings elsewhere. That is one course of battle. Another option would be to prioritize the investments and try to fund some of them at a smaller level, recognizing that some of them could increase in later years. Those are two main options we are now considering.

Los Angeles Times, 4-16:(A)22.

5

[On the problem of attacking the Federal budget deficit at a time when the government also wants to spend on needed programs]: The problem is, we have made in this [Clinton] Administration a fundamental commitment to pay the mortgage on our national economy [bring down the deficit]. We have also made a fundamental commitment . . . to pay the mortgage on the house, to also pay for repairing the roof, and pay for health-care bills. The one thing that we cannot accept is the effort to take money from paying for the health-care needs of this country, and putting it to paying the mortgage. We think that it undermines the basic effort that this Administration is all about.

To reporters, Nov. 19/
The Christian Science Monitor, 11-22:6.

Lewis F. Payne, Jr.
United States Representative,
D-Virginia

6

[On the proposed NAFTA]: There's a lot of conflicting information out there. The management of companies come to us very much in favor of NAFTA because it will open markets and opportunities and consequently provide more jobs. Then we talk to the workforce of the same company that sees NAFTA as a threat to themselves and fellow workers. As it comes closer to a vote, the pressure is increasing. The stakes are high.

The Washington Post, 9-28:(A)21.

Ross Perot
Industrialist;
1992 independent
Presidential candidate

1

[On President Clinton's economic proposal]: I can't understand the details of the plan . . . Right now, it's like an artist's sketch for a house. You and I look at it and say that's a beautiful house, but we don't know how many bedrooms are in it, we don't know how many bathrooms are in it, we don't know if it's heated by electricity or gas, we don't know where the plumbing is.

Broadcast interview/
"This Morning," CBS-TV, 3-2.

2

Our [tax] money must be accurately accounted for in an audited quarterly financial report which will allow the people to see whether or not our elected servants are performing on-budget and on schedule—as promised. We must also eliminate all the government's accounting tricks. To assure that these plans materialize as promised, pass a term-limitation law for Congress as part of the tax plan. If the financial forecast plans which they generated do not materialize on schedule, this law limiting the number of terms Congressmen can serve would automatically take effect and remain in force.

Broadcast address to the nation/
NBC-TV, 3-21.

3

At the same time we're creating free-enterprise zones in the inner cities, we're negotiating NAFTA, which will take the very jobs that are most apt for the inner cities and ship them down to dollar-an-hour labor in Mexico. While we're shifting jobs to Mexico, we're putting an additional tax burden on small business in health care and new regulations—environmental, you name it—and we are having family-leave [requirements]. If you're in business, all you have to do is go south of the border and leave all that behind you.

Interview, Dallas, Texas/
U.S. News & World Report,
5-17:43.

4

The [proposed] North American Free Trade Agreement is another in a long series of one-sided trade agreements that damage our ability to create and keep jobs in the United States. [Foreign lobbyists] must not be allowed to dictate the future of working Americans.

Aug. 13/
The New York Times, 8-14:25.

5

[Arguing against the proposed NAFTA]: I've been accused of looking in this rearview mirror. That's right. I'm looking back at reality. And here is what I see after many years. Mexican workers' life, standard of living and pay has gone down, not up. After many years of having U.S. companies in Mexico, this is the way Mexican workers live all around big new U.S. plants [in slum conditions] . . . [With U.S. companies operating plants in Mexico,] you would think the standard of living of the Mexican worker would begin to come up. Instead, it continues to go down by design. Thirty-six families own over half the country . . . Eighty-five million people work for them in poverty. U.S. companies, because it is so difficult to do business in this country, can't wait to get out of this country and go somewhere [such as Mexico] and, if possible, get labor that costs one-seventh of what it costs in the United States.

Broadcast interview,
Washington, D.C./
"Larry King Live," CNN-TV, 11-9.

Pete Peterson
United States Representative,
D-Florida

6

[On the Congressional debate on NAFTA]: This has been one of the most dishonest debates on any issue I have ever seen in my life. Everything is exaggerated on both sides. There is too much misinformation . . . There is so much speculation, so many claims and counterclaims, it is difficult to find independent data to support anything.

The Christian Science Monitor,
11-17:4.

Kevin P. Phillips
President,
American Political Research
Corporation

1

[Criticizing the argument put forth by President Clinton's advisers who say he can raise taxes on the middle class without reneging on last year's campaign promises not to do so because he had actually said he would not raise their taxes "to pay for my programs"]: At the most recent count, only 800,000 Americans were lawyers, and I don't think the 248 million or so who are not lawyers are going to buy a caveat stuck on in the middle of a passionate plea to the middle-class voters that they should vote for him because he was going to save them. Talk about reading his lips! His lips were all over the United States for a year telling people how the middle class was being hammered by unfair taxes. And now he comes up with a lawyer's loophole, a Yale Law School special, to make them forget all that? No way.

The New York Times, 1-26:(A)16.

2

[On President Clinton's economic plan]: This budget is the end product of a surprising number of political miscalculations by the White House, in which they have lost many of their budget battles, and so we have wound up with a much less growth-oriented package. You've got a package with too many taxes and too much deficit reduction at a time when the economy is weakening and you've got more defense cutbacks coming. So this budget could take a weak economy and kick it down into the cellar.

Los Angeles Times, 7-12:(A)12.

Robin Pinkley
Assistant professor
of organizational behavior
and business policy,
Southern Methodist University

3

[On labor-management negotiations and strikes]: Negotiation is an exchange of value. But many unions are not talking value language.

Instead, what they're doing is talking about loss, loss, loss, threat, threat, threat, threat. In this market, it just doesn't work. When you frame it in terms of loss, the other side responds by digging in their heels, and they become real contentious. They're less likely to settle. And when they do settle, they demand greater value.

The Christian Science Monitor,
11-24:3.

Jack Pitney
Political scientist,
Claremont McKenna College

4

If [President-elect] Clinton decides to cut [Federal] spending, that will directly influence every state, because a large part of the Federal budget consists of grants to states. If he tries such things as raising taxes, it will be harder for states to raise their own taxes on top.

The Christian Science Monitor,
1-8:3.

Lewis T. Preston
President, International Bank
for Reconstruction and Development
(World Bank)

5

The developing countries have become a powerful force in the world economy. They are projected to contribute about one-third of the growth in world GDP over the next five years. Over the last five years, they have accounted for more than a quarter of the increase in global imports. Trade among the developing countries is growing rapidly. Their markets also represent the fastest-growing trade areas for many developed nations—including the United States. This highlights the fundamental importance of [the proposed] NAFTA and, on a global scale, the fundamental importance of free trade. There should be no doubt that NAFTA holds great potential to boost wages and living standards for all parties concerned.

Before World Bank Group's Board
of Governors, Sept. 28/
The Washington Post,
9-30:(A)22.

Don Ratajczak
Economist,
Georgia State University

1

I have a rule of thumb that I will cancel subscriptions to economics journals if I go for a whole year without being able to understand at least one article. I've finally gotten to that point with some of them. In trying to make economics scientific, they have made it not useful.

Los Angeles Times, 1-8:(A)21.

Robert B. Reich
Secretary of Labor-designate
of the United States

2

The American workforce is coming to be the American economy. That is the way you begin to define the American economy—in terms of skills and capacities of the people who are here . . . Unskilled and untrained Americans are losing out. If not competing with low-wage workers abroad, they increasingly are competing with new technologies here at home, which are rapidly replacing routine work of all kinds.

At Senate Labor Committee hearing
on his nomination,
January/Nation's Business, March:24.

Robert B. Reich
Secretary of Labor
of the United States

3

[On the growing trend toward the use of temporary, contingent workers]: These workers are outside the traditional system of worker-management relationships. As the contingent workforce grows—as many people find themselves working part time for many different employers—the social contract is beginning to fray.

Interview/Time, 3-29:44.

4

We have built up in this country since the 1930s a system of employment relationships, guaranteed by law and guided by business practices that have become norms. The state courts have essentially codified entire areas of workplace law having to do with everything from unjust

dismissals through areas of labor-management relationships such as family and medical leave, which many of the states pioneered before the Federal legislation was passed. [But today], many people think this system needs fundamental rethinking.

Interview/Time, 3-29:46.

5

[On the growing trend toward temporary, part-time jobs]: Unless people [workers] feel that they will be valued over the long term, they may be more reluctant to go the extra mile, to think a little harder, to contribute. In the same way, if the employer feels this is not a long-term relationship, the employer may be more reluctant to invest in on-the-job training of that worker. There are companies that traditionally were very, very careful about laying off workers because they were so concerned about their corporate culture. Now they just fire people, sometimes with very little notice.

Interview/Time, 3-29:47.

6

Even if we're seeing major productivity improvements in one sector, the consequences for [overall] wages may be negative unless workers who are displaced by the productivity improvements get good jobs somewhere else.

Interview/
U.S. News & World Report,
3-29:41.

7

[Supporting a Clinton Administration proposal to ban companies' ability to hire permanent replacement workers during a labor strike]: This legislation is all about closing the book on the 1980s. This was a very devisive issue and led to the disintegration of trust between labor and management in the last decade. You can't create a genuine partnership when one partner feels that there's a loaded gun aimed at its temple . . . The practice of permanent striker replacement became a prominent feature of American labor relations only in the last dozen years. [By ban-

(ROBERT B. REICH)

ning it now,] we can start to concentrate on the [labor-management] solutions of the future and not on the problems of the past.

Congressional testimony,
Washington, D.C., March 30/
Los Angeles Times, 3-31:(A)1,26.

1

The American worker has every right to feel insecure, worried. Because, you see, these big companies are shrinking. And not only are the big companies shrinking, but you have international trade, you have technology, you have military downsizing. A lot of people are not able to get jobs. There's very high unemployment. They're worried about their future and their kids' futures. And even if they had jobs, what we see is that the average income, in terms of wages and benefits of the average American, is not going up. In fact, over the past 15 years, even if you've got a job, it is actually trending downward. So Americans all over—they're insecure about jobs. They're insecure about health care. Those are the things that the Clinton Administration was put into office to deal with.

Interview, April 7/
The Washington Post, 4-8:(A)20.

2

[Defending the proposed NAFTA]: People ask: If there's a wage differential, if it's cheaper to get labor in Mexico, why do American companies stay here [in the U.S.]? And they do stay here. The reason is we have . . . a superb infrastructure—communications systems, highway systems. We have . . . a skilled labor force. We have equipment, machinery. We have a stable government. We have all sorts of systems in place that make it desirable to produce goods in the United States. If low wages were the key to where manufacturers located . . . Bangladesh and Haiti . . . would become the manufacturing capitals of the world.

Before Senate Finance Committee,
Washington, D.C., Sept. 21/
The Washington Post, 9-22:(A)22.

3

I am questioning whether we have gone too far in corporate downsizing. Cutting payrolls may not be the most effective way of improving corporate performance. There are a lot of non-financial criteria that don't show up on a balance sheet and are hard to get your hands on.

Before Council of Institutional Investors,
New York, N.Y./
The New York Times, 10-12:(C)2.

Robert D. Reischauer
Director, Congressional Budget Office

4

[On NAFTA]: Boosting trade with Mexico will create a few [U.S.] jobs in this machine-tool factory and a job in that advertising agency. Circulation in this magazine will rise, and the financial district of New York will have a new job here and there. It will all largely be invisible. But when the glass factory in Toledo closes or the textile plant in South Carolina or the furniture manufacturer in North Carolina [closes] because those low-wage jobs move to Mexico, it will be highly visible, and it will be attributable to NAFTA. Or at least people will blame NAFTA for it.

The New York Times, 9-15:(A)12.

Alice M. Rivlin
Deputy Director-designate,
Federal Office
of Management and Budget

5

[On Federal deficit reduction]: We have to stop living beyond our means. In the end, everybody will have to give up something. We'll have to have shared sacrifice to solve this problem.

At Senate Government Affairs
Committee hearing on her nomination,
Washington, D.C., Jan. 13/
Los Angeles Times, 1-14:(A)20.

Russell Roberts
Professor of economics,
Olin School of Business,
Washington University

6

When tax rates go up, you encourage dishonesty [in tax reporting]. People don't like to be

(RUSSELL ROBERTS)

dishonest, but when it gets too expensive to be honest, unfortunately they are going to be a little less honest than they were before.

The Christian Science Monitor,
4-1:9.

Douglas Ross
Assistant Secretary
for Employment and Training,
Department of Labor
of the United States

1

The old ideal of job security being attached to a particular job and a particular employer is essentially gone. All of us are now in a condition where, if we want to be successful, we have to manage our employment lives ourselves. And clearly we are not in a situation, in most communities, where we have systems in place to enable people to do that.

Los Angeles Times, 10-6:(A)12.

Pedro Rossello
Governor of Puerto Rico

2

[On the proposed NAFTA]: It will affect Puerto Rico negatively in some areas, there's no question about it. In apparel, for example, our sector of manufacturing is very vulnerable and will be negatively impacted by NAFTA. [But] we're sort of looking back and saying that there's no other way the U.S. can go [but to approve NAFTA]. If you look at what's happening in the different markets worldwide, more and more they're going to intraregional trade. The natural market for the U.S. is the Americas, or it will be hurt in its economic development.

Interview/
USA Today, 11-11:(A)13.

Dan Rostenkowski
United States Representative,
D-Illinois

3

[Saying President Clinton needs to make his tax plan more politically palatable for it to pass in Congress]: You've got to get some people out there suggesting to the American people that this is good for the country and that corporations and small businesses see in this bill an attractiveness. I think the Administration, never having written a tax bill, doesn't realize that you have to get supporters out there.

To reporters,
Washington, D.C., May 12/
The Washington Post, 5-13:(A)12.

Martin O. Sabo
United States Representative,
D-Minnesota

4

[Criticizing the Republicans' alternative proposals to President Clinton's economic plan]: If they had their way, they'd have us back to gravel roads. Their approach reflects a very, very restrictive view of government, and they want to make sure the wealthy don't pay more in taxes. In the process, that leaves us with a larger [Federal budget] deficit.

The Washington Post,
3-19:(A)18.

Paul S. Sarbanes
United States Senator,
D-Maryland

5

It would be a sad irony for the country to have voted to end the gridlock in economic policy between the Congress and the President, only to find it replaced with a new gridlock between an Administration and a Congress committed to stronger growth, and a Federal Reserve determined to restrain growth by keeping its foot on the monetary brakes.

Los Angeles Times, 1-28:(A)14.

Robert Schaen
Former comptroller,
Ameritech Corporation

6

The days of the mammoth corporations [with their huge permanent workforces] are coming to an end. People are going to have to create their

(ROBERT SCHAEN)

own lives, their own careers and their own successes. Some people may go kicking and screaming into the new world, but there is only one message there: You're now in business for yourself.

Time, 3-29:47.

Charles L. Schultze
Senior fellow,
Brookings Institution;
Former Chairman,
Council of Economic Advisers
to the President
of the United States
(Jimmy Carter)

1

[On the positive effect on the economy of proposed government spending on U.S. infrastructure repairs and updating]: All this stuff is going to be gradual. You have to think in terms of decades, which is not to say it shouldn't be done. You have to tell people to be realistic, and they should understand that Rome wasn't built in a day.

The New York Times, 2-15:(C)3.

2

[On criticism that President Clinton's policy of "investment" is really just another word for "spending"]: My advice would be, don't pay any attention to whether or not something's labeled an investment; look at its merits. Some items that aren't investment are meretorious, and vice versa.

The Washington Post,
3-1:(A)4.

Donna E. Shalala
Secretary of Health
and Human Services
of the United States

3

We can't afford as a nation—not because of money but because of our social fabric—to have large numbers of people who are not working. We

have to mainstream everybody. No matter what their circumstances when they were growing up. Part of that is knowing that after they're finished with school, everybody in this country gets up and goes to work.

Interview/
Los Angeles Times, 7-18:(M)3.

Alan K. Simpson
United States Senator,
R-Wyoming

4

[On President Clinton's economic plan]: Pure pork, and metric tons of it. This is the same old crap right back through F.D.R.

Washington, D.C., March 31/
USA Today, 4-1:(A)4.

5

Democrats can't function without [imposing] taxes. They are institutionally, genetically incapable of functioning without taxes.

Los Angeles Times, 8-3:(A)13.

Allen Sinai
Chief economist,
The Boston Company

6

[On President Clinton's economic plan]: The Administration has taken a big chance, because the deficit-reduction plan could depress economic growth well beyond the next Presidential election. The package is going to take a chunk of growth out of the economy, and that is simply the price we have to pay for getting our house in order.

The Washington Post, 8-6:(A)15.

Jim Slattery
United States Representative,
D-Kansas

7

The worst nightmare for people like me is we vote for tax increases, and then see entitlements explode and gobble up all the savings.

Newsweek, 5-31:20.

John D. Steinbruner
Director of foreign-policy studies,
Brookings Institution

1

The dominant foreign-policy issues for the new [Clinton] Administration is economic performance. Its main mandate to look at domestic economic performance can't be dealt with outside the context of the global economy, large pieces of which are in real trouble.

Los Angeles Times, 2-18:(A)13.

Susan Sterne
Economist,
Economic Analysis Associates

2

Very few people even forecast inflation anymore. Everyone assumes that it will stay at 3 percent. [But] consumers are already showing a willingness to accept higher prices, whether that is apparel that suddenly sells at full price, or GM announcing mid-year car-price increases, or housing prices firming.

At conference on inflation,
New York, N.Y./
The Washington Post, 3-11:(D)12.

David A. Stockman
Former Director,
Federal Office of Management
and Budget

3

The question is, what will [President] Clinton do about the two big promises that he made during [last year's election] campaign? The first was to restore fairness, as Democrats define it, to the tax system and the economy overall, and put in an adequate level of public investment. That is a doable promise. The second was to cut the budget deficit in half while shielding the middle class from any tax increases or benefit reductions. That promise can't be kept. The math simply is prohibitive. So how will the Clinton Administration craft a program that somehow addresses the real-world facts that they're facing? . . . If he follows the [former President George] Bush pattern and hangs on to campaign promises that are not consistent with reality, he'll have a very difficult time.

Interview/Newsweek, 2-1:70.

Donald Straszheim
Chief economist,
Merrill Lynch & Company

4

It is important that we start to get some better employment data. In the last analysis, people with jobs and income spend. Those who don't, won't.

The Christian Science Monitor,
4-1:8.

Peter Sutherland
Director General,
General Agreement
on Tariffs and Trade

5

It is essential that the United States, the [European] Community, Japan and Canada provide the launching pad for the takeoff of [trade] negotiations in [the forthcoming G-7 meeting in] Tokyo. Rhetoric about the importance of the Uruguay Round is not good enough. I am a facilitator, but I cannot facilitate a lack of will . . . Protectionism [in Europe] is a recipe for making Europe an industrial graveyard, a museum piece, paralyzed by inefficiencies. Look at the failure of the industries we've tried to protect—steel and shipyards. It's a basic fact that open trade has been positive for the world. The Uruguay Round cannot, at this stage, start trying to impose social and environmental legislation on developing countries. It's time to stop pointing fingers and seeking excuses. The alternative to open multilateral trade could be terrible rifts both within the developed world, and between the developed world and developing countries.

Interview,
Geneva, Switzerland, July 1/
The New York Times, 7-2:(C)1,2.

6

It is high time that governments made clear to consumers just how much they pay for decisions to protect domestic industries from import competition. The effects of protection almost always fall most heavily on the poorest sections of society. It is they who . . . have to spend the highest proportion of their household budget on

(PETER SUTHERLAND)

necessities like clothing, footwear and basic food products. It is exactly in these areas that protection is most common and intense.

Los Angeles Times, 8-16:(D)2.

1

[On the recent GATT trade agreement]: Today, the world has chosen openness and cooperation instead of uncertainty and conflict. I am convinced that today will be seen as a defining moment in modern economic and political history.

Dec. 15/
Los Angeles Times, 12-16:(A)16.

Mike Synar
United States Representative,
D-Oklahoma

2

[Supporting President Clinton's proposed energy tax based on BTUs]: Nobody likes taxes. [But] the fact is, if you look at all the taxes that were [considered], including the carbon tax, the gasoline tax and the VAT tax, the BTU tax fits the bill for what has been the driving theme of the Clinton economic program: one, honesty in the numbers of revenues, and two, it fairly distributes the burden.

The Christian Science Monitor,
5-24:3.

Alexander Trotman
Chairman-designate,
Ford Motor Company

3

We [the U.S.] have a long-standing trade imbalance with Japan, and two-thirds of it is automotive and parts. Instead of talking $30-odd-billion, which is what the automotive imbalance is, we should think of it as 20,000 to 30,000 American jobs per $1-billion. Then maybe more people would be interested in the subject. That job loss is the "sucking sound" that [industrialist] Ross [Perot] should have been talking about. There has been an enormous trans-

fer of U.S. jobs to Japan over the past 20 years. That's what the trade deficit is about.

Interview, Oct. 5/
USA Today, 10-6:(B)2.

Norman True
Director,
Institute for Research
on the Economics of Taxation

4

[Criticizing Clinton Administration proposals to increase tax rates for wealthy individuals]: The top 1 percent are the most productive people in the country. If you think this will have no effect on their contribution to the economy's progress, then you have to assume they are very peculiar human beings.

The New York Times, 2-20:13.

Laura D'Andrea Tyson
Chairman,
Council of Economic Advisers
to President of the United States
Bill Clinton

5

If you compare the advanced industrial countries, and you look at their tax burdens relative to gross domestic product, the U.S. is at the bottom. There is no simple relationship between the level of taxes a nation pays and how fast it grows . . . There is no *simple* relationship. That doesn't mean you don't want to look at the kind of taxes you impose.

Before House Budget Committee,
Washington, D.C., February/
Working Woman, August:67.

6

The market does many things very well, but there is a rationale for the government doing things that the market doesn't do very well. The role of the Council of Economic Advisers to help evaluate when there is a defensible role for a government policy and whether government policy in pursuit of that objective is efficient.

Interview, Washington, D.C./
The New York Times, 3-15:(A)8.

(LAURA D'ANDREA TYSON)

1

[When it comes to government aid or intervention in the private sector,] I'm cautious, as well as activist, and the cautious part is serious. I do understand that even when there is a compelling case to be made [for government intervention], it's very hard to design the ideal policy. And it is very hard to get the politics right, so that you end up with a policy that you really want.

Working Woman, August:68.

2

[On President Clinton's economic plan]: This is about living standards. It means higher living standards by the end of this decade. But it's a very slow process. I want to make clear that we're talking about reversing course over time. The returns primarily come in the form of higher productivity growth and higher income growth for the average American family . . . We consider it a two-part strategy. The first thing is to stabilize the rate of growth of debt compared to the rate of growth of the economy. A continually growing debt relative to the size of the economy is a sign that we don't have control of the financial situation. The second is to not just stabilize the debt but to bring it down . . . That is a process that's going to take much more time. One way is to use the findings of the national performance review of the Vice President to better organize the government, to think about where further cuts in spending could be made. Second, is to deal with health-care reform.

Interview, Aug. 4/
USA Today, 8-5:(A)11.

Dirk Van Dongen
Co-chairman,
Tax Reform Action Coalition

3

[Criticizing possible Clinton Administration plans to increase corporate taxes]: Everyone knows that we have to create more jobs because we have a relatively fragile [economic] recovery. This proposal [to increase corporate taxes] is counter-productive because it takes away from businesses the very asset they need to create jobs: their surplus dollars.

The New York Times, 2-15:(C)1.

Ted Van Dyk
Democratic Party consultant

4

[On big labor's opposition to NAFTA, which was just passed by the House]: They threw all their forces into this and made it a defining issue of labor's strength. They got themselves painted as rear-guard oppositionists to modernism. They got themselves trapped as negativists.

The New York Times, 11-19:(A)11.

Richard Vedder
Professor of economics,
Ohio University

5

My view of unemployment is simple. It happens when workers are too expensive for employers to hire.

The Christian Science Monitor,
12-6:1.

Henry A. Waxman
United States Representative,
D-California

6

[On the Clinton Administration's proposed Federal budget]: Every Democrat has to understand that whatever complaints he has about the budget, failure to pass a bill would be a terrible blow to the idea that the Democratic Party—with a President in the White House and a majority in Congress—can govern.

Los Angeles Times, 5-21:(A)19.

Bob White
President,
Canadian Labor Congress

7

All of this talk about . . . work reorganization has to take into consideration the real quality of work life of the workers. We recognize change. But part of that is understanding how change affects the worker, not just how it makes a company more competitive.

Interview/
The Christian Science Monitor,
2-17:8.

131

Pete Wilson
Governor of California (R)

1

I respectfully but strongly urge President-elect Clinton to follow his instincts and let us benefit from the North American Free Trade Agreement [between the U.S., Canada and Mexico]. If ratified by Congress, it promises vast new markets and new jobs on both sides of the border.

State of the State address,
Sacramento, Calif., Jan. 6/
Los Angeles Times, 1-7:(A)20.

2

All public programs begin not in this chamber [the legislature] but in the sweat and toil of working men and women. Jobs make all else possible.

State of the State address,
Sacramento, Calif., Jan. 6/
The Christian Science Monitor,
1-8:3.

3

[Government should] help create the climate that encourages investment . . . We [in California] have prospered beyond our numbers because people had the guts to experiment in the marketplace. We need to give incentives for small businesses, because that's where our growth is now. The last thing government should do is provide . . . training for jobs that don't exist.

The Christian Science Monitor,
3-24:12.

Julie Wright
Secretary of Trade
and Commerce of California

4

We are used to thinking of international trade as "You buy this, we buy that," when [in fact] it has gone far, far beyond these old patterns. [For example,] California-Israeli trade is much more than export-import . . . Israel now develops products that we in California manufacture and sell. California companies are considering Israel as a manufacturing base for the European Community. Israeli firms are interested in investing in California, and Israeli and California companies are looking at a substantial number of export-oriented joint ventures and licensing ventures. For California, Israel can provide a competitive edge in the U.S. market and in the world market.

Los Angeles Times, 5-7:(A)5.

Alan Zuckerman
Executive director,
National Youth Employment
Coalition

5

When young people look around and see no one working, many reach the conclusion that they don't have a chance of getting a job which will support them. It is difficult for family, friends or teachers to convince young people that there is [a] payoff for doing well or remaining in school.

The Christian Science Monitor,
5-26:7.

Education

Lamar Alexander
Former Secretary of Education
of the United States

1

By 1994-95, we'll have national standards that will affect every classroom in America. The idea of giving parents choices [of] which schools to send their children to] has gained enormous momentum. The idea of freeing teachers from so many regulations, that's gaining momentum, too. All of this is in the right direction . . . But the structures of elementary and secondary education are still in a time warp.

Interview/USA Today, 3-17:(D)6.

2

[Supporting school choice for parents through the use of government-supplied vouchers]: This is inevitably going to pass [in the U.S.]. This is the Berlin Wall of American political issues. One day, [opposition to vouchers is] going to collapse, and one day in America low- and middle-income children will have the same choice as rich people.

The Washington Post, 9-30:(A)8.

Walter H. Annenberg
Philanthropist;
Former United States Ambassador
to the United Kingdom

3

[On his plans to fund projects aimed at improving public schools]: Nothing is as important philanthropically as improvement at the precollegiate level. Improvement there can bring about improvement in citizenship, and that can bring about improvement in government. That's what moves me.

Interview, St. Davids, Pa./
U.S. News & World Report,
11-1:20.

4

[On his recently announced $500-million gift to public education]: I am deeply troubled by the violence in some grade schools and high schools and, if this continues, it will not only erode the educational system but will destroy our way of life in the United States. We must ask ourselves whether improving education will halt violence. If anyone can think of a better way, we may have to try that. But the way I see this tragedy, education is the most wholesome and effective approach.

At White House ceremony honoring
him for the gift,
Washington, D.C., Dec. 17/
The New York Times, 12-18:8.

William J. Bennett
Former Secretary of Education
of the United States

5

Values can and should be taught in schools without fear of violating the separation of church and state, without fear of accusations of proselytizing. Such teaching is not only appropriate, it is essential in our time . . . I believe the most important responsibility we have now is the moral education of our young. It is a time-honored belief, from Thomas Jefferson to the present, that schools should be places that teach kids how to read, write, count, think—*and* develop reliable standards and morals.

Interview/
Christianity Today, 9-13:33.

6

[Supporting school choice for parents through the use of government-supplied vouchers]: We've tried just about everything the establishment suggested [to improve the public schools]: More money. Smaller classes. New social services. New math. We've tried all the gimmicks the last 20 years and things have gotten worse. The only thing left on the table is this "radical notion" of choice.

USA Today, 10-20:(A)2.

Marian Bergeson
Superintendent-designate
of Public Instruction
of California

1

Schools don't serve in isolation. You have to deal with support services: law enforcement, the court system . . . if you're ever going to move away from the crime and the drugs and the kind of battlegrounds that exist around our schoolyards. It doesn't stop at the gate. What happens in the community eventually gets into the classroom. In order to have a safe learning environment, you're going to have to bring in law enforcement. We can't tolerate the gang warfare and the gang graffiti when it's costing the community resources. I mean, that money could go into positive efforts at setting up parks and playgrounds and things for kids . . . If you have a city that simply can't deal with the external factors—crime, violence—you're going to find a community that can't deal with its classroom problems.

Los Angeles Times, 3-16:(E)2.

Erich Bloch
Former director,
National Science Foundation

2

No doubt about it, [research universities] have supported part of their research with tuition funds . . . Research has become the prime reason for [the university's] existence. At one time it was education.

The Atlantic, March:34.

Leon Botstein
President, Bard College

3

Students through the 1960s accepted the idea that higher education was about trying on the clothes of adulthood, so they eagerly accepted responsibility for their actions. If they got involved with someone, if they got drunk, if they hurt someone, they sought to take responsibility. Today's students believe they are not responsible; quite the opposite, they feel they are *owed* something—an entitlement to a reward from distress. And when they are hurt, they are more prone to call themselves "victims." Life, as the theologians have taught us for a long time, is inherently victimizing. So when something goes wrong, a student feels empowered to distribute the blame elsewhere . . . Rather than say, "This is my life; I take responsibility," the reaction today is, "I have suffered; I wish to be entitled to some reparation." And where the puritan character really comes out is in the desire for punishment, a public flogging of a presumed wrongdoer . . . So the final message of higher education becomes not, "Life is tough, unfair, tricky, difficult, complex; ergo, learn to take responsibility and live with it," but [rather], "All problems in your life can be reduced to the task of exacting redress."

Panel discussion,
Columbia University/
Harper's, September:42.

Ernest L. Boyer
President,
Carnegie Foundation
for the Advancement of Teaching

4

We can debate curriculum and graduation requirements, but in the end, what we have to do is find a way to hold on to our talented teachers.

Newsweek, 4-19:47.

5

What's been missing is a unified vision of school renewal. Time is running out on school reform. The coming decade may be our last. If we do not find a way to focus our efforts and to give energy and direction to keep our priorities, public confidence will diminish and the structure we call public education will continue to decline.

The Christian Science Monitor,
4-26:12.

William E. Brock III
Chairman,
Wingspread Group
on Higher Education;
Former Secretary of Labor
of the United States

6

We have issued this "wake-up" call to alert the leadership of the nation's colleges and universi-

(WILLIAM E. BROCK III)

ties that they must rethink their basic assumptions and how they go about their business. Too much of higher education and education at every level seems to be organized for the convenience of educators.

The Christian Science Monitor,
12-13:9.

George Butterfield
Deputy director,
National School Safety Center

1

Many suburban areas are in denial about the possibility of violence happening in their schools. But more and more, we find that this is an issue crashing in on administrators. Schools have to change their approach to doing the business of education . . . Many of the stabbings and shootings [in schools] start with somebody bumping somebody else in the hallway—or just a perceived disrespect. Students out there have a wide belief that if someone has shown you disrespect, just about the only way to deal with that shame is to fight, to be aggressive. Unless they learn some alternatives to that kind of approach, it's just going to continue to escalate.

The Christian Science Monitor,
4-19:6.

Daniel S. Cheever
Chairman,
Coalition for Student Loan Reform

2

[Criticizing the Clinton Administration's desire to have the student loan program taken over directly by the Federal government, thereby eliminating banks from the process]: The Senators [who voted against a complete government takeover] have shown the proper caution that should be taken in moving into the uncharted waters of direct lending. Ever-decreasing estimates of savings from direct lending and the Department of Education's poor administrative track record make shifting to full-blown direct lending without an adequate test an extremely risky proposition.

Los Angeles Times, 6-12:(A)2.

Bill Clinton
President of the United States

3

[On the importance of two-year technical colleges]: For the majority of people who do not go on to a four-year college, it is imperative that we join the ranks of the other high-wage countries and provide a system by which 100 percent of them at least know they have the opportunity to move into a program like the one that you have been a part of.

To graduating students
at New Hampshire Technical College,
May 22/
The Christian Science Monitor,
5-24:4.

Hillary Rodham Clinton
Wife of President
of the United States Bill Clinton

4

We must always uphold the idea of our colleges as incubators of ideas and havens for free speech and free thought . . . We must be careful not to cross the line between censuring behavior we consider unacceptable and censoring. We have to believe that in the free exchange of ideas, justice will prevail over injustice, tolerance over intolerance and progress over reaction.

At University of Pennsylvania commencement,
May 17/
The Washington Post, 5-18:(A)8.

James P. Comer
Educator, Child Study Center,
Yale University Medical School

5

This thrust toward [national education] standards is crazy. The belief that if schools knew what they were supposed to do . . . They [do] know what they are supposed to do; [national standards are] not going to improve anything. It's a continuation of the previous [Bush] Administration's thrust. What they are claiming is people do anything in schools because there's no standard, no established agreement about what they should be doing. Well, that's not the reason kids aren't achieving in school. The reason kids aren't

(JAMES P. COMER)

achieving has to do primarily with relationship issues. You have people teaching their own kids at home—in a way, with no standards—who are preparing them to go to Harvard.

Interview/Essence, December:140.

Walter Denham
Manager for
Mathematics Education,
California Department
of Education

1

[On a survey which shows many California students are below the national average in mathematics proficiency]: To have 52 percent below the basic level on what are extremely modest requirements is pretty discouraging. One never likes to be below the median, but even if we were above it, we wouldn't be satisfied. The national averages are still way less than students can accomplish and less than they need for when they are adults.

Los Angeles Times, 4-9:(A)23.

Maureen DiMarco
Secretary of Child Development
and Education of California

2

[On school districts that spend too much money]: The responsibility of the state is to equitably fund education at the local level. But I don't think you can hold the state up as the bad guy when a thousand other school districts manage their resources and don't make commitments beyond their funding. I don't think the state has the obligation to say to a school district that is spending its money far too fast, "Well, that's okay. We'll take care of it." That's not fair to the other kids in the state. And I'm not against teacher salaries being higher—don't hear that. I think it's something we need to have an absolute commitment to. But I don't think you can spend money you don't have.

Interview/
Los Angeles Times, 1-10:(M)3.

Joseph Duffey
President,
American University

3

We need to reinvent the university. [U.S. universities are] vulnerable because we have said that character is not related to education, [that] we're dealing in knowledge, not morals . . . We really got caught up in the designer-college spirit, a race for prestige based on assets.

Interview/
The Washington Post, 2-27:(A)9.

Bill Eadington
Director, Institute for
the Study of Gambling
and Commercial Gaming,
University of Nevada, Reno

4

[On state-run lotteries whose proceeds are designated for education]: The education establishment does not like to be dependent on sales of a commodity, which the lottery is, for a good portion of their funding. The vagaries of the demand for that commodity would then affect the revenues coming into education. And lotteries have experienced quite a bit of fluctuation, particularly in the last three years.

The Christian Science Monitor,
8-16:10.

Joseph Fernandez
Chancellor,
New York City School System

5

The problems [in schools] are very similar in most urban areas. You have a growing disparity between the haves and the have-nots. Many of the problems schools face are directly related to poverty. They are directly related to people not seeing any kind of hope at the end of the tunnel, the inability of people to get housing and jobs and good health services. All of that impacts the schools. I recently looked at a survey done in California that said the biggest [school] problem in the mid-1950s was chewing gum, speaking out of turn. Today the biggest problems in our

(JOSEPH FERNANDEZ)

schools are guns, weapons, dealing with substance abuse and gangs.

Interview, New York, N.Y./
Los Angeles Times, 5-4:(A)5.

James O. Freedman
President, Dartmouth College

1

Next to the military, universities are the institutions that have brought people of different races together . . . [Institutions of higher education] are the vehicles for upward mobility.

Interview, Dartmouth College/
The Christian Science Monitor,
5-25:10.

Ellen V. Futter
President, American Museum
of Natural History;
Former president,
Barnard College

2

[On her new position as museum head after having previously run a college]: What possible relationship is there between a premier women's college like Barnard and a preeminent scientific museum such as this? The answer is simple: They both concern endangered species.

At reception for her at Americum Museum
of Natural History,
New York, N.Y., Dec. 1/
The New York Times, 12-3:(A)13.

James Gallagher
Professor,
University of North Carolina;
President,
National Association
for Gifted Children

3

It's politically correct right now to say that a heterogeneous classroom is somehow "equitable." But if you put all your 30 youngsters in one classroom—those with disabilities, those with learning problems, plus the gifted—and you

don't provide the teacher with any special support, then you're throwing classrooms back to the '50s, instead of the year 2000.

Newsweek, 11-15:67.

David Gardner
Former president,
University of California

4

I think we profess to have high expectations for our students and our schools, but we're willing to settle for much less. We talk a good fight about wanting to have excellent schools when in fact we're content to have average ones . . . What I see is a slow, steady erosion of public regard for the public schools and in some respects a psychological abandonment. [But] I think we ought not to be discouraged. We were 20 years going down and it shouldn't be surprising if we're 20 years coming back. We're only halfway there.

Newsweek, 4-19:46.

Howard Gardner
Professor of education,
Graduate School of Education,
Harvard University

5

Most communities still think that the success of the school is someone else's concern—and that school problems occur in other persons' districts. Bond issues are regularly voted down. Teachers are universally bad-mouthed, even though the wretched conditions under which many work are not known.

Newsweek, 4-19:47.

John P. Gould
Dean,
Graduate School of Business,
University of Chicago

6

A dean is not a chief executive and you don't get to run things by announcement. The faculty is like a bunch of independent entrepreneurs working in one place, and you are dealing with people who are by training skeptical. My first line of strategy has been to try to at least convince

(JOHN P. GOULD)

people not to block innovative activities by others.

Interview/
The New York Times, 3-30:(C)4.

William H. Gray III
President,
United Negro College Fund

1

[On the financial difficulties of private black colleges]: When you're talking about these schools, you're talking generally about who's a half-inch off the edge, who's one inch off the edge, and who's six inches off the edge. If you take even the best private [black] colleges and compare them with their white counterparts, even they aren't doing very well economically.

The New York Times, 1-2:7.

Daniel Greenberg
Director,
Sudbury Valley School,
Framingham, Mass.

2

[On his school's adherence to "alternative education" ideas, which give more freedom to students in the learning process]: We adhere to the idea that the best and only significant learning takes place when you're self-motivated. We're not interested in the learning that takes place when somebody else is forcing you to do it.

The Christian Science Monitor,
12-27:12.

Sheldon Hackney
President,
University of Pennsylvania;
Chairman-designate,
National Endowment
for the Humanities
of the United States

3

Among the values I hold dear is a belief that a university ought to be open to all points of view, even if some of those views expressed are person-

ally abhorrent. I take some pride in having protected the right to speak of diverse controversial figures . . . The university should belong to all its members and not be the exclusive domain of any particular person, group or point of view.

At Senate Labor and Human Resources
Committee hearing on his nomination,
Washington, D.C., June 25/
The New York Times, 6-26:6.

Pat Henry
President,
National Congress
of Parents and Teachers

4

We are beginning to understand that to improve education we have to improve the quality of life of the children coming to school. That's a big plus. We have never been a nation that placed its highest priority on its children. That, too, accounts for the state of education in the past. But schools more and more are realizing that it may be necessary to spend a little money giving parents some of the skills they need to help raise their children in a positive way.

Interview/USA Today, 3-17:(D)6.

Gerald Holton
Professor of physics
and the history of science,
Harvard University

5

Parents [of American students] . . . are convinced that their own children are going to come through [school], just because they're good kids—no matter how little work they actually do. That's very different from the Japanese, or Chinese, or Taiwanese, Israeli parents, where no matter how well the kids do, the parents are after them to do better.

Newsweek, 4-19:48.

William Kilpatrick
Professor of education,
Boston (Mass.) College

6

In the late '60s and early '70s, educators convinced themselves that there was an easier

(WILLIAM KILPATRICK)

method [to teach character], which I call the decision-making method: Students would make up their own minds about right and wrong. The important thing that got left out was the whole business of habit formation, which is essential to character formation. Moral education is not just a matter of talking or having discussion or debate; it's a matter of practice and habit.

Interview/Christianity Today, 10-4:70.

Rotan E. Lee
President, Philadelphia (Pa.)
Board of Education

1

As an Afro-American, I don't think there is anything wrong with schools being populated by one ethnic group if that ethnic group lives in that community and wants their schools to facilitate their cultural or linguistic interests.

The New York Times, 3-1:(A)10.

Henry M. Levin
Economist
and education specialist,
Stanford University

2

[Calls for increased education as an answer to bad economic conditions] have been so convincing that there has been little call for evidence. It is simply assumed that much of the economic challenge has education at its roots and that more education and higher test scores will solve the problem . . . [But] we have a lot of over-education relative to the capacity of the economy. This view is very unpopular. It doesn't win adherence from industry, which uses the excuse that kids aren't well-enough educated, or with educators who want to increase investment in schools. But I'm not sure sheer numbers of new credentials are called for.

Mother Jones, Sept.-Oct.:59,60.

Edward A. "Monk" Malloy
President,
University of Notre Dame

3

The great danger to Catholic universities is that they will take the route of Harvard, Princeton

and Yale, that they will shuck off their religious identity as they become more academically sophisticated and mature.

U.S. News & World Report,
10-4:122.

Deborah McGriff
Superintendent of Schools
of Detroit, Mich.

4

The problem in American education is not "urban education." It's that even many of the best students in the country can't compete globally.

Interview, Detroit, Mich./
The Christian Science Monitor,
3-16:13.

5

We're moving away from this notion that there's one best [education] system—one size fits all. But our challenge seems to be in taking schools that are successful and replicating them so that we can have a system that is successful.

The Christian Science Monitor,
4-26:13.

Ira Mehlman
Spokesman, Federation for
American Immigration Reform

6

Our position is that [immigrants] are overwhelming many school systems. The schools have reached a point where they just can't absorb any more new immigrants and provide a quality education for any of the children. Let's face it: The resources just aren't there.

The Washington Post, 7-28:(A)12.

Yolanda Moses
President,
City College of New York

7

I'm talking about a core curriculum that all students take that looks at the history of the world

(YOLANDA MOSES)

from all perspectives, that looks at history, political science, in a way that is inclusive, so that it includes all voices and is not just told from one particular viewpoint . . . In the diversity discussion, the differences are not just whether or not Plato and Aristotle were the only contributors to Western civilization but what influence have African philosophers had, for example, on Western civilization, so the diversity of ideas is exponentially more exotic than it was before.

Interview/
The New York Times, 9-14:(A)17.

Barry Munitz
Chancellor,
California State University

1

[On the economic problems of his and other university systems]: The ticking bomb under the social fabric of the state is that just as the demographic profile is changing, we are saying to those coming to the school door that the rules are changing. We just can't do that. And not just because it will make those people angry. From a crass, economic view, that's the next generation of the work force. They have to be educated and trained. It's a particular dilemma for us, because we are training three out of four of the K-through-12 teachers in the state, and one out of nine in the entire nation! So all of those people who are worried about what's happening in the public schools have got to confront our ability to educate the educators. We're in danger of undermining the social assumption that if you've worked hard in California and paid your taxes, a quality education will be available for your children at a reasonable cost. If you start to get the signal that contract has disappeared, you question other aspects of your relationship to the state. That intangible rip in the social fabric worries me.

Interview,
Long Beach, Calif./
Los Angeles Times,
10-17:(M)3.

David Noble
Professor of history,
York University (Canada);
Co-founder,
National Coalition
for Universities
in the Public Interest

2

Corporations sponsor research at universities to use public tax dollars to defray the cost of developing marketable inventions and to spread the risk of failure. They're not building the buildings, or paying for the education of the staff, or supporting the students, or the library, or the land, or the accumulated prestige and knowledge of the university. If they had to replicate these resources in-house, it would cost them orders of magnitude more than what they're paying . . . Just as Americans should be concerned about the regulation of the oil under the ground and the timber above it, they should also be concerned about this precious and irreplaceable asset—what some call intellectual capital. We have no quarrel with universities acting in any way they want so long as they don't take public funds. But when they do—and nearly all do—to ask the question, "What's in it for the public?" is not only legitimate, it's essential democratic behavior.

The Atlantic, March:34,44.

Francois Orivel
Director,
Economics of Education
Research Institute (France)

3

Does it have to be government that controls education? . . . Those countries that have taken public responsibility for education are not always the ones that have achieved the best results. For example, some African countries made the mistake of nationalizing all the private [educational] networks in the first decades of independence. The more privately run higher education is, the more public resources can be allocated to primary schooling . . . One of the arguments that has done the most harm to the development of educational systems in the Third World is the idea that if education is private it is less equitable,

(FRANCOIS ORIVEL)

and if it's public it's more democratic . . . In countries where education is entirely public—India, Bangladesh or Nepal—access to second-level education is rationed and to higher education even more so. Who goes to secondary school and university [in those places]? Not the poor classes.

Panel discussion/
The Christian Science Monitor,
9-8:12.

Adama Ouane
Researcher,
United Nations Educational,
Scientific and Cultural
Organization

1

Those countries where education works are countries that have gotten beyond a certain level of development. But then look at Sri Lanka, which is very backward and yet has a remarkable educational system. One thing is certain—the training of human resources is capital for development.

Panel discussion/
The Christian Science Monitor,
9-8:12.

Lewis J. Perelman
Senior researcher,
Discovery Institute

2

The very notion of traditional education will become obsolete. The new technologies that are now being developed will enable people of all ages and social conditions to learn anything, anywhere, at any time. Learning will not be based, as it is today, on mechanisms of selection and exclusion. Diplomas will disappear. Instead, people will get certificates—the same way we get driver's licenses—to show potential employers that they have specific skills, talents or knowledge.

Interview/
The Christian Science Monitor,
9-22:9.

Colin L. Powell
General, United States Army;
Chairman, Joint Chiefs of Staff

3

[With high-school ROTC programs,] all you have to do is send this Major or Lieutenant Colonel and a couple of Sergeants into a school anywhere and put some uniforms on these kids; that's structure. You put [the students] all in a uniform, they all look alike. That takes care of the Nikes, it takes care of all the fancy clothes, it takes care of all the other crap we're wasting money on our kids with. And it does wonders.

Interview, Washington, D.C./
U.S. News & World Report,
9-20:51.

Diane S. Ravitch
Former Assistant Secretary
for Educational Research
and Improvement,
Department of Education
of the United States

4

We divide classes into winners and losers. The winners are told to learn chemistry so they can go to college. The losers are given some watered-down version of general science; just learn enough to work in McDonald's, because that is where you are going to end up anyway.

Mother Jones, Sept.-Oct.:57.

Bruce Reed
Deputy Assistant-designate
to President-elect Bill Clinton
for Domestic Policy

5

People tend to think being a Rhodes scholar is a bigger deal than it really is. I think most Rhodes scholars are lucky people—luckier than smart . . . If I can talk on background for a moment, the stereotype of the Rhodes scholar is someone who keeps index cards on every person he meets, and is always looking for an angle, another way to succeed. Unfortunately, that stereotype is largely true. The one thing that makes me uncomfortable about the whole Rhodes-scholar shtick is that it tends to perpetuate self-promotion—

WHAT THEY SAID IN 1993

(BRUCE REED)

which I find somewhat distasteful, in others or in myself.

Interview/
The Washington Post, 1-7:(C)2.

Robert B. Reich
Secretary of Labor
of the United States

1

[On skill standards developed as a guide to help students choose specific non-four-year schools for employment training]: I see the skill standards offering a way for the non-college bound student, who either can't afford it or doesn't feel that he or she wants to go to a regular four-year university, to utilize either the community-college system, technical-college system, proprietary-college system in a way that gives more guidance to those students as to what they're actually buying, what they're getting. Because they can see that industry has helped create specific areas of competence [that] industry feels it needs and so that they know in effect what kind of training they get . . . It provides a very powerful signaling mechanism to the high-school guidance-counseling community as to what kinds of skill competencies are in demand, where you can get the best training for those skill competencies. It gives students who are not going on to college a career path, a potential career route with training and a certification at the end.

Before Senate Labor and Human Resources
Committee, Washington, D.C., Feb. 24/
The Washington Post, 2-25:(A)22.

Condoleezza Rice
Provost-designate,
Stanford University

2

What's the opposite of multiculturalism [in education]? There's no place in the world for monoculturalism. I would like to think a student leaving Stanford appreciates Duke Ellington and Beethoven with the same fervor. I don't see culture as a prison where you are born and have to stay.

Interview, Palo Alto, Calif./
The New York Times, 6-23:(B)6.

Richard W. Riley
Secretary of Education
of the United States

3

I and the President [Clinton] are opposed to [government] vouchers to be used in the private schools. We support all innovative concepts to make schools exciting and different within public schools. We want to make the public schools exciting, creative places, but we don't favor public dollars going to private schools . . . [Vouchers] would absolutely kill what we're talking about. And that is making the public school system the same as Sidwell Friends [a private school] in quality. If a local school district wants to do something like that, we're not into controlling what they do. But that's not in our agenda. It would kill public schools slowly. Now, I have no negative feelings whatsoever about good private schools. And there are some great private schools out there. But to have money shipped off the public system into that would be a real mistake.

Interview/
USA Today, 3-25:(A)13.

4

The Federal government's role in providing leadership as a partner in education reform has not been updated or clearly redefined in 30 years. We're talking about a new relationship between the Federal and state government, one of partnership.

The Christian Science Monitor,
4-23:2.

5

[On a study showing a great many American adults score low on literacy]: It's bound to be a shock when you look at the complexity of our economic system, and the requirements that a person has to have to function well in that system, and to say that 90 million adults in this country don't have the skills to do that.

Sept. 8/
Los Angeles Times, 9-9:(A)1.

142

James Rosenbaum
Education researcher,
Northwestern University

1

Over and over we find the relationship between high-school grades and unemployment, earnings and job quality is practically zero. If you interview employers, they say they don't use anything in the high-school transcript in hiring, with the possible exception of attendance records. We have set up a system with no incentives to do well in school.

Mother Jones, Sept.-Oct.:59.

Neil L. Rudenstine
President,
Harvard University

2

[On education 60 years from now, in 2053]: Liberal-arts education will fare better than expected in the first half of the 21st century. Society will finally have remembered that lawyers and doctors can be wiser for having read Shakespeare and Tolstoy, as can engineers and economists for having studied the arts.

Interview/
U.S. News & World Report, 10-25:72.

George Rupp
President,
Columbia University

3

[Saying the undergraduate program is more important to his university than the research aspect]: Offering an unsurpassed undergraduate education ties this university together in a way that nothing else does. It's important that this institution has a sense of itself that's more than just the sum of it parts.

Interview, New York, N.Y./
The Christian Science Monitor,
12-7:14.

James W. Schmotter
Dean, College of Business
and Economics,
Lehigh University

4

[On education 60 years from now, in 2053]: The MBA will no longer exist. Corporations, not universities, will provide education and training. It will be lifelong and tailored to the needs of corporations.

Interview/
U.S. News & World Report,
10-25:73.

Albert Shanker
President,
American Federation of Teachers

5

[Comparing President-elect Clinton's education appointments with those of the outgoing Bush Administration]: [Clinton] has put a lot of people who have a passionate interest in education into Cabinet and sub-Cabinet positions. I'm sure that we'll have some disagreements and some arguments. But there's a difference between having a disagreement with somebody who is out to kill you [as in the Bush Administration] and having a disagreement with somebody where you know that your goals are the same but you've got some different opinions on how to get there. In one case, it's a life-or-death struggle; in the other case, it's a family feud.

The Christian Science Monitor,
1-11:12.

6

[On the poor educational showing of many well-to-do students in U.S. schools when compared with students in foreign schools]: Why is it that kids who are not only well-fed but probably over-fed, and who are among the most affluent kids who ever walked the face of the earth, are learning very, very little compared to youngsters in other industralized countries?

Los Angeles Times, 4-9:(A)29.

7

I'd find a substitute for school boards. Basically, what we need to have is superintendents and principals who will let the professionals [teachers] do what works. We need to get the political interference with teachers off their backs. And we need to really professionalize teaching by making it much tougher to get in, and increasing the rewards.

Newsweek, 4-19:49.

Ted Sizer
Chairman,
Coalition of Essential Schools

1

One starts by asking people to think of education not as something that is delivered to people but as something that is provoked in people. Right now, schools have curriculums that have lists of answers. Kids don't work hard in school; they're fed things. [And] the silence about probably the most important teacher in the culture— television—is absolutely deafening. We don't know how to tackle it yet.

Interview/
USA Today, 3-17:(D)6.

H. Patrick Swygert
President,
State University of New York,
Albany

2

[On the trend of public colleges and universities soliciting private funds because of cutbacks in government support]: This is the new world of higher education and it's going to be the way it is for the foreseeable future. We've got to run faster and work harder and smarter not just to stay even, but if we want to move forward in even modest increments, we're going to have to have outside support.

The New York Times, 3-29:(A)1.

James D. Watson
Biologist;
Winner, 1962 Nobel Prize
in Physiology and Medicine

3

[On his advice to students]: Don't learn too much—you'll just delude yourself. Focus. Concentrate. The most important thing I learned in graduate school was from a professor who told me most of the work being done by the faculty was bad.

At Sidwell Friends School,
Washington, D.C., March 9/
The New York Times, 3-10:(A)11.

Richard West
Dean, Stern School of Business,
New York University

4

[On choosing a business school]: Find out what a school is actually doing about innovation and new programs. Don't just go by what the [college] catalogs say. Look for evidence that the faculty really knows what is going on in courses other than their own. It's the equivalent of asking engineers working on the front end of a car if they know what's going on in the back end. If they don't, it's dollars to doughnuts the car won't be very well-made. If you find that in the same course each section is using a different text, you should be suspicious about the degree to which the program has a holistic quality.

Interview/U.S. News & World Report, 3-22:56.

Hayden White
Professor of the history
of consciousness,
University of California,
Santa Cruz

5

We used to think of culture as something outside the domain of politics. But culture has now become a site of very severe political contestation. That means that any scholar who's worth his or her salt is going to be very self-conscious about the political and social implications not only of the work they do but the conditions under which they do their work.

Los Angeles Times, 7-15:(A)18.

Pete Wilson
Governor of California (R)

6

To fix our schools, we must also free our schools. We must free them from the tangle of state rules and regulations that distract teachers, principals and superintendents from their central mission: educating our children. I'm sure, given the freedom to focus solely on what's best for our kids, each of you could construct a better school than the one created piecemeal through thousands of rules and regulations written by politicians in [the state capital].

To education administrators, Sacramento, Calif.,
Jan. 28/Los Angeles Times, 1-29:(A)1.

The Environment • Energy

Bruce Babbitt
Secretary of the Interior
of the United States

1

I think the Pacific Northwest, the timber crisis up there, is going to be the test case for my Department and for this [Clinton] Administration. And I'm very confident that if we can get everybody down around a table, coordinate the Federal response, that we can set aside areas to protect not only the spotted owl but the salmon run and all the rest of the wildlife up there and, at the same time, get the logging industry back on its feet by saying there are areas and there are techniques. You don't have to clear-cut every last tree in order to sustain the timber industry. We can use new logging techniques, provide job retraining and do both.

Broadcast interview/
"Today," NBC-TV, 2-9.

2

We must get control of the Endangered Species Act process by pro-active front-end administration of that Act. And what that means is, rather than focusing on single species as they spiral toward extinction, we need to step back and look at the entire ecosystem and ask, is it possible to intervene before the crisis? Is it possible to look at habitat management that will prevent that crisis, to do it on the basis not just of one species but of the entire ecosystem? There have been some successes in some parts of California, and elsewhere, with that approach. It does, however, require an added emphasis on the scientific capacity of the agency. In describing those particular issues, I think I draw you inevitably toward a larger conclusion, and that is that this [Interior] Department needs a scientific research capacity that transcends the needs of individual agencies.

Before House Natural Resources Committee,
Washington, D.C., Feb. 16/
The Washington Post,
2-17:(A)18.

3

As I float around the Department [of the Interior], summoning people, saying what are we doing, I make an extraordinary set of discoveries . . . I find that our effort, our scientific effort, to try to get the information, solid, consistent, across ecosystems and multi-species, is nonexistent because each agency [within the Department] is looking at its little postage-stamp jurisdiction . . . Now, what I have [found], after roaming the halls for a couple of weeks and sort of hanging around with some of you and others, it becomes crystal clear that that won't work, that what we need to do in this country is to mount a systematic assessment to deploy science across jurisdictional lines to do the kinds of surveys that will provide us the information from which people can make land-use decisions.

Before Environmental Grantmakers Association,
Washington, D.C., Feb. 25/
The Washington Post, 2-26:(A)22.

4

For 12 years [under Republican Administrations, the] Interior [Department] has been the center of the Washington anti-environmental movement. [But] the Department is full of people who came to Interior because they wanted to conserve the natural heritage, not attack it. [But with me as the new Secretary,] they are now liberated.

Newsweek, 3-29:25.

5

[On Georgia-Pacific Corporation's agreement to help protect the habitat of a woodpecker while continuing its foresting operations]: It's a demonstration that it is possible on a large cooperative scale to find that balance between the imperative to create jobs in forest production and the imperative to protect the environment . . . in advance of the crises, in advance of the litigation scenarios that we've seen so often in the past.

The Christian Science Monitor,
4-21:8.

(BRUCE BABBITT)

1

Of this you can be certain: 1993 will be the year of reform for public land and water. The [Clinton] Administration is solidly committed to land-use reform, and the question is not if these changes will occur, but how they occur.

At National Press Club,
Washington, D.C., April 27/
The Washington Post, 4-28:(A)7.

2

[On the Clinton Administration's increased grazing fees and regulations on the use of Federal land in the West]: It's about our commitment and our responsibility to live more lightly on the land. It's about asserting our American heritage, the landscape, the resources and the culture that constitutes the American West.

Aug. 9/
The New York Times, 8-10:(A)1.

Dan Becker
Environmental analyst,
Sierra Club

3

[Saying President Clinton's proposals to control "greenhouse gas" emissions are not strong enough]: The plan we're hearing about is one that [former President] George Bush could have produced. It has no hammers, no substantial requirements. And the numbers don't add up: You can't get dramatic benefits from throwing pennies at a program and not requiring anything of industry. This plan would not be a "clarion call." It would be a broken promise.

Sept. 29/
Los Angeles Times, 9-30:(A)18.

Carol M. Browner
Administrator-designate,
Environmental Protection Agency
of the United States

4

I hope my tenure [at the EPA] will mark a new era in communication between the EPA and America's business community, between en-

vironmentalists and business leaders . . . [The] adversarial relationship creates damaging delays in the regulatory process, and often, unnecessarily harms business without significantly aiding the environment.

At Senate Environment and Public Works
Committee hearing on her nomination,
Washington, D.C., Jan. 11/
The Washington Post, 1-12:(A)11.

Carol M. Browner
Administrator,
Environmental Protection Agency
of the United States

5

[On the high cost of the environmental "Superfund" program to clean up hazardous-waste sites]: The most vexing question of all: How clean is clean? Should cleanups allow some contamination to remain if public health is protected, or should all sites be restored to their original state, no matter what the cost? Should the level of cleanup of land and ground water be dependent to some extent on the post-cleanup use of those resources?

Senate testimony,
Washington, D.C./
The Christian Science Monitor,
5-25:2.

John Bryson
Chairman,
Southern California
Edison Company

6

Competitors like Germany and Japan can produce a unit of economic output for roughly half the energy we [the U.S.] use. Energy efficiency will lead not only to technological development, but to economic growth and environmental improvement. It will provide the basis for producing the next generation of globally competitive U.S. products and services.

At economic conference convened
by President-elect Bill Clinton,
Little Rock, Ark./
The Christian Science Monitor,
1-12:12.

Robert Bullard
Professor of sociology,
University of California,
Riverside

1

All over the country, working people in cities have organized themselves into civic groups and neighborhood associations to address the [local environmental] issues, whether it's fighting a facility or the cleanup of a waste dump, or even garbage pickup. I have identified over 200 organizations of people of color actively involved in environmental issues in their communities. It's unfortunate that the larger society has not come to understand the diversity now within the environmental movement.

The Christian Science Monitor,
1-7:8.

Bill Clinton
President
of the United States

2

[On the controversy over logging and the forest environment in the Pacific Northwest]: Thousands of jobs are at stake, but the very ecostructure of the Pacific Northwest is also at stake. The parties on both sides have been paralyzed in court battles . . . One of the problems has been that the United States itself has taken different positions across the agencies. So the first thing I hope to do is to be able to at least adopt a uniform legal position for the United States. The second thing I want to do is go out there, along with the Vice President [Gore], and listen, hammer out the alternatives and then take a position that I think will break the logjam. The position—it may be like my economic program: It'll probably make everybody mad. But I will try to be fair to the people whose livelihoods depend on this and fair to the environment that we are all obligated to maintain . . . Everybody may be somewhat disappointed, but the paralysis now gripping the lives of the people out there is totally unacceptable.

News conference,
Washington, D.C., March 23/
The New York Times,
3-24:(A)7.

Barry Commoner
Director,
Center for the Biology
of Natural Systems,
Queens (N.Y.) College

3

[Criticizing a Clinton Administration proposed expansion of a system whereby companies can sell their "pollution rights," which would be set and limited by the government, to other firms which may not be able to meet the government's pollution limits]: The only way to deal with the remediation of the environment is to prevent the production of the pollutant at its point of origin. What the entire trading program is based on is the *production* of pollution—you can't have a market unless you have a pollutant to trade. It's an absolute residue of the Reagan-era which violates everything we know from experience: that the only way we can reduce pollution is by preventing it.

Los Angeles times, 9-9:(A)5.

Howard Golub
Acting Director
and Chief Engineer,
Interstate Sanitary Commission

4

[Saying a 1988 Federal law banning ocean dumping of waste did little to solve the problem of contaminated beaches in the Northeast because the real culprit is over-burdened sewer systems]: A sewer system isn't sexy. It's expensive to fix, and nobody wants to hear about it. So people focused on what they understand—and they understand that [ocean-dumped] sewage and the sea don't seem nice together.

The New York Times, 3-22:(C)8.

Mikhail S. Gorbachev
Former President
of the Soviet Union

5

The fact that [the world's leaders] came to the [1992] Rio Summit [on the environment] means that politicians are beginning to understand that we have reached a watershed in our relationship

(MIKHAIL S. GORBACHEV)

with the environment. Last November, 1,500 scientists, including 100 Nobel prize-winners, stated at a conference that if things go on like this, within decades our biosphere will suffer irreversible damage. I think this realization will change the way politicians think.

Interview,
Kyoto, Japan/Time, 9-6:53.

Al Gore
Vice President-elect
of the United States

1

[On the Environmental Justice Act]: It empowers the citizens of a local community victimized by high concentration of environmental threats with the ability to intervene in ongoing proceedings—siting decisions and so forth—and it empowers them with the ability to get scientific help in analyzing the nature of the threat posed . . . Where there is a large concentration of pollution sources in a particular neighborhood, this will make it possible to look at the cumulative threat to the air and the water. In other words, it takes the point of view of the people instead of the smokestack. This really needs to be passed. It also represents a bridge between the civil-rights movement and the environmental movement, and there's a lot of traffic going in both directions across that bridge.

Interview/
The Christian Science Monitor,
1-12:9.

Ladd Greeno
Senior vice president,
Arthur D. Little, Inc.,
consultants

2

[In the environmental debate,] nobody is satisfied. The public wants better environmental performance, and they want it now. Businesses, on the other hand, are spending vastly increased amounts of money and time on environmental issues than they were a few short years ago, but they are frustrated by government regulations

that too often result in a misdirection of efforts and priorities.

The Christian Science Monitor,
12-27:14.

Walter J. Hickel
Governor of Alaska (R)

3

[On a proposal to allow the killing of wolves in Alaska so that caribou and moose herds would expand for the benefit of hunters]: For Alaskans, the wolf is a magnificent animal, one to be respected and admired. But we do not have the luxury of mistaking a wolf for Lassie or Rin Tin Tin . . . You can't just let nature run wild.

Los Angeles Times, 1-13:(A)5.

Paul Kennedy
Political analyst

4

[There are] urgent environmentalists who say, "What we need to do is to totally transform our lifestyle by banning the automobile, getting on a bike, stopping industrialization in the developing countries, returning to the age of candlelight." But that has no chance whatever with the American public, which can't even accept a 10-cent gasoline tax.

Interview/
Mother Jones, May-June:59.

Roger Kennedy
Director,
National Park Service
of the United States

5

It doesn't embarrass me a whit to try to reduce our responsibilities to public lands to a moral position . . . I believe our national parks are chosen places and that we have a moral imperative to take care of those places.

Interview,
Washington, D.C./
Los Angeles Times,
8-16:(A)14.

Andy Kerr
Director of conservation
and education,
Oregon Natural Resources
Council

1

When so little of the virgin forest is left . . . environmentalists are not in a position to compromise. The forest has been compromised all it can.

The Christian Science Monitor,
4-5:2.

Fred Krupp
Executive director,
Environmental Defense Fund

2

[Supporting President Clinton's order that the Federal government use paper products with a higher recycled content]: What may be different about this is that paper recycling is vested with enormous importance, because average Americans have come to understand that one of the first things they can do to align their life with the environmental ethic is to recycle paper. I'm hoping that the public's enthusiasm—whether from inner-city residents who will benefit from jobs or from suburbanites who care deeply about recycling—will help the the President again understand that what's good for the environment makes good politics.

Oct. 20/
Los Angeles Times, 10-21:(A)18.

Joseph S. Larson
Director,
Environmental Institute,
University of Massachusetts,
Amherst

3

While wetlands make up only 5 percent of the land surface area of the coterminous United States, their importance to the health, welfare and safety of our citizens is highly important . . . When coastal storms move on shore at low tide, coastal wetlands can provide a measure of storm buffering. But more importantly, and fully demonstrated in recent East Coast hurricanes, coastal wetlands are areas of high risk for human habitation and development. Maintaining these wetlands in their natural state by prohibiting development avoids major individual and public financial losses.

Before Senate Committee on
Environmental and Public Works,
Washington, D.C., Sept. 15/
The Washington Post, 9-17:(A)20.

Robert Lee
Sociologist,
University of Washington

4

[Saying the effects of environmental regulations and restrictions on timber harvesting in forests for ecological reasons have been hard on logging communities]: We are moving into a process that looks a lot like what happened in the inner cities. We are seeing the collapse of families, disintegration of families, disintegration of communities, homelessness, stranded elderly people, people whose lives are in disarray from substance abuse.

The Christian Science Monitor,
4-5:2.

Thomas Mignanelli
President,
Nissan Motors U.S.A.

5

We need some kind of fuel tax or energy tax. It's long overdue. Everybody yells and screams up front; when you live with it for awhile, it's not a problem.

USA Today, 2-19:(A)11.

George Miller
United States Representative,
D-California

6

The environmental movement is pulsating out there in the neighbordhoods. People are learning about their neighborhoods and the environment. They're expanding both in their knowledge and in their willingness to take actions—and they're having success.

The Christian Science Monitor,
1-12:9.

149

Jurgen Moltmann
Professor of theology,
University of Tubingen
(Germany)

1

We have the qustion of the destruction of nature. The whole life system of the Earth has been brought out of balance by humanity, and may die. Year after year hundreds of species of plants and animals become extinct. The ozone layer is being destroyed. The soil is increasingly poisoned. If we cannot change these trends, we may be part of the collective suicide of humanity. Therefore, we need a new ecological theology.

Interview/
Christianity Today, 1-11:33.

Hisham Nazer
Minister of Petroleum
of Saudi Arabia

2

[Criticizing attempts by Western countries to decrease the use of oil through environmental and economic regulations]: Given the role of Saudi Arabia in the world of oil, it is not very helpful to see the industrialized countries implementing one policy after another to undermine international oil trade and consequently market stability . . . Saudi Arabia is a major stabilizing force in the oil market. We are investing billions of dollars to increase our production capacity to assure the world of adequate supplies in the years ahead. If demand is deliberately suppressed, then it would not be surprising if oil producers reassess the compatibility of their policies with the evolving policies and trends on the demand side.

At Cambridge Energy Research
Associates conference,
Houston, Texas/
The Christian Science Monitor,
2-12:8.

Wayne Pacelle
Director, Fund for Animals

3

[On the threatened economic boycott of Alaska which forced that state to shelve plans to allow the killing of wolves as a means of preserving herds of animals for hunters]: We recognize that [an economic boycott] is a political tool that needs to be cautiously exercised. But we also knew that reasoning would not appeal to [Alaska Governor] Walter Hickel and that the state legislature would not do anything because of the hunting lobby. We felt [the tourism] industry was dependent upon wildlife-sensitive people. They can't have it both ways. If they want tourist dollars from people in the lower 48 states, they have to respect their values . . . It's one of the issues that struck a deep chord.

The Washington Post,
1-8:(A)8.

Carl Pope
Executive director,
Sierra Club

4

[President Clinton's proposed 1994 Federal] budget contains important increases in funding for energy efficiency and renewable energy sources, decreases in funding for nuclear energy, and a new tax on energy. But important public-lands programs and the Environmental Protection Agency will suffer again next year. This budget does not reflect an advancing environmental agenda on all fronts.

The Christian Science Monitor,
4-13:2.

Frank P. Popoff
Chairman,
Dow Chemical Company

5

We must ensure that the polluter pays. Be they private citizens; be they businesses—large or small; be they government agencies; they must pay rather than pass on, postpone, or try to duck the environmental impact of their actions.

At economic conference convened
by President-elect Bill Clinton,
Little Rock, Ark./
The Christian Science Monitor,
1-12:12.

Paul C. Pritchard
President,
National Parks and
Conservation Association

1

What happens in the next few years could decide whether the [national] parks will become mass entertainment and recreation centers or whether they will function as quiet campuses of the nation's largest outdoor university.

Los Angeles Times, 8-16:(A)14.

William K. Reilly
Former Administrator,
Environmental Protection Agency
of the United States

2

It is far past time when we become mature enough as a nation to address an environmental issue, mobilize to support it, and do so without acting in an emergency atmosphere. Not everything is a crisis that has to be corrected tomorrow. And we need to make clear that cost considerations are relevant to any remedy.

The New York Times, 3-26:(A)11.

Felix G. Rohatyn
Senior partner,
Lazard Freres & Company,
investment bankers;
Chairman, Municipal
Assistance Corporation
of New York

3

I'm for [an increase in the Federal] gasoline tax as a national-security measure to reduce dependence on foreign oil, second, as a conservation measure, and third, as a revenue-raising measure. The biggest luxury this country indulges in is its over-use of energy.

The New YorkTimes, 1-2:13.

Urvan R. Sternfels
President,
National Petroleum Refiners
Association

4

[Criticizing a Clinton Administration proposal to increase taxes on oil]: This is a very heavy penalty. Clearly, they are trying to get people to move to other forms of energy, but it will have a horrendous effect on the industrial economy, especially those with oil as a principal fuel, such as trucking and aviation.

The Washington Post, 2-18:(A)26.

Jonathan Turley
Professor of law,
and director of
Environmental Crimes Project,
George Washington University

5

[Saying a Federal fine imposed on Louisiana-Pacific Corporation for falsifying reports on pollution from its plants is too lenient a punishment]: This case is a prime example of how a company can dominate a market by avoiding the costs of complying with environmental laws. They have enjoyed a long period of high profits and rapid expansion because of their falsification of records and misleading of regulators. To allow Louisiana-Pacific to simply internalize those costs now and not face criminal liability sends a message to industry that environmental violations remain simply the cost of doing business.

The New York Times, 6-3:(A)14.

Timothy E. Wirth
Under Secretary of State
of the United States

6

President Clinton is deeply committed to moving population to the forefront of America's international priorities. He understands the cost of excessive population growth to the health of women, to the natural environment and to our hopes for alleviating poverty. He believes that America cannot stand aside as the world confronts one of the largest challenges of this century and the next.

Speech, United Nations,
New York, May 11/
The New York Times,
5-12:(A)6.

Jay Ziegler
Spokesman for the
Department of the Interior
of the United States

1

[Saying there is a problem of polluted Federal lands]: We are acutely aware of the serious management problems on the public lands that are before us—the problems that 12 years of neglect have left to be addressed. We're committed to addressing these issues seriously, to doing better. And some of this costs money. That's going to be a serious issue.

Sept. 20/
Los Angeles Times,
9-21:(A)11.

Government

William J. Althaus
Mayor of York, Pa.;
President,
United States Conference
of Mayors

1

[Republicans] talk about tax-and-spend Democrats. [But] the nature of government is taxing and spending. What is at issue is what it's spent on.

The Washington Post, 5-26:(A)6.

Ross K. Baker
Political scientist,
Rutgers University

2

The Senate has been a swamp in which many a Presidential program has sunk without a trace after breezing through the House . . . [As Democratic President Clinton is finding,] a Senate Democrat is simply not as sure a Democratic vote as a House Democrat.

Los Angeles Times, 3-27:(A)6.

Robert S. Bennett
Lawyer;
Former Special Counsel
to the U.S. Senate Ethics
Committee

3

[On independent counsels assigned to investigate wrongdoing by government officials]: There's an old saying: Beware of the lawyer with one case. The trouble with independent counsels is that you give one case and enormous power to a single individual, and the pressures to find wrongdoing are overpowering. You don't get much credit saying that nothing wrong occurred.

U.S. News & World Report, 11-8:47.

William J. Bennett
Former Secretary of Education
of the United States

4

I believe in what's been called "statecraft as soulcraft." The government is a bully pulpit; the government can be a teacher in a vital national seminar. What it teaches it teaches by example— first, through the words and actions of the President and others, and second, through how it runs its programs. It teaches through the kinds of behavior it rewards and encourages, [and] the kinds of behavior it discourages.

Interview/
Christianity Today, 9-13:32.

David Boaz
Scholar, Cato Institute

5

[Saying he does not support the massive kind of inauguration and pre-inauguration festivities planned for President-elect Clinton]: We have aggrandized our Presidency. What we're doing now is putting on a coronation instead of an inauguration . . . It's not what our founders intended. I guess I like the tradition of the old one slipping quietly out of town and the new one slipping in. I think that's a healthy attitude. The idea of an earlier era—that the ascension of a new person into the Presidency was not that important—was a better one for a democracy.

USA Today, 1-15:(A)2.

John Boehner
United States Representative,
D-Ohio

6

[On his calling in safety inspectors to check his House office, which had numerous safety hazards]: I called for these inspections to illustrate two points. One, to demonstrate that many of the rules and standards [that the government] imposes on the private sector are nothing more than a regulatory nightmare . . . And two, the hypocrisy of a Congress which forces these regulations and standards on the productive sector of our economy and yet exempt themselves from these very same rules.

The Christian Science Monitor,
2-23:3.

David L. Boren
United States Senator,
D-Oklahoma

1

The fact that [Congress] was not and is not working has given rise to both immense frustration on the part of members of Congress and to outrage amongst the American public. Last year's election—including the drive toward term limits, the [Ross] Perot [Presidential] candidacy and the largest number of new members being elected to Congress in almost 50 years—showed how strongly the American people feel about the status quo here in Washington.

At Joint Committee on the
Organization of Congress hearing,
Washington, D.C., Jan. 26/
Los Angeles Times, 1-27:(A)5.

2

[Saying he will work for Congressional reform by pushing ethics, cutting lobbyists' influence, etc.]: I'm going to call it like I see it. I'm not going to hesitate to put my colleagues on the spot . . . I'm not interested in doing something cosmetic, just so we can say we passed Congressional reform. It's got to be meaningful. I'd rather lose, and go down fighting for something meaningful, than to win on something that's just going to be incremental.

Interview/
The Christian Science Monitor,
2-9:1.

Alan Brinkley
Professor of history,
Columbia University

3

[Saying he does not agree with some critics who do not support the massive kind of inauguration and pre-inauguration festivities planned for President-elect Clinton]: Rituals by definition are always excessive, and this is a ritual. It's just a form of ceremony that gives people a sense of connection with government. I think that's healthy and valuable.

USA Today, 1-15:(A)2.

Dale Bumpers
United States Senator,
D-Arkansas

4

[On the increase in political scandals]: When I was growing up, all the salacious stuff I found was about Hollywood stars. First thing you know, it became commonplace in Hollywood. And that's when the focus began to turn to Congress and, to a lesser extent, the Executive Branch . . . Constituents care, and they can make you sorry. And they can be pretty vindictive.

Interview, Nov. 3/
The New York Times, 11-4:(A)7.

Robert C. Byrd
United States Senator,
D-West Virginia

5

[Criticizing Senator Bob Packwood's refusal to turn over certain parts of his personal diaries to the Senate Ethics Committee which is investigating charges against him of sexual harassment]: None of us is pure or without flaws, but when those flaws damage the institution of the Senate, it is time to have the grace to go [resign]. Senator Packwood has chosen to do the opposite . . . [He] has chosen to protect himself at the expense of the Senate and has even resorted to the use of certain revelations [in his diaries that may involve other Senators in scandals] that give every appearance of an attempt to intimidate the Senate and the committee charged with investigating allegations of improper conduct which may reflect upon this body.

Before the Senate,
Washington, D.C., Nov. 2/
The Washington Post, 11-4:(A)19.

6

The Senate is larger than any one of its members. When the duly elected representatives of the people gather together in this hallowed chamber, they become much more than the combined intellects, talents and idiosyncracies of 100 people. They become the living, breathing manifestation of the spirit and soul of the people of the nation . . . We who assemble here in our

(ROBERT C. BYRD)

official capacities embody the hopes, the dreams, the aspirations, the wisdom and the shortcomings and the flaws of the people we serve. We have been selected by our fellow citizens and entrusted with their sacred rights and personal liberties. Service in this body is a supreme honor. It is also a burden and serious responsibility. Members' lives become open for inspection and are used as examples for other citizens to emulate . . . Every time that one of us tarnishes the Senate by not living up to the title and high calling of Senators, we are hurting much more than ourselves or our families or even the constituents we serve. Every time that a member brings less than honor to this chamber, a little more of the marble of the people's trust is chipped away from this institution.

Before the Senate,
Washington, D.C., Nov. 2/
The Washington Post, 11-4:(A)19.

Ben Nighthorse Campbell
United States Senator,
D-Colorado

1

[On being a Senator besieged by reporters and lobbyists]: [It is] like being attacked by a plague of locusts. Now I know what a grain of wheat feels like.

The New York Times, 8-7:28.

2

[On his being an unconventional Senator, such as in his dress]: I've never believed that to be part of America, we all have to look alike, dress alike, talk alike and ride around in black limousines. Unfortunately, there's a stereotype for the "Senatorial look." But I don't think you have to have a Senatorial look to get things done.

Interview/
The Washington Post, 9-20:(A)17.

Jesse Choper
Professor,
University of California-Berkeley
Law School

3

[Saying the Senate Ethics Committee may be within its rights in demanding that Senator Bob

Packwood turn over his personal diaries because of allegations against him of misconduct]: [For the diaries to be exempt from subpoena,] you have to show some Constitutional immunity, some privilege against self-incrimination or free speech or freedom of association. As a general proposition, a court can subpoena records that contain reference to criminal conduct.

Time, 11-8:42.

Henry G. Cisneros
Secretary of Housing
and Urban Development
of the United States

4

[On the weak financial safeguards at HUD]: It's like a car without headlights. It doesn't mean it's going to go off the road, but it enhances your chances of not making the next curve.

Interview,
Washington, D.C., March 10/
The New York Times, 3-11:(A)13.

Bill Clinton
President-elect
of the United States

5

[As President,] to be preoccupied with the institution of the Presidency keeps you from thinking about the people who sent you there and the problems they have. I really do get up every day and just put one foot in front of the other and not think about "it" as if it were some disembodied thing. I'm just going to do the very best I can and try to have a wonderful time doing it.

Interview, Little Rock, Ark./
Time, 1-4:37.

6

There's [something] I've learned about governing that the most famous Governor of the 20th century said, Franklin Roosevelt. We ought to be about bold experimentation, which means we ought to try things, and if they don't work we ought to stop them and try something else. It worked pretty well for America at one time, in different circumstances. I think it would work

155

(BILL CLINTON)

pretty well again today. These are the lessons that I want to bring from the Statehouse to the White House. My goal as President will be to bring to this city a new spirit of innovation, and to work to empower all of you, all the more to continue your own innovation.

To Governors and former Governors,
Washington, D.C., Jan. 19/
The New York Times, 1-20:(A)10.

1

It would be irresponsible for any President of the United States ever not to respond to changing circumstances. Every President . . . and especially the ones who really did a good job . . . had to change some of their positions in response to changing circumstances.

Los Angeles Times, 1-20:(A)6.

2

The President has to strike a fine balance. I have to get enough facts and spend enough time to really feel a high level of self-confidence in decisions I'm going to make. But, on the other hand, I can't see everybody, I can't make every decision. I have to have real discipline, knowing what paper not to read, what people not to see. I really do care about this. When I was Governor, the longer I served, the more I delegated.

Interview, Little Rock, Ark./
U.S. News & World Report,
1-25:42.

3

I spent more time picking a Cabinet than any President in history. I believe it was time well spent. I think Presidents have been hurt by picking Cabinets with people who wind up being virtual strangers, who had very little to do with their campaigns, who weren't on the same wavelength as they. I was looking for excellence, general philosophical agreement and diversity. And we got that.

Interview, Little Rock, Ark./
U.S. News & World Report,
1-25:42.

Bill Clinton
President of the United States

4

This beautiful capital, like every capital since the dawn of civilization, is often a place of intrigue and calculation. Powerful people maneuver for position and worry endlessly about who is "in" and who is "out," who is up and who is down, forgetting those people whose toil and sweat sends us here and pays our way. Americans deserve better. I say to all of you here: Let us resolve to reform our politics, so that power and privilege no longer shout down the voice of the people.

Inaugural address,
Washington, D.C., Jan. 20/
The New York Times, 1-21:(A)10.

5

[On his wife, Hillary]: I think that in the coming months the American people will learn, as the people of our state [Arkansas] did, that we have a First Lady of many talents, but who most of all can bring people together around complex and difficult issues to hammer out consensus and get things done. Of all the people I've ever worked with in my life, she's better at organizing and leading people from a complex beginning to a certain end than anybody I've ever worked with in my life.

Washington, D.C., Jan. 25/
Los Angeles Times, 1-26:(A)1.

6

Over the past decade, the best American businesses have had to reorder themselves and revitalize themselves. They've had to reduce layers of bureaucracy, give people on the front lines the freedom to innovate and do more with less to better serve their customers. Well, the taxpayers of this country are our [government's] customers, and we intend to follow those methods of modernization to increase our services to them and to do it at an affordable cost so that this money can be put to more productive purposes.

Announcing White House staff reductions,
Washington, D.C., Feb. 9/
The Washington Post, 2-16:(A)11.

(BILL CLINTON)

1

When I became President, I was amazed at just the way the White House worked . . . in outmoded ways that didn't take maximum advantage of technology and didn't do things that any business would have done years ago.

Newsweek, 3-1:31.

2

We intend to redesign, to reinvent, to reinvigorate the entire national government. [To do it,] we will turn to Federal employees for help. They know better than anyone else how to do their jobs if someone will simply ask them and reward them for wanting to do it better.

The Washington Post, 3-19:(A)29.

3

[On his first few months in office, during which he has had problems getting his programs through Congress, including a Republican filibuster in the Senate]: After spending three months getting banged around in this town, I can understand a little more about [the game of] hockey than I did before I came here. Hockey is a tough game. It's a hard-hitting sport. It does have one virtue, though: There's a penalty for delay of game. I wish we had that rule in the Senate.

At ceremony honoring the champion
University of Maine hockey team,
Washington, D.C., April 19/
The Christian Science Monitor,
4-21:9.

4

When people say to me, "Well, what did you do in your first 100 days [as President]?" I say, "What did the other guys do in their first 100 days?" . . . If people thought that I'd be President and 90 days later every [election-] campaign commitment I made would be written into law and everybody's lives would be changed, I think that's just not realistic. You have to have a realistic feeling about how much time it takes to change and how long it takes to have an impact on it.

Before Newspaper Association of America,
Boston, Mass., April 25/
The Washington Post, 4-26:(A)1,7.

5

[On suggestions that he has been working on too many issues at the same time]: I do think that I may have over-extended myself, and we've got to focus on big things. I'm used to a legislative environment where, as Governor [of Arkansas], I worked up all these initiatives, I put them into the pot and then we worked them through the Legislature. It's almost like we are supposed to do one, maybe two, things at a time in Congress. And I think that I have been pushing too hard trying to get everything done.

Interview/
The New York Times, 4-28:(A)8.

6

[On criticism that he has moved too slowly on Presidential appointments during his first 100 days in office]: This may surprise you, if you've been reading the press reports, but . . . our Administration has in 100 days nominated 172 people for consideration by the Senate. At the same point in their Administrations, President [Ronald] Reagan had named 152 people and President [George] Bush had named 99. By any measure, we're doing a fairly good job in staffing up the Administration with high-quality folks.

At U.S. Dept. of Justice,
Washington, D.C., April 29/
The New York Times, 4-30:(A)10.

7

[On being President compared with his previous post of Governor of Arkansas]: The thing I find more difficult, with the exception of my morning run, is just the opportunity that I used to take, in a very consistent way, to kind of keep in regular touch with people. I always found that was much more valuable than polling or all that kind of stuff. You know, polls come and go. You get a real sense of people's lives and the language they speak and the way they look at the world when you can relate to them in kind of an unstructured way that I could always do as Governor and even as a candidate for President. It's just much more difficult now.

Interview, Washington, D.C./
U.S. News & World Report,
5-3:43.

(BILL CLINTON)

1

When President [John] Kennedy occupied [the White House], nearly three-quarters of the American people believed that their leaders would tell them the truth and that their institutions worked and that problems could be solved . . . A year or two years could go by, people [in government] could be working on something with maybe only slightly measurable progress, but the country felt that it was moving forward. That is what we have to restore today, a sense that it can be done, and it cannot be done by the President alone, but the President has to keep saying that, that faith is a big part of this.

News conference, Washington, D.C., May 14/
The New York Times, 5-15:8.

2

Some, but not all, in the national Democratic Party have placed too much faith in the whole politics of entitlement—the idea that big bureaucracies and government spending, demanding nothing in return, can produce the results we want. We know that is simply not true. [Similarly,] some, but not all, in the national Republican Party have practiced the politics of abandonment—of walking away from common concerns like dropping test scores, or rising crime rates, or an insufficient infrastructure . . . Well, that's not right either. We have to move beyond entitlement and abandonment.

Speech, Milwaukee, Wis., June 1/
The Washington Post, 6-2:(A)7.

3

[The new Government Performance and Results Act is] an important first step in the efforts to reform the way the Federal government operates and relates to the American people . . . The law simply requires that we chart a course for every endeavor that we take the people's money for, see how well we are progressing, tell the public how we are doing, stop the things that don't work, and never stop improving the things that we think are worth investing in.

At signing of the Act,
Washington, D.C., Aug. 3/
The Washington Post, 8-4:(A)15.

4

Back East [in Washington], where I work, "consensus" is often turned into "cave in"; people who try to work together and listen to one another instead of beat each other up are accused of being weak, not strong. I miss you [in state government]. I miss this [being a state Governor]. I miss the way we make decisions. I miss the sort of heart and soul and fabric of life that was a part of every day when I got up and went to work in a state capital. Somehow, we've got to bring that back to Washington.

Before National Governors' Association,
Tulsa, Okla., Aug. 16/
The New York Times,
8-17:(A)7.

5

[On his continuing contacts with people he knew in Arkansas when he was Governor there]: The President can live not only a hectic and busy but an isolated life in a way that the Governor of a small and highly personalized state like Arkansas can never do. When I get down, there's always my friends from home who kinda buck me up. A lot of them are far more likely to have what you might call the "real answer to the problem." They often serve as a kind of little yellow light, if they sense something is going wrong that hasn't gotten out of hand.

Interview/
U.S. News & World Report,
11-29:31.

6

I think most Americans do know that I'm trying to face the hard problems and work on them and taking them one right after the other, trying to make some progress. But I think it is more difficult for them to feel a personal connection with me because there are more filters in our communications. And that's frustrating. I'm dealing with a government that's much bigger and that often puts out conflicting messages. Of course, I just got started.

Interview/
U.S. News & World Report,
11-29:34.

(BILL CLINTON)

1

Part of my job is to be a lightning rod. Part of my job is to lift the hopes and aspirations of the American people, knowing that as long as you're trying to lift hopes and lift aspirations, you can never fully close the gap between what you're reaching for and what you're actually doing . . . One of the things that I underestimated when I became President was the actual power of the words coming from the bully pulpit of the White House to move the country. I overestimated my capacity [to] get things done in a hurry in the Congress. But when I read the other day in the *Los Angeles Times* that I had the best record of any President in 40 years, I said, "Pity the others."

At Georgetown Medical Center,
Washington, D.C., Dec. 1/
The New York Times, 12-2:(A)12.

2

[Saying he must make compromises with the left and the right in order to move ahead with his programs]: When you produce policies that embody these values of opportunity and responsibility and community in a democratic society that elects people to Congress and that requires the President to work with the Congress, that requires the accommodation of various interests all across the country in the private sector and requires a partnership with people at the state and local level. Having the best ideas in the world does not free you of the obligation to make difficult decisions.

Before Democratic Leadership Council,
Washington, D.C., Dec. 3/
The New York Times, 12-4:8.

3

What bothers me are not big things and bad news. I like it when people come in and disagree here. I get frustrated when I think that something is wrong with the system, and so we're not doing our best for the American people. I don't think I should ever lose my temper, but when I do, it's because of some process screw-up. If there's something wrong with the way we're organized or

something that keeps us from doing [our best], that's what drives me nuts.

Interview, Washington, D.C./
Time, 12-13:42.

4

I think the trick of being in public life in this day and age, when there is always going to be a lot of clamor and criticism, is to be able to take all this barrage of criticism seriously but not personally. In other words, you have to listen to the people who are criticizing you because they're right sometimes. And Benjamin Franklin said long ago: Our enemies are our friends, for they show us our faults.

Interview,
Washington, D.C./
Time, 12-13:42.

5

[On Presidential appointments]: It takes too long to get anybody appointed [and confirmed]. People who are independent and who have led interesting lives may be able to get elected to public office but may not be able to get appointed to anything. It's just ridiculous. And thoughtful people in both parties recognize it. I'm trying to think of a device we can employ next year to get a good, fresh bipartisan look at the whole appointments process.

Interview,
Washington, D.C./
Time, 12-13:42.

6

The success of a President, in part, is going to depend on the time that they're in [office]. And some of our failed Presidents, had they been President at a different time, might have actually been quite good. And some of our greatest Presidents were great just for the moment at which they lived. Had they served at a different time, they might have fallen in a different category.

Interview,
Washington/
U.S. News & World Report,
12-13:37.

Hillary Rodham Clinton
*Wife of President-elect
of the United States
Bill Clinton*

1

[On the prospects for the forthcoming Clinton Administration]: [An important concern] is whether, given the high expectations and the need for change [in the country], you can work out the right balance between moving forward and not getting caught up in politicizing everything you do, so that you have a chance substantively to make some things work before people get distracted and thrown into a frame of mind of skepticism or loss of will. I think that is an endemic problem now in our society, this whole short-term fixation that we've got and the incapacity to plan for the long run and to have a vision of where you're going and to try to stay the course to get there.

*Interview, Little Rock, Ark./
Time, 1-4:36.*

Dan Coats
*United States Senator,
R-Indiana*

2

There are many people here [in Washington] who only view the issues before them from a political standpoint. Their analysis of an issue and the conclusions they draw are based solely on their own political career or the people they represent. Unfortunately, the norm is to see very little discussion and conclusions based on a principle that supercedes the political.

*Interview/
Christianity Today, 3-8:70.*

Charles Colson
*Columnist;
Former Special Counsel to the
President of the United States
(Richard M. Nixon)*

3

Though [some] might argue that government can inspire and create public virtue—that statecraft is soulcraft—I respectfully disagree. I believe virtue is something that grows from within,

not something enforced from above. The law does have a role in moral instruction. But the roots of our moral life go deeper than laws and bills. Government programs can feed the body; they cannot touch the soul. They can punish behavior; they cannot transform hearts.

*At National Press Club,
Washington, D.C., March 11/
Christianity Today,
8-16:32.*

Charles L. Cragin
*Chairman,
Federal Board
of Veterans' Appeals*

4

[On fixed-term government appointees, who are not automatically replaced when a new Administration takes office]: If you have a body that is not a policy-making body and it is critically important that it be perceived as applying a rule of law and not be subject to political considerations, one way you can address and respond to those sorts of requirements is through [fixed-] term appointments . . . Why take a person who has been doing a phenomenally good job that everybody is satisfied with and say, "We're sorry, you can't do your job again. I'm not permitted to reappoint you"?

*The Washington Post,
2-1:(A)17.*

John C. Danforth
*United States Senator,
R-Missouri*

5

[Criticizing the controversial demand of the Senate Ethics Committee for the complete personal diaries of Senator Bob Packwood, who is accused of sexual harassment by a number of women]: Regardless of what one might think of the charges against Senator Packwood, this is a blockbuster precedent, and it goes to the fundamental issue of civil liberties. As a matter of fundamental fairness, we cannot agree to a subpoena that is this broad for any reason.

*The New York Times,
11-3:(A)11.*

Michael K. Deaver
Former Director
of Communications for former
President of the United States
Ronald Reagan

1

I think it's clear that [President Clinton] is undisciplined when it comes to focusing on one thing. He has an interest in so many things. That's one of Clinton's problems. One of the things [former President Ronald] Reagan was criticized for was that he was disinterested. He was. He was stubbornly disinterested. You could get him to engage in only one or two things at a time . . . When someone brings up gays in the military or something else, Clinton should say: "I don't want to talk about that. I want to solve the economic problem before I talk about anything else." That worked for us [in the Reagan Administration] for the first four or five years.

Los Angeles Times, 4-19:(A)10.

Dennis DeConcini
United States Senator,
D-Arizona

2

[On voting against one's own party in the Senate]: You try to please; we politicians are pleasers. When you can't please and it's your party, you just stand on what you think is right and hope it turns out right. Sometimes you pay a price . . . either way.

June 25/
The Washington Post, 6-26:(A)9.

Robert J. Dole
United States Senator,
R-Kansas

3

We've got enough [government] mandates on employers . . . We're good at mandates because we've discovered that the government's broke, and the best way to do it is to mandate the states or mandate employers. And employers have limits, too, on how much they can absorb without losing jobs or shutting down their businesses.

Interview, Washington, D.C.,
July 26/USA Today, 7-27:(A)9.

Pete V. Domenici
United States Senator,
R-New Mexico

4

The framers [of the Constitution] never intended the Senate to be as controlled, as much a bloc-voting institution, as the House. The House is the hot coffee cup and the Senate is the saucer that cools it.

The Washington Post, 7-14:(A)12.

Joycelyn Elders
Surgeon General
of the United States

5

[On the criticism she has received since she went to Washington for her confirmation hearings]: I came there as prime steak, and now I feel like low-grade hamburger.

Interview/USA Today, 9-10:(A)13.

Anna G. Eshoo
United States Representative,
D-California

6

[On her first few months in office]: What I'm struck with is this continuing, ongoing perception that so many people have. They think you move here and plant yourself inside the Beltway and that you have all sorts of leisure time, but you don't. I have been working seven days a week since I was sworn in . . . Moving from a five-member county Board of Supervisors to the largest legislative body in the country is an adjustment. Where once I spoke to department heads, I now speak to Cabinet Secretaries and the White House. It is at once exhilerating, serious, sobering and extraordinarily challenging.

Interview/
Los Angeles Times, 6-3:(A)5.

Susan Estrich
Professor of law,
University of Southern California

7

[On the effect of radio and TV talk shows on the political process]: Talk shows [are] like town

(SUSAN ESTRICH)

meetings. When an issue takes hold with the people, you don't need a formal political process for the country to reach a decision. [In the case of Zoe Baird, whose controversial nomination for U.S. Attorney General was recently withdrawn,] they reached it on their own, without leadership from Washington, and communicated that decision to the talk shows and television shows, and the matter was concluded within a few days.

Time, 2-1:28.

J. James Exon
United States Senator,
D-Nebraska

1

[On President Clinton's problems in dealing with Congress]: The President has come out of a very small state [as Governor of Arkansas] with a very small legislature controlled by his own party . . . I suspect that the President, with all his smarts, does not fully understand the workings of Congress.

Los Angeles Times, 1-29:(A)1.

Harris W. Fawell
United States Representative,
R-Illinois

2

It has been said that if one dies and goes to heaven and wants to come to Earth and have eternal life, come back to a Federal program. [They] just go on and on.

Before the House,
Washington, D.C., Aug. 6/
The Washington Post, 8-31:(A)17.

Vic Fazio
United States Representative,
D-California

3

If you're into symbolism on cutting [government] spending, there's nothing better than killing a big project—especially if it's not in your district.

USA Today, 6-24:(A)4.

Jim Florio
Governor of New Jersey (D)

4

I look forward to the day when public servants who follow the dictates of their conscience are not regarded as heroes worthy of awards, but simply as men and women who are worthy of the offices to which they've been entrusted.

Accepting "Profile in Courage"
award at John F. Kennedy Library,
Boston, Mass., May 24/
The New York Times, 5-25:(A)9.

Thomas S. Foley
United States Representative,
D-Washington;
Speaker of the House

5

[Today] there are a lot of entrepreneurs in Congress, individuals who have their own political organizations, who have their own fund-raising activities, who don't depend on a national Administration or party, and who can be quite independent.

Interview, Washington, D.C., Aug. 6/
The Christian Science Monitor, 8-9:14.

Bill Frenzel
Fellow, Brookings Institution;
Former United States Representative,
R-Minnesota

6

[On how President Clinton should treat Congress if he wants to get his programs through]: Congress needs to be fondled and schmoozed and does not like to be dealt with like an ordinary acquaintance. It takes constant personal attention if you want to get your program dealt with successfully. Mr. Clinton has not yet learned that.

Los Angeles Times, 5-24:(A)17.

Charles Fried
Professor of Constitutional law,
Harvard University;
Former Solicitor General
of the United States

7

[On whether it is proper for President Clinton to appoint his wife, Hillary, to head his health-

(CHARLES FRIED)

care reform task force]: Presidents have, since the beginning of the Republic, chosen all kinds of people, without official jobs and statuses, to give them advice. The fact that this particular adviser happens to be someone the President is married to doesn't change that. The President can get advice from an astrologer, if he wants. Making a Constitutional case out of it is not the point. I see nothing different about giving Hillary Clinton this job than [naming industrialist] Peter Grace to chair the Grace Commission or anything else like that. Now, it is entirely possible to argue that the wisdom behind the [anti-nepotism] law extends to this case. That may be. But that's not a legal argument—that's an argument of prudence.
Interview/
Los Angeles Times, 3-21:(M)1.

Richard A. Gephardt
United States Representative,
D-Missouri

1

We learned in the [recent] budget debate that it is hard for the country to take on more than one debate and issue at a time. You lose the edge and the focus. But we don't live in a perfect world, and it's not always possible to get the big debates isolated.
The New York Times, 8-31:(A)1.

George Gerbner
Professor,
Annenberg School
of Communication,
University of Pennsylvania

2

[Saying President Clinton's forthcoming inauguration is being too commercialized]: This sort of thing sends a message that everything is for sale in our country, even the Presidency. The parade and swearing-in of the President are public [events] that must be preserved for public purposes, not expropriated for private uses.
The Washington Post,
1-15:(F)5.

David Gergen
Counsellor to
President of the United States
Bill Clinton

3

I think we [in the Federal government] live lives of privilege. We are all paid extraordinarily well. We all live well. We have lots of power and perks. And if you go around the rest of the country, you see a country that is falling apart for most people. I don't mean to get up on my high horse about it, but I feel strongly we're playing games.
Interview/Vanity Fair, August:170.

Stephen Gillers
Professor of legal ethics,
New York University
Law School

4

[Criticizing Senate Ethics Committee demands that Senator Bob Packwood turn over his personal diaries because of allegations against him of misconduct]: By definition, a diary is a conversation with yourself. Allowing the state to get your diary is allowing the state to get into your mind.
Time, 11-8:42.

John Glenn
United States Senator,
D-Ohio

5

Rarely in our history have calls for governmental reform come together in such a positive way. We now have what may be just the right mix of political consensus and public pressure to successfully overhaul the government.
At Senate Government Affairs
Committee hearing,
Washington, D.C., March 11/
The Washington Post, 3-12:(A)21.

6

[Supporting changes in the Hatch Act to permit Federal employees more rights to engage in partisan political activity]: I want to have civil-service protection, I truly do, but I want it to be

(JOHN GLENN)

fair. That's the only thing this [bill] does; and all these dire portents [about what such reforms will do to the independence and non-partisan perception of Federal workers by the public] that are drawn up with regard to this bill are just ridiculous.

The Washington Post, 7-12:(A)13.

Janlori Goldman
Director,
Project on Privacy
and Technology,
American Civil Liberties Union

1

[Saying the Senate Ethics Committee is going too far by demanding Senator Bob Packwood's complete personal diaries as part of its investigation into sexual harassment charges against the Senator]: We need a legal recognition that diaries are of a highly personal nature, and that the Senate Ethics Committee must follow traditional rules of relevancy before they can get access to personal records. We think that the principles of the Fourth Amendment should apply, even though this is not a traditional Fourth Amendment case in which a warrant was issued.

The New York Times, 11-3:(A)11.

W. Wilson Goode
Former Mayor
of Philadelphia (Pa.)

2

Public service is a noble profession that needs people of honesty, integrity, commitment and vision. Know it will be hard, because you will be different. Fight for your position. Don't give an inch. Don't compromise your principles for the sake of political expediency. Even when an overwhelming number don't believe in what you stand for, don't give up . . . This can only happen when we have politicians who are motivated not by selfish interest, but by the larger interests of the community.

Interview/
Christianity Today, 4-5:25.

Al Gore
Vice President
of the United States

3

May we all [in government] not just listen, but truly hear. May we all not just see, but truly understand. And may we all reach deep into our own hearts to summon the will to take action, to keep our commitment to the kind of democracy and the kind of government that never forgets its roots or responsibilities, that remembers it was forged by the courage and vision and ideas of the people it was meant to serve.

At luncheon with members of Congress,
Washington, D.C., Jan. 20/
The New York Times, 1-21:(A)7.

4

It is time for the quality revolution—which swept corporate America over the last 15 years but somehow bypassed the Federal government—to be brought into the daily lives of Federal employees. We are going to deliver services to the American people in a high-quality, low-cost manner.

At U.S. Dept. of Housing
and Urban Development,
Washington, D.C., March 26/
The Washington Post, 3-27:(A)10.

5

[On his plans for overhauling and streamlining the Federal bureaucracy]: We're going to talk about the success stories in government until it gets to the point that success in government is no longer regarded as a contradiction in terms, an oxymoron.

At meeting outlining the Clinton
Administration's plans for evaluating
Federal-government performance,
Washington, D.C., April 15/
The Washington Post, 4-16:(A)23.

6

[On being Vice President]: It has been even more enjoyable than I anticipated, although there is a lot more to it than I anticipated. I've always

(AL GORE)

worked hard, but I've never worked this hard. There's just one thing right after another, and the constant intensity of the disputes which come into the White House is something that's hard to appreciate until you are a part of it.

Interview/USA Today, 7-16:(A)4.

1

It has become a cliche to criticize the Federal government: People call it bloated, bureaucratic, wasteful. Of course, they get that impression because it is all too accurate. While American business has spent much of the last 15 to 20 years reinventing itself . . . Washington has preserved its outmoded ways. Our work has a short-term deadline but a long-term goal: to create government that works better and costs less.

Before National Governors' Association,
Tulsa, Okla., Aug. 15/
USA Today, 8-16:(A)4.

2

I think that the ground has shifted and many who are traditionally cynical about the prospect for system changes [in government] are going to be surprised by the amount of support for rock 'em, sock 'em, shake 'em up—sweeping changes of this kind . . . The way the government operates presently steps on the toes of the American people. We're going to lift that dead weight off their toes . . . Any effort to change the culture of a large organization will take time, perhaps eight to 10 years.

Interview,
Washington, D.C., Sept. 6/
Los Angeles Times, 9-7:(A)17.

Phil Gramm
United States Senator,
R-Texas

3

If lawmakers are going to catch hell no matter what they do, they'll normally do the right thing.

Time, 9-27:15.

4

[On complaints about how Congress operates]: The system is the way it is because it creates a lot of chiefs and few Indians. And everybody wants to be a chief.

The Washington Post, 10-21:(A)18.

Stanley B. Greenberg
Chief public-opinion analyst
for President of the United States
Bill Clinton

5

Passage of programs by themselves does not guarantee success [in making government work]. There has to be restructuring of the American economy . . . There has to be health care that is secure . . . There has to be a government that is leaner and more efficient. [Clinton] has to show government can be successful. That's the way out of this mess—the way we can create a new coalition.

Los Angeles Times, 7-1:(A)18.

6

What Clinton is saying is, government has to intervene to allow people to have an essential level of [economic] security so they can better cope with change. We are talking about broad-based security—something essential for everybody so they can deal with a changing world as individuals and that we as a country can deal with a changing world.

Los Angeles Times, 10-6:(A)12.

Morton Halperin
Senior associate,
Carnegie Endowment
for International Peace

7

[On regulations Congress puts on the Executive Branch, such as the Boland Amendment and the Arms Export Control Act]: The problem with general laws like these is that the Executive Branch is supposed to be bound by them, but that doesn't make individuals who violate them liable, criminally or civilly. The truth is that Congress was not as explicit as it should have been about making violations [of these laws] a criminal offense . . . [But] whatever Congress expected or tolerated in the past, it is now saying very clearly to government officials, "You can tell the truth or refuse to testify [before Congress on these matters]. What you can't do is deceive or lie to Congress."

The Christian Science Monitor,
1-5:3.

Lee H. Hamilton
United States Representative,
D-Indiana

1

When you begin to talk about [Congressional] reform, you immediately move into very technical areas. We're talking about process, and the public is going to judge us by results—but the two are clearly linked. If the process is faulty, you can't get the best results . . . The criticism made is that [the reform being considered] is not bold enough. But it is important that the perfect not be made the enemy of the good.

The Washington Post, 11-26:(A)29.

Stephen Hess
Senior fellow,
Brookings Institution

2

[On President-elect Clinton and the new Congress]: Initially, it's going to be a very good Congress. You start with a new President with lots of proposals in his basket. And that in itself is terribly important. The President is the motor force in Washington.

The Christian Science Monitor,
1-4:1.

3

I think [Presidential] inaugurals are really not that important. They're like cotton candy: colorful and tasty for a moment.

USA Today, 1-20:(A)2.

4

The notion that since [President] Clinton is a Democrat and Congress has a Democratic majority, they would walk in lockstep to a glorious future [isn't true]. The process . . . is based on compromise. A President presents his program. The legislature and the opposition present theirs. Ultimately, if the President succeeds, the end product is more like what he proposed than what anyone else proposed. I find it powerfully strange that compromise is being used as a dirty word by people who should know better, and that the President is being faulted for compromise.

The Christian Science Monitor,
5-21:2.

Michael Huffington
United States Representative,
R-California

5

[On his first few months in office]: What I've learned is that the way the system works can be appalling at times. The American people would be amazed at some of the things that go on . . . This [the Federal government] is not a well-run organization. I can understand why. You have over half the Congress who are lawyers. Lawyers don't know how to run a business. They are very good at writing laws but terrible at running Congress.

Interview/
Los Angeles Times, 6-3:(A)5.

Nancy Johnson
United States Representative,
R-Connecticut

6

For a woman to run for Congress, much less get elected, is the exception to the rule. We got there because we have already demonstrated leadership and commitment and strength in a way that our male colleagues haven't necessarily had to demonstrate . . . We didn't get to where we are because we are women. We got there because we're capable leaders.

Cambridge, Mass./
The Christian Science Monitor, 5-3:14.

Roger W. Johnson
Administrator-designate,
General Services Administration
of the United States

1

[On his being a Republican named to head the GSA in a Democratic Administration]: I have throughout my career been concerned principally about issues as opposed to partisanship. I will take whatever action I need to take to move issues forward . . . The test is the issues, the test is logic, the test is performance.

At Senate Governmental Affairs
Committee hearing on his nomination,
Washington, D.C., June 8/
The Washington Post, 6-9:(A)17.

Daniel Kemmis
Mayor of Missoula, Mont.

2

I [have] a lot of skepticism [about] the national government. I have a great deal of doubt about the national government's ability to function effectively as a democracy . . . What was most troubling to me about the movie [*J.F.K.,* about the assassination of President John Kennedy] was that it seemed to take the attitude that we had elected a President who had given us hope. Then, because of the machinations of a few evil men, that hope had been destroyed and that if only those men had not been so evil, all would have been well. That attitude is a profound escape from reality, which many of us are deeply engaged in. There is a . . . very substantial danger that going to this new [Clinton] Presidency with much the same attitude, we are simply setting ourselves up for a loss of hope or a dashing of hope.

At Claremont McKenna College,
March 25/
Los Angeles Times, 3-26:(B)2.

Jay C. Kim
United States Representative,
R-California

3

[On his first few months in office]: This job is different. I don't have to worry about generating profit. All my staff salaries are being paid by taxpayers. All I have to do is spend. What kind of a job is this? No wonder those guys want to be here 50 years. All they have to do is spend.

Interview/
Los Angeles Times, 6-3:(A)5.

James B. King
Director-designate,
Federal Office
of Personnel Management

4

[Saying Federal workers have received an unfair "shower of abuse"]: Somehow there's been an image created that if you could [do something else], you [would], and if you can't, you go into government. That's the thing we can turn around. [Public service] is an honorable profession. [College graduates should be able to say,] "Mom, Dad, I've decided to go into government work," and not have them look at them as someone that's failed their family, their community, their education that they struggled to receive. That's the part that is the disgrace and that's not the fault of the public employee.

Before Senate Government Affairs Committee,
Washington, D.C., March 30/
The Washington Post, 3-31:(A)17.

William Kristol
Chief of Staff
to Vice President
of the United States
Dan Quayle

5

[On the many entertainment personalities who have come to Washington for the inauguration of President Clinton]: Having watched Hollywood descend upon Washington in the last couple of days makes me more convinced than ever that [Vice President Quayle] was right. Hollywood's utter preoccupation with image, and their disdain for real problems and real issues, is amazing even to those of us who have been around Washington for a while—and Washington, in itself, isn't exactly focused on reality.

The New York Times, 1-20:(A)11.

Bernard Kulik
Assistant Administrator
for Disaster Assistance,
Small Business Administration
of the United States

1

I must raise the question of whether we, all of us, are really serious about the idea of [government] reform, or are we merely paying it lip service . . . Is Congress really ready to give the agencies the budgetary and accounting flexibility they need to become more efficient? And are government employees really ready to change parts of the current civil-service system to recognize outcomes rather than longevity and size?

At Congressional hearing
on governmental reform,
Washington, D.C./
The Washington Post, 7-22:(A)29.

Everett Ladd
Professor of political science,
University of Connecticut;
Executive director,
Roper Center for
Public Opinion and Research

2

As government has gotten bigger, public dissatisfaction with its performance has increased. But the public still wants something done, and doing something will always beat out doing nothing.

USA Today, 3-26:(A)7.

Patrick J. Leahy
United States Senator,
D-Vermont

3

I don't have any great hopes [about Congressional reform] until [members] are willing to give up what they perceive as great power and influence, when it's not. A lot of people around here who love to be called "Mister Chairman" don't have anything much to do with what gets done around here.

The Washington Post,
10-21:(A)18.

Charles Lewis
Executive director,
Center for Public Integrity

4

These people—the big law firms, the associations, the big corporation lobbyists—are the permanent ruling class here [in Washington]. And they are guys who always back both horses [in a Presidential election]; they contributed to both candidates [President Bush and President-elect Clinton], threw parties at both conventions, and so on. This [Presidential inauguration] week, they'll kick in some more, because they know that putting up $100,000 or so is chump change in relation to what they'll get back. The President [Clinton] remembers who helped pay for his inaugural, who his friends are.

The New York Times, 1-18:(A)8.

5

[On a former Clinton Administration transition-team member who is now a lobbyist but who Clinton says is not breaking requirements that former transition members not lobby government agencies for at least six months]: This is why people distrust Washington—all these narrow legal interpretations. It all speaks to how tough it is to handle influence-peddling. It's like trying to dam a creek with chicken wire. If you want to get around these rules, you can probably find some way to [do] it.

The New York Times, 4-9:(A)10.

Joseph I. Lieberman
United States Senator,
D-Connecticut

6

[On the politically active public, who communicate with and put pressure on Congress regarding specific issues]: The danger—we don't have it yet—is hyperactive democracy. The check on it is us [in Congress]. We have to have the sense of fairness to listen but the guts to do what's right, even if it goes against your phone calls.

The Washington Post,
2-1:(A)10.

Joseph E. Lowery
President,
Southern Christian
Leadership Conference

1

[Opposing state-run lotteries]: [A lottery] perpetuates the something-for-nothing, quick-fix, get-rich-quick psychology. It's a very negative message, and it is miseducating people about how you support worthy causes.

The Christian Science Monitor,
8-16:11.

G. Calvin Mackenzie
Chairman,
Department of Government,
Colby College

2

[On First Lady Hillary Clinton's large influence in the Administration]: It's totally unprecedented. All Presidents have said their spouses are advisers to them, with caveats. Bill Clinton doesn't use caveats. This is the beginning of redefining the role of the First Lady.

March 10/
The Washington Post, 3-11:(A)18.

John D. Macomber
Former Chairman,
Export-Import Bank
of the United States

3

[On the National Performance Review report on efficiency and management in the Federal government]: People who look at the National Performance Review and only see program cost-cutting and workforce reductions do not yet understand what is going on in the world . . . They reflect the old way of thinking about the Federal government as a collection of budget items. The last 10 years in the private sector have taught us that lower costs and leaner structures are not ends or goals in themselves; they are the consequences of well-managed, mission-driven organizations.

The Washington Post, 9-14:(A)19.

Thomas E. Mann
Director of governmental studies,
Brookings Institution

4

[On charges that the Clinton Administration is trying to tackle too many issues at once]: It is inevitable a new Administration's plate will be filled with more than just the top-priority item or items. That's especially true when party control of the White House changes. It's all well and good to say that what matters for Clinton is the economic package first and the health-care package second, and those should be his priorities, and most of his energies and public campaigning should go into those programs. But the reality is that other things have to be done, and life goes on. He cannot distance himself from all those efforts.

Los Angeles Times, 4-19:(A)10.

5

Congress has become hypersensitive to public sentiment. They monitor it; they cultivate it; they react to it instantaneously. It makes it so much more difficult for the body to suspend its intense connection to the political world and to figure out how to do the right thing.

The New York Times, 11-4:(A)7.

Mike Mansfield
Former United States Senator,
D-Montana

6

[In Congress,] the comity among members in both houses has been reduced to a considerable degree . . . and individualism to a certain extent . . . has replaced it. The sound bites on the TV. One-liners. Things of that sort.

Interview,
Washington, D.C., March 15/
The Washington Post, 3-16:(E)4.

David Mason
Authority on Congress,
Heritage Foundation

7

A lot of the . . . problems that people complain [to Congress] about are created by Con-

(DAVID MASON)

gress. In fact, bad laws get Congressmen re-elected. They pass a bad law, and the regulations are stupid or inconsistent or whatever, and people have to come to them for help.

The Christian Science Monitor,
3-23:3.

Mary Matalin
Co-host, "Equal Time," CNBC-TV;
Former deputy campaign manager
for former President
of the United States
George Bush's
1992 re-election campaign

1

There used to be a presumption that it was unusual for a President not to get two terms. Now it's unusual to get the two terms. In the end, it hinges on the economy. But there is also something intangible in the evaluation of a President, which we used to call character.

Interview/
"W" magazine, August:111.

Michael McConnell
Professor of law,
University of Chicago (Ill.)

2

When the government becomes such a huge part of our cultural life, so that it controls the schools, it controls the practice of medicine, it controls much of higher education, it controls television channels, it controls funding for the arts, and has so many employees, and has so much property—at that point if we say that the government is going to be scrupulously secular, it ceases to be so neutral . . . It's much more imperative now than at the founding [of the country] to ensure that the understanding of neutrality is not secular, but pluralistic.

Christianity Today, 10-25:23.

Howard P. "Buck" McKeon
United States Representative,
D-California

3

[On his first few months in office]: I've learned a lot. I really didn't understand how Congress

worked . . . The system seems designed to keep us so busy running around that you feel you are accomplishing something. I see a lot of people here who are working real hard but not accomplishing anything. We need to be able to distinguish between doing and accomplishing.

Interview/
Los Angeles Times, 6-3:(A)5.

Thomas F. McLarty III
Chief of Staff to
President of the United States
Bill Clinton

4

I don't see my role as advocating or shaping policy. I see it just the contrary: to make sure the President has the best information he can get to make the best decision he can.

USA Today, 3-19:(A)2.

5

I can see the concern about [the Clinton Administration] overloading the agenda, and we are mindful it can be a problem. But we have a President who understands the issues and has definite ideas about what he can do for the country. [Clinton] knows he can't do everything, but he's engaged and he's willing to tackle the tough issues, and sometimes that sets up a President for being less than successful on every issue he addresses.

Los Angeles Times, 4-19:(A)10.

Kweisi Mfume
United States Representative,
D-Maryland

6

[Arguing against giving the President line-item-veto power over Congressional bills]: Even the most naive student of Constitutional history knows that no legislator since the beginning of this nation has come to the point that we are at today, and that is to give away, to cede unto the Executive Branch, those powers.

Washington, D.C., April 29/
The New York Times, 4-30:(A)10.

Barbara A. Mikulski
United States Senator,
D-Maryland

1

[Supporting the Senate Ethics Committee's controversial demand for the personal diaries of Senator Bob Packwood, who is accused of sexual harassment by a number of women]: We are not the Senate Select Committee on Voyeurism. We have no prurient interest in this information. The question is whether the Senate will retreat from our commitment to a serious investigation. Will the Senate demonstrate that we can investigate and, if necessary, discipline our own?

At Senate Ethics Committee hearing,
Washington, D.C., Nov. 1/
The New York Times, 11-2:(A)1.

James Moran
United States Representative,
D-Virginia

2

[Arguing against a six-year limit for Congressional committee chairmen]: I think the change that people are looking for is for the Congress to get things done . . . They want to see action. They want to see their members working for them, and the fact is that if their members have been working for them for six years or 10 years, or whatever, they want to keep those members. The same thing in the House of Representatives: If the chairman is doing a good job, it seems to me that he or she ought to be kept in office and kept in their position. If they're not doing the job, then we ought to move against it. But this kind of arbitrary [six-year] limit doesn't necessarily give you the most effective leadership that we have available to us.

Broadcast interview, Jan. 5/
The Washington Post, 1-7:(A)30.

William A. Morrill
Former Assistant Secretary
for Planning and Evaluation,
Department of Health,
Education and Welfare
of the United States

3

[On the National Performance Review report on efficiency and management in the Federal government]: One key National Performance Review recommendation calls for performance agreements between the President and his department and agency heads. If these agreements include institutional reform objectives, have important consequences for the official, and are extended to the sub-Cabinet, real improvements could result. Basically, political appointees—like civil servants—should be charged and held accountable on a regular basis so that they leave the institution they serve more effective when they depart than when they arrive.

The Washington Post, 9-14:(A)19.

Yasuhiro Nakasone
Former Prime Minister
of Japan

4

With the Cold War gone and Russia no longer the enemy, strong leadership [in many governments] is going from centripetal to centrifugal. It is being dispersed, [resulting in something] more like the Japanese consensus-oriented type rather than the crisis type.

Time, 7-12:44.

Richard M. Nixon
Former President
of the United States

5

It's the responsibility of a leader to educate the people so they will support what needs to be done. Putting it more simply, you don't take people where they want to go; you take people where they ought to go.

Interview, Moscow, Russia/
The New York Times, 2-19:(A)4.

6

When the rest of the world is turning away from big government, we shouldn't be turning toward it. The problem with "reinventing government" [as the Clinton Administration terms it] is that they want government to be doing better the things that government shouldn't be doing in the first place.

Interview, Park Ridge, N.J./
The New York Times, 12-6:(A)11.

Jim Nussle
United States Representative,
R-Iowa

1

[On why House members move around the floor frequently, talking to other members while speeches are going on]: Constituents ask, "Why can't you stop talking in the chamber?" Well, we [members] never see each other [outside the chamber]. Members of Congress do not have the time to communicate among themselves enough . . . We don't spend enough quality time talking and learning about each other, which would bring the institution and the country closer together.

The Christian Science Monitor,
4-13:3.

Norman J. Ornstein
Fellow,
American Enterprise
Institute

2

There are lots of people in the Democratic Party who want as many issues as possible closed to amendments, reasonable or otherwise. The House is, and should be, a majoritarian institution. The majority should be able to rule it. But there is a balance to be struck between majority control and minority rights.

The Christian Science Monitor,
4-27:3.

Bob Packwood
United States Senator,
R-Oregon

3

[Criticizing the Senate Ethics Committee's demand for his complete personal diaries as part of its investigation into sexual harassment charges against him]: Grand juries are not licensed to participate in an arbitrary fishing expedition [into personal papers]. A subpoena recipient cannot put his entire life before the court.

The New York Times,
11-3:(A)11.

Ross Perot
Industrialist;
1992 independent
Presidential candidate

4

[On United We Stand, America, the organization that supported his Presidential bid last year and which will now become a political watchdog group]: We want to recreate a government that comes from the people, not at the people. Our challenge is not to criticize the President or the Congress but to create an environment out here in the grass-roots of America—and, believe me, we will have a bullhorn.

News conference,
Dallas, Texas, Jan. 11/
Los Angeles Times, 1-12:(A)13.

5

All over corporate America we're downsizing, cutting back, making lean, mean fighting machines. Here [in the U.S. Congress]—fat, bloated, increasing—you know, add another floor to the gym, put in more tennis courts, keep the music going. And we the suckers out here just keep paying for it. Employees of standing committees in the House of Representatives have increased 55 percent since the tax-and-budget summit. Somebody better point out which way is up and which way is down. Senate employee benefits—now, here's one I love. As you well know, these folks are supposed to be our servants. They go there to work for us. All the benefits they have, whether it's medical, whether it's retirement, whether it's you-name-it, are better than the people they serve. Well, since we decided to tighten our belts at the tax-and-budget summit, they've increased their benefits by 44 percent. Who's paying for it? Go home and look in the mirror.

News conference,
Dallas, Texas, Jan. 11/
The Washington Post, 1-12:(A)16.

6

[Saying he is glad he isn't President]: I'm very thankful I do not have to deal with this. It's the worst job in the world. It is comparable to getting

(ROSS PEROT)

up every morning, climbing into a barrel and having everybody in the world beat on the barrel with a stick, a baseball bat.

*At National Press Club,
Washington, D.C., March 18/
The Washington Post, 3-19:(A)19.*

1

We must rebuild a strong moral and ethical base in our great country, and we must start by holding our elected servants to the highest possible standards. All of [us] must stop asking, "What's in it for me?" The only question we must ask is: "What is right for our country?" After watching the abuse of power in Washington for years and years, the American people understand that they, as the owners of this country, must reassert control over their servants in Washington.

*Broadcast address to the nation/
NBC-TV, 3-21.*

2

We created the Royal Presidency—bulletproof limos and airplanes—under the guise of the Cold War. And now the Cold War is over. Isn't it interesting we keep all the trappings.

USA Today, 10-11:(A)2.

3

People feel their Congressman shouldn't accept anything from lobbyists. Just keep it simple. A lobbyist can give you ideas, but he [shouldn't] buy you lunch, take you on a trip, pay your greens fees. When you have government and campaign reform, then you can focus on what's good for the country.

*U.S. News & World Report,
12-20:19.*

Kevin P. Phillips
*President,
American Political Research
Corporation*

4

We're already seeing signs of over-extension [by the Clinton Administration]. The ineptitude of the Administration on a couple of early issues, the proliferation of foreign-policy problems and a lack of adequate staffing throughout the government combine to create a need to tighten down to a couple of achievable priorities. Unfortunately, that's easier said than done.

Los Angeles Times, 4-19:(A)10.

John E. Porter
*United States Representative,
R-Illinois*

5

[Calling for a limit of six years for Congressional committee chairmen]: The proposal is that committee chairs be limited to six years on the job and that after that time they give up the chairmanship. I think the American people decided in [the] November [1992 election] that they wanted change, and they wanted change in business as usual in Washington. And having a chairman who serves 15, 20, 30 years on the job builds the iron triangles that cause the gridlock in Washington. I think people said they wanted change, and this I think is a very good way to address it. It doesn't require amending the Constitution. It doesn't even require the President's signature. All we have to do is change the House rules and limit ourselves to six years as the chair of a committee.

*Broadcast interview, Jan. 5/
The Washington Post, 1-7:(A)30.*

Dan Quayle
Vice President of the United States

6

[On President-elect Clinton's plans to eliminate the White House Competitiveness Council, which is currently headed by Quayle and which watches for over-regulation of business by government]: If he doesn't keep the Competitiveness Council, he better have something pretty close to it, because otherwise the bureaucracy will run all over him and his Administration . . . They may change the name, but he has to have something here [in the White House] to ride herd on the unelected bureaucracy, which does not necessarily have his interests at heart.

*Interview,
Washington, D.C., Jan. 12/
The Washington Post, 1-13:(A)4.*

WHAT THEY SAID IN 1993

Bruce Reed
*Deputy Assistant to
President of the United States
Bill Clinton
for Domestic Policy*

1

[On President Clinton's proposed pay freeze for Federal employees]: We're not singling out Federal workers. We are trying to let the American people know that if there's going to be a contribution, the Federal government is going to go first. We want Federal workers to know that their lives are going to get better, their jobs are going to get better under a Clinton Administration. They're going to have more sane decisions, fewer managers telling them what to do, fewer daily hassles, and a more-rewarding work life. I don't think anybody likes having their pay held back, but over the long haul it will be worth it.

The Washington Post, 3-19:(A)29.

Leo Ribuffo
*Historian,
George Washington University*

2

[On the new Clinton Administration's orders to trim government perks and staffs]: This is an early attempt to play to the politics of symbolism. I don't think this is going to count for very much and it may backfire . . . It looks so manipulative and symbolic. How can you tell after three weeks how many people you need?

The Washington Post, 2-10:(A)19.

Elliot L. Richardson
*Former Attorney General
of the United States*

3

[In recent years,] lawyers at [the U.S. Department of] Justice have been co-opted [by the Executive Branch] to find legal rationalizations for policies adopted by the White House. The Department should not be the law office for the Administration in power, but the embodiment of the fair and honorable administration of justice.

Time, 2-15:29.

John D. (Jay) Rockefeller IV
*United States Senator,
D-West Virginia*

4

There is nothing so beautiful to me as an enraged public focused on an issue.

*July 29/
Los Angeles Times, 7-30:(A)18.*

David H. Rosenbloom
*Member, National Academy
of Public Administration*

5

[Arguing against revising the Hatch Act to give Federal employees more rights to engage in partisan political activities]: Whatever partisan political activity is permitted off duty would, for many, become the expected behavior. Those in the civil service would soon come to believe that better assignments, promotions and bonuses depend in part on partisan political activity. Equally destructive of morale and motivation would be a growing concern that not being promoted or given a preferred assignment was due to engaging in political activity for the unsuccessful party or candidate or for not participating at all. This is no way to attract and retain a high-quality civil service.

*Before Senate Governmental
Affairs Committee,
Washington, D.C., April/
The Washington Post, 7-12:(A)13.*

William V. Roth, Jr.
*United States Senator,
R-Delaware*

6

[Arguing against revising the Hatch Act to give Federal employees more rights to engage in political activities]: Are we really prepared to allow Federal employees to become campaign managers and party leaders? If so, we must be prepared to deal with the abuse which is sure to follow, along with the public's belief that politics has once again crept into the non-partisan administration of government.

*The Christian Science Monitor,
7-19:14.*

William Schneider
Analyst,
American Enterprise Institute

1

[State] Governors are the least-safe incumbents in American politics. People hold Governors responsible for everything that goes wrong.

The Christian Science Monitor,
12-27:8.

Patricia Schroeder
United States Representative,
D-Colorado

2

I have the kind of career that, if you're bored, you're probably brain-dead. No two days are ever the same.

Working Woman, November:52.

H. Norman Schwarzkopf
General,
United States Army (Ret.)

3

[On the Federal government]: [Washington, D.C.] is the only place you can run 10 miles in a straight line and still be at the scene of the crime . . . And we all know Congress is the world's largest adult day-care center.

At Video Software Dealers
Association convention/
USA Today, 7-16:(A)13.

Donna E. Shalala
Secretary of Health
and Human Services
of the United States

4

I've been running institutions for almost 15 years. For the most part, I've had to cut and refocus, as opposed to adding. [In government,] there are limits to what you can spend. I did indeed start out as a flaming liberal. And I still have those values. But as an administrator, I've been seasoned. I didn't come here expecting additional resources. I was trained in graduate school to be a Cabinet officer in the [Lyndon] Johnson Administration. I was trained in life to

be a Cabinet officer in the [current] Clinton Administration.

The Washington Post, 4-15:(C)4.

John Sharp
State Comptroller of Texas

5

The principle that drives people to govern is the same in city councils, state legislatures and the Federal government. The only difference in Washington is that they've got a bigger mess.

Los Angeles Times, 4-17:(A)11.

Christopher Shays
United States Representative,
R-Connecticut

6

[On Congress's exemption of itself from many of the laws it passes]: By exempting ourselves from laws, we are depriving members of the opportunity to experience firsthand the effects of the legislation we adopt.

The Christian Science Monitor,
2-23:3.

Alan K. Simpson
United States Senator,
R-Wyoming

7

[Arguing against giving the Senate Ethics Committee authority to subpoena the personal diaries of Senator Bob Packwood, who has been accused of sexual harassment by a number of women]: In my years of practice, I have never seen [a resolution] like it [the subpoena-authority resolution] . . . Do you hear the key word anywhere in it, the word "relevant" [in describing the diary material that can be subpoenaed]? . . . That is what Senator Packwood is trying to get at [in refusing to turn over his diaries], and the staff of the Senate Ethics Committee refuses to "get it," and they do not get it, and that is the legal issue of "relevance." You cannot do this. You cannot have a subpoena like this unless it is relevant. You insert the word "relevant" in this subpoena and I will vote for [the authorization]. Just put it right there—"all *relevant* diaries, journals";

(ALAN K. SIMPSON)

stick that in there and you have my vote for a sure shot. Senator Packwood may not like that, but I will like it as a lawyer. That is the issue. That is where we are. Insert that word in there—"all *relevant* diaries and journals" . . . Put that word in there and then go ahead with your work.

Before the Senate,
Washington, D.C., Nov. 2/
The Washington Post, 11-4:(A)19.

Dick Simpson
Professor of political science,
University of Illinois, Chicago

1

[On the proliferation of "special districts" as a part of state and local government systems]: If I gave a class project on how to invent a bad system of government, I wouldn't be able to come up with one worse than this, short of totalitarianism.

Los Angeles Times, 5-26:(A)1.

Theodore H. Sorensen
Former speechwriter
for the late President
of the United States
John F. Kennedy

2

Having looked at a lot of [Presidential] in-augural speeches at one time in my life—some of our most successful Presidents gave dreadful inaugural speeches—I have to conclude they're not critical to one's success . . . Compared to choosing the right policies and choosing the right people, choosing the right speech is minor.

USA Today, 1-20:(A)2.

George Stephanopoulos
Senior Adviser to
President of the United States
Bill Clinton

3

Part of the risk of [a President] trying to do big things and trying to achieve large change is that

you often have to accept what appears to be more compromise because you set out such a big goal.

Interview,
Washington, D.C., Aug. 3/
The Christian Science Monitor,
8-4:3.

Bob Stone
Project Director,
National Performance Review

4

Our Federal agencies were designed in the 1930s as copies of modern Industrial Age America. Things are different today. The country has seen the transformation from the Industrial Age to the Information Age. We're trying to bring the government into the Information Age and the 21st century.

Los Angeles Times, 8-17:(A)5.

Stanley G. Tate
Former Chairman-designate,
Resolution Trust Corporation
of the United States

5

[On his decision to withdraw his candidacy for RTC Chairman after months of Congressional inaction and allegations against him of impro-prieties]: Washington is a vicious city, with all kinds of hidden agendas. It is a city full of rumors, allegations and accusations, without much, if any, regard for truthfulness or factuality.

News conference,
Washington, D.C., Nov. 30/
Newsweek, 12-13:17.

Dennis Thompson
Specialist on
Congressional ethics,
Harvard University

6

[On the Senate Ethics Committee's controver-sial demand for the personal diaries of Senator Bob Packwood, who is accused of sexual harass-ment by a number of women]: There are two competing issues: his privacy and the public's interest in the integrity of Congress. As the facts

(DENNIS THOMPSON)

of this case are played out, institutional integrity should prevail.

USA Today, 11-1:(A)1.

Mona Van Duyn
Poet Laureate
of the United States

1

All our lives, we literary people have sat evaluating politicians on TV, and before TV— the older ones of us—reading what they said, and saying, "Oh my God! What cliches! Dreadful use of language! What meaningless rhetoric!" Because we're trained with words . . . [But] much as one detests the insensitivity, the lying, the grossness, et cetera, [that] one mostly sees in politicians, it is clear that not the poets but the politicians have to save the world.

Interview, Washington, D.C./
The Washington Post, 1-5:(C)3.

Wellington E. Webb
Mayor of Denver, Colo.

2

[On his habit of frequently walking the streets of his city]: Walking allows me to have constant contact with my base, the people . . . I do more walking than most people. That's my style of government. It allows me to get out of the office and deal with people in the streets and communities and neighborhoods. And whatever is on people's minds, they bring it to me. Walking keeps me in touch with people.

Interview, Denver, Colo./
Ebony, December:30.

L. Douglas Wilder
Governor of Virginia (D)

3

[On government deficits, such as that faced by his state]: The challenge before us should not be made trivial by vague references to "doing more with less" or "cutting the fat out of the budget." Rather, the challenge is about identifying those programs, activities or services that we are prepared to do without—and we need to be frank and honest and candid in saying so.

Before Virginia General Assembly
money committees,
Richmond, Va., Aug. 23/
The Washington Post, 8-24:(A)1.

Timothy E. Wirth
Under Secretary of State
of the United States;
Former United States Senator,
D-Colorado

4

[On his working in the State Department]: I have found it fascinating in dealing with a very large and very, very sophisticated and subtle bureaucracy. The State Department has developed to an art-form the capacity to say no. But if you figure out how to use the State Department to get all these incredibly good elements going with you, you can have enormous impact. You can have a great success.

Interview/The New York Times, 7-8:(A)9.

Law • The Judiciary

Nan Aron
Executive director,
Alliance for Justice

1

[On President Clinton's having to appoint a successor to retiring U.S. Supreme Court Justice Byron White]: Clinton's appointment will have a tremendous impact. White has been a reliable vote on the conservative side. His retirement whittles away at the conservative stronghold on the Court and allows Clinton to begin fashioning a Court that brings another viewpoint.

The Christian Science Monitor,
3-22:9.

Zoe Baird
Attorney General-designate
of the United States

2

While there will be partisan issues, [the Justice Department] should not be a partisan department. The Department's purpose is to use law to protect the American people and to use law to enforce the rights of the American people—their civil rights, their rights to economic fairness, their rights to a cleaner environment, their rights to security from crime.

At Senate Judiciary Committee
hearing on her nomination,
Washington, D.C., Jan. 19/
The New York Times, 1-20:(A)12.

Daniel J. Boorstin
Historian;
Librarian-emeritus of Congress
of the United States

3

The standard Oxford [University] course in the honors school of jurisprudence was about half in legal history and Roman law. I enjoyed that. I enjoyed Roman law; I enjoyed legal history and jurisprudence. You see, you don't prepare for the bar in England merely by getting a law degree. You had to enter one of the Inns of Court if you were going to become a barrister.

Interview/Humanities, Jan.-Feb.:7.

Francis A. Boyle
Professor of law,
University of Illinois

4

In any litigation, you ask for the stars, and if you get the sun and the moon, you are quite happy.

Interview,
The Hague, Netherlands, Sept. 13/
The New York Times, 9-14:(A)4.

James Bredar
United States Public Defender
for the District of Maryland

5

To the many who from time to time ask and wonder, "How can you represent people who you know are guilty?" I say I can do it, and I am fulfilled doing it because, by representing them, and by representing all the others who are only marginally guilty, and the still others who may be guilty of only part of that with which they have been charged, and the still others who are guilty of nothing and have been falsely accused, by representing all of these people vigorously, I keep you and me free.

At his investiture, Feb. 5/
The Washington Post, 3-5:(A)20.

James C. Cacheris
Chief Judge,
United States District Court
for the Eastern District
of Virginia

6

High ceilings add a great deal to the dignity and decorum of a courtroom. Psychologically, trying a case in a large-ceiling courtroom can make a big difference. People come in angry, and you can keep their feelings under control if you give them some room.

Interview/
The Washington Post,
12-6:(A)14.

Bill Clinton
President of the United States

1

[On his having to name a replacement for retiring U.S. Supreme Court Justice Byron White]: I think that there are few decisions a President makes which are more weighty, more significant and have greater impact on more Americans than an appointment to the Supreme Court. [I will] try to pick a person who has a fine mind, good judgment, wide experience in the law and in the problems of real people, and somebody with a big heart.

To reporters, Georgia, March 19/
The Washington Post, 3-20:(A)1.

2

I will not ask any potential Supreme Court nominee how he or she would vote in any particular case. I will not do that. But I will endeavor to appoint someone who has certain deep convictions about the Constitution. I would not, for example, knowingly appoint someone that did not have a very strong view about the First Amendment's freedom-of-religion, freedom-of-association and freedom-of-speech provisions. And I strongly believe in the Constitutional right to privacy; I believe it is one of those rights embedded in our Constitution, which should be protected.

News conference,
Washington, D.C., March 23/
The New York Times, 3-24:(A)7.

3

[On his nomination of Ruth Bader Ginsburg for the U.S. Supreme Court]: I decided on her for three reasons. First, in her years on the bench she has genuinely distinguished herself as one of our nation's best judges, progressive in outlook, wise in judgment, balanced and fair in her opinions. Second, over the course of a lifetime in her pioneering work in behalf of the women of this country, she has compiled a truly historic record of achievement in the finest tradition of American law and citizenship. And finally, I believe that in the years ahead, she will be able to be a force for consensus-building on the Supreme Court, just as she has been on the Court of Appeals, so that our judges can become an instrument of our common unity in the expression of their fidelity to the Constitution . . . Ruth Bader Ginsburg cannot be called a liberal or conservative. She has proved herself too thoughtful for such labels. As she herself put it in one of her articles, and I quote: "The greatest figures of the American judiciary have been independent-thinking individuals with open but not empty minds—individuals willing to listen and to learn. They have exhibited a readiness to re-examine their own premises—liberal or conservative—as thoroughly as those of others."

Announcing the nomination,
Washington, D.C., June 14/
The New York Times, 6-15:(A)15.

William C. Cobb
President,
W.C.C.I. Consultants

4

[Saying law firms must find ways to bring down their charges to clients as a means to increase business and bring back clients who have left]: What law firms should not do, if they want to survive, is play the part of the old buffalo hunters. When buffalo become scarce, buffalo hunters can come up with a better way of hunting, they can hunt something else, or they can nurture the buffalo they have. Buffalo hunters cannot sit in bars waiting for the buffalo to return on their own. They won't.

The New York Times, 10-22:(B)11.

Mario M. Cuomo
Governor of New York (D)

5

[On being a U.S. Supreme Court Justice, a post President Clinton may be considering him for]: It's about as luxurious a life as you can imagine, intellectually. All you have to do is listen, think, conclude and write. It's heaven. That's one theory. [Another theory is,] they put you in this big room. They slam this mahogany door shut. And you're dead.

Interview/Newsweek, 3-29:23.

(MARIO M. CUOMO)

1

[On his taking himself out of the running to be the next new U.S. Supreme Court Justice]: Some people have speculated that I would be more pleased by the rough-and-tumble of politics than the solitary confinement of the Court. That's not true. It was not a question of deciding that I wouldn't enjoy the Court. The law is a wonderful life and it's an aspiration I've always had. I can't think of a more pleasant way to spend a lifetime than being free to work on the law, unfettered by polls, elections and the need to raise money. Someone told me, "You really like to slug it out with the legislature." That's ridiculous. What am I—perverted? . . . It's just that when the moment came that might have been the opportunity to be on the Court, I concluded very swiftly that, apart from what I would enjoy most, the place I could do the most good is here [as Governor of] New York.

Interview/Newsweek, 4-19:50.

James Dator
Political scientist,
University of Hawaii

2

[Sixty years from now, in 2053,] disputes will be settled in "courthouse-less courts" with judges, lawyers and the disputing parties linked electronically. Witnesses will appear by holographs, and computers will help judges and lawyers make decisions.

Interview/
U.S. News & World Report,
10-25:74.

Alan M. Dershowitz
Professor of law,
Harvard University Law School

3

How do we put truth back into the legal profession? Judges lie, then lawyers lie, then clients lie. Sixty years from now, technology will make it harder to lie.

Interview/
U.S. News & World Report,
10-25:74.

John J. Duncan, Jr.
United States Representative,
R-Tennessee

4

[Saying too many expensive Federal courthouses are being built]: You don't need one courtroom for every judge, [or] 14 courtrooms for seven judges. There are judges all over this country in state courts who share courtrooms, and it doesn't kill anybody. Federal courthouses are some of the most expensive construction around, and it would behoove us to try to save some money.

The Washington Post, 12-6:(A)14.

Richard Freeman
Presiding Administrative Judge
of the Oklahoma State Courts

5

[On a new Oklahoma law allowing judges to carry guns in response to an increase in violence in courtrooms]: We're not frantically trying to grab guns and shoot everyone in sight. We're just wanting to provide an element of caution to the thing. It's a sign of the times. There used to be respect for the law, and even criminals would not think of causing trouble in the courthouse. Those days are over.

The New York Times, 4-23:(B)10.

Ruth Bader Ginsburg
Judge,
United States Court of Appeals
for the District of Columbia

6

The effective judge will strive to persuade and not to pontificate. She will speak in "a moderate and restrained voice," engaging in a dialogue with, not a diatribe against, co-equal departments of government, state authorities, and even her own colleagues . . . In writing for the court, one must be sensitive to the sensibilities and mindsets of one's colleagues, which may mean avoiding certain arguments and authorities, even certain words. Should institutional concerns affect the tone of separate opinions, when a judge finds it necessary to write one? . . . Measured motions seem to me right, in the main, for Consti-

(RUTH BADER GINSBURG)

tutional as well as common-law adjudication. Doctrinal limbs too swiftly shaped, experience teaches, may prove unstable.

At New York University Law School,
March 9/
The New York Times, 6-15:(A)15.

Ruth Bader Ginsburg
Judge,
United States Court of Appeals
for the District of Columbia;
Associate Justice-designate,
Supreme Court
of the United States

1

[As a nominee for the Supreme Court,] I expect to be asked in some detail about my views of the work of a good judge on a High Court bench . . . Chief Justice [William] Rehnquist offered one I keep in the front of my mind: A judge is bound to decide each case fairly in a court with the relevant facts and the applicable law even when the decision is not, as he put it, what the home crowd wants.

At the announcement of her nomination,
Washington, D.C., June 14/
The New York Times, 6-15:(A)15.

2

It would be wrong for me to say or preview in this legislative chamber how I would cast my vote on questions the Supreme Court may be called upon to decide. A judge sworn to decide impartially can offer no forecasts, no hints, for that would show not only disregard for the specifics of the particular case, it would display disdain for the entire judicial process.

At Senate Judiciary Committee hearing
on her nomination,
Washington, D.C., July 20/
The New York Times, 7-21:(A)1.

3

My view of the civil-rights laws conforms to my views concerning statutory interpretation

generally—that is, it is the obligation of judges to construe statutes in the way that Congress meant them to be construed. Some statutes, not simply in the civil-rights area but the antitrust area, are meant to be broad charters: the Sherman Act. The Civil Rights Act states grand principles representing the highest aspirations of our nation to be a nation that is open and free, where all people will have opportunity. And that spirit imbues that law, just as free competition is the spirit in the antitrust laws. And the courts construe statutes in accord with the essential meaning that Congress had for passing them.

At Senate Judiciary Committee hearing
on her nomination,
Washington, D.C., July 22/
The New York Times, 7-23:(A)8.

James Graves
Mississippi circuit court judge

4

Nobody wants to make excuses for criminal defendants, but what everybody ought to desire is a system that says, if a white man steals a car and gets five years for it, then a black man who steals a car ought to get five years for it. And I think having African-American judges in the judiciary brings a certain sensitivity and a sense of how devastating injustice can be.

The Christian Science Monitor,
5-19:6.

Charles S. Haight, Jr.
Judge,
United States District Court
for the Southern District
of New York

5

[On delays in payments to juries due to Federal spending cutbacks and the resulting postponing of trials]: It's an appalling problem. What just makes me sick at heart is that we are simply not able to do the nation's business. Fully recognizing that the [Federal budget] deficit is out of control, I think there is a quantum difference between deciding whether to fund or close a military base or put more money into cancer research, and funding the courts. This is

(CHARLES S. HAIGHT, JR.)

not choosing between one aspect of spending or another; this is saying one of the branches of government is out of business. This is about litigants being disenfranchised.

The New York Times, 4-9:(B)10.

William M. Kunstler
Lawyer

1

One of the criticisms of me is, "You're a show-boat," "You're a publicity-seeker," and to some extent that has the ring of truth. I enjoy the spotlight, as most humans do, but it's not my whole *raison d'etre.* My purpose is to keep the state from becoming all-domineering, all-powerful. And that's never changed.

Interview/
The New York Times, 7-6:(A)12.

Patrick J. Leahy
United States Senator,
D-Vermont

2

[On President Clinton's task of appointing a replacement for retiring U.S. Supreme Court Justice Byron White]: If I were asked for advice, I'd tell the President: "When you name this person, think of someone whose name will stand out in the history books." The public impression [is] the Court is becoming increasingly politicized . . . If it were solely a political statement or reflected the interests of one political interest group, that would badly diminish public respect for the Court.

USA Today, 3-29:(A)10.

Elaine Martin
Professor of political science,
Eastern Michigan University

3

A good judge is a good judge, and generally race or gender doesn't make any difference. But on the cutting edge of law, where things are changing, it's more uncertain; then I think you'll see that when women or minorities are present, there's a different perspective.

The Christian Science Monitor, 5-19:6.

Blane R. Prescott
Partner,
Hildebrandt management
consulting company

4

[On the trend away from "billable hours" as the standard method of charging by law firms]: Clients are talking about fixed fees, capped fees, fee estimates, contingent fees and discounts. They want to see a budget, something that will give them a better idea in advance of what a law firm's services will cost. They want to discuss that budget and how it was developed . . . [And due to the abundance of lawyers and the shrinking number of clients,] clients are getting what they want.

The New York Times, 10-22:(A)1.

Janet Reno
Attorney General
of the United States

5

I want to approach [civil-justice reform] in a non-partisan, careful, thoughtful way through the creation in the Department of Justice of something akin to the old Office of Justice Improvement—an office where we can focus on the issues of civil-justice reform without buzz words, without labels and without political debate . . . I have a commitment to this area as one of the most important that the Department of Justice can undertake . . . All lawyers [must face the issue of] how complicated we have made our laws, what we have done to ensnarl the American people in bureaucratic rules and regulations that make access to services or compliance with the law sometimes difficult, if not impossible.

At conference at U.S. Chamber of Commerce,
Washington, D.C./
Nation's Business, June:10.

6

We [in the legal profession] must explain our actions . . . not in obscure legalese, but in the small old words we all understand. Too often, lawyers have made the law a mystery; we must make it a lamp that shines the way.

Vogue, August:263.

(JANET RENO)

1

Lawyers have got to start teaching the people what the law is about—not in the terms of Roman numerals or alphabets or titles this-or-that, or this act or that act or some acronym, but in words that people can understand: right and wrong and justice and time and efficiency.

At American Bar Association convention,
New York, N.Y./
The New York Times, 8-9:(A)9.

Dirk Roggeveen
Senior litigation attorney,
Institute for Justice

2

[On the "independent-sovereigns" doctrine, which permits both state and Federal trials of the same defendant for the same crime]: In the early days of the republic, when the Federal government wasn't very active in criminal prosecution, it didn't bother people that defendants who were tried by a state for robbery were later tried by the Federal government for piracy on the same facts. But the [independent-sovereigns] doctrine is potentially more troubling today, when in a number of areas the Federal government has criminal statutes that are almost identical to state laws. Now there's talk of Federal domestic-violence laws that probably will track some state laws almost word for word.

The Christian Science Monitor,
3-15:12.

Antonin Scalia
Associate Justice,
Supreme Court
of the United States

3

[Criticizing the belief that the U.S. Constitution can be used to remedy all societal ills]: That attitude used to be confined just to law professors and judges. "The Constitution is whatever we say it is . . . pass it on" . . . [But] the American people now feel that if there is anything that we feel dearly about, it must be in the Constitution . . . We will squeeze it in somewhere . . . My view is that [the Constitution] contains a

limited number of guarantees. The meaning does not expand or contract over time. It is not everything in the world. It is very little in the world, as a matter of fact. If you read the Bill of Rights, what does it contain? Certainly not everything that is good and true and beautiful . . . I am a textualist. I am not a nut.

Before Association of American Publishers,
Washington, D.C., March 26/
The Washington Post, 3-27:(A)5.

William W. Schwarzer
Director,
Federal Judicial Center

4

[On Federal sentencing guidelines]: The guidelines say you have to sentence the offense and not the offender. What bothers Federal judges so much is that you can't sentence an offense. You have to sentence an offender.

The New York Times, 8-6:(B)10.

M. Dwayne Smith
Chairman,
department of sociology,
Tulane University

5

[On recent acts of violence in courthouses]: Courthouses are no longer removed from what's going on in the outside world. The emotions that generate the violence we see in courthouses now are exactly the kind of emotions that account for a majority of the homicides in the United States.

The New York Times, 1-26:(A)8.

Laurence H. Tribe
Professor of
Constitutional law,
Harvard University

6

[On retiring U.S. Supreme Court Justice Byron White]: Justice White has almost from the beginning been a person who didn't develop doctrines or frameworks or ways of looking at things that would influence other Justices. As a result, he has been among the least influential. If he is replaced by anyone with a more systematic

(LAURENCE H. TRIBE)

approach, that could over time be more influential of other Justices.

The Washington Post, 3-20:(A)13.

Raymond Trombadore
Chairman,
disciplinary committee,
New Jersey Bar Association

1

[Saying the legal profession's self-disciplinary proceedings should be open to the public]: Secrecy always breeds suspicion, particularly when the system you are asked to accept as trustworthy is a system of self-regulation. You can't ask people to trust something which they cannot see . . . If we want the public to respect the system of lawyers' [self-] regulation as a system that has integrity, then I think we've got to permit them to see its functions.

The Washington Post,
1-15:(A)18.

Lawrence E. Walsh
Independent Counsel
investigating the Iran-contra scandal;
Former president,
American Bar Association

2

[Criticizing President Bush's recent granting of pardons to a number of persons convicted or implicated in the Iran-contra scandal]: I was surprised. I had heard it was possible, but I couldn't conceive that President Bush would do it. It's hard to find an adjective strong enough to characterize a President who has such contempt for honesty—and such a lack of sensitivity to the picture of a President protecting a Cabinet officer who lies to Congress. Using the pardon power to help a friend and other associates from the [Ronald] Reagan Administration shows a disdainful disregard for the rule of law. It gives the impression that people in high office with strong political connections can get favored treatment. And I think that is a terrible impression for the President of the United States to give.

Interview, Oklahoma City, Okla./
Newsweek, 1-4:16.

Politics

Lamar Alexander
Secretary of Education
of the United States

1

I've been to 100-plus communities in the last 18 months, California 20 times. And I've got a picture of this country that I didn't have before. The country is filled with anxious people who would like some help understanding what's going on and what we ought to do . . . Our Party—the Republican Party—has been talking in the language of 1964 and 1980 and not in the language of the '90s. Parties, when they do that, get ushered out to refresh themselves, which is what's happened to us.

Interview, Washington, D.C./
The Christian Science Monitor,
1-19:12.

Thomas H. Andrews
United States Representative,
D-Maine

2

[Criticizing what he says is Clinton Administration efforts to "buy" votes for NAFTA by offering wavering Congressmen incentives such as "pork" projects for their districts]: I've been asked in so many ways: What do you need; what will it take? We do a great disservice to this country when we make this a matter of pork-barrel auctioneering or making it an issue of what threats will we respond to. Both sides do it.

The Washington Post, 11-1:(A)7.

Haley Barbour
Chairman,
Republican National Committee

3

[On President Clinton's low ratings in public-opinion polls and a series of controversies surrounding his handling of various issues since taking office]: Every time he digs himself a hole—and that's been pretty often—it makes a little mound for us [Republicans] to stand on. He has done more to unify the Republican Party in 120 days than I'll do in four years, if I last that long.

The New York Times, 5-24:(A)12.

4

[On industrialist Ross Perot, who ran for President as an independent last year]: One of the things Ross Perot's [popular] campaign showed is that if you give people something to be for, and a chance to participate, they'll knock down your door.

June 21/USA Today, 6-22:(A)6.

Evan Bayh
Governor of Indiana (D)

5

[On the anti-incumbent mood in recent elections]: The burden of proof used to be on the challenger; today, it's almost on the incumbent. You've got to show you can make a difference in tangible terms that people can relate to in their daily lives.

The New York Times, 11-4:(A)1.

Paul Begala
Political Adviser
to President of the United States
Bill Clinton

6

[On the supporters of industrialist Ross Perot, who ran for President last year as an independent]: They ought to be called "independent voters," not "Perot voters." His ability to reach those independent voters is compromised by his inability to articulate a positive message or a substantive message. Mr. Perot will find they're increasingly independent of him as well.

Nov. 10/
The Washington Post,
11-11:(A)8.

William J. Bennett
Former Secretary of Education
of the United States

1

[On President Clinton's political problems and low public-opinion poll ratings]: As people say in the South, the boy's a mess. He doesn't know who he is or where he is.
The New York Times, 6-4:(A)12.

2

The two sacramental objects of [the Clinton] Administration, from what I can tell, are taxes and condoms. They like them all. They like them all the time. They even like them when they don't work.
USA Today, 8-6:(A)13.

Wayne L. Berman
Former Counsellor
to the Secretary of Commerce
of the United States
in the George Bush
Administration

3

[President] Clinton has overcome the chief flaw of Democrats of the last generation: They talked "left," legislated "left," and were therefore "left" with no appeal to most Americans. What Clinton is doing is feinting to the center but legislating to the left.
Time, 3-15:49.

Merle Black
Political scientist,
Emory University

4

[On the perception that President Clinton waffles and changes his mind too often on policy and appointments]: There may soon be a widespread belief in Washington that any deal with Clinton needs three witnesses, because he doesn't deliver. And that really undermines his ability to influence other politicians.
Los Angeles Times, 6-14:(A)12.

Richard N. Bond
Chairman,
Republican National Committee

5

Our job [as Republicans] is to win elections, not cling to intolerances that zealots call principles, not to be led or dominated by a vocal few who like to look good losing. That is a sure path to disaster.
At Republican National Committee meeting, St. Louis, Mo., Jan. 29/ The New York Times, 1-30:28.

David L. Boren
United States Senator,
D-Oklahoma

6

The vicious race to raise money [for election campaigns] has made us part-time Senators and full-time fund-raisers. [Senators who] came here idealistic, wanting to render a public service . . . have been turned into panhandlers on the street, for sale to the highest bidder on the auction block because they have to figure out how to raise $4-million to get re-elected.
Los Angeles Times, 6-9:(A)23.

Bill Bradley
United States Senator,
D-New Jersey

7

[On industrialist and political activist Ross Perot for criticizing NAFTA]: I think that, you know, he is clearly using this as an organizing vehicle for his own party. He wants to essentially be a third—run a third—party that challenges Democrats and Republicans, and this [anti-NAFTA campaign] is simply an organizing tool for him and for his organization. There is no question in my mind to that.
News conference, Sept. 20/ Los Angeles Times, 9-21:(A)9.

John B. Breaux
United States Senator,
D-Louisiana

8

[President Clinton] really has to govern as he campaigned—as a mainstream moderate. I'm

(JOHN B. BREAUX)

willing to do everything I can to help him reach that goal of being a new Democrat, a mainstream Democrat, because that's where the future of this Party and this country lies . . . After you become President, the normal pressures from the left become very active and very visible. People who really didn't support Bill Clinton in the primaries at all now feel that since he is a Democratic President, he has to follow the same rules that old-style Democrats were used to.

Interview/
Los Angeles Times,
5-29:(A)24.

George Bush
President of the United States

1

[On his future plans, having lost re-election in 1992]: I don't really know what I will be doing. You see, my problem is, I thought I was going to win, so I didn't do any defense planning, you might say. I plan to put something back into society, and not at the head table, not always in the glamour, certainly not with a lot of news attention—try to be a useful citizen back in Houston, Texas, and in Maine. And then I'll figure it out.

Somalia, Jan. 2/
The New York Times, 1-4:(A)6.

George Bush
Former President
of the United States

2

[On how history will treat him, considering he lost his re-election bid in 1992]: It takes years to take the full measure of any Presidency, and that's all right with me, because I am very quietly confident that history will be a kinder and gentler judge than the jury of 1992.

Before National Restaurant Association,
Chicago, Ill., May 23/
Los Angeles Times,
5-24:(A)15.

Jimmy Carter
Former President
of the United States

3

[On industrialist Ross Perot, who ran for President as an independent in 1992 and who is now a critic of President Clinton]: Unfortunately in our country now, we have a demagogue who has unlimited financial resources and who is extremely careless with the truth, who is preying on the fears and the uncertainties of the American public. And this must be met, because this powerful voice can be pervasive even within the Congress of the United States unless it's met by people of courage who vote and act and persuade in the best interests of our country.

At President Clinton's signing of
supplemental agreements to NAFTA,
Washington, D.C., Sept. 14/
The New York Times, 9-15:(A)12.

Dick Cheney
Former Secretary of Defense
of the United States;
Former United States Representative,
R-Wyoming

4

[On President Clinton]: He strikes me as a guy with a good set of basic political skills in terms of his intellect. He's every inch the activist. When I try to identify what he believes, that's about all I can come up with—an activist role for government.

Interview/
U.S. News & World Report,
10-25:40.

Bill Clinton
President-elect
of the United States

5

[On the 1992 Presidential election, which he won by a plurality]: If it had been a two-person race [between him and President Bush], the popular [-vote] margin would have been greater, but the electoral margin might have been slightly tighter. It's hard to calculate because some states were so close. I think what I have a mandate to do

(BILL CLINTON)

from the people who voted for Clinton and [independent Ross Perot], and some of the people even who voted for Bush, is to try to make the government work again, to strengthen the economy to solve problems, to represent the people at large rather than just the people who are organized and have great wealth.

Interview, Little Rock, Ark./
Time, 1-4:34.

1

[On charges that he has already broken some of his election-campaign pledges]: The American people would think I was foolish if I said, "I will not respond to changing circumstances." I think that it would be irresponsible for any President of the United States ever not to respond to changing circumstances. Every President, as far as I know, who's held this office, and especially the ones who really did a good job, have had to answer questions like this, because they had to change some of their positions in response to changing circumstances.

News conference,
Little Rock, Ark., Jan. 14/
The Washington Post, 1-15:(A)16.

2

We'll do our best never to forget who put us in the White House: people like you along the roads of America. Never to forget what this election was all about, that there were too many men and women who were working hard and falling further behind . . . that we could not allow our children to be the first generation of children to grow up to a future worse than their parents'. That will be our guiding, driving missions.

Warrenton, Virginia, Jan. 17/
USA Today, 1-18:(A)2.

Bill Clinton
President of the United States

3

I intend to come forward with a proposal that will end the use of "soft money" in Presidential

[election] campaigns, in the next few days. We're working on it now. We're working on trying to hammer it out with the friends of campaign finance reform in both houses of the Congress. I will attempt to do it in a different way that will at least enable the parties to raise sufficient funds to involve grass-roots people and empower people to participate in the political process; but I think that we should do away with this soft-money issue and make a lot of other changes as well, and we're working on it.

News conference,
Washington, D.C., March 23/
The New York Times, 3-24:(A)7.

4

[On his performance as President since he took office]: Look what's happened in four months. We had a major foreign-policy challenge in Russia right after I got in office. If [Russian President Boris] Yeltsin had got beaten in Russia and a militant regime had returned, we would have had to turn around with the defense budget. A lot of bad things could have happened to America. The United States went to work, organized the rest of the world, supported Yeltsin. He won the election. We're back on track there making this world a safer place. That's my Number 1 job. I think that's pretty impressive. The Congress passed a resolution committing to do a budget that reduced the [Federal] deficit by $500-billion on time for the first time in 17 years. Congress passed the family-leave bill they've been fooling around with for eight years to guarantee people some time off without losing their jobs. They passed the motor-voter bill they'd been fooling around with for years. No one now asks, "Are we going to reduce the deficit?" The question is, how much and how? No one now asks, "Are we ever going to do anything about health care?" The question is, when and exactly what are we going to do? I think that's a pretty good record for four months.

Broadcast "town meeting,"
Washington, D.C./
"CBS This Morning," CBS-TV, 5-27.

5

If I worried about the poll ratings, I'd never get anything done here. The only thing I'd remind

(BILL CLINTON)

you is, for 12 years we've seen politicians in the Congress and the Executive Branch worry about their poll ratings every month, and then at the end of every four years things are a lot worse. If things are better at the end of the period that I was given to serve, then the poll ratings now won't make any difference; and if they're not, they won't make any difference. So my job is to do my job and let the chips fall where they may.

News conference,
Washington, D.C., May 14/
The New York Times, 5-15:8.

1

[On criticism that he is mingling with celebrities too much]: Has the Administration gone Hollywood? The answer to that is: no, heck no, never, no, never—never.

Broadcast "town meeting,"
Washington, D.C./
"CBS This Morning," CBS-TV, 5-27.

2

This is the most decisive Presidency you've had in a very long time on all the big issues that matter. And I might say, all the heat we're getting from people is because of the decisions that have been made, not because of those that haven't.

News conference,
Washington, D.C., June 15/
The New York Times, 6-16:(A)1.

3

[On Vice President Al Gore]: When the record of this Administration is written, one thing will go down in the history books: There will never have been a Vice President in the history of the Republic who played such a constructive role in helping to advance the public interest.

Los Angeles Times, 7-27:(A)5.

4

[Calling for Congress to unite behind his programs]: In the long run, we cannot succeed in an endless season of partisan bitterness and rancor and bickering. If some of us have to make hard choices while others stand aside and hope that the house collapses, nothing will in the end get done.

At signing of his economic bill,
Washington, D.C., Aug. 10/
The Washington Post, 8-11:(A)4.

5

[Saying there is an anti-incumbent mood in the country, demonstrated by this week's elections which saw a number of high-profile Democratic Mayors and Governors voted out of office]: The voters are not yet happy with the pace of economic renewal, social reunification in this country. They're worried about crime and they're worried about all these other social problems we've got. And I think it's also a sense they have that government's not yet working for them. And all that is right. I think that all people who are in [office], if they want to stay in, are going to have to work together until we produce economic results.

To reporters, Nov. 3/
Los Angeles Times, 11-4:(A)25.

6

When historians look at this first year [of his Presidency], they will be hard-pressed to find many first years of Presidencies that equal ours.

Broadcast interview,
Washington, D.C./
"Meet the Press," NBC-TV, 11-7.

7

[On the controversy earlier this year regarding a $200 haircut he allegedly received from a celebrity stylist on Air Force One at Los Angeles Airport]: That was something that really struck a raw nerve at home [in Arkansas] because nobody [there] believed that I would pay $200 to see the cow jump over the moon or that I would keep anybody waiting [it was alleged some planes couldn't land while he was getting the haircut]. So they all called, but they said, "God, if he's really done that, he's really lost it. He's gone

(BILL CLINTON)

Washington." We told them I didn't do it, so they felt better about that.

Interview/
U.S. News & World Report,
11-29:34.

1

I have fought more damn battles here for more things than any President has in 20 years, with the possible exception of [former President Ronald] Reagan's first budget, and not gotten one damn bit of credit from the knee-jerk liberal press. I am sick and tired of it, and you can put that in the damn article.

Interview/Newsweek, 11-29:25.

2

[Saying the Democratic Party must embrace middle-class Americans]: We must fight their fight. We must give voice to their concerns. We must give them the chance to build security while embracing change. And above all, we must honor those basic values of opportunity, responsibility and community, of work and family and faith. This is what it means, in my view, to be a "new Democrat." I was proud to campaign as one; I'm proud to govern as one.

Before Democratic Leadership Council,
Washington, D.C., Dec. 3/
The New York Times, 12-4:8.

3

I think the nature of the times in which we live preclude [politicians] from getting astronomical [public-approval] ratings unless you [in the press] decide to canonize them.

Dec. 8/USA Today, 12-9:(A)4.

4

[Criticizing new allegations that he was involved in extra-marital affairs when he was Arkansas Governor and improperly used the power of his office to cover them up]: The only relevant questions are questions of whether I

have abused my office, and the answer is no. We've otherwise responded clearly to the allegations that were made, and I just don't think I should say any more about it . . . The American people gave me a four-year contract. In the political environment in which we're living today, we've seen repeatedly that painful, personal things can be alleged by anybody at any time. That's just, I guess, part of the deal.

Broadcast interview,
Washington, D.C./
National Public Radio, 12-22.

Hillary Rodham Clinton
Wife of President
of the United States Bill Clinton

5

[Criticizing new allegations that her husband was involved in extra-marital affairs when he was Arkansas Governor and improperly used the power of his office to cover them up]: I find it not an accident that every time he is on the verge of fulfilling his commitment to the American people and they are responding—whether it's forging ahead in the polls in New Hampshire [during the primaries] or now with very high popularity—out comes yet a new round of these outrageous, terrible stories that people plant for political and financial reasons.

Interview,
Washington, D.C., Dec. 21/
The New York Times, 12-22:(A)10.

Robert J. Dole
United States Senator,
R-Kansas

6

The Democrats have had a lock on [Congress] for 40 years. If people are frustrated with Congress, they shouldn't be frustrated with us [Republicans] unless they give us a chance . . . If the Perot voters [those who supported independent Presidential candidate Ross Perot in the 1992 election] want to help, they can help us in 1994 to change the Congress [by electing more Republicans]. If we don't do any better than the Democrats, then kick us out. If they're upset with

(ROBERT J. DOLE)

Congress . . . I think they ought to attribute it to the right party.

At Republican National Committee meeting, Chicago, Ill., July 9/ The Washington Post, 7-10:(A)6.

Thomas S. Foley
United States Representative, D-Washington; Speaker of the House

1

I don't believe eliminating political action committees [PACs] is good [campaign-finance] reform. In many cases, they pose far less of a problem than individual contributions might because individual contributions are often difficult to trace and they are often insufficiently identified.

June 17/USA Today, 6-18:(A)10.

Wendell H. Ford
United States Senator, D-Kentucky

2

When most Americans think about what is wrong with the political process, they can think of only three things: money, money and more money. Political reform must occur if we are to reconnect the American people with their government.

Los Angeles Times, 6-9:(A)23.

Geoffrey Garin
Democratic Party consultant

3

[On industrialist Ross Perot, who ran for President last year as an independent and who continues to remain popular]: It turns out he's more than just an "anti" vote. He has the support of a lot of people who genuinely have concluded that they no longer can believe in conventional politicians . . . I don't know what he has in mind ultimately, but so far he's managed to set himself up as the Good Housekeeping Seal of Approval when it comes to government reform

and fiscal responsibility. The challenge for [President] Bill Clinton is to bring about that reform and responsibility, which the voters genuinely want, without making Perot seem overly important. If he can do that, Perot will begin to slip into the political background.

The New York Times, 3-15:(A)7.

David Gergen
Counsellor to President of the United States Bill Clinton

4

[On the effect on Democratic President Clinton's staff of Gergen's joining the Administration, considering that he has worked for Republicans in the past]: If I had worked my tail off [for Clinton] during [last year's election] campaign, and some guy [like himself] who had worked for Republicans came into my chain of command, I would be anxious. And it's as big a surprise for me as it is for them. Some of them think this is a liver transplant and I'm the liver.

Interview/Time, 6-14:25.

Newt Gingrich
United States Representative, R-Georgia

5

Our [Republican Party] goal should be cooperation without compromise. Our role in the minority [in Congress] is to offer new ideas, to offer intelligent criticism of their [Democrats'] dumb ideas, and to cooperate when we have common ground.

Interview/The Atlantic, June:27.

Al Gore
Vice President of the United States

6

Political change has sometimes been described as the metaphor of a sailboat tacking against the wind. When one side comes up out of the water, it's a vivid image. That image and that metaphor remind me very much of what happened in the [House chamber] last night [when most Democrats applauded President Clinton's economic

191

(AL GORE)

speech and most Republicans were cool toward it]. I saw the mirror image of it during the beginning of the [former President Ronald] Reagan era, when one side of the chamber stands and applauds wildly and the other side sits with their hands folded in their laps. Visually, the image is very much that of a great ship changing course, with one side out of the water and the other, sort of sinking.

To reporters,
Washington, D.C., Feb. 18/
The New York Times, 2-19:(A)9.

Judd Gregg
United States Senator,
R-New Hampshire

1

Other than [Senator] Bob Dole, we [Republicans] have no one of national stature [as a possible 1996 Presidential candidate]. As long as [independent industrialist] Ross Perot is filling the role a Republican should be filling—carrying the case against [President] Bill Clinton's policies to the country—we will remain diffuse.

The New York Times, 5-24:(A)12.

Peter Hart
Democratic Party
public-opinion analyst

2

[On whether well-known military people would make good politicians nowadays when they leave the service]: The hardest thing is that [after they leave the military] they no longer have that aura. Once they take off the stars and the cap, a stupid answer is still a stupid answer.

U.S. News & World Report,
9-20:52.

Stephen Hess
Senior fellow,
Brookings Institution

3

[On President-elect Clinton's campaign promises]: Like many past Presidents, he's come smack up face to face with reality. He's in a little more trouble than many past Presidents only because he's made more promises and the promises have been more specific. [But] the American people give a new President a fair amount of wiggle room. Since they don't believe their promises in the first place, it's very hard for them to get upset when they break their promises.

The Washington Post, 1-13:(A)13.

4

[On the controversy over President Clinton having his hair cut by an exclusive celebrity hair stylist]: The President should remind himself that the people who elected him get their hair cut, not styled, by barbers named Ed, not Cristophe, and they pay in cash, not personal-services contracts.

Time, 5-31:21.

Robert Holsworth
Political scientist,
Virginia Commonwealth University

5

It would be a very unusual precedent if people are removed from office after a campaign for lying because they stretched the truth, or told outright falsehoods, during the campaign. By that standard, one would have to remove a good percentage of the politicians, and one would spend a lot of time trying to distinguish between ignorance and falsehood.

The Christian Science Monitor,
5-12:2.

Jesse L. Jackson
Civil-rights leader

6

[President Clinton] thinks we'll [blacks] have nowhere to go except with him in [the election in] '96. Well, that's what other Democrats thought when they talked the talk but then didn't deliver. Those guys, like [New Jersey Governor Jim] Florio [who recently lost his re-election bid], fooled us the first time around. We weren't fooled the second time. Florio didn't lose because the black vote was repressed [by his Republican

(JESSE L. JACKSON)

opponents]. He lost because blacks were depressed, and didn't vote.

Time, 12-13:40.

Frank Jordan
Mayor of San Francisco, Calif.

1

The political arena is not a pleasant one. It's a brutal game where perception is more important than reality. I don't like it at all. I fight it and resist it every day . . . I never do what I think is "politically right" for me; I do what is best for the city—and that is not understood [by political enemies]. I don't care about political posturing.

Interview, San Francisco, Calif./
The Christian Science Monitor,
5-25:3.

David Keene
President,
American Conservative Union

2

[President Clinton's economic] speech [to Congress] was a terrible mishmash of outdated liberal principles . . . This is a President who believes all good flows from government.

At Conservative Political Action Conference,
Washington, D.C./
The Christian Science Monitor,
2-22:2.

Jack Kemp
Former Secretary of Housing
and Urban Development
of the United States;
Former United States Representative,
R-New York

3

[Calling for Republican Party unity]: We should be like Abraham and Lot. We've got to stop carping at each other and work together as kindred spirits. Let there be no enmity between tribesmen.

At Conservative Political Action Conference,
Washington, D.C., Feb. 20/
The Christian Science Monitor,
2-22:2.

4

The statement was made at the [1992] Republican [national] convention that those people who didn't think like us were not part of the country. That was offensive to me. Some of this attitude comes from my football career; some of my very best friends are people who tried to knock my head off on the football field; they were my friends off the field. We'd beat the heck out of each other on Sunday, or try to. I wish political debates could take place in that type of arena, more Marquis of Queensberry rules than alley-cat rules. But unfortunately, politics is all too often an alley fight, not something done out in the open where people debate the issues fairly and let the American people judge.

Interview/
American Heritage, October:59.

Larry King
TV and radio talk-show host

5

[On 1992 independent Presidential candidate, industrialist Ross Perot]: In a weird kind of way, people miss him. It won't be as fervent as in the heat of the campaign, but there will always be interest in Ross Perot. Whatever that potion is that goes into a television screen and beams out to make people attracted to him, Perot has it.

The New York Times, 1-8:(A)10.

Lane Kirkland
President,
American Federation
of Labor-Congress
of Industrial Organizations

6

I stand here with no present doubt that, in the fullness of time, when President Clinton must stand for re-election against the kind of candidate the other [Republican] party can be counted upon to cast up—another front man for the government of the privileged few, for the few and by the few—the trade-union movement will be there with him, fighting shoulder-to-shoulder for a better tomorrow.

At AFL-CIO convention,
San Francisco, Calif., Oct. 4/
The Washington Post, 10-5:(A)13.

Helmut Kohl
Chancellor of Germany

1

The essence of politics is [for government leaders] to carry out things the electorate might not immediately understand.

The Christian Science Monitor,
5-25:19.

William Kristol
Republican Party strategist;
Former Chief of Staff
to former Vice President
of the United States Dan Quayle

2

[President] Clinton has so identified himself with the cultural left, with taxpayer funding for abortion, and gays in the military, that he's left a lot of room for us [Republicans] in the middle. We can oppose [racial] quotas without seeming Neanderthal on civil rights and favor restrictions on abortion without seeming anti-women.

The New York Times, 5-24:(A)12.

Everett Ladd
Professor of political science,
University of Connecticut;
Executive director,
Roper Center for Public
Opinion and Research

3

[On the recent election defeats of a number of black Mayoral candidates in big cities that have had black Mayors for many years]: It's not that racial antipathy has increased, but that many white voters no longer feel they owe a black candidate a vote or support. In the first stage, there was a sense of guilt or recognition that blacks were so shut out from opportunities in electoral life, that whites, especially more moderate and liberal whites, tended to be particularly inclined to give a black a vote. That's past.

USA Today, 11-5:(A)2.

Rush Limbaugh
Political talk-show host
and commentator

4

[On whether he would consider going into politics]: The countryside is strewn with the carcasses of many media types who thought they could get elected. Ten percent makes you Number 1 in the media, [but] 10 percent and you're a laughingstock in politics.

Interview/
U.S. News & World Report,
8-16:35.

Trent Lott
United States Senator,
R-Mississippi

5

[President Clinton] talked a good game [when he was a candidate in last year's election] campaign, but he sounds just like another tired old Democrat so far. The first week, we had the Zoe Baird-Attorney General [appointment] fiasco; the next week we had the homosexuals in the military. The next week he talked about immigrants with AIDS coming into the country. Now he's talking about a budget package that doesn't cut spending and raises taxes. That's an unbelievable series of events.

Feb. 16/
The Washington Post, 2-17:(A)7.

Susan Manes
Vice president,
Common Cause

6

PACs give to legislators who are in a position to affect their interests. PACs are at the heart of making this system one that's stacked against challengers [to incumbents].

USA Today, 8-24:(A)4.

Thomas E. Mann
Director of governmental studies,
Brookings Institution

7

I think [President] Clinton got caught up in the excitement of governing during his first 100 days [in office]. He got so involved in indulging his interest in different aspects of policy that he forgot about the politics of selling it. He thought that his policy discussion sessions inside the White House were sufficient. But they were not.

(THOMAS E. MANN)

Not enough was being conveyed to the public about what exactly his Presidency was up to.

The New York Times, 5-15:9.

Mike Mansfield
Former United States Senator,
D-Montana

1

[In politics,] you should never take yourself too seriously. If you win in politics, you don't win on the basis of your charm, or your education, or your good looks. There are a thousand people out there who know more than you do, who could probably do a better job, but they didn't get the breaks. And recognize there are two sides to almost every issue. Sometimes, the other side is right—it doesn't do any harm to listen.

Interview,
Washington, D.C., March 15/
The Washington Post, 3-16:(E)4.

Mary Matalin
Co-host,
"Equal Time," CNBC-TV;
Former deputy campaign manager
for former President
of the United States
George Bush's
1992 re-election campaign

2

A [political election] campaign is definitely war. It's fun if you're winning. It's not fun if you're not. It's very high stakes. You're fighting for something you believe in and there's a real live enemy and no second place. It's not like basketball and football. There are real-life consequences; and if you lose, it makes a big difference.

Interview/
"W" magazine, August:111.

3

I've worked hard in steel mills and beauty shops and stopped learning. But in politics you never stop learning. Even though we lost [the Presidential election], the cause was rewarding.

Working Woman, November:53.

4

Politics [today] is a multimillion-dollar industry. It used to be a bunch of guys in a back room smoking cigars. That cliche was real. Now a bunch of people make a bunch of money. What was intended to reform politics and make it accessible to the masses—the diminution of party bosses through campaign-finance reform—has turned politics over to the technocrats. A lot of people who do it could be working for [Cuban President Fidel] Castro [for all they care]. It's just a business. It's a technology. And *those* are the people I don't like.

Interview, New York, N.Y./
Lear's, December:14.

George J. Mitchell
United States Senator,
D-Maine

5

[On the Clinton Administration's proposal for reforming political-campaign financing]: There are cynics who will oppose it, who question our motivation. They cannot believe that incumbents would propose legislation to make election contests more fair. What the cynics ignore is the effect the current campaign-finance system has on our system of government. The American people no longer have confidence in the political process.

Washington, D.C., May 7/
The New York Times, 5-8:7.

Sam Nunn
United States Senator,
D-Georgia

6

[On his disagreements with President Clinton, who is also a Democrat]: I want to help Bill Clinton every time I think he's anywhere near the mark. But . . . on important matters when I disagree with him, I feel I have an obligation to my constituents, and to my own sense of duty, my conscience . . . I don't view myself as trying to pull him one way or the other. I try to express my own views. If he agrees, then I think it's great. If he doesn't agree, that's his privilege.

Interview/
The Washington Post, 5-3:(A)4.

Paul H. O'Neill
Chairman,
Aluminum Company of America

1

I have one lingering uneasiness that [President Clinton's] sense about what to do will be tempered by those who know too much about political suicide. I told him at the economic conference in Little Rock he ought to act like he was going to be a one-term President, and that by doing that, he would insure himself of a second term.

Interview/
The New York Times, 3-1:(C)12.

Timothy J. Penny
United States Representative,
D-Minnesota

2

[President Clinton is] a great consensus leader, somebody who will rally a group once they've got agreement and happily run with it. But he's not a leader to take a strong position and make it happen by sheer force of will.

Los Angeles Times, 7-31:(A)17.

Ross Perot
Industrialist;
1992 independent
Presidential candidate

3

[On his new watchdog organization, United We Stand, America]: We're going to be organizing every city, town and neighborhood across the country, and we are going to give the American people a voice. We will stick together; one for all and all for one.

News conference,
Dallas, Texas, Jan. 11/
The New York Times, 1-12:(A)1.

4

[Saying President Clinton may involve the U.S. in the conflict in Bosnia as a diversion from domestic problems in the U.S.]: My biggest concern is that anytime things get complicated in this country, we like to start a war. The first 100 days

[of Clinton's Presidency] didn't go well. Everything's in disarray . . . The [campaign] promises are imploding. So it's a good time to distract the American people. You have all these interesting forces at work. When you're shutting down the defense industry, you can get a little war going. When you're downsizing the military, you get a little war going . . . The one advantage of conflict overseas would be to divert the American people's mind. You can go home at night and watch smart-bombs going down air shafts again.

Interview/
The Washington Post, 5-8:(A)16.

5

In war there are rules. Even mud wrestling has rules. Only politics has no rules.

U.S. News & World Report,
5-17:41.

6

[On whether he has plans to pursue the Presidency again, as he did in 1992]: As far as having any personal agenda, I don't have one except to get the [country's] problem[s] solved. We feel very strongly that we don't have four years to wait, that we need to work night and day now to build and strengthen our country. I have an obligation to all these people in United We Stand [his support group] to provide them with the leverage. See, they insist that I never say never. So I won't.

Interview, Dallas, Texas/
U.S. News & World Report,
5-17:43.

7

[On President Clinton]: [He is] still doing things the Arkansas way [where he was Governor], like trying to give the [White House] travel business as a political payoff. See? Now, that's just straight out of Arkansas. Now he's learned the hard way you can't do that. Then, bringing your cousin in and bringing the travel agency in that bailed you out when you were broke in your campaign. That's fine in Arkansas. That's not fine in Washington . . . What we have here is

(ROSS PEROT)

a person who does not have the background or experience for the most difficult job in the world which we, the American people, have elected him to fill. If you were interviewing him for your company, and you had a medium-sized company, you wouldn't consider giving him a job anywhere above middle management.

Broadcast interview, Dallas, Texas/
"Talking with David Frost," PBS-TV,
5-28.

Kevin P. Phillips
President,
American Political
Research Corporation

1

[On President Clinton's core advisers]: This is a crowd that doesn't have the stature to demand sacrifice [by the public]. These are people who spent [the] Vietnam [war] in Oxford [England]; they are $500,000 lawyers who hire illegal immigrants as baby-sitters; they are hotshot lobbyists. This group has no understanding of the kind of sacrifices made every day by the $26,000-a-year couple in Peoria, Illinois. They don't speak the language of the older generation that fought in World War II or the language of the under-30 generation that hasn't shared in the circumstances of the [baby-] boomers.

Time, 2-1:29.

2

The [political] right has no credibility on economics. It will be very difficult for a conservative movement to pretend to be populist while it still safeguards the interests of the top one-tenth of 1 percent. What is much easier to see coming into the vacuum is a [industrialist Ross] Perot-type mixture of conservatism and liberalism that touches on all the soft points of the interest groups and the foreign lobbyists and the whole paranoid streak. An awful lot of people may say the whole thing needs to be blitzed.

Interview/
Mother Jones,
May-June:60.

Harold R. "Red" Poling
Chairman,
Ford Motor Company

3

[On President Clinton]: I have been impressed by this man. In my meetings with him, he exhibited a broad knowledge of a wide range of issues. He listens very carefully and is very much a people-oriented person. He pays attention to what you are saying, and he takes the time to do it. That not only impresses me, it literally amazes me.

Interview/
The New York Times, 3-1:(C)12.

Jack Quinn
Chief of Staff
to Vice President
of the United States Al Gore

4

[On the perceived victory of Vice President Gore in a recent debate with industrialist and political gadfly Ross Perot]: [Those who think Gore] pulled the rug from under Perot [should remember that] with $3-billion, Perot can buy a new rug. Perot's not always exquisitely careful with the facts, so there's always a danger that he can affect the debate, and not for the better.

The New York Times, 12-10:(A)12.

Charles B. Rangel
United States Representative,
D-New York

5

The difference between "race" and "ethnicity" [in elective politics] is that historically when everyone was out competing, they knew at one time their name would get on the ballot. First, the Irish had to wait for the white Anglo-Saxons, and the Italians had to wait for the Irish, and the Jews had to wait for the Italians. But you knew that, with party tickets, when your time came, you'd get it. Then they threw away the old rule book because who was up next? The blacks. While Jews could have pride in seeking a Jew, and the Irish could have pride in [the late President John] Kennedy, when the blacks in Chicago had pride and sought Harold Washington [for

(CHARLES B. RANGEL)

Mayor], the white Democrats went bananas and found an unknown—a Jew, I think—to run against him as a Republican. What does that mean? Is that ethnicity? I don't think so.

The New York Times, 10-18:(B)11.

Ronald Reagan
Former President
of the United States

1

This is a night to celebrate because, as you dine together, Democrats are making the mistakes that guarantee Republicans will be in the White House for the next 25 years.

At Republican Party dinner/
USA Today, 5-14:(A)13.

Edward J. Rollins
Former co-chairman,
National Republican
Congressional Committee

2

[To foes of President Clinton]: Just hold his coat. He won [the 1992 election] and he's got sufficient votes in Congress to do whatever he wants. Wish him well for the good of the country. And the moment he falters, be prepared to put the kick in his side on the way down.

The Washington Post, 3-26:(A)19.

Warren Rudman
Former United States Senator,
R-New Hampshire

3

We'd like to change the "background music" of the next [Republican national] convention [by not having the Party take stands on abortion and other sensitive social issues]. Social issues are volatile and emotional. They touch on religious beliefs; they're not rational. They're things you should keep out of politics.

The Christian Science Monitor,
5-5:3.

Larry J. Sabato
Professor of government,
University of Virginia

4

[On unusual election ballot propositions, such as the recent one involving a police officer's right to carry a ventriloquist's dummy policeman with him on his beat]: I have followed politics as though it were my life for 25 years, and I have never heard of anything as silly as this. It just goes to prove the electoral process is for everyone, kooks included.

Los Angeles Times, 11-4:(A)32.

Jim Slattery
United States Representative,
D-Kansas

5

[On the politically active "religious right"]: From the standpoint of delivering votes, they're more influential than the bankers, more influential than the real-estate industry and as powerful as a single labor union in America. Their source of power is the ability to communicate with their followers, and the fact that in many parts of the country, they can generate a lot of phone calls and public interest.

The Washington Post, 2-1:(A)10.

Louise M. Slaughter
United States Representative,
D-New York

6

[Criticizing President Clinton for backing away from his proposed BTU tax after extracting votes for it from members of Congress]: I remember the President telling us specifically that if we went out on a limb over the BTU tax, he would be there with us. But now we don't even know where the limb is.

Time, 6-21:23.

George Stephanopoulos
Director of Communications
for President of the United States
Bill Clinton

7

[Saying President Clinton wants to encourage small donations to political campaigns]: We're

(GEORGE STEPHANOPOULOS)

trying to make sure that we limit the amount of money in politics. We will be doing that by having strict spending limits. We also want to make sure people have adequate opportunity to participate in campaigns. And we'll continue to balance those interests.

March 25/
The Washington Post, 3-26:(A)11.

John H. Sununu
Former Chief of Staff
to President of the United States
George Bush

1

[On outgoing President George Bush]: Some people think that a lot of the changes of the last three years—the collapse of Communism, changes in Latin America, some of our domestic programs—would have happened regardless of who was in the White House. That's dead wrong. George Bush pushed and tugged to get these things off dead center. He gets the credit.

The New York Times, 1-20:(A)10.

Al Swift
United States Representative,
D-Washington

2

[On the difficulty in coming up with an effective election-finance reform plan]: We have rural areas, we've got suburban districts, we've got urban districts, we have "super-urban" districts like New York and Los Angeles. We have more minorities who tell us they . . . raise money differently. We have more women who argue they raise their money very differently from men. The effort to get a one-size-fits-all kind of reform runs into this enormous problem in the House.

Interview/
The Christian Science Monitor,
10-26:4.

Ruy A. Teixeira
Scholar,
Brookings Institution

3

[On the Federal "motor-voter" bill, which will allow people to register to vote when they renew

their driver's license]: Given what we know about states where motor-voter has already been implemented, you're really looking at a five to 10 percentage-point increase in [voter] turnout, and that's at the most. A lot of these people are somewhat disconnected from political issues and the political process. There's no guarantee that they're going to go out and vote just because you sign them up.

The New York Times, 3-18:(A)12.

Dan Thomas
Political scientist,
University of Iowa

4

[On President Clinton's first 100 days in office]: There was little doubt in the public mind that [then-President] Ronald Reagan's agenda was Reagan's agenda in the sense of it representing an authentic . . . identity. There was, quite obviously, no such certainty for [then-President] George Bush. One hundred days into the Clinton Presidency, one wonders anew, "Who is Bill Clinton and what does he want to do with his Presidency?"

The Washington Post, 4-29:(A)1.

Paul E. Tsongas
Former United States Senator,
D-Massachusetts

5

It'll be interesting to see if the Republicans can get themselves past the [divisive] abortion issue. If they can do it, they will be formidable. If not, they'll be an asterisk.

The Christian Science Monitor,
5-4:4.

Ben Wattenberg
Senior fellow,
American Enterprise Institute

6

[On President Clinton]: Here he is 10 days into his Administration, and all the signals he is sending are the opposite of what he conveyed in [last fall's election] campaign. It's worse than wrong; it's stupid.

The New York Times, 2-2:(A)7.

199

Ralph Whitehead
Professor of journalism,
University of Massachusetts

1

[President Clinton] has tried to present the ideas of the elite to ordinary people, and he has tried to present ordinary people to the elite. He can speak wonk, and he can speak American. [But] on the campaign trail [last year], he had [political adviser] Jim Carville, who had no trouble making himself understood in barrooms. He needs people in the Administration who will do the same.

Time, 2-1:29.

David C. Wilhelm
Chairman-designate,
Democratic National
Committee

2

We ought to take the 500,000 people who donated to the [Democratic] Party in this [last year's] general-election campaign. We need to turn that into five million. We need to be truly a grass-roots party, truly a party that reaches into every nook and cranny of this country . . . I think the Democratic National Committee will emerge as the principal vehicle for how President Clinton can communicate outside the Beltway. That's an enormous job, but it's a very important part of the mission of the DNC to create an environment in which he can succeed.

Interview, Little Rock, Ark., Jan. 15/
The New York Times, 1-16:7.

David C. Wilhelm
Chairman,
Democratic National Committee

3

[On last year's Democratic Party victory in the Presidential election]: We just out-organized, out-hustled, out-campaigned, out-worked and just plain outdid the other team [the Republicans]. And as a result, we won.

At post-Presidential-inaugural party,
Washington, D.C., Jan. 21/
The New York Times, 1-22:(A)9.

4

The way to build a [political] party—the party, the Democratic Party—is to organize around ideas. People don't get involved in campaigns or in politics for the greater glory of the party, or even for the greater glory of the candidates. They do it if the party is saying something that is relevant to their everyday lives . . . The vision of building a party that is truly a party of the people has to be associated with the promotion of ideas. If not, the party is a pretty dry and uninteresting place.

Interview, Washington, D.C./
Los Angeles Times, 3-7:(M)3.

Social Welfare

Gary L. Bauer
President,
Family Research Council

1

If you look at the last 30 years, as a culture we have removed any form of being judgmental about out-of-wedlock pregnancy, as well as a host of other things. While at first glance that may seem to be kind, the fact is that when a society has increasing rates of illegitimacy, it is headed for the rocks of decline.

The New York Times, 12-2:(B)4.

Douglas Besharov
Resident scholar,
American Enterprise Institute

2

[Criticizing President Clinton's proposal to expand the earned income tax credit]: It opens the door to a whole new realm of entitlements that I think is quite unhealthy. This in effect puts half of all American families on a semi-welfare program. We can't provide that kind of subsidy for half of all families without major increases in taxation.

March 5/
The Washington Post, 3-6:(A)12.

Jimmy Carter
Former President
of the United States

3

We have two Americas—two Atlantas, two Washingtons, two New Yorks, two Chicagos, and so forth. One is fairly affluent and the other is destitute, with high levels of crime and poverty, homelessness and unemployment. We ought to emphasize on a global basis the importance of economic rights . . . I am not talking about welfare checks. I am talking about food and clothing, a place to sleep and something to do that's productive.

Interview/
USA Today, 6-14:(A)13.

Henry G. Cisneros
Secretary of Housing
and Urban Development
of the United States

4

[On working at HUD]: At the end of the day, you're exhausted. But it has nothing to do with what you need to accomplish in the real world . . . This is an Alice in Wonderland world. No human being could ever consciously create something this gridlocked and mazed.

The New York Times, 3-15:(A)7.

5

I think one of the things America has to address very, very squarely is whether or not we can live with continued vast spatial separations between the poorest of our populations, concentrated in public housing in central cities, and the vast differences that exist across our urban geography to the suburbs, which are essentially white. What we've got to do is break up the concentrations by making it possible for people to live in newly designed, thoughtfully scaled public housing, negotiated with outlying communities, because many of the problems . . . are a symptom of large concentrations of poor people with few role models and no lift.

Broadcast interview, April 11/
The Washington Post, 4-15:(A)29.

6

HUD's management of its [housing] inventory has been abysmal. The physical condition of many properties are deteriorating; others have been overrun by drug trafficking and crime. The truth is stark: HUD has in many cases exacerbated the declining quality of life in America.

Before Senate Banking, Housing
and Urban Affairs Committee,
Washington, D.C., June 22/
The New York Times, 6-23:(A)10.

(HENRY G. CISNEROS)

1

I think that for a Department whose name begins with "Housing," there can be no higher priority than housing people who are unhoused.

Interview,
Washington, D.C., Oct. 13/
The Christian Science Monitor,
10-14:3.

Bill Clinton
President of the United States

2

[On the earned income tax-credit feature of his economic plan]: This plan rewards work over welfare by lifting out of poverty every parent with children at home who choose full-time work over lifetime welfare. We do this through the earned-income tax credit, which reduces taxes for 20 million working families and households earning less than $27,000. It does this without creating a new government bureaucracy and simply using the tax code. This sends an enormously powerful message to the people who struggle against great odds to raise themselves and their families. It empowers them; it says we're on the side of people who work and care about their children. It's pro-work, it's pro-family, and it is a crucial first step to one of my most important priorities: ending welfare as we know it.

Broadcast address to the nation,
Washington, D.C., Aug. 3/
The New York Times, 8-4:(A)10.

3

[On babies born to single mothers]: If someone becomes pregnant and decides to have a baby rather than have an abortion, that may be a moral decision. So I wouldn't say that everybody who becomes pregnant out of wedlock who has a baby is immoral. But I believe that this country would be a lot better off if children were born to married couples. Remember the Dan Quayle speech [in which the then-Vice President criticized TV character Murphy Brown for having a baby out of wedlock]? There were a lot of very good things in that speech. [Quayle's]

Murphy Brown [reference] was a mistake; it was too cute because this woman is not symbolic of the real problem in society. [But] would we be a better-off society if babies were born to married couples? You bet we would.

Interview, Washington, D.C./
Newsweek, 12-13:35.

4

[On Federal entitlement programs for senior citizens, such as Social Security and Medicare]: I think it's important to point out that behind every one of these entitlements, there is a person. It's not just organized interest groups—there are people who believe they are literally entitled to receive something back that they paid into. It is the middle-class entitlements that have united us and brought us together, that also have the strongest constituencies. These programs are very important in human terms. Thirty-four million people go to see a doctor, or get medical care, because of the Medicare program. Social Security has changed what it means to be old. [Americans] should not view this whole program as welfare. It is not a welfare program. We should be very sensitive about the fact that this is something that has worked. Because of these programs we are a healthier people. We treat our elderly with great dignity. This is a huge deal.

At conference on Federal spending,
Bryn Mawr, Pa., Dec. 13/
The New York Times, 12-14:(A)12.

Hillary Rodham Clinton
Wife of President
of the United States Bill Clinton

5

The culture of poverty in this country has become institutionalized to an extent that is surprising to me and many others. Poverty has been with us since the beginning of time, and in many cultures there is permanent underclass with all the problems that that suggests. It is contrary to the American ethos and history of progress that we would see that developing and becoming institutionalized in our country. There is nothing new about having poor people in our midst. What is very new is that we now have the institutionalization of that culture of poverty in ways that are

(HILLARY RODHAM CLINTON)

difficult to reconcile with the whole concept of upward mobility, change, the American dream. And so those observers . . . who point that out as one of our major problems are absolutely right.

Interview, Washington, D.C./
Newsweek, 2-15:22.

Marian Wright Edelman
President,
Children's Defense Fund

1

I wish that more of my pro-choice [on abortion] friends were vocal on investments in the early years of life, and also that all those pro-life [anti-abortion] proponents were consistent with their concern for life after birth. There are many more people speaking out on abortion than there are on helping homeless children. I am deeply concerned that we are getting used to homeless children.

Interview, Washington, D.C./
Lear's, March:131.

Joycelyn Elders
Surgeon General-designate
of the United States

2

We [in the U.S.] do the sorriest job of any country in the world providing family planning. We're always running around hollering and screaming about abortion—and abortion is not the issue. The issue is providing family-planning services for all women who need them. Right now, the rich have them, but we don't care about the poor.

Los Angeles Times, 3-8:(E)1.

Mike Espy
Secretary of Agriculture
of the United States

3

We need to come to a better understanding about how poverty can be eradicated. Poverty has adamantly outlived the "War on Poverty," the New Deal and the Great Society; it has defied

the "Reagan Revolution" and [former President George] Bush's "kinder, gentler." Poverty is here and it is stronger . . . We have got to do it better.

At conference sponsored by
The Employment Network,
Washington, D.C., Feb. 16/
The Washington Post, 2-17:(A)2.

Amitai Etzioni
Sociologist,
George Washington University

4

[On life 60 years from now, in 2053]: On television, single parenting is suddenly chic. More middle-class whites are having children out of wedlock, and many children are being brought up by hired hands and a bewildering rotation of boyfriends and girlfriends. Sixty years ago [in 1993], people understood that children need the loving care of their parents. Will it take another 60 years to understand that again?

Interview/
U.S. News & World Report,
10-25:70.

Jim Florio
Governor of New Jersey (D)

5

I think that welfare, no matter how well-intentioned, has failed. It failed the people it was supposed to help because, instead of rewarding work, it trapped them in poverty and dependency. And it failed the taxpayers who, year after year, have been asked to foot the bill.

The New York Times, 9-20:(A)7.

Richard A. Gephardt
United States Representative,
D-Missouri

6

[Criticizing Republicans in Congress for questioning how to finance Federal relief for flooded areas of the Midwest and thus delaying that relief]: When you have unforeseen emergencies and circumstances that demand immediate action, you don't stop everything and go through

(RICHARD A. GEPHARDT)

a budget process. Not today, not when people are out of their houses. Not when people are un-employed. Not when people are working day and night putting up sandbags to save their lives.

Los Angeles Times, 7-28:(A)13.

W. Wilson Goode
Former Mayor
of Philadelphia (Pa.)

1

[We] need to examine carefully three central concerns: hunger, inadequate clothing and home-lessness. We can begin to alleviate these prob-lems without getting the government involved. To fight a drug war, you have to involve the govern-ment. To rebuild major parts of our cities, you have to involve the government. But not to address the problem of hunger. Not to provide adequate shelter for homeless families. Shelter is available in churches, in properties owned by churches, in facilities churches can lease out. There is enough clothing in our closets to clothe all the people who don't have adequate clothing—clothing we don't need and will never wear again. But what do we do? We sell this clothing at garage sales.

Interview/
Christianity Today, 4-5:25.

Vincent Gray
Director,
Department of Health
and Human Services
of the District of Columbia

2

I just don't think there are simplistic answers to what causes homelessness. But I know there is no point in getting a job for a person who is actively smoking crack [cocaine].

The Christian Science Monitor,
12-7:6.

Andrew Hacker
Professor of political science,
Queens (N.Y.) College

3

I'm about the only one who says that what we call welfare is one of the greatest successes this country has ever had. The typical woman on welfare is not a career welfare person. She's one of the millions of black and white women who has been on it for a while because they needed that kind of help, needed a couple of months or a year to put their lives together after the man left, before they went back to work. Welfare saved their lives.

Interview/Lear's, March:24.

Nicholas Lemann
National correspondent,
"The Atlantic" magazine

4

In a world historical context, poverty has never been put on the front burner. When [former President] Lyndon Johnson got up in January 1964 and declared a war on poverty, that was an extremely unusual event. It would be very hard to find any leader in any country at any time who did that. It takes an alignment of the planets to confront these issues head-on. To make matters worse, the Republicans created a wildly exag-gerated view of the "misdeeds" of the war on poverty and sold it to the American people. I wish [President Clinton] would start turning around the perception that anti-poverty pro-grams don't work . . . Millions of people have left the inner-city ghettos since 1970, and it's been a success story. That's what we should aim to do. We should aim to improve conditions in the ghetto to enable people to leave and get into the mainstream of American life.

Interview/
Mother Jones, March-April:7.

Alvin F. Poussaint
Associate professor
of psychiatry,
Harvard University
Medical School

5

[There's] a change in attitude about babies. We don't regard them as precious anymore. We don't protect them as much. We express more of our rage at them, we beat them up, and even kill them. We use them as pawns in our struggles with mates. We've been having a rash of murder-

(ALVIN F. POUSSAINT)

suicides all over the place—men killing their wives and children. It's also an indication of a breakdown in the transition of child-rearing skills from one generation to the next.

Interview, New York, N.Y./
Lear's, February:16.

Robert B. Reich
Secretary of Labor
of the United States

1

[On the Clinton Administration's plan for a summer jobs program for disadvantaged youths]: Giving a poor kid a job and some tutoring over the summer doesn't work miracles. Calling the eight to 10 weeks a failure because it fails to alone improve a young person's chance to lead a productive life is like condemning the school lunch program because it doesn't end malnutrition. An effort like this must be judged by its modest goal—in this case, to help poor kids retain over the summer what they learned before, and to give them a modicum of structure, discipline and work experience.

Los Angeles Times, 4-8:(A)5.

Robert D. Reischauer
Director,
Congressional Budget Office

2

[On the earned income tax credit, which President Clinton proposes to expand]: It really doesn't help you put bread on the table week after week. Nor does it clearly tie your work effort to your reward from work ... What it has become is very much like a winning lottery ticket at the end of the tax year.

The Washington Post, 3-6:(A)13.

3

Cutting entitlements sounds painless. But when you examine the specifics, you realize this is the third rail of American politics.

The New York Times, 6-8:(A)1.

Alexander Sanger
President,
Planned Parenthood
of New York City

4

[On government paying certain expenses of pregnant teenagers]: We policy-makers really don't understand young people. It's inevitable that one person's compassion becomes another's incentive. We want to take care of the child and the teen mother, but that can lead to teens looking at it as an incentive, a ticket out of the home. Their apartment is paid for by the city, they receive welfare and food stamps. So how do we do one without the other? We are all wrestling with that.

The New York Times, 12-2:(B)4.

William Donald Schaefer
Governor of Maryland (D)

5

I want to start the debate on how we can humanely reduce the number of children who are born to parents who cannot provide for them or who will not provide for them. I [am] worried about parents who won't accept responsibility for their children and who expect the state to be the provider. I have been in public office for more than 30 years, and in that time I've seen welfare rolls continue to grow. One reason is we haven't done enough to prevent unwanted pregnancies. Another reason is that we need to make parents more responsible for the children they have ... No one has ever accused me of not caring for people, of not wanting to help. But we have a runaway welfare system in this state, and the easiest thing in the world would be for me to leave it to the next guy to worry about.

State of the State address, Jan. 14/
The Washington Post, 1-15:(A)20.

Donna E. Shalala
Secretary of Health
and Human Services
of the United States

6

The thing that you have to remember about HHS is that there never is going to be a clear winner or clear losers. It's a complicated agency with complicated constituencies, and it's how we manage our way through that and get some things done that people will, in the end, judge our success or failure as an Administration. No issue is ever going to be pure for us. If I wanted something like that, I should have taken a smaller agency where there were some more straight-forward decisions, where you could just reverse a bunch of things the [former George] Bush Administration did; and walk away.

Interview/
Los Angeles Times, 7-18:(M)3.

1

We [in government] have to rework our programs so what they do is increase people's responsibilities for themselves, for their own lives; empowering them to go out, get off the public dole and go to work . . . It's a fundamentally different way for government to think. It involves people taking more responsibility for their lives, particularly low-income people, that have been beaten down over the years. It involves a change in culture. Asking the government to help you for short periods of time is different than asking the government to take care of you for the rest of your life.

Interview/
Los Angeles Times, 7-18:(M)3.

Judith Wallerstein
Director,
California Children
of Divorce Study

2

[On her study which concluded that children do not "get over" their parents' divorces]: We got angry letters from therapists, parents and lawyers saying we were undoubtedly wrong. They said children are really much better off being released from an unhappy marriage. Divorce, they said, is a liberating experience. [But] divorce is deceptive. Legally, it is a single event, but psychologically, it is a chain—sometimes a never-ending chain—of events, reloca-

tions and radically shifting relationships strung through time, a process that forever changes the lives of the people involved.

Interview/The Atlantic, April:65.

Maxine Waters
United States Representative,
D-California

3

This nation has always struggled with how it was going to deal with poor people and people of color. Every few years you will see some great change in the way that they approach this. We've had the war on poverty that never really got into waging a real war on poverty. There are those who say there was a backlash from white, middle-class Americans that didn't want to fund a war on poverty. It's no secret [that Democratic President] Bill Clinton did not campaign on a war-on-poverty idea. He talked a lot about the middle class, which a lot of us didn't like. But we didn't have a lot of choices [for President in 1992], did we?

Interview/
Los Angeles Times, 5-16:(M)3.

Cornel West
Professor of religion
and director of Afro-American
studies program,
Princeton University

4

I think young people need love, care and concern; on the other hand, they need economic opportunity, jobs and decent education. Those two are not identical but they are inseparable. You simply cannot live a life of any meaning and purpose without effective ties and supportive networks in your life. The hopelessness is often tied to a sense of rootlessness, no connections, no linkages. That's the cultural side. The economic side is, when there's massive unemployment, when there's decrepit education, the very notion of there being some sense of possibility, opportunity, wanes. The combination of these produces a level of self-destruction we've never seen in this country. It takes the form of a cold-hearted and mean-spirited disposition toward the world,

(CORNEL WEST)

toward one's own self. If one's self has no worth, then others have no worth. If one has no property, then other people's property has no worth.

Interview, Los Angeles, Calif./
Los Angeles Times, 5-9:(M)3.

Pete Wilson
Governor of California (R)

1

[On the problem of illegal immigrants in his state]: Enough people to fill a city the size of Oakland [Calif., almost 400,000] got past the border patrol over the past four years. The almost $3-billion in state tax dollars we are required to spend by Federal law on services for illegal immigrants is causing us to be unable to spend [on], and in some cases to [have to] cut, needed services for legal residents. We are required to provide prenatal care, obstetrics, delivery and postnatal care to illegals. I asked the Legislature for some kind of care for working-poor mothers— women who are not eligible to receive Medicaid—and they gave me what I wanted but cannot give me the funding because instead we are spending almost $3-billion on various services for illegals. To me, it is terribly unfair and wrong to be spending state tax dollars for illegal immigrants and declining it to working poor who are legal residents.

Interview, Los Angeles, Calif./
The Christian Science Monitor,
10-4:12.

Transportation

Langhorne M. Bond
Former Administrator,
Federal Aviation Administration

1

[Saying air-traffic controllers who were fired in 1981 for striking, and banned from being rehired, should now be taken back by the FAA]: [The strike] was a tragic mistake and we should never forget. But forgiveness is another thing. It is time for that . . . President Clinton has spoken in favor of Americans who live by the rules, and the strikers broke the rules [against striking]. They have had to accept the consequences of their act. They have been out of work for 12 years. I say, enough is enough. The punishment now fits the crime. They should once again be eligible to work for FAA.

Before Air Traffic Control Association,
March 22/The Washington Post, 3-22:(A)5.

Bob Carr
United States Representative,
D-Michigan

2

[Expressing reservations about Federal funding for a proposed high-speed rail system]: Everybody knows I'm a high-speed rail skeptic. There's a lot of hype and romance . . . I get real worried anytime I hear somebody devoted to the *mode* rather than to *transportation*, moving people and goods.

News conference,
Washington, D.C., April 28/
The New York Times, 4-29:(A)16.

Bill Clinton
President of the United States

3

[Announcing an alliance between the Federal government and the auto industry to develop the car of the future]: We intend to do nothing less then redefine the world car of the next century, to propel the [U.S.] auto industry to the forefront of world automobile production.

Washington, D.C., Sept. 29/
The Washington Post, 9-30:(A)1.

4

[On his intervention in the strike between flight attendants and American Airlines, which resulted in the parties agreeing to binding arbitration and an end to the strike]: I want to encourage all the people involved in the American Airlines family to now return to work together without any bitterness and with a spirit of mutual respect as they attempt to work through these issues through binding arbitration. This company and its employees are a very important part of the American economy, a very important part of the airline sector that has been troubled for the last couple of years and that is a very important part of our high-tech future.

News conference,
Washington, D.C., Nov. 22/
The New York Times, 11-23:(A)1.

David Cole
Director,
Office for the Study
of Automobile Transportation,
University of Michigan

5

[On Ford's claim to have had the Number 1 selling car in the U.S. in 1992]: A lot of people care about who is Number 1. It symbolizes the comeback of the American car company. American products are far more competitive than they were a few years ago, when the Japanese had superior quality and fit-and-finish.

The Christian Science Monitor,
1-8:8.

Robert L. Crandall
Chairman, AMR Corporation
(American Airlines)

6

[Criticizing the U.S. Transportation Department's approval of a $300-million investment in USAir by British Airways]: [The agreement] will have an adverse impact on the U.S. international trade balance. Moreover, it will shift

(ROBERT L. CRANDALL)

passengers, revenue, profits and jobs from U.S. carriers to British Airways at a time when the U.S. economy and U.S. workers need active and vigorous support.

March 15/
The New York Times, 3-16:(C)9.

David Davis
Editor,
"Automobile" magazine

1

[Saying claims by U.S. automobile makers such as Ford that they have increased their market share against imports is misleading because of all the financial incentives they have been offering]: [Ford's best-selling-car victory] doesn't change the automobile universe one bit. The hollow claim that "We're Number 1" only proves they're willing to give away the store.

The Christian Science Monitor,
1-8:8.

Al Gore
Vice President
of the United States

2

[On the Clinton Administration's new 10-year venture with the Big 3 car manufacturers to develop an automobile that gets three times today's gasoline mileage]: We think it's an enormous breakthrough. The goal has been consciously set at a point that lies beyond what we know how to do with current systems. Advances like this, a threefold increase in performance, are taken for granted over a 10-year period in the computer industry. Up until now there has been an assumption that only incremental change is possible in an industry like the auto industry. These three CEOs [of the Big 3] are rewriting the book . . . We have a strategic interest as a nation in meeting the goal we've set in this program. It's an act of patriotism but also an act of good business sense, because I predict this will result in breakthroughs that are likely to position our American auto industry to dominate the growing world market in the next century.

Interview, Sept. 28/
The New York Times, 9-29:(C)1,4.

Edwin Harper
President,
Association of American Railroads

3

The advantages of high-speed rail passenger service probably will never be expressed in terms of profitability. [But] the social benefits can be enormous in terms of reducing energy use, helping the environment, easing congestion and preserving the nation's transportation infrastructure.

The New York Times, 4-29:(A)16.

Denise Hedges
President,
Association of Professional
(airline) Flight Attendants

4

[On the recent American Airlines flight-attendants' strike]: It is critical and mandatory that management recognizes contributions of employees as a corporation's most valuable resource. While it's understood that business needs to be competitive, employees need recognition.

USA Today, 11-26:(A)11.

Herbert D. Kelleher
Chairman, Southwest Airlines

5

The [airline] industry historically has been profit-poor. The fact that the industry makes a little money is meaningless. The industry needs to make a lot of money. In the next decade, it'll need to spend $150-billion on new jets and renovation of airports. You cannot do that with a 2 percent net profit margin.

Interview, Aug. 25/
USA Today, 8-26:(B)2.

John McTague
Vice president
for technical affairs,
Ford Motor Company

6

[On the U.S. automobile industry in the 1980s]: I thought they were a bunch of Neanderthals. They were in trouble [because of foreign competition], they were way behind the tech-

(JOHN McTAGUE)

nological curve, they didn't have a hell of a lot of future and they deserved themselves. These guys were a bunch of losers. The U.S. auto industry [in the 1980s] was the kind of place you didn't want to be [working in].

Time, 12-13:65.

Federico F. Pena
*Secretary of Transportation
of the United States*

1

Generally speaking . . . most studies indicate that rail requires some kind of government involvement. My answer to that is, if it's a matter of public policy that we want to ensure that people can move efficiently, then there is a role for it. We do it today. We do it with Amtrak.

*Interview/
The Washington Post, 2-20:(A)11.*

2

My philosophy is that we ought to have competition in the airline industry. Three carriers alone is not good for competition in our country. On the other hand, what happened was we went through a period of deregulation and we were not very thoughtful about monitoring what was happening. So now we're trying to work through all of that . . . The range of issues are everything from looking at bankruptcy laws; looking at the effects of deregulation; looking at the aircraft-manufacturing industry; looking at tax relief. The question of capital. The issue of foreign investment. Do you know we have a law that allows foreign ownership of U.S. carriers? Should we rewrite that? Should we renew it? Should we change it? What should be our unified global strategy as we go about renegotiating bilateral agreements? All of those issues are going to be in the mix.

*Interview, March 10/
USA Today, 3-11:(A)11.*

3

[Saying the Clinton Administration supports the emergence of small, new airlines]: While we

will do whatever we can to support our existing carriers, so, too, will we do whatever we can to make sure fledgling carriers have a fair shot.

The New York Times, 5-19:(A)1.

4

[On the trend toward hostile relations between the airline industry and government-operated airports over such issues as landing fees]: The airline industry is experiencing financial stress. The cities and airport authorities have their own stresses, and the tensions between the parties . . . will be played out in a different atmosphere than in the last decade.

*Washington, D.C., Dec. 1/
Los Angeles Times, 12-2:(A)3.*

Joseph Phillippi
*Automobile analyst,
Lehman Brothers, investments*

5

[Saying Japanese cars have lost the sales advantage they had over U.S. cars in the past]: When there was a $500, even a $1,000, price difference between a domestic car and an import, the customer would say, "Well, it costs more, but I know I'm getting Japanese-level quality so I'll pay the extra bucks." Now with so many pressures on consumers, and with the price differential $2,500 or more, that suddenly adds up to serious money in the minds of many [buyers], and they're switching [to U.S. cars].

*U.S. News & World Report,
6-14:72.*

John Robson
*Former Chairman,
Civil Aeronautics Board
of the United States*

6

Once the government starts sticking its finger into the airline market, it's only a short step before you start regulating prices or routes or both. The fact of the matter is, there aren't very many good ways to manage a contraction.

The Washington Post, 2-23:(A)8.

Felix G. Rohatyn
Head of financial-status group,
Federal Commission
to Ensure a
Strong Competitive
Airline Industry

1

None of us has ever been exposed to an industry that plays such a role in the survival and financial life of the country as the airline industry . . . [and] it is so weak that [it] could not survive another shock, such as another war in the Middle East.

At U.S. Department of Commerce,
Washington, D.C./
The Washington Post, 7-8:(D)9.

Frank Shrontz
Chairman, Boeing Company

2

Back in the early days of the 707 [airliner], we [aircraft manufacturers] thought planes would last 10 years. Then, we got up to 15, 20 and 25, and now we are up to 30-year-old airplanes. Part of the reason they stay in service that long is because the new airplanes—even though they are more efficient, more comfortable—are not sufficiently so to force out those old planes.

Interview/
The Washington Post, 2-22:(A)9.

John F. Smith, Jr.
Chief executive officer,
General Motors Corporation

3

[The problem at GM and other U.S. automobile companies in the 1980s] was never the people. It was the screwed-up structure we had. We had to change it. It took us years to understand that. You go through a denial phase. Ford went through its own changes a lot earlier than we did, and is very good today. Chrysler really went to the wall and got its act together. We [at GM] had a history I'd like not to repeat. Now we'd like to get this baby fixed.

Time, 12-13:69.

Laura D'Andrea Tyson
Chairman,
Council of Economic Advisers
to President of the United States
Bill Clinton

4

[On Federal involvement in the aircraft industry]: This is an industry where there's no point in history—and unlikely to be any point in the future—in which outcomes in that industry are not influenced by government policy. That has to do with the nature of the industry. It tends to be, by its own making, influenced by government, and it tends also to have a major dual-use character [civilian and military] so that the government always will be involved either to try to make the market more competitive, to develop more than one supplier, or they'll always be involved because the major commercial aircraft producers are also the companies used for major military aircraft. So that [is] one [area] where we've already had industrial policy, and we always will.

Interview, Washington, D.C./
Los Angeles Times, 3-28:(M)3.

John Wallace
Project development manager,
electric-vehicle program,
Ford Motor Company

5

[On development of electrically powered cars]: We're mandating a completely new industry to come into being . . . But I don't expect any major breakthroughs. It's more like football: You get three yards at a time. We'll have to slog it out.

The Christian Science Monitor,
11-22:7.

Stephen M. Wolf
Chairman, United Airlines

6

[Announcing the cutting of 2,800 jobs at United]: [The airline industry] has developed into one of this country's major foreign-trade successes, and makes a major contribution to our national security. The national investment in this

WHAT THEY SAID IN 1993

(STEPHEN M. WOLF)

strategic industry is now at serious risk [because of the economic conditions in the industry], which has dangerous implications for our economy and our international competitiveness . . . The fundamental flaws in our industry . . . threaten our long-term financial health . . . This chaotic environment leaves us no choice but to take considerable and difficult steps to reduce our losses and ensure the long-term viability of United.

Jan. 6/
The Washington Post,
1-7:(A)1,18.

Jerry Abramson
Mayor of Louisville, Ky.;
President, United States Conference
of Mayors

1

[On being a Mayor in recent years]: Along with picking up the trash and catching criminals, you had to learn to be creative and innovative in attracting investment. You had to say, "If my community is going to be competitive, my schools have to be good, my city's skills-training has to be the best." That pushes you into a whole new dimension you never had 20 years ago, and it takes a lot of energy to keep it up. It's not like in the [movie] *The Last Hurrah* anymore, where you'd cut a lot of ribbons and smoke a few cigars. Those days are gone forever, and how long you can keep up the pace today changes from Mayor to Mayor. For a lot of these folks, the satisfaction is simply not there anymore.

The Washington Post, 10-11:(A)15.

David Axelrod
Democratic Party
political consultant

2

[On recent Republican Mayoral election victories in big cities such as New York, where Rudolph Giuliani was victorious]: Generally, where Republicans succeed is where Democrats offer them an opportunity [by fielding weaker candidates]. If the Democratic Party in New York had a candidate, whether white or black, who was identified like [Democrats Richard] Daley [of Chicago] and [Edward] Rendell [of Philadelphia] and [Michael] White [of Cleveland] with municipal reform, there wouldn't have been a place in this race for Giuliani.

Los Angeles Times, 11-4:(A)23.

Donald J. Borut
Executive director,
National League of Cities

3

The last decade has been a very difficult time for cities. Mayors realize they can't be heroic anymore. They can't come in and solve all the problems . . . [Being a Mayor is] an enormously demanding job, and to expect someone to make a lifetime career of it is unrealistic. They're on the cutting edge of dealing with the worst problems imaginable, and they can't run from hard decisions . . . They're scrutinized all the time, they're dealing with intractable problems and they get below-market pay. For what? The right to make decisions that are going to tick off half the people.

The Washington Post, 10-11:(A)15.

Bill Bradley
United States Senator,
D-New Jersey

4

It was less than a year ago that we watched Los Angeles explode in disorder across our television screens, followed by a parade of people saying it was time to do something about our cities. And, of course, nothing happened . . . We've had 12 years of neglect [of cities]. The fact of the matter is, cities are sicker and poorer than ever. We can't wait until the next urban crisis to start doing something.

At House subcommittee hearing,
Washington, D.C./
The Washington Post, 5-26:(A)6.

Tom Bradley
Mayor of Los Angeles, Calif.

5

I think term limits nationally, at state and local levels, will result in some problems for government agencies. When it takes you two years just to find the doors in City Hall, it makes it difficult to do your job. When a city has term limits, constituencies are denied the rise of their representatives through the power structure to positions of authority.

Interview, Los Angeles, Calif./
The Christian Science Monitor,
7-1:2.

Henry G. Cisneros
Secretary-designate
of Housing and Urban Development
of the United States

1

You can't solve problems of urban neighborhoods or rural communities by thinking just about HUD or . . . any single department. We've got to find ways to integrate resources so they work. For example, it's not enough to talk about housing in a neighborhood—we need to work with the Justice Department on matters of crime.
USA Today, 1-11:(A)9.

Henry G. Cisneros
Secretary of Housing
and Urban Development
of the United States

2

[On whether investment should be in bettering run-down areas of cities, or in the people who live there now so they can get out]: You must do both, because if you invest just in the people and their capabilities, then you leave behind whole areas of America, valuable real estate, physical stocks, massive investments, central-city areas which are wastelands.
The Washington Post, 2-24:(A)13.

William D. Eggers
Director, privatization center,
The Reason Foundation

3

[On recent elections in which a number of big cities with liberal Mayors elected new Mayors with a more centrist political stance]: Look around the country and what we're witnessing is the beginning stages of what will be the most fundamental reshaping of city halls since the Progressive Era ushered out Boss Tweed and Tammany Hall.
Los Angeles Times, 11-4:(A)23.

Thomas Ferguson
Political scientist,
University of Massachusetts,
Boston

4

When [Federal] budget crunches come, the cities get pushed to last. And when the government turns its back on cities, the business community generally follows suit.
The Christian Science Monitor,
4-28:4.

Frank Jordan
Mayor of San Francisco, Calif.

5

[On his city budget plan]: I've got a package that no one is going to like because it hits all sides equally. I'm laying people off, raising taxes, freezing salaries, reopening contract talks. A good politician tries to protect some constituency. I haven't done that.
Interview, San Francisco, Calif./
The Christian Science Monitor,
5-25:3.

Larry Ledebar
Director,
Center for Urban Studies,
Wayne State University

6

Cities and their suburbs grow and prosper together or they decline together . . . The model of a declining central city and prosperous suburbs is a very short-term one; it doesn't prove viable over the long term.
The Christian Science Monitor,
11-4:6.

Richard Moe
President,
National Trust
for Historic Preservation

7

I think communities and neighborhoods are richer for having older structures. There is nothing more sterile than to go into a totally new community and see nothing but steel and glass . . . [Mixing in] older structures not only is aesthetically pleasing, but it gives us a sense of where we came from as a community and a nation. Sometimes people see preservation as kind of frivolous; it's not. It's important to the livability of our communities . . . There is more

(RICHARD MOE)

to a community than bricks and mortar; there is really an element of spirit.

Interview, Washington, D.C./
The Christian Science Monitor,
5-14:12.

Mitchell Moss
Director,
Urban Research Center,
New York University

1

[On recent election victories by big-city Mayoral candidates with a centrist, rather than liberal, outlook]: Every generation produces a new cult of city governance. Now we are going through a new version of the reform era, with business practices brought into government. Whether it's privatization or less patronage, it's less government rather than more.

Los Angeles Times, 11-4:(A)23.

Ed Rendell
Mayor of Philadelphia, Pa.

2

[On his receiving praise for positively turning around the Philadelphia city government]: We've done nothing that other Mayors haven't done. We have just confronted problems in a way that maybe is novel because we've been forced to do it all at once. But privatization didn't start in Philadelphia . . . Reasonable contracts that cut the financial burden of cities didn't start with Philadelphia . . . We are a city that has raised taxes about 10 times in 11 years. If we don't raise taxes, that will allow us to have the opportunity to develop and grow our economy; but if we have to raise taxes again, you can forget it. People will be flooding out of this city.

Interview/
Los Angeles Times, 7-15:(A)5.

Shelby Steele
Professor of English,
San Jose (Calif.)
State University

3

There's no point in waiting for the government to redevelop [run-down urban] areas because it cannot possibly afford it. This is one of the biggest illusions we have now in American life, that we can somehow rebuild the inner cities for the people who live there. It simply cannot be done. It's an absurdity. We don't have those resources.

Interview/
Mother Jones, Jan.-Feb.:6.

Wellington E. Webb
Mayor of Denver, Colo.

4

My staff, as well as my kids, say I'm "fiscally tight." But it works. These are difficult times for cities. Nobody is coming to our rescue.

Interview, Denver, Colo./
Ebony, December:32.

PART TWO

International

Foreign Affairs

Mumtaz Ahmad
Professor of political science,
Hampton (Va.) University

1

[On concern about the spread of Islamic fundamentalism around the world]: The most important thing to remember is that not all Islamic revivalist movements are fundamentalist, that not all fundamentalists are political activists, and that not all political activists are radicals. There are very respectable Islamic fundamentalist movements in major Muslim societies that are part of the mainstream and part of the democratic electoral process, and that want to operate within a constitutional framework.

Time, 3-15:34.

Madeleine K. Albright
United States Ambassador/
Permanent Representative
to the United Nations

2

If there is one overriding principle that will guide me in this job, it will be the inescapable responsibility ... to build a peaceful world and to terminate the abominable injustices and conditions that still plague civilization.

Feb. 1/Time, 5-17:74.

3

We are in a period where all the kind of ways that we used to talk about nation-states and sovereignty are changing. There are beginning to be very ill-defined questions about what's internal and external ... Fewer and fewer issues are specifically internal affairs. Those redefinitions are evolving ... What is going to be harder are definitions of what are civil wars and what are cross-border wars, and how sovereignty defines all of that.

Interview, New York, N.Y./
Los Angeles Times, 5-2:(M)3.

4

The one thing about being U.S. Ambassador to the UN, I think, is, clearly, to have this job at this time is the luckiest and most fascinating thing that's ever happened to me, because it is a moment when the United States government believes that working within the United Nations is good and positive and useful.

Interview, New York, N.Y./
Los Angeles Times, 5-2:(M)3.

5

This [U.S. Clinton] Administration believes that whether an operation is multilateral or unilateral, whether the troops are U.S. or foreign, young men and women should not be sent in harm's way without a clear mission, competent commanders, sensible rules of engagement and the means required to get the job done.

At National War College,
Washington, D.C., Sept. 23/
Los Angeles Times, 9-24:(A)13.

6

The UN emerged from 40 years of Cold War rivalry overweight and out of shape. Today, the UN peacekeepers need reformed budget procedures, more dependable sources of military and civilian personnel, better training, better intelligence, better command and control, better equipment and more money.

At National War College,
Washington, D.C., Sept. 23/
Los Angeles Times, 9-24:(A)13.

Stephen Ambrose
Director, Eisenhower Center, University
of New Orleans (La.)

7

[Outgoing U.S. President George] Bush did a credible job as the American President who was

(STEPHEN AMBROSE)

lucky enough to be in office when the Cold War came to an end and the Berlin Wall came down. The debate among historians will center around those events, the big events of his Presidency. The debate will be: What did he do to bring those about? Was it just dumb luck to be there, or did he make a meaningful contribution? Did he react appropriately? Did he take advantage of opportunity? It all depends how it turns out.

The Christian Science Monitor,
1-19:4.

Kofi Annan
Undersecretary General
of the United Nations
for Peacekeeping Operations

1

People say that [international] peacekeeping is a growing business. We'd like to see it go the other way . . . I'll be very happy if we can resolve some of these issues and go home . . . I think we, as [UN] peacekeepers, have to be patient and persistent . . . It's not always possible to know when you are going to get a break . . . when people who have been fighting suddenly decide they have had enough.

Interview/
The Christitan Science Monitor,
6-16:7.

Les Aspin
Secretary of Defense-designate
of the United States

2

[With the end of the Cold War,] the super-power rivalry is gone. The stakes do not automatically go up every time the United States decides to use force. In [the] Vietnam [war of the 1960s and '70s], American policy-makers kept escalating our involvement because they were afraid of what our allies and adversaries would think and do if we withdrew.

U.S. News & World Report,
1-11:18.

J. Brian Atwood
Administrator, Agency for
International Development
of the United States

3

If you look at what is causing failed states, you'll find that it is population growtn, environmental degradation, the lack of economic growth and a total absence, in light of all the other three, of democracy and human rights.

Interview/
U.S. News & World Report,
11-29:40.

Bandar bin Sultan
Saudi Arabian Ambassador
to the United States

4

Media coverage and serious public discussion here [in the Western world] are out of focus when they use the label of "Islamic Fundamentalists" as to the various violence-prone groups currently causing trouble in parts of the Middle East and elsewhere. With their blatant extremism, such groups are actually doing violence to basic Islamic teachings—and certainly to Islam's good name. What they are really concerned with most is not Islam, but economic and other grievances or, more often, dead-end power for themselves. But please keep in perspective that these extremists are a very small fraction of the overall Islamic community. They are not at all in the historical or present Muslim mainstream.

Before International Road Federation,
Laguna Niguel, Calif., Aug. 19/
Los Angeles Times, 8-20:(B)2.

C. Fred Bergsten
Director,
Institute for International Economics
(United States)

5

The end of the Cold War has devalued the importance of traditional military and security issues. Economic issues are now the driving force of domestic affairs as well as overall international relations, and therefore a critical component in what kind of people are chosen to lead.

Los Angeles Times, 1-19:(H)14.

Joseph R. Biden, Jr.
United States Senator,
D-Delaware

1

[For the most part, State Department officials] aren't very inclined to want to deal [with terrorism and crime]. Most go to Georgetown School of Foreign Policy or the Fletcher School or Woodrow Wilson School, and their desire is not to be involved in law enforcement. They'd much rather carry treaties that have to do with arms control or the environment in their briefcases.

April/
The Washington Post, 7-22:(A)29.

John R. Bolton
Senior fellow,
Manhattan Institute
(United States);
Former Assistant Secretary
for International
Organization Affairs,
Department of State
of the United States

2

[Saying there are limits to the UN's peace-keeping capabilities]: The United Nations is overloaded. The demands on the organization have outpaced its capabilities. It has been the victim of its friends who have asked it to do too much.

The Washington Post, 6-15:(A)1,17.

Boutros Boutros-Ghali
Secretary General
of the United Nations

3

The reaction against the United Nations everywhere in the world shows that at last the United Nations is being active. You need patience, political imagination and time to make peace, and you also have your ups and downs.

News conference,
Addis Ababa, Ethiopia, Jan. 5/
The New York Times, 1-7:(A)4.

4

[On recent U.S. criticism of the way he is handling the job of UN Secretary General]: It is healthy. It proves that the United Nations is active. It proves that the United Nations takes positions. And I welcome all those criticisms. I may not share their point of view, which is normal, but I welcome them . . . If you take no action at all, certainly everybody will be quite happy with you.

Interview,
United Nations, New York/
Los Angeles Times, 3-6:(A)11.

5

The international community must take over from the states that fail to fulfill their [human-rights] obligations. Where sovereignty becomes the ultimate argument put forward by authoritarian regimes in order to conceal their abuse of men, women and children, such sovereignty . . . is already condemned by history.

At World Conference on Human Rights,
Vienna, Austria, June 14/
The Washington Post, 6-15:(A)15.

6

It must be understood that there will be failures as well as successes [by the UN]. The UN is not a magic wand. The problems before us cannot be solved quickly. Staying power is crucial. If the forces of chaos and corruption conclude that the United Nations is short of breath, they will prevail simply by waiting for the world to turn its attention elsewhere.

News conference,
New York, N.Y., Sept. 27/
The New York Times, 9-28:(A)4.

7

I am only the [UN] Security Council's servant, though not always its humble one . . . To put it bluntly, I have no power, no independence. You [the UN membership] are free to send the troops or not to send the troops. You are free to pay the money or not to pay the money. So unless I obtain your good will, I will not be able to do your

221

(BOUTROS BOUTROS-GHALI)

work . . . [In this job,] you're damned if you do and damned if you don't. If you're not trying to be authoritarian, they'll say there has to be a re-arrangement of your administration, that there has to be a strong United Nations. Et cetera, et cetera. And when you try to have a strong United Nations, they say you are becoming a general and a Pharoah.

Interview/
The New York Times, 10-16:1,7.

Bill Bradley
United States Senator,
D-New Jersey

1

[On U.S. President Clinton's push to have NAFTA passed by Congress]: It's the most important foreign-policy decision in the Clinton first term. It has profound implications for his ability to lead in the world.

At debate sponsored by
"U.S. News & World Report"/
U.S. News & World Report,
11-15:65.

Zbigniew Brzezinski
Counsellor,
Center for Strategic
and International Studies
(United States);
Former Assistant
to the President
of the United States
(Jimmy Carter)
for National Security Affairs

2

The world [today] is much more likely to be turbulent and tense, creating minimal stability . . . The 1970s were the period of maximum danger [for the West]. This is the period of maximum complexity.

The Christian Science Monitor,
1-5:4.

3

There'll be no clarity to the [international political] picture, as there has been in recent decades. It'll be much more confused, with both right and left as well as nationalism, ethnicity and religion increasingly interacting and clashing.

Los Angeles Times, 2-18:(A)13.

4

The essence of being a Churchill is to take difficult choices up front. The essence of Chamberlainism . . . is to defer, to obscure, and to propitiate.

Interview, Washington, D.C./
The Christian Science Monitor,
4-29:14.

George Bush
President of the United States

5

[On U.S. President-elect Bill Clinton]: I am one who wants very much to see Governor Clinton succeed as President . . . When I say to my [foreign] friends [such as French] President [Francois] Mitterrand that I believe he will find Governor Clinton a good man to work with on these important [global] problems, I can say that from the heart.

To reporters, Paris, France, Jan. 3/
The Washington Post, 1-4:(A)18.

Warren Christopher
Secretary of State-designate
of the United States

6

I do believe that the discreet and careful use of force in certain circumstances, and its credible threat in general, will be essential to the success of our diplomacy [in the forthcoming U.S. Clinton Administration]. [But] we cannot re-spond ourselves to every alarm. I want to assure the American people that we will not turn their blood and treasure into an open account for use by the rest of the world.

At Senate Foreign Relations Committee
hearing on his nomination,
Washington, D.C., Jan. 13/
Los Angeles Times, 1-14:(A)8.

Warren Christopher
Secretary of State
of the United States

1

American foreign policy in the years ahead will be grounded in what President Clinton has called the three pillars of our national interest. First, revitalizing our economy; second, updating our security forces for a new era; and third, protecting democracy as the best means to protect our own national security while expanding the reach of freedom, human rights, prosperity and peace. Our watchword always must be action, not reaction; timely prevention rather than costly cure.

Before House Appropriations Subcommittee,
Washington, D.C., March 10/
The Washington Post, 3-12:(A)22.

2

[Saying U.S. Embassies should be truthful in reporting human-rights violations by American-backed local forces, and not lie about them as seems to be indicated in new documents about El Salvador during the civil war there]: With my long interest in human rights, I want to make sure that the State Department in the future accurately reports human-rights conditions in the countries where we have Embassies. I think that the reporting by [U.S. diplomatic] officers there should be candid and honest and direct, and it should not be molded to fit political concerns . . . This is not a witch hunt. It is not a determination to try to find out whether somebody made a mistake in the past on our part, but to try to make sure that in the future our human-rights reporting is accurate; that an opportunity for the dissent of younger officers is available; and that when people testify here before the Congress, they are doing it based on what our assessment is, what our most honest assessment is in the countries where we have Embassies and representatives . . . We give priority to declassifying these documents where we can, barring some overwhelming national interest. And embarrassment is not a national interest.

Before Senate Appropriation
Foreign Operations Subcommittee,
Washington, D.C., March 30/
The Washington Post, 3-31:(A)18.

3

[The U.S. is] undertaking the role of the world's most prominent power. But we have to be careful; we have to jealously guard that power. If we were really threatened by something, if our national interests were at stake—for example, if somebody was invading us—of course we'd act alone . . . But there's a hierarchy of interests that are involved . . . We can't do it all. We have to measure our ability to act in the interests of the United States, but to save our power for those situations which threaten our deepest national interest, at the same time doing all we can where there's a humanitarian concern.

Interview, Washington, D.C.,
May 26/The Washington Post,
5-27:(A)45.

4

[Calling for a tougher world stance against human-rights abuses]: Those who desecrate these rights must know that they will be ostracized. They will face sanctions. They will be brought before tribunals of international justice. They will not gain access to assistance or investment . . . We must sharpen the tools of human-rights diplomacy to address problems before they escalate into violence and create new pariah states.

At United Nations World Conference
on Human Rights,
Vienna, Austria, June 14/
Los Angeles Times, 6-15:(A)14.

5

[Multilateralism] is warranted only when it serves the central purpose of American foreign policy, to protect American interests. This country will never subcontract its foreign policy to another power or another person.

Speech, New York, N.Y., Sept. 20/
The New York Times, 9-23:(A)4.

6

In protecting our vital national interests, this [U.S. Clinton] Administration is doing extremely well. Our support for [Russian President Boris]

(WARREN CHRISTOPHER)

Yeltsin; our involvement in the Middle East peace process; what we've done in [nuclear] non-proliferation with Russia, China, North Korea; promoting global economic growth. President Clinton's leadership doesn't have to give anything away to [former] President [George] Bush, and that's putting it mildly.

> *Interview,*
> *Washington, D.C., Oct. 8/*
> *Time, 10-18:46.*

1

One of the jobs of policy-makers is to make sure to keep our eye on the ball and make a steady focus on the big issues. Not be thrown off our course by the small issues . . . In this world of instantaneous communication . . . the whole world can see events that happen in a small country in Africa or some place in Asia. Naturally, Americans are drawn to this. [The Clinton policy will be to emphasize] the big issues on which we're working, on which we've made very considerable achievements.

> *Interview, Oct. 28/*
> *USA Today, 10-29:(A)2.*

Bill Clinton
President-elect
of the United States

2

This is a very troubled world we live in. We are seeing the flip side of the wonder of the end of the Cold War. The bipolar world gave the U.S. and the Soviet Union a limited capacity to contain some of what we are now witnessing in Bosnia [the ethnic conflict there]. I'm worried about what is happening in Russia. I think it's all eminently predictable that there would be some setbacks.

> *Interview, Little Rock, Ark./*
> *Time, 1-4:36.*

3

I still think our first priority is to rebuild America at home, economically and otherwise. I

still intend to do those things which I laid out in the [Presidential-election] campaign to try to increase our investment focus, to try to make us more competitive, to try to generate jobs and raise incomes. But a part of my job, especially now at this moment in our history, is not only to tend to these fires that have been burning, but also to develop an approach to the world which will permit us to have a post-Cold War world that is a good place for freedom and democracy and market economics, and which supports global growth and minimizes global misery. I just think that's a part of the job [of being President].

> *Interview,*
> *Little Rock, Ark., Jan. 13/*
> *The New York Times, 1-14:(A)8.*

4

The foreign policy of my Administration will be built upon three pillars. First, we will make the economic security of our own nation a primary goal of our foreign policy. Here in America we cannot sustain an active engagement abroad without a sound economy at home . . . Second, our foreign policy will be based on a restructuring of our armed forces to meet new and continuing threats to our security interests and the international peace . . . Third, my Administration's foreign policy will be rooted in the democratic principles and institutions which unite our own country and to which so many now around the world aspire. The spread of democratic values has given the hope of freedom to millions all across the world who have endured decades of oppression. Whenever possible, we will support those who share our values because it is in the interests of America and the world at large for us to do so.

> *To diplomats,*
> *Georgetown University, Jan. 18/*
> *The New York Times, 1-19:(A)8.*

Bill Clinton
President of the United States

5

Foreign aid is unpopular in every country in the world, and it's always been unpopular here [in the U.S.]. I realize that the responsibility is

(BILL CLINTON)

on me to communicate to the American people any kind of [aid] package I propose and to justify it. That's my responsibility, and I intend to assume it.

Little Rock, Ark.,
March 29/USA Today, 3-30:(A)4.

1

During the Cold War, our foreign policies largely focused on the relations among nations. Our strategies sought a balance to keep the peace. Today our policies must also focus on relations *within* nations, on a nation's form of governance, on its economic structure, on its ethnic tolerance. These are of concern to us for they shape how these nations treat their neighbors as well as their own people, and whether they are reliable when they give their word.

Before American Society of Newspaper Editors,
Annapolis, Md., April 1/
The New York Times, 4-2:(A)6.

2

There is no clear dividing line between domestic and foreign policy. The end of the long, twilight [Cold War] struggle does not ensure the start of a long peace . . . Now, not fear, but vision must drive our investment and engagement in this new world.

Before American Society of Newspaper Editors,
Annapolis, Md., April 1/
USA Today, 4-2:(A)4.

3

We learn again and again that the world has yet to run its course of animosity and violence. Ethnic cleansing in the former Yugoslavia is but the most brutal and blatant and ever-present manifestation of what we see also with the oppression of the Kurds in Iraq, the abusive treatment of the Baha'i in Iran, the endless race-based violence in South Africa.

At dedication of Holocaust Memorial Museum,
Washington, D.C., April 22/
The New York Times, 4-23:(A)14.

4

[U.S.] involvement in multilateral efforts need not be open-ended or ill-defined. We can go abroad and accomplish some distinct objectives and then come home again when that mission is accomplished . . . Some will ask why we must so often be the ones to lead. Well, of course we cannot be the world's policeman, but we are and we must continue to be the world's leader. That is the job of the United States of America.

Welcoming U.S. troops back from
peacekeeping in Somalia,
Washington, D.C., May 5/
The Washington Post, 5-6:(A)40.

5

Ultimately, the key for reforming the United Nations, as in reforming our own government, is to remember why we are here and whom we serve. It is well to recall that the first words of the UN Charter are not, "We, the governments," but "We, the peoples of the United Nations." That means in every country the teachers, the workers, the farmers, the professionals, the fathers, the mothers, the children from the most remote village in the world to the largest metropolis—they are why we gather in this great hall. It is their futures that are at risk when we act or fail to act. And it is they who ultimately pay our bills.

At United Nations,
New York, Sept. 27/
The New York Times, 9-28:(A)4.

6

In recent weeks in the [UN] Security Council, our nation has begun asking harder questions about proposals for new peacekeeping missions. Is there a real threat to international peace? Does the proposed mission have clear objectives? Can an exit point be identified for those who will be asked to participate? How much will the mission cost? From now on, the United Nations should address these and other hard questions for every proposed mission before we vote and before the mission begins.

At United Nations, New York, Sept. 27/
The New York Times, 9-28:(A)4.

(BILL CLINTON)

1

[On criticism of his handling of foreign policy]: It's easy for people who don't have these responsibilities to use words like "naive" or this, that or the other thing. The truth is we're living in a new and different world, and we've got to try to chart a course that is the right course for the United States to lead, while avoiding things that we cannot do or things that impose costs in human and financial terms that are unacceptable for us.

News conference,
Washington, D.C., Oct. 14/
The New York Times, 10-15:(A)5.

2

[Criticizing attempts by some in Congress to restrict his ability to commit U.S. troops to the conflicts in Haiti, Bosnia and elsewhere without prior Congressional approval]: I want to resist, and I urge the Senate not to vote for, things which unduly infringe on the President's power . . . All I can tell you is that I think that I have a big responsibility to try to appropriately consult with members of Congress in both parties in a wide way whenever we are in the process of making a decision which might lead to the use of force. I believe that. But I think that, clearly, the Constitution leaves to the President, for good and sufficient reasons, the ultimate decision-making authority.

Interview,
Washington, D.C., Oct. 18/
The New York Times, 10-19:(A)1,4.

3

[Following World War I,] we [the U.S.] neglected during a careless peace what had been so dearly won in a relentless war. We turned our backs on the rest of the world. We ignored new signs of danger. We let our troops and arms fall out of readiness. We neglected opportunities for collective security in our own national interests. We succumbed to the siren song of protectionism and erected walls against peaceful commerce with other nations. Soon, we had a Great Depression and soon that

depression led to aggression and then to another world war, one that would claim a half-million American lives. Let us today resolve [that] we will not shrink from the responsibilities necessary to keep our nation secure and our people prosperous.

Veterans Day address at Arlington
National Cemetery, Nov. 11/
The New York Times, 11-12:(C)17.

4

More than ever, our security is tied to economics. Military threats remain, and they require our vigilance and resolve; but increasingly, our place in the world will be determined as much by the skills of our workers as by the strength of our weapons, as much by our ability to pull down foreign trade barriers as our ability to breach distant ramparts.

At Asia-Pacific Economic Cooperation conference,
Seattle, Wash., Nov. 19/
The New York Times, 11-20:5.

5

[On the proliferation of nuclear-bomb material in the post-Cold War world]: I think it is fair to say that there is somewhat more disarray in the system, by which not only nuclear but other weapons of mass destruction are capable of being produced and distributed, than there was [during the Cold War]. In other words, the bipolar [the West vs. Soviet Union] world had a little more discipline, certainly on the nuclear side.

Interview, Washington, D.C./
Newsweek, 12-13:35.

Kresimir Cosic
Deputy Croatian Ambassador
to the United States

6

[Working in an Embassy is] not the diplomatic life you read about in the books, with chauffeurs and big parties. In this business, whenever there is a crisis everyone has to focus on solving the crisis. Of course, that puts you behind on everything, so you're permanently in crisis.

The New York Times, 5-18:(A)1.

Ralf Dahrendorf
Anglo-German historian

1

[The current ethnic conflict in] Yugoslavia is a symbol of something that will be present everywhere. I suspect we will live in a world of tribalism, which means intolerance within and enmity without.

U.S. News & World Report, 1-18:56.

Michael Dewar
Deputy director,
International Institute
for Strategic Studies
(Britain)

2

[On U.S. President Clinton]: We started with a clear impression of a man with a lack of knowledge, background and depth when it comes to foreign policy. Now that's been followed by a lack of decision-making.

Newsweek, 5-24:23.

Robert J. Dole
United States Senator,
R-Kansas

3

[On suggestions that UN Secretary General Boutros Boutros-Ghali is telling the U.S. what to do in such places as Bosnia, where an ethnic war is taking place]: The last time I checked, the American people did not elect Boutros-Ghali to run U.S. foreign policy. And while it may be tempting to toss things in Boutros-Ghali's lap in view of the many domestic problems and challenges we face, we need to remember that American strength is derived not only from our economic power and military muscle, but from our leadership abroad.

Before National Governors' Association,
Tulsa, Okla., Aug. 17/
The Washington Post, 8-18:(A)25.

Peter F. Drucker
Professor of social sciences
and management,
Claremont (Calif.) Graduate School

4

[U.S. President] Clinton can be guaranteed to be a failure in international affairs because

nobody can be anything else. Nobody can predict what's going to happen tomorrow. Nor can you be prepared for it.

Interview, Claremont, Calif./
The Christian Science Monitor,
8-26:12.

William Durch
International security specialist,
Henry L. Stimson Center
(United States)

5

The most pessimistic aspect of the [international] arms-sale story is that most of the budding conflicts today are the result of the weapons scattered around the world during the Cold War, mainly the lower-end arms with which the world has become awash courtesy of the past half-century. The breadth and depth of armament in general is already such that you can't expect to dampen or avoid conflict because people don't have guns, which might have been true of the first half of the century.

Los Angeles Times, 8-17:(H)5.

Lawrence S. Eagleburger
Secretary of State
of the United States

6

[Saying the incoming U.S. Clinton Administration should avoid trying to impose U.S. ethical standards on foreign countries it deals with]: [Current U.S.] President Bush resisted this tendency throughout his Presidency, often at great political cost [at home]. But because of his commitment to working with, and maintaining leverage over, governments that his critics deemed [only] worthy of punishment and isolation . . . he was able consistently to forge international coalitions under UN auspices to address critical challenges to world peace and stability.

Before Council on Foreign Relations,
Jan. 7/
Los Angeles Times, 1-9:(A)4.

7

We are in the middle of a global revolution, a period of change and instability equaled in modern times only by the aftermath of the French and Russian revolutions. The status quo everywhere is under siege.

*Before Council on Foreign Relations,
Jan. 7/
Los Angeles Times, 2-18:(A)13.*

Michel Foucher
*Director,
European Geopolitical
Observatory (France)*

1

Since the [1991 Persian] Gulf war, a certain directorate has begun to function in international affairs, encompassing the permanent members of the [UN] Security Council, and then Germany and Japan. Although no one uses the name, this "directorate" was put into place by [former U.S. President George] Bush. [Current U.S. President] Clinton is demonstrating by his early consultations with Russia that he intends to pursue it, and [French President Francois] Mitterrand understands the necessity of continuing in that direction, and with France very present.

The Christian Science Monitor, 3-8:3.

Robert M. Gates
*Former Director
of Central Intelligence
of the United States*

2

[Spying is] a risky business, and every now and then one of those operations is going to blow up in your face. But if you want to know more about proliferation and terrorism, you have to take risks. Congress and the Executive Branch have accepted that. But when one of those operations blows up, they also have to remember it.

Newsweek, 4-12:32.

Newt Gingrich
*United States Representative,
R-Georgia*

3

The fact is, [with the Cold War over and the Soviet Union no more], we [in the U.S.] can afford a fairly ignorant Presidency now. It'll just be a mess. [U.S. President Clinton] is entering a world which is tactically more dangerous but strategically safer. Twenty or thirty little messes [around the world] can be very debilitating. You can bleed to death from lots of little cuts.

Interview/The Atlantic, June:28.

Mikhail S. Gorbachev
*Former President
of the Soviet Union*

4

[Sixty years from now, in 2053,] the political map will have changed greatly. Perhaps the very model for coexistence among states will be replaced by interstate formations. Our very understanding of democracy will probably change. But I would like to believe that the meaning of "the power of the people" will not change, and this power will be realized fully.

*Interview/
U.S. News & World Report,
10-25:73.*

Alan Greenspan
*Chairman,
Federal Reserve Board
(United States)*

5

[On countries in the East which are in transition from a Communist-controlled economy to a free market]: A formal legal structure which defines and protects property rights and trade through the laws of contract and bankruptcy must pre-exist before a viable sophisticated market economy can emerge from the remnants of a centrally planned one. Even now, many potential [outside] investors in these newly emerging economies fear that a signed contract, which has the force of law and is backed by the police powers in the West, is nothing more than an autograph in some economies of the East. In addition to a legal structure, a functioning market economy also requires a number of business professions, professions that have no purpose and hence no existence in a centrally planned system. I speak of accountants, auditors and marketing spe-

(ALAN GREENSPAN)

cialists, all those professions whose activities are an integral part of the mechanism of production and distribution in a market economy, functions which are accomplished by state orders . . . in a centrally planned economy.

At State Department conference
for business executives,
Washington, D.C., Oct. 20/
The Washington Post, 10-22:(A)22.

Lee H. Hamilton
United States Representative,
D-Indiana

1

You can't use military power without strong public backing. Even during the Cold War, when the U.S. security situation was more urgent and perilous, most interventions [overseas by the U.S.] were fiercely debated [at home].

The Christian Science Monitor,
2-3:2.

Hurst Hannum
Specialist in international law,
Fletcher School of Law
and Diplomacy,
Tufts University (United States)

2

The temptation [for outside parties] just to walk away [from a conflict] where no one wants to stop fighting is getting stronger and stronger. It's only been in the last couple of years that the UN has been thinking about taking this active, aggressive role in going in and essentially forcing settlements. Nobody's been very good at that, and the UN really isn't any better.

The Christian Science Monitor,
6-15:4.

John G. Healey
Executive director,
Amnesty International

3

We always thought that once we got rid of Communism, it'd be a nice world. But instead,

things are worse. Human rights remains a daily struggle in every country in the world, including this one [the U.S.].

Los Angeles Times, 2-28:(M)1.

Stanley Hoffmann
Chairman,
Center for European Studies,
Harvard University
(United States)

4

[Saying U.S. President Clinton has not been controlling American foreign policy as strongly as he should]: [Secretary of State Warren] Christopher is, above all, an excellent negotiator and diplomat, but there is a difference between being a negotiator who carries out policy and setting policy. If the President is not the person who is setting the policy, then one needs either in the NSC or in the State Department someone who can set the policy. There's kind of a vacuum there.

The New York Times, 6-1:(A)3.

Ernest F. Hollings
United States Senator,
D-South Carolina

5

[On Geneva, Switzerland, as a site for international conferences and negotiations]: Everybody likes to go to Geneva. I used to do it for the Law of the Sea conferences. And you'd find these potentates from down in Africa, you know, rather than eating each other, they'd just come up and get a good square meal in Geneva.

Washington, D.C./
The New York Times, 12-16:(A)18.

Jesse L. Jackson
American civil-rights leader

6

[On the U.S. Clinton Administration's foreign-policy record]: We hosted the Middle East peace signing, [but] we did nothing to make it happen. Haiti has made us blink. If we can't get past Haiti and Bosnia, then maybe we can't get past North Korea. To be a superpower does require resolve. You have to use it or lose it.

Interview/
U.S. News & World Report,
12-27:82.

Max Kampelman
Former United States diplomat

1

I think the world was ready for a [U.S. President] Bill Clinton leadership [in foreign policy], but Bill Clinton wasn't ready. Our President has a capacity to lead, but he started out falling flat on his face.

Time, 7-12:43.

Mickey Kantor
United States Trade Representative

2

Because [Bill Clinton is] the first American President elected since the end of the Cold War, he views the world differently than any President we've ever had. The President and other people around him have talked about this a lot. There is a generational change, and it comes at a time when the world is changing enormously.

The Washington Post, 4-20:(A)6.

Julius Katz
Former Deputy United States
Trade Representative

3

For all the frustrations of the multilateral system, you keep coming home to it. We're a world power with interests in every corner of the globe, and we need global rules to advance them.

U.S. News & World Report,
12-13:79.

Bilahari Kausikan
Director,
East Asia and Pacific Bureau,
Foreign Ministry of Singapore

4

For the first time since the Universal Declaration [of Human Rights] was adopted in 1948,

countries not thoroughly steeped in the Judeo-Christian and natural-law traditions are in the first rank [economically]. That unprecedented situation will define the new international politics of human rights. It will also multiply the occasions for conflict.

Newsweek, 11-29:47.

5

The traditional notion of sovereignty [of nations] is being eroded by the influence of television, environmental concerns and the United Nations. This tension is the defining characteristic of our time. There is a false debate on whether human rights is relative to a country's conditions or whether they are absolute. Of course, there are universal values, but the core of the values is smaller than the West believes. The debate is over the way that international norms are set, and that depends on the global distribution of power.

The Christian Science Monitor,
12-15:12.

John Kerry
United States Senator,
D-Massachusetts

6

[On the proliferation of "mafias" around the world]: Organized crime [is] the new Communism, the new monolithic threat.

Newsweek, 12-13:20.

Henry A. Kissinger
Former Secretary of State
of the United States

7

We [the U.S.] have an unusual approach to foreign policy as a nation, which we take for granted. If you read what American Presidents have said since the turn of the century about foreign policy . . . [most Presidents] have prided themselves that America has no interest in the world. Whenever we've done something, we've said it's selfless, we don't do it for ourselves, we do it for mankind, we do it for principle, we do it for law, we do it for anything

(HENRY A. KISSINGER)

other than the American national interest . . . The question we have to answer is: For what purposes can American military force be used without our getting ourselves into the position of world policeman and yet contributing to world peace?

Speech sponsored by Town Hall of California,
Los Angeles, Calif., July 19/
Los Angeles Times, 7-23:(B)2.

Andrei V. Kozyrev
Foreign Minister of Russia

1

There is a simple fact that Russia and the United States are two nuclear giants which can pose a mortal threat to each other. This of course is true only due to the legacy of distorted vision of each other and the lethargy of reason which was with us in the Cold War. This lethargy of reason brought up the monsters of mutual fear, hostility and distrust. The main reason for a suicidal frame of mind and the resulting confrontation was of course the Soviet totalitarian system. But it is also true that this is fed by hegemonic designs and unfortunate schemes, be it *Pax Americana* or *Pax Sovietica* or claims which we see today for religious or ethnic exclusivity.

At American University,
Washington, D.C., March 24/
The Washington Post, 3-26:(A)24.

Anthony Lake
Assistant to President
of the United States
Bill Clinton
for National Security Affairs

2

Public pressure for [American] humanitarian engagement [overseas] increasingly may be driven by televised images, which can depend in turn on such considerations as where CNN sends its camera crews. But we must bring other considerations to bear as well—cost feasibility, the permanence of the improvement our assistance will bring, the willingness

of regional and international bodies to do their part and the likelihood that our actions will generate broader security benefits for the people and the region in question.

At Johns Hopkins School
of Advanced International Studies,
Sept. 21/
The New York Times, 9-22:(A)18.

3

While there will be increasing calls on [the U.S.] to help stem bloodshed and suffering in ethnic conflict [in the world], and while we will always bring our diplomacy to bear in such conflicts . . . there will be relatively few intra-national ethnic conflicts that justify our military intervention. Ultimately, on these and other humanitarian needs, we will have to pick and choose, although we will always do our best.

At Johns Hopkins School
of Advanced International Studies,
Sept. 21/
The Washington Post, 9-22:(A)16.

4

Geography and history always have made Americans wary of foreign entanglements. Now economic anxiety fans that wariness. Calls [from] the left and right to stay at home rather than engage abroad are reinforced by the rhetoric of the neo-know-nothings.

At Johns Hopkins School
of Advanced International Studies,
Sept. 21/
The Washington Post, 9-22:(A)16.

5

Our interest in democracy and markets do not stand alone. Other American interests at times will require us to befriend and even defend non-democratic states for mutually beneficial reasons. Our strategy must also view democracy broadly. It must envision a system that includes not only elections but such features as an independent judiciary and protections of human rights. Democracy and human rights are inseparable. Our strategy must also respect diversity. Democracy and markets can come in many legitimate variants. Freedom has many faces.

At Johns Hopkins School
of Advanced International Studies,
Sept. 22/
The Christian Science Monitor,
9-29:19.

John le Carre
Author;
Former member
of British Intelligence

1

What we've seen again and again [in intelligence organizations], when there's been a Watergate or there's been something else, is this curious mixture that includes the real zealots who believe they can repair the inadequacies of the democratic system by doing unofficial things. They think they're the heroes. Then you see the total misfits who need to take shelter in secret rooms and who actually get off being secretive. It is actually only very excited, over-stimulated men on very short sleep, together with all the toys of supersecrecy and the helicopters and the special passes, that inevitably produce irrational behavior. But those people, when they began, were ordinary guys; they were like us. Noel Annan, who was in British intelligence for years, said nobody should be allowed to do it more than three years, that one way of keeping an intelligence service sane is to have it run entirely by temporary people.

Interview/Time, 7-5:33.

Ernest Lefever
Senior fellow,
Ethics and Public Policy Center
(United States)

2

There is a growing tendency to rely on the United Nations, but there is no such thing as

UN power in reality. There is only the power of the member states.

The Washington Post, 6-15:(A)17.

Joseph I. Lieberman
United States Representative,
D-Connecticut

3

[In the U.S.,] it isn't hawks and doves anymore. It's internationalists and isolationists. The question is, are you prepared to use force in behalf of principles, or just to protect the national interest. Traditional liberals are more ready to use force for a principle, as in Bosnia. Traditional conservatives are ready to use force where there is a national interest, as in the Persian Gulf. And some of us are prepared to use force in both cases.

Los Angeles Times, 1-13:(A)7.

Liu Hua-qiu
Deputy Foreign Minister
of China

4

[Arguing against countries requiring specific human-rights standards for other countries]: Other countries have no right to interfere. The right of each country to formulate its own policies on human-rights protection in light of its own conditions should . . . be respected and guaranteed.

At United Nations World Conference
on Human Rights,
Vienna, Austria, June 15/
Los Angeles Times, 6-17:(A)6.

Edward Luck
President,
United Nations Association
of the U.S.A.

5

[On recent UN peace-keeping operations in various countries]: The Security Council nations have ordered up a whole slew of new operations when they don't have deep national interests in the outcomes. You get a great credibility gap because they often don't have the political will to back up the resolutions.

The Washington Post, 6-15:(A)17.

Richard G. Lugar
United States Senator,
R-Indiana

1

[President Clinton has abandoned] American leadership and decisiveness [in the world] in favor of "multilateralism" and the desire to pursue consensus. The President has given the impression of lacking a policy of his own, seeking, instead, to gauge what will sell. How many potential aggressors . . . will now feel that they can defy the international community with impunity—that the West is all bark and no bite?

Before Overseas Writers Club,
Washington, D.C., June 24/
Los Angeles Times, 6-25:(A)16.

Barbara MacDougall
Secretary for External Affairs
of Canada

2

In many situations [of conflict in today's world], we just cannot wait any longer for the beginnings of political settlement before acting, nor can we allow ourselves to be held hostage by factions which see no advantage in peace. Intervening [in foreign conflicts] without being invited by all parties to a dispute has made the job of attaining peace riskier, both politically and militarily.

The Washington Post, 4-27:(A)10.

Lewis Mackenzie
General,
Canadian Armed Forces;
Former Commander,
United Nations forces
in Bosnia-Herzegovina

3

The UN charter says, don't get involved in internal situations. Yet here we are sending troops into Bosnia, into Somalia, both civil wars. There are no clearly defined political objectives. And once the [UN] peacekeepers are in the field, the political and diplomatic work to support them is not done.

Interview/
World Press Review, October:15.

Michael Mandelbaum
Foreign-policy specialist,
School of Advanced
International Studies,
Johns Hopkins University
(United States)

4

[On the forthcoming G-7 summit in Tokyo]: What we have in Tokyo is a meeting of the world's strongest countries but the world's weakest leaders.

Time, 7-12:42.

Abdelhamid Mehri
Secretary general,
National Liberation Front
of Algeria

5

[Criticizing Western governments for their support of dictatorships and authoritarian regimes in Third World countries]: The masses see Western attitudes as a continuation of Western aggression. When it comes to Western values such as human rights, social justice and democracy, the West hesitates to believe they are valid for the Third World.

The Christian Science Monitor,
4-28:11.

Jose-Maria Mendiluce
Chief,
United Nations refugee program
in the former Yugoslavia

6

[On the UN relief effort in the conflict in what used to be Yugoslavia]: Maybe our greatest success here has been that for the first time we have established the principle that the world community has the right to humanitarian intervention in a country during wartimes. We are using all the tools we have to penalize those who use force against others. We aren't doing enough, but we have established a very important new direction.

Interview, Belgrade, Yugoslavia/
The New York Times, 5-18:(A)6.

George J. Mitchell
United States Senator,
D-Maine

1

The fundamental policy of the United States regarding our role in the post-Cold War world should be addressed in a comprehensive manner rather than by a series of piecemeal actions, or reactions, to particular international situations.

News conference,
Washington, D.C., Oct. 22/
The Washington Post, 10-23:(A)5.

Richard M. Nixon
Former President
of the United States

2

The latest Gallup Poll I saw found 4 percent of American people care about foreign policy—any foreign policy. Last week we had another example—[President] Clinton appeared on a town meeting in Michigan, a national town meeting, where he took questions, no holds barred. There was only one question about foreign policy . . . In view of that, any politician is going to say, "Well, I'm going to concentrate on domestic policy." But it's the responsibility of a leader to educate the people so they will support what needs to be done. Putting it more simply, you don't take people where they want to go; you take people where they ought to go.

Interview, Moscow, Russia/
The New York Times, 2-19:(A)4.

Augustus Richard Norton
Political scientist,
Boston University
(United States);
Former United Nations specialist
on the Middle East

3

[Saying there will be a wide-ranging impact of the recently signed Israel-PLO mutual-recognition agreement]: Skeptics have argued that the end of the Cold War is back to the future, to a horrible period of internecine conflict and bloodshed [in the world]. But today's

dramatic handshake [between Israeli Prime Minister Yitzhak Rabin and PLO leader Yasir Arafat] on the White House lawn offered a very different conclusion, and that is that the rules have changed on the international scene. And while we have tired of cliches like the "new world order," we really are living in a new age, when conflicts deemed long insoluble will yield to resolution, in an age when great-power adversaries will see the wisdom of stability and peace.

Sept. 13/
Los Angeles Times, 9-14:(A)12.

4

The state system—with its armies and diplomatic privileges and sovereignty—survives. But parallel to the state system now is a system of non-sovereign or non-state actors, sometimes local but sometimes crossing boundaries, because the communications revolution has enabled them to maneuver around state restrictions and laws and surveillance . . . Sustaining democracy requires more than just reforming laws to open up the political system or creating a large middle class. It also requires opening up political space where contending opinions are given a voice. The real home of democracy is civil society, because without a vibrant and autonomous civil society, elections no matter how pristine, no matter how mechanically perfect, are unlikely to produce durable results.

Los Angeles Times, 10-12:(H)4.

Shimon Peres
Foreign Minister
of Israel

5

For the last 75 years, the American foreign policy, as the European foreign policy, was basically busy with the threat of the Soviet Union, the military and ideological threat. Now [with the dissolution of the Soviet Union] all of us lost an enemy, but we have discovered a problem. And in the heart of the new agenda will be the political issues, the human issues, the issues of life and death and sickness. And

(SHIMON PERES)

we have really to rearrange our thinking and our work in accordance with the new agenda.

Broadcast interview/
"Good Morning America,"
ABC-TV, 2-17.

1

World history would never have been what it is without the strength and the generosity of the United States. When in war, they're on your side. When at peace, they're at your service and never asking for a return but peace and freedom . . . We do not have any real opportunities to say a simple word to the American people: Thank you for what you are to all of us.

News conference,
Washington, D.C., Sept. 13/
U.S. News & World Report,
9-27:16.

Colin L. Powell
General, United States Army;
Chairman, Joint Chiefs of Staff

2

The debates that we're seeing now about unilateralism and mutlilateralism or isolationism and interventionism and the other "isms" are somewhat silly and they miss the point. The point is that history and destiny have made America the leader of the world that would be free. And the world that would be free is looking to us for inspiration.

At National Press Club,
Washington, D.C., Sept. 28/
The New York Times, 9-29:(A)9.

Muammar el-Qaddafi
Chief of State of Libya

3

[U.S. President] Clinton and I belong to the same democratic camp. Clinton is the new generation. He does not look down on Third World people as inferior.

Interview/USA Today, 7-7:(A)4.

William B. Quandt
Senior fellow,
Brookings Institution
(United States)

4

[Saying there will be a wide-ranging impact of the recently signed Israel-PLO mutual-recognition agreement]: There's now a sense that the 21st century is around the corner and that you can either be part of it—which means being part of processes taking place globally—or you'll be left behind with real crosses to be borne, as Bosnia is now bearing [with its ethnic war]. If your economy is going to boom, then you have to be part of the world economy. If your political system is going to be legitimate, then you have to allow participation. And if you're not going to waste your resources, then you have to have peace with your neighbors.

Los Angeles Times,
9-14:(A)12.

Juan de Dios Ramirez Heredia
Spanish member
of European Parliament

5

I believe that nationalism is exclusionary and, like all exclusionary sentiments, it puts up defenses against the differences of others. In this sense, it is dangerous. When nationalisms arise that are fundamentally political rather than cultural, when they are defending artificial differences, they bring in their wake wars and confrontations and pain for humanity. However, it is important not to confuse the nationalism that leads to the tragedy of war . . . with the legitimate right of peoples to defend their own identities. There is a right to be different, to defend a common history and a common tradition, a common language and a common culture. This is an attitude that deserves the respect and the understanding of the majority peoples.

Interview,
Brussels, Belgium/
Los Angeles Times,
2-28:(M)3.

Bert Rockman
Political scientist,
University of Pittsburgh
(United States)

1

I think there hasn't been a lot of thinking about foreign policy [in the U.S. Clinton Administration] . . . There's no big foreign-policy thinker in their entourage, no liberal Henry Kissinger.

The Christian Science Monitor,
4-2:4.

Brent Scowcroft
Former Assistant
to the President
of the United States
(George Bush)
for National Security Affairs

2

It is a traditional American mistake [to play down foreign policy]. But if you look at the consequences in this century that have arisen from the U.S. turning its back on a world situation . . . it seems to me that a concentration on foreign policy to prevent a World War II, a cold war . . . , what have you, is worth an enormous investment.

To reporters/
The Christian Science Monitor,
10-8:4.

Cornelio Sommaruga
President,
International Committee
of the Red Cross

3

[On the forthcoming International Conference for the Protection of War Victims]: We are asking participants to make a public commitment to end the [wartime] massacre of civilians, summary executions, systematic torture of detainees, inhuman conditions of detention, the starvation or forced displacement of populations, indiscriminate use of arms, the plundering of humanitarian aid and the murder of personnel working under the emblems of the Red Cross and Red Crescent . . . The practice of war

has undergone a change for the worse. Civilian populations are becoming with ever greater frequency the hostages of warlords. We also observe a marked increase in sexual violence . . . I am struck by a degree of savagery that neither I nor my colleagues in the field have ever witnessed before.

Los Angeles Times, 8-30:(A)8.

John Temple Swing
President,
Foreign Policy Association
(United States)

4

Not since the 1920s has this country been faced with the crisis of what to do about the leadership role that has been thrust upon it. In the 1920s, it was World War I; in the 1990s, it is the end of the Cold War. The risk of turning inward and ignoring the world outside is no longer an option for this country when 20 per cent of our jobs are dependent on exports.

Aug. 5/The New York Times, 8-6:(B)10.

Peter Tarnoff
Under Secretary
for Political Affairs,
Department of State
of the United States

5

[On the U.S. Clinton Administration's new policy as to when and where to use U.S. force and influence in the world]: Our economic interests are paramount. [The U.S. must] define the extent of its commitment and make a commitment commensurate with those realities. This may on occasion fall short of what some Americans would like and others would hope for. [For example, in the current conflict in Bosnia] we simply don't have the leverage, we don't have the influence . . . to bring to bear the kind of pressure that will produce positive results . . . We're talking about new rules of engagement for the United States. There will have to be genuine power-sharing [with other countries] and responsibility-sharing.

At Overseas Writers Club,
Washington, D.C., May 25/
The Christian Science Monitor,
6-18:19.

Margaret Thatcher
Former Prime Minister
of the United Kingdom

1

There just isn't any way of isolating yourself or insulating yourself in the world today. It's no good saying that you'll serve only your domestic policy, because you're just a part of [the world]. So, what is your foreign policy? You just have to have leadership in the world. It's no good relying on the United Nations. It's no good thinking that [UN] resolutions—some of which are ambiguous because they can't get agreement on them if they're clear—are an effective substitute for action.

Interview, Los Angeles, Calif./
Los Angeles Times, 11-28:(M)3.

Volodymyr Tolubko
Deputy of Ukrainian Parliament

2

The U.S. is rudely inteferring . . . in everyone's affairs throughout the world, because it appears that any point on planet Earth is "vitally significant for America."

The Christian Science Monitor,
5-12:7.

Marghareta Af Ugglas
Foreign Minister of Sweden

3

[On a U.S. official's remark that American foreign policy will become scaled back and less interventionist]: What the United States says about its own role is very important. It is really tragic to give a signal to the world that you are not prepared to pursue your leadership. What does that tell the future dictators of the world?

Interview/
The New York Times, 6-1:(A)3.

Sergio Vieira de Mello
Adviser to Sadako Ogata,
United Nations High Commissioner
for Refugees

4

[Saying the UN's refugee efforts are being overwhelmed today]: In the past, crises seemed to occur one by one. Today, so many crises are happening simultaneously that keeping the plight of displaced persons within manageable bounds seems almost impossible . . . The biggest danger with simultaneous crises is that our organization no longer has the time to conceive a global plan for managing potential migrations. What we are sure of is that we alone are not equal to the task.

World Press Review, November:47.

Jusuf Wanandi
Director,
Center for Strategic
and International Studies
(Indonesia)

5

The decline of the United States is not in power, but [in] the will to really get involved militarily. If you [in the U.S.] see 20 people dead on CNN, you chicken out. What leadership is that?

U.S. News & World Report,
11-22:36.

Alexander Watson
Assistant Secretary
for Inter-American Affairs,
Department of State
of the United States

6

The democracies oriented toward an [open-] market policy make the best partners for commerce and investment, are the best guarantors of the rights of their citizens, and offer the best prospects for long-term stability and economic growth.

Speech, Caracas, Venezuela, Dec. 2/
The Christian Science Monitor,
12-15:24.

Timothy E. Wirth
Under Secretary of State
of the United States

7

What do you do about a country like Peru where the President [Alberto Fujimori] usurped all the functions of democratic government? One school of thought says we [the U.S.] should cut off all aid. Another—to which I subscribe—says that it's important to work with them and try to move them back into the column of working democracies. So we cut off their military aid, but we kept giving them humanitarian aid as a carrot, and slowly they seem to be moving in the right direction. There's no magic formula. You can't say that if a country gets caught in X number of drug interdictions plus Y number of human-rights abuses and Z torture cases . . . you fit a certain formula, and we can't give you aid. You have to look further down the road at whether there is a capacity and a will to change.

The Washington Post, 5-5:(A)28.

Manfred Woerner
Secretary General,
North Atlantic Treaty Organization

1

What is the consequence of the failure of the international community to deal successfully with a major crisis, such as ex-Yugoslavia? Shall we abandon our objective of building a new international order based on human rights, the rule of law and democracy? Shall we renounce our goal of a new, more democratic, just and peaceful European order? Shall we give up our concept of interlocking institutions before we have even had a chance to implement it fully? Shall we just leave the world to the forces of disorder and limit ourselves to safeguarding our own national borders and security, or at most, to attempting to contain the crisis spots so as to prevent them from spreading? My answers are clearly no. We simply cannot afford such passivity, not only because it goes against our principles and morals, but also because it goes against our national self-interests. In the world of today you simply cannot live in security surrounded by chaos.

Before International Institute
for Strategic Studies,
Brussels, Belgium, Sept. 10/
The Wall Street Journal,
9-14:(A)20.

2

If there is one lesson from history, it is that the sooner one stands up to a bully, the less the force required and the fewer the risks encountered. To the extent that our democracies prove their resolve, they are less likely to be challenged.

Before International Institute
for Strategic Studies,
Brussels, Belgium, Sept. 10/
Los Angeles Times, 9-11:(A)15.

3

Political solutions and diplomatic efforts [to end conflicts] will only work if backed by the necessary military power and the credible resolve to use it against an aggressor.

Before International Institute
for Strategic Studies,
Brussels, Belgium, Sept. 10/
Los Angeles Times, 9-11:(A)15.

R. James Woolsey
Director-designate
of Central Intelligence
of the United States

4

In many ways, today's threats are harder to observe and understand than the one that was once presented by the U.S.S.R. . . . Yes, we have slain a large dragon [the now-defunct Soviet Union]. But we live now in a jungle filled with a bewildering variety of poisonous snakes. And in many ways, the dragon was easier to keep track of.

At Senate Select Committee on
Intelligence hearing on his nomination,
Washington, D.C., Feb. 2/
Los Angeles Times, 2-3:(A)10.

5

If someone involved in intelligence, with respect to an overseas party, let's say, learns of activity that is against the interests of the United States, there is, I think, in the intelligence community often an inclination to watch and wait and to understand, because the next

(R. JAMES WOOLSEY)

time . . . one might learn something more. And that next thing one learns might be something that is truly vital to the interests of the country. And the mindset of those who are involved in prosecuting crimes on behalf of the United States is, of course, quite different. They both are legitimate interests.

At Senate Select Committee on Intelligence hearing on his nomination, Washington, D.C./ The Washington Post, 2-15:(A)23.

Boris N. Yeltsin
President of Russia

1

Everything used to be measured in terms of the number of nuclear warheads [a country had], how big a country was or how small it was. At present, when two-thirds of the nuclear warheads [in the U.S. and Russia] will be destroyed, the criteria will be entirely dif-

ferent. No one country will have to dictate how this or that region of the world should proceed.

To reporters, Moscow, Russia, Jan. 25/ Los Angeles Times, 1-26:(A)4.

Philip Zelikow
Professor of public policy, Harvard University (United States); Former member, National Security Council of the United States

2

I think the vision of a new world order is still a good one. But since the new (post-Cold War) world is so messy, the U.S. and other leaders of the free world need to define very clearly just what interests they are prepared to defend . . . [But] we don't really pick them. History picks them. And we have to decide which challenges we're going to meet. If you make poor choices, you will have failure.

USA Today, 10-11:(A)4.

Mohammed Farah Aidid
Somali factional leader

1

[Criticizing U.S. military intervention in the conflict in Somalia]: The Somali National Alliance [Aidid's political organization] stands for peace, justice, equality and democracy. The U.S. pursued, promoted and encouraged . . . destructive policies and, as a result, merciless military operations which massacred hundreds of Somalis were launched. We do not see any viable reason for the deployment of more U.S. troops.

News conference,
Mogadishu, Somalia, Oct. 14/
The New York Times, 10-15:(A)6.

2

[On the U.S. military intervention in Somalia]: The solution of the Somali problem lies with the Somali people, as [U.S.] President Clinton stated, and the Somalis should be left alone to find peaceful and lasting solutions for their problems. The international community should play the role of catalyst and provide the necessary assistance to Somalia to end their fight.

News conference,
Mogadishu, Somalia, Oct. 14/
The Washington Post, 10-15:(A)29.

Madeleine K. Albright
United States Ambassador/
Permanent Representative
to the United Nations

3

[Saying the U.S. will offer $100-million in aid to Somalia if the warring factions there agree to make peace]: These funds will be used for humanitarian assistance and rehabilitation projects in those regions where progress on political reconciliation and security has been made. These funds will be made available if and only if Somalis makes real progress in creating a secure environment and reconciling politically.

We urge other donors to participate actively in this effort . . . If Somali leaders demonstrate their own commitment to peace, which is a prerequisite for development, international donors will respond.

At United Nations,
New York, Nov. 19/
The New York Times, 11-20:3.

Benny Alexander
Secretary general,
Pan-African Congress
(South Africa)

4

[Criticizing the ANC for selling out blacks in its negotiations with the South African government]: We are convinced that the regime and the ANC are going to get married and give birth to a baby named neocolonialism.

Feb. 15/
Los Angeles Times, 2-16:(A)13.

Les Aspin
Secretary of Defense
of the United States

5

The danger now [in the unrest in Somalia] is that unless we return security to south Mogadishu, political chaos will follow . . . Other warlords would follow [fugitive warlord Mohamed] Aidid's example. Fighting between the warlords would ensue. And that, of course, is what brought the famine to massive proportions in the first place. The danger we're dealing with here is that the situation will return to what existed before the United Nations sent in its troops [last year].

At Center for Strategic
and International Studies,
Washington, D.C., Aug. 27/
The Washington Post,
8-28:(A)1.

Roelof F. Botha
Foreign Minister
of South Africa

1

[Saying the U.S.'s stand against South African apartheid should not lead it to sympathy for the ANC]: I can understand there is a sentiment [toward the ANC in the U.S.]. It would be a pity if that continues much longer . . . It was one thing to fight apartheid. But what must be emphasized now is whether those who opposed apartheid support democratic values. [For example,] where does the United States government really stand [on the ANC's alliance with the Communist Party of South Africa]?

Interview, Pretoria, South Africa/
The New York Times, 3-18:(A)4.

Boutros Boutros-Ghali
Secretary General
of the United Nations

2

[Saying the current UN-backed, U.S.-led military intervention in Somalia is to ensure delivery of food and medicine in that famine- and conflict-ridden country, not to gain political advantage]: The Cold War is finished. Nobody [from the outside] wants control over Somalia. I can assure you that humanitarian relief was the only aim of the intervention . . . Some Somalis believe Somalia has strategic importance. That's not true . . . No one is interested in Somalia, not for strategic reasons, not for oil, not for gold . . . There can be a real *drama* [tragedy] some day: The world could forget Somalia in a few minutes.

News conference,
Addis Ababa, Ethiopia, Jan. 5/
Los Angeles times, 1-6:(A)6.

3

[The crisis in] Somalia showed the world the terrible consequences of the collapse of a [UN] member state. There was no government. There was no law. There was no order. There was death . . . The United Nations intervened because it was morally compelled to do so. We, the United Nations, are rebuilding Somalia. We must show that collective action can be an active force for good, not merely a defensive shield against evil.

At United Nations, New York/
The Washington Post, 10-9:(A)17.

Bill Bradley
United States Senator,
D-New Jersey

4

[Criticizing how U.S. forces, some of whom have been killed, have been used during the current peacekeeping operation in Somalia]: A series of ad hoc decisions, divorced from any overall strategy, led our troops into an ill-defined, poorly planned and open-ended mission. The [U.S. Clinton] Administration plan keeps American troops on the ground and at risk, but provides far too little force to pacify Mogadishu door by door, block by block.

Before the Senate,
Washington, D.C., Oct. 14/
The New York Times, 10-16:6.

George Bush
President of the United States

5

[On the U.S.-led military intervention in Somalia aimed at allowing the delivery of food and medicine to the starving population of that conflict-ridden country]: I determined that only the use of force could stem this human tragedy in Somalia. The United States should not stand by with so many lives at stake, and when a limited deployment of U.S. forces, buttressed by the forces of other countries and acting under the full authority of the United Nations, could make an immediate and dramatic difference—and do so without excessive levels of risk and cost.

At U.S. Military Academy,
West Point, N.Y., Jan. 5/
The New York Times, 1-6:(A)5.

George Bush
Former President
of the United States

6

[Saying he is concerned about U.S. forces getting involved in military conflict in Somalia,

(GEORGE BUSH)

where he sent troops last year to help the starving population]: The [original] mission was to go in and save lives. People were starving, and American troops went in there and they opened the supply lines and they took food in. They weren't fighting. And I just hope that we don't get that mission messed up now, that we don't start getting off into an equation where we don't know the answer to those three questions [what is the mission, how to accomplish it, and how to get out].

At Castle Hills Elementary School,
San Antonio, Texas, Oct. 13/
The Washington Post, 10-14:(A)22.

Mangosuthu Gatsha Buthelezi
President,
Inkatha Freedom Party
of South Africa;
Chief of the Zulu people

1

[Saying a new South African Constitution should be finalized, containing certain guarantees such as regional autonomy, before a national election date is set]: Once there is a craze about elections, everyone will forget everything else, and I think that's a recipe for disaster in this country. If we don't entrench the powers and functions of regions before the elections, then we are asking for trouble. We'll have the same experience as Angola.

South African broadcast interview,
June 23/
Los Angeles Times, 6-24:(A)4.

2

[On next year's scheduled South African elections, in which for the first time blacks will be able to fully participate]: The election date is made a kind of high hype, which we all must strive for regardless of whether we've got a Constitution . . . [or] whether we'll be able to put in place the preparations which are needed for people, most of whom are illiterate or semi-literate black people who've never participated in an election. But of course, the elec-

tion now, as stated by the international community including [the U.S.], is something you must go through come rain or come sunshine, which concerns me very much, because . . . when I cast my eyes toward Angola and see that there were [international election] monitors there, but it went to pieces.

Interview, Ulundi, South Africa/
U.S. News & World Report,
11-29:48.

Benjamin F. Chavis, Jr.
Executive director,
National Association
for the Advancement
of Colored People
(United States)

3

We have concerns about the [U.S.] Clinton Administration's policy or lack of policy, toward Africa and the Caribbean. We believe that this is an opportunity for the Clinton Administration to correct the past 12 years of bad policy toward Africa by the [Ronald] Reagan and [George] Bush Administrations. Certainly, the President has a lot on his plate, but from an African-American perspective, considering the massive outpouring of votes that went to the Clinton ticket [in last year's election], there was high expectation that there would be a change in policy.

Los Angeles Times, 4-17:(A)6.

Dick Cheney
Secretary of Defense
of the United States

4

[On the U.S. policy of treating the warlords of Somalia, who are responsible for the current conflict and famine in that country, as legitimate authorities]: Well, if not those people, who would you have dealt with? We don't, I think in any way, sanction what they may have done in the past by dealing with them, but it has been important to establish a relationship up front in order to have no organized military opposition to our [famine-relief] activities there, and it's been very successful. And the

(DICK CHENEY)

reason we've had so few casualties—only one American killed, a few injured—has been because of, I think, the careful way in which we did establish those relationships up front to preserve our neutrality and objectivity among the clans.

Interview,
Washington, D.C., Jan. 4/
The Washington Post, 1-5:(A)11.

Warren Christopher
Secretary of State
of the United States

1

[Saying the U.S. supports the government of Angolan President Jose Eduardo dos Santos, and not UNITA, the rebel group trying to overthrow dos Santos and which the U.S. supported in the past]: We intend to remain actively engaged in promoting a negotiated settlement that enables all the people of Angola to enjoy the benefits of democracy. We hope UNITA will be a part of the government we recognize; we continue to believe there can be no military victory in Angola—and the United States will not support those who pursue a military solution.

Before African-American Institute,
Washington, D.C., May 21/
The Washington Post, 5-22:(A)16.

Bill Clinton
President of the United States

2

[On his decision to recognize the government of Angola over objections of UNITA, the formerly U.S.-supported rebel group that is fighting that government]: The Angolan government by contrast [with UNITA] has agreed to sign [a] peace agreement, has sworn in a democratically elected National Assembly and has offered participation by UNITA at all levels of government. Today we recognize those achievements by recognizing the government and the republic of Angola.

To reporters,
Washington, D.C., May 19/
Los Angeles Times, 5-20:(A)9.

3

[Defending a U.S.-backed UN attack on a Somali warlord who is said to be responsible for ambushing and killing UN peacekeepers in conflict- and starvation-plagued Somalia]: With this action, the world community moves . . . to underscore its commitment to preserve the security of UN forces. If UN peacekeepers are to be effective agents for peace and stability in Somalia and elsewhere, they must be capable of using force when necessary to defend themselves and accomplish their goals.

USA Today, 6-14:(A)1.

4

[Saying the U.S. could continue its role in trying to restore order in Somalia]: I have to remind my fellow Americans, and all the people of the world who have an aversion to the events of the last two weeks [military confrontations between U.S./UN forces and Somali militias], not to forget that over 300,000 [Somalis have] lost their lives there, were starved, were murdered, were subject to incredibly inhumane conditions because of the chaotic and lawless behavior of the people who had authority . . . [We should support the Somalis until they can] take control of their own affairs in peace and dignity and without starvation and murder. We don't want to do something that rewards the very conduct we went to Somalia to put an end to.

Washington, D.C., Sept. 17/
The New York Times, 9-18:5.

5

[On U.S. military involvement in Somalia]: [We did not send more than 11,000 troops to Somalia] to prove we can win military battles. No one seriously questions the fact that we could clean out that whole section of Mogadishu [controlled by warlord Mohammed Aidid] with minimum loss to ourselves if that's what we wanted to do. The reports today say that 300 Somalis were killed and 700 more were wounded in the firefight that cost our people their lives last week. That is not our mission. We did not go there to do that . . . It

(BILL CLINTON)

is not for the United States or for the United Nations to eliminate whole groups of people from having a role in Somalia's future.

News conference,
Washington, D.C., Oct. 14/
Los Angeles Times, 10-15:(A)6.

Richard Cobb
Leader of U.S. delegation
at fund-raising conference
for Somalia

1

While we have come together here to pledge our commitment to a relief and rehabilitation plan for [famine- and conflict-plagued] Somalia, I want to stress the United States's views that any commitments made here are contingent upon the successful efforts of Somalis to engage in peaceful, sincere political negotiations. Continued episodes of violence that disrupt concerted world efforts now under way to help Somalis could lead eventually to [the world] saying no to Somalis' request for assistance.

Addis Ababa, Ethiopia, March 12/
Los Angeles Times, 3-13:(A)22.

Herman J. Cohen
Assistant Secretary
for African Affairs,
Department of State
of the United States

2

[The government of Zaire is] basically a clan, a family of cousins acting like the Mafia in Sicily, making these illegal deals, siphoning the money off cobalt and copper revenues. [President] Mobutu [Sese Seko] requires a huge cash flow. He has to keep the family afloat. In effect, he has about three thousand to four thousand dependents, including women and children [and the military]. It's essentially his own tribe. The attitude is: "We've got to all hang together. If we don't, we're dead."

The Atlantic, August:25.

T. Frank Crigler
Former United States Ambassador
to Somalia

3

[Criticizing the use of U.S. forces in Somalia against local warlords rather than for protection of humanitarian aid for civilians]: We are turning triumph into tragedy, applying brute military force to a situation that calls for quiet diplomacy, patient mediation, steadiness and understanding. [Permitting U.S. forces to become involved in conflicts with local warlords] has cast U.S. combat troops in the ugly role of airborne bullies whose aim is to force peace on the Somalis at gunpoint.

Before House Foreign Affairs
Subcommittee on Africa,
Washington, D.C., July 29/
The Washington Post, 7-30:(A)15.

Frederick W. de Klerk
President of South Africa

4

[On the end of apartheid in South Africa and the coming majority rule]: I'm not changing the very essence of a philosophy; I'm broadening democracy. It is not as if we are moving from the dark ages where there was no form of democracy suddenly into a new system. I'm not moving from Communism to free-market enterprise. We have a basically sound economy. South Africans have been prepared for the final process of reconciling with each other, of becoming part of one entity and one nation, over a long period.

Interview/Time, 6-14:37.

5

We [whites] asked for power-sharing [in a new black-majority-ruled South Africa], and we will get it in the transitional period in a government of national unity. We believe it would be necessary to have a form of power-sharing also in terms of a final constitution, but we have a totally open mind as to how that should be structured. I do not think a permanent form of enforced coalition can be written into a final constitution. But we need more than

(FREDERICK W. DE KLERK)

five years to ensure that the various components of our community will all feel secure and that they need not fear suppression or the misuse of power. We must ensure that there will never be domination again in South Africa. I'm not talking about minority vetoes but about preventing the misuse of power to the detriment of minorities.

Interview/Time, 6-14:36.

1

[On the just-approved new South African Constitution, guaranteeing the rights of all races and ethnic groups]: This is a historic day. A new Constitution has been born that can ensure a peaceful transition that will lay the foundation for a proper democracy. There has been a process of give and take, and we have made concessions. But all the fundamentals are there.

Interview, Nov. 16/
The Christian Science Monitor,
11-17:1.

2

[On the ending of apartheid in South Africa, which will culminate in a non-racial election in April, 1994]: [The election will] not be about blacks or whites, or Afrikaners and Xhosas [or] apartheid or armed struggle. It will be about future peace and stability, about progress and prosperity, about nation-building. Five years ago, people would have seriously questioned the sanity of anyone who would have predicted that [ANC president Nelson] Mandela and I would be joint recipients of the 1993 Nobel Peace Prize.

Speech upon receiving Nobel Peace Prize,
Oslo, Norway, Dec. 10/
The New York Times, 12-11:6.

Jan Eliasson
Under Secretary General
for Humanitarian Affairs
of the United Nations

3

[On the UN's famine-relief operations in Somalia]: Due to the security needs, the international community is spending $10 on military protection for every dollar of voluntary humanitarian assistance in Somalia, even if the 1993 Relief and Rehabilitation Programs were to be fully funded. Unless sufficient funds are provided for rehabilitation activities, there is a risk that the military operation can be perceived as an end in itself, rather than as a means of ensuring security for rehabilitating the country's infrastructure and forging reconciliation.

Before UN Economic and Social Council,
Geneva, Switzerland, July 21/
The Washington Post, 7-22:(A)22.

Richard Goldstone
South African judge;
Chairman,
South African Commission
of Inquiry Regarding the
Prevention of Public Violence
and Intimidation

4

If one thing has surprised me it's the large number of people who are capable of committing horrible acts of violence in this society [South Africa]. I suppose I was, innocently, of the view that it was only a very few people, on the fringes of society, who could take an automatic weapon and mow down innocent men, women and children. And the number of incidents—train violence, violence generally involving killing and injuring and maiming innocent people—happens with much horrible frequency that I think that surprised me more than anything. I was really surprised at human conduct more than anything else.

Interview,
Johannesburg, South Africa/
Los Angeles Times, 3-21:(M)3.

Chris Hani
General secretary,
Communist Party
of South Africa

5

Whether we like it or not, whites are South Africans like ourselves. They took power away from us [blacks] and oppressed us, but we

(CHRIS HANI)

didn't get into the struggle to destroy the white group. We want to convince whites that democracy is better than apartheid, that . . . they will continue having a better life and a more normal life. They won't fear the blacks they've feared for years. Whites are beginning to realize that changes are inevitable, and they are learning to live with changes. I stay in a conservative part of Johannesburg called Boksburg, and my kids have not been harassed. I've had no problems. I'm an optimist, and it may take some time, but political democracy will triumph.

Interview/Newsweek, 4-19:33.

Mohammed Hardi
Minister of the Interior
of Algeria

1

The people aren't with the government [in Algeria], and one of the reasons is that we made promises to the people, and they didn't find them to come true. From the beginning, they created an Algeria for the benefit of 10 percent of the Algerians to the detriment of the other 90 percent, and there came the moment where we are today: an Algeria full of people who possess absolutely nothing. Now, people want two things. They want, first, that social justice be established. And second, they want everyone who stole their heritage to be punished.

Interview/
Los Angeles Times, 1-11:(A)6.

Jonathan Howe
United Nations envoy
to Somalia

2

[On U.S. and UN actions in violence-and hunger-plagued Somalia]: The U.S. did a great job over here [in pacifying Somalia over the last five months]. Now the UN has a much larger task. It has to take a whole country that has basically broken down into total anarchy and bring it to its feet . . . People are sick of rule by the gun and extortion. We have to seize this moment now and put guns in the hands of a legitimate police force [instead of the current "warlords"].

USA Today, 6-18:(A)7.

Ikram ul-Hasan
Brigadier General,
Pakistani armed forces

3

[On the unrest in Somalia, where he recently commanded Pakistani peacekeeping forces under UN jurisdiction]: [Somali fighters have] lost all human values. There's no respect for a man, the life of a man. It has degenerated to such an extent that it will require intense amounts of time, education and bloodshed to get those values back.

Interview, Mogadishu, Somalia/
The Washington Post, 11-3:(A)11.

Ahlud Jama
Former Chief
of Somalia's National Police

4

[On the recent U.S. military intervention as peacekeepers in Somalia's civil war]: The expectation was very high with the arrival of the American-led troops that they would rid our country of all these weapons, but the job appears to be only half-done. The most important thing was to carry out disarmament, and the Americans stopped short on that. So that expectation remains unfulfilled.

Los Angeles Times, 5-5:(A)9.

Bill Johnson
Political scientist,
Oxford University (England)

5

[On the increasing political divisions within South Africa, which will have blacks voting for the first time in next year's scheduled elections]: We could be seeing the beginning of the disintegration of South Africa as a single state. After all, it has only been a single state for 80 years. If parties perceive that there is going to

(BILL JOHNSON)

be a weak center, it is to be expected that regional groupings will try to seize more power.

At conference on democracy,
Johannesburg, South Africa/
The Christian Science Monitor,
7-28:2.

Robert B. Johnston
Lieutenant General,
United States Marine Corps;
Commander,
U.S. forces in Somalia

1

This city [Mogadishu, Somalia,] has been destroyed to a degree such as I have never seen anywhere in my career. Bandit activity is almost part of the culture. They often resolve disputes at the end of a gun, and I'm not sure we can legislate that away with our presence no matter how long we stay.

Mogadishu, Somalia/
Los Angeles Times, 1-19:(H)5.

2

[On the end of U.S. control of relief efforts in famine-and conflict-plagued Somalia]: It was one thing to see it on TV and see it in the newspaper, but quite another thing to witness the effects of famine first-hand, to feel it, smell it, to look into the eyes of children who were completely emotionless, instinctively struggling to survive. Now the famine is behind them. They have learned to smile. It's a good feeling to have been part of that, to make it so different.

Mogadishu, Somalia, May 4/
The New York Times, 5-5:(C)22.

Robert B. Johnston
Lieutenant General,
United States Marine Corps;
Former Commander,
U.S. forces in Somalia

3

[Criticizing the recent switch in the mission of U.S. forces in Somalia from famine relief to

going after warlord Mohammed Aidid, which resulted in loss of U.S. lives]: Whether you like Aidid or not . . . in the Somalis' eyes he is a leader. You don't just take on Aidid, you take on his entire clan. And that entire clan will fight to the death . . . It was a gross miscalculation. I think we've since acknowledged that and turned that around.

Before House Armed Services Committee,
Washington, D.C., Oct. 21/
USA Today, 10-22:(A)8.

Amin Khalifa
Leader,
National Council of Sudan

4

[On the civil war in his country]: When [rebel leader John] Garang went to the World Council of Churches, he used to say the war is between Muslims in the north and Christians in the south. Naturally, they assisted him. When he used to go to the East Bloc, he would talk about the proletariat fighting against the forces of imperialism. Naturally, they helped him, too. He would go to the West and say, "Help us in the democratization of Sudan." He would go to South Africa and say the war in Sudan is an ethnic war; we are black and they want to impose themselves on us. Actually, the war in the south of Sudan is not a religious war; it is not an ethnic war; it is a political one, over the question of the identity of the Sudanese people. We don't want to say we are 100 percent Muslim. We are a multi-religious, multi-cultural, multi-lingual country, and we are going to have to find a way of living together.

Los Angeles Times, 4-10:(A)14.

Nelson Mandela
President,
African National Congress
(South Africa)

5

When we [South African blacks] win an election, we don't then gain power. We merely hold political office. To gain power means that we should have control of the civil service, of the South African police, of the South African

(NELSON MANDELA)

Defense Force, of business. That is going to take some time for us to achieve.

Interview,
Johannesburg, South Africa, Jan. 17/
The New York Times, 1-18:(A)3.

1

Forty years of apartheid [in South Africa] have been like 40 years of war. Our economy and our social life have been completely devastated, in some respects beyond repair. That was the situation in Europe after the end of the last World War. What the Western world did was to mobilize their resources and introduce Marshall Plan aid to ensure that the countries of Europe devastated by the war recovered. What we expect—and this is a matter which I'm going to raise with [U.S.] President Clinton—is that the Western world, led by the U.S., should ensure that massive measures of assistance are given to the people of South Africa so we can address their expectations.

Interview/Time, 6-14:36.

2

[On South Africa's ruling National Party and next year's scheduled elections]: Their concept of democracy is different from yours and mine. We have already encountered this problem in their concept of power-sharing, which to them means the party that loses the elections should continue to govern. Now we have moved them away from that, and they are coming to accept our concept of a government of national unity which is based on majority rule. We are saying all political parties with a substantial following should be included in government, so we can face problems together.

Interview/Time, 6-14:36.

3

We believe the moment has come when the United Nations organization and the international community as a whole should take steps of the decisive advances that have been made

to create a just setting for the victory of the cause of democracy in [South Africa] . . . To give added impetus to this process, to strengthen the forces of democratic change, and to help create the necessary conditions for stability and social progress, we believe that the time has come when the international community should lift all economic sanctions against South Africa. We therefore extend an earnest appeal to you, the governments and peoples you represent, to take all necessary measures to end the economic sanctions you imposed and which have brought us to the point where the transition to democracy has now been enshrined in the law of our country.

Before United Nations Special
Committee Against Apartheid,
New York, N.Y., Sept. 24/
The New York Times, 9-25:5.

4

[On the just-approved new South African Constitution, guaranteeing the rights of all races and ethnic groups]: We have reached the end of an era. We are at the beginning of a new era. Whereas apartheid deprived millions of our people of their citizenhiip, we are restoring that citizenship. Whereas apartheid sought to fragment our country, we are reuniting our country.

At signing of the Constitution,
Kempton Park, South Africa,
Nov. 18/
Los Angeles Times, 11-18:(A)1.

5

The expectations of our people [South African blacks] are quite understandable, because they can see that their white counterparts are enjoying privileges and rights which are denied to them. [We need] an economy that is not only vibrant but which is able to address the just demands of all its people. The huge gap between black and white that exists, and that has existed for generations, will only lead to further conflict. And therefore it is our duty to insure that the living standards of all our people—the dispossessed, the poor, the weak.

(NELSON MANDELA)

the marginal—are raised to the same level as the white minority.

Speech on eve of receiving
Nobel Peace Prize,
Oslo, Norway, Dec. 9/
The New York Times, 12-10:(A)8.

1

[On the ending of apartheid in South Africa, which will culminate in non-racial elections in April, 1994]: Let a new age be born! [April will be a time when] all humanity will join together to celebrate one of the outstanding human victories of our century. This triumph will finally bring to a close a history of 500 years of African colonization that began with the establishment of the Portuguese empire.

Speech upon receiving
the Nobel Peace Prize,
Oslo, Norway, Dec. 10/
The New York Times, 12-11:6.

2

[Criticizing the idea of a homeland for those South African whites who want one]: We have no hostility against Afrikaners . . . We are prepared for some sort of compromise. [But] the problem with a volkstaat [a white homeland] is that it reopens the whole ethnic question, and we are not going to do that.

Speech at fund-raiser,
Rustenburg, Transvaal, South Africa/
U.S. News & World Report,
12-27:70.

Mike McCurry
Spokesman for the
Department of State
of the United States

3

[Criticizing Nigeria's military government for annulling the country's recent election results]: According to independent Nigerian monitoring groups and outside observers, the election was orderly, fair and free from any serious irregularities. The Nigerian press, public and leading civilian politicians view the election as the most successful in Nigeria's history and have called upon the military to release and respect the results [which would have turned the government over to civilian rule]. The failure on the part of the military regime to respect the will of the Nigerian people . . . will have serious implications to U.S.-Nigerian relations.

June 23/
Los Angeles Times, 6-24:(A)8.

4

We deplore the continuing crisis in Zaire and hold President Mobutu [Sese Seko] responsible for a situation which puts at risk the lives and welfare of millions of his countrymen and the stability of an entire region . . . It is abundantly clear to objective observers that President Mobutu bears responsibility for the continuing political impasse, economic deterioration and human suffering. We call on him once again to allow the transition [to a new government] to proceed or bear full responsibility for the consequences.

Washington, D.C.,
July 21/
The New York Times, 7-22:(A)4.

Abdelhamid Mehri
Secretary general,
National Liberation Front
of Algeria

5

We cannot deny the phenomenon [of the popularity of Islam in Algeria]: The longer they hesitate in applying democracy [allowing moderate Islamists to be involved in the political process], the more the [Algerian] authorities isolate themselves from the people. Regimes weaken themselves by saying that there can be no democracy in the face of such a phenomenon.

The Christian Science Monitor,
4-27:6.

Meles Zenawi
President of Ethiopia

1

[Addressing Somali leaders whom he holds responsible for the conflict and famine in Somalia]: You stand now before the Somali people, the international community and history and the principal engineers of the tragedy in Somalia. I am saying this not to apportion blame but to underscore the need for you to measure up to the demands of your people, to transcend your clan animosities and to allow the strong patriotic streak in every one of you to flourish. I am saying this to convey the message to you that you must lead the way in the resurrection of Somalia, a country that has collapsed in front of your eyes because of your failure to keep the family quarrel within acceptable limits.

At conference on Somalia,
Addis Ababa, Ethiopia, Jan. 4/
Los Angeles Times, 1-5:(A)8.

Hosni Mubarak
President of Egypt

2

[Accusing Sudan of training international terrorists]: The Sudanese deny it, but the [training] camps are there. They are farms. They take people not only from Egypt but also from Saudi Arabia, Algeria, Morocco, Tunisia and even from Uganda. They act as if they are workers on these farms. But under this umbrella they teach them about explosives and about firearms.

Time, 8-30:30.

John P. Murtha
United States Representative,
D-Pennsylvania

3

[Saying the UN is delaying its takeover of responsibilities for peacekeeping in Somalia following the current U.S.-led military intervention there to alleviate the conflict and famine]: The biggest disappointment we have found is the UN is doing nothing. The UN is dragging its feet. The impression we get from all the people we've talked to is they should be in here as real players at this stage . . . I'd like to see the Americans out of here as soon as possible, because the longer we're here, the more involved we get. The more involved we get, the longer the deployment will be, the more they'll depend on us.

News conference,
Mogadishu, Somalia, Jan. 10/
The New York Times, 1-11:(A)4.

Robert B. Oakley
United States Special Envoy
to Somalia;
Former U.S. Ambassador
to Somalia

4

[Saying Somalia has for too long depended on other countries for aid]: They have always been masterful at cornering foreign assistance. This country has lived off the dole for as long as I can remember. In future, Somalis will have to work harder at earning it rather than getting it.

Press briefing, Mogadishu, Somalia/
The New York Times, 3-3:(A)4.

5

[On the U.S. military intervention in famine- and conflict-plagued Somalia]: I compare our mission to taking someone with hysterics and slapping him out of it. There will be violence in Somalia for a long time, but it will be low-level violence. The cycle [of anarchy and starvation] has been broken.

Time, 5-17:42.

Olusegun Obansanjo
Former Head of State
of Nigeria

6

[On skepticism about whether the Nigerian military, as it has promised, will turn over the country to civilian rule after the forthcoming elections]: I've stopped believing what [military leader General Ibrahim] Babangida says. I only believe what Babangida does. This is an Administration that when it says "Good morn-

(OLUSEGUN OBANSANJO)

ing," people will look out of the window four times to ascertain the time of the day before they respond.

Interview, Ota, Nigeria/
The New York Times, 6-8:(A)5.

Muammar el-Qaddafi
Chief of State of Libya

1

[Saying his country welcomes guerrilla leaders from around the world]: Libya acts according to its interests. Our interests mean we meet [guerrilla leaders such as] Abu Nidal, Abu Abbas, Ahmed Jibril, Abu Mussa and all real Palestinian leaders and those of the true resistance . . . We are the mecca of freedom fighters, and their natural ally. We are the first to welcome them, from Ireland to the Philippines.

Speech at rally in Libya, Dec. 16/
The New York Time⁻, 12-18:3.

Randall Robinson
Executive director,
TransAfrica (United States)

2

Africa needs economic assistance, and we [the U.S.] ought to be there with it. We ought to receive African leaders as we receive leaders from other parts of the world, because that's an important American indication of our concern and active support. We ought to see from [U.S.] President Clinton more interest in a country for which we are in a major way historically responsible—Liberia . . . Liberia is a shattered country. There's no situation in Africa for which we have more responsibility than that one. We've got a responsibility to help Liberia right itself . . . Disappointingly, with the exception of the Angola policy, it is very difficult to see the difference between President Clinton and [former U.S.] President [George] Bush.

Interview/
USA Today, 7-12:(A)11.

Salim Ahmed Salim
Secretary General,
Organization of African Unity

3

[On the unrest in Somalia]: We cannot make peace for the Somali people, nor can we impose it upon them. The people of Somalia have to reconcile if peace is to be restored to their country.

At conference on Somalia,
Addis Ababa, Ethiopia, Nov. 29/
The New York Times, 11-30:(A)7.

Jonas Savimbi
Leader, National Union for the
Total Independence of Angola
(UNITA)

4

[On foreign criticism of his rebel force which is attempting to overthrow the Angolan government]: The loss of international support will not stop us from achieving our objectives if we feel we are doing the right thing in terms of our own evolution. In the 34 years of my political career, I won some support and I lost some . . . You cannot dominate it [the international community].

Interview, Huambo, Angola/
The Christian Science Monitor,
4-16:1.

Helen Suzman
Former member
of South African Parliament

5

[On next year's South African election, in which blacks will have the right to vote]: There is no culture of democracy in any party standing for election, except my own [the Democratic Party]. But it can be developed. Once in power, one hopes the ANC will acquire those values, especially if a free press and free association are guaranteed in the [new] Constitution.

Interview,
Washington, D.C./
The Washington Post, 11-10:(C)4.

251

Morgan Tsvangirai
General secretary,
Zimbabwe Congress
of Trade Unions

1

To a greater extent, reconciliation [between whites and blacks in Zimbabwe] has worked . . . [But] there is resentment [among blacks] against the continued economic power of the whites. There is no discernible method of translating the political power of blacks into economic power. Whites still are the managers. They are the owners of the bulk of the wealth. Blacks are the servants.

The New York Times, 8-30:(A)4.

Desmond M. Tutu
South African Archbishop;
Winner,
1984 Nobel Peace Prize

2

[On the joint award of the 1993 Nobel Peace Prize to South African President Frederik de Klerk and ANC leader Nelson Mandela]: Here we have two men—one white and one black. One [de Klerk] who stood at the head of a racist government but contributed to peace . . . The other [Mandela], who had spent many years in prison fighting for peace and freedom, contributed through his dignity and magnanimity.

The Christian Science Monitor,
10-18:2.

Chima Ubani
General secretary,
Campaign for Democracy
(Nigeria)

3

We were advocates of total economic sanctions [against] South Africa, and we believe the sanctions were the main reason why apartheid is giving way to democracy there. It should be no different for Nigeria. [Foreign economic sanctions] will place hardship on the people [of Nigeria], but there is no freedom without sacrifice.

Time, 9-6:41.

David Welsh
Professor of political science,
University of Cape Town
(South Africa)

4

We now have [in South Africa] a liberal democratic [non-racial] Constitution, which is supported by 80 percent of the population. To have expected more was always utopian and romantic. I think there is a fair chance that the adoption of the new Constitution will lower the stakes of political conflict and prevent the election blowing the roof off the society. But it is bound to be messy and flawed.

The Christian Science Monitor,
12-23:4.

Frank R. Wolf
United States Representative,
R-Virginia

5

[Saying the world isn't paying attention to the starvation in Sudan]: [The churches] flooded my office concerning Nicaragua, and all. But now, when people are dying in southern Sudan, I hear silence from the mainline Christian community. Where is the media? Where is the [U.S. TV program] *20/20,* where is [the U.S. TV program] *60 Minutes* and all those people? Where are they? Because [Sudan] is so difficult to get to, no one is covering it.

Speech/
The Washington Post, 4-8:(A)2.

The Americas

Sergio Aguayo
President, Mexican Academy
of Human Rights

1

I'm hopeful we'll finally see the [Mexican] Judicial Police under control. But their behavior is tied to the authoritarian system—a system which by its nature needs a blunt instrument. Is the government willing to surrender its instrument of coercion? Can the police force be "born again" ethically? I respect [new Mexican Attorney General Jorge] Carpizo, but I have my doubts if one man can change this culture.

The Christian Science Monitor,
1-14:2.

Ricardo Alarcon
Foreign Minister of Cuba

2

[On the hostile U.S. attitude toward Cuban President Fidel Castro's regime and the American economic sanctions against his country]: We are used to a systematic display of hostility toward Cuba from successive American Administrations. We are perfectly prepared to continue facing similar hostile posturing in the future . . . With an enormous effort and with sacrifices, we can stand up to this. But there are going to be cutbacks and shortages.

News conference,
Madrid, Spain, Jan. 12/
The New York Times, 1-13:(A)4.

Miguel Alfonso
Member,
Cuban government delegation
to United Nations
Human Rights Commission

3

Don't look for freedom of expression in Cuba because you won't find it. But what about the right to life—the most basic of human rights? Here [in Cuba], there is the right to food, to health care, to education. How many people are alive today in Cuba because of the [Communist] revolution? Compare the life expectancy of Guatemalans and Cubans and tell me whose human rights are being violated.

The Christian Science Monitor,
11-4:8.

Oscar Arias (Sanchez)
Former President
of Costa Rica

4

The greatest challenge to democracy in Latin America—not just in Central America—is to prove democracy works. We don't want to arrive at the end of this century with new dictators. But democracy must deliver the goods. For democracy to deliver the goods we need to eliminate economic distortions, and the [military] is one of the greatest distortions and obstacles to economic growth.

The Christian Science Monitor,
1-7:6.

5

The United States should realize that [its] economic blockade against Cuba has been counterproductive from both a political and a human point of view. The elimination of this form of political pressure will make the Cuban government fully responsible for the current problems faced by that country. At the same time, it will prevent the further deterioration of the education or health systems, the continuation of which will condemn the Cuban people to malnutrition and disease. A country so sensitive to the sufferings that military conflicts inflict upon civil populations must recognize the injustice of abandoning a society to misery for political ends. Lifting the economic embargo against Cuba will also serve the interests of the United States and Latin America. After such a significant step for the Americas as NAFTA, there is no justification for prolonging this futile attack against social welfare and free trade.

Speech, Washington, D.C., Dec. 3/
The Washington Post, 12-8:(A)22.

Jean-Bertrand Aristide
Exiled former President
of Haiti

1

What we need [in Haiti] is the professionaliza-tion of the military, the separation of the soldiers from the police, if we are to have democracy. Of course we need an army, but one which will not kill people—3,000 people were killed after the coup [which ousted him in 1991]—but protect their human rights. My country is like broken glass; it has to be put together again by the inter-national community. We are talking about a mili-tary with 7,000 men, which has 40 percent of the national budget. We have a rate of 85 percent illiteracy. We have eight doctors for every 10,000 Haitians.

Interview/
The Washington Post, 1-5:(A)2.

2

[On the possibility of his returning to Haiti, from which he was exiled in a 1991 coup]: I am quite sure that if [Haitians] stay home and remain mobilized, not remain passive, and don't leave the country . . . with the commitment made by [U.S.] President-elect Clinton, jointly with the last steps taken by the UN and OAS, we will soon see the changes we are looking for.

Voice of America broadcast,
Jan. 11/
The Washington Post, 1-13:(A)18.

3

[With the forthcoming U.S. President Clinton Administration,] there is no doubt we will have democracy back in Haiti. When we have democracy back in our country, the Haitians will stay [instead of trying to flee by sea to the U.S.]. We won't have to suffer not knowing whether we will lose them in the sea . . . I encourage them to stay, but I cannot blame them for leaving. The military is killing too many of them, and they are fleeing from that death. From one side to the other side, they are moving from death [in Haiti] to death [in the sea].

Interview, Atlanta, Ga., Jan. 13/
USA Today, 1-14:(A)9.

David Barrett
Former Premier
of British Columbia, Canada

4

[On the new Reform Party, which had a strong showing in the western part of Canada during the recent national election]: This vote was a sort of finger in the eye of this system from the west. Psychologically, the Reformists tapped into western separatism. But what they really are is a populist party on the right, getting votes from the poor and money from the rich by promising to protect the two from each other.

The New York Times, 10-28:(A)6.

Lloyd N. Bentsen
Secretary of the Treasury
of the United States

5

[Supporting the proposed U.S.-Canada-Mexico free trade agreement]: We don't know who [Mexican President Carlos Salinas's] successor is going to be [when he leaves office next year]. I grew up on that border. The United States was always the colossus of the North, and Mexican politicians got elected attacking the United States. Now the country wants to work with us, and that is an incredible change. We can't lose the opportunity.

Interview,
Washington, D.C., April 1/
The New York Times, 4-2:(C)4.

Ray Bishop
Secretary general,
Panamanian Syndicate
of Employees of United States
Armed Forces

6

[On the scheduled turnover of control of the Panama Canal from the U.S. to Panama at the end of the century and the effect on Panamanian employment when the U.S. pulls out its bases]: We have a treaty [mandating the U.S. pullout], and that is something we cannot hide from, because once 1999 comes we'll be down to zero Americans and zero jobs. The problem is that the Panamanian government is not ready for this kind of responsibility. This is going to be the mess of the century.

The New York Times, 7-23:(A)4.

Michael Bliss
Professor of history,
University of Toronto (Canada)

1

[On the government of new Canadian Prime Minister Jean Chretien]: This Canadian Administration is going to be more prickly than the last one was, more concerned about asserting Canadian interests and reminding the U.S. that it is an independent nation with a mind of its own.

The Christian Science Monitor,
11-19:7.

Robert C. Bonner
Administrator,
Drug Enforcement Administration
of the United States

2

[On Colombian drug traffickers]: They have insinuated themselves into exerting undue influence over the political process, and there is a very grave threat that these organizations will become so powerful you would have a "narco-democracy" in Colombia, that is, a system actually influenced and controlled by drug traffickers.

Interview, Washington, D.C./
The Washington Post, 3-9:(A)14.

Rafael Caldera
President-elect of Venezuela

3

[On his victory in the just-held Presidential election]: We've passed through one of the most difficult periods in history. We are going to unite our efforts so that there is true democracy, not a corrupt and injust democracy. We will have a just democracy that serves the legitimate interests of the community and serves as an example for the other people of this continent.

Victory speech,
Caracas, Venezuela, Dec. 5/
The Christian Science Monitor, 12-7:1.

4

I am against this epidemic of privatizations [of government enterprises] by people who consider that everything will be resolved by selling everything that we have.

News conference, Dec. 6/
The New York Times, 12-7:(A)3.

Rafael Leonardo Callejas
President of Honduras

5

I am the third elected President [of Honduras], and that shows civilian power is above military power. We civilians elect our governments, and each President has more preeminence and more authority over the military than his predecessor.

Interview/
The Washington Post, 6-2:(A)24.

Kim Campbell
Minister of Defense of Canada

6

What are the things that unify us [Canadians]? What are our goals? What are we as a country? It sometimes seems to boil down to nothing more than our social programs, and I think—no, no, no! We have a social and political culture that's quite remarkable, ways of doing things that we've worked out over the years that have been dictated by geography, a small population, certain senses of historical connectedness that gave us a sense of obligation to one another.

Interview, Boston, Mass./
The Christian Science Monitor,
3-31:13.

Kim Campbell
Prime Minister of Canada

7

[On her redesigning Canada's government]: It is crucial to close the distance between Canadians and their government. Canadians want their government to help them, not hinder them, in the process of economic renewal. A smaller Cabinet is a more effective instrument to discuss, decide, to lead.

News conference following her
swearing-in as Prime Minister,
Ottawa, Canada, June 25/
Los Angeles Times, 6-26:(A)4.

Jorge Casteneda
Mexican political scientist

1

[On the proposed NAFTA, which Mexican President Carlos Salinas supports]: A majority in the U.S. House of Representatives agrees that this is in the United States's best interest. [But] there has been no such debate here [in Mexico]. After all we've given up, if the net result of five years of this economic model is 1 percent growth and a prediction of 3 percent growth next year— is this such a good deal for Mexico? Salinas won. But is he right?

The Christian Science Monitor,
11-19:16.

Fidel Castro
President of Cuba

2

[On his long leadership of Cuba]: Time passes, and marathon runners get tired. This has been a very long race—too long. I feel I am a slave of the revolution.

To reporters/Time, 3-8:18.

3

[Criticizing the U.S. economic embargo against Cuba because of its human-rights record]: Those that blockade us have excellent relations with Argentina, where 100,000 people have been "disappeared." We have no death squads here killing children who are homeless and hungry just to clean them from the streets [such as occurs in Brazil].

The Christian Science Monitor,
11-4:8.

Dick Cheney
Former Secretary of Defense
of the United States

4

[On the political crisis in Haiti]: There are some problems you're not going to solve. If you put [U.S.-backed deposed President Jean-Bertrand] Aristide back in there, he won't last very long. He'd probably be assassinated, unless you're willing to put a hell of a lot of American troops in there to protect him. I would not put American lives at risk to try to fix Haiti.

Interview/
U.S. News & World Report,
10-25:40.

Warren Christopher
Secretary of State
of the United States

5

[On Haiti, where the legally elected government was ousted in a coup in 1991]: We're going to keep working to make sure that international observers get into Haiti and that we can take steps toward the restoration of democracy . . . It's a frustrating and very tough situation, but those who hold illegal power there should know that they're swimming against the tide of history and that they will not prevail.

To reporters,
Washington, D.C., Feb. 5/
The Washington Post, 2-6:(A)8.

6

[On U.S. President Clinton's reneging on his campaign promise to end the previous Bush Administration policy of turning away Haitian boat people trying to get to U.S. shores]: I think our Haitian policy is the one that's soundest at the present time. I don't suppose you'd want anybody to keep a campaign promise if it was a very unsound policy.

Broadcast interview/
"Meet the Press," NBC-TV, 2-28.

Bill Clinton
President-elect
of the United States

7

[On his meeting with Mexican President Carlos Salinas during which they discussed NAFTA]: I reaffirmed my support for the North American Free Trade Agreement, and my conviction that there are some issues still outstanding between our two nations that needed to be addressed—including the labor issues and environmental issues and others. I don't believe the

(BILL CLINTON)

agreement needs to be reopened. I do believe that there need to be other agreements. I would like to see this wrapped up in a timely fashion, but I want these other issues addressed.

News conference,
Austin, Texas, Jan. 8/
The New York Times, 1-9:8.

1

[Urging Haitians not to try to come to the U.S. by boat as a result of 1991's military coup in Haiti]: Those who . . . leave Haiti for the United States by boat will be stopped and directly returned by the United States Coast Guard. To avoid the human tragedy of a boat exodus, I want to convey this message directly to the Haitian people: Leaving by boat is not the route to freedom . . . The practice of returning those who flee Haiti by boat will continue, for the time being, after I become President.

Voice of America radio address,
Jan. 14/
The Washington Post, 1-15:(A)16;
Los Angeles Times, 1-15:(A)23.

Bill Clinton
President of the United States

2

The North American Free Trade Agreement . . . began as an agreement [between the U.S. and] Canada, which I strongly supported, which has now led to a pact with Mexico as well. That agreement holds the potential to create many, many jobs in America over the next decade if it is joined with others to ensure that the environment, that living standards, that working conditions are honored, that we can literally know that we are going to raise the condition of people in America and in Mexico. We have a vested interest in a wealthier, stronger Mexico. But we need to do it on terms that are good for our people.

At American University,
Washington, D.C., Feb. 26/
The Washington Post,
2-27:(A)8.

3

To those who have blocked the restoration of democracy [in Haiti, following 1991's military coup], I want to make it clear in the strongest possible terms that we will not now or ever support the continuation of an illegal government in Haiti and that we want to step up dramatically the pace of negotiations to restore President [Jean-Bertrand] Aristide [who was ousted in the coup] under conditions of national reconciliation and mutual respect for human rights with a program of genuine economic progress. Any opposition, any delay, will only result in stronger measures taken by the United States and more difficulty and hardship for the people of Haiti who have been the innocent sufferers in this whole sad saga.

To reporters,
Washington, D.C., March 16/
Los Angeles Times, 3-17:(A)6.

4

[On the political crisis in Haiti]: During the past few days, we have witnessed a brutal attempt by Haiti's military and police authorities to thwart the expressed desire of the Haitian people for democracy . . . There are important American interests at stake in Haiti and in what is going on there. First, there are about 1,000 American citizens living in Haiti or working there. Second, there are Americans there who are helping to operate our Embassy. Third, we have an interest in promoting democracy in this hemisphere, especially in a place where such a large number of Haitians have clearly expressed their preference for a President [Jean-Bertrand Aristide, who was elected, then deposed in a coup, and who the U.S. is trying to reinstall]. And finally, we have a clear interest in working toward a government in Haiti that enables its citizens to live there in security so they do not have to flee in large numbers and at great risk to themselves to our shores and to other nations . . . The military authorities in Haiti simply must understand that they cannot indefinitely defy the desires of their own people as well as the will of the world community. That path holds only suffering for their nation, and international isolation for themselves.

News conference, Washington, D.C.,
Oct. 15/The New York Times, 10-16:4.

(BILL CLINTON)

1

[Supporting the return to Haiti of President Jean-Bertrand Aristide, who was ousted from office in a 1991 coup]: [If Aristide's opponents] believe that all they have to do is wait out Aristide and everything will somehow be all right, and that the international community will put up with the reestablishment of a Duvalier-like [dictatorial] regime there, in plain violation of the overwhelming majority of the people of Haiti [who elected Aristide], I think they are just wrong.

To reporters, Oct. 28/
The Washington Post, 10-29:(A)32.

Fernando Collor (de Mello)
President of Brazil

2

The elites were always uncomfortable with my program. I wanted to open the markets, end protectionism, and end the paternalistic relationship between the state and private enterprise. I wanted a government of transformation, of social and structural change, and this provoked very strong opposition. These people used as their banner the issue of morality. But there is *nothing* there . . . We have to reaffirm that—and this is extraordinary—Brazil is enjoying the broadest freedom since the creation of the republic. It's important to note that despite all that has happened, the institutions of democracy are consolidating, that the democratic process is unassailable.

Interview/
Vanity Fair, February:135,136.

Alfredo Cristiani
President of El Salvador

3

[On a UN commission's report charging human-rights abuses by the Salvadoran military during the civil war in the 1980s]: As far as promoting reconciliation, we think the Truth Commission report does not fulfill the desires of the majority of Salvadorans [today]. That desire is to forgive and forget the painful past that has caused so much suffering.

San Salvador, El Salvador, March 18/
The Washington Post, 3-19:(A)47.

Ramiro de Leon (Carpio)
President of Guatemala

4

Fortunately, within the [Guatemalan] Army, there is an understanding that it is time to prepare for peace, time to prepare for working professionally within a democratic system. That is not something that is so easy, because for many years that is not how [the military's] role was performed. Still, I am very certain that this is the way I will govern. Otherwise, I would prefer not to govern.

Interview,
Guatemala City, Guatemala, June 7/
Los Angeles Times, 6-8:(A)10.

Herve Denis
Minister of Culture
and Information of Haiti

5

[Saying the current military government of Haiti, which ousted the democratically elected government in a 1991 coup, would give up power if the U.S. ordered it to]: We know that the army will not move without being told, one way or another by their master [the U.S.]. The army has been built by the United States during the occupation period, 1915 to 1934. And the army is the instrument of the domination by the United States of Haiti. That's their thing; that's their instrument, that's their institution, and everybody knows in Haiti that the high officers of Haiti belong to the [U.S.] CIA or the Pentagon.

Interview,
Washington, D.C., Dec. 3/
The Washington Post, 12-6:(D)9.

Robert J. Dole
United States Senator,
R-Kansas

6

[On exiled former President of Haiti Jean-Bertrand Aristide, who the U.S. is trying to reinstall after he was ousted in a coup in 1991]: I don't think he'd win any blue ribbons in most places. I think he has a lot of shortcomings. He was elected. We didn't see a lot of democracy in the eight months he was there, but I assume that,

(ROBERT J. DOLE)

you know, he'll go back if it can be done peaceably. But I wouldn't risk any American lives to put Aristide back in power and try to force democracy on Haiti where there's no real record of democracy in the past—I don't know how long—way back in the 1930s or before.

Broadcast interview/
"Face the Nation," CBS-TV, 10-17.

Eduardo Frei, Jr.
President-elect of Chile

1

[On his victory in Chile's Presidential election]: Democracy has triumphed. Chile has triumphed. We will create the room and opportunity for the poor and disadvantaged of this country to grow. We will reach the 21st century as a developed nation with humanity and solidarity.

Victory speech,
Santiago, Chile, Dec. 11/
The Christian Science Monitor,
12-13:4.

Alberto K. Fujimori
President of Peru

2

[On his seizing almost dictatorial powers in Peru last year]: Today we have 95 percent of the Shining Path [guerrillas] leadership behind bars. By 1995, the Shining Path will be completely eradicated as an organized group. There's a close relationship between the fight against terrorism and the fight to restore economic growth. No amount of foreign aid, no economic plan—no matter how well designed—will have a beneficial effect if terrorism is not stopped . . . What has been demonstrated is that here in Peru the people want a strong government that creates social and economic order. People want a government that gives security to all the population and that gives guarantees to investors. I am confident that Peru is going to be one of Latin America's most developed nations in a few years.

Interview,
Lima, Peru, April 4/
The New York Times, 4-6:(A)3.

Cesar Gaviria (Trujillo)
President of Colombia

3

[On the decline in his popularity as guerrilla and narcotics violence has escalated in his country]: The government had a tough year . . . Even with great institutional changes it is very difficult for a government to remain popular while violence of such dimensions persists. All these periods of transformation produce some euphoria at first and disenchantment later.

Interview/
The Washington Post, 2-24:(A)16.

Daniel Goldstein
Senior analyst,
Grupo Financiero Serfin
(Mexico)

4

[On the controversy over NAFTA in the U.S.]: The [Mexican stock] market is oversensitive. The whole signing and ratification of NAFTA has been oversold. Every time somebody sneezes, the market goes up or down, depending on who is doing the sneezing . . . Do we really need NAFTA to be signed and ratified at this point? We've been living NAFTA for the past three or four years. Companies have been gearing up, investing and building their infrastructures here. Do you think they're going to stop just because NAFTA doesn't go through?

The Washington Post, 7-3:(A)11,14.

Al Gore
Vice President
of the United States

5

[Calling for a "Western hemisphere community of democracies"]: We, the sovereign states of the Americas, share the same obligation—to create nations in which all have equal access to land, jobs and education—and together we dream of a future in which no person is exploited for the well-being of a few . . . We will seek to make explicit the convergence of values that is now rapidly taking place in a hemisphere community of democracies, increasingly inte-

(AL GORE)

grated by commercial exchange and shared political views.

Speech,
Mexico City, Mexico, Dec. 1/
Los Angeles Times, 12-2:(A)10.

1

[We should] rethink the way we deal with the new Latin America . . . to make explicit the convergence of values that is now rapidly taking place in a hemispheric community of democracies . . . These developments [NAFTA and the opening-up of Latin American markets to trade and development] are harbingers of a future in which the U.S. commercial and financial future will become increasingly entwined with the Americas—not only with Mexico and Canada, but with the countries of Central America, the Caribbean and South America as well.

Speech,
Mexico City, Mexico, Dec. 1/
The Christian Science Monitor,
12-15:24.

Monica Heller
Sociolinguist,
Ontario Institute for Studies
in Education (Canada)

2

The basis of Quebec nationalism is that we need a state to be able to function in French. The ideology of bilingualism, by contrast, is that you can be French anywhere in Canada.

The Washington Post, 4-7:(A)21.

John Kirton
Specialist in
U.S.-Canadian relations,
University of Toronto (Canada)

3

[On U.S.-Canadian relations under new Canadian Prime Minister Jean Chretien, who replaced Brian Mulroney]: [With Mulroney,] you had an unparalleled intensity of interaction between our two countries at the highest level,

and a real personal warmth and understanding. Canada was important and well-liked by [former U.S. Presidents Ronald] Reagan and [George] Bush. Now we're seeing the end of that high-level political access—and along with it goes the assumption of Canada's relevance and a favorable disposition on the American side.

The Christian Science Monitor,
11-19:7.

Lawrence Kudlow
Chief economist,
Bear, Stearns & Company
(United States)

4

The Mexican government is in a strong financial position, with a balanced budget, declining indebtedness, declining tax rates, and a Constitutional mandate to maintain the purchasing power of the peso. Looking forward, Mexico is likely to continue opening its markets . . . creating growing exports and investment. Having had five years of rising economic prospects, Mexico is likely to carry out the smoothest and fairest election in its history in August, 1994.

The Christian Science Monitor,
11-19:11.

Frank LaRue
Director,
Guatemala Center
for Legal Action
in Human Rights

5

I don't think the political structure of Guatemala has changed. The military and business community still control the country. Pragmatists in the Army are opening space for political debate. But the Army is still very much in control . . . The Guatemalan state should be able to function freely without military influence. The military shouldn't be the leading faction. But if you go to isolated villages in the Ixcan, there are no schools, no hospitals, no state presence except for the Army garrison.

The Christian Science Monitor,
7-20:7.

Robert Malval
Prime Minister of Haiti

1

My government has one goal: restore democracy as of today. My government has one duty: put an end to human-rights violations as of today. My country has one dream: to reconcile the country with itself.

At ceremony installing him as Prime Minister,
at Haitian Embassy,
Washington, D.C., Aug. 30/
Los Angeles Times, 8-31:(A)7.

2

We [in Haiti] don't ask for much. We ask only for the means to break out of the vicious circle of abject poverty so we can hope finally to break down the fatalism of our misery.

Before Organization of American States,
Washington, D.C., Aug. 30/
The Washington Post, 8-31:(A)20.

3

[Calling on the military to give up control of Haiti and return the government to himself and exiled elected President Jean-Bertrand Aristide, who he says have access to $29-million in Haiti's frozen accounts in the U.S.]: You cannot hold power only through violence, crimes and corruption, because the state is so bankrupt [financially] it is like a cow which has no more milk. So what's the use? In a bureaucratic state like ours, the people who sign the checks are the ones who are in power no matter what. [The military] may have the guns, but if they do not have the pen to sign the documents, well, then, they can destroy the country but they are not running it.

Interview,
Port-au-Prince, Haiti, Oct. 21/
The Washington Post, 10-22:(A)25.

Paul Martin
Minister of Finance of Canada

4

People [in Canada] can't say consistently that there's a problem with [government] deficits but solve it on somebody else's back. What people have to understand is that there can be no sector of the economy that is sacrosanct. If there's pain, then it's going to have to be shared equally.

The Christian Science Monitor,
12-27:2.

Judy Maxwell
Associate director,
School of Policy Studies,
Queen's University (Canada);
Former Chairman,
Economic Council of Canada

5

[On Canada's debt problem]: We're in a situation where the inexorable geometric progression of the interest on the interest on the interest is something we really have to worry about. The ratio of debt to GDP is higher in this country [than in the U.S.] and is rising much more quickly . . . Canada is pretty much up against its taxing limits . . . [The U.S.] is not.

Interview, Ottawa, Canada/
The Christian Science Monitor,
4-14:9.

Grant McCracken
Cultural anthropologist,
Royal Ontario Museum (Canada)

6

My sense is that the budget cuts we're going to see in the public sector and social supports [in Canada] in the next decade are going to be astonishing and will fundamentally change the nature of public life and political relations in Canada . . . This could spell the end of Canadian civility as we know it.

The Christian Science Monitor,
12-27:2.

Mike McCurry
Spokesman for the
Department of State
of the United States

7

[On the possibility of improved relations between the U.S. and Cuba]: We need to see fundamental changes in Cuba and its approach to

(MIKE McCURRY)

human rights, to democracy, to a range of conditions before there can be further discussions of how best to change this relationship. We have been fairly clear that we expect there to be real democratic change in Cuba as a necessary precondition for any type of dialogue with the United States.

The Washington Post, 7-31:(A)18.

Brian Mulroney
Prime Minister of Canada

1

[On the military government in Haiti, which took power in a 1991 coup]: People [in the U.S. and Canada] are going to have to decide whether we allow this travesty to take place in our own back yard, or whether we deploy some assets to make certain that the duly elected President of Haiti [Jean-Bertrand Aristide, who was ousted in the coup] is restored and that a constitutional democracy is allowed to survive and not be extinguished on an island, a little poor island off our own shores.

To reporters,
Washington, D.C., June 2/
The New York Times, 6-3:(A)5.

Dee Dee Myers
Press Secretary
to President of the United States
Bill Clinton

2

[On reports that Jean-Bertrand Aristide, who the U.S. is trying to get reinstalled as President of Haiti, is mentally unstable]: In our dealings with President Aristide, he has been rational and responsible. He has had the best interest of his people at heart, he has lived up to the commitments that he has made, and I would remind you that he is the duly elected leader of that country [he was ousted in a coup in 1991]—democratically elected leader—and so it is our judgment, based on our experience with him, that he is fully qualified to serve as the President of Haiti.

The New York Times, 10-23:3.

John Pammett
Chairman,
department of
political science,
Carleton University
(Canada)

3

[On Canada's forthcoming national election]: What's important politically is the public perception of whether the economy is improving or not. The general perception in the country is that the economy isn't improving. People judge this for themselves by their job situation and their own purchasing power . . . I find it hard to see the economy improving in a way that the [ruling] conservatives will be able to ride that to re-election. What will hurt them is that if you look back to 1984, the big issue in that election was unemployment. The conservatives' promise then was "jobs, jobs, jobs." Unfortunately for them, jobs, jobs, jobs is still the issue.

The Christian Science Monitor,
6-28:6.

Evans Paul
Mayor of Port-au-Prince,
Haiti

4

[On the failure of the U.S. and UN to act to remove the military government of Haiti, which in 1991 ousted Haiti's elected President, Jean-Bertrand Aristide]: We are asking ourselves a lot of questions about the negotiations themselves. Is the strategy adopted the best or is it deceptive, really aimed at something else? We do not understand how it is that the little Haitian army can hold off the whole world. It is hard to understand how the illegitimate government has the power to defy the United States and United Nations . . . The country is in the process of crumbling away. People are losing confidence in the negotiating process, and that could lead to violence. But so far we have seen no difference between [U.S. President] Clinton and [former U.S. President George] Bush, except that Clinton has put on a better show.

The Washington Post,
5-27:(A)38.

Jaime Paz Zamora
President of Bolivia

1

The real big privatization that's taken place [in Bolivia] in the past four years has been in people's minds. Most people today are thinking in terms of private initiative. In the old days, it used to be all state companies. The economic structure of the country has been privatized. That's the single biggest change in my country during my term of office.

The New York Times, 7-19:(A)5.

Rene Emilio Ponce
Minister of Defense
of El Salvador

2

[On a UN report accusing the Salvadoran military of human-rights abuses during the civil war in the 1980s]: We consider the report to be unjust, incomplete, illegal, unethical, partial and insolent. [It] defrauds the hope and faith of all Salvadorans, all of us who were expecting a serious and impartial document that might contribute to healing the wounds generated in 12 years of war.

Broadcast address to the nation,
San Salvador, El Salvador, March 23/
Los Angeles Times, 3-25:(A)6.

Rene Emilio Ponce
Former Minister of Defense
of El Salvador

3

[Defending the Salvadoran military against charges of human-rights abuses during the 1980s civil war against rebels who were trying to overthrow the government]: Let us reflect for a moment: Did the [rebels] achieve their objectives like the Marxists in Managua [Nicaragua] and Cuba? Has a Communist system been established here? Were the armed forces defeated militarily in order to change our democratic system? The answer to all of these questions is no.

At Salvadoran Military Academy,
July 1/
Los Angeles Times, 7-2:(A)6.

Randall Robinson
Executive director,
TransAfrica (United States)

4

[Criticizing U.S. President Clinton's policy of returning Haitian boat people to Haiti in order to reduce the flow of Haitians seeking asylum in the U.S.]: Clinton said [former U.S. President George] Bush's [same] policy was inhumane and cruel. Now he has embraced that policy. The Bush policy was a racist policy. It remains a racist policy under Clinton.

Los Angeles Times, 4-17:(A)7.

Gert Rosenthal
Executive Secretary,
United Nations Economic Commission
for Latin America
and the Caribbean

5

[On the possibility that the U.S. House of Representatives may not pass the proposed NAFTA]: [The failure to pass NAFTA] would be very negative for Latin America. The United States has been advocating for many years the benefits of free trade. After 40 years, Latin America is convinced, and opens up unilaterally. Now, at this stage of the game, [the U.S. tells] us they made a mistake? That sends a pretty confusing signal.

The Washington Post, 11-13:(A)20.

Pedro Rossello
Governor of Puerto Rico

6

I'm an advocate for [U.S.] statehood for Puerto Rico, and so is my [New Progressive] Party. We feel that Puerto Rico fulfills all the requirements to be a state. The only thing missing is that the people of Puerto Rico petition it . . . From a purely democratic perspective, as American citizens we should have all the rights, privileges and responsibilities [of citizens]. Also, we look at ourselves in the context of opening up the Latin American part of the Americas. We share with the Latin American nations a heritage and language, and if the U.S. is to develop a leadership within the Americas, it will need those skills.

Interview/USA Today, 11-11:(A)13.

Carlos Salinas (de Gortari)
President of Mexico

1

The broad consensus that exists today in Mexican society in favor of [NAFTA] is based on the perception that this is a just and balanced accord. In Mexico's case, the fact that a broad majority of the population now supports a new type of relationship with the United States is something that has not been present for generations. To understand the significance [of this reversal of attitude], one merely has to recall the complex and at times traumatic history of the U.S.-Mexican relationship. Only a few years ago, anti-U.S. rhetoric was an easy route to popularity.

Oct. 7*/
The Washington Post, 10-8:(A)33.

2

We [in Mexico] are unavoidably neighbors of the greatest world power at the end of the Cold War [the U.S.]. History has taught us to be profoundly zealous of our territorial integrity, of our will to endure as a sovereign nation . . . The defense of sovereignty demands a Mexico that is internally strong and also united.

State of the Union address,
Mexico City, Mexico, Nov. 1/
The Christian Science Monitor,
11-3:3.

Elisardo Sanchez (Santa Cruz)
Cuban political dissident

3

[Saying the U.S. is wrong to isolate Communist Cuba, whose government he opposes]: We [in Cuba] are only 90 miles away from you [in the U.S.], and whatever happens in Cuba will have serious national-security consequences for the United States. It is time to realize that by maintaining open hostility, the United States is helping [Cuban President Fidel] Castro. The external enemy is the best friend of the totalitarian dictator . . . The embargo against Cuba is not the cause of the country's problems. They result from three decades of neo-Stalinist policies, and this is what will cause Castro's down-

fall. The boxer who fights in a rigid style is more easily beaten. Change is coming to Cuba, and if Washington could learn to be more flexible, its opponent would fall of his own accord.

Interview, Miami, Fla./
The New York Times, 8-3:(A)5.

Jaime Serra (Puche)
Mexican economist;
Leader of Mexican delegation
at North American Free Trade
Agreement negotiations

4

There are two ways to look at NAFTA. You may see it as a zero-sum game—where one wins and the other loses; or you may see it as a positive-sum game—where both parties win. Every one of the 23 independent studies on NAFTA that I know of demonstrate that it is a positive-sum game. They say there will be job creation in the three countries [U.S., Canada, Mexico] due to the synergy of the three countries' economies. This would make the region more competitive vis-a-vis other regions . . . Those who say NAFTA is a zero-sum game . . . [say that] low wages determine exports [and therefore Mexico's exports will benefit most at the expense of the U.S. and Canada. But] if low wages could determine the behavior of exports, there would be no country with low wages. Countries like Haiti would be a true export power. Ironically, if you take a look at the export products that sell in the United States, you'll see they come from Japan and Germany—both high-wage countries.

Interview, Mexico City, Mexico/
Los Angeles Times, 8-1:(M)3.

Wayne Smith
Fellow,
Center for International Policy
(United States);
Former Chief of U.S. Interest Section
in Cuba

5

[Saying the U.S. should improve its relations with Cuba]: It is rather depressing. Here the Cubans are moving in the direction we said we

(WAYNE SMITH)

wanted them to move . . . [But] it begins to appear [the U.S. Clinton Administration is] wasting this chance. [Cuba] has done virtually everything we used to ask them to do. They got their troops out of Africa, they are not supporting revolution anywhere in the world, and Cuba-Russia military ties are practically non-existent. And the principal human-rights activist [in Cuba] says U.S. policy doesn't help the situation. If there were a reduction in tension, then a lot more could happen.

The Washington Post, 7-31:(A)18.

David Stewart
Political scientist,
University of Alberta (Canada)

1

Changing leaders is something Canadians view as almost creating a new party. Canadians identify parties by their leaders, so that if you change the leader it almost creates a new party in the eye of the beholder.

The Christian Science Monitor,
8-25:3.

Robert G. Torricelli
United States Representative,
D-New Jersey

2

[On a UN-sponsored report accusing the Salvadoran military of human-rights abuses during a time when then-U.S. President Ronald Reagan's Administration was telling Congress the opposite]: This Congress 10 years ago established a process whereby President Reagan would certify that improvements were being made in human rights in order to continue [U.S.] military aid to El Salvador. It now is abundantly clear that Ronald Reagan made those certifications in defiance of the truth. If [government officials] testified they had no knowledge of killings when they did, they better not have said it under oath. [We] will review every word uttered by every Reagan Administration official . . . I,

for one, will not be content until we know the whole truth about our own attempt to cover up these abuses from the Congress and the American people.

At House Western Hemisphere
Subcommittee hearing,
Washington, D.C., March 16/
The Washington Post, 3-17:(A)28.

George Vest
Former United States Ambassador
to El Salvador

3

[On U.S. support for the Salvadoran government during the civil war there in the 1980s, despite charges of human-rights abuses committed by the Salvadoran military]: In principle, in my heart, I'm with the people who wanted human rights to be our sole priority. But in the real world, you don't have the luxury of having an absolute choice. The essential test is: to what extent did the [U.S.] policy succeed? This policy hasn't succeeded totally, but it's made some progress. El Salvador is a much better place to live than it was when all this started.

July 15/
Los Angeles Times, 7-16:(A)8.

Frantz Voltaire
Chief of Staff
to Haitian Prime Minister
Robert Malval

4

[Saying Malval intends to resign because, despite his being the ostensible democratic Prime Minister of Haiti, the real power remains with the military leaders who took over in a 1991 coup that ousted the elected government]: The fiction of our [democratic] government comforts everyone. It allows the international community to avoid facing up to the reality here and it allows the army to avoid its responsibilities. Meanwhile, the situation in the country just rots.

Interview,
Port-au-Prince, Haiti, Dec. 1/
The New York Times,
12-2:(A)8.

Alexander Watson
Assistant Secretary
for Inter-American Affairs,
Department of State
of the United States

1

[On U.S. policy toward Cuba now that the Cold War is over]: We can neither ignore nor negotiate away the human and political rights of the Cuban people. There will be no upgrade in relations until rights are respected.

The Christian Science Monitor,
11-4:8.

Clifton R. Wharton, Jr.
Deputy Secretary of State
of the United States

2

Our marching orders [from U.S. President Clinton] are to engage with Latin America and the Caribbean to strengthen democracy and expand prosperity [there] . . . Human rights is the core of our policy. The United States will direct its aid and influence in every way possible to enable the nations of this hemisphere to advance human rights and strengthen the democratic institutions which promote the rule of law.

Before Council of the Americas,
Washington, D.C., May 3/
The Washington Post, 5-4:(A)15.

Graham White
Political scientist,
University of Toronto (Canada)

3

[On the unpopularity of the Senate, the upper house of the Canadian Parliament, which recently gave its members a $6,000 increase in expense allowances]: People are having a tough time in the private and public sectors, and the Senate seems to many like a resting home for old political hacks. When people see everybody else tightening their belts, and the Senators go and do this, it looks bad.

The Christian Science Monitor,
7-20:7.

Michael Wilson
Analyst,
Heritage Foundation
(United States)

4

[On the U.S. Clinton Administration's trying to return Jean-Bertrand Aristide to the Presidency of Haiti, from which he was removed by a coup in 1991]: I think we're making the mistake of promoting Aristide's interest over the interests of [the U.S.]. I think it's a mistake to equate him with the restoration of human rights and democracy . . . It's important for [the Clinton Administration] to realize Aristide is not going to return. [Haiti] is so polarized and there is this kind of gang mentality. There are no institutions that promote civilian control of the army, or promote democracy or economic freedom.

The Christian Science Monitor,
1-15:2.

Ruben Zamora
Vice President
of the Legislative Assembly
of El Salvador

5

The [Salvadoran] armed forces are faced with a historic dilemma, the same as the rest of the country. The dilemma is whether we start on the road toward demilitarization or whether we stay a militarized society, and that would lead us back to war sooner or later.

The Washington Post, 1-12:(A)12.

6

[Saying the military has too much influence in El Salvador's government]: We have a crisis and the question is: Who is running the country, a Defense Minister who resigned or the President who has not yet accepted his resignation? Is the military power subordinate to the civilian power, or is the civilian power merely decorative? . . . The military is trying to hang on to 60 years of privileges. They do not want to understand the country has changed, and it has changed for better, not for worse.

The Washington Post,
3-26:(A)30.

(RUBEN ZAMORA)

1

The [UN-sponsored] peace agreement [ending the civil war in El Salvador] means the deepest political transition in modern Salvadoran history. The country in the last 14 months has changed more than the previous 60 years. Basically, we see four processes taking place in the country. One is from war to peace . . . A second . . . is from a militarized society into a demilitarized society. The military had been dominating our society for the last 60 years and the peace agreement is the main instrument for changing that. This transition is going on, but there is a lot of opposition on the part of the military . . . Then there is a third level of transition that I would say is even deeper than the other two. Because it is a transition in the way political power has been conceived and exercised in Salvadoran society . . . From the very beginning in our society, power has always been an instrument for excluding other people . . . Negotiation, consenting policies, give and take—this is out of our political culture.

Interview, Boston, Mass./
The Christian Science Monitor,
4-2:7.

Asia and the Pacific

Joseph F. Ada
Governor of Guam

1

[Urging U.S. commonwealth status for Guam]: Guam is a colony of America, with all that the term implies. We are a colony, one of the last, in a world which for the most part has turned away from the idea that colonies should exist . . . Even today, although we go through the motions of electing our own legislature and Governor, the [U.S.] Federal government reserves to itself the right to overrule all of our laws, overthrow our government and unilaterally establish any law over our people that it wishes, without restriction.

At conference on U.S. territories,
Washington, D.C., Feb. 9/
The Washington Post, 2-10:(A)14.

Kazuo Aichi
Member of Japanese House
of Representatives

2

Both [the U.S. and Japan] suffer from a perception gap. Japan still acts as if it is the younger brother of the United States, unable to act without U.S. initiative, studying every move of the U.S. so as to learn from "older brother." The United States seems to continue to live in the 1950s, when it had the economic resources to take global initiatives and could expect others to follow without consultation. As Japan introduces political reform, we will be able to approach the U.S. as a true partner. Certainly, this will be [a] healthier situation than what exists now. But I must say I am concerned as to whether the Americans can make this adjustment in perception. The first step to developing a mature, equal partnership requires that both recognize each other as a partner and that each is literate in the other's economic, political and social structures. The United States must learn how to become a partner.

Before Asia Society,
Washington, D.C., March 18/
The Washington Post, 4-1:(A)22.

Desmond Ball
Analyst, Strategic
and Defense Studies Center,
Australian National University

3

For many [Asian] countries, China is emerging as the greatest security concern in the region. Its military buildup is the fastest in the region and . . . bears a major proportion of the responsibility for the buildups elsewhere in the region.

The Washington Post, 3-31:(A)21.

Max Baucus
United States Senator,
D-Montana

4

[U.S. President-elect Clinton has the opportunity of] leading the nations of the world in convincing China that it cannot continue its destabilizing policies on trade, human rights and arms sales . . . Each year the nations of the world can less afford to isolate China. One in every five people in the world now lives in China. Its sheer size means that it will play a significant role in the world's political, economic and environmental affairs. Breaking ties with China would only hand its future over to the hard-line Marxists who sent the tanks into Tiananmen Square. It would not help the cause of democracy, improve trade relations or further the cause of arms control.

Before Business Coalition
for U.S.-China Trade,
Washington, D.C., Jan. 7/
The Washington Post, 1-8:(A)18.

Paul Beaver
Publisher,
"Jane's Defense Weekly"

5

Whether you want to call it an arms race is an emotive term, but there is certainly a continued buildup taking place is Asia. There is definitely no peace dividend and everyone in the region is increasing their defense spending.

Los Angeles Times, 3-23:(H)1.

Benazir Bhutto
*Former Prime Minister
of Pakistan*

1

I have symbolized for the people of Pakistan a democratic, liberal and egalitarian country. That is why I have retained their respect and affection . . . I know the people of Pakistan are with me. I know in a free election, the people of Pakistan would vote for me. But I know there are powerful elements who oppose what I stand for, and they will go out of their way to prevent the people of Pakistan from having me as Prime Minister.

*To reporters/
The Christian Science Monitor,
5-11:7.*

Joseph R. Biden, Jr.
*United States Senator,
D-Delaware*

2

[U.S.] engagement [with China] is fine if our diplomacy makes clear to China that we have no higher international priority than preventing nuclear and missile proliferation. But our policy must have a bottom line. An endless dialogue would allow China's leaders to . . . [reap] an enormous surplus from the American consumer market and a dangerously irresponsible profit from the global arms bazaar.

*Oct. 29/
The Washington Post, 11-1:(A)6.*

Boutros Boutros-Ghali
*Secretary General
of the United Nations*

3

[Saying Japan should play a larger role in UN peacekeeping efforts]: If you are an important country, you have important responsibilities. And Japan is a great power, a major country. My message to Japan is that we need more assistance, we need more involvement, we need more attention to what is done by the UN.

*Before Japan National Press Club,
Tokyo, Japan, Feb. 18/
Los Angeles Times, 2-19:(A)10.*

Richard A. Brecher
*Director of
business advisory services,
United States-China
Business Council*

4

American companies are working the China trade issue more aggressively than ever before because the commercial stakes are so much higher this year. The pressure from the Chinese is not overt, but it's generally understood that all these big business deals will die overnight if [China's most-favored-nation trade status with the U.S.] is revoked. Everything we [Americans] are selling, they [the Chinese] can buy from someone else.

The New York Times, 5-7:(C)2.

Warren Christopher
*Secretary of State
of the United States*

5

[On whether the U.S. will renew China's most-favored-nation trade status]: It is my hope we can go forward with MFN this year, but conditioned on their making very substantial progress [in human rights]. Whether that program will be enough to justify going forward, whether the [U.S.] Congress will find the trend to be in the right direction, is something that will have to evolve over the next several weeks and months. It is not the preferred solution, I think, to isolate China further.

*Before House Appropriations Subcommittee,
Washington, D.C., March 10/
The Washington Post, 3-11:(A)25.*

6

Asia buys more from us [the U.S.] than any other region in the world. Our trading relationship is the strongest of any region in the world. It gives [U.S. President Clinton] an opportunity to emphasize that we intend to remain a Pacific power; to emphasize that we will maintain our security relationships in the Pacific; and that we feel a responsibility to provide leadership in the Pacific. Our forward basing will continue in the Pacific.

*To reporters, Tokyo, Japan, July 6/
Los Angeles Times, 7-7:(A)6.*

269

WHAT THEY SAID IN 1993

(WARREN CHRISTOPHER)

1

Some have argued that democracy is some-how unsuited for Asia and that [the U.S.] emphasis on human rights [in Asia] is a mask for Western cultural imperialism. They could not be more wrong. The yearnings for freedom are not a Western export; they are a human instinct.

*At meeting of Association
of Southeast Asian Nations, July/
The Christian Science Monitor,
12-15:12.*

Chua Beng Huatt
*Professor of political science,
National University of Singapore*

2

America never really had the clout to influence Asia. It lost influence on economics and in security, and now only has a moral stance on human rights.

*The Christian Science Monitor,
12-15:12.*

Bill Clinton
President of the United States

3

The persistence of the [trade] surplus the Japanese enjoy with the United States and with the rest of the developed world can only lead one to the conclusion that the possibility of obtaining real, even access to the Japanese market is some-what remote.

*News conference,
Washington, D.C., March 23/
The New York Times, 3-25:(C)1.*

4

The world needs a strong Japan. The world needs a strong United States. The world needs these two countries to cooperate. And it can only happen if we are making real progress on this [U.S.-Japan] trade deficit . . . Let's not paper this over. There are still differences between the [Japanese] Prime Minister [Kiichi Miyazawa] and me about what we should do. I recognize that these are complex issues, but the simple fact is

that it is harder to sell in Japan's market than in ours. America is accepting the challenge of change and so, too, must Japan.

*News conference,
Washington, D.C., April 16/
The New York Times, 4-17:1,4.*

5

[On his decision to grant China a continuation of most-favored-nation trade status with the U.S. despite China's poor human-rights record]: In order for a country to trade with us, they have to get what's called "most-favored-nation status" in order to have big trade. China is a huge trading partner of ours. We have, I think, now our second-biggest trading deficit with China, just behind Japan. They've got one of the fastest-growing economies in the world. They're moving away from Communism to market economics very quickly. They still put political prisoners in jail. They still, we think, have used prison labor to make products. And we have some other prob-lems with them. The issue is, should we revoke [MFN] or should we put conditions on it. I basically have decided to extend most-favored-nation status for a year because I want to sup-port modernization in China. And it's a great opportunity for America there. But I want to make it clear to them that there has to be some progress on human rights and the use of prison labor. Our trade disputes and our disputes about arms sales—I'm going to take [them] out of this issue and negotiate directly with them.

*Broadcast question-and-answer session,
Washington, D.C./
"CBS This Morning," CBS-TV, 5-27.*

6

The United States has no more important bilateral relationship than our relationship with Japan. We are strategic allies, and our futures are bound up together.

*Tokyo, Japan, July 6/
Los Angeles Times, 7-7:(A)6.*

7

Some have argued democracy is somehow unsuited for Asia . . . that human rights are rela-

270

(BILL CLINTON)

tive, that they simply mask Western cultural imperialism. I believe those voices are wrong. It is not Western urging or Western imperialism, but the aspirations of Asian people themselves that explain the growing numbers of democracies and democratic nations in this region. It is an insult to the spirit and hopes and dreams of the people who live here to assert that anything else is true.

At Waseda University (Japan),
July 7/
Los Angeles Times, 7-7:(A)7.

1

[On U.S.-Japanese relations]: We have built a vital friendship. We continue to anchor this region's security and to fuel its development. Japan is an increasingly important global part- ner in peacekeeping, in promoting democracy, in protecting the environment, in addressing major challenges in this region and throughout the world. Because our relationship has been built on enduring common interests and genuine friend- ship, it has transcended particular leaders in each country, and it will continue to do so.

At Waseda University (Japan),
July 7/
The Washington Post, 7-8:(A)14.

2

Even as we move through the sixth year of [U.S.] defense cuts, we are not reducing our base presence in Japan, we are not reducing our base presence in [South] Korea. We are strengthening our military presence in Asia and in the Pacific. We reaffirm our security commitments to Japan and to [South] Korea and to all our other allies in this region. And we intend to press to see that the [nuclear] non-proliferation treaty's regime is fully observed, including having the interna- tional observers [in North Korea, which may be developing atomic weapons]. That is the posi- tion that the United States takes, and I think that we have to adhere to it very firmly. North Korea has not yet declined to comply [with the treaty, so] let us continue the negotiations. Until there is

a rupture that seems final, I don't think we should talk about what would happen at that point.

News conference at G-7 summit,
Tokyo, Japan, July 9/
The New York Times, 7-10:5.

3

When you examine the nature of the Ameri- can security commitment to [South] Korea, to Japan, to this region, it is pointless for [North Korea] to try to develop nuclear weapons. Because if they ever use them, it would be the end of their country.

To U.S. troops,
South Korea, July 11/
The New York Times, 7-12:(A)2.

4

[On the recent meeting between the U.S. and Asia-Pacific nations]: If you ask me to sum- marize in a single sentence what we've agreed, it is this: It is that the Asian-Pacific region should be a united one, not divided. We are helping the Asia Pacific to become a genuine community: not a formal legal structure but rather a community of shared interests, shared goals and shared com- mitment to mutually beneficial cooperation.

The Washington Post, 11-22:(A)1.

Kenneth S. Courtis
Chief economist,
Deutsche Bank Capital Markets
(Asia) Ltd.

5

[On Japan]: A country that has had a trade surplus year in and year out since 1960 is a coun- try that is structurally under-consuming.

The Washington Post, 4-15:(D)16.

Deng Xiaoping
Senior leader of China

6

[On China and Taiwan]: The two sides must be unified. If Taiwan engages in "one China, one Taiwan" or in Taiwan independence, if it colludes with foreign forces to interfere in

(DENG XIAOPING)

China's internal affairs, we'll have no choice. We'll have to use force to solve the Taiwan question.

Speech/
The New York Times, 4-12:(A)6.

John M. Deutch
Under Secretary
for Acquisition and Technology,
Department of Defense
of the United States

1

The current North Korean capability in tactical ballistic missiles and the future possibility that these missiles can carry nuclear, chemical or biological warheads is one of the major security dangers of the future. The threat will be in this area for a long time.

Tokyo, Japan, Sept. 22/
Los Angeles Times, 9-23:(A)31.

Rudi Dornbusch
Economist,
Massachusetts Institute
of Technology (United States)

2

There are no major obstacles to continued growth in Asia: Savings rates are high, access to external capital is plentiful, and the world trading system is staying open. Asia cannot fail to do well.

The Christian Science Monitor,
12-3:11.

J. Malcolm Dowling
Economist,
Asian Development Bank
(Philippines)

3

Japan has taken Western technology and figured out how to produce it better and cheaper, and to do it in Asian countries. But the Japanese don't want Southeast Asia and China to do the same thing. They want them tied to Japanese technology. It's like the prey of the black widow spider: By the time you realize you're in the web, it's too late.

The Christian Science Monitor,
12-1:13.

Peter Drysdale
Executive director,
Australia-Japan Research Center
(Australia)

4

For people with vision, the idea of a free-trade arrangement in the Asia-Pacific [area] has got to be the defining idea for the Pacific century.

The Christian Science Monitor,
11-17:10.

David Goodman
Professor,
Murdoch University (Australia)

5

We all grew up with the assumption that a democracy is sustained by a middle class, but does a middle class demand a democracy? Our evidence [in Asia] would tend to suggest that is not true. What we are hearing is that the new rich want a system that works; they are not so worried about who is making the decisions. The pattern that I think is most likely to emerge in Asia is one of quasi-democracies, where one party dominates. In China, it will probably be the Communist Party.

World Press Review, August:25.

Toyoo Gyohten
Chairman,
Bank of Tokyo (Japan)

6

When the Cold War was over, we were extremely happy. But while Europe and the Western Hemisphere enjoy a high degree of political stability, Asia is more complex. What we are going to see in this part of the world is a coexistence of several world powers.

The Christian Science Monitor,
4-7:4.

Alexander M. Haig, Jr.
*Former Secretary of State
of the United States*

1

[Criticizing the U.S. policy of trying to get China to improve its human-rights record]: How dare we go around telling the rest of the world [to live according to U.S. human-rights standards]. I think the time has come to take a different tack here. And [the 1989 violent government crackdown on pro-democracy demonstrators in Beijing's] Tiananmen [Square] is a long way behind us.

*Interview, Beijing, China/
The New York Times, 10-28:(A)6.*

Han Sung Joo
*Foreign Minister
of South Korea*

2

Our security need will continue with or without unification [with North Korea]. For regional balance, as well, we need the United States in the [region]—in the security, political and economic areas . . . I don't expect any strong clamor [in the U.S.] to reduce the American presence in the area and in Korea. It is in the interest of the United States to have Korea as a strong ally in this area where there is a lot of competition going on among the major powers—Japan, China and, I suppose, Russia . . . And even in an economic sense, it is not a loss to the United States. It costs less for the United States to keep troops here than at home.

*Interview,
Seoul, South Korea, March 5/
Los Angeles Times, 3-6:(A)4.*

Abdul Basit Haqqani
*Secretary for United States
and Europe,
Ministry of Foreign Affairs
of Pakistan*

3

[On U.S. suggestions that Pakistan is a terrorist state because of its alleged supplying

of arms and training to guerrillas fighting India in Kashmir and its support for Sikh militant separatists in Punjab]: Pakistan is not that kind of country at all. What exactly is Pakistan being accused of? At best, it is accused of providing material support, weapons and training . . . Which is exactly what we and the U.S. were doing in Afghanistan.

Los Angeles Times, 4-9:(A)5.

Robert D. Hormats
*Former Assistant Secretary
for Economic Affairs,
Department of State
of the United States*

4

The Chinese, in particular, understand now that the United States needs their market. Fifteen years ago, our entire relationship with China was geo-strategic. They were a card to play against the Soviets. Now it is geo-economic. They know we need them as a market for exports, not a card to play. That gives them a lot more leverage when we make demands on them about human rights. [U.S. President] Clinton will be meeting with a much more self-confident Chinese leadership than any President in the past.

The New York Times, 11-19:(A)7.

Morihiro Hosokawa
Prime Minister of Japan

5

It is time to candidly admit that Japan has so far put its highest priority on economic development and has not paid sufficient attention to improving the quality of life for each and every person . . . I intend to work vigorously for expanded domestic demand and improved market access and for such consumer-oriented policies as rectifying the disparity between domestic and international prices and promoting deregulation.

*Before Japanese Diet (Parliament),
Tokyo, Japan, Aug. 23/
The New York Times, 8-24:(A)5.*

6

[On the wide-ranging changes he is proposing for Japan's economic and political system]: In

(MORIHIRO HOSOKAWA)

the modern history of Japan, there were three instances of major change. One was the visit by Commodore Perry [in the 1850s], and the ensuing Meiji Restoration. The second major change was the end of World War II [and the U.S. occupation] . . . This time around, for the first time in the modern history of this country, the major change is being generated from inside. This by itself, I believe, is a remarkable thing, almost revolutionary.

Interview,
Tokyo, Japan, Sept. 24/
The New York Times, 9-25:3.

Jiang Zemin
Chairman,
Communist Party of China

1

As for the way that China deals with the so-called democracy activists, this is an internal Chinese matter. But when foreign countries do not understand us, we believe in dialogue. We are opposed [to foreign countries] applying pressure. Applying pressure against China is undesirable and ineffective. On matters that cannot be resolved immediately, we should seek common ground while reserving differences. China has always resolved these [democracy-activist] matters according to China's legal system.

Interview, Beijing, China/
U.S. News & World Report,
3-15:60.

2

[On China's arms sales to other countries]: We always abide by three principles: The transfers must contribute to the strengthening of the recipient countries' legitimate self-defense capabilities. They must not harm the peace and security of the regions concerned. And we do not use arms transfers to interfere in the internal affairs of other sovereign nations. In quantitative terms, the volume of arms sold by China is, in a relative sense, extremely small. If we compare China's arms sales with those of developed countries, using a vivid Chinese expression we would

say that it's like the novice magician meeting the Grand Wizard. [The amount of China's arms exports is as small as the world's supply of] phoenix feathers and unicorn horns.

Interview, Beijing, China/
U.S. News & World Report,
3-15:60.

3

[On reunification of China and Taiwan]: In order to see an early end to the state of separation, both sides should undertake contacts and peaceful negotiations as early as possible. I personally believe that if we can sit down and talk, we will surely be able to find a method acceptable to both sides. We advocate achieving national reunification as soon as possible through peaceful methods. But we do not promise not to use military force. This is absolutely not directed against the Taiwanese people. This is mainly directed against the forces of Taiwanese independence and foreign interference. If Taiwan were to become independent or if foreign forces were to split China, we would absolutely not sit by and watch. We would take drastic measures to resolutely defend the state's sovereignty and territorial integrity and to protect the fundamental interests of the entire Chinese people, including our 20 million Taiwanese compatriots.

Interview,
Beijing, China/
U.S. News & World Report,
3-15:60.

Sidney Jones
Director, Asia Watch

4

Most of the political violence [in Cambodia] is by the SOC [the government]. Cambodian human-rights organizations are terrified, not of the Khmer Rouge [rebels], but of the current government. There are absolutely no good guys. Regardless of who wins the [upcoming] elections, it's going to be bad news for most Cambodians.

The Washington Post,
2-15:(A)34.

Bob Kapp
Director,
China Relations Council
of Washington State
(United States)

1

[On the forthcoming meeting of the Asia-Pacific Economic Cooperation forum, at which the U.S. will try to improve its trading relationship with that area]: If policies are improved and enhanced, then we're all going to do better: More people will get work, and more people will have money in their pockets. Does the [U.S.] shoe-repair shop on the corner benefit tomorrow from what APEC did yesterday? Of course not. But if APEC contributes to enhanced economic relations throughout the Pacific Rim, the shoe-repair person will ultimately benefit as well.

USA Today, 11-12:(A)6.

Bilahari Kausikan
Director,
East Asia and Pacific Bureau,
Foreign Ministry of Singapore

2

Japan has always been "in" Asia but is still not "of" Asia. It has had only ad hoc responses to issues that come up and lacks a consensus on a partnership with Asia.

The Christian Science Monitor,
12-15:13.

Paul Keating
Prime Minister of Australia

3

[On his Labor Party's recent national re-election]: I wanted to win again, to be there in the 1990s, to see Australia prosper, as it will. We have turned the corner; the growth is coming through. We will see ourselves as a sophisticated trading country in Asia and we've got to do it in a way where everybody's got a part in it.

Victory speech, March 13/
The Christian Science Monitor,
3-15:6.

4

[Calling for Australia to become a republic and cut its ties to the British monarchy]: We need to be in every sense, including the symbolic one, our own masters. It is why the affirmation of our nationhood is central to our psychology . . . The fact is, Australia will be taken more seriously as a player in regional affairs if we are clear about our identity and demonstrate that we really mean to stand on our own feet, practically and psychologically.

Speech,
Sydney, Australia, April 28/
The Christian Science Monitor,
4-30:7.

5

[On freer trade in the Asia-Pacific area]: What I think APEC portends is half the world's [output] being allowed to move more freely between member states so that by taking away impediments to trade and investment and harmonizing standards, we can actually pick up the velocity of trade and investment in this part of the world.

News conference, October/
The Christian Science Monitor,
11-17:10.

Kim Young Sam
President of South Korea

6

[On his being inaugurated as South Korea's first President without military connections]: Deep in my heart, I have a vision of a new Korea . . . a freer and more mature democracy. We have had to wait for this moment for 30 long years. At last we have established a government by the people and of the people of this land.

Inaugural address,
Seoul, South Korea, Feb. 25/
The Washington Post, 2-26:(A)29.

7

[South] Korea is situated between advanced countries and developing countries in terms of its economic status. So we are in a position to be able to promote a smooth dialogue with both advanced countries and developing countries . . . The United States regards Korea as an

(KIM YOUNG SAM)

important country. So does Japan. And China cannot ignore us. So all important countries of the world cannot continue treating our country as they did when we had illegitimate military governments. After I took office as President, the international opinion toward Korea changed. Unlike the past 32 years, we are morally proud.

Interview, Seoul, South Korea/
Los Angeles Times, 11-14:(M)3.

1

[On negotiations between his country and North Korea]: My position is this: North Korea should discharge its international obligations first—that is, accept International Atomic Energy Agency special inspections [to determine if North Korea is developing atomic weapons] and also show its sincerity in conducting meaningful dialogue with South Korea. These conditions are what North Korea must meet before demanding any concessions from its partners. My position will not change. It is firm.

Interview, Seoul, South Korea/
Los Angeles Times, 11-14:(M)3.

Lee Hong Koo
Former South Korean Ambassador
to the United Kingdom

2

[On the U.S. Clinton Administration's increasing attention to Asia]: The [former U.S. President George] Bush generation grew up in the tradition of the Atlantic Community, whereas Clinton seems free of the traditions that make it automatic to focus on Europe. I am sure he is not trying to replace Europe, but we believe he wants a more balanced view and feels free to do so . . . There is no legacy of communal fellowship in Asia-Pacific. It is not like the European Community, where you faced a common enemy together. It is much more of a Wild West situation where you have to persuade each country to come along on each issue.

The New York Times,
11-19:(A)7.

Lee Kuan Yew
Former Prime Minister
of Singapore

3

[Saying Japan needs to be more open to other Asians]: Because of culture and language, [the Japanese] don't have the empathy and ease of relations with other peoples, which Americans have . . . The best [Asian] students . . . are not going to Japan but to America. They bring back fond memories of days at college there and the friendships struck there, which will be carried into business and political life . . . That may not be easy for Japan. It is the nature of the culture.

The Christian Science Monitor,
12-15:13.

Winston Lord
Assistant Secretary-designate
for East Asian and Pacific Affairs,
Department of State
of the United States

4

Today no region in the world is more important for the U.S. than Asia and the Pacific. Tomorrow, in the 21st century, no region will be as important.

At Senate hearing on his nomination,
Washington, D.C./
The Christian Science Monitor,
6-9:4.

Winston Lord
Assistant Secretary
for East Asian and Pacific Affairs,
Department of State
of the United States

5

We will seek cooperation with China on a range of issues, [but] Americans cannot forget [China's crushing of pro-democracy demonstrations in Beijing in 1989]. The United States therefore should conduct a nuanced policy toward Beijing until a more-humane system emerges. Shunning China is not an alternative. We need both to condemn repression and preserve links with progressive forces which are the foundation of our longer-term ties.

The Christian Science Monitor, 4-30:3.

(WINSTON LORD)

1

[U.S.] President Clinton has made reviving the domestic economy his number 1 priority. Asia and the Pacific are now the most lucrative terrain for American exports and American jobs, and therefore the most relevant region of the world for the President's domestic economic agenda.

The New York Times, 11-19:(A)7.

Lu Ping
Director,
Hong Kong and Macau Affairs Office
of China

2

[Criticizing Hong Kong Governor Chris Patten's proposal to introduce more democracy into Hong Kong, which China is scheduled to take over in 1997]: In the history of Hong Kong, Chris Patten will stand condemned as a criminal for all eternity.

News conference,
Beijing, China, March 17/
The Washington Post, 3-18:(A)29.

Minoru Makihara
President,
Mitsubishi Corporation
(Japan)

3

The political turmoil [in Japan] now is probably inescapable in the process of realizing political reform, which I think is essential for the future of Japan. I hope the result will be a system where the electorate is given clear alternatives. On the other hand, if the political scene remains confused, it will affect the confidence of the customers and market, and will not be good for companies like ourselves . . . Several of the new opposition leaders are quite responsible people. They are advocating decentralization and deregulation, and I respect what they are trying to do.

Interview/
The New York Times, 7-14:(A)4.

Kiichi Miyazawa
Prime Minister of Japan

4

[On U.S. President Clinton's remarks that the Japanese often say yes when they mean no]: I think this yes or no thing is something I myself might say. You all remember, don't you, "Yes, we have no bananas"? That reminded me of that particular song. The more I think about it, the more that is the way we converse, we Japanese.

News conference,
Tokyo, April 12/
The New York Times, 4-13:(A)4.

5

[Saying that Japan may need *gaiatsu*, pressure from the outside, to change its trade practices that cause consternation for its trading partners]: A certain pressure that we should do something to correct this . . . is the way we try to accommodate ourselves . . . I'm not trying to justify the *gaiatsu*, but . . . that is the way we try to learn from you [the U.S.] the rules of the game . . . It's a reflection of our history and tradition. It is like your mother telling her child to do this or not do that—otherwise your neighbor might laugh at you. This is the way of education in this country.

News conference,
Tokyo, Japan, April 12/
The Washington Post, 4-13:(A)1.

6

We must nurture this [U.S.-Japan trade] relationship with a cooperative spirit based upon the principle of free trade. This cannot be realized with "managed trade" nor under the threat of unilateralism [tariffs, sanctions, etc.]. Our relationship must be a plus-sum relationship, not a zero-sum one.

News conference,
Washington, D.C., April 15/
The New York Times, 4-17:4.

Murdiono
State Secretary of Indonesia

7

[Criticizing a recent U.S. Senate vote to link further U.S. arms sales to his country with

277

(MURDIONO)

Indonesia's improving its human-rights record]: We are a free and sovereign state, and the government of Indonesia will probe the possibility of buying aircraft from other nations in line with our needs. The purchase of weapons will also not depend on a single country but can also be from other countries which understand our problems and still trust us.

Los Angeles Times, 9-24:(A)5.

Nursultan A. Nazarbayev
President of Kazakhstan

1

[Saying there was a too-rapid change to the free-market system in his country and that significant state control must be restored]: The over-hasty destruction of the old when the new has not yet been built usually leads to economic chaos and decline, which discredits the new, democratic ideas.

Speech, January/
The New York Times, 3-2:(A)3.

Richard M. Nixon
Former President
of the United States

2

[Saying the U.S. should not yet normalize relations with Vietnam]: Until Hanoi not only fully accounts for the [U.S.] MIAs [during the war of the 1960s and '70s] but also ceases its brutal treatment of those who were aligned with the U.S. during the war, and until North Vietnam complies with the other terms of the Paris Peace Accords [which ended the war], it would be a diplomatic travesty and a human tragedy to go forward with normalization.

Memo in response to questions by
U.S. Senate Committee on POW-MIA Affairs*/
Los Angeles Times, 1-9:(A)12.

Saparmurad A. Niyazov
President of Turkmenistan

3

Why should I create something [in Turkmenistan] just so you can call me a "democrat"? The

society is not yet ripe enough for creation of political parties . . . We have censorship, but not for the sake of crushing dissent. We don't want political strife.

Interview,
Ashkhabad, Turkmenistan/
The Christian Science Monitor,
3-25:7.

4

We don't deny that the toughest period [for his country] was when the Soviet Union [of which Turkmenistan used to be a part] collapsed. [But] we didn't start to copy things done elsewhere [in other former Soviet republics]. Everyone's mistake was that they listened to what the West told them about how to build a democratic society, and all started to shout slogans of democracy instead of creating the basis for a democratic society. Moscow showed us a bad example—that you have to make noise, shout, go out into the streets, criticize all the past and grab power. That worked for some people. But our position was to deeply think over the transition period. In Western Europe and America it's easy to judge us—you've forgotten your transition period.

Interview,
Ashkhabat, Turkmenistan/
Los Angeles Times, 8-23:(A)8.

Masao Okonogi
Professor of international relations,
Keio University (Japan)

5

If there is no U.S. military force in Asia, there can be no stability in the region.

The Christian Science Monitor,
4-7:4.

Michel Oksenberg
President,
East-West Center (United States)

6

The big unknown [in an economically changing China] is how strong the central government will be in terms of distribution of income. Interprovincial tensions over the distribution of

(MICHEL OKSENBERG)

resources have been an important part of Chinese politics since the Communists came to power. Those tensions, swept under the rug in the past by a secretive regime, have now become more open.

The Christian Science Monitor,
4-2:1.

Chris Patten
Governor of Hong Kong

1

[On Chinese criticism of his plans for final British-administered democratic elections in Hong Kong before it comes under Chinese sovereignty in 1997]: It's difficult to understand why a government of 1.1 billion people that embarked on a hugely successful opening-up of its economy should be worried about proposals that hardly represent a huge leap toward democracy in Hong Kong, where there are 6 million people. I think my proposals are extremely modest—if I hadn't been attacked so strongly by China, I'm sure that some people would have said excessively modest. It's difficult to comprehend how such proposals can be regarded as a worry by the Chinese leadership . . . The arrangements for the last elections under British sovereignty have to be fair. We're not proposing a much more rapid pace toward democracy, but I don't think it would be conducive to political stability if I was to agree to arrangements that plainly try to skew the elections in [Beijing's] favor.

Interview,
Washington, D.C./
Los Angeles Times, 6-6:(M)3.

Nancy Pelosi
United States Representative,
D-California

2

[Arguing against extending U.S. most-favored-nation trade status for China unless that country improves its human-rights situation]: A lot of people who have juicy deals with China do not want to do anything [about stopping MFN]. They talk about the loss of face [for] the Chinese

leaders but forget about the loss of face [for] the people who died in [the pro-democracy demonstrations in Beijing in 1989]. America needs to make a decision—to decide what it stands for. It would be a cruel hoax if we said that the Cold War was about freedom and democracy but it was really about access to cheap labor markets.

The Christian Science Monitor,
4-30:3.

Clyde V. Prestowitz, Jr.
President,
Economic Strategy Institute
(United States)

3

I think Japan will remain a formidable [economic] competitor and will recover nicely [from its present slump], but it won't have the 10-foot-tall, totally invincible characteristics that it looked like it had in the 1980s. Japanese fundamentals remain pretty solid and Japanese industry will come out more efficient; they're slimming down and rationalizing. Having said that, I don't think we'll see the same kind of wild, unbridled investment, either domestically or overseas, that we saw in the '80s.

The Washington Post, 4-12:(A)14.

Qian Qichen
Foreign Minister of China

4

After the end of the Cold War, military industries in some countries lost their markets. They need to find new markets. That is the reason why they create the opinion that China poses a threat and that there is tension in the Asia-Pacific region—to promote sales of their arms.

News conference,
Beijing, China, March 23/
Los Angeles Times, 3-24:(A)4.

Moeen Qureshi
Interim Prime Minister
of Pakistan

5

The deep malaise from which [Pakistan's] society and economy suffers today is not the

(MOEEN QURESHI)

result of the action of one Administration. It is the cumulative consequence of both the actions and inaction on the part of the governments over the last two decades.

The Christian Science Monitor,
9-1:9.

Robert RisCassi
General, United States Army;
Commander of U.S. forces
in South Korea

1

North Korea is no longer manageable. We are increasingly concerned that North Korea could slide into an attack as an uncontrollable consequence of total desperation or international instability.

Senate testimony,
Washington, D.C., April 21/
The Christian Science Monitor,
5-10:8.

Alan Romberg
Authority on East Asia,
Council on Foreign Relations
(United States)

2

I don't see China becoming a superpower rivaling or threatening the U.S. in the foreseeable future. Beijing has repeatedly said it has no intention of becoming a superpower or replacing the former Soviet Union. [U.S. policy] will seek to engage China constructively. In post-Cold War Asia, what's needed are confidence-building measures so that the region's powers and smaller nations feel comfortable with one another.

World Press Review, April:15,16.

Bhabani Sen Gupta
Analyst,
Center for Policy Research
(India)

3

[On recent confrontations between the Indian government and Hindu activists]: The battle of

Delhi is over, but the war certainly isn't over. This confrontation between democratic secularism and Hindu nationalism will continue for the rest of the decade . . . What is at stake is the parliamentary political process. A new generation of politicians has come up that has no confidence in [the British] parliamentary model and don't even understand the model. We're paying a terrible price for that.

Los Angeles Times, 2-27:(A)5.

Norodom Sihanouk
King of Cambodia

4

[On the elections in Cambodia last May]: To receive this noble result, the Cambodian nation had to face great difficulties. Cambodian people have suffered a lot for liberal democracy. From now on, the Cambodian people are masters of their own destiny. There remains only one problem, the problem of Khmer Rouge [rebels]. We will do our best to try to resolve that problem militarily or peacefully.

To reporters following his coronation,
Phnom Penh, Cambodia, Sept. 24/
The New York Times, 9-25:3.

Neil H. Snyder
Professor of free enterprise,
University of Virginia

5

[On the world 60 years from now, in 2053]: How can the United States ensure that *it* is granted most-favored-nation trading status with China, which will be the world's lone superpower?

Interview/
U.S. News & World Report,
10-25:72.

Nathaniel Thayer
Professor,
School of Advanced
International Studies,
Johns Hopkins University
(United States)

6

I don't know who's advising [U.S. President Clinton]. But every time he opens his mouth

(NATHANIEL THAYER)

[about Japan], he talks on one matter—and that's trade—and he says the Japanese are screwing us. [As a result, when the Japanese Prime Minister visits Washington soon,] he'll be in a defensive mode. He'll probably back off the airplane.

Los Angeles Times, 4-12:(A)11.

Yoko Tomiyama
Chairman,
Consumers Union of Japan

1

[On the forthcoming national election in Japan]: From my point of view, the entire political movement seems to be lacking any debate over policies. The only debate is over whether or not they will pursue political reform, and even there it's not clear what kind of political reform they are talking about. There aren't any policy debates on what everyday life should be, on peace, on the environment. This [election] is a chance for us consumers and voters to generate our own policies and politics. We should not just follow the people in power.

Interview/The New York Times, 7-14:(A)4.

Jusuf Wanandi
Director,
Center for Strategic
and International Studies
(Indonesia)

2

[With its increasing military force, China] could become a rogue in [Asia] . . . China thinks that the West, especially the U.S., is not accepting her natural position in the region and would like to prevent her from becoming a powerful country in the Asia-Pacific by intervening in her domestic political affaira through efforts like human rights and democracy.

The Washington Post,
3-31:(A)21.

Xu Xin
Chairman,
China Institute
for International
Strategic Studies

3

China has not stationed a single soldier on the Korean Peninsula since [1958]. I would appreciate it if your country [the U.S.] were to withdraw all its troops from South Korea. With the disintegration of the Soviet Union, there has been tremendous change in the situation. So it probably is worthwhile for your country [also] to re-evaluate whether you should continue your military presence in Japan. We would also like the Korean Peninsula to become a non-nuclear zone.

Interview/
U.S. News & World Report,
3-15:61.

Europe

Paul Arthur
Professor of politics,
Ulster University
(Northern Ireland)

1

[On the ethnic conflict in Northern Ireland]: I used to go to conferences with academics from [other areas of conflict such as South Africa and the Middle East]. It was always said the world's three intractable problems are [apartheid in] South Africa, [the Arab-Israeli conflict in] the Middle East and Northern Ireland. I noticed that the participants from the other two would go away and say: As bad as the situation in Johannesburg or Jerusalem is, at least there's some people who want to make it different. Part of our problem in Northern Ireland is we think we're unique. And if they can make progress in South Africa and the Middle East and we can't, that just proves how unique we are.

The New York Times, 11-1:(A)1.

Les Aspin
Secretary of Defense
of the United States

2

We can't take [American] public support for a U.S. troop presence in Europe for granted. It hinges on how relevant NATO remains in the new era. And to remain relevant, NATO's forces must be able to respond to the challenges of the new era. These include the challenges of peace-keeping and peace enforcement operations. But NATO forces also must be prepared to deter and defeat aggression against Western interests beyond the NATO boundaries.

Before International Institute
for Strategic Studies,
Brussels, Belgium, Sept. 12/
Los Angeles Times, 9-13:(A)4.

Edouard Balladur
Prime Minister of France

3

[On differences between France and the U.S. on GATT and NATO]: We have the right to

defend our interests while remaining good friends and allies. We must not mix all these problems together. There are problems of trade, and there are problems of security . . . I hope we can learn that there are big differences between them.

Interview, Paris, France, Nov. 29/
The Washington Post, 11-30:(A)22.

Mykhailo Batih
Deputy of Ukrainian Parliament

4

I think it is obvious that the political situation has changed dramatically since we first declared that Ukraine would get rid of all its nuclear weapons. This was before anyone in Russia made territorial claims on parts of Ukraine and, before [Russian President Boris] Yeltsin's request for special military authority over the whole former Soviet Union. In today's situation it would be naive to rush into this without considering our security interests.

The Christian Science Monitor,
3-8:6.

Kurt Biedenkopf
Premier of Saxony, Germany

5

One thing that's very important for the Germans is to be pulled out of the niche protecting them from international responsibility. Germans were never particularly happy with [former Chancellor] Helmut Schmidt's observation that they were economic giants and political dwarfs, but they felt rather comfortable with that position.

The Washington Post, 7-28:(A)14.

Lars Bille
Political scientist,
University of Copenhagen
(Denmark)

6

[On the forthcoming referendum in Denmark on the Maastricht treaty calling for more Euro-

(LARS BILLE)

pean unity]: There is no enthusiasm. Those who plan to vote "yes" say they will do so because they see no alternative, because Denmark can't stand alone, or because they fear a "no" would push unemployment that's already 12 percent even higher. Only about 10 percent say "yes" because they see any positive development from the idea of European unity.

The Christian Science Monitor,
4-30:6.

Boutros Boutros-Ghali
Secretary General
of the United Nations

1

[Saying Germany should lift its ban on participating in UN peacekeeping operations]: After all, you [Germany] are the third most important country in the world. We need the full participation of Germany in peacekeeping, peace-making, peace-enforcing and peace-building operations if we want a strong United Nations.

News conference, Bonn, Germany,
Jan. 11/
The New York Times, 1-12:(A)7.

Zbigniew Brzezinski
Counsellor,
Center for Strategic
and International Studies
(United States);
Former Assistant
to the President
of the United States
(Jimmy Carter)
for National Security Affairs

2

[On the current confrontation between Russian President Boris Yeltsin and the Russian Parliament, which he recently ordered dissolved]: The critical point is that the crisis is systemic, national and historic. Systemic in the sense that the old system has fallen apart, but the new one has not taken shape. National in the sense that Russia is in the process of defining itself, and the question remains open whether it would be a

nation-state or whether it will seek again to be an empire. It is historic in the sense that it reflects yet another of the periodic, very deep crises of Russian identity and condition.

Interview/USA Today, 9-27:(A)13.

George Bush
President of the United States

3

Today, as we meet on Russian soil, home to 1,000 years of heritage and history, to a people rich in scientific and creative talent, I want to assure the Russian people on behalf of all Americans, we understand that Russia faces a difficult passage. We are with you in your struggle to strengthen and secure democratic rights, to reform your economy, to bring to every Russian city and village a new sense of hope and the prospect of a future forever free. Let me say clearly, we seek no special advantage from Russia's transformation. Yes, deep arms reductions, broader and deeper economic ties, expanded trade with Russia—all are in the interest of my country. But they're equally in the interest of the Russian people.

News conference,
Moscow, Russia, Jan. 3/
The New York Times, 1-4:(A)6.

Anton Buteiko
Chief foreign-policy adviser
to Ukrainian President
Leonid M. Kravchuk

4

[Arguing against a strengthening of the Commonwealth of Independent States, the loose confederation of independent republics that used to be part of the now-defunct Soviet Union]: Ukraine cannot accept the transition of the CIS into a new supranational structure. It would be little more than a revival of the Soviet Union.

Jan. 21/
Los Angeles Times, 1-22:(A)12.

Viktor S. Chernomyrdin
Prime Minister of Russia

5

Which is the greater evil [in Russia]—industrial decline or unrestrained price growth and

283

inflation? The answer is simple. The former is bad and the latter is very bad. The principal threat we face today is hyper-inflation, which is leading us to catastrophe. We must curb inflation first and begin to tackle other pressing problems later.

Speech, Jan. 28/
Los Angeles Times, 1-29:(A)18.

Jacques Chirac
Mayor of Paris, France;
Leader, Gaullist Rally
for the Republic Party of France

1

[Addressing voters who just elected a conservative-dominated government in France]: You have expressed your rejection of socialism, but above all you wanted another policy to fight unemployment and all forms of exclusion. You wanted . . . to build Europe according to our hopes and our interests.

March 28/
The Washington Post, 3-29:(A)12.

Warren Christopher
Secretary of State
of the United States

2

[Calling for U.S. aid to Russia]: Bringing Russia, one of history's most powerful nations, into the family of peaceful nations, will serve our highest security, economic and moral interests. For America and the world, the stakes are just monumental. If we succeed, we will have established the foundation for our lasting security into the next century. But if Russia falls into anarchy or lurches back into despotism, the price that we pay could be frightening. Nothing less is involved than the possibility of renewed nuclear threat, higher defense budgets, spreading instability, the loss of new markets, and a devastating setback for the worldwide democratic movement . . . With great courage [the Russians] are attempting to carry out three simultaneous revolutions. First, transforming a totalitarian system into a democracy. Second, transforming a command economy into one based upon free markets. And third, transforming an aggressive, expansionist empire into a peaceful modern nation-state. If they succeed in this tremendous experiment, we will all succeed.

Before Chicago (Ill.) Council
on Foreign Relations, March 22/
The New York Times, 3-23:(A)7.

Jack Clark
British member
of European Parliament

3

[On European companies that are moving production to countries with cheaper costs within the European Community now that EC economic union has taken effect]: Job losses are the painful consequence of this necessary restructuring in the current difficult economic situation. The ability to concentrate production on one site . . . is the very essence of the single market.

Los Angeles Times, 3-3:(A)1.

Bill Clinton
President of the United States

4

The perils facing Russia and other former Soviet republics are especially acute and especially important to our future, [because] reductions in our defense spending, that are an important part of our economic program over the long run here at home, are only tenable as long as Russia and the other nuclear republics pose a diminishing threat to our security and to the security of our allies and the democracies throughout the world. Most worrisome is Russia's precarious economic condition. If the economic reforms begun by [Russian] President [Boris] Yeltsin are abandoned, if hyperinflation cannot be stemmed, the world will suffer.

At American University,
Washington, D.C., Feb. 26/
The Washington Post, 2-27:(A)8.

5

[On political and economic reforms in Russia]: In the end, the Russian people will have to

(BILL CLINTON)

resolve this for themselves, and I hope they'll be given the opportunity to do that in some appropriate fashion . . . I do not believe that we [the U.S.] can be decisive in the sense that we can determine the course of events in Russia or, frankly, in the other republics of the former Soviet Union with which we also have a deep interest. But I do believe that we are not bystanders. For one thing, I don't think that this country can do what it needs to do, in any acceptable time frame, in moving to a successful economy, unless we move to act across a whole broad range of areas.

News conference,
Washington, D.C., March 23/
The New York Times, 3-24:(A)6.

1

The United States has three interests in our cooperation with Russia. One, is to make the world a safer place; to continue to reduce the threat of nuclear war and the proliferation of nuclear weapons. Two, is to support the development of democracy and freedom for the people of Russia—it is a vast and great country—and, indeed, for all of the Commonwealth of Independent States. And three, is to support the development of a market economy. At every step along the way, with or without [Russian President Boris] Yeltsin in authority, from now, I suppose, till the end of time, or at least for the foreseeable future, the United States will have those interests. And we will be guided by those interests.

News conference,
Washington, D.C., March 23/
The New York Times,
3-24:(A)6.

2

[Supporting U.S. aid to Russia]: If we provide more food aid, that helps our farmers. If we can find a way to help to privatize more [Russian] businesses . . . that helps us. If we can find a way to help them run their energy business better . . . it gives us a market for our pipeline products. If we can find a way to help them con-

vert their nuclear power plants . . . that could put a lot of our folks at work.

Broadcast interview,
Washington, D.C., March 24/
The Washington Post, 3-25:(A)27.

3

As long as there are reformers in the Russian Federation and the other states leading the journey toward democracy's horizon, our strategy must be to support them. And our place must be at their side. Moreover, we and the Russian people must not give up on reform simply because of the slow pace of economic renewal . . . The burning question today is whether Russia's economic progress, whether Russia's democratic progress, will continue or be thwarted. I believe that freedom, like anything sweet, is hard to take from people once they've had a taste of it. The human spirit is hard to bottle up again. And it will be hard to bottle up again in Russia.

Before American Society of Newspaper Editors,
Annapolis, Md., April 1/
The New York Times, 4-2:(A)6.

4

If Russia were to revert to imperialism or plunge into chaos, we would need to reassess all our plans for defense savings. The danger is clear if Russia's reforms turn sour, if it reverts to authoritarianism or disintegrates into chaos. The world cannot afford the strife of the former Yugoslavia replicated in a nation as big as Russia, spanning 11 time zones, with an armed arsenal of nuclear weapons that is still very vast.

Before American Society of Newspaper Editors,
Annapolis, Md., April 1/
Los Angeles Times, 4-2:(A)12.

5

[On U.S.-Russian relations]: The contrast between our promising new partnership and our confrontational past underscores the opportunities that hang in the balance today. For 45 years, we pursued a deadly competition in nuclear arms. Now we can pursue a safe and steady cooperation to reduce the arsenals that have

(BILL CLINTON)

haunted mankind. For 45 years, our nation invested trillions of dollars to contain and deter Soviet Communism. Now the emergence of a peaceful and democratic Russia can enable us to devote more to our own domestic needs. The emergence of a newly productive and prosperous Russia could add untold billions in new growth to the global economy.

News conference,
Vancouver, Canada, April 4/
The New York Times, 4-5:(A)5.

1

[On the current unrest in Russia pitting President Boris Yeltsin against recalcitrant members of Parliament]: The United States must support Yeltsin and the process of bringing about free and fair elections. We cannot afford to be in the position of wavering at this moment or backing off or giving any encouragement to people who clearly want to derail the election process and are not committed to reform in Russia.

To reporters,
Washington, D.C., Oct. 3/
The Washington Post, 10-4:(A)16.

2

[Criticizing the extremist views of Vladimir Zhirinovsky, whose nationalists received a large public vote in the just-held Russian Parliamentary election]: I think no American, indeed no citizen of the world, who read [his] comments could fail to be concerned . . . [But] I think it's important to recognize that we don't have any evidence at this time that the people who voted for that party were embracing all those comments or, indeed, may have even known about them. I believe this was clearly a protest vote fueled by people who have been in—many of them—in virtual economic free fall. I think it's important at this moment not to overreact. Do I think that this means there will be a big new dangerous direction in Russian policy? I don't think there's any evidence to support that.

News conference,
Washington, D.C., Dec. 15/
Los Angeles Times, 12-16:(A)12.

Robert Conquest
Senior research fellow,
Hoover Institution,
Stanford University
(United States);
Former British diplomat

3

[On today's Russia, following the breakup of the Soviet Union]: The monster has died, but its stinking corpse is still around. What do you do with this enormous dead tyrannosaurus? The results are still there, the total failure to keep up the infrastructure—the buildings, the sewers, the roads, and so on. It's left a very nasty stench behind, including, of course, the stench of [the nuclear-plant disaster at] Chernobyl . . . I think one of the remarkable things about present-day Russia is that practically nobody talks Marxism or Stalinism. Even the conspirators who tried the [failed] coup de'etat [against the reform government in 1991] didn't mention Marxism or socialism in their manifesto. They just spoke of restoring order and preserving the borders of the old union. But you never know. In a very dangerous situation, some sort of totalitarian group might gain power.

Interview/Humanities, May-June:10.

Michel Crozier
French sociologist

4

[On the loss of support for France's ruling Socialist Party]: The French are feeling extraordinary disappointment in a Socialist Party that came to power attacking the right for its inability to address unemployment and promising to do something about it . . . All the French remember is that when [the Socialists] arrived there were 1.5 million unemployed, and now there are 3 million.

The Christian Science Monitor,
2-10:7.

Amedeo de Franchis
Deputy Secretary General,
North Atlantic Treaty
Organization

5

Today, the strategic situation in Europe is practically the reverse of that which brought

(AMEDEO DE FRANCHIS)

NATO into existence. The Warsaw Pact has disappeared. Not only the ideological threat has gone, but also the military threat. The country which threatened us all in massive ways, the Soviet Union, has dissolved. Never in history has an alliance [NATO] succeeded so completely . . . But at the same time, we can [ask] the question: With the enemy gone, is NATO needed anymore and, if so, why? . . . In a nutshell, Communism has lost, but democracy has not yet won. In this type of environment of instability, we have every reason to preserve a collective-security system that has really proven to be extremely efficient.

> *Speech sponsored by Los Angeles (Calif.)*
> *World Affairs Council, April 6/*
> *Los Angeles Times, 4-9:(B)2.*

Ghijs de Vries
Dutch member
of European Parliament

1

[On the European Parliament]: It is extraordinary that 12 countries—countries that were at war for centuries, that fought two wars against each other this century, that still harbor deep prejudices against each other—have agreed to be bound by legislation passed not by unanimous vote but by majority vote.

> *Los Angeles Times, 3-2:(H)4.*

Herman Diligensky
Political scientist,
Institute for World Economics
and International Relations
(Russia)

2

[On the current deadlock in the Russian government between President Boris Yeltsin and his foes, which is stalling reform]: If the current situation continues, it would further weaken central authority, and it follows that power would devolve to Russia's regions and autonomous republics. It could mean the breakup of Russia. We can have a central government that doesn't wield any power . . . something like China of the 1920s: a warlord era.

> *The Christian Science Monitor, 4-29:6.*

Ulf Dinkelspiel
Minister of
European Community Affairs
and Foreign Trade of Sweden

3

We recognize that over time the EC intends to develop a common defense. [And although Sweden is traditionally a neutral country,] we will not stand in the way of such a development. Time will tell where we end up, but you will see us very active in the debate on European security.

> *The Christian Science Monitor,*
> *5-12:8.*

Ingemar Dorfer
Security-policy adviser,
Foreign Ministry of Sweden

4

Sweden is becoming truly European [in outlook] again, and not just some exotic UN nation floating around like a self-proclaimed moral power. Swedes used to smugly say, "We agree to disagree [with the rest of the world]"; but now we agree, which is a position I prefer.

> *The Christian Science Monitor,*
> *4-28:7.*

Yegor T. Gaidar
Deputy Prime Minister
of Russia

5

[On the surprisingly large vote for an ultra-nationalist group in Russia's just-held elections for Parliament]: Fascism and Communism are not synonymous. Fascism is what comes after disappointment in Communism. This historic risk cannot be underrated.

> *News conference,*
> *Moscow, Russia, Dec. 13/*
> *The New York Times, 12-14:(A)6.*

Dermot Gallagher
Irish Ambassador
to the United States

6

[On the new negotiations between Britain and Ireland on the future of Northern Ireland]: The

(DERMOT GALLAGHER)

Irish Prime Minister spelled out very clearly that he has no intention to . . . seek to impose unity of Northern Ireland [with Ireland] against the wishes of a majority of people in Northern Ireland because, after all, what we are trying to do is bring together the peoples of Ireland, north and south. The barriers, the division, the gulf is in the minds of people. It's not pieces of ground we're trying to bring together. It's people who are Irish people and who are divided at this time in their political allegiance, some looking to Britain, some looking to Ireland. It is the role of those of us who believe in the coming together of the two traditions to convince, through political dialogue and through peaceful means, that that is the way forward. We all have to learn how to share the one small island.

Broadcast interview/
"MacNeil/Lehrer NewsHour," PBS-TV, 12-15.

Norbert Gansel
Member of
German Bundestag (Parliament)

1

[In Germany,] the ideals of social democracy are in crisis. We lack strong personalities and the readiness to run a personal risk. The people are searching for answers that no one in Bonn is willing or able to give. The problem is, German politics cannot appeal to a national dream as [Americans] can. There is no German dream. There is only German nightmare.

Interview, Bonn, Germany/
The Washington Post, 5-5:(A)26.

Nigel Gault
Economist,
DRI/McGraw Hill (Britain)

2

Germany's cost structure is an enormous burden. We're seeing throughout German manu-facturing industries a rethinking of where to locate production facilities, and they are deciding in some cases that they cannot afford to produce in Germany anymore. They are deciding that one of the places they want to produce in the future is Eastern Europe.

The New York Times, 5-11:(C)2.

Kiro Gligorov
President of Macedonia

3

[On the difficulty his country is having in being recognized by the world following its separation from Yugoslavia]: We are a small state of 2 million with practically no army, not a member of NATO. What danger do we represent? We have offered a treaty, a mutual guarantee of borders . . . When the EC set out requirements for recog-nition, it created a commission to investigate which of the Yugoslav republics fulfilled those requirements: human rights, non-violence, and so on. Only Slovenia and Macedonia met the requirements. Yet we still are not recognized.

Interview, Skopje, Macedonia/
The Christian Science Monitor,
1-5:7.

Mikhail S. Gorbachev
Former President
of the Soviet Union

4

If you compare the goals put forward by today's authorities [in Russia] and what was put forth by Gorbachev—reform of property relations, transition to political pluralism via democracy, recognition of dissident thought, reform of the Union—have you heard anything new from today's reformers? You haven't.

Interview, Moscow, Russia/
Los Angeles Times, 1-7:(A)1.

5

If things were to get worse [in Russia], if the desire of the people is for Gorbachev to leave everything to deal again with the problems of Russia, then I am ready to do my duty. I recently realized that people don't want me to distance myself from the internal problems of the coun-try, and I will not do so . . . People expect the Federal government [of Russia] to come up with clear policies, but [President Boris] Yeltsin does not talk of economic, financial and foreign-policy problems. He does not mention the standard of living of people which has returned to that of the 1970s. We must start from there, as people are paying too high a price.

Italian broadcast interview, March 21/
Los Angeles Times, 3-22:(A)6.

(MIKHAIL S. GORBACHEV)

1

[On Russian President Boris Yeltsin's relations with the Congress of People's Deputies]: The Congress wanted to do some irreversible damage to the President. The Congress did not succeed. The President, too, wanted actually to dismiss the Congress. It is not proper for the President to do such things. Neither side can win outright, and that's good. Thank God for that. We don't need victors in this situation.

Interview, Calgary, Canada/
Time, 4-5:27.

2

I think you [the U.S.] have to invest in the new Russia, in our common future. I mean not just financial investment. I mean, also, political investment. You should support the process of reform. You should support all those who are realistic. Don't just look at those people waving the red banners. This is not Russia's mood.

Interview, Calgary, Canada/
Time, 4-5:27.

3

[On the forthcoming referendum in Russia on public support for President Boris Yeltsin]: What we need is not a referendum but a new election . . . The executive and legislative branches of government [in Russia] are not able to cooperate. They're not capable of uniting their efforts. And this disagreement, this confrontation is affecting our public opinion. And this is happening at a time when Russia is standing at the threshold of crucial decisions. The authorities at the Federal level cannot remain as they are now, and therefore I very much support the idea of an early election. So what we need is not [a] referendum, a plebiscite or a poll. We just would waste time. And time is very dear to us.

Broadcast interview/
"CBS Morning News," CBS-TV, 4-12.

4

The current politicians [in power in Russia], many of them are pygmies. They have nothing to say. They have no policy, domestic or foreign. They cannot govern the country. They are steeped in lies. They are all connected with Mafia-like structures. They are plundering the country [of its raw materials] . . . I can't believe that [Russian President Boris] Yeltsin is instructing these people to do this . . . but [they] have the President's blessing. And I think it shows the kind of person he is, the scale of his personality . . . It is you in America [who support Yeltsin], you don't really want to sort things out. You think it is either Yeltsin or the bad guys . . . no one else. Very profound analysis. Amazingly profound analysis . . . People in the West tend to support Yeltsin just because he is for private property . . . Does that mean he is a democrat? Why is [the West] making these incantations . . . supporting Yeltsin, Yeltsin, Yeltsin? They're making Yeltsin believe that he's been acting correctly these past two years . . . when in fact we are on the verge of disintegration.

Interview, Moscow, Russia/
The Washington Post, 10-13:(B)8.

5

[Saying Russian President Boris Yeltsin should strive for a Parliament of varied views and not one made up only of those who support him]: I would like this thought to reach [the Yeltsinites]: Democracy is not convenient; it's not fun to be shoved, controlled, required to give accounts, continually questioned. I know; I myself introduced this pluralism. I caught hell from it, but I kept silent because this was kasha I cooked myself. But if the Parliament does not reflect society, its mood, then it will be Communist, neo-Bolshevik, it will allow only one scheme. This will be an imposition again. And what kind of democracy is that?

Interview, Moscow, Russia/
The New York Times, 11-3:(A)3.

Al Gore
Vice President
of the United States

6

[Saying Poland is a model for other East European countries in moving from Communism

(AL GORE)

to freedom]: In Poland the signs are, after all, a lot better than elsewhere. Travelers from the rest of Eastern Europe come to Poland to catch their breath. The Poles are keeping the promises . . . I am here to state my faith in the proposition that the future belongs to Poland's resolve to seek a democratic society, where differences among people are celebrated, not feared.

Warsaw, Poland, April 20/
Los Angeles Times, 4-21:(A)6.

1

[Criticizing the extremist views of Vladimir Zhirinovsky, whose nationalists received a large public vote in the just-held Russian Parliamentary election]: Let me say clearly for myself and on behalf of the [U.S. Clinton] Administration and on behalf of our country, [that] the views expressed by Zhirinovsky on issues such as the use of nuclear weapons, the expansion of borders and the treatment of ethnic minorities are reprehensible and anathema to all freedom-loving people in Russia, in the United States and everywhere in the world.

Interview,
Moscow, Russia, Dec. 15/
Los Angeles Times, 12-16:(A)12.

Pavel Grachev
Minister of Defense of Russia

2

[Saying the Russian nuclear weapons that have remained in Ukraine since the breakup of the Soviet Union should be moved to Russia]: By its practical . . . actions, the military leadership of Ukraine, without much publicity, is striving to retain the nuclear weapons. At the same time, the security of the weapons on Ukrainian territory is deteriorating. We [Russians] are not allowed to change parts and systems in time, to carry out routine maintenance. The supervision by our scientists of the status of the nuclear warheads designed by them is impossible. In a word, there is a problem here and a very serious one.

Interview/
The Christian Science Monitor,
6-9:2.

Povilas Gylys
Foreign Minister of Lithuania

3

[Saying his government has reversed the cool attitude toward Russia that the previous Lithuanian government maintained since independence in 1991]: Our policy is based on an absolutely different philosophical and psychological premise. We have never made expressions that would humiliate or offend Russia. Our philosophy is to let things go, to let events take their natural flow. There is no pressure of any kind . . . The recent [Russian] troop withdrawal [from Lithuania] is really a turning point. To Russia it means the end of dominance in this region, and to us it means that the possibility of military intervention here is now very small. It is a victory for Lithuania, a victory for the Baltic countries, and in my opinion even a victory for the Russians. It is a victory over their own evil side, which is the most difficult kind of victory. They can feel better, morally, now.

Interview/
The New York Times, 9-4:5.

Vaclav Havel
Former President
of Czechoslovakia

4

Democracy is truly born with difficulty. We [in Czechoslovakia] had 20 years of a democratic state between the two wars, and very quickly [after 1989] there was a renewal in this country of new democratic mechanisms that resided somewhere in the lower strata of the social memory. But because that democracy is young and fresh, it carries a higher degree of danger. Mediocre people often surface due to their own ambition. It's possible to observe a lack of a detached vision—the famous Czech irony does not function here. The politicians are all terribly serious, and they very quickly renewed one of our worse traditions, Czech contentiousness. And one can observe in political life much that can be ascribed to ambitiousness, to dilettantism.

Interview,
Prague, Czech Republic/
Esquire, February:89.

Vaclav Havel
President of the Czech Republic

1

[Saying the West is bowing too much to Russia in its reluctance to allow Eastern European countries to become full members of NATO]: Any dialogue on associate or observer status [in NATO] is welcome but cannot exclude our eventual full membership. We will continue to express our opinion at the top of our voice . . . The ghost of Yalta is not present but there is a danger of its re-apparition. Just because Russia does not want our countries to join NATO should not be considered a return to Yalta but rather a danger of it . . . The Czech Republic, like Poland, Hungary and Slovakia, wants full membership in NATO. We don't believe our membership endangers Russia in any way. We believe NATO should seek good relations with countries of the Commonwealth of Independent States. Our entry into NATO would not bring the enemy closer to Russia but would bring democracy closer to Russia.

News conference,
Warsaw, Poland, Oct. 21/
The New York Times, 10-22:(A)6.

Francois Heisbourg
Director, International Institute
for Strategic Studies (Britain)

2

European nation-states were born in the 19th century as part of a process of nation-building. Today, we're witnessing a reverse process; ethnicization and the disintegration of nation-states. This is virgin territory for security thinking. The test bed is how we cope with events in Yugoslavia. It's very difficult to see how international organizations would operate if ethnicity supersedes the logic of traditional nation-states.

U.S. News & World Report,
6-14:63.

Nicholas Henderson
Former British Ambassador
to the United States

3

It is quite right that Europe has not produced a common entity [to represent its political and security interests], that it has not produced something that can act coherently in the world. Now, whether America would really like it if Europe had strong leadership is another question.

The Washington Post, 2-8:(A)15.

Regine Hildebrandt
Minister for Social Affairs,
Women, Family Life and Labor
of Brandenburg, Germany

4

[Following the unification of East and West Germany,] a lot of people in the east don't have work, and they're hurting. Fifty percent of people in the east have lost all or part of their income, so they can't share all these new things. And people who rely on welfare are very unhappy, especially retired people and single mothers. They can't buy a magazine or ride the streetcar because it's too expensive. For them, unification has been very negative. When a person in eastern Germany loses a job, it means much more than in the west. Under our old system, the workplace was the center of life. That's where your sports club was, that's where you organized your vacations and your trips to the theatre or museum, that's where your doctor was, that's where you went whenever you had a problem. When the workplace suddenly closes, people are left without any mooring at all.

Interview, Brandenburg, Germany/
The New York Times, 11-20:4.

Stanley Hoffmann
Chairman,
Center for European Studies,
Harvard University
(United States)

5

You're dealing with very weak governments and a genuine leadership problem in the three main West European countries [Germany, Britain and France]. The main fear I see is tied to recession and the growing xenophobia it has touched off. It's not limited to Germany, though it's depressing it should reappear there after 45 years of democratic government.

U.S. News & World Report,
6-14:53.

Serhiy Holovaty
Member of Ukrainian Parliament
and its Commission
for Foreign Affairs

1

[Saying Ukraine will not give up its nuclear weapons lightly]: As someone with influence in Parliament on this issue, I can tell you that Ukraine has been so burned by Russia in financial and economic matters, that after a year of this we will not lightly give up any more assets. We would never give up the nuclear weapons now, at least without something in return. We don't want to be the fool. The U.S. needs to understand this, to take into account the psychological factor.

Interview/
The New York Times, 1-7:(A)6.

John Hume
Member of British Parliament
from Northern Ireland;
Leader, Social Democratic
Labor Party

2

Given that the British government has stated it cannot defeat [Northern Ireland's] IRA and that the IRA has stated it cannot defeat the British government, my simple Irish mind tells me the logic of that is that the only thing that'll solve the problem is dialogue.

Broadcast interview/
The New York Times, 11-4:(A)4.

Josef Janning
Deputy director,
research group on Europe,
University of Mainz
(Germany)

3

In Germany, at least, people are thinking about their job security, while published opinion is wondering about the future course of Russia, and neither one sees how the EC can have a major impact on those concerns. People are seeing such issues less in European and more in national terms.

The Christian Science Monitor,
10-28:3.

Wojciech Jaruzelski
Former Prime Minister
of Poland

4

[On Poland's current change from Communism to capitalism]: Richness and prosperity is good as long as it's amassed in an honest way. But in a period of rapid transition like we've gone through, with all kinds of loopholes and players gathering fortunes without any real work—that has nothing in common with a normal, healthy capitalist system. It's like capitalism at an early stage, in the 19th century. It's run amok and it's dangerous. It could lead to social outbursts. These 45 years of Communism—regardless of all the mistakes that were made and the failure to really build up the country—still, it's 45 years. You can't just eliminate it from history in one swoop. Most people worked hard. They became accustomed to social security. Now we have this great Polish romanticism—everything up to 1939 was good, and everything after 1939 was bad. Well, the period between the wars wasn't so hot.

Interview, Warsaw, Poland/
The New York Times, 3-4:(A)1.

A. H. Rinnooy Kan
President,
Federation of Netherlands
Industry

5

If you'd asked me a couple of years ago about [Europe's economic] future, I would have said it looked excellent. We were on the verge of European integration, and that alone was going to give a big boost to growth rates. But now the outlook everywhere is somewhat more gloomy. You're catching us at a bad moment.

The Washington Post, 4-12:(A)14.

David Kern
Chief economist,
National Westminster Bank
(Britain)

6

The European labor market is less flexible and mobile than that of the United States. It's much

(DAVID KERN)

easier in Europe to make the decision not to work. The support systems have been more generous. That might be the sign of a civilized society, but it also might make the unemployment problem that much worse.

The Washington Post, 2-27:(A)9.

1

The aspiration that the political establishment has had in positioning Britain as one of the leading geopolitical players is increasingly untenable. We have to devote resources in the defense area that are increasingly out of line with our economic base.

The Washington Post, 8-6:(A)25.

Ruslan I. Khasbulatov
Speaker of the
Supreme Soviet of Russia

2

[Criticizing Russian President Boris Yeltsin's assumption of emergency powers]: [Yeltsin's measures are an] attempt at usurping power cloaked in anti-Communist rhetoric, the verbiage of the struggle against the renascent hydra of Communism in Russia. [But it really represents the] failure of the economic policy pursued by the President. A direct threat of the return to the worst times of neo-totalitarianism is looming over the country. It is clothed in democratic rhetoric, the threat of dictatorship. This situation dictates an unequivocal solution, the repeal of all un-Constitutional decisions and return to the path of search for concord.

Before Russian Parliament,
Moscow, Russia, March 21/
The New York Times, 3-22:(A)4.

3

[Criticizing the economic reform program supported by Russian President Boris Yeltsin]: I would like Russians to think over one question: During the past three years of this economic policy, has your life become better or worse? I want the people to know there were other options

and ways of carrying out reform in a more successful fashion. It is no secret to anyone today that the President is not up to his job and keeps violating the Constitution and the laws. He has reverted to the kind of activity that comes natural to him—being the first secretary of a regional Communist Party committee. But life is not going to end on April 25 [the date of a referendum on Yeltsin's rule]. It will be only the beginning of a more serious life.

Interview/Time, 4-26:36.

Henry A. Kissinger
Former Secretary of State
of the United States

4

I am not deeply worried about the return of Communism [to Russia]. But I am concerned that very few Russians can accept the disintegration of what they had been working on for 400 years, which was the expansion of Russia from the area around Moscow, to the shores of the Pacific, to the center of Europe [and] the gates of India. If you watch carefully, you'll see a number of worrisome phenomenons. You'll see that there are still Russian armies in every one of the former republics of the Soviet Union. They are neither withdrawing nor does the international community say anything about it because they don't know what to do about it . . . I am not passing judgment now . . . All I'm saying is that we must not delude ourselves that we can repeat the experience of the Marshall Plan on the territory of the former Soviet Union.

Speech sponsored by Town Hall
of California,
Los Angeles, Calif., July 19/
Los Angeles Times, 7-23:(B)2.

Egon Klepsch
President
of the European Parliament

5

[The European] Parliament is the only European Community institution directly elected by the people. Otherwise, the democratic structures of the Community are lacking. The more power the Community accumulates, the more

293

(EGON KLEPSCH)

important it is for us [in Parliament] to play a major role.

Los Angeles Times, 3-2:(H)4.

Helmut Kohl
Chancellor of Germany

1

We [Germany] are a land whose pensioners are growing ever younger and whose students are becoming ever older. With ever shorter working lives, ever shorter working weeks and ever longer vacations, our competitiveness is in danger. A successful industrial nation . . . can't organize itself into a collective amusement park.

Before German Parliament,
Bonn, Germany, March 25/
Los Angeles Times, 3-26:(A)5.

2

It cannot be stressed often enough [that] a substantial [U.S.] military presence should remain in Europe in order to meet the alliance's tasks now and in the future. [American voters] may not understand this, but the essence of politics is to carry out things the electorate might not immediately understand.

The Christian Science Monitor,
5-25:19.

3

[In Germany today, there is] all this moaning and whining. No other country would have responded to its unification, a gift of history, with so much public brooding. [Despite] unprecedented prosperity, [Germans] react with excessive nervousness or even hysteria to the slightest fluctuations and changes.

The Washington Post, 6-28:(A)15.

4

[On Germany's economic and welfare system]: We have become too expensive . . . We have the oldest students, the youngest pensioners and the idlest machines. People are living

beyond their means. The time for change has come.

Speech, September/
U.S. News & World Report,
10-25:44.

5

[Supporting European unity]: In the long term, I am firmly convinced that this is also a question of war and peace. It's a grave mistake if people think the horrific pictures from the [ethnic war in] the former Yugoslavia are limited to that area of Europe, or that racism, nationalism, chauvinism and xenophobia in other parts of Europe and in Germany have been banished once and for all . . . What we have accomplished economically together in the European Community will last only if we bolster it politically. A kind of super free-trade zone is not enough. We need political union.

Before German Parliament,
Bonn, Germany, Nov. 11/
The New York Times, 11-12:(A)5.

Andrei V. Kozyrev
Foreign Minister of Russia

6

Despite political tension in Russia, there is no reason needed to underestimate the dramatic and crucial moment in its political development nor to panic or predict civil war. Yes, there is a strong resistance to change. This comes from the path over the old Bolshevik system of power, which is fighting for survival and really for *revanche.* Hence, the attempts to reject such basic notions and conditions of democracy as referendum on land ownership, on the fundamentals of the new Constitution, and calls for reverting to the policies of confrontation with the outside world.

At American University,
Washington, D.C., March 24/
The Washington Post, 3-26:(A)24.

Leonid M. Kravchuk
President of Ukraine

7

[Saying Ukraine will not give up its nuclear weapons lightly]: I have a right to defend the

(LEONID M. KRAVCHUK)

interests of my people. We should not be "accused" of defending the interests of my people; we should not be pressured in the mass media. I see these reports that Ukraine is trying to play on something, to speculate on this. No. It wants a just resolution of this issue. We want not to look foolish, not to get applauded for giving up our missiles and, then forgotten.

Interview/
The New York Times, 1-7:(A)6.

Horst Krenzler
Director General
for External Relations
of the European Community

1

[On West European companies that are increasing their manufacturing in East Europe due to lower wages there]: We are bound to see production moving away to areas where production costs are lower. And it is a problem we are going to have to grapple with for the next 10 to 15 years . . . We see the first signs in textiles and steel, but it is something that is going to become much more acute when we bear in mind that wage costs are lower in the [East] by a factor of more than 1 to 10.

To European Parliament panel,
April/
The New York Times, 5-11:(C)2.

Valentin Kuptsov
Former Secretary,
Central Committee,
Communist Party
of the Soviet Union

2

[Criticizing the anti-Communist reforms and Western tilt of Russian President Boris Yeltsin]: From morning to night, television shows the American way of life. It is a humiliation of [Russia]. Foreigners used to speak to us as [though we were] representatives of a great power. Now they have forgotten us. [But] we can straighten this country out. When a Communist promises to do something, he does it. We don't make political lies.

USA Today, 3-15:(A)6.

Denis Lacorne
Scholar, Centre d'Etudes
et de Recherches Internationales
(France)

3

[On the current controversy in France over free speech and press limits]: For the first time, the French political system has been forced to examine issues of freedom of speech and freedom of the press in a context similar to the First Amendment debates that have been going on for 200 years in the United States . . . We [in France] admit limits to freedom of speech that do not exist in the United States. Neo-Nazis could not hold demonstrations in France, nor could an overtly racist organization like the KKK hold demonstrations here. Defamation laws are also much different in France, where the truth is not a defense if it involves the invasion of privacy.

Los Angeles Times, 5-17:(A)4.

Otto Graf Lambsdorff
Leader,
Free Democratic Party
of Germany

4

[On fears about extremist views espoused by Vladimir Zhirinovsky, whose party won a large vote in Russia's recent Parliamentary election]: One parallel does exist [with Germany 70 years ago]. We have ridiculed [Adolf] Hitler, we have laughed at Hitler, we have called him a fool and a lunatic. Yet he had written in 1923 in *Mein Kampf,* absolutely everything he did after coming to power. Now we think everything Zhirinovsky wrote and said is ridiculous.

The Christian Science Monitor,
12-23:2.

Rene Lasserre
Center for Information
and Research on
Contemporary Germany (France)

5

[The current European monetary] crisis will not be the departure into a rationalization of economic policies, but an alert to reverse a focus on purely national concerns that has been build-

(RENE LASSERRE)

ing over the last 18 months. There will be a rethinking of monetary union as envisioned in Maastricht [a treaty aimed at European unity] that will result in quicker union among a hard core of continental countries. These countries, and Germany especially, have profited too much from monetary stability to give it up.

The Christian Science Monitor,
8-17:1.

John le Carre
Author;
Former member
of British intelligence

1

[Saying Western intelligence overestimated the former Soviet Union's capabilities]: I think it was a failure of intelligence and, in a curious way, a failure of common sense. The overkill of coverage was so immense that they literally started counting the cows twice, that when you have huge amounts of data coming in, it's very easy to lose count as simply as that. But the failure of common sense is absolutely weird in its stupidity. Any good journalist who'd been living in Moscow in the later years of [former Soviet leader Leonid] Brezhnev would know that nothing worked anymore. The knight was dying inside his armor, and somehow that human perception never made itself felt in intelligence analyses.

Interview/Time, 7-5:32.

David M. Maddox
General and European Commander,
United States Army

2

[Saying the total U.S. forces based in Europe should not drop below 100,000]: I think there is considerable concern that we stop there . . . You hear [even] from key eastern Europeans [former Communist nations] that they want a U.S. presence here, and presence does not mean a couple Americans to them. I think that enough has happened in the world that we have rationalized the 100,000. People agreed to it, but clearly we're extremely sensitive about what kind of

structure there would be below 100,000, and would it be meaningful, credible or large enough to have the United States in a position of leadership in the [NATO] alliance.

Interview, Heidelberg, Germany/
The New York Times, 8-3:(A)8.

Alain Madelin
Minister of Economic Development
of France

3

France's economic culture is not that of a market economy or free trade. We have a market economy and we are free-traders, but we still do not adhere intellectually to these ideas. And at moments of fear, such as now, the instinct is to look to the state and be suspicious of the market.

Interview/
The New York Times, 11-30:(C)1.

John Major
Prime Minister
of the United Kingdom

4

NATO most certainly has a continuing role. The Soviet Union has collapsed; that is true. [But] that doesn't mean the West has to neglect the essential guardian of its security. Nor do I believe it would be wise to do so. I know there are moves within the European Community to raise the Europeans' profile in defense . . . First, it is indisputably right that Europe should bear a great proportion of the cost in money and manpower of its own defense within Europe. But it would be folly to invent any defense structures that damaged NATO or subtracted from NATO in any way. I can tell you emphatically that it is not and will not be the British government's policy. We are strong supporters of NATO. No Soviet Union, you say? Who knows what will happen in the future?

Interview/USA Today, 2-23:(A)13.

5

It would be a mistake to equate the special [U.S.-British] relationship simply to a personal relationship [between their respective] leaders

(JOHN MAJOR)

. . . There are some [links] that are tangible and some that are intangible. The intangible links are links of blood and history and instinct. The tangible links are a common outlook and almost invariably a common perception of international problems . . . That has been an instinct over quite a few generations. If the United Kingdom is in difficulties, it expects to find the United States by its side. And if the United States is in difficulties and is looking for international support, I think its first instinct is to see if the United Kingdom is by its side—and, generally, it will be.

Interview/USA Today, 2-23:(A)13.

1

[I envision a European Community extending] right from Britain up to the doorsteps of Russia. I am not going to sit back and be told that that is not a vision worth fighting for because I happen to believe that it is.

Interview/
The Washington Post, 3-5:(A)27.

2

[On reports that he is depressed because of declining popularity among voters]: I am fit. I am well. I am here—and I'm staying . . . I'll tell you what I am tired and weary of—I am weary of gossip dressed up as news, malice dressed up as comment, and fiction reported as fact . . . I was planting delphiniums when [his wife] Norma rushed into the garden waving a newspaper. "It says here you are tired and weary." This, mind you, after something in excess of three hours digging.

To Conservative Party women,
June 4/
The New York Times, 6-5:3.

3

[On U.S.-British relations]: I do not, myself, use the term "special relationship." I do think there is a natural alliance of interests between the United Kingdom and the United States, and I think that remains, and I think that is going to remain in the future. That does not mean that on each and every issue we will take precisely the same view. And that has not been the case in the past; it was not the case in the [former U.S. President Ronald] Reagan/[former British Prime Minister Margaret] Thatcher years, it was not the case in earlier years. There have often been shades of different opinion. But the broad perspective that we both have upon the world is remarkably similar; the way in which we approach problems is similar; the outcome that we want in international problems is almost invariably similar . . . Ask yourself the fundamental question: If the United States, in difficulty, wanted to look for someone who would be likely to line up on their side of their fence, where would they look? And ask the question of the British: If they wanted to look around the world to find someone who would be likely to line up on their side, where would they look? Push aside the froth and bubble and answer that question and then we can get on with serious matters.

Interview, London, England/
Los Angeles Times, 6-20:(M)3.

4

[On Britain's economic problems]: I don't want us having some magnificent invention and then having it developed by Japan, Europe or the United States. I want it developed here, so I need the people with the practical skills here, and I must create the climate in which people are prepared to go out and use their manual skills—building roads, building bridges, plumbing, building houses, whatever it may be with exactly the same attraction as they would go into the City [the financial world]. When we reach a situation where I can find an average couple with a youngster having [passed his exams], who say to that youngster going to university, "We are as happy if you go out and do something like building bridges as we are if you go into a job that will lead you to become Governor of the Bank of England!"—then we will have achieved something of value for this country. I put it in those personal terms, but I feel passionately about that. We have sold ourselves short and it is time we change.

Interview, London, England/
Los Angeles Times, 6-20:(M)3.

(JOHN MAJOR)

1

The [European] Community's share of world markets has declined by about a fifth since 1980. If we had been as good at creating jobs as other industrial countries over the same period, there would be nine million more people in work in the Community today.

At EC summit meeting,
Brussels, Belgium, Oct. 29/
The New York Times, 10-30:4.

2

[On an agreement between Britain and Ireland, aimed at ending the ethnic violence in Northern Ireland, which includes a provision that the IRA may join in peace talks if they cease their terrorism]: Our message is clear and it is simple. There is no future in violence. There is a fair and democratic future for all those who want to enter the political process. We believe that it is now up to those who used or supported violence to take that opportunity. The door is open to them. They won't have a better opportunity, and they don't have a better option.

To reporters,
London, England, Dec. 15/
Los Angeles Times,
12-16:(A)1.

Michael Mandelbaum
Foreign-policy specialist,
School of Advanced
International Studies,
Johns Hopkins University
(United States)

3

I would go with [Russian President] Boris Yeltsin, even if he behaves undemocratically in the short term. He is a democrat; most of the [Russian] Parliamentarians are not. He was elected democratically; they were not. And he favors market and democratic reforms, while they do not.

Newsweek,
3-22:39.

Valery L. Manilov
Deputy Secretary,
Russian Security Council

4

Russia reconfirms its principle of non-use of nuclear weapons against any state except in cases when nuclear or non-nuclear allied forces would lead an aggression against Russia. [This is] in complete accord with the world practices [of the U.S. and other nations].

Nov. 3/Los Angeles Times, 11-4:(A)1.

Sergei Markov
Political scientist,
Moscow State University
(Russia)

5

We [in Russia] do not live in a democratic country—it is authoritarian. It may be soft [authoritarian], pro-Western and pro-market, but it is still authoritarian. The structure of government depends most not on Parliament but on the President and the games around the President.

U.S. News & World Report,
12-27:67.

Ann McCann
Administrator,
Peace People (Northern Ireland)

6

[On the ethnic violence in Northern Ireland]: In some way, people are beyond shocking. It's like [the ethnic violence in] Yugoslavia: The horrible things add up until they overwhelm everybody. You can almost smell the fear. The eeriness of it. People don't go out on the streets. They don't move. They don't do anything. They just stay indoors and feel afraid.

The New York Times, 11-1:(A)4.

Francois Mitterrand
President of France

7

[On the efforts of the French and German governments to prevent devaluation of the franc]: The speculators have no chance to win. They will

298

(FRANCOIS MITTERRAND)

be forced to pay because the political will exists to hold the line against them. If we do not resist, the European Monetary System would break up, and it would inflict a serious blow to the cause of Europe.

To journalists/
The Washington Post, 1-8:(A)12.

1

I would like to see the European Community give itself common rules to protect its industries from foreign goods produced in social conditions that cause such imbalance in the costs of production that we cannot long put up with the competition.

The New York Times, 7-1:(A)4.

Dominique Moisi
Associate director,
Institute for International Relations
(France)

2

[On the new conservative-oriented French government]: This is a government of popular, competent and reassuring individuals. It's a team that says to the French people, "It's not the right that has come to power, but honesty, modesty and energy."

The Christian Science Monitor,
4-1:6.

Luis Moreno
Political sociologist,
Institute for Advanced
Social Studies (Spain)

3

[On the Socialist Party's expected loss of its governing majority in the forthcoming election in Spain]: This election indicates another leap forward, but the end of Spain's transition will be when a conservative takes power and governs . . . The majority of Spaniards is still center-left, but they are tired of 11 years of Socialist government.

The Christian Science Monitor,
6-4:6.

Alexei Morozov
Deputy Foreign Minister
of the Republic of Karelia,
Russia

4

[On the increasing autonomy of many of Russia's republics]: Russia can no longer be a centralized state in the way we were before. If anyone thinks that everything can be ruled from Moscow, this is quite an illusion . . . If the center can't find a compromise with the regions, Russia can cease to exist as a state. This is the most terrible thing that could happen.

The Washington Post, 5-25:(A)12.

Vitaly V. Naumkin
Deputy director,
Institute of Oriental Studies
(Russia)

5

[On the friction in relations between Russia and Turkey]: Historical memory is one of the most decisive things in modern history, particularly in this part of the world. Most of the wars Russia fought were with Turkey. Turkey was a permanent enemy of Russian domination in the Caucasus, the Black Sea basin, and in the steppes.

The Christian Science Monitor,
9-13:10.

Richard M. Nixon
Former President
of the United States

6

I've been around a long time; I knew [former Soviet leaders] Khrushchev, Mikoyan, Kosygin, Brezhnev, Gromyko and so forth. There's an interesting thing about Russian leaders, and that includes the current crop—I have yet to meet one who is a weak one. They are strong, very strong. Believe me, they are strong. Perhaps it's the system; perhaps it's in the genes. I would say that under the circumstances, because they are so strong, it's quite remarkable that this revolution [of reform] has occurred in a peaceful way.

Interview, Moscow, Russia/
The New York Times, 2-19:(A)4.

(RICHARD M. NIXON)

1

[On U.S. aid for Russia]: Without our help, [Russian President Boris Yeltsin] will certainly fail. The choice we have here is between Yeltsin with his weaknesses and an alternative. Having met all the players, I can say there's not one of them that would not be worse. They are strong men and they are able men, but all of them would slow down economic reforms . . . I think [U.S. President] Clinton is making a gutsy call [in supporting aid to Russia], really the mark of a leader. There's no question a majority of the American people at this time would oppose aid to Russia. Clinton realizes that if the Yeltsin government goes down, it means the peace dividend is down the tube and the [U.S.] defense budget has to be increased by billions of dollars.

Interview/Time, 4-5:27.

2

To paraphrase [Winston] Churchill, the free market is the worst economic system except for all the others. But the central question in Russia is: Can democratic capitalism provide progress better than Communist capitalism, the kind they have in China? . . . If democratic capitalism fails in Russia, that will be water on China's wheels.

Interview,
Park Ridge, N.J./
The New York Times, 12-6:(A)11.

Sam Nunn
United States Senator,
D-Georgia

3

It's a mistake . . . to act as if everybody [in Russia] who's not in favor of what [Russian President Boris] Yeltsin is now doing is an old-line Communist. [The U.S. should] certainly support him . . . as the only nationally elected leader. But there are other people that we ought to be talking to. It's not Yeltsin exclusively.

Broadcast interview/
"Meet the Press,"
NBC-TV, 3-21.

Ian Paisley
Member of British Parliament
from Northern Ireland

4

[On the ethnic violence in Northern Ireland, such as took place recently in the Shankhill Road section of Belfast and in the town of Greysteel]: There's no difference between the tears of Protestants and the tears of Roman Catholics. These murders come from Hell, and they lead to Hell. How many more Shankhill Roads must we have, how many more Greysteels must we have, to bring about the ripening of the time [for peace]?

Before British House of Commons,
London, England, Nov. 1/
The Washington Post, 11-3:(A)10.

Dmytro Pavlychko
Chairman,
Foreign Affairs Committee,
Ukrainian Parliament

5

[Saying Ukraine owns the nuclear arsenal on its soil left there when the Soviet Union broke up]: If we do not say these weapons are ours, then we have no right to exchange these weapons for security guarantees and compensation. Ukraine will move toward arms reductions and START will be ratified. Only our enemies can say that Ukraine wants to become a nuclear state and brandish a nuclear truncheon.

July 2/
The Washington Post, 7-3:(A)24.

Milan Popovic
Yugoslavian psychiatrist;
Former dean,
Department of philosophy,
Belgrade University

6

We are in a macho war culture, in which to be good is a sign of feebleness, to be tolerant is traitorous. It is very important that people at the top be tolerant, humanistic and so on, at a time like this, and that is not the case here. During the past two years, politicians have achieved a cohesion of the people and the nation with paranoid

(MILAN POPOVIC)

anxiety, creating a self-image among the Serbs as a group in danger from outside enemies, both real and imagined. If there are not sufficient enemies outside the country, you can find them in your own circles—people who think or act differently.

Los Angeles Times, 3-27:(A)13.

Juan de Dios Ramirez Heredia
Spanish member
of European Parliament

1

Sadly, Germany has had to wash away for many years the image of a country that was truly horrible. This belongs to the recent past, but it is the past. It is not fair in this time—1993—to identify a past of repression and ignominy and crimes against humanity with the German people who are there now. But I have to admit that when one sees on television or in the newspapers the pictures of those young men, neo-Nazis, covered with swastikas that recall the horrors of the past, it makes our blood run cold.

Interview, Brussels, Belgium/
Los Angeles Times, 2-28:(M)3.

Peter Reddaway
Professor of political science
and international affairs,
George Washington University

2

[The Russian central government] is so gridlocked and corrupt that the [U.S.] Clinton Administration will make terrible mistakes if it continues to consult overwhelmingly with it, rather than with the people in the regions and provinces who are really running Russia.

U.S. News & World Report,
3-29:30.

Lord Rees-Mogg
Member of British
House of Lords;
Former editor,
"The Times" (Britain)

3

[British Prime Minister John Major is] a very depressing chap. He takes a decision, often gets it

wrong, goes through with it with great obstinacy, and then panics and abandons his position. That's the A-B-C of John Major.

The New York Times, 8-11:(A)5.

Michel Rocard
Former Prime Minister
of France

4

[On reforming France's Socialist Party]: What we need and what I urge you to join is a vast, open and modern movement, outward-looking, rich in diversity and even encouraging it; a movement gathering all those who share the same values and hold the same goal of transforming society. It will embrace ecologists, centrists loyal to our social traditions and reformed Communists.

To Socialist Party supporters,
Montlouis, France/
The Washington Post, 2-26:(A)28.

5

[On the popularity of the two "ecology parties" in French politics]: When the French can no longer find the springs of their identity in a social class, nor in a religion, nor in a profession, nor in a generation or a level of income, what is left to identify with? What surrounds them immediately? Their environment.

Speech/
The Washington Post, 3-6:(A)30.

Sergei M. Rogov
Chairman, Center for
National Security Problems,
U.S.A.-Canada Institute
(Russia)

6

[On the current standoff between Russian President Boris Yeltsin and Alexander Rutskoi, who has assumed the title of Russian President following Yeltsin's recent dissolution of Parliament]: These are two guys who are quite ready to shoot at each other. In the final analysis, you have two individuals fighting for the same chair. It's a very dangerous situation, especially when

301

(SERGEI M. ROGOV)

the prize is power none of them could dream of two years ago.

Sept. 22/
Los Angeles Times, 9-23:(A)24.

Oleg Rumyantsev
Leader,
Social Democratic Party
of Russia

1

[The word "sovok" means] a special mentality brought up by the Soviet system with all its anti-intellectualism, xenophobia, traditionalism and conservatism . . . We [in Russia] are not facing a revival of the Communist Party, or a Communist takeover. We are facing the return of the "Soviet mentality," a return to the mentality of the "sovok." The political crisis has been aggravated because the conflict between the radical and liberal reforms, on the one side, and the culture and psychology of a "sovok" has aggravated.

News conference/
The Christian Science Monitor,
3-24:1,4.

Stephan Russ-Mohl
Professor of communications,
Free University of Berlin
(Germany)

2

[On recent scandals in the German government]: The political discussion here is rapidly moving away from policy toward an emphasis on corruption—a personalization of politics that we have not had before . . . This is all very minor stuff compared to what's going on in Italy. But the public seems to take it very seriously. If it keeps going like this, we could get a similar trend as in Italy, with ministers resigning every week.

Los Angeles Times,
The Washington Post, 4-1:(A)34.

Alexander V. Rutskoi
Vice President of Russia

3

[On how the Russian government should be run]: Military people have an excellent formula, which civilians dislike for some reason. There are five conditions which must be met to secure progress in tackling any job. The first is sizing up the mission. The second is that you must estimate your capabilities. Then comes taking a decision. And lastly, the system of execution and control over execution. If our ministries learned how to follow these conditions, the reform would proceed with clockwork precision. But whenever I say this I am immediately branded an anti-marketeer and anti-democratic. I am a marketeer and a democrat. Only I believe there is a need to think first, then act. If a pilot does otherwise, he will simply crash.

Interview/
Los Angeles Times, 3-27:(A)17.

4

[Criticizing Russian President Boris Yeltsin's reform program]: People are tired of what is happening. We call these "reforms," expecting that they should open up a path to a better life. But the results of these reforms are all minus. There is not a single economic indicator that shows an improvement in people's living conditions or successes in [economic] transformations.

Speech/Los Angeles Times, 3-27:(A)17.

5

[Saying he would run for the Russian Presidency if current President Boris Yeltsin were to leave office]: I have enough strength, I fully understand the situation and, without doubt, I will put forward my candidacy. I want only one thing: to stop this corrupt and criminal chaos [in Russia] that is called "reforms."

Interview/
The Washington Post, 4-21:(A)21.

6

The political circles around [Russian President] Boris Yeltsin . . . are persistently pushing the President toward coercive action. Consequently, they are pushing the country to the brink,

(ALEXANDER V. RUTSKOI)

behind which lies blood, violence, chaos and the collapse of Russian statehood.

The Christian Science Monitor,
8-20:3.

Dmitri B. Ryurikov
Assistant to
Russian President
Boris N. Yeltsin
for National Security Affairs

1

[The] changes [in Russia] are fundamental. During one year and a half, you can record fundamental achievements such as, for example, turning former adversaries into partners, giving a serious boost to reduction of nuclear weapons and missile arsenals to two-thirds, fundamental agreements with the United States. There were principal changes in relations with major democratic countries. We became partners and set a goal of friendship. Russia became a member of the democratic community of states. All this in a short period of time, and achieved largely by a foreign policy that is a policy of a different state—that is striving to become a democratic state.

Interview,
Washington, D.C./
Los Angeles Times, 9-5:(M)3.

Wolfgang Schaeuble
Parliamentary Leader,
Christian Democratic Union
of Germany

2

[On Germany's decision to curb its liberal asylum law]: We have tried everything short of changing the Constitution. We can no longer take in two-thirds of Europe's asylum-seekers. This decision is crucial for the internal peace in our country.

Debate in the German Bundestag (Parliament),
Bonn, May 26/
The Washington Post,
5-27:(A)44.

Erwin Scheuch
Sociologist,
Cologne University
(Germany)

3

[On recent anti-immigrant violence in Germany]: Nothing has changed in [German] attitudes toward people of different cultures. Britain and France [which acknowledge their multicultural societies] are former empires, but Germans are entirely European. Anything outside of Europe for them is close to Mars.

Newsweek, 6-14:39.

Pierre Schori
Member of
Swedish Parliament;
Former Secretary of State
of Sweden

4

This [Swedish] government says it wants to stress our "European identity" in foreign policy, but that is code for merely following where the rest of Western Europe leads. We are letting our involvement with the rest of the world slide, and to that extent I think the world doesn't recognize Sweden anymore.

The Christian Science Monitor,
4-28:7.

Eduard A. Shevardnadze
President of Georgia

5

If Russia tries to reconstruct the [Soviet] empire, it will be destroyed. That is why the fate of Georgia is associated with Russian democracy . . . [A] democratic Russia is not a threat to Georgia . . . When the economy of Russia transfers completely into a free-market economy, I think that will change the point of view and perspective of people a lot.

Interview,
Tbilisi, Georgia/
The Christian Science Monitor,
12-13:13.

Andre Shleifer
Economist,
Harvard University
(United States);
Adviser to the government
of Russian President
Boris N. Yeltsin

1

[Saying Western aid to Russia should be targeted at privately owned businesses]: If you spend all your money on stabilization and none on privatization, you stabilize socialism. Unless Russia becomes a market economy, it will remain addicted to aid.

The Washington Post, 5-7:(A)27.

Krzysztof Skubiszewski
Foreign Minister of Poland

2

If Poland joins NATO, it won't bring any problems. If Poland joins, the security of Europe will be strengthened. There are no questions of being involved in any strife in the region. We have no minority problems; we have no border claims; and we have stable frontiers and good relations with our neighbors, Germany, Russia and Ukraine.

The New York Times, 8-26:(A)3.

Dick Spring
Foreign Minister of Ireland

3

[On U.S. attitudes toward the violence in Northern Ireland]: It's crucial that politicians in the States would understand that we've got to show tolerance on this island for different traditions; and that, ultimately, means compromise. You can't have winners and losers. It's a lot more complicated than "Brits Out" or "Up the Rebels." That attitude doesn't represent the attitude of modern Ireland. It's got to be a peaceful resolution by consent of the people of the island, north and south.

Interview,
Dublin, Ireland/
The New York Times, 3-3:(A)5.

Strobe Talbott
United States Ambassador-at-Large
to the former Soviet republics

4

[The] basic story of what is going on in that part of the world [Russia and the former, now independent, Soviet republics] is actually quite simple. It's a historic struggle that pits those who brought down the Soviet Communist system against those who would like to preserve its vestiges, if not to restore its very essence . . . In short, it pits reform against reaction. And that struggle is going to last for a very long time, certainly for decades. We have an immense stake in the outcome of that struggle.

To business group, Washington, D.C./
Newsweek, 5-10:43.

Boris Tarasyuk
Deputy Foreign Minister
of Ukraine

5

[On U.S. pressure on Ukraine to rid itself of nuclear weapons]: The Ukrainian-American relationship in these last few months has become the hostage of the nuclear issue. I am deeply convinced that this pressure has caused an increase and a strengthening of the forces who support a nuclear Ukraine. Thus, this pressure has had the reverse effect than the result expected by the U.S. Administration.

Kiev, Ukraine/
The Christian Science Monitor,
5-12:7.

Levon Ter-Petrosyan
President of Armenia

6

We proceed from the assumption that in this unstable situation [in the newly independent nations of the Caucasus region that used to be part of the Soviet Union], this transitional period, Armenia could not risk its security, could not leave a security system created over decades [and dominated by Russia]. The Russian presence in the Caucasus is a factor for stability. If Russia left completely, a very serious vacuum would be

(LEVON TER-PETROSYAN)

created, and other forces would try to fill this vacuum—Turkey and Iran.

Interview, Yerevan, Armenia/
The Christian Science Monitor,
12-13:13.

Margaret Thatcher
Former Prime Minister
of the United Kingdom

1

[On Russia's difficulties following the breakup of the Soviet Union]: When any empire breaks up, there are always great problems—more so with an evil empire, because it suppressed so many feelings . . . What I am critical of is that we [in the West] should have done more to help on the fundamentals. It's quite a mistake to think that because Communism is at an end, democracy or peace has broken out [in Russia and the former Soviet republics]. It hasn't . . . The amount of [Western] money that's gone in hasn't gone in the right way. It would be far better if we put all our efforts into a request to the [International Monetary Fund] to have a real currency board and a proper central bank, right at the beginning. You can't build a confident people without a confident currency.

Interview, Los Angeles, Calif./
Los Angeles Times, 11-28:(M)3.

Helmut Turk
Austrian Ambassador
to the United States

2

With the dissolution of the bipolar European system, the European Community has emerged as the central political force on the continent . . . The success of the Community is based on the fact that the existing state system in Europe no longer corresponds to the needs of today. To resolve the problem arising from increasing interdependence requires of sovereign states a pooling of resources and an unprecedented level of solidarity . . . Public-opinion polls in many European Community countries indicate, however, that skepticism and distrust of the integra-

tion process is widespread . . . [But] the new security challenges that Europe faces today . . . can only be resolved through collective efforts in the framework of international institutions.

Before Los Angeles (Calif.) World
Affairs Council, July 7/
Los Angeles Times, 7-9:(B)2.

Alparslan Turkes
Leader, Nationalist Action Party
of Turkey

3

When I look at events in Russia and the other [now-independent] republics which were under Soviet imperialism, I find the Russians trying to establish their old czarist imperialism in these countries again. I told many Russians that, "You have to change your attitude and your relations with those nations which were under your dominance . . . You have to accept equality and respect toward other nations and people."

Interview/
The Christian Science Monitor,
9-13:11.

Boris Usik
Director,
Stalingrad Battle Museum
(Russia)

4

[On the current increase in visitors to his museum, which commemorates the World War II Battle of Stalingrad in 1943]: The loss of faith in *perestroika* [Russia's recent restructuring program] and market reforms has caused people to look back to the past. If *perestroika* and market reforms had been more successful, then people would be looking forward, instead of behind.

Interview, Volgograd, Russia/
The Christian Science Monitor,
9-10:9.

Jan Vanous
Authority on
Eastern European economies

5

The West naively thought that all that had to be done in [East Europe] was to throw in some aid

(JAN VANOUS)

and sit back. The bad news is that if you restructure the East you will have to restructure the West. If the businessmen of the East start behaving like capitalists, they will cause a lot of pain in the West . . . Ultimately, the EC will have to reconcile its political desire to help former Communist countries with the economic reality that its concessions on market access have been small. They are just too greedy.

The Washington Post, 4-27:(C)1,6.

Volkan Voral
Senior adviser
to Turkish Prime Minister
Tansu Ciller;
Former Turkish Ambassador
to Russia

1

In Russia, there is debate and there is some suspicion as to the intentions of the former Soviet republics. First, they have to accept the fact that these republics are becoming independent. Independence does not necessarily mean hostility to Russia. We do not want to see a confrontation between Russia and the Central Asian republics. We also do not want that Russia or any other country should dictate terms to them and give them stark choices.

Interview, Ankara, Turkey/
The Christian Science Monitor,
9-13:10.

Stephanie Wahl
Sociologist,
Institute for Society
and Economics (Germany)

2

[On the controversy over expanding Germany's military role in the world]: Of course, we'd rather stay as we were before the Berlin Wall came down, like a plant grown in a greenhouse, big and strong, but never exposed to wind and rain. We had an army, but it was just play; it wasn't really being a soldier. Now we have to decide: do we do it for real? That's very hard.

The Washington Post, 4-3:(A)19.

Lech Walesa
President of Poland

3

[On Poland's just-held Parliamentary elections in which Walesa's old archenemies, former Communists, were victorious]: I have no choice [but to accept the results and form a government with those people]; democracy is not a joke. If the nation wants it, it surely has to be that way.

Interview, Sept. 19/
Los Angeles Times, 9-21:(A)7.

Norbert Walter
Chief economist,
Deutsche Bank (Germany)

4

[On Germany's economic and welfare system]: The system is a fair-weather arrangement. For demographic reasons, it can only end in catastrophe. Our over-burdened welfare state lies at the heart of the problem.

U.S. News & World Report,
10-25:44.

Peter Weilemann
Deputy director of research,
Konrad Adenauer Foundation
(Germany)

5

For two years, we [western Germans] talked about kick-starting the eastern [German] economy as if it wasn't attached to us. Now it's dawning that we're all in the same boat, and if they [in the east] are in trouble, so are we.

Los Angeles Times, 3-26:(A)5.

Paul Wilkinson
Director, Research Institute
for the Study of Conflict
and Terrorism (Britain)

6

[On the IRA's campaign of planting bombs in England to force Britain out of Northern Ireland]: They calculate that the havoc they create will be an extra lever on the British government to change its policy. Disrupting commercial cen-

(PAUL WILKINSON)

ters, the railway network and industrial complexes does great harm to business and industry. The IRA considers that, in terms of publicity, one bomb in England is worth 20 in Belfast.

The Christian Science Monitor,
3-3:6.

Manfred Woerner
Secretary General,
North Atlantic Treaty Organization

1

I think it's a measure of the importance of NATO that our former enemies [in the Soviet bloc] wish to join the alliance. Why? Because once you're in, you feel safe. If you're out, you feel less safe. So it proves the value of NATO as the key factor of stability in an unstable environment . . . [NATO has] found two new missions that no other organization can fulfill: providing forces for peacekeeping efforts and projecting our blanket of stability for those nations of Eastern Europe and the former Soviet Union.

Interview,
Brussels, Belgium/
Los Angeles Times, 4-2:(A)5.

2

[NATO] has changed more than any other international institution in the last few years. We have adopted a new strategy and force posture. We have started to strengthen our European pillar. We have established close relations with our former adversaries through NACC, and we have started participating in crisis management beyond our borders. So the slogan "out of area or out of business" is out of date. We are acting out of area and we very much are in business. Still, we need to further adapt the alliance to play its role in stabilizing Europe.

Before International Institute
for Strategic Studies,
Brussels, Belgium, Sept. 10/
The Wall Street Journal,
9-14:(A)20.

Gennadi I. Yanayev
Former Vice President
of the Soviet Union

3

[On his facing trial for treason for his part in the 1991 failed coup that temporarily ousted Soviet President Mikhail Gorbachev]: I am still a Communist, and even in jail I will continue my political activity. I do not intend to bury myself alive. I will keep struggling for the system that we have lost and for the restoration of the Soviet Union.

Interview,
Moscow, Russia, April 13/
Los Angeles Times, 4-14:(A)8.

Boris N. Yeltsin
President of Russia

4

There have been accusations that our Foreign Minister's orientation is pro-Western, that he is always looking left and cannot turn his head to the right. It seems to me that now our policy is more or less balanced. After all, we are a Euro-Asian state . . . We do not want axes, triangles or blocs. We would not wish for an alliance with India to the detriment of other countries. I would call this policy the specialty of the new Russia.

News conference,
Moscow, Russia, Jan. 25/
The New York Times, 1-26:(A)4.

5

Crime has become problem Number 1 [in Russia]. Crime has acquired such a scale and character that it poses a great danger for individuals and for the entire Russian state . . . Corruption in the organs of power and administration is literally corroding the state body of Russia from top to bottom.

To law-enforcement officials,
February/
The Christian Science Monitor,
5-10:12.

6

[Saying Russia should have special powers to put down ethnic conflicts in the now-independent

(BORIS N. YELTSIN)

republics of the former Soviet Union]: The world community is increasingly coming to understand Russia's special responsibility in this difficult task. I think the moment has come when responsible international organizations, including the United Nations, should grant Russia special powers as a guarantor of peace and stability in the region of the former union. Russia has a heartfelt interest in stopping all armed conflicts on the territory of the former Soviet Union.

Before Civic Union,
Moscow, Russia, Feb. 28/
The New York Times, 3-1:(A)1.

1

Only a [Russian] President chosen by the people can implement tough but necessary measures. No reform can survive without these tough measures. Do Deputies realize that neither the Congress nor the Parliament nor any other body are bold enough to implement these measures? . . . Today, in the present situation, it is strong Presidential power that ensures guarantees for the implementation of reforms.

Before Congress of People's Deputies,
Moscow, Russia, March 11/
The New York Times, 3-12:(A)5.

2

It must be acknowledged that [Russia's] economic crisis was aggravated by our [his Administration's] mistakes—insufficient social orientation of the reforms, inadequate support by the state of new forms of management and of the new level of owners in the production sphere, absence of an efficient anti-inflation policy and excessive reliance on foreign aid.

Before Congress of People's Deputies,
Moscow, Russia, March 26/
The New York Times, 3-27:5.

3

All our problems are rooted not in the conflict between the Executive and Legislative Branches of power, not in the conflict between the President and the Congress [of People's Deputies]. The essence is somewhere else—it is deeper. It is in the profound contradiction between the people and the former Bolshevist anti-people system which has not yet disintegrated, which today again seeks to regain its lost power over Russia.

Broadcast address to the nation,
Moscow, Russia/
The Washington Post, 3-27:(A)14.

4

[On the forthcoming referendum in Russia on his leadership]: It is up to us to persuade the citizens of the Russian Federation that if they do not vote in favor of confidence on the 25th of April, they will be dealing a major blow not only upon Russia but also upon the United States of America, upon the other countries of the world. This would be a loss to democracy, a loss to freedom, a rollback to the past, a return to the Communist yoke. There is no alternative to Yeltsin. Perhaps there will be one tomorrow, but certainly not today.

News conference,
Vancouver, Canada, April 4/
USA Today, 4-5:(A)8.

5

[On the reforms he supports which have swept across Russia in the last few years]: People quickly get used to freedom, to independence. They have shorn fear and start to acquire dignity . . . Yesterday I was in Kuzbass. People told me that they no longer have to suffer the humiliation as before of standing in long lines at shops with empty shelves, though of course prices bite [deeply] . . . To put a yoke on people again will only be possible by using unlimited, inhuman force, only by unprecedented repression.

News conference,
Moscow, Russia, April 14/
The Christian Science Monitor,
4-15:6.

6

[On the recent public referendum which backed his rule]: Everybody must understand

(BORIS N. YELTSIN)

that the President, the government and the policy of reforms now enjoy the protection of the people. All decisions contradicting the will of the people, no matter who adopts them, should not be carried out and should be canceled. The Congress and the Supreme Soviet must make their choice— either to back the President's and government's course or to confront the people directly.

Speech, April 29/
The Christian Science Monitor,
4-30:7.

1

[On the Russian Parliament's opposition to many of his political and economic reforms]: Parliament has begun to work against the interests of the people and increasingly threatens Russia's security. I can only regret that the [Parliament building], the White House, where two years ago Russian citizens defended freedom and democracy, has become a bulwark of revanchist forces.

News conference,
Moscow, Russia, Aug. 19./
Los Angeles Times, 8-20:(A)6.

2

[On the improving relations between Russia and Poland]: There is no room for hegemony and *diktat,* the psychology of a "big brother" and a "little brother," in new Russian-Polish relations . . . An entire era is coming to a close. The time when Polish leaders traveled to Moscow for advice, or on the other hand, Moscow leaders went to Warsaw to give advice on what to do, is gone.

To reporters,
Warsaw, Poland, Aug. 25/
Los Angeles Times, 8-26:(A)10.

3

[Announcing his dissolving of the Russian Parliament]: Power in the Supreme Soviet of Russia has been seized by a group of persons who have turned it into the headquarters of irrecon-

cilable opposition . . . Being the guarantor of the security of our state, I am obliged to propose a way out of this deadlock. I am obliged to break this ruinous, vicious circle . . . People should come to the Russian Parliament who will not indulge in political games at the people's expense, but instead primarily create the laws that Russia needs so badly. More competent, educated and democratic people should fill the Russian Parliament. I believe that such people exist in Russia. I believe we shall find them and we shall elect them.

Broadcast address to the nation,
Moscow, Russia, Sept. 21/
The New York Times, 9-22:(A)8,9.

4

[On his decision to dissolve the Russian Parliament]: The security of Russia and her peoples is more precious than formal compliance with contradictory regulations created by the legislature. The measures that I have to take as President are the only way to protect democracy and freedom in Russia, to defend reform and the still-weak Russian market.

Broadcast address to the nation,
Moscow, Russia, Sept. 21/
The Washington Post, 9-22:(A)28.

5

[On his recent use of force to crush an uprising against him in Parliament]: This alarming and tragic night taught us many lessons . . . Everything that has happened and is happening in Moscow is a pre-planned, armed mutiny. It is organized by Communist revenge-seekers, Fascist chieftains, some former deputies and representatives of soviets [councils]. While holding sham negotiations, they accumulated forces, brought together bandit groups of mercenaries inured to killing and arbitrariness.

Broadcast address to the nation,
Moscow, Russia, Oct. 4/
The Christian Science Monitor,
10-5:4.

6

[On the proposed new Russian Constitution]: Skeptics say a majority of people won't be able to

(BORIS N. YELTSIN)

make sense of this Constitution, that its text is too complicated for them. It's true that a simple man may not understand all the legal subtleties. But I'm sure people have already figured out the main principles of this Constitution . . . that the human being is the supreme value, not a class or a nation. Russia has not had a Constitution like that so far.

Broadcast address to the nation,
Moscow, Russia, Nov. 9/
The Washington Post, 11-10:(A)35.

Vladimir V. Zhirinovsky
Leader,
Liberal Democratic Party
of Russia

1

We are not anti-Semites. But our voters are tired of seeing so many non-Russian announcers on television . . . [Anti-Semitism] is provoked by Jews themselves. We Russians have never been anti-Semites ourselves.

The Christian Science Monitor, 12-15:18.

2

[On his personal heroes]: My political ideals are all in Russia . . . But as far as Western politicians are concerned, I prefer Bismarck and Frederick the Great in Germany, de Gaulle in France, Roosevelt in the U.S.A. and, recently, Margaret Thatcher in Great Britain and maybe Benazir Bhutto in Pakistan—a woman that has won elections twice; that is very important.

Interview, Dec. 20/
The Christian Science Monitor, 12-24:9.

Todor Zhivkov
Former President,
and former General Secretary
of the Communist Party,
of Bulgaria

3

I am the first leader of a Communist party of the Warsaw Pact to denounce the system because it entered into contradiction with socialist ideals. Nobody but Todor Zhivkov denounced it. [Former Soviet President Mikhail] Gorbachev repeated *"perestroika," "perestroika"* [reform] all the time, but did nothing. We in Bulgaria began to do away with the system. The main economic reforms that began freedom for some private enterprise bear Todor Zhivkov's signature. The first decree for market reform was signed by me. The later governments used these reforms.

Interview,
Boyana, Bulgaria/
The New York Times, 7-9:(A)6.

Valery D. Zorkin
Chairman,
Constitutional Court of Russia

4

Only a strong legal authority can save Russia. But the power of that authority is not in imposing an "absolute" truth on the rest, not in crushing a political opponent. The power and wisdom of that authority is its ability to negotiate, search for and find reasonable compromises.

Los Angeles Times, 2-9:(H)4.

THE ETHNIC CONFLICT IN THE BALKANS

All of the quotations in this sub-section relate to the ethnic civil war which broke out following the self-declared independence in 1992 of the Yugoslavian republics of Bosnia-Herzegovina and Croatia. In this conflict, Bosnian Serbs, with support from Yugoslavian Serbs, aim to conquer Muslim territory in Bosnia to form a larger Serbian-ruled area. The fighting has also involved Croatia.

Morton I. Abramowitz
President, Carnegie Endowment
for International Peace
(United States)

1

The Muslim side—the weakest side—has a Hobson's choice—either to accept division [ethnic partition] or to be ground down because the West is unwilling to help except through cheap rhetoric.

The New York Times, 6-19:4.

Madeleine K. Albright
United States Ambassador/
Permanent Representative
to the United Nations

2

The [U.S.] Clinton Administration will not recognize—and we do not believe the international community will recognize—any deal or effort to grant immunity to those accused of war crimes [in the Balkan conflict]. Governments will be obliged to hand over for trial [by the UN] those indicted who are within their jurisdiction. If they refuse, the states may be subject to sanctions and the indicted will become international pariahs, trapped within the borders of their countries.

Before International Rescue Committee,
New York, N.Y., Nov. 2/
The New York Times,
11-3:(A)4.

Diego Arria
Venezuelan Ambassador/
Permanent Representative
to the United Nations

3

[Urging the UN not to approve attempts to carve up Bosnia with Bosnian Serbs keeping most of the territory they have conquered]: [While Bosnia] would pay an extremely high price [under such proposals], the international community will definitely pay an even higher one in moral and political terms . . . The [Serb] aggressor's triumph will surely diminish all of us in the [UN] Security Council. I trust that tomorrow when contemplating the devastation of the remains of what used to be a beautiful country . . . we will not have to be reminded of Shakespeare's lament in *Henry V:* "Shame and eternal shame, nothing but shame."

At United Nations,
New York, Aug. 24/
Los Angeles Times,
8-25:(A)7.

Reginald Bartholomew
United States Special Envoy
to the Balkans

4

The military and human horror has to stop now. Bosnian Serbs have to do it now . . . If they [the Serbs] persist in their actions [against

Bosnian Muslims], the international community will make of Serbia a pariah state for as far ahead as we can see.

April 14/
Los Angeles Times, 4-15:(A)8.

Joseph R. Biden, Jr.
United States Senator,
D-Delaware

1

The United States must lead the West in a decisive response to Serbian aggression [against Bosnia], beginning with air attacks on Serb artillery everywhere in Bosnia and on Yugoslav National Army units in Serbia that have participated in this international crime. From talks with the most informed U.S. military officials, I am confident it would not require the introduction of a major Western ground force to deny the Serbs the victory toward which they are now headed in the face of Western apathy.

Washington, D.C., April 16/
Los Angeles Times, 4-17:(A)17.

2

[On Serbia's attacks on Bosnia]: The West . . . has appeased [Serbian President Slobodan] Milosevic for so long that he has no reason to respond to our blandishments and our threats. The world [must] stop bemoaning the fact that all our options are bad ones. They *are* all bad ones. We've got to pick a couple.

At Senate Foreign Relations
Committee hearing,
Washington, D.C., April 20/
Los Angeles Times, 4-21:(A)4.

3

[Addressing U.S. Secretary of State Warren Christopher, saying the Europeans are not doing enough to help the Bosnians against Serbian aggression]: Let me put it plainly. You are required to speak diplomatically; I am not. I cannot even begin to express to you my contempt for a European policy that is now asking us

to participate in what amounts to a codification of the Serbian victory . . . After [the Europeans] held our coats on Kuwait and Somalia, they are asking us to put in a few thousand troops on the ground in order to have the right to speak and in order to help implement their new idea of "safe havens" for the Bosnians. Let us not mince words. European policy is based on cultural and religious indifference, if not bigotry. And I think it's fair to say that this would be an entirely different situation if the [Bosnian] Muslims were doing what the Serbs have done, if this was Muslim aggression instead of Serbian aggression.

At Senate Foreign Relations
Committee hearing,
Washington, D.C., May 11/
The Washington Post, 5-12:(A)24.

Boutros Boutros-Ghali
Secretary General
of the United Nations

4

We have as an objective the withdrawal of the Serbs [from the areas of Bosnia they have taken by force], and if they will not withdraw, then we'll have to take the necessary measures. I believe that if, after whatever ought to be done, we find that we are not able to obtain their [the Serbs'] withdrawal, then there is only one solution, which is enforcement. [In that case, UN members] must be ready to send troops on the ground.

Broadcast interview/
"This Week With David Brinkley,"
ABC-TV, 3-7.

George Bush
President of the United States

5

Sometimes, the decision not to use force, to stay our hand, I can tell you it's just as difficult as a decision to send our soldiers into battle. The former Yugoslavia, well, it's been such a situation. There are, we all know, important humanitarian and strategic interests at stake there, but up to now it's not been clear that the application of limited amounts of force by the United States and its traditional friends and allies would have had the desired effect, given the nature and the complexity of that situation. Our assessment of the situation in the former Yugoslavia could well change if and as the situation changes. The stakes could grow. The conflict could threaten to spread. Indeed, we are constantly reassessing our options and are actively consulting with others about steps that might be taken to contain the fighting, protect the humanitarian effort and deny Serbia the fruits of [its] aggression [against Bosnia].

At U.S. Military Academy,
West Point, N.Y., Jan. 5/
The New York Times, 1-6:(A)5.

3

The continuing destruction of a new United Nations member [Bosnia] challenges the principle that internationally recognized borders should not be altered by force . . . Bold tyrants and fearful minorities are watching to see whether ethnic cleansing is a policy the world will tolerate. If we hope to promote the spread of freedom, if we hope to encourage the emergence of peaceful ethnic democracies, our answer must be a resounding no.

Washington, D.C.,
Feb. 10/
The Washington Post, 8-19:(A)24.

Warren Christopher
Secretary of State-designate
of the United States

1

I believe the future of Europe is at stake in Bosnia. Already the problems in Bosnia and the rest of the former Yugoslavia are ricocheting around the Balkans and Europe . . . Failure to introduce sufficient [outside] military force into the Bosnian equation will, I fear, prolong the agony and allow the conflict there to grow and threaten our national-security interests.

At Senate Foreign Relations Committee
hearing on his nomination,
Washington, D.C., Jan. 13/
The Washington Post,
8-19:(A)24.

4

We must today admit frankly a fact that now haunts our search for peace: The West missed too many opportunities to prevent or contain this suffering, bloodshed and destruction when the conflict was in its infancy. The lesson to be learned from this tragedy is the importance of early and decisive engagement against ethnic persecution and aggressive nationalism.

To NATO foreign ministers,
Brussels, Belgium,
Feb. 26/
Los Angeles Times, 2-27:(A)4.

Warren Christopher
Secretary of State
of the United States

2

This conflict may be far from our shores, but it is not distant to our concerns. The world's response to the violence in the former Yugoslavia is an early and crucial test of how it will address the concerns of ethnic and religious minorities in the post-Cold War world.

To reporters, Feb. 10/
Newsweek, 4-26:37.

5

Let me put that situation in Bosnia in just a little broader framework. It's really a tragic problem. The hatred between all three groups—the Bosnians and the Serbs and the Croatians—is almost unbelievable. It's almost terrifying, and it's centuries old. That really is a problem from hell. And I think that the United States is doing all we can to try to deal with that problem. [But] the United States simply doesn't have the means to make people in that region of the world like each other.

Broadcast interview/
"Face the Nation,"
CBS-TV, 3-28.

WHAT THEY SAID IN 1993

(WARREN CHRISTOPHER)

1

We are prepared to commit our military forces to implement a peace settlement entered into consensually and in good faith by the [warring] parties. But we will not use our military forces to impose a settlement in the Balkans.

Before House Foreign Affairs Committee,
Washington, D.C., May 18/
The Washington Post, 5-19:(A)24.

2

Bosnia is a human tragedy, a humanitarian—just a gross—grotesque humanitarian situation. But it is not [like] a confrontation between the United States and Russia. It does not affect our vital national interests except as we're concerned about humanitarian matters and except as we're trying to contain it.

Broadcast interview/
"MacNeil-Lehrer NewsHour," PBS-TV, 6-1.

3

[On the quick Western recognition last year of the independence of the former Yugoslav republics of Bosnia and Croatia, which some say led to the current conflict]: There were serious mistakes made in the whole process of recognition, quick recognition, and the Germans bear a particular responsibility in persuading their colleagues and the European community. We [the U.S. Clinton Administration] were not in office at that time, but many serious students of the matter think the beginning of the problems we face here today stem from the recognition of Croatia and thereafter of Bosnia.

Interview, June 16/
USA Today, 6-17:(A)11.

4

[On what the U.S. can do about the conflict]: I feel now and probably should have stated more clearly very early, though I felt it very early, that the only reliable way to stop the killing there or impose a solution was through the massive use of ground troops . . . I think there was a long period

in which many Americans had the feeling, I call it an illusion, that air power could solve this problem. Now, I happen to think [U.S.] President Clinton made exactly the right decision in feeling that we should not put in ground troops, because it would require hundreds of thousands of ground troops. And, believe me, they would have been to a large extent American troops . . . [But] if I had articulated more clearly the fact that no solution would have been successful except with the use of massive numbers of ground troops . . . that might have been some help in the debate. But I'm not sure it would have convinced those who still feel so sincerely and so deeply that the United States somehow should solve this problem. I call them the "do something" people.

Interview/
U.S. News & World Report,
7-5:24.

5

[Indicating the U.S. will not use military force to end the conflict]: That's a tragic, tragic situation in Bosnia . . . It's the world's most difficult diplomatic problem, I believe. It defies any simple solution. The United States is doing all that it can consistent with our national interest . . . Our national interest . . . is in humanitarian relief, to the extent that we can provide it, coupled with preventing the spread of the conflict [and] doing all we can to make sure that those who are involved in evil conduct there realize that they will be subject, as people, to war-crimes trials and, as nations, to continuing sanctions.

News conference,
Washington, D.C., July 21/
Los Angeles Times,
7-22:(A)8.

6

[Threatening the use of NATO air strikes against the Serbs]: The international community simply cannot accept the laying of siege of cities and the continuous bombardment of civilians. It's time now for the Serbs to stop their strangulation of Sarajevo and the other cities in Bosnia. They'd be well advised to take very seriously what we're doing here . . . We are ready to take the action that needs to be taken.

To reporters,
Aviano Air Base, Italy, Aug. 6/
Los Angeles Times, 8-7:(A)4.

1

This winter, the snows have come early to Bosnia and the humanitarian crisis has deepened. Whatever we do to help, it will not be enough. So long as the armed conflict continues, it is not humanly possible to end the suffering of the people of Bosnia . . . The only answer is to bring the fighting to an end, and the only means to that end is a negotiated settlement.

To Foreign Ministers of the
Conference on Security and
Cooperation in Europe,
Rome, Italy, Nov. 30/
The New York Times, 12-1:(A)9.

Bill Clinton
President of the United States

2

I think it will be very interesting for the world to look and see if the Serbians are willing to negotiate in good faith in a process that they have embraced when it suited their short-term strategic interests. I hope that they will support it over a longer term. We'll see . . . [But] the United States cannot proceed here unilaterally. We need the support of the Europeans, who are much closer to the situation and who will be much more immediately impacted by any further adverse instability in the Balkans than we would.

Washington, D.C., March 5/
The New York Times, 3-6:4.

3

[On what the U.S. can do to end the conflict]: I think we have an interest in standing up against the principle of "ethnic cleansing." If you look at the turmoil all through the Balkans, if you look at the other places where this could play itself out in other parts of the world, this is not just about

[Serbian aggression against] Bosnia. On the other hand, there is reason to be humble when [considering military action against] the former Yugoslavia. You have only to look at the topography of the country to realize we have a very limited hand to play . . . I have operated from the beginning under the assumption that whatever is done must be done within the framework of a multilateral cooperation, that this is not something the United States could effectively do alone.

News conference,
Washington, D.C., April 16/
The New York Times, 4-17:5.

4

[On the possibility of U.S. military intervention]: If the United States takes action, we must have a clearly defined objective that can be met, we must be able to understand it, and its limitations must be clear. The United States should not become involved as a partisan in a war. With regard to the lifting of the arms embargo [on Bosnia to allow that country to defend itself against the Serbs], the question obviously there is, if you widen the capacity of people to fight, will that help to get a settlement and bring about peace or will it lead to more bloodshed, and what kind of reaction can others have that would undermine the effectiveness of the policy? But I think both of them deserve some serious consideration along with some other options we have.

News conference,
Washington, D.C., April 23/
The New York Times, 4-24:5.

5

Before I agree to put one American soldier [in the Balkans], I will obviously speak not only to [the media] but directly to the American people about it. There has been enormous loss of life under especially brutal conditions there, and it is a very politically unstable part of the world which has significant potential for a wider war. And so the United States has tried to work with our allies . . . in an attempt to get the parties together so that we can present a united front, and so that

(BILL CLINTON)

we can keep the pressure up to end the killing but also to stop the prospect of a much wider war, which could cause much more trouble, much more instability.

To reporters,
Washington, D.C., May 3/
Los Angeles Times, 5-4:(A)10.

1

I have never advocated the United States unilaterally sending troops to Bosnia to fight on one side or the other of a civil war. But I think there is much more that we can do to induce the parties to stop the fighting, to do what we can to stop this idea of ethnic cleansing, murdering people, raping children and doing terrible acts of violence because of people's religion. We want to try to confine that conflict so it doesn't spread into other places and involve other countries, like Albania and Greece and Turkey, which could have the impact of undermining the peace in Europe and the growth and stability of democracies there. That's quite a different thing than what happened [with U.S. intervention in Vietnam in the 1960s and '70s], where the United States essentially got involved in what was a civil war on one side or the other.

At Fenton High School,
Bensenville, Ill., May 11/
The Washington Post, 5-12:(A)24.

2

[On the possibility of using Western air power to help Bosnian Muslims who are under siege by the Serbs]: The position of the United States is still that the best use of the air option is as a backup to buying time to better equip the Bosnians to defend themselves. I wouldn't rule out any option. I'm not ruling out that option, but I'm not ruling it in, either . . . The purpose of any of this, I might add, is not to bring the United States or the world community into the conflict on the side of the Bosnian Muslims. It is to try to stop their slaughter, to end the violence and to restore a reasonable political solution which permits peace within the borders of Bosnia and

stops the spreading of the conflict. That's another issue. You have to be very sensitive. When people talk about air power, not only do you have to be able to see the end of the day, we have to remember what the role of the United States and the world community here is. It is not to enter conflict on the side of the Muslims. It is to—from the point of view of the United States anyway— to try to end the conflict, end the ethnic cleansing, restore some reasonable political solution and stop the spreading of the conflict.

Interview,
Washington, D.C., May 13/
The Washington Post, 5-14:(A)10.

3

Because Bosnia was created as a separate legal entity, it is both a civil war, where elements of people who live within that territory are fighting against one another, and there has been aggression from without—from the Croatians and from the Serbs, principally from the Serbs. The inevitable but unintended impact of the [UN] arms embargo [against the Bosnian Muslims] has been to put the United Nations in the position of ratifying an enormous superiority of arms for the Bosnian Serbs that they got from Serbia. Our interest is in seeing, in my view at least, that the United Nations does not fore-ordain the outcome of a civil war. That's why I've always been in favor of some kind of lifting of the arms embargo—that we contain the conflict and that we do everything we can to move to an end of it and to move to an end of ethnic cleansing.

News conference,
Washington, D.C., May 14/
The New York Times, 5-15:8.

Jacques Delors
President,
European Commission

4

[On the West's response to the conflict]: We should not have stated on the outbreak of hostilities that we would not use force. Even if military intervention was debatable, it made little sense to signal to the warring factions that they would not have to face the military might of the West. In

(JACQUES DELORS)

other words, without a plausible threat to use force, we needlessly undermined the credibility of our warnings and ultimatums.

*Before International Institute
for Strategic Studies,
Brussels, Belgium, Sept. 10/
Los Angeles Times, 9-11:(A)15.*

Michael Dewar
*Deputy director,
International Institute for
Strategic Studies (Britain)*

1

[Saying outside military intervention would be impractical to try to stop the conflict]: The original mistake was recognizing Bosnia-Herzegovina as an independent state in the first place . . . Unfortunately, there are no effective military solutions to the Bosnian crisis. Perhaps the unpalatable truth is that when a people are determined to fight each other, there is precious little that the outside world can do to help.

Los Angeles Times, 5-17:(A)8.

Robert J. Dole
*United States Senator,
R-Kansas*

2

[Saying there is a lack of decision by the U.S. as to what to do about the conflict]: [American policy] is a sham. All we're doing is standing by while the Serbs mop up Bosnia and divide it into 11 little pieces and slaughter all the women and children. In my view, that's not a policy.

*Broadcast interview/
"Meet the Press," NBC-TV, 4-18.*

3

[Criticizing U.S. agreement to a plan to provide "safe havens" for Bosnian Muslims]: [It] offers little if any hope of ending the war in Bosnia. Moreover, it amounts to writing off Bosnia as a state by ratifying the status quo [of Serbian military victories] on the ground.

*The Christian Science Monitor,
5-25:2.*

4

My view is [U.S. President Clinton] ought to call the world leaders together. This [conflict] is an international tragedy, and there ought to be . . . an international meeting somewhere, maybe right here, and the President ought to get up and provide the leadership to do something . . . It's too important just to let it drift on . . . I don't suggest we can take on everybody's problem in the world, but at least we ought to address it on a high enough level that we've demonstrated an effort to try to deal with it. I think that's missing . . . If we're going to be the leader of the free world, we ought to be the leader of the free world.

*Interview,
Washington, D.C., July 26/
USA Today, 7-27:(A)9.*

Bill Fenrick
*Commander, Canadian Navy;
Lawyer, United Nations
War Crimes Commission*

5

I'd like it if the war was over, if there was no question of who was the winner and who the loser. I'd like it if there was a nice big court where we could take those responsible, with lots of policemen. But it's not clear who's going to win, or even what "winning" in this war would mean. So I don't think that what we're going to end up with is a Nuremberg II.

*To reporters,
Sarajevo, Bosnia-Herzegovina, April 25/
The New York Times, 4-26:(A)4.*

Ejup Ganic
*Vice President
of Bosnia-Herzegovina*

6

[Rejecting the idea of dividing Bosnia into separate ethnic states as a way of ending the conflict]: Partition is not an option for us. Agreeing to partition is like allowing someone to come to your house, move into more than half the rooms, steal your furniture, kill and rape your daughters and then tell you to sign on the dotted line. We just can't say yes to that.

*July 7/
The Washington Post, 7-8:(A)10.*

John Glenn
United States Senator,
D-Ohio

1

[Expressing reservations about possible U.S. military intervention in the conflict in Bosnia]: You don't go into a situation like this halfway; you don't just bomb a few artillery sites. All that does is satisfy your conscience and it doesn't mean a wit. What do we do next? What do we do after they [the Serbs] finish laughing at us? It's like a little bit of pregnancy; there's no such thing.

The Washington Post, 4-29:(A)35.

Patrick Glynn
Resident scholar,
American Enterprise Institute

2

[The conflict] was a manageable problem some months ago. There were small actions that could have been taken [by the West] to prevent this. But once it became clear what was taking place, once we had footage of concentration camps, reports of genocide and rape camps and torture on a massive, systematic scale, it was really incumbent upon the world to do something. And that was last summer. Our failure to do it is going to be a blot on our historical record, both the United States and Europe . . . Often it seems as though Western democracies are short on courage. It takes courage to stand up against evil people like the Bosnian Serb militants. People just aren't as good as perhaps they should be.

Interview/USA Today, 4-20:(A)11.

Paul A. Goble
Senior associate,
Carnegie Endowment
for International Peace
(United States)

3

What Bosnia is about is changing borders. If the West acquiesces to a new map achieved by force in Yugoslavia, why shouldn't 4.5 million Russians in northern Kazakhstan change that border by violence and join Russia? [By not stopping the aggression in Bosnia,] what we in the West are saying is, "We don't care." That's a

dangerous answer in a part of the world where political borders don't correspond to ethnic borders. The day after the Serbs take Sarajevo, any Russian leader who stands up and says, "We have to create a Greater Russia," will be listened to.

Los Angeles Times, 5-17:(A)10.

Lee H. Hamilton
United States Representative,
D-Indiana

4

[Saying U.S. President Clinton must completely spell out for Congress the details of any plan for U.S. intervention in the conflict]: The ordinary members of Congress are really frustrated. They're crying out for more information; they want to hear the goals and the objectives and the costs articulated . . . There are a lot of things that have to be done before military action begins. We've got to be very sure of what our interests are, what our objectives are, what the costs are going to be, what we can achieve, and how we can get out.

Broadcast interview/
"Meet the Press," NBC-TV, 5-9.

Ernest F. Hollings
United States Senator,
D-South Carolina

5

[Arguing against U.S. bombing of Serbs to try to end the conflict]: I hear Hitler's plan [of bombing Britain in World War II] all over Washington—that we bomb [the Serbs], that we'll bring them to the peace table. I think that will steel their will . . . and we'll all end up feeling stupid because it's not going to do what's intended.

At Senate Appropriations Subcommittee hearing,
Washington, D.C., April 27/
The Washington Post, 4-28:(A)16.

Larry Hollingworth
Senior United Nations
refugee official in Sarajevo,
Bosnia

6

[Denouncing the Serbian shelling of the Bosnian city of Srebrenica]: I hope that the mili-

(LARRY HOLLINGWORTH)

tary commander who ordered the firing on Srebrenica burns in the hottest corner of hell . . . [Those] who loaded the weapons and fired the shells—I hope they have nightmares forever more; I hope their sleep is punctuated by the screams of the children and by the cries of the mothers.

To reporters, April 13/
The Washington Post, 4-14:(A)23.

Alija Izetbegovic
President
of Bosnia-Herzegovina

1

[Saying Western air strikes should be used against Serbian forces attacking Bosnia]: When we have to choose between agony and surgery, it might be better for [Bosnia] to accept the surgery. I think [Bosnia] can be saved by the surgery, but it cannot stand the continued agony.

To reporters,
Washington, D.C., Jan.. 8/
Los Angeles Times, 1-9:(A)10.

2

The killing of the [Bosnian] civilian population [by the Serbs] is continuing, the towns are still under siege and people are now being killed also by starvation and exposure to cold . . . [Western] military intervention is already late by half a year. At least 1,000 people are killed daily. If the international community fulfilled its obligations to [a member] state that is being attacked, every day 1,000 lives could be saved.

News conference,
Geneva, Switzerland, Jan. 25/
Los Angeles Times, 1-26:(A)6.

3

If anybody asked me today what was the most important thing, I would say that the survival of my people is more important than the survival of the country. I cannot sacrifice my people [Bosnian Muslims] for the sake of saving the country. But by saving my people, I believe we

can eventually save the country. We could decide to fight on for the sake of the country, but then we might not have people to live in it.

At conference on an international peace plan,
Sarajevo, Bosnia, March 14/
The New York Times, 3-15:(A)3.

4

[Criticizing the international arms embargo against his country]: The arms embargo deprives Bosnia of the right to legitimate defense because, in practice, it affects only Bosnia. Those countries that want to maintain the embargo are seeking the capitulation of Bosnia and are accepting the primacy of force over law in international relations. The arms embargo cannot be defended from a moral, political or military point of view.

News conference,
Copenhagen, Denmark, June 21/
The New York Times, 6-22:(A)4.

5

[Rejecting a proposal to end the conflict in his country by dividing it into separate Muslim, Serb and Croat states]: You may take this statement of mine as an appeal to the American government and people, to help preserve the multi-ethnic and multi-religious state that Bosnia and Herzegovina has always been. Any support, particularly in military terms, would be welcome [whether it be from the U.S. or Europe, but] I think my message can be much better understood by the United States, because it represents a multicultural and multi-ethnic state.

News conference,
Sarajevo, Bosnia, July 9/
The New York Times, 7-10:3.

6

[Criticizing a proposal to partition his country into three ethnic republics, but saying it may be necessary as an interim step toward ending the conflict there]: It is our duty in these days to save what can be saved of Bosnia. This may give us the opportunity to save all of Bosnia in the future. We have to divide. We have to do it either at the

(ALIJA IZETBEGOVIC)

negotiating table or on the battlefield. I think it is better to do it at the negotiating table.

> *Before Bosnian Parliament,*
> *Sarajevo, Bosnia, Aug. 27/*
> *Los Angeles Times, 8-28:(A)1.*

1

[Saying the UN should either militarily defend Bosnia or lift the arms embargo against his country]: Defend us or let us defend ourselves. You have no right to deprive us of both.

> *At United Nations,*
> *New York, Sept. 7/*
> *The New York Times, 9-8:(A)3.*

2

[On suggestions of partitioning Bosnia's capital of Sarajevo as a means to end the conflict]: I'm here to tell you that we don't have any intention, nor shall we ever accept, dividing Sarajevo.

> *News conference,*
> *Sarajevo, Bosnia, Dec. 3/*
> *The New York Times, 12-4:5.*

John Paul II
Pope

3

How can we keep silent today—the day of peace—before the . . . atrocious drama being relentlessly played out in Bosnia-Herzegovina? Who will be able to say, "I did not know"? No one can consider that this tragic situation is not their affair, a situation which humiliates Europe and seriously compromises the future of peace. Leaders of nations, men and women of good will, with my heart overflowing with sorrow, I appeal once more to each one of you: Stop this war! Put an end, I beg you, to the unspeakable cruelties whereby human dignity is being violated and God, our just and merciful Father, is being offended.

> *Easter address,*
> *Vatican City, April 11/*
> *Los Angeles Times, 4-12:(A)4.*

David Kanin
Chief analyst for Yugoslavia,
Central Intelligence Agency
of the United States

4

I believe we are moving toward a greater Serbia, a greater Croatia and a greater Albania as a result of this war. The issue [for the U.S.] is whether to manage it or ignore it. We are not trying to manage it. We're just ignoring it.

> *Panel discussion at Woodrow Wilson Center,*
> *Washington, D.C./*
> *The New York Times, 12-22:(A)3.*

Radovan Karadzic
Leader, Bosnian Serbs

5

Right now, we [Serbs] have a state made by our own forces and our own enterprise [won by attacks on Bosnia's Muslims]. We have territory and authority. This was our objective, and we've got it.

> *Interview/*
> *U.S. News & World Report,*
> *2-1:60.*

6

[Saying the conflict in Bosnia will lead to a separate Serbian state on what is now Bosnian territory]: There will be a Serbian republic once and for good, and anybody who wants to deal with us has to take that into account. Serbs have decided to have their own province that will be independent.

> *May 18/*
> *The New York Times, 5-19:(A)6.*

7

[Saying the Muslim-led government of Bosnia should accept partition of the country into separate ethnic states in order to end the conflict there]: If the Muslims are for war, we [Serbs] have to totally defeat them. If they are for peace, we are ready to assure them safe territory in a confederal state.

> *July 7/*
> *The Washington Post, 7-8:(A)10.*

Muhammed Kresevljakovic
Mayor of Sarajevo,
Bosnia-Herzegovina

1

[On his country's decision to halt UN food shipments to Sarajevo even though attacking Serbs have cut off normal supplies]: Our primary intention is to show that at the end of the 20th century, in Europe, people are starving to death, in places where the media doesn't see them. This is a policy of extermination of [Bosnian] Muslims [by Serbs], and we think the world should do something about it.

Sarajevo, Bosnia, Feb. 12/
The New York Times, 2-13:5.

Zlatko Lagumdzija
Deputy Prime Minister
of Bosnia-Herzegovina

2

[The UN has said it would use all necessary means to get relief supplies to Muslims, but] "all necessary means" has been interpreted as meaning that the United Nations has to beg the Serbs to let the convoys pass. As far as the Bosnian government is concerned, "all necessary means" should mean that the United Nations places a convoy on the road, warns the Serbian forces that it is coming up the road, and tells them, "If you attempt to block the road, you will be removed, by force if necessary."

Interview, Feb. 15/
The New York Times, 2-16:(A)3.

Sergei Lavrov
Deputy Foreign Minister
of Russia

3

It is impossible in this conflict to determine who is right and who is wrong. An arithmetical approach to suffering is utterly irrelevant.

News conference, Moscow, Russia, Feb. 24/
The Washington Post, 2-25:(A)14.

Slaven Letica
Croatian author; Former aide
to the President of Croatia

4

There is the possibility that Croatia could reintegrate by economic means, could win by buying time and buying an opportunity for Western support . . . by changing the structure of government, opening the media and promoting human rights. But this is the optimistic scenario. We can also imagine a catastrophic one—war lasting forever, without end. The most awful flow of awful events one could imagine.

Los Angeles Times, 7-8:(A)10.

Edward Luck
President,
United Nations Association
of the U.S.A.

5

[Saying the West should be willing to use military force to try to end the conflict]: The willingness to use force . . . can be a persuasive argument in diplomacy. I think in Bosnia to a certain extent [force and diplomacy] have been decoupled . . . I'm not so confident that there's going to be a diplomatic solution that is just and viable and durable unless there is a real perception, a deep one, among the various groups in Yugoslavia that the alternative is some kind of international military intervention. It doesn't mean that one invades or that you get into a quagmire, but that there is a willingness, particularly among the Europeans, to raise the stakes if necessary . . . The big stick just hasn't been there.

The Christian Science Monitor,
1-15:4.

John Major
Prime Minister
of the United Kingdom

6

There is no easy option [for the West]. One might as well face the reality: You either put in several hundred thousand troops and hold the combatants apart, or you continue to try and find a diplomatic solution and ameliorate the humanitarian difficulties. There is no middle way.

Interview,
London, England/
Los Angeles Times, 6-20:(M)3.

321

Petar Mandic
Former professor of education,
Sarajevo University
(Bosnia-Herzegovina)

1

I blame politicians—[Muslim, Serbian] all of them. So long as nationalism was kept out of our politics, we were able to live together. As soon as the virus was introduced, it spread uncontrollably. Now all I hear are lies. I am a Serb, but no one is right. They are all wrong. Nationalism is a cheap "answer" which solves nothing.

Interview, Sarajevo, Bosnia/
U.S. News & World Report,
2-15:60.

John McCain
United States Senator,
R-Arizona

2

[Expressing reservations about sending U.S. forces to intervene in the conflict]: We need to be honest about one central fact: We have no way to predict the size, length and casualties of a peacemaking effort. If we find ourselves involved in a conflict in which American casualties mount, in which there is no end in sight, in which we take sides in a foreign civil war, in which American fighting men and women have great difficulty distinguishing between friend and foe, then I suggest that American support for military involvement would rapidly evaporate.

Before the Senate,
Washington, D.C., April 21/
The New York Times, 5-5:(A)8.

3

[On whether the U.S. should intervene militarily in the conflict]: [Americans] are gripped by two genuine but conflicting emotions—the horror of the Holocaust [in World War II] and the tragedy of [U.S. military intervention in] Vietnam. There is an understandable guilt we all feel about having done nothing to stop the Holocaust, but there is also the question of whether there is a viable U.S. involvement [in Bosnia] that will bring about what we want to achieve.

The Washington Post, 4-29:(A)35.

4

[Criticizing a reported plan by U.S. President Clinton to bomb Serbian artillery positions]: I believe it's a "feel-good" policy—you know, we'll just bomb, and if it doesn't work then we'll think of something else. That just smacks of sophistry. It smacks of total irresponsibility to say, "Just go ahead and bomb, and if that fails . . . we'll have to escalate," or, as the other argument goes, if it fails we're no worse off than we were before. But the U.S. cannot afford to fail. We're the world's superpower. The situation *would* be worse if we failed—in my view, considerably worse.

Interview,
Washington, D.C., May 4/
The Washington Post, 5-5:(B)4.

Mike McCurry
Spokesman for the
Department of State
of the United States

5

Is Bosnia horrifying, troubling? It is no more horrifying or troubling than the instances around this globe where populations, because of civil strife . . . face these kind of humanitarian disasters.

The Washington Post,
11-13:(A)6.

Donald McHenry
Former United States Ambassador/
Permanent Representative
to the United Nations

6

The problem is that at this stage people still believe that they can obtain their objectives by force. Until they reach the point where they conclude that they can't, they are not going to be inclined to negotiate. As harsh as it may seem, the situation may have to deteriorate further before the parties will see that their best interests are served by a settlement.

The Christian Science Monitor,
2-3:4.

Jose-Maria Mendiluce
Chief,
United Nations
refugee program
in the former Yugoslavia

1

[On the limited Western response to the conflict]: There is an attitude in the West that war is raging three hours from Venice [Italy] only because Balkan people are fundamentally different from other Europeans. That is a very dangerous mistake, because it is leading Europeans to become immobilized and to think only about their new cars and their beach holidays. When I look at far-right groups emerging in various European countries, including some that have enjoyed electoral successes, I realize that Yugoslavia-type conflicts could easily break out there. All it takes is an economic crisis and a few cynical politicians who blame it on immigrants or poor people or people who are somehow different. Here you see how easily it is for cynical leaders to stir up hatred by spreading lies in the media and fomenting provocations on the ground. The rest of Europe is not immune to this kind of manipulation. It could happen in Britain or France or Germany or Spain.

Interview,
Belgrade, Yugoslavia/
The New York Times, 5-18:(A)6.

Slobodan Milosevic
President of Serbia

2

[Saying the conflict is not the fault of the Serbs but of the Bosnians who, he says, want to set up an Islamic republic in cooperation with Turkey]: You know what Turkish authorities said? "A new Ottoman Empire again, from the Chinese Wall to the Adriatic coast" . . . I think [Turkish President Turgut] Ozal said that many times . . . There is a campaign in the whole media to define Serbs as terrorists, killers, murderers. It is a very distorted picture . . . We are doing our best to support peace.

Interview,
Belgrade, Yugoslavia, April 5/
The Washington Post, 4-6:(A)16.

Miodrag Mitic
Chief Legal Officer,
Foreign Ministry of Yugoslavia

3

Yugoslavia cannot be held responsible at all for the course events have taken on the territory of the former Yugoslav Republic of Bosnia-Herzegovina, nor for any crimes, including the crime of genocide [against Bosnian Muslims]. The Federal Republic of Yugoslavia has no paramilitary of any kind, either within or out of its territory.

At World Court,
the Hague, Netherlands, Aug. 26/
The New York Times, 8-27:(A)4.

Daniel Patrick Moynihan
United States Senator,
D-New York

4

[Criticizing U.S. agreement to a plan to provide "safe havens" for Bosnia Muslims]: We are legitimating genocide [by the attacking Serbs]. The moral basis of the world international order in the aftermath of Bosnia is weakened as it has not been since the 1930s.

May 23/
The Christian Science Monitor,
5-25:2.

Daniel Nelson
Director,
graduate programs
in international studies,
Old Dominion University
(United States)

5

There are only two ways this [conflict] is ultimately going to end, and negotiations isn't one of them. Either there's going to be a total military victory by the Serbs and the Croats [over the Bosnian Muslims], or the West . . . will have to intervene significantly to deny them that victory.

The Christian Science Monitor,
3-8:4.

323

Mario Noblio
Croatian Ambassador/
Permanent Representative
to the United Nations

1

[Arguing against lifting the UN-imposed arms embargo on Bosnia]: We don't believe that bringing more arms into the region would bring more peace. We need a pragmatic political solution which will stop the fighting. We need a Switzerland of the Balkans, not a new Lebanon in the area.

The Christian Science Monitor,
6-28:2.

David Owen
European Community mediator
in the Balkan conflict

2

[Criticizing the Bosnian Serbs' rejection of a peace plan to end the conflict]: I think that confrontation is now inevitable and will be faced up to by the world community. It will be faced up to economically, politically, and if [the Bosnian Serbs] continue [to fight], in my view, militarily. They collectively have decided to pursue the war, and they will be held accountable by the world for that decision.

Belgrade, Yugoslavia, April 26/
The Christian Science Monitor,
4-27:1,4.

3

Negotiators can do their utmost, but they do not have the power to deliver. That comes from the governments [of the Western countries]. There's no use passing resolutions of the [UN] Security Council if you don't have the means to back them up, and there's no use piling on rhetoric when you don't mean it in terms of action . . . There won't be any final victory for any of the warring parties. Sensible Serbs know that the Muslim population [of Bosnia], having been forced to take up arms and having been forced to choose an identity which in many ways they didn't in the past have and didn't seek, will not give up.

Sarajevo, Bosnia, June 4/
Los Angeles Times, 6-5:(A)21.

4

There is a sense in which I am outraged by the inability to weigh in the scales the pure horror [of this conflict], in terms of death, of mutilation. I am driven to try to get a peace. I believe peace is in the service of humanity. It may not be the peace I want, but it will be peace. I have said to myself, do not let yourself become so blunted that you no longer become indignant about this. In the privacy of your heart, you've got to still feel angry. Furious. Outraged. Even if you don't allow yourself to show it.

Interview, England/
The New York Times, 12-29:(A)3.

Milan Panic
Former Prime Minister
of Yugoslavia

5

No [U.S.] military intervention in Yugoslavia. We don't need another Vietnam. Their proposal of surgical bombing is absolutely the same as surgical bombing [during the war in] Vietnam, and we know what happened there. We need to embrace the Serbs for peace . . . We have to bring the peace at any price. Serbs are for peace. Croats are for peace, too. Muslims are for peace. Who is for this senseless killing, fighting, raping? It is bad leaders desperate to take power . . . You cannot stop killing with more killing.

Interview/
USA Today, 4-29:(A)13.

6

Yugoslavia is in our thoughts because of the civil war in one country [Bosnia], but the entire region must be considered as a whole if we wish to achieve peace, stability and prosperity. There are many good reasons for considering the south-eastern European region as a whole . . . Ethnic groups are spread through several countries. There is a problem when people identify more with their ethnic group than their country . . . It is terrible that there are leaders in power in 1993 who can put forth a concept such as "ethnic cleansing." Freedom must be won again and again. Not everyone supports the idea of democracy . . . The world has been understandably

(MILAN PANIC)

stunned and horrified by the cruel and heartless attack upon civilians. But moral outrage alone does not end wars. There must also be realistic policies that address the issues. That is why I say over and over again that only ann evenhanded, regional approach can bring an end to this conflict.

At speech sponsored by Los Angeles (Calif.)
World Affairs Council,
Beverly Hills, Calif., June 8/
Los Angeles Times, 6-11:(B)2.

Vesna Pesic
Director,
Center for Anti-War Action
(Yugoslavia);
Founder, Civic Alliance Party
of Yugoslavia

1

What distinguishes us from other opposition groups and parties [in Yugoslavia] is our double agenda—*for* democracy and *against* nationalism. Many people talk about democracy, but you cannot implement democratic values and institutions within the framework of aggressive nationalism and war [against Bosnia]. You cannot be silent about the horrors of bloodshed and ethnic cleansing and the destruction of cities and villages and places of worship and claim that you are a democrat. You cannot call yourself a democrat if you are only seeking democracy for your ethnic community. We raise our voices against such thinking and against those who inflame national feelings and fears in their own struggles for power.

Before National Endowment for
Democracy (United States), April 27/
The Christian Science Monitor,
5-14:18.

Zarko Puhovski
Professor of philosophy,
Zagreb University (Croatia)

2

[On the government of Croatian President Franjo Tudjman]: I don't think you can rightly

say there is a dictatorship here. The worst moves Tudjman could do would be supported by a majority of the population. The real problem we have here is absolutism. There is no real parliament and no real government.

The New York Times, 12-21:(A)6.

Poul N. Rasmussen
Prime Minister of Denmark

3

[On the difficulty in getting Europe to act on the Balkan conflict]: Without a common enemy in Moscow, it isn't so easy to coordinate our efforts. Can we get weapons through to the Muslims [in Bosnia]? If we do, will they be able to fight effectively? What about the peacekeeping troops already there? Will we bring the Croats back into full-scale conflict? Will the war spread to Kosovo and Macedonia? Will the Russians decide to help their Slavic cousins?

Washington, D.C./
The New York Times, 5-10:(A)6.

Malcolm Rifkind
Secretary of Defense
of the United Kingdom

4

[On the possibility of the West using air strikes against Serb forces]: There are 15,000 UN troops in Bosnia who have managed to save 400,000 civilians from starving to death. If the air strikes are launched, what will become of them? We must ensure that any new action does not jeopardize what we have done or make us lose more than we have gained.

To reporters/
The Washington Post, 5-18:(A)17.

Muhamed Sacirbey
Bosnian Chief Delegate
to the United Nations

5

[On the possibility of politically dividing Sarajevo as a way to end the conflict]: Frankly, I find any division of Sarajevo to be repugnant, the re-creation of Berlin. But, on the other hand, the people of Sarajevo have to survive the consequences of the world not coming to their aid to lift

(MUHAMED SACIRBEY)

the siege; and if division is what the world deems, somehow by default, to be necessary, then we're going to try to save lives.

Geneva, Switzerland, Dec. 2/
The New York Times, 12-3:(A)6.

Raymond Seitz
United States Ambassador
to the United Kingdom

1

The worst possible outcome from Bosnia would be to make an essentially Balkan problem into a transatlantic problem. We and our allies may not agree on all options. But we should not permit disagreement to erode or undermine the indivisibility of our joint security. In an unhappy, ironic way, Bosnia has demonstrated that there is no genuine European security without an American presence, and so long as the United States maintains its vigorous role in Europe, even at reduced levels, the dangers of widening instability are remote.

Los Angeles Times, 6-4:(A)5.

Vojislav Seselj
Leader,
Serbian Radical Party
(Yugoslavia)

2

[Warning the UN not to intervene in the conflict]: If they want to win this war, they better send 200,000 soldiers and bring many thousands of coffins with them. If planes come from Italian bases to bomb us, then Italy is going to be devastated by Serbian rockets. When the bombing of Bosnia begins [by UN forces], all United Nations soldiers will immediately be killed.

At Serbian rally,
Loznica, Yugoslavia, May 13/
The New York Times, 5-14:(A)4.

John M. Shalikashvili
General, United States Army;
Chairman,
Joint Chiefs of Staff

3

[On the possible use of U.S. troops in a peacekeeping role in the conflict]: The United

States has stated that if there is [a peace] agreement, and it is a just agreement, and all three parties [Serbs, Muslims and Croats] sign up to it, and not just the leadership but that there's indication . . . down to the warlords [that] there's the willingness to implement that agreement, and if it's implementable with military forces, [then] the United States would be willing to, in . . . consultation with [the U.S.] Congress, to participate in such an operation.

Press briefing, Washington, D.C., Dec. 14/
The Washington Post, 12-15:(A)14.

George P. Shultz
Former Secretary of State
of the United States

4

[Saying the U.S. should intervene with military force]: When you try to conduct diplomacy without power and the other side is using force, as in the Bosnia situation, you wind up making a fool of yourself . . . The [UN] Secretary General [Boutros Boutros-Ghali] has said, "Don't use force because the negotiations still might succeed." I say this man must be on some other planet. Force is already being used [by Serbs against Bosnian Muslims] 24 hours a day. It's counterforce that's missing.

Interview, April 26/
The New York Times, 4-27:(A)14.

Haris Silajdzic
Foreign Minister
of Bosnia-Herzegovina

5

[Asking for international help to end the conflict]: Bosnia-Herzegovina is everything that human rights are not. It is a bloodbath on the conscience of the international community. I demand on behalf of the participants [at this human-rights conference], on behalf of humanity—because this is a crime against humanity—to take all measures to stop the genocide [in Bosnia] in at least the one town of Gorazde. This is the test. If this is not done, I don't think there will be any credibility left for any one of us in the international community.

At United Nations World Conference
on Human Rights, Vienna, Austria, June 15/
Los Angeles Times, 6-16:(A)6.

(HARIS SILAJDZIC)

1

The problem of ex-Yugoslavia, I must admit, is a problem of deep primitivism. The vacuum left by the Communists was filled with ultra-nationalism, with masses of people disoriented, displaced, physically and mentally . . . They are disillusioned, they start looking for a familiar pattern or face, and they find a leader that speaks in very short sentences of the past as a future. The problem is that it's partly a clash between culture and non-culture. You can imagine what is in the hearts of people when they want to destroy Dubrovnik, Vukovar, Sarajevo, Mostar. That's emptiness. That's why they want to level everything down, whatever is culture, civilization. Level everything down . . . I think we are looking at very bad times in Europe to come. This is the beginning . . . When I said last year that we are stepping into a very dangerous period, everybody said, "That's too far-fetched; everything is okay." I don't think everything is okay. I think there is a big undercurrent of racism in Europe. I think we are repeating 1938.

Interview,
Zagreb, Croatia/
Los Angeles Times, 7-12:(A)10.

Immo Stabreit
German Ambassador
to the United States

2

[Saying the U.S., not Europe, should take the lead in dealing with the Balkan conflict]: I've been saying this again and again, and you will hear this from Europeans: The United States of America does have—whether you like it or you don't—a leadership position in this thing. What you have is the one remaining superpower, with a very large and also very mobile military instrument. I know the prevailing view here in the U.S. at the beginning was of the European steward. While Europe has been going as far as it can, for anything going beyond that they need your leadership.

Interview/
USA Today,
5-4:(A)13.

Margaret Thatcher
Former Prime Minister
of the United Kingdom

3

I suggest that we revive what was a previous policy, talked about but not implemented, of arming the Bosnian Muslims, who've been prevented from getting arms to defend themselves by a United Nations resolution. It is totally and utterly wrong to stop people from defending themselves against a highly armed aggressor, and we should reverse that . . . You cannot just let this go on. This is not right for the West . . . America was right in the first place to expect Europe to deal with this. It's within Europe's sphere of influence, and it should be within Europe's sphere of conscience . . . Either you allow the present slaughter, massacre, maiming, ethnic cleansing to go on, or you attempt not to appease the aggressor [Serbia] but to fight him. And you fight him not by us fighting but by the Bosnians being armed to fight, and also by using our air cover . . . The aggressor's taken the view that, yes, we [the West] have the weapons but we haven't the resolve to use them. Let that not be the message from the free world to any other evil dictator.

Broadcast interview/
"This Morning," CBS-TV, 4-14.

4

I was appalled at the lack of [Western] action [to stop the fighting in] Bosnia. I thought that [the former U.S. Bush Administration] was entitled to think that Europe would deal with it. [But] Europe goes to consensus, and consensus is the negation of leadership. They're now congratulating themselves that they haven't got involved, which, to me, is horrific . . . Has the West the weapons? Yes. All of them. The latest. Any surgical strike, anywhere in Yugoslavia, and in Serbia. Can you get them there? Yes. Good heavens! There were three aircraft carriers bouncing about in the Adriatic. So, yes, we had all the weapons. Yes, we have them there. [But] would we use them? No. For us to have failed on resolve, under those circumstances, is the disgrace of the latter half of the 20th century.

Interview, Los Angeles, Calif./
Los Angeles Times, 11-28:(M)3.

Franjo Tudjman
President of Croatia

1

How can the world continue to watch the barbaric developments that are taking place [in Bosnia], the destruction of villages and towns [by Serbs] and the suffering and the death of people, of women and children? We have reached a point where something must be done . . . The Serbs have sustained this aggression because, in my view, Western diplomats committed the error . . . of saying there would be no military intervention. However, if the sanctions [against Serbia] were made more severe and combined with air strikes, I believe such combined action would be successful . . . I believe air strikes . . . would be sufficient and that no ground forces would be required.

Interview/
U.S. News & World Report,
5-3:54.

Hans van den Broek
Commissioner for External Affairs
of the European Community

2

[On Europe's failure to act decisively in the conflict]: The image of the European Community has suffered grievously from our failure to resolve this ghastly conflict on our doorstep. The absence of a credible EC threat to use military force has resulted in European impotence and the need for ultimate U.S. involvement, a pattern too familiar in European history.

Los Angeles Times, 6-4:(A)5.

Guenter Verheugen
German Legislator

3

[Criticizing Germans who call for their country to be involved in NATO attacks on Serbia]: What's going on in the brains of [German] politicians who make such suggestions is incomprehensible to me. That is irresponsible adventurism. For months, in Germany now, there has been no discussion of foreign policy, but only of when, where and under what conditions the German military can be sent off, as if foreign policy consisted of military expansionism.

The Washington Post, 4-16:(A)21.

Karsten Voigt
Director of foreign policy,
Social Democratic Party
of Germany

4

[Expressing concern that non-intervention by the West in the conflict could result in a wider war]: We will watch the ethnic cleansing of Vojvodina, which is already under way; then we will watch the ethnic cleansing of Sandjzak; and then we will watch the ethnic cleansing of Kosovo. Conflict in Kosovo raises the likelihood of an international war, dragging in Albania, which has security arrangements with Turkey; while the destabilization of Macedonia could easily bring in Greece and Bulgaria.

Los Angeles Times, 5-17:(A)10.

Jon Western
Former Eastern Europe analyst,
Intelligence and Research Bureau,
Department of State
of the United States

5

[On reports he reviewed, when he worked at the U.S. State Department, about atrocities committed by Serbs against Muslims]: I spent the better part of a year reading daily accounts. When you sit down and plot these daily events over a map or over the course of time, what you come up with is a pattern of systematic slaughter of civilians. This isn't civilians caught in a crossfire. This isn't the euphemistic collateral damage. This is a systematic effort on the behalf of Serbs to kill, to move populations out of territory they want.

Interview,
Washington, D.C., Aug. 25/
The New York Times, 8-26:(A)5.

The Middle East

Haidar Abdel-Shafi
Chief Palestinian delegate
at Arab-Israeli peace negotiations

1

[On Israeli-Palestinian violence in Israel and the occupied territories]: We are all mindful, painfully so, that violence begets violence. We feel ourselves being pulled deeper and deeper into that cycle. That Israel responds with disproportionate force, excessive force, leads Palestinians to resort to more force . . . Our people's confidence in the peace process diminishes as they see the violence around them increase. It gets harder and harder to continue that process. And this, too, unfortunately, leads to greater violence.

Los Angeles Times, 3-27:(A)15.

2

[Saying Jerusalem should not be under Israeli sovereignty]: What would we [Palestinians] have without Jerusalem? The Palestinian problem is the heart of the Middle East conflict, and Jerusalem is the heart of the Palestinian problem.

Los Angeles Times, 7-10:(A)3.

Abu Ali Mustafa
Deputy general secretary,
Popular Front for the
Liberation of Palestine

3

[Criticizing PLO chairman Yasir Arafat's signing of a mutual-recognition agreement with Israel]: There are, of course, certain difficulties we will face in opposition to Arafat's policy. Arafat will be supported politically and economically by many powerful groups and countries. And that will give him a power base beyond his Fatah faction. But this, in turn, will give our ongoing operation its own mechanism. In time, it will give birth to new forces, even within his own faction, that will see Arafat more and more as a traitor. And these new forces will combine into a single new force—a reborn PLO.

Interview, Damascus, Syria, Sept. 12/
Los Angeles Times, 9-14:(H)5.

Bassam Abu Sharif
Senior adviser to
Palestine Liberation Organization
chairman Yasir Arafat

4

I want to tell all the Israeli public, I assure them that we want to establish peace with Israel, that we want to establish our state in the West Bank and Gaza, and that we recognize Israel and its right to live in peace and cooperation with its Arab neighbors. Let me take this opportunity to tell the Israeli government and the Israeli people, we [have] renounced terrorism, we will be against terrorism, and we will cooperate to fight terrorism.

Israeli Television interview,
Tunis, Tunisia, Sept. 3/
The New York Times, 9-13:(A)5.

5

[On the pending Israel-PLO mutual-recognition agreement allowing Palestinian self-rule in the West Bank and Gaza]: This is not a peace agreement with Israel. This is a first step in the transfer of authority to a Palestinian self-government, and it is linked in stages whereby the Israelis should complete their withdrawal from the occupied territories and the Palestinians will have their national independence. To certain people, this is not acceptable. Those who are for the peace process and criticize this agreement have a point of view that the step-by-step approach is not the right way. But the overwhelming majority [of Palestinians] support president Arafat and realize the step-by-step plan is the best way to reach a peace agreement with Israel, based on a two-state solution.

Interview/Los Angeles Times, 9-4:(A)11.

Madeleine K. Albright
United States Ambassador/
Permanent Representative
to the United Nations

6

[On the recent U.S. missile attack on Iraqi intelligence headquarters in Baghdad in response

(MADELEINE K. ALBRIGHT)

to an alleged Iraqi government-sponsored plot to kill former U.S. President George Bush]: I come to the [UN Security] Council today to brief you on a grave and urgent matter, an attempt to murder a President of the United States by the intelligence service of the government of Iraq, a member of the United Nations. Even by the standards of an Iraqi regime known for its brutality against its neighbors and its own people, this is an outrage . . . As [U.S.] President Clinton indicated last night, this was a direct attack on the United States, an attack that required a direct United States response. Consequently, President Clinton yesterday instructed the United States armed forces to carry out a military operation against the headquarters of the Iraqi Intelligence Service in Baghdad. We responded directly, as we are entitled to do, under Article 51 of the United Nations Charter, which provides for the exercise of self-defense in such cases. Our response has been proportional and aimed at a target directly linked to the operation against President Bush. It was designed to damage the terrorist infrastructure of the Iraqi regime, reduce its ability to promote terrorism, and deter further acts of aggression against the United States.

At United Nations,
New York, June 27/
The New York Times,
6-28:(A)5.

Mahmoud Aloul
Member,
Fatah Revolutionary Council

1

[Saying even those in the Arab world who disagree with the recent Israel-PLO mutual-recognition agreement allowing Palestinian self-rule in the West Bank and Gaza need to go along with the pact]: The accord is like a one-way train going to Gaza and Jericho. There are no stations on the way, and no other train may pass for a very long time. You are either on the train or you are left behind in the wilderness.

U.S. News & World Report,
12-27:37.

Joseph Alpher
Director,
Jaffee Center for Strategic Studies,
Tel Aviv University (Israel)

2

[On the current difficulty in implementing the recent Israel-PLO mutual-recognition agreement allowing Palestinian self-rule in the West Bank and Gaza]: The Israeli emphasis is on security, while the Palestinian emphasis is on political state-building. You can really see all the issues of controversy through that prism. When you look at the borders and border crossings, it is strikingly clear. Here [PLO leader Yasir] Arafat needs to make a point about state-building; here Israel cannot concede security—which is why it has become such a difficult problem.

The Washington Post,
12-24:(A)11.

Abdullah Alshayeji
Chairman,
department of political science,
Kuwait University

3

[On Kuwait's new democratically elected National Assembly]: I'm afraid that this Assembly, in its very energetic crusade to uncover, to unmask and to reform, is going faster than the government would like. The government is really being lynched by the Assembly, and when you're being lynched you're not going to enjoy it. The government can put up with this cold war for a while, but, for the first time, there's talk around the country that this Assembly could be suspended . . . We have to be very careful. We are not politically and democratically entrenched here. There's a lack of political consciousness. And the intelligentsia in Kuwait is very concerned now. The people are saying, "What has the Assembly done for me as a Kuwaiti? They haven't gotten me a higher salary. They haven't helped me get my house in seven years instead of 12." I'm really concerned now. Some people are starting to say this summer may be the turning point.

Los Angeles Times,
4-10:(A)5.

Hussein Amin
Former Egyptian Ambassador
to Algeria

1

[Saying the growth of Islam may present a threat to Arab governments]: Encouraging [even] moderate Islam is not wise. It creates a broad base of religiosity from which the young easily jump to extremism whenever they feel economic or social grievances. I believe freedom should not be given to the enemies of freedom.

The Christian Science Monitor,
4-27:6.

Yasir Arafat
Chairman, Palestine
Liberation Organization

2

[On the current violence between Palestinians and Israelis in Israel]: To stop all this, risks must be taken by both sides. We all must understand that the greatest risk for our respective peoples is if the peace process grinds to a halt. Then the cycle of violence would be unstoppable, risking chaos and Balkanization of our whole region. Free elections for a representative [Palestinian] assembly are essential to providing a way out . . . We sincerely hope that the Israelis will move confidently toward the coming negotiations with the idea of elections in mind. We ache for the day of self-governance legitimated by elections, when we will have a system of laws and even a structure of discipline and law enforcement. Anyone who then acts in the name of the Palestinians will do so with responsibility or will be held accountable . . . Palestinian rejectionists in their frustration continue to engage in acts that violate what we [the PLO] have been trying to accomplish . . . I am sure they will fail, however, since most Palestinians today believe that the achievement of comprehensive peace and success in attaining interim self-government and ultimately statehood leading to confederation cannot be achieved without a peaceful, negotiated resolution with the Israelis.

Interview,
Tunis, Tunisia/
Los Angeles Times, 4-15:(B)7.

3

The denial of the Palestinian people's right to self-determination and grave violations of Palestinian human rights over decades provides us with the most striking example of double standards in the implementation of human rights. The very clear support accorded to Israel by the U.S.A. and other states can only but encourage Israel to persist in its policies of aggression, occupation . . . and violation of human rights.

At United Nations World Conference
on Human Rights, Vienna, Austria, June 15/
Los Angeles Times, 6-17:(A)6.

4

[On the pending Israel-PLO mutual-recognition agreement allowing Palestinian self-rule in the West Bank and Gaza]: In light of the new era marked by the signing of the Declaration of Principles, the PLO encourages and calls upon the Palestinian people in the West Bank and Gaza Strip to take part in the steps leading to the normalization of life, rejecting violence and terrorism, contributing to peace and stability and participating actively in shaping reconstruction, economic development and cooperation.

Letter issued Sept. 9*/
Los Angeles Times, 9-10:(A)12.

5

[On the pending Israel-PLO mutual-recognition agreement allowing Palestinian self-rule in the West Bank and Gaza]: There has been a change [in the Middle East]. The same change which happened in Eastern Europe and the fall of the Berlin Wall. Nobody expected it, but it happened. We are now after the Cold War and we need new calculations and new vision. By this which we are about to do tomorrow [signing the agreement], our people are taking their place on the political map, and also on the geographical map, in this new world order . . . The final status [of the Palestinian-Israeli relationship] will lead to a complete, independent Palestinian state which will confederate with Jordan according to the free choice of the two peoples. It is coming.

Interview en route to Washington, D.C.,
Sept. 12/
Los Angeles Times, 9-13:(A)8.

(YASIR ARAFAT)

1

[On the pending Israel-PLO mutual-recognition agreement allowing Palestinian self-rule in the West Bank and Gaza]: The Palestinian state is within our grasp. Soon the Palestinian flag will fly on the walls, the minarets and the cathedrals of Jerusalem.

Time, 9-13:39.

2

[On the signing of an Israel-PLO mutual-recognition agreement allowing Palestinian self-rule in the West Bank and Gaza]: Now as we stand on the threshold of this new historic era, let me address the people of Israel and their leaders, with whom we are meeting today for the first time, and let me assure them that the difficult decision we reached together was one that required great and exceptional courage. We will need more courage and determination to continue the course of building coexistence and peace between us. This is possible and it will happen with mutual determination and with the effort that will be made with all parties on all the tracks to establish the foundations of a just and comprehensive peace. Our people do not consider that exercising the right to self-determination could violate the rights of their neighbors or infringe on their security. Rather, putting an end to their feelings of being wronged and of having suffered an historic injustice is the strongest guarantee to achieve coexistence and openness between our two peoples and future generations.

At signing ceremony for the agreement,
Washington, D.C., Sept. 13/
Los Angeles Times, 9-14:(A)8.

3

[On being a Palestinian]: Maybe a lot of you do not know what it is to be a refugee, to be a refugee as myself. Homeless, stateless, even without identity cards. This is the Palestinian tragedy from the day of birth to the grave.

At National Press Club,
Washington, D.C., Sept. 14/
The Washington Post, 9-15:(A)24.

4

[On his recent signing of an Israel-PLO mutual-recognition agreement allowing Palestinian self-rule in the West Bank and Gaza]: Our Arab nation at this historic point needs to transcend the past, with all its pains and hardships, and face the future more strong and united, so our nation can deal strongly with the new world order as it is being crystallized, and so that it will not be at the expense of our people . . . The agreement which we have reached, dear brothers, is only a starting step to laying down a transitional solution, which must be based on the withdrawal of [Israeli] occupation . . . from our territories and holy Jerusalem . . . Comprehensive peace can only be realized through a final solution and the establishment of similar solutions for all Arab areas.

To Arab League foreign ministers,
Cairo, Egypt, Sept. 19/
Los Angeles Times, 9-20:(A)6.

5

[On his recent signing of an Israel-PLO mutual-recognition agreement allowing Palestinian self-rule in the West Bank and Gaza]: We face very difficult problems. We start from zero. The infrastructure of Gaza has been destroyed. We need help, not only from our brothers and friends but also from those who want real peace in this area. Peace is a Palestinian need, but it is also an Israeli, an American, a Russian and an Arab need. Every power in the world has a strategic interest in this area because it has so much oil.

Interview, Washington, D.C./
Time, 9-27:32.

6

[Now that Israel and the PLO have signed a mutual-recognition agreement allowing Palestinian self-rule in the West Bank and Gaza,] Israel and all the Arabs are in need of a Marshall Plan for the whole area. Right now, we [Palestinians] have to start from zero. For our first year [of self-rule], we need $1.7-billion at least. We have [commitments for only] $500-million. I also hope we will see more money from the

(YASIR ARAFAT)

[Persian] Gulf [states]. I just met with a very important delegation from the American Jewish Congress. I even have a delegation of 10 [Israeli] Likud [Party] members coming to see me . . . There is no turning back.

Interview, Tunis, Tunisia/
U.S. News & World Report,
11-8:58.

1

[Jerusalem] should be the capital for two states, with the Christian and Muslim [holy places] under our supervision, under [religious] institutions like the Islamic Waqf. The Wailing Wall can be under the Jewish rabbis. We are not looking for a Berlin Wall in Jerusalem.

Interview, Tunis, Tunisia/
U.S. News & World Report,
11-8:58.

Hanan Ashrawi
Palestinian representative
at Arab-Israeli peace negotiations

2

[On the Israeli Parliament's decision to lift its ban on Israeli contacts with the PLO]: This is a positive and important first step. We hope it will lead quickly to the dialogue that must take place between Israel and the PLO. It is always our position that nothing is to be gained by non-communication or boycotts. Peace is made between enemies and between parties who can deliver.

Jan. 19/
Los Angeles Times, 1-20:(A)16.

3

The heart of the Palestinian people is in Jerusalem—and nowhere else. Without it as our capital, there will be no settlement. But our claim is not to Jewish neighborhoods, but those that are and were Arab. Jerusalem we can share [with the Israelis]. So far, however, Israel does not even agree to discuss it.

Los Angeles Times, 7-10:(A)3.

4

[On the recent Israel-PLO mutual-recognition agreement allowing Palestinian self-rule in the West Bank and Gaza]: We have finished the easy part. Now we have the task of giving reality to the basic agreement we reached. We have become partners in peace and no longer adversaries in conflict. So we congratulate [Israeli] Prime Minister [Yitzhak] Rabin and his government on this victory.

East Jerusalem, Israel, Sept. 23/
Los Angeles Times, 9-24:(A)12.

Hafez al-Assad
President of Syria

5

[Criticizing the PLO for signing a mutual-recognition agreement with Israel allowing Palestinian self-rule in the West Bank and Gaza]: As for why Israel was successful [in this matter], it is because we lost. And we lost because the wall of Arab coordination was affected by what happened. We have been hurt because the Arab parties had been acting in coordination, and [the PLO's] causing a gap in the Arab wall is not in the Arabs' interest or in the interest of the Palestinians. Any of these parties acting alone will be weaker than if all the Arab parties were moving together . . . I would hope that this agreement could give the Palestinian brothers what they deserve. But if you want me to count for you the holes in this agreement, I will give you the agreement itself, and if you read it with concentration and precision, you will not need to ask me . . . Every point in this deal needs another deal of its own, and that deal in turn needs even more discussions and negotiations . . . The Palestinian-Israeli agreement will not affect Syria's position on peace. We want to realize a just and comprehensive peace for the area . . . and we know that the peace process must be pursued in two directions, not just one.

News conference, Cairo, Egypt,
Sept. 22/Los Angeles Times, 9-23:(A)4.

Ahmed Baqer
Member of Kuwaiti Parliament

6

Since Kuwait was liberated with the help of the superpowers [in 1991's Persian Gulf war which

(AHMED BAQER)

ousted Iraq from Kuwait], it's ridiculous to say now we can depend on ourselves. The superpowers must work to see Kuwait independent until it can defend itself. This, of course, could be a matter of some years. And, until that time, Kuwaitis fear only one thing: that the superpowers may change their minds.

Los Angeles Times, 1-28:(A)4.

Amatzia Baram
Senior lecturer,
Haifa University (Israel);
Specialist on Iraq and Syria

1

[On Iraqi President Saddam Hussein's defying Western orders to keep out of the no-fly zone in southern Iraq]: Saddam is trying to show that he has not weakened and that he is not giving up the south, which is the source of two-thirds of Iraq's oil and its outlet to the [Persian] Gulf. He thinks the time is ripe with the changing of the guard at the White House, given [U.S.] President-elect Clinton's commitment to [American] domestic affairs and because of America's involvement in Somalia and possibly Bosnia. Saddam is anxious to avoid a military confrontation. The question is how far Saddam is prepared to go and whether he will know when and where to stop.

Los Angeles Times, 1-12:(H)1.

Yossi Beilin
Deputy Foreign Minister
of Israel

2

Israel's expectations are that the Middle East conflict will be very high on the American agenda . . . and we believe that American involvement is vital to the [Arab-Israeli] negotiations. [U.S. President] Clinton's actions so far do demonstrate a readiness to be involved and an understanding that it is needed . . . Whether we like it or not, without American help there will be no peace in the Middle East. Just formal direct negotiations [between Israel and the Arabs] are not enough to conclude an agreement.

The Christian Science Monitor,
1-27:7.

Meron Benvenisti
Israeli historian

3

[On the recent Israel-PLO mutual-recognition agreement allowing Palestinian self-rule in the West Bank and Gaza]: For us to finally recognize [PLO chairman Yasir] Arafat from the outside is one thing. I can say hello to him on the street. But that is not all. Now he is coming into my house. We are going to share some of the rooms. And he needs space, and that is going to be the difficulty at all levels. Because we are not just talking about physical space. We are talking about everything. It is much more complicated than [Israel's] peace treaty with Egypt. There, space was being divided. Here it is being shared.

The New York Times, 9-15:(A)1.

Abdullah Bishara
Secretary General,
(Persian) Gulf Cooperation Council

4

[Saying Kuwait no longer has a reason to be scared of Iraq, which was forced out of Kuwait in 1991's Persian Gulf war]: [Kuwaitis are] scared for no reason. Kuwait today is more solid and its independence and legitimacy are more certain than before August of 1990 [when Iraq invaded and took over Kuwait]. Before August, Kuwait lived off good will, and now there's a realization that good will is no good in international politics, especially when you have a monster as a neighbor.

Los Angeles Times, 1-28:(A)4.

John R. Bolton
Senior fellow,
Manhattan Institute;
Former Assistant Secretary
for International Organization Affairs,
Department of State
of the United States

5

Even at the height of [1991's Persian Gulf war], when we had Iraqis running in every direction and . . . nothing but sand between us and

(JOHN R. BOLTON)

downtown Baghdad, we never had any thought in our mind of militarily going in and taking [Iraqi President] Saddam [Hussein] out . . . [Even Kuwait, which Iraq had invaded,] asked us not to do anything that would jeopardize the territorial integrity of Iraq. Certainly our allies in the region feared the consequences of Iraq breaking up, because nobody could predict what that could be.

USA Today, 7-2:(A)7.

George Bush
Former President
of the United States

1

[On his being honored by Kuwait for the U.S.-led Operation Desert Storm which forced Iraq out of Kuwait in 1991]: Mere words cannot express how proud I am to be here with you on the hallowed ground of Kuwait. It gives me tremendous personal satisfaction to know that, together, we really made history. Together, we stood up to naked aggression [by Iraq] and proved once again that the thirst for freedom will always overwhelm those who seek to quench it with the bitter brine of tyranny.

At dinner in his honor,
Kuwait, April 14/
The Washington Post, 4-15:(C)9.

Warren Christopher
Secretary of State-designate
of the United States

2

[On Iraqi President Saddam Hussein]: I think you look back at the past history of the man, what he's done to his people in the past, what he's doing now. I don't expect any great change in his behavior, and I think we'll have a problem with him starting next Thursday [when the Democratic Clinton Administration takes power in the U.S.], just as the Republicans have.

Broadcast interview/
"This Week With David Brinkley,"
ABC-TV, 1-17.

Warren Christopher
Secretary of State
of the United States

3

No one should doubt the resolve of the United States [in the Persian Gulf area]. As long as the people of this region are subject to the threat of aggression, our friends can rely on the steadfast vigilance of the United States.

Kuwait, Feb. 22/
USA Today, 2-23:(A)10.

4

Iran is one of the principal sources of support for terrorist groups around the world. [That and] their determination to acquire weapons of mass destruction, I think, leaves Iran as an international outlaw . . . When I was in the Middle East, I found that to be a common judgment among many of the leaders that I met with, that Iran was greatly feared at the present time because of their support for terrorist groups, which they have not in any way disavowed.

Before Senate International Operations
Subcommittee, Washington, D.C., March 30/
The New York Times, 3-31:(A)3.

5

Iran must understand that it cannot have normal commercial relations [with the rest of the world] . . . on the one hand, while trying to develop weapons of mass destruction on the other . . . Iran's economy is in trouble. Iran will be vulnerable to concerted pressure from the West if it is clear that we seek strictly defined changes in its behavior.

News conference,
Luxembourg, June 9/
Los Angeles Times, 6-10:(A)8.

6

[Saying the world's nations should provide funds to the West Bank and Gaza areas in which Palestinians will soon have self-rule according to

WHAT THEY SAID IN 1993

(WARREN CHRISTOPHER)

the recent Israel-PLO agreement]: The international community must move immediately to see that the agreement produces tangible improvements in the security and daily lives of Palestinians and Israelis . . . All agree that we must take immediate steps to address the high rate of unemployment that robs families of hope and fuels extremism. All roads and other permanent improvements must be developed quickly. We must also act now to provide assistance in public administration, tax collection and social services.

At Columbia University,
New York, N.Y., Sept. 20/
Los Angeles Times, 9-21:(A)4.

Bill Clinton
President-elect
of the United States

1

[On recent provocations by Iraqi President Saddam Hussein against U.S.-led forces and UN resolutions in place since 1991's Persian Gulf war]: Certainly based on the evidence we have, the people of Iraq would be better off if they had a different ruler. But my job is not to pick their rulers for them. I always tell everybody I am a Baptist. I believe in death-bed conversions. If he wants a different relationship with the United States and the United Nations, all he has to do is change his behavior . . . The main thing is that we cannot do anything to give him or anyone else the slightest indication that we are wavering. If I knew what was motivating him . . . Is he sticking it to [out-going U.S. President] Bush [who led the Persian Gulf war against Iraq] at the end? Is he trying to test me? Does he just not understand the American people? I just don't know. Since I don't know that, all I can do is deal with what I can see, and that is his conduct. I would not rule out anything, except to say that I have no intention of seeing our nation back away from the adherence to the [UN] guidelines.

Interview,
Little Rock, Ark., Jan. 13/
The New York Times, 1-14:(A)9.

Bill Clinton
President of the United States

2

[On the pending Israel-PLO mutual-recognition agreement allowing Palestinian self-rule in the West Bank and Gaza]: We've been up the hill and down the hill before with the Middle East, but these people are really working at it, and I think their hearts as well as their minds are in it. I think we should keep our fingers crossed. We're just a sponsor of this process. They will have to make the agreement. And I think that there's reason for hope.

At White House Rose Garden photo session,
Washington, D.C., Sept. 2/
The New York Times, 9-3:(A)6.

3

[On the signing of an Israel-PLO mutual-recognition agreement allowing Palestinian self-rule in the West Bank and Gaza]: Throughout this century, bitterness between the Palestinian and Jewish people has robbed the entire region of its resources, its potential and too many of its sons and daughters. The land has been so drenched in warfare and hatred that conflicting claims of history etched so deeply in the souls of the combatants there, that many believe the past would always have the upper hand . . . Now the efforts of all who have labored before us bring us to this moment, a moment when we dare to pledge what for so long seemed difficult to even imagine: that the security of the Israeli people will be reconciled with the hopes of the Palestinian people, and there will be more security and more hope for all . . . Together, let us imagine what can be accomplished if all the energy and ability the Israelis and the Palestinians have invested into your struggle can now be channeled into cultivating the land and freshening the waters, into ending the boycotts and creating new industry, into building a land as bountiful and peaceful as it is holy.

At signing ceremony for the agreement,
Washington, D.C., Sept. 13/
Los Angeles Times, 9-14:(A)8.

4

[Saying the U.S. is not weakening its support for Israel following the recent signing of an

(BILL CLINTON)

Israel-PLO mutual-recognition agreement]: All the progress yet to be made depends upon the conviction of the people of Israel that they are secure and that making peace [with the Arabs] makes them more secure. So I don't think anyone in the Arab world should want me to do anything that makes the Israelis feel less secure.

Arabic Television interview,
Washington, D.C./
Los Angeles Times, 9-15:(A)14.

1

The position of the United States has been, number one, that I believe [Israeli] Prime Minister [Yitzhak] Rabin wants a comprehensive peace in the Middle East; number two, that in order to do it, he has to have the support of the people of Israel, which means we have to implement the present [mutual-recognition] agreement between Israel and the PLO, we have to continue to make progress in opening up other Arab nations' attitudes toward Israel, we have to continue to make progress on the other tracks, and I think there has to be some time in which [Rabin] can work out whatever his situation is with his parliamentary body [the Israeli Knesset, where there is some opposition to his agreement with the PLO].

News conference,
Washington, D.C., Oct. 25/
The New York Times, 10-26:(A)3.

2

[On the slowness so far of the PLO in setting up economic and security operations in the West Bank and Gaza areas it will now govern as a result of the recent Israeli-PLO agreement]: I wish that the pace had been more rapid, but I think it is important to recognize that the PLO itself, by its very nature, by the nature of its organization and its activities over the last many, many years, has never had the responsibility of going through the mechanics that have to be discussed in this agreement. You know—how do the lights get turned on in the morning, how is the food distributed, how are the houses built, how

are these things done. So I think, in fairness, I would be quite concerned if I thought that the fact that we're a little bit slow in the pace here was the result of some sort of deliberate desire to undermine an accord they had just signed off on. At the present moment, I really believe it is more a function of the whole organization not being organized for or experienced in the work in which they must now engage.

News conference,
Washington, D.C., Nov. 12/
The New York Times, 11-13:4.

Irwin Cotler
Authority on human rights,
McGill University (Canada)

3

Israel is expected to live up to standards no other nation is asked to observe . . . [Then it is] portrayed as an anti-human-rights metaphor. Israel emerges as the new Antichrist.

U.S. News & World Report,
4-26:64.

Yael Dayan
Member of Israeli Knesset
(Parliament)

4

[On the recent Israel-PLO mutual-recognition agreement allowing Palestinian self-rule in the West Bank and Gaza]: The end of the conflict will mean we [Israelis] can be comfortable in our own skin. We can stop being worriers, missionaries, occupiers. We can be Middle Eastern, Mediterranean; we can eat watermelon and sit under our fig trees, while also producing the best computers and medical equipment in the world.

Time, 9-20:38.

Ronald V. Dellums
United States Representative,
D-California

5

[Criticizing the recent U.S. missile attack on an intelligence center in Baghdad in retaliation for Iraq's alleged plot to kill former U.S. President George Bush]: No nation, especially an

(RONALD V. DELLUMS)

unrivalled superpower [the U.S.], should presume to use unilateral force to seek to vindicate the rule of international law. Had [U.S. President Clinton] sought my counsel, I would have urged him to take further diplomatic action . . . We must move past the time in human affairs when violence is the first recourse of statecraft.

The Washington Post, 6-28:(A)13.

Edward P. Djerejian
Assistant Secretary
for Near Eastern and
South Asian Affairs,
Department of State
of the United States

1

Both [U.S.] President Clinton and Secretary of State [Warren] Christopher have gone on record regarding the importance of continuing [U.S.] aid to Israel and Egypt at the current levels. We remain steadfast in our commitment to direct substantial foreign-aid resources to the security of Israel, to support for Egypt's vital role in the stability and security of the region, and to promotion of comprehensive and lasting peace in the Middle East.

Before House Foreign Operations Subcommittee,
Washington, D.C., March 8/
The New York Times, 3-9:(A)6.

Rolf Ekeus
Chief, United Nations
Special Commission on Iraq

2

[Saying that, despite an international effort to destroy Iraq's weapons of mass destruction, the country could revive its nuclear and chemical-weapons programs in the future]: The capabilities are there; the supply system, including banks and payments, is there. The day the oil embargo is lifted, Iraq will get all the cash. With the cash, the suppliers and the skills, they will be able to re-establish all the weapons programs. It may grow up like mushrooms after the rain.

At meeting sponsored by Washington
Institute for Near East Policy,
Washington, D.C., March 24/
Los Angeles Times, 3-25:(A)12.

Saeb Erekat
Deputy head of Palestinian
delegation to Arab-Israeli
peace negotiations

3

The first thing that comes to mind if we want to move to final status [of the Israeli-occupied West Bank and Gaza] is Jordanian-Palestinian relations; and here confederation is not only the most promising but something that appeals deeply to many of our people.

July 16/
Los Angeles Times, 7-17:(A)4.

Abraham Foxman
Executive director,
Anti-Defamation League
of B'nai B'rith

4

[Saying the U.S. Jewish community is concerned about U.S. President-elect Bill Clinton's appointing a number of former Jimmy Carter Administration officials to his foreign-policy team]: When you look at the people appointed to the top foreign-policy jobs, there is a lingering concern about Carterism. The Jewish community was disturbed and distressed about the Carter Middle East policy, because it was simplistic, preachy and involved holding Israel to standards that were unreasonable, given the neighborhood it lives in . . . All of those [Clinton appointees] who will be dealing with Israel come from that background. In fairness, though, they are all distinguished public servants, and they will be working with [Vice President] Al Gore and Defense Secretary Les Aspin [in the new Clinton Administration], who have been known for their open and strong support of Israel.

The New York Times, 1-5:(A)8.

5

[Calling for continuing strong U.S. support for Israel following the recent signing of an Israel-PLO mutual-recognition agreement allowing Palestinian self-rule in the West Bank and Gaza]: The greater the risk Israel takes, the greater the reassurance it needs from its friend and ally that it will be supportive. It's a need Israel has domes-

(ABRAHAM FOXMAN)

tically, and in its bilateral relations with the Arab world, so they don't think Israel is dealing out of weakness or being forced or pressured by the United States.

Los Angeles Times, 9-15:(A)14.

Jacob Frenkel
Governor, Bank of Israel

1

In Israel's economic history, the real jumps in GNP have come with the big flows of immigrants. This [current flow] is a huge increase—a 12 percent increase in the labor force—and what fantastic quality! It is a historic opportunity for us, a quantum leap.

Los Angeles Times, 3-7:(D)3.

Robert M. Gates
*Former Director of the
Central Intelligence Agency
of the United States*

2

[On criticism that U.S.-led forces in 1991's Persian Gulf war did not go into Baghdad and capture Iraqi President Saddam Hussein, instead of stopping after Iraq had been pushed out of Kuwait]: People say, "Well, the 24th mechanized division was right there and just could have shot to Baghdad," and so forth. Well, that assumes that Saddam Hussein would have gone out and waited on his veranda for them to arrive. And our experience in trying to find [Panamanian leader Manuel] Noriega in Panama—a country that was a lot smaller and where we knew a lot more—made us skeptical that it would be so easy just to get Saddam. We also realized that if our forces went on to Baghdad and brought about a change of regime, then we would have created the circumstances for the kind of Vietnam-like morass that everyone was so concerned about . . . My hope is that at some point, as Iraqis continue to pay the price for Saddam's refusal to change behavior in a way that would allow the UN to lift sanctions and make these [U.S.] raids stop, the Iraqi people will decide that this guy is too high an overhead

for them to bear. He has brought enormous destruction down on Iraq in the past dozen years. The pain he has inflicted on his own people is awesome, far more than anything the [Persian Gulf war] coalition or the West ever did.

*Interview/
USA Today, 7-7:(A)11.*

Shlomo Gazit
*Researcher,
Jaffee Center for Strategic Studies,
Tel Aviv University (Israel)*

3

[On Israel's current attacks on Lebanon in response to attacks on Israel by Lebanon-based Hezbollah guerrillas]: This is still small potatoes, but in the Middle East small potatoes can grow into something enormous. The situation is dangerous. It could explode into a larger conflict; it might quickly destroy the whole [Arab-Israeli] peace process . . . Nothing in the Middle East finishes the way you expect.

Los Angeles Times, 7-27:(A)8.

4

[Saying PLO leader Yasir Arafat wants to move too fast following the recent signing of an Israel-PLO mutual-recognition agreement allowing Palestinian self-rule in the West Bank and Gaza]: Arafat wants already to see symbolic elements of a Palestinian state, and this is totally unacceptable. Not that there won't be a Palestinian state at the end. But this is an open-ended issue under the agreement, not one to be taken up now.

The New York Times, 12-16:(A)3.

Dan Gillerman
*Chairman,
Federation of Israeli
Chambers of Commerce*

5

[Criticizing Israel's plans to close off the occupied territories and prevent Palestinians from entering Israel to work, because of recent Palestinian violence against Israelis]: Talk of reducing the number of Arab laborers is un-

(DAN GILLERMAN)

realistic because market forces are stronger and people will go to where labor is cheaper. It is in the interests of Israel to see the quality of life and standard of living in the territories rise as quickly as possible, so instead of having a powder keg next to us, we have an economic partner next to us. People who are well-fed and employed don't throw stones and go into the streets, and don't wage war.

The Washington Post, 4-1:(A)39.

1

[Saying Israel's closing off the occupied territories has shown the country's dependence on the labor of Palestinians, who can no longer cross into Israel to work]: We have become very dependent and very complacent, and in doing so we have put our economy, certainly agriculture, seriously at risk . . . We are at war [with Palestinian violence against Israelis], and during war you mobilize all your forces. If we asked people to dig trenches, they would. So why not ask them to work in construction and agriculture? In the long run, this could be a blessing.

Los Angeles Times, 4-10:(A)3.

Al Gore
Vice President-elect
of the United States

2

[On whether the U.S. should do business with Iraqi President Saddam Hussein]: The phrase "do business" implies normal relations, and the answer to that is "no." We will have trouble from Iraq so long as Saddam Hussein and his regime are in power.

Broadcast interview/
"Meet the Press," NBC-TV, 1-17.

Mordechai Gur
Deputy Minister of Defense
of Israel

3

[On the pending Israel-PLO mutual-recognition agreement allowing Palestinian self-rule in

the West Bank and Gaza]: During the negotiations, we will determine the conditions, means and methods that will allow the IDF to reach any corner to make sure that we can carry out our responsibility for the safety of all Israelis. We are not leaving the whole area. We are only redeploying.

The New York Times, 9-3:(A)6.

Richard Haass
Former Director
for the Mideast,
National Security Council
of the United States

4

[On the recently signed Israel-PLO mutual-recognition agreement allowing Palestinian self-rule in the West Bank and Gaza]: I'm bullish about prospects for democratic institutions among Palestinians. They're highly literate, bourgeois people in the positive sense of that word. I'm confident that democracy can take hold. And if it does, it'll have a powerful impact, by example but also because Palestinians are everywhere in the Arab world. So it's not an isolated example. And people throughout the Mideast are also going to be watching.

Los Angeles Times, 9-14:(A)12.

Nizar Hamdoon
Iraqi Ambassador/
Permanent Representative
to the United Nations

5

Iraq does not recognize the no-fly zone [an area of Iraq that U.S.-led forces do not permit Iraqi aircraft to enter] because it was not a UN job. It was imposed by the three Western powers and, based on that, Iraq reserves all its rights to do whatever it wants at the time it deems necessary.

To reporters, Jan. 7/
The New York Times, 1-8:(A)6.

Hamid Youssef Hammadi
Minister of Information
of Iraq

6

[Saying his government hopes new U.S. President Clinton will have a less-hostile attitude

(HAMID YOUSSEF HAMMADI)

toward Iraq]: We hope that President Clinton would seek to establish a relationship of equality that ensures legitimate interests between Iraq and the Arabs on the one hand and the U.S. on the other . . . I also hope that Mr. Clinton would not keep [former U.S. President] Bush's group in the State Department and Defense Department, because they are "yes" men who only read Bush's lips.

Baghdad, Iraq, Jan. 20/
Los Angeles Times, 1-21:(A)18.

Rafik al-Hariri
Prime Minister of Lebanon

1

Under no circumstances whatsoever will we accept the permanent settlement of a part of the Palestinian people on our [Lebanon's] territory. Lebanon is for the Lebanese, Palestine is for the Palestinians.

Sept. 4/
The Christian Science Monitor, 9-8:6.

David Harris
Executive vice president,
American Jewish Committee

2

[On the pending Israel-PLO mutual-recognition agreement allowing Palestinian self-rule in the West Bank and Gaza]: It may represent the first breakthrough on the Palestinian front in a century, and it creates a certain optimism. There's a great deal of confidence in [Israel's Yitzhak] Rabin Administration. I think that Israel feels now that risk of aggressive peacemaking presents more opportunity and less risk down the road than the alternative of simply maintaining the status quo with its endless cycles of war, terrorism and hostility.

The New York Times, 9-3:(A)7.

David Hartman
Director,
Shalom Hartman Institute
for Jewish Studies (Israel)

3

Jerusalem does not let people forget they are connected to history. Even if they are not reli-

gious, deep down each side views the city as "who is God working with in history?"

U.S. News & World Report,
11-8:56.

Chaim Herzog
President of Israel

4

[On the current Arab-Israeli peace negotiations]: Things in the Middle East develop according to the rules of the Middle East market. You don't put down the price [asked] immediately. You don't pay what you're asked for. You bargain. You walk away. You break off. You look annoyed. It takes a long time before you finally do a deal. I would estimate that within the next year or so we will have reached somewhere.

Interview, Jerusalem, Israel/
The New York Times, 5-4:(A)4.

Chaim Herzog
Former President of Israel

5

[On the recent Israel-PLO mutual-recognition agreement allowing Palestinian self-rule in the West Bank and Gaza]: It is yet to be proved that this is one of the great moments of history. But certainly it is one of the great opportunities.

Time, 9-20:40.

Robert E. Hunter
Director of European studies,
Center for Strategic
and International Studies
(United States)

6

[On the threat by U.S.-led powers to respond against Iraqi President Saddam Hussein's attempts to violate the Persian Gulf-war peace accords and regulations]: This is all part of the continuing war of wills to try to show the people in the region and potential enemies of Saddam Hussein that, yes, we haven't forgotten about him and we're still trying to get rid of him. He's been struggling for two years to paint himself as David to our Goliath. If he can say, "See, they continue to pick on me," that helps him at home.

The Christian Science Monitor,
1-8:4.

341

Hussein ibn Talal
King of Jordan

1

[Criticizing recent U.S.-led air attacks on Iraq in response to that country's provocations against UN resolutions placed on Iraq following 1991's Persian Gulf war]: I feel deep anger [about the U.S.-led attacks], which I believe is what is felt by Arabs throughout the Arab world. Nobody can be happy with the use of force in this region. And as far as Iraq is concerned, we are with the Iraqi people.

Jan. 18/
Los Angeles Times, 1-19:(A)10.

2

[On the effect on autocratic rulers in the Arab world of the recent Israel-PLO peace agreement]: There is no doubt that the rug will be pulled from under the feet of many a leader in the region who used the confrontation with Israel to aspire to or justify his own power ... True [Arab] unity can only happen when there is pluralism and freedom of expression so that we can deal with each other on a people-to-people basis. Then the relationships mean something and are not based on the whims or moods of unaccountable leaders.

Interview/
Los Angeles Times, 10-28:(B)7.

3

[On his country's relations with Israel]: In the past, one might say we've been the best of enemies. In the context of peace, I think the possibilities available [now that Israel and the PLO have signed a peace agreement] are unbelievable for joining together to secure a better future for everyone. Obviously, economic [cooperation] is one dimension. Some people here say they are afraid. Members of this school had their run for years and haven't very much to show for it. I have no fear whatsoever. This is a period of very rapid movement. Still, you can't formulate a peace treaty before we see a resolution of all the problems leading up to that.

Interview, Amman, Jordan/
U.S. News & World Report,
11-8:55.

4

[On democracy in Jordan]: We are still at an early stage of pluralism. It's going to take time to evolve from 22 parties to a smaller group with programs that can attract people. But democracy in Jordan is here to stay.

Interview, Amman, Jordan/
U.S. News & World Report,
11-8:55.

Saddam Hussein
President of Iraq

5

[On U.S.-led military attacks on Iraqi targets in response to Iraq's defiance of UN resolutions imposed on it following 1991's Persian Gulf war]: This is the new chapter in the "mother of all battles." If the enemy continues its military aggression, or even it if stops, it is the final and decisive chapter which will be the end of all chapters.

Speech, Jan. 17/
The New York Times, 1-18:(A)4.

6

We and all of humanity consider this [anti-war] aspect of [U.S. President] Clinton's personality to be a mark of strength. The problem is whether the information and advice given to him would keep him on this path ... or he would take another after becoming President. Is he ready to listen to the viewpoint of Iraq? If he is ready, I simply believe that we can pave the way for building new relations based on mutual respect ... regardless of what has happened in the past.

At meeting with former U.S. Attorney General
Ramsey Clark, Baghdad, Iraq, Feb. 13/
The Washington Post, 2-15:(A)29.

Martin Indyk
Senior Director for Near East
and South Asian Affairs,
National Security Council
of the United States

7

The current regime [of President Saddam Hussein] in Iraq is a criminal regime, beyond the

(MARTIN INDYK)

pale of international society and, in our judgment, irredeemable.

Speech, May/
The Christian Science Monitor,
7-14:1.

Ahmed Jibril
Leader, Popular Front
for the Liberation of
Palestine-General Command

1

[Criticizing the pending Israel-PLO mutual recognition agreement]: First, the armed struggle [against Israel] will be intensified and, secondly, the revolution will be purified of people like [PLO leader Yasir] Arafat. They have betrayed the cause of liberating Palestine and uprooting Zionism.

Beirut, Lebanon/
Los Angeles Times, 9-10:(A)14.

2

[Criticizing PLO chairman Yasir Arafat's signing of a mutual-recognition agreement with Israel]: I have not said that I will personally kill Arafat. I said our Palestinian people will not be lenient with Arafat, who has given up 90 percent of the Palestinian land. Therefore, he will be dishonored by the Palestinian people . . . And when Arafat is killed, the accord will fade away.

Interview,
Damascus, Syria, Sept. 12/
Los Angeles Times, 9-14:(H)5.

David Kay
Former United Nations
weapons inspector in Iraq

3

[On Iraqi President Saddam Hussein's current provocations against UN resolutions placed on Iraq following 1991's Persian Gulf war]: The U.S. policy has no conceptual basis for how to move Iraq out of "cheat and retreat" mode, and the challenge for [incoming U.S. President] Clinton is how to get beyond this and hold out to

Saddam Hussein that, if he abides by the resolutions, we can talk about a new relationship and, if he doesn't, we're going to hit him hard.

Interview/
Los Angeles Times, 1-19:(A)12.

Robert Kelly
Chief United Nations
nuclear inspector in Iraq

4

[Saying 1991's Persian Gulf war has destroyed most of Iraq's nuclear-weapons capability]: Literally billions of dollars worth of effort has been destroyed. That's why we say the program from before the war is dead . . . All of the critical facilities have been destroyed; virtually all of the critical equipment . . . has been destroyed. [But] if Iraq would choose to restart a nuclear-weapons program, they would probably do it faster than anyone else in the world because they have a lot of experience under their belt.

Baghdad, Iraq/
Los Angeles Times, 6-30:(A)11.

Gilles Kepel
Professor of Arab studies,
Institute of Political Science
(France)

5

[On PLO chairman Yasir Arafat's plans to negotiate with the Israeli government, which is looking toward allowing Palestinian self-government in the West Bank and Gaza]: Arafat has taken a risk greater than that of [the late] Egyptian President [Anwar] Sadat when he traveled to Jerusalem in 1977. The PLO support in Gaza has eroded enormously in favor of the [militant anti-Israeli] Hamas and fundamentalist movements, and it is not even clear if Arafat will be able to set foot there. New elites now exist on the ground in Gaza and the West Bank.

The New York Times, 9-3:(A)6.

Edward Luck
President, United Nations Association
of the U.S.A.

6

Iraq provokes a military confrontation and then it gives in. All this does is tell the West

(EDWARD LUCK)

that . . . the only thing Iraq pays attention to is the use of military force. If you go back to the negotiations before [1991's Persian] Gulf war, military force was the one thing that [Iraqi President] Saddam Hussein seemed to respect.

The Christian Science Monitor,
1-19:4.

John Major
Prime Minister
of the United Kingdom

1

[Criticizing suggestions that the U.S.-led coalition should have gone to Baghdad and captured Iraqi President Saddam Hussein at the end of 1991's Persian Gulf war]: Should they really have gone right into Baghdad and dragged Saddam Hussein out by the heels? A very agreeable thing to say in retrospect, maybe . . . Apart from the fact we had no international mandate to do it, it would have been a bloodbath for both the Iraqis and for the allies. And what would have happened had we done it? We would have created an Arab martyr with no certainty of who or what would have replaced him. If you look at his [current] position, he's a man standing on a patch of sand with the water increasingly lapping over it. There have been a number of coup attempts; they've failed. He's surrounded by the fanatical few. He's ruthless. His country is suffering. I don't know how long he can continue, but it is not our job to bring him down. It's the Iraqis' job.

Interview/
USA Today, 2-23:(A)13.

Tarik Moayyid
Minister of Information
of Bahrain

2

This [Persian Gulf] region is moving [toward democracy], and the tide is moving. Those who don't move with it will lose their heads. Those who do change with it will prosper, along with their people.

Los Angeles Times, 4-10:(A)5.

Abdullah al-Mohammadi
Director, Committee for the
Promotion of Virtue
and the Prevention of Vice,
Jidda, Saudi Arabia

3

[On his "religious police," who are given the authority to crack down on un-Islamic behavior in Saudi Arabia]: Crime is derived from a mutation of human morals, and if we can protect and promote moral behavior, crime will not be able to take root . . . We are fighting against an infusion of vice. Magazines and papers, even shirts, are imported with sexually arousing pictures. We have a big problem with illegal pornographic videos. And a few of the foreigners who come to work have evil intentions, such as prostitution.

The New York Times, 1-6:(A)4.

Amre Moussa
Foreign Minister of Egypt

4

The situation in the [Persian] Gulf is not good. It is precarious. The security [situation] is still not addressed . . . The security of the Arab countries of the Gulf is essential for us, and we are not going to keep silent if [it] is threatened.

Interview/
The Washington Post, 4-6:(A)17.

Hosni Mubarak
President of Egypt

5

[On criticism that his government isn't more democratic]: The public opinion should be ed-u-ca-ted. This country was under pressure for years and years, so when you open the gate for freedom, you will find many terrible things taking place. If you have a dam and keep the water until it begins to overflow, and then you open the gates, it will drown many people. We have to give a gradual dose so people can swallow it and understand it.

Interview,
Cairo, Egypt, Oct. 11/
The New York Times, 10-12:(A)3.

Richard W. Murphy
Former Assistant Secretary
for Near Eastern
and South Asian Affairs,
Department of State
of the United States

1

While we [the U.S.] don't want to see one nation dominating the [Persian] Gulf, for better or worse there *is* one nation dominating the Gulf. It's us.

Newsweek, 1-25:43.

Laurie Mylroie
Scholar,
Washington Institute
for Near East Policy
(United States)

2

[On Iraqi President Saddam Hussein]: Watching him on Iraqi television when I was there in November, it was stunning to see his self-confidence and his arrogance, and his evident pleasure in public adulation, however obviously coerced. Bombing [by U.S.-led forces in response to Iraqi violations of the Persian Gulf-war peace requirements] isn't going to change that much. It has very limited utility.

The New York Times, 1-9:5.

Said Naggar
Egyptian economist

3

The present political system [in Egypt] is out of tune with the times. You cannot postpone [reform] forever on the basis of [fear] of Islamic fundamentalism; it may be with us for 200 years. I fully understand [the government's] fears. They are afraid that if this question is opened, the Islamic fundamentalists could inspire some provisions in a reform Constitution that would make it a semi-Islamic Constitution—which is not in the best interests of the country. The best answer to this fear is not to say we close the door to further democratization. Islamic fundamentalism is a fact of life . . . History tells us you cannot kill an idea by repression. Ideas have to be killed by ideas.

The Washington Post, 3-15:(A)15.

Hanna Nasir
President, Birzeit University,
Israeli-occupied West Bank;
Member,
Palestine National Council

4

[On his return after being exiled by Israel in 1974]: Israel would like me to say I am grateful to be back. In fact, I am still angry. I am angry over my deportation—the way I was bundled into a jeep, driven through the night in handcuffs and a blindfold, dropped across the border in Lebanon and never charged with a crime or even given an explanation. And I am angry that, almost two decades later, the Israelis' occupation continues, that they still deport people in the same way and that they are not called to account for their actions. If I had a hope, it was that I would return to a free and independent Palestine. Alas, we are still occupied and we are still oppressed . . . I am a former member of the PLO's executive committee, as are two other returnees, and the Israelis know and accept this. Many more returnees are present or former members of the Palestine National Council and of its central committee. With us here and in other ways, Israel has moved to *de facto* recognition of the PLO. The Israelis may have finally come to understand that the PLO is not in Tunis [Tunisia] but here on the West Bank and in the Gaza Strip. The PLO has to be dealt with if the Palestinian problem is to be resolved and if there is to be peace.

Interview, Birzeit,
Israeli-occupied West Bank/
Los Angeles Times, 5-25:(H)2.

Benjamin Netanyahu
Former Deputy Foreign Minister
of Israel;
Former Israeli Ambassador/
Permanent Representative
to the United Nations

5

[On the change in Israeli politics which will result in the direct election by the people of the next Prime Minister]: For the first time, the candidate for Prime Minister will get his mandate from the people, not through deals done in back rooms, under the table and behind others' backs. For the first time, the electorate will decide who leads this country, who takes responsibility, who has the authority . . . [The current system in Israel] is not a system for a modern democracy, for the 21st century, for the challenges that Israel faces. I don't want to say that it is undemocratic, but it is inherently unstable and promotes bickering, infighting and back-stabbing. We need a bill of rights, we need a constitutional framework, we need to give people a real say in their government, we need to give them good government.

Los Angeles Times, 2-2:(H)1,5.

1

[On his running for the leadership of Israel's Likud Party]: The country [Israel] is on fire [with anti-Israeli violence by Palestinians], the knife-wielders are running rampant in the streets. In the face of such a [Labor Party] government, such a failure, the question is who can replace it—and as quickly as possible. I am here . . . I am the only one who can replace it. I am the only one who can return Likud to government.

Israeli broadcast debate/
Los Angeles Times, 3-23:(H)2.

Benjamin Netanyahu
Leader, Likud Party of Israel;
Former Deputy Foreign Minister
of Israel

2

We can fight [anti-Israeli] terror. We know how to, and we will do it. [But] if [members of Prime Minister Yitzhak Rabin's current Labor Party government] don't know how, they should step aside . . . We [the Likud Party] will, through parliamentary and other means, organize to topple this government as soon as possible.

At rally,
Tel Aviv, Israel, March 25/
Los Angeles Times, 3-26:(A)23.

3

[On Israel's ruling Labor Party]: This government says that it is impossible to fight the

knifings, that it is impossible to fight [anti-Israeli Arab] terrorism. How do they put it? "Terrorism has only one solution: a political solution." In other words, there is no solution to terrorism except retreat.

At rally,
Tel Aviv, Israel, March 25/
The New York Times, 3-26:(A)2.

4

It's now an open secret that this [Labor Party] government [of Israel] is willing to give up all of the Golan Heights and to create the foundations of an armed Palestinian state. You think this will lead to peace? We know that it will lead to disaster.

Before Israeli Knesset (Parliament),
Jerusalem, Israel, May 10/
Los Angeles Times, 5-11:(A)8.

5

[Criticizing the Israeli government's moves toward Palestinian self-government in the West Bank and Gaza]: If you think you are not creating a mini-Libya in Jericho and a mini-Teheran in Gaza, then you are not living in the Middle East. Behind the back of the [Israeli] people, this government is establishing the bridgeheads for a Palestinian state.

Los Angeles Times, 8-31:(A)6.

6

[Addressing and criticizing Israeli Prime Minister Yitzhak Rabin for signing an Israel-PLO mutual-recognition agreement allowing Palestinian self-rule in the West Bank and Gaza]: You are preparing the way for a Palestinian state. This agreement abandons security of Israeli citizens and gives it to the hands and "good intentions" of [PLO leader] Yasir Arafat. The hope [for peace] is common to all, but policy we don't make on hope alone, and we don't make on faith alone, but first and foremost on security.

In the Israeli Knesset (Parliament),
Jerusalem, Israel, Sept. 21/
The Washington Post,
9-22:(A)26.

Hazem Nusseibeh
Jordanian historian

1

[On the recent Israel-PLO mutual-recognition agreement allowing Palestinian self-rule in the West Bank and Gaza]: The Arabs are entering a new era of clear-minded realism. There is a realization now that war [with Israel] is out of the question, and that empty slogans don't win peace. We missed so many chances in the past by not giving considerations to all aspects of what was on offer.

The Christian Science Monitor,
9-15:3.

Ehud Olmert
Member of Israeli Knesset
(Parliament);
Former Minister of Health
of Israel

2

[Criticizing the pending Israel-PLO mutual-recognition agreement allowing Palestinian self-rule in the West Bank and Gaza]: I have two main concerns. One is the fact that this was done with official representatives of the PLO. Israel was reluctant to negotiate with the PLO and to recognize it for a long period. Our argument was twofold: First, the PLO is the most active supporter of terror against Israel. How can Israel seriously act against terror if it recognizes those who are waging the war of terror? The other reason was that the PLO is identical to a Palestinian state. For a very, very long period of time, Israel, and even the international community, agreed that the creation of a Palestinian state will establish a mortal danger to Israel.

Interview, Aug. 30/
Los Angeles Times, 8-31:(B)7.

Shimon Peres
Foreign Minister of Israel

3

[On the pending Israel-PLO mutual-recognition agreement allowing Palestinian self-rule in the West Bank and Gaza]: We want to live with [the Palestinians] in peace. They are human beings just like us. We don't want to control them,

to degrade them, to humiliate them. They are not four-legged creatures; they are not in bottles [like insects]; they are not animals; they are people like us. And we will live with them in peace.

Before Israeli Knesset (Parliament),
Jerusalem, Israel, Aug. 30/
Los Angeles Times, 8-31:(A)6.

4

[Addressing critics of the pending Israel-PLO mutual-recognition agreement allowing Palestinian self-rule in the West Bank and Gaza]: You are the men of yesterday. The world has changed. There is no conflict between America and the Soviet Union. There is no supply of weapons from the Soviet Union to the Arab countries. We bring news to the younger generation that after 100 years of terror, there is no return to the same situation [of Palestinian-Israeli antagonism]. Rather, we will start 100 years of understanding and living together, each people with its flag, each people with its book of prayer.

Before Israeli Knesset (Parliament),
Jerusalem, Israel, Aug. 30/
The Washington Post, 8-31:(A)14.

5

[Saying that, despite other changes in Israeli-Palestinian relations, Jerusalem will remain Israel's capital]: This is our only capital, and for them it is their never-never capital. They can dream—we deny no one his dreams—but united Jerusalem is and will remain Israel's eternal capital.

September/
Los Angeles Times, 10-6:(A)10.

6

[On the pending Israel-PLO mutual-recognition agreement allowing Palestinian self-rule in the West Bank and Gaza]: I thought in my heart not only about the great revolution that has occurred among us, but also about the great revolution that has taken place within the PLO. Don't make little of that. We are not recognizing the PLO of yesterday but, rather, the PLO of today.

To Labor Party members
of Israeli Parliament/
Los Angeles Times, 9-10:(A)14.

347

(SHIMON PERES)

1

[Criticizing Israeli opponents of the pending Israel-PLO mutual-recognition agreement allowing Palestinian self-rule in the West Bank and Gaza]: People prefer remembering rather than thinking. In memory, anything goes. [But] people must start buying tickets for the new century.

Interview/Newsweek, 9-13:26.

Norman Podhoretz
Editor,
"Commentary" magazine
(United States)

2

[Criticizing the pending Israel-PLO mutual-recognition agreement allowing Palestinian self-rule in the West Bank and Gaza]: This is the first step toward the establishment of a Palestinian state, which I think will happen sooner rather than later. And far from being a cause of peace and stability, I think it will be the cause of another war. As I see it, the Palestinians have finally decided to adopt the so-called phase strategy, which calls for getting a foothold to begin with, a state in phase 2, and then using the state as a launching pad for a final assault [against Israel].

The New York Times, 9-3:(A)7.

Jerrold Post
Political psychologist,
George Washington University
(United States)

3

[On Iraqi President Saddam Hussein's provocations against U.S.-led forces assigned to enforce UN resolutions against Iraq following 1991's Persian Gulf war]: Desert Storm [the war] was really the greatest humiliation of [Hussein's] entire career. [In his view,] there simply had to be a vindication, for himself and his own people, to say that Iraq, and Saddam, did not lose—"We are still in power while [U.S. President] George Bush is going out."

Jan. 13/
USA Today, 1-14:(A)2.

Yasir Abed Rabbo
Director of information,
Palestine Liberation Organization

4

To achieve real, stable [Israeli-Palestinian] peace necessarily demands mutual recognition. Peace between the courageous requires that courageous steps be taken. I don't think that it is impossible that there will be a meeting between [Israeli Prime Minister Yitzhak Rabin and PLO chairman Yasir Arafat] sometime soon.

Israeli Army Radio interview/
Los Angeles Times, 8-30:(A)1.

Yitzhak Rabin
Prime Minister of Israel

5

If the message the Arabs get is that they can use the [UN] Security Council to coerce Israel to do as they wish, then I tell you that there is absolutely no chance for peace with them. Whoever fails to grasp this basic fact of life fails to understand the ABCs of international relations.

To Israeli Labor Party members,
Jan. 28/
The New York Times, 1-30:3.

6

An [Israeli] agreement with Syria is a favorable strategic change for Israel. An [Israeli] agreement with the Palestinians is a political agreement, public relations.

Israeli broadcast interview/
U.S. News & World Report,
2-22:38.

7

We are ready to withdraw the Israeli armed forces on the Golan Heights to secure and recognized boundaries. But we will not negotiate the geographic dimension of the withdrawal before we know what we are getting for it. [Israel wants] open boundaries [with Syria] for movement of people and goods, diplomatic relations . . . and policies by the two governments that will encourage normalization of relations between people.

Interview, Jerusalem, Israel/
The Washington Post, 3-12:(A)19.

(YITZHAK RABIN)

1

If the state of Israel wants to reach a political solution [to the Arab-Israeli conflict], it has to understand there are enemies to this solution, especially among terrorist organizations, first and foremost the Islamic extremist organizations. I have no doubt that the terrorist organizations and the enemies of Israel draw encouragement from the fact that [the current rash of anti-Israeli violence by Palestinians] creates among Israelis a mood of fear.

Israeli TV broadcast,
Washington, D.C., March 16/
Los Angeles Times, 3-17:(A)4.

2

[On the current anti-Israeli violence by Palestinians]: I have no hocus-pocus solution, no magic cure, no simple answer, and that is just the way it is . . . This is a difficult period, but we will get through it . . . When and how precisely, I can't say. But we will, we will, I know we will.

Los Angeles Times, 3-27:(A)15.

3

[On his decision to close the borders between Israel and the occupied territories]: My goal is to reduce in stages, as fast as possible, the number of Palestinians working in Israel. It is this intermingling which allows them to endanger our security.

March 29/
The Christian Science Monitor,
4-6:7.

4

What will we [Israelis] learn [from the Holocaust of World War II]? We will learn to believe in a better world. But most important, we will not trust in others any longer, generous as they may be: only us, only ourselves. We will protect ourselves.

April 18/
The New York Times, 4-19:(A)4.

5

Today, after 50 years, we [Jews] have enough power and spiritual energy . . . to protect our new home [Israel] against its enemies, enough to grant asylum to those persecuted, enough to repel all those who conspire against us . . . We swear to you [victims of Nazi concentration camps in World War II], as long as we live, as long as Israel as a nation is alive, such a tragedy will never happen again. We will defend every Jew in every corner of the Earth at any price. Your blood has not been shed in vain.

At the former Auschwitz concentration camp,
Poland, April 20/
Los Angeles Times, 4-21:(A)6.

6

I don't see the permanent solution in a [Palestinian-Jordanian] confederation, since a confederation is between two sovereign states. Whoever says a confederation between Jordan and the Palestinians says, first of all, a Palestinian state. And I oppose that.

May 4/
Los Angeles Times, 5-5:(A)4.

7

[In the Arab-Israeli peace talks,] there was and there will be a struggle over [the status of] Jerusalem. We [Israelis] are determined . . . that Jerusalem will remain united, under Israeli sovereignty, and stay the capital of the Jewish people and the state of Israel forever.

At dedication of new City Hall,
Jerusalem, Israel, June/
Los Angeles Times, 7-10:(A)3.

8

[On Islamic militants]: They will not tolerate any presence of any foreign, non-Islamic entity in the Middle East. They will fight all the moderate Arab regimes. [And] have no illusion: They will not hesitate, whenever needed outside the Middle East, to use terror.

To reporters,
Paris, France/
The New York Times, 7-3:4.

(YITZHAK RABIN)

1

[On Israel's current attacks on Lebanon in response to attacks on Israel by Lebanon-based Hezbollah guerrillas]: Only if the attacks against our communities in the north [of Israel] are stopped will you [Lebanese] return to your homes in the south [of Lebanon]. We believe the Prime Minister of Lebanon, his army and his people, are capable of doing this. We call on Syria to use its influence to prevent Hezbollah from acting against us . . . We are sorry for the suffering of the Lebanese population moving in these days, even as we speak, on the roads [to get away from the Israeli] attacks. But as long as one resident of [the northern Israeli town of] Kiryat Shemona is still sitting in the [bomb] shelter, the operation [against Hezbollah] will go on.

Before Israeli Knesset (Parliament),
Jerusalem, Israel, July 28/
Los Angeles Times, 7-29:(A)1,10.

2

[On the pending Israel-PLO mutual-recognition agreement allowing Palestinian self-rule in the West Bank and Gaza]: We stand on the verge of a great opportunity. There is movement along the whole Arab front in readiness for peace. There are big obstacles, there are difficulties, but I am convinced the horizons for peace are open . . . A solution to the problem with the Palestinians is a solution for the focus of the Arab-Israeli conflict. What has been achieved . . . is a big step forward in moving Israel toward peace with the neighboring countries, first and foremost with the Palestinians . . . There will be criticism, and people will talk about problems here and problems there. But big acts cannot be done without programs and without reasonable risks . . . We committed ourselves not just to talk about peace, but to make peace.

To members of Israeli Parliament,
Jerusalem, Israel, Aug. 30/
Los Angeles Times, 8-31:(A)1,6.

3

[Defending the pending Israel-PLO mutual-recognition agreement allowing Palestinian self-rule in the West Bank and Gaza]: Peace is not made with friends. It is made with enemies who are not at all nice. I will not try to beautify the PLO. It has been our enemy, and it is still our enemy. But negotiations are carried out with enemies.

To members of Israeli Labor Party,
Sept. 9/
Los Angeles Times, 9-10:(A)14.

4

[On the pending Israel-PLO mutual-recognition agreement allowing Palestinian self-rule in the West Bank and Gaza]: I believe that there is a great opportunity of changing not only the relations between the Palestinians and Israel but to expand it to the solution of the conflict between Israel and other Arab countries and other Arab peoples. It is an historic moment that, hopefully, will bring about an end to 100 years of bloodshed and misery between the Palestinians and Jews, and Palestinians and Israel.

At signing of preliminary agreement,
Jerusalem, Israel, Sept. 10/
The New York Times, 9-11:1.

5

[On the pending Israel-PLO mutual-recognition agreement allowing Palestinian self-rule in the West Bank and Gaza]: This is a new chapter for people everywhere. We're going to breathe a little fresh air from now on. We've done the right thing. History will record it.

USA Today, 9-10:(A)2.

6

[On the signing of an Israel-PLO mutual-recognition agreement allowing Palestinian self-rule in the West Bank and Gaza]: Let me say to you, the Palestinians, we are destined to live together on the same soil in the same land. We, the soldiers who have returned from battles stained with blood; we who have seen our relatives and friends killed before our eyes; we who have attended their funerals and cannot look into the eyes of their parents; we who have come from a land where parents bury their children; we who

(YITZHAK RABIN)

have fought against you, the Palestinians, we say to you today in a loud and a clear voice: Enough of blood and tears. Enough! We have no desire for revenge; we harbor no hatred toward you. We, like you, are people—people who want to build a home, to plant a tree, to love, live side by side with you in dignity, in affinity, as human beings, as free men. We are today giving peace a chance and saying to you—and saying again to you—enough. Let us pray that a day will come when we all will say farewell to the arms. We wish to open a new chapter in the sad book of our lives together, a chapter of mutual recognition, of good-neighborliness, of mutual respect, of under-standing. We hope to embark on a new era in the history of the Middle East.

At signing ceremony for the agreement,
Washington, D.C., Sept. 13/
Los Angeles Times, 9-14:(A)8.

1

[On criticism in Israel of his signing a mutual-recognition agreement with the PLO allowing Palestinian self-rule in the West Bank and Gaza]: There are those who are trying to paint the future of the Israeli state in apocalyptic colors because of the Palestinians. But there is nothing more wrong than describing the Palestinians as a threat to the existence of Israel . . . Palestinian ter-rorism has never been, is not now and will not be a threat in the future to the existence of the state of Israel. It is, to be sure, a troublesome threat that injures and is painful and leads to the loss of life of Israeli soldiers and citizens; but it does not and cannot threaten Israel's existence.

Radio interview,
Jerusalem, Israel, Sept. 15/
Los Angeles Times, 9-16:(A)9.

2

[On the recently signed Israeli-Palestinian peace agreement]: We have done something. We expect not only to give but to get something in return, and not only from those who signed the agreement. The time has come, for their part, for Arab countries to come and say, "You have done

something. We will change our relations with you." This is what Israel expects.

Alexandria, Egypt, Sept. 19/
The Washington Post, 9-20:(A)12.

3

[On his recent decision to sign an Israel-PLO mutual-recognition agreement allowing Pales-tinian self-rule in the West Bank and Gaza]: It became truthfully clear over time that the one and only address for decision [on the Palestinian side] was PLO headquarters in Tunis. It would have been possible to act like an ostrich; it would have been possible to lie to ourselves; it would have been possible to hide in the sand; it would have been possible to deceive ourselves . . . We have decided not to act as such. [While the PLO is] an organization of terror and destruc-tion that has known no mercy, an organization that sent the murderers of children against us, we cannot choose our neighbors or our enemies, not even the cruelest among them. We only have what there is: the PLO, which fought against us and we fought against them.

Before Israeli Knesset (Parliament),
Jerusalem, Israel, Sept. 21/
The Washington Post, 9-22:(A)25.

4

[Saying the U.S. should stay out of Israel-PLO talks on implementing recently signed peace agreements]: We initialed the agreement in Oslo with the Palestinians, the PLO, without any sponsors. We do not need uncles, fathers, grand-mothers and grandfathers. This is a respon-sibility *we* took on together and *we* have to imple-ment it.

Jerusalem, Israel, Dec. 3/
The New York Times, 12-4:4.

5

[On the Israel-PLO mutual-recognition agree-ment he recently signed allowing Palestinian self-rule in the West Bank and Gaza]: When I decided to run for Prime Minister [last year], I believed that the coincidence of events on the international scene, in the Middle East, in Israel, were ripe to achieve two goals: peace and security, and changing the order of national priorities for the people of Israel—not to look at the [occupied] territories [the West Bank and Gaza] as the main issue. At least 96 percent of Israeli Jews live on sovereign Israeli soil, within the green lines, including united Jerusalem. The future of Israel depends much more on what that 96 percent of Jews and about 1 million non-Jewish Israeli citizens will achieve in their economy, social progress, cultural and scientific achievements.

Interview, Tel Aviv, Israel/
Time, 9-27:33.

Hashemi Rafsanjani
President of Iran

1

The Iraqi government's biggest mistake was that it turned its back on the people and disregarded them. When a government is representative of its people, no enemy would dare have bad intentions against them.

Issahan, Iran, Jan. 14/
The New York Times, 1-15:(A)5.

2

[On Iranian-U.S. relations]: If the United States forms its policy, we do not see any reason for continued severance of relations . . . Before talks, there must be good will . . . In general, the United States should first prove its good will so that a decision can be made. Our policy is not one of making enemies. On the contrary, by making efforts to solve the problems and eliminate obstacles to friendship, we move in the direction of improving relations with world countries.

News conference,
Teheran, Iran, Jan. 31/
Los Angeles Times, 2-1:(A)1,9.

3

Iran has suffered from terrorism more than any other country. We know that terrorism does not serve our interests, neither domestically nor internationally. We have respect for Hezbollah [Lebanon's Iran-backed Party of God, which has been accused of terrorist acts] as concerns the liberation of their land occupied by Israel. But if Hezbollah commits terrorist acts, we do not accept that, and we condemn it. As for involvement in terrorism by the Iranian government, if you can show one piece of evidence, please make it known to everybody. We should all cooperate to prevent terrorism.

Interview, Teheran, Iran/
Time, 5-31:48.

4

As a result of what Israel has done, a nation, the people of Palestine, has been ruined; about 4 million Palestinians are refugees throughout the world. We do not consider it right that Palestinians should forever be deprived of returning to their homeland. We don't say that "you who have come to Israel should leave this land." The world should adopt a position that would allow Palestinians to return to their homeland and create a system in which people can live freely together. If there is not enough room for everybody, priority should be given to Palestinians, not to Jews who are being taken to Israel.

Interview, Teheran, Iran/
Time, 5-31:51.

5

I'm a revolutionary figure; I was involved in the struggle and spent almost all the young years of my life in prison. In our culture, both extremes are rebuked: We believe that people should be moderate. When I defend revolution, you say I'm a hard-liner. When I say we would like to have cooperation with the West, you say I'm being moderate. That's because you don't know Iran. As far as we are concerned, they go together.

Interview, Teheran, Iran/
Time, 5-31:51.

Ariel Rosen-Zvi
Dean of law,
Tel Aviv University (Israel)

6

[On Israel's political system]: Rarely has a country undertaken such fundamental political

(ARIEL ROSEN-ZVI)

change short of a war or economic collapse. And these structural changes will bring in other changes, including the breakdown of the old parties and the start of new ones, a repositioning by everyone on the major issues and a rethink about the role of religion in Israel.

Los Angeles Times, 2-2:(H)1.

Saud Nasser al-Saud al-Sabah
Minister of Information
of Kuwait

1

[On the current military and economic pressure on Iraqi President Saddam Hussein by the U.S. and UN resulting from 1991's Persian Gulf war]: It is difficult to really answer [the] question where Saddam will turn his anger because Saddam is being now cornered from every aspect, politically and militarily, and his internal situation is in serious trouble. Every time Saddam Hussein is in serious trouble, he turns in anger on his neighbors.

News conference,
Kuwait City, Kuwait, Jan. 17/
The New York Times, 1-18:(A)5.

Mohammed Said Sahaf
Foreign Minister of Iraq

2

Iraq affirms that it is not responsible for the safety of [UN inspection flights, which have taken place since 1991's Persian Gulf war in accordance with cease-fire resolutions] inside Iraqi airspace in case of a mistake or a misunderstanding, God forbid. This is because all the barrels of guns in Iraq, even on the popular level, are aimed so as to defend Iraq's skies and sovereignty. U.S., British and French warplanes . . . are violating Iraqi airspace in an open aggression which is not accepted by Iraq.

Baghdad, Iraq,
Jan. 15/
Los Angeles Times,
1-16:(A)1.

Hisham Shawi
Former Iraqi Ambassador
to Canada

3

[On his defection to the West due to his opposition to Iraqi President Saddam Hussein] Today, Iraq suffers from a reign of terror and misery unprecedented in its long history. It has no laws, no freedoms. Citizens do not enjoy even the most rudimentary of human rights. It is the law of the jungle.

News conference,
London, England, Aug. 24/
Los Angeles Times, 8-25:(A)4.

Shimon Shetreet
Minister of Economics
of Israel

4

[On the pending Israel-PLO mutual-recognition agreement allowing Palestinian self-rule in the West Bank and Gaza]: This agreement is the beginning of a process, while the [1978] peace treaty [between Israel and] Egypt was the conclusion of a process with everything ready in front of you. Here, you have so many questions open. How will security arrangements be secured? What direction are we going in, overall? What will be the nature of this Palestinian entity? Is it going to be associated with Jordan, or is it going to be separate? There are important questions that have not been clarified . . . There are too many questions, in fact, that haven't been clarified.

Los Angeles Times, 9-10:(A)14.

Abdullah Sheyaji
Professor of political science,
Kuwait University

5

[Kuwait's] reliance on the Americans [for protection] is a fact of life right now. But there are some who have had it with the U.S. The argument is, will the reliance on the U.S. undermine our independence in foreign policy, domestic policy, oil policy? The answer is yes. When you need somebody so badly, he's going to call the shots, not you.

Los Angeles Times, 1-28:(A)4.

(ABDULLAH SHEYAJI)

1

[On Kuwait's reluctance to help finance the new Palestinian self-rule in the West Bank and Gaza]: It's really the wrong time for us to put our hands in our pockets. We have a difficult problem. We have wiped out more than half of our investment portfolio, and we have been hit by deficits. So, for us in Kuwait, it's a double whammy. [And] how do you explain [such an aid request] to the average Kuwaiti, male or female, who [during 1991's Persian Gulf war in which the PLO supported Iraq's invasion of Kuwait] saw a Palestinian questioning a Kuwaiti at a checkpoint, or torturing a Kuwaiti, or acting as the Iraqis' Fifth Column during the occupation? How do we reconcile our grudge?

Los Angeles Times, 10-1:(A)11.

Ben-Ami Shiloni
Specialist on Asia,
Truman Institute,
Hebrew University (Israel)

2

[On Israel's diplomatic and economic talks with North Korea, aimed at dissuading the North Koreans from selling missiles to Iran]: Better than putting our faith in new anti-missile weapons and better than pre-emptive military action is preventing delivery of these Scud-D missiles to Iran and other states, if we can. If Iran makes it worth North Korea's while to develop these weapons, let us [Israelis] try to make it more profitable not to.

Los Angeles Times, 6-26:(A)3.

Zalman Shoval
Director, international
relations department,
Likud Party of Israel;
Former Israeli Ambassador
to the United States

3

The strength of the American Jewish community is in its unity. I strongly recommend to Israeli politicians that we not treat American Jews the way Leninists would, saying those who are not for us are against us. American Jews are entitled to their opinions and to express them [on the Middle East situation], but at the end of the day, they should support Israel's elected and legitimate government because that government has to make the decisions, especially regarding security.

Los Angeles Times, 7-27:(H)2.

Azmi Shuebi
Member of Palestinian delegation
and PLO steering committee
at Arab-Israeli peace negotiations

4

[Israeli Prime Minister Yitzhak] Rabin's problem, as we see it, is that he wants to be sure, absolutely sure, about security [for Israel], so he is always focusing on the end result [of peace talks with the Arabs] although insisting that he is discussing the interim stage. Everyone has his eyes on the second phase—we are clear that we want a Palestinian state—and that makes negotiating the interim period of autonomy very difficult. We feel that if we could provide assurances about the final result, we could then conclude an interim agreement.

Aug. 16/
Los Angeles Times, 8-17:(A)6.

Ephraim Sneh
Member of Israeli Knesset
(Parliament)

5

[Saying the U.S. is not taking the threat from Iran seriously enough]: The intelligence community in the United States is aware of the danger, and the military establishment is aware, but I'm worried the political establishment might be influenced by the mood which says keep away from Iran. Iran is the Bermuda Triangle of American politics.

The Washington Post, 3-13:(A)14.

Shubert Spero
Professor of Jewish thought,
Bar Ilan University (Israel)

6

[On the current anti-Israeli violence by Palestinians]: The people of Israel have a perfect right

(SHUBERT SPERO)

to be furious with their present government. From the Prime Minister [Yitzhak Rabin] on down . . . we have seen gross insensitivity to our personal security needs to a degree unprecedented in the entire conflict-ridden history of this country. At this point, it is difficult to say whether it emanates from sheer stupidity or masks devious dishonesty . . . But it is certainly and in great measure the inevitable outgrowth of the irresoluteness of several Israeli governments.

Los Angeles Times, 3-27:(A)15.

Jalal Talabani
Leader,
Kurdistan Front of Iraq

1

[Criticizing the U.S. for not giving monetary aid to those opposing Iraqi President Saddam Hussein]: I think for a long time the Americans were waiting for a military coup against Saddam, but I don't think that's possible anymore. To revolt against a monster like Saddam Hussein, you need a very high morale. You need to pay the troops and feed the troops after they come over to your side. So I personally am not expecting any military coup now . . . The United States is not sincere in helping the Iraqi people topple Saddam Hussein. I was all along believing the U.S. was in favor of eliminating Saddam Hussein. But now, I doubt it.

Interview, Damascus, Syria/
Los Angeles Times, 4-24:(A)15.

Walid al-Tamimi
Leading member,
Association of Iraqi Democrats

2

[Criticizing recent U.S. attacks on Iraqi targets, saying they only strengthen Iraqi President Saddam Hussein's hold on the country]: What is the objective of all this? Is it to destroy a few Iraqi missiles here or a factory there, or to kill a few civilians, in order to "frighten Saddam into line?" He will never, never give up; the man is beyond redemption. I am shocked when I hear [U.S. President] Bush or [British Prime Minister John] Major saying they are "delivering Saddam a message." Saddam couldn't care less about Iraqi people's lives and property. They are the most disposable items he possesses. If you destroy a factory he built or a weapon he bought, he isn't going to be upset; he is going to use it to his advantage. And that's just what he's doing.

The Christian Science Monitor,
1-20:1.

Yoash Tsiddon-Chatto
Former member of
Israeli Knesset (Parliament)

3

[On Israel's political system]: Everyone was able to see what we have doesn't work. Our system brings political paralysis . . . But getting anything done about it was next to impossible. The big parties were caught in a deadlock with one another—reform had to be politically neutral and give neither an advantage—and the small parties had vested interests against any real change. And there was public apprehension that change would be for the worse, no matter how bad things were . . . The biggest barrier to political reform is the refusal of the ultra-religious and their parties to yield the enormous powers they have. They want control from birth to death, even though two-thirds of the country does not agree with them.

Los Angeles Times, 2-2:(H)1,5.

Harry Wall
Jerusalem director,
Anti-Defamation League
of B'nai B'rith

4

If [Arab-Israeli] peace happens, the [U.S.] Clinton Administration will need to broker it, and brokering it will require an activist approach at the highest levels of U.S. foreign policy. But the Clinton Administration will appraise that effort carefully. The upside is a historic opportunity, and Bill Clinton would benefit politically. The downside is that it will require leaning on Israel, and that could mean the same loss of support among American Jews that other mediators suffered. The current dissonance could discour-

(HARRY WALL)

age President Clinton from making peace in the Middle East a priority.

Los Angeles Times, 7-27:(H)2.

R. James Woolsey
Director of Central Intelligence
of the United States

1

[On the possibility that Iraq will be able to resume development of nuclear weapons despite their destruction in the Persian Gulf war and continued UN sanctions and inspections]: Military force can slow nuclear-weapons development programs in the short term but cannot permanently stop [them] . . . Without international scrutiny, continued inspections, Iraq probably could rebuild, with available expertise, its nuclear-weapons program and manufacture a device in about five to seven years.

Before Senate Governmental Affairs Committee,
Washington, D.C./
The New York Times, 10-19:(A)17.

David Yahav
Colonel,
and Deputy Advocate-General,
Israeli Army

2

[Saying Israeli soldiers in the occupied territories are held to a high standard of behavior despite being in hostile areas]: The soldiers are under pressure, they are under attack in a hostile environment, and our dilemma is to what extent we should pursue a standard criminal investigation [of soldiers accused of killing Palestinians] when the troops are in such difficult circumstances. In a war, there aren't such criminal investigations and soldiers aren't court-martialed for causing death through negligence. Yet, [here] we investigate every killing and we're tough on the soldiers. Despite the more difficult conditions, our open-fire regulations follow the same legal principles that govern the police in Israel and in Western countries where there is no war.

The New York Times, 5-24:(A)3.

David Yerushalmi
President,
Israel Export Corporation

3

In Israel, people still don't believe that capitalism works better than socialism, and for that reason we will never get an across-the-board transformation of the Israeli economy. I think we can prove it, though, and in the process get real growth that brings in investment, creates jobs and promotes change . . . [Israel should be] pulled out of its socialist lethargy and into the competition of the global market with the profitability that would bring.

Los Angeles Times, 5-16:(D)5.

James Zogby
President,
Arab American Institute
(United States)

4

[On Iraqi President Saddam Hussein's provocations against U.S.-led forces assigned to enforce UN resolutions against Iraq following 1991's Persian Gulf war]: If he's testing this [U.S. Bush] Administration or the next [the incoming U.S. Clinton Administration], it's an act of absolute foolishness that will only result in more suffering. Hussein is the odd man out. He doesn't seem to get it.

USA Today, 1-14:(A)2.

5

[Because of the recent Israel-PLO peace agreement,] there's a spirit of reaching out, and it has spread broadly across both communities. We are one-time adversaries who are now colleagues . . . I have a stake [now] in seeing that Israel's aid does not get cut. Anybody who raises the question of cutting aid to Israel puts the peace process at risk.

The Christian Science Monitor,
10-19:2.

PART THREE

General

The Arts

Jane Alexander
Actress;
Chairman-designate,
National Endowment for the Arts
of the United States

1

The very essence of art . . . is to hold the mirror up to nature. The arts reflect the diversity and variety of human experience. The artist often taps into the very issues of society that are most sensitive.

At Senate Labor and Human Resources
Committee hearing on her nomination,
Washington, D.C., Sept. 22/
Los Angeles Times, 9-23:(F)3.

2

I have a vision for the arts in this country. That vision is that every man, woman and child find the song in his or her heart. I see the arts as part of the solution to our problems and not, in any way, part of the problem. The arts are life-enhancing and bring joy. Through the arts, we release the very best that is in our imaginations, and it is through our imagination that we draw the map for our future. Through the arts, we learn the discipline of a skill and the accomplishment that comes from collaboration. The arts are a community issue. They bring together, they do not rend asunder.

At Senate Labor and Human Resources
Committee hearing on her nomination,
Washington, D.C., Sept. 23/
Daily Variety, 9-27:23.

3

Let me talk about what the arts do. Absolutely, people have the right to reject the arts. But my hunch is if there are any old people, any young people, any people that want to feel that sense of joy that only comes with either achieving something artistically or through a vicarious experience, then they'll want and support the arts.

Interview, Oct. 12/
The New York Times, 10-16:12.

Betty Allen
President,
Harlem School of the Arts,
New York, N.Y.

4

[On criticism that the arts are elitist]: The word "elite," in its original sense, was not negative, but regrettably it has come to be perceived as such. People assume the arts are the outgrowth of something aristocratic—that music, dance, theatre and art are intended for the rich . . . The arts, and those who are professionals in the arts, are perceived as elitist; but the arts are surely for everyone to enjoy . . . The attitude that music, dance, theatre and the visual arts are for and about rich people only stems from external perceptions of artists and the fields they work in. The positive attitude toward artistic excellence comes from the artist's peers. The negative attitude proceeds from those outside the world of the arts, and not always without envy. Artists look only for the opportunity and challenges of their art. They do not single themselves out, but, having a certain talent, can no more live without expressing and refining that talent than they can live without breathing.

At Curtis Institute of Music
commencement,
May 7/
Opera News, November:22.

Richard Avedon
Photographer

5

A photograph is like a word in a sentence. The pictures put together become a sentence. And then they can become a paragraph. I've never been able to express everything I know about the subject in one photograph. By editing the pictures and interweaving them in an almost symphonic form, I have enough images to tell my full story.

Interview/
The New York Times,
2-15:(B)3.

Stephanie Barron
Curator of 20th-century art,
Los Angeles County (Calif.)
Museum of Art

1

[Supporting a Clinton Administration proposal to expand a tax break for people who contribute art to museums]: If this goes through, this could be the best news for American museums, especially in light of increased Federal, state, municipal and private fiscal cuts. Tax incentives are the most significant resource [that] museums—large and small—can use to encourage donations of works of art to build collections and to keep great works of art from being traded in salesrooms.

Los Angeles Times, 2-20:(A)19.

Ilse Bing
Photographer

2

[On why she has not taken pictures since 1959]: Every art medium has a classic period, when the work is self-contained with no reference to anything else. For music, it was the time in the 18th century of Haydn and Mozart; for painting, the 15th century of the Renaissance. In photography, the classic period was the 1920s through the 1950s, before the trend to multimedia. [When that period ended,] I realized that everything moves, nothing stays and I should not hold on.

The New York Times, 3-8:(B)5.

Daniel J. Boorstin
Historian;
Librarian-emeritus of Congress
of the United States

3

I think that so many of the great works of art are the byproducts of particular people's miseries. There's almost an antithesis between happiness and creativity. Each artist must have his own kind of dissatisfaction with what he sees.

Interview/Humanities, Jan.-Feb.:10.

James Lee Burke
Author

4

Humility is something that an artist *must* have, or he won't endure as an artist. His creative powers will dissipate as soon as he sees himself as an end in himself. He will no longer be able to write with what Faulkner called "the pity and compassion that is the mark of all great art."

Interview/
Writer's Digest, January:40.

Bill Clinton
President of the United States

5

[The arts and humanities] have enabled Americans of all backgrounds and walks of life to gain a deeper appreciation of who they are as individuals and who we all are as a society. Stirring our minds and our senses, stimulating learning and collective discourse, the arts and humanities teach us in ways that nothing else can about the vastness and the depth of human experience.

At National Medal of Arts ceremony,
Washington, D.C., Oct. 7/
The Washington Post, 10-8:(D)1.

6

There are few things more powerful in any time or place than culture. The ability of culture to elevate or debase is really profound.

Speech to entertainment-industry personnel,
Beverly Hills, Calif., Dec. 4/
The New York Times, 12-6:(A)7.

Clement Greenberg
Art critic

7

I've been charged with reducing everything to the question of quality. And I do—if you want to call that a reduction . . . I don't pay any attention to [the artist's] intentions. Take a classical Greek sculpture that portrays a god, or a Persian miniature that was done under the patronage of some ruler. In the end, we don't look at them because of why they were done; we look at them because they work so well as art . . . Leon Golub, for instance, has painted paintings charged with moral and political feelings. I presume to think that what he wants most to hear, really, is that the paintings are good. I always go back to the evidence of my eye.

Interview/Newsweek, 4-19:66.

Sarah Greenough
Curator of photography,
National Gallery of Art,
Washington, D.C.

1

Photographers these days are concerned about computer-generated imagery. If the negative resides in the computer, and 8-by-10 prints, or slides, or a 30-by-40-inch print can be produced year after year [by this method], where is the hand, the eye, the artist in the process? This is not to say [computer image-making] is good or bad, but photographers know the change has to be dealt with . . . Photographers in their 40s are used to working with negatives and making a print of some kind because the whole process is fascinating. They still have that love of the technique, of getting the perfect expression on paper. And it may be that the generation in their teens now won't want to have that photo to hold. They will be more interested in having it stored in a computer.

Interview, Washington, D.C./
The Christian Science Monitor,
4-22:11.

Edythe Harrison
Founder, Virginia Opera,
Norfolk, Va.

2

Beginning with [former U.S.] President [Jimmy] Carter, we have been given the idea that anyone banging on a tin can was producing art. We were made to feel that we should be ashamed of Western civilization. I feel our first responsibility is to protect the artist. After that, we have to provide excellence and, above all, accessibility.

Opera News, November:24.

David Hockney
Painter

3

I think you can't have art without play. Picasso always understood that. I think you can't have much human activity of any kind without a sense of playfulness. I don't know of any good art that's boring—in music, poetry or painting. Isn't that why Shakespeare is so exciting?

Interview/
The Christian Science Monitor,
12-10:13.

Christopher Hogwood
Orchestra Conductor

4

I think . . . of the classical arts rather like hospitals, in the sense that hospitals fill a crucial need in a civilized society. The classical arts nurture and heal the spirit in a comparable way. They are comparably indispensable.

Interview/
The Washington Post, 6-26:(B)6.

Thomas P. F. Hoving
Former director,
Metropolitan Museum of Art,
New York, N.Y.

5

The craft movement . . . is the fine-arts movement of the late 20th century. Fifty years from now people will way, "Oops, crafts were really the fine arts of the time." Five years ago, the Louvre put on a show called "Magicians of the Earth," which gathered work from so-called crafts-people from all over the world and mixed them with contemporary artists and painters. There was no competition at all; these guys from Patagonia and the Eskimos whipped all the high-priced, fancy painters and sculptors right off the map.

Interview, Boston, Mass./
The Christian Science Monitor,
1-20:14.

Yousuf Karsh
Portrait photographer

6

I wouldn't have minded photographing the most disapproved-of person in the world. Because I'm a historian. I'm not a judge. I'm not a critic of character. I would photograph anyone—anyone, absolutely, without any reservation. It would be wonderful to have photographed some

WHAT THEY SAID IN 1993

of these questionable characters throughout history.

Interview, Ottawa, Canada/
Los Angeles Times, 3-16:(H)4.

Jonathan Katz
Executive director,
National Assembly
of State Arts Agencies

1

[Criticizing Congressional action that could cut NEA arts funding by 5 percent]: It is disappointing to see this kind of action because it doesn't have any of the effect that is intended—balancing the [Federal] budget and fiscal accountability. It has the opposite effect, considering the Endowment is distinguished among Federal agencies with a 20 percent return in jobs, contracts and services.

July 15/
The Washington Post, 7-16:(C)2.

Christopher Knight
Art critic,
"Los Angeles Times"

2

[In the arts,] you still run up against the sissy factor: Culture is only paid lip service because it's considered the insignificant province of women and gays, which is what allowed [political commentator] Patrick Buchanan and his ilk to beat up on the NEA.

Newsweek, 1-18:19.

Leon Kossoff
British painter

3

Initially, I pick my subjects because I find them visually exciting, but after I've drawn and painted something for a while I often discover that it played some role in my life. Take Christ Church [which he has painted frequently], for instance. I spent my early childhood not far from Christ Church and must've passed it countless times when I was very young; and I'm sure my

desire to paint it related to a need to work through something to do with my childhood. Exactly what that is or why I want to address it, I don't know. When I began working on this church, I thought it would take me two years, but I wound up spending seven years on it—and I still don't feel that I know that church. One never really finishes with a subject; what happens is I'll feel I've examined it sufficiently for the time being, and that feeling creates room in my mind for another subject to creep in.

Interview, Los Angeles/
Los Angeles Times, 5-13:(F)9.

Harvey Lichtenstein
President and executive producer,
Brooklyn (N.Y.) Academy of Music

4

I don't think of myself as making trends at all. My watchword has been "follow the artists." They're the ones in the front lines doing the work. What I want *not* to do is to get involved in ideology in the arts. Real artists create work in many forms—and one is not better than another.

Dance Magazine, March:64.

Roy Lichtenstein
Painter

5

My style [of painting] is an unartistic style that imitates printing and mechanical sources. It's supposed to look like a fake . . . A head composed of lines or dots or yellow hair is completely unrealistic, but it's taken not only as real, but people impute feelings to these configurations. They think, this is a sad girl or a happy man, without realizing how artificial the whole thing is.

Interview, New York, N.Y./
The Christian Science Monitor,
10-19:12.

Michael Medved
Film critic;
Co-host, "Sneak Previews," PBS-TV

6

There is this idea in Hollywood, which I hear constantly, that it's the obligation of the artist to

(MICHAEL MEDVED)

challenge society, to shake it up, to be a heretic. This is part of the 20th-century disease. This idea in modernism that art must be harsh, shocking, horrifying has produced the degeneration of contemporary art in almost every field. And now it has reached popular culture. As recently as 1939, the movie business still held up the *old* ideal of artistic achievement, which was touching people's hearts, touching people's spirits, giving people hope, optimism and, at times, tragedy. They always sought to connect with an audience. Now the most respected films are often very expensive films that have no chance of making a dime since they refuse to make that connection with the audience.

Interview/
Christianity Today, 3-8:24.

Ivo Pogorelich
Pianist

1

I personally do not believe in the concept of the *Wunderkind.* There are no self-made men in [the] arts. You must have the knowledge that you inherit from your teachers and the masters of the past; only then can you begin building on that foundation. You have to be able to re-create before you can create.

Interview, Pasadena, Calif./
Los Angeles Times, 1-13:(F)12.

Ned Rifkin
Director,
High Museum, Atlanta, Ga.

2

People come to expect these big [art] shows, when they may be missing profound experiences they can get from smaller exhibitions, from permanent collections or modest loan exhibitions of very special material. It feeds that part of people's need not to miss the big movie of the summer when there may be this wonderful little foreign film down at an old movie house.

The New York Times, 9-7:(B)2.

Sebastiao Salgado
Photojournalist

3

It's not the photographer who really does the picture, but the person in front of you who gives a gift. And it's your relationship that makes things come out stronger.

Interview/People, 5-17:96.

Michael Shapiro
Director,
Los Angeles County (Calif.)
Museum of Art

4

Museums are a reflection of the cultures in which they reside; whatever challenges we face, they are not unique to ourselves but reflective of a set of national issues that even the best-endowed American museums are facing.

Interview/
Los Angeles Times, 4-12:(F)5.

James D. Wolfensohn
Chairman,
Kennedy Center
for the Performing Arts,
Washington, D.C.

5

[We must] make sure that the next generation is properly educated in the performing arts. The point of view which I take is that the arts for our kids are not an optional extra; they're essential to their development. It's the one thing that transcends cultural backgrounds. It's one thing which is unifying.

Interview, Washington, D.C./
The New York Times, 4-5:(C)10.

Udo Zimmermann
Composer, Conductor;
Intendant, Leipzig Opera
(Germany)

6

It's important to understand that art is not just a metaphor for Utopia; it's an actual life aid. It protects our inner world. It's a part of our culture, a part of human life.

Opera News, August:25.

Journalism

Cathleen Black
President,
Newspaper Association
of America

1

[On newspapers' entry into electronic services because of competition and a decline in advertising-revenue growth]: The last three years were a clarion call to editors and publishers to understand the changing economics of the marketplace. That tremendous jolt has encouraged people to expand and explore because the old way of doing business . . . is not enough.

The Christian Science Monitor,
12-23:8.

David Broder
Political columnist,
"The Washington Post"

2

[On the importance of the White House press corps to the President]: You can talk to Omaha or Portland or Los Angeles on any given day, [but] if you want to get your story out day by day, you really have to deal with the White House reporters.

Los Angeles Times, 9-15:(A)11.

Tom Brokaw
Anchorman, NBC News

3

[On CBS using Dan Rather and Connie Chung as co-anchors on their evening newscast]: It's not my style to comment on what the other networks are doing. I don't have a problem emotionally with a co-anchor. But I don't think there's room for it in 22 minutes. One of the reasons these [network evening newscasts] work is that you've got a single authority figure—male or female— that drives through the 22 minutes. This back-and-forth, back-and-forth between co-anchors gets in the way of a strong linear newscast.

Interview, New York/
Los Angeles Times, 9-9:(F)11.

4

The biggest change [in TV news in the past 10 years] is that there's more of it on the air. Second, there's more competition. Third, technology makes it possible to get on the air from almost anywhere at any time. The fourth big change is the financial pressures. And they all play against each other. Because the competition is greater and because the overall network TV business is not what it once was, we have to be more resourceful now and we have to work harder at story selection.

Interview,
New York, N.Y./
Los Angeles Times, 9-9:(F)1.

Ronald Brownstein
Political reporter,
"Los Angeles Times"

5

In the same way that CNN has speeded up the news cycle, [weekend TV political talk shows have created] an incredible acceleration of the judgment cycle. Everybody is competing . . . to render the definitive judgment.

Los Angeles Times, 9-16:(A)22.

Hodding Carter
News columnist
and commentator

6

The top journalists move in packs with the affluent and powerful in Washington. They swarm with them in the summer to every agreeable spot on the Eastern Seaboard. When any three or four of them sit down together on a television talk show, it is not difficult to remember that the least-well-paid of these pontificators make at least six times more each year than the average American family.

Interview/
Los Angeles Times, 4-1:(A)19.

Henry G. Cisneros
*Secretary of Housing
and Urban Development
of the United States*

1

[Criticizing the press for reporting new allegations that President Clinton was involved in extra-marital affairs when he was Arkansas Governor and improperly used the power of his office to cover them up]: One really has to ask the fundamental question of the press itself: "What is the point here? What are we trying to do?" Is it . . . just to search and destroy, slash and burn, and follow every lead that ever comes along about anyone in public life? If so . . . we do great damage to the Presidency and, in so doing, to the country.

*Broadcast interview/
"Meet the Press," NBC-TV, 12-26.*

Eleanor Clift
*White House correspondent,
"Newsweek" magazine*

2

[On President Clinton's negative press coverage early in his Administration]: [The] overall tone of the press coverage was about 30 percent more negative than it needed to be because of the animosity that was felt toward Clinton and the people around him [due to the Administration's seeming anti-press attitude]. The level of hostility in the pressroom, I think, was extraordinary.

Los Angeles Times, 9-17:(A)18.

Bill Clinton
President of the United States

3

I have long since given up the thought that I could disabuse some of you [in the press] of turning any substantive decision [I make] into anything but political process.

*To the White House press corps/
USA Today, 6-18:(A)13.*

4

[On his frequent appearances on TV interview programs and at other public venues while holding fewer press conferences]: You know why I can stiff you [the news media] on the press conferences? Because [TV talk-show host] Larry King liberated me from you by giving me to the American people directly.

*Before Radio and Television
Correspondents Association/
Los Angeles Times, 9-15:(A)11.*

Michael K. Deaver
*Former Director
of Communications
for the President
of the United States
(Ronald Reagan)*

5

[The Clinton Administration's] inattention to the White House press corps is coming home to roost. It's one thing to deal with the [out-of-town] media, but you'd better deal with the people who are at your back door 24 hours a day. If not, when you have a problem, the media are ready to jump on it.

*U.S. News & World Report,
6-7:26.*

Umberto Eco
Italian author

6

The press is becoming more and more sensationalist and is becoming enslaved to the TV. In Italy, all the newspapers are becoming like the [sensationalist] *New York Post*. They are no longer interested in what happens in the world but only in what the other media have said about the world: the media speaking about the media . . . This is masturbatory. It is sexual perversion.

World Press Review, November:30.

Stuart Ewen
*Professor of communications,
Hunter College*

7

We're witnessing the development of global news networks that are beholden to no particular nation or state. I don't think we know yet what the cultural implications of that are.

Los Angeles Times, 7-18:(Calendar)85.

Clay Felker
Former editor,
"New York" magazine

1

My philosophy [as a magazine editor] is that you have faith in the writer's point of view. You pick the writers you believe in and give them their freedom. As opposed to most editors who want to mold the writers into what they want, make them a tool of the editors.

Interview, New York, N.Y./
The Washington Post, 3-27:(G)4.

Max Frankel
Executive editor,
"The New York Times"

2

[On criticism that *The New York Times* printed a front-page article saying that dresses were getting shorter]: Don't tell me that's not important. When hemlines go up, industries rise and fall. Why isn't that news? Because somebody didn't get up and have a press conference yesterday and announce that as of tomorrow morning skirts are going up? To catch a trend at the right moment is the most important thing we [in the media] can do.

Esquire, March:108.

Dorothy Gilliam
Columnist,
"The Washington Post";
President,
National Association
of Black Journalists

3

[Saying there is a lack of opportunity for blacks to climb the ladder in journalism promotions and management]: White editors talk and talk of diversity, but they don't walk the walk. Some of them are not willing to share power. That's really what we're talking about. You've got blacks in top positions everywhere else. Why is journalism so slow?

The Washington Post,
8-14:(A)6.

Pete Hamill
Author, Journalist

4

One of the great dangers of journalism is that you see so much horror that the true emotional impact begins to dissipate. You see two murders, and the subject is murder. But if you see 2,000 murders, you develop a certain amount of callousness, and you begin to handle them in a professional way. You have to somehow keep an amateur's eye alive and use the professionalism to be able to convey that. It's tricky. I don't cover many homicides anymore. Not because I think homicide isn't an important subject, but because I've seen so many of them that I'm afraid of that part of it. I've seen so many I don't know if I can bring anything fresh to it.

Interview/
Writer's Digest, September:46.

Hendrik Hertzberg
Executive editor,
"The New Yorker" magazine

5

The demand for definite-sounding, pugnacious opinions [by journalists on the political scene] far outstrips the supply of same that are grounded in any kind of reality. There's a huge sucking vacuum of op-ed pages and [political] TV shows . . . This huge maw has to be fed.

Los Angeles Times, 9-16:(A)22.

Brit Hume
White House correspondent,
ABC News

6

We live in a time when the worst thing that can be said about a journalist in Washington is that he or she is not "tough."

Los Angeles Times, 9-15:(A)10.

Ellen Hume
Executive director,
Barone Center on the Press,
Politics and Public Policy,
Harvard University

7

The news was much more upbeat in the 1940s and 1950s when [the] nation's political leaders

(ELLEN HUME)

were treated by the journalists with deference and respect. What changed everything were the lies of Watergate, the Vietnam war, the Iran-contra scandal and Iraqgate. Now journalists are locked into the negative assumption that the government and political leaders are lying much of the time . . . [There is a constant] cynical framework [that] doubtlessly feeds the public's cynicism and distrust of its political leadership—and of the piranha press corps which seems willing to devour anyone, at any time, for frivolous infractions as well as for serious ones.

At University of Texas/
Los Angeles Times, 3-31:(A)17.

John King
White House correspondent,
Associated Press

1

I spend enormous amounts of mental energy to break a story that, three days later, no one cares who got it first. Could I do better journalism if I didn't, every now and then, have to go with reckless abandon to get it five minutes before somebody else? Yeah, I could. But it's part of how we get our charge . . . It's how we make names for ourselves. It's probably childish, but I get a kick when CNN has to interrupt is programming to say, "According to the Associated Press, [President] Clinton is going to . . . "

Los Angeles Times, 9-17:(A)18.

Maxwell King
Executive editor,
"Philadelphia Inquirer"

2

Newspaper editors [are] groping for ways to be more relevant to readers, [and] all sorts of dumbing down of newspapers is taking place, all kinds of silly gimmicks are being employed . . . I think it's real simple . . . If you want to be relevant to readers, you've got to write about what really matters to them.

Interview/
Los Angeles Times, 4-1:(A)18.

Michael Kinsley
Co-host,
"Crossfire," CNN-TV

3

[Arguing against government officials attending dinners given by the press]: [It is] ethically corrupt for the press. Here are these people you're supposed to be covering, at least skeptically, and you're brown-nosing them to "please come to our table so we can impress our boss."

The Washington Post, 3-11:(C)9.

Edward Kosner
Editor,
"Esquire" magazine

4

Magazines that have been around for a while have to find their voice and adapt to new times. The ones that don't adapt successfully don't survive. The subjects have to be right. The writers have to be right. The covers have to be interesting.

On his being named editor of "Esquire,"
Sept. 21/
The Washington Post, 9-22:(C)1.

Bill Kovach
Curator, Nieman Foundation,
Harvard University;
Former journalist

5

A newspaper is a habit, an intimate relationship. It's one of the few things from the outside that people will carry into the bathroom with them. So that newspaper has got to be comfortable. The more it has to reintroduce itself—[to change, to try to increase readership]—the more its readers get nervous. And that is dangerous.

Esquire, March:106.

Andrew Lack
President, NBC News

6

I think all of the broadcast networks have taken a bit of a shot from CNN. CNN has gone to town

367

(ANDREW LACK)

making deals for coverage where we were concentrating on other areas of our business. I think CNN has done a very good job of getting the word out that when there's a crisis, they have the news. But I don't think they've done as good a job at programming their news. We're producing news as well as gathering it. Why shouldn't NBC or ABC or CBS News have a leg up in this area? . . . Part of the reason for cutbacks at the networks in recent years was that there was too much fat for too few outlets . . . It's up to us to find ways to program the news.

Interview,
New York, N.Y./
Los Angeles Times, 5-14:(F)20.

Bob Lichter
Director,
Center for Media
and Public Affairs

1

[On the trend toward gossip, scandals and controversy aimed at journalists and others in the news media]: This is a continuation of what happens when journalists become public personalities. The news is a part of pop culture now, so the people who bring you the news are pop-culture figures.

The New York Times, 10-18:(C)7.

Robert K. Massie
Historian, Biographer

2

My problem when I was a journalist was always that I didn't have enough space. I always wanted to go deeper into the causes and describe the personalities more completely. Of course, in *Newsweek* I couldn't do that. So I moved on to magazines where I could do more, where I could write 4,000 or 5,000 words. But I still didn't have enough space. So I was sort of a goner as far as journalism was concerned.

Interview/
Writer's Digest, February:37.

Susan Milligan
Reporter,
"New York Daily News"

3

[On White House press briefings]: They won't tell you the simplest things. They wouldn't even tell us their salaries, which is public record. George [Stephanopoulos, President Clinton's Communications Director] will never answer the question you ask. He just answers the question he wants to answer, which I guess is standard flack mode.

The Washington Post, 2-17:(A)17.

Andrea Mitchell
White House correspondent,
NBC News

4

[On the Clinton Administration's dealings with the press]: There's definitely a generation gap between some of the reporters and [Clinton's] staff. [The White House staff is] younger, they're looser, they're less impressed with the way things have always been done in Washington. They know what works for Bill Clinton, they've figured out how to use him as a salesman and they've also figured out how to go over the heads of the Washington press corps.

The Washington Post, 4-1:(D)2.

Dee Dee Myers
Press Secretary to
President of the United States
Bill Clinton

5

[On questions regarding her stature at the White House, which seems to some observers to be lower than that of White House Communications Director George Stephanopoulos, who is handling some of the traditional duties of a Presidential Press Secretary]: It's interesting to me that people have so much trouble with this relationship. They can only understand it through the prism of their experience. This isn't how it was done in the [George] Bush Administration and therefore "there's something wrong with it."

The Washington Post, 4-1:(D)2.

Allen H. Neuharth
Founder, "USA Today";
Chairman, Freedom Foundation

1

There aren't many readers left who will read a dull gray newspaper . . . The younger generation . . . wants a maximum of news and entertainment in a minimum amount of space and time.
Los Angeles Times, 1-26:(E)2.

2

There is no question that the general public is far more disenchanted with the media in general—and has been for the last several years—than at any time in my memory . . . I'm on the speaking circuit . . . journalism schools, university campuses, everything from furniture manufacturers and sellers to accountants, meatpackers . . . and without an exception, the thing that those people want to complain about or talk about or argue about is the bias of the media.
Interview/
Los Angeles Times, 3-31:(A)1,17.

W. Russell Neuman
Professor of communications,
Fletcher School of Law,
Tufts University

3

[Saying electronic technology will replace the daily newspaper in the future]: This will be such a cultural shift that it may be that the current generation of professional journalists and publishers who have ink in their veins will have to die off before the next generation realizes that the newspaper industry is no longer a newspaper industry.
The Christian Science Monitor,
8-26:13.

Mitch Odero
Deputy editor,
"The Standard" (Kenya)

4

Sedition laws still exist [in Kenya] which say the journalism profession shouldn't cause disaffection within the government. The media,

which interprets a multi-party system as checks and balances, therefore, go all out with criticism. Then that amounts to causing disaffection against the government and has landed many editors in court.
The Christian Science Monitor,
9-30:19.

Geneva Overholser
Editor,
"Des Moines Register"

5

One of the pieces of the conventional wisdom these days is that we [in the press] used to be objective and now we're not. I reject that emphatically. I think the people who are saying that aren't looking at the "used to be." I also think that they tend to be responding to very successful manipulation of public opinion about the media by . . . politicians.
Interview/
Los Angeles Times, 3-31:(A)17.

Maynard Parker
Editor,
"Newsweek" magazine

6

There's no question that in Washington, the press—and particularly the big mules of the press, particularly the White House press corps—want to be catered to [by those in government].
Los Angeles Times, 9-17:(A)18.

Howell Raines
Editorial-page editor,
"The New York Times"

7

[On criticism of his blunt editorials which some see as overly harsh on those who are the targets]: I understand when people don't want to see their names in the paper as advocates of a bad idea, but the fact is it's not personal. It is not harmful to amuse the reader with a turn of phrase or witty line, as long as it's fair comment . . . In the newsroom you really work hard to separate opinion from what you're doing. People outside the business may say we don't do it very well, and no one's perfect; but on this paper and many other papers it is a serious undertaking. [However,] editorial writing is a polemical exercise. It is the celebration of opinion.

Interview, New York, N.Y./
The Washington Post, 5-10:(B)4.

Dan Rather
Anchorman, CBS News

1

There is some danger . . . in [being] sucked into believing that it is our job [in the news media] to be popular. We all understand that you want to sell newspapers [and] I want people to watch CBS News programs; but it's worth remembering that if you do your job as a conscientious professional journalist . . . you are going to have to ask unpopular questions, you are going to have to report on stories that a lot of people don't particularly want to see or hear. I think the soul, the very core, of . . . a journalist is to understand that that's his duty. I hear an awful lot of talk about popularity in journalism these days and not quite enough talk about duty.

Interview/
Los Angeles Times, 3-31:(A)17.

2

[On public distrust of the news media]: I don't think it helps anybody in journalism to point fingers and make accusations along the lines of, "Your end of the boat is sinking." There's no such thing as "Your end of the boat is sinking." If the boat is sinking, then we're all sinking—the boat in this case being our reputation, our credibility with the public.

Interview/
Los Angeles Times, 4-1:(A)18.

3

[In TV news,] it's the ratings, stupid, don't you know? They've got us putting more fuzz and wuzz on the air, cop-shop stuff, so as to compete not with other news programs but with entertainment programs—including those posing as news programs—for dead bodies, mayhem and lurid tales.

Newsweek, 10-11:19.

Eugene Roberts
Former editor,
"The Philadelphia Inquirer"

4

[Saying newspapers are cutting back too much on costs]: I think we're at a crossroads. Newspaper companies have got to come to realize that you can't increase profits and increase profits into infinity without putting your franchise into jeopardy. And that's exactly what many newspapers have become, franchises . . . It's folly and lunacy even to think that readers don't notice . . . And furthermore, it's more than a question of noticing. When they think their newspaper is less complete than it once was, they become less dependent on it. They think, "Well, I can't really rely on my local paper for news."

Los Angeles Times, 1-26:(E)2.

Walter Robinson
City editor,
"The Boston Globe"

5

[On his newspaper's being sold to *The New York Times*]: Being owned by *The New York Times* is about as good as you can do, but being independent is a lot better and we have lost that.

June 10/
Los Angeles Times, 6-11:(A)17.

Larry J. Sabato
Professor of government,
University of Virginia

6

[On President Clinton's poor relations with the press]: How in the world did it come to this so quickly? A very high degree of mutual hostility has developed in record time. The President has obvious contempt for the press—not just anger. In return, many of the senior press people are furious, and all of these things matter.

Los Angeles Times, 5-28:(A)10.

Van Gordon Sauter
President, Fox News

1

We're [the news media] no longer as trust-worthy as we used to be; we're no longer as credible as we used to be; we're no longer as committed to the viewer or reader as we used to be. There is [between the press and the public] a repository of good will, but it's very much on loan, and I think some people are really beginning to doubt the value of that loan . . . Look at *Newsweek* magazine. Look at *Time* magazine. The subjectivity that just runs through them I find absolutely stunning. If you look at *The New York Times, The Boston Globe, The Washington Post* . . . the [political] liberalism of those papers manifests itself in their news columns, not just on their editorial pages.

Interview/
Los Angeles Times, 3-31:(A)17.

2

[Many in the news media have become so] arrogant . . . so damned stuffy and self-important and self-righteous and, in effect, sort of removed from the daily concerns of people that it was easy for people to go to other sources [of news] that just seem to be more real. [Many traditional journalists today] think that they somehow have been anointed by some higher power to bring "The Truth" to the peasantry. And the peasantry is saying, "Up yours."

Interview/
Los Angeles Times, 4-1:(A)19.

Yuri Shchekoehikhin
Journalist,
"Literaturnaya Gazeta"
(Russia)

3

[Saying that before government censorship of newspapers was lifted several years ago, Russian journalism was more interesting because of the bitter relationship between the government and the media]: For the greater part of my journalistic career, I had been so used to the fact that without the censor's stamp no issue of the newspaper could be printed, that the past few uncensored years have seemed a lot less significant and much less rich in impressions.

U.S. News & World Report,
11-29:49.

Richard M. Smith
Editor-in-chief,
"Newsweek" magazine

4

There are so many pundits [in journalism] now that the race to be first with a judgment is a pretty frenetic one. Particularly if you look at the world of television political talk [shows] these days, the emphasis is on who can say the most dramatic, outrageous, "bold" comment that attracts the most attention . . . The ability to get genuine news scoops out of the White House, with however many hundreds of people are covering that place, is limited. It's much easier [for a journalist] to make the most outrageous analytical point in hopes of getting noticed for that.

Los Angeles Times, 9-16:(A)22.

James Squires
Former editor,
"Chicago Tribune"

5

Today, with few exceptions, the final responsibility for newspaper content rests with the business executive in charge of the company, not the editor.

Los Angeles, Calif./
Los Angeles Times, 1-26:(E)2.

George Steinbrenner
Owner, New York "Yankees"
baseball team

6

I remember something my father told me. He said, "Remember, the most perishable item on the back porch is not the milk and not the eggs. Those things will last three days. The most perishable item is the newspaper. What's a big story today is gone tomorrow."

Interview/
Los Angeles Times, 9-28:(C)2.

George Stephanopoulos
Director of Communications
for President
of the United States
Bill Clinton

1

[On press briefings at which he presides]: You just have to get into the spirit of it when they ask a question where they know you're not going to answer. It's like an existential dilemma. The risk is that you look stupid, but that doesn't matter. You can't announce something before the President has announced it.

The Washington Post, 2-17:(A)17.

Mitchell Stephens
Chairman,
Department of journalism,
New York University

2

[On the recent embarrassment of NBC News for using staged and deceptive reporting]: What happened at NBC was very good. Every now and then journalists need a reminder to be straight, to stick to the facts, and not do things on the cheap. That's especially important in television news now, where competitive pressures are very great.

The Christian Science Monitor,
3-9:13.

Richard B. Stolley
Editorial director,
Time, Inc.

3

[On *People* magazine, of which he was the first managing editor when it was founded in 1974]: I knew we would be dealing with what in those early days was going to be pretty hairy stuff. It was a new kind of intimate reporting, with information about prominent men and women in all fields that other magazines were not getting and probably would not print if they did. This kind of personal reporting has become so prevalent today that it's hard to remember, or even believe, that it did not really exist before, at least not in the way we proposed to do it . . . *People* made the responsible but unrelenting study of personality and behavior a legitimate and even essential part of American journalism. I say that with full knowledge of how some of our competitors have debased the craft we developed and perfected. We are not responsible for what our success has encouraged others to fail at. Week after week, *People* has made the contribution to our society and our profession that serious journalists want to make.

People, 2-15:1.

Gay Talese
Author; Former journalist

4

We [at *The New York Times,* where he worked as a reporter in the 1950s and '60s] knew we were above the people who were running things. What we had written would last in the world maybe eleven minutes, but what a terrific thing those eleven minutes were. You were making what happened news. It was the greatest job in the the world, the happiest time in my life. Let me tell you, when I left that building, I wept.

Esquire, March:106.

Elizabeth Thoman
Founder, Center for
Media and Values

5

[On TV "reality" series]: These shows have all the ambience of a news show. They portray themselves as news. They have anchors or hosts or voiceovers. That's not like a movie, where a story unfolds. The reason that it's hard for people to distinguish [between news and "reality" programs] is that it took a decade for the broadcast news world to slowly disintegrate. Up until the '70s, news was still considered a public service to inform the nation.

Interview/
Los Angeles Times, 3-13:(F)15.

Helen Thomas
White House correspondent,
United Press International

6

[Saying the Clinton Administration should allow government officials to attend dinners

(HELEN THOMAS)

given by the press, which is now prohibited because of ethical considerations]: These are evenings of really good fellowship. We do mix and mingle. It's important that we [in the press] get to know these [government] people. To think of people as friends and colleagues, why not? Do you have to make an enemy of everyone?

The Washington Post, 3-11:(C)9.

1

[On the Clinton Administration's stand-offish attitude toward the press]: We have no sense of the White House anymore, no sense of the vibes, the spirit. Everything is closed off.

U.S. News & World Report,
6-7:26.

2

In this age of instant communications, [reporters must be able to reach the Presidential Press Secretary or his deputy] at any hour. There are some questions that really won't wait. We don't walk into their offices if the doors are closed; [but] we wait till they come out and try to ambush them or buttonhole them.

Los Angeles Times, 9-15:(A)11.

Ed Turner
Executive vice president,
Cable News Network

3

[Thirty-five years ago,] we [in the news media] were then highly regarded [by the public]. We were looked up to. We were the subjects of admiration, sometimes even awe. Now, we are often despised.

Interview/
Los Angeles Times, 3-31:(A)1.

R. Emmett Tyrrell
Editor,
"American Spectator"

4

When I walk into a roomful of journalists, what they espouse [political liberalism] is so similar

that I could die from the boredom of it. One of the problems with journalists in this town [Washington] is they all seek approval. I'm delighted [that as editor of the conservative *American Spectator*] I never have to seek approval. Every once in a while, I sort of sneak out and seek disapproval. Who's going to fire me?

Interview/
The Washington Post, 12-24:(C)2.

Eudora Welty
Author

5

[*Life* magazine once] asked me if I would go on a news story [as a photographer], and I did it, and they used the pictures. But I *hated* the experience. It amounted to using somebody, the subject of the picture. It was so heartless, and I remember sending them the whole roll of film— you couldn't choose which picture they would use—and I wrote and asked them, "Please, use something nice." I was completely out of my element . . . The fault was not *Life* magazine's; the fault was journalism itself, which demanded things I didn't want to give to it. I felt that I was hurting somebody. I didn't like being part of it . . . I just wasn't made for journalism.

Interview,
Jackson, Miss., September/
American Way, 12-1:96.

Judy Woodruff
Anchorwoman,
Cable News Network

6

Women are judged more on appearance than men are, and in television [news] it's exaggerated. If I'm doing an interview and my hair looks messy, or my makeup is too made up or not enough made up, or my lipstick is the wrong color, or my earrings look weird, people notice. I'm conscious of that.

Interview/
The Washington Post, 6-7:(D)4.

373

Literature

Maya Angelou
Author, Poet

1

Poetry is really closer to our hearts and our tongue than we admit. But we employ poetry at critical moments of our lives. When we fall in love, we employ poetry to try to explain ourselves. Not everybody has written poetry, but just the way we talk to explain ourselves is poetic. When we are distressed, it is poetry that we employ. When we make supplication to God, in meditation or in praise, we employ poetry. It is so close to us, and it allows us to describe ourselves at our most profound and our most elemental.

Interview/
USA Today, 1-18:(A)13.

2

[On her writing a poem for President Clinton's inauguration]: The writing of poetry is so private, so reclusive, one has to really withdraw inside one's self to a place that is inviolate. But when a whole country knows that you are writing a poem, it is very hard to withdraw. Even on an airplane, people would pass by my seat and say: "Mornin', finish your poem yet?"

Interview/Ebony, April:72.

John Banville
Irish author

3

What I try to do is to give to prose the kind of denseness and thickness that poetry has. [W. H.] Auden said you cannot half-read a poem. You can look at a picture and be thinking of something else. You can listen to a piece of music— you can be at the opera and be making love to somebody in a box. But a poem—you either read it or you don't. I would like to think that with my novels, you either read them or you don't.

Interview, Cork City, Ireland/
Publishers Weekly, 11-15:56.

Daniel J. Boorstin
Historian;
Librarian-emeritus of Congress
of the United States

4

In some ways it's more daunting to write a non-fiction work than fiction because if you write a fictional work, you can keep the reader in suspense as to whether the central figure is a hero or a villain. But if you're writing non-fiction, everybody knows how it turned out, so you have a problem of creating drama and suspense.

Interview/Humanities, Jan.-Feb.:6.

Robert Boswell
Author

5

The writer's job is to embrace the next impossible task . . . I'm just trying to be honest and decent, to be true to the people I love and the things I hold dear, which includes literature—*the story.* Because I believe that storytelling is crucial to humans for existence, that in very complex ways it helps us to see our own lives with more clarity.

Interview, Las Cruces, N.M./
Publishers Weekly, 1-25:66.

Paul Brodeur
Author

6

[On publishers selling books at deep discount to large store chains]: It's so shortsighted and stupid, it hurts to think about it. God help the publishers if some of these chains go out of business. Where are they going to be, having discounted all this stuff like peanut butter? They are crazy not to do everything in their power to keep the quality bookstores that we've got in business, because that's how you encourage reading. But look who owns these [publishers]—big, vast combines interested in the bottom line. That's why there is not editing anymore. I'm just a writer, but you can't find any senior editors in

(PAUL BRODEUR)

New York, who have been in the business 25 years, and don't in their heart of hearts deplore what has happened to the industry.

Interview, Cape Cod, Mass./
Publishers Weekly, 8-30:71.

Frederick Busch
Author

1

Conduct your fiction [writing] as you would a love affair: Write fast and furiously and hard. But then, later, come back to the work and rewrite it with the cold precision—the awful distance—of a divorce lawyer.

The Writer, August:3.

Robert Olen Butler
Author

2

[On his winning the 1993 Pulitzer Prize in fiction]: I've been publishing books since 1981. I've had a loyal, important but very small following who've really listened to me, but I haven't had many sales, and I still don't get reviewed very widely. So a long time ago, I learned that the only way to avoid madness was to just turn on the computer every morning and do my work and not think about the prizes, the critics, how many readers there are. So then I'm in a position when this sort of thing happens, it comes as an absolute shock, on the one hand, and then on the other hand, to my deepest self it seems like the most natural thing in the world.

Interview, Lake Charles, La./
The New York Times, 4-20:(B)1.

Rita Dove
Poet Laureate
of the United States

3

Poetry is language at its most distilled and most powerful. It's like a bouillon cube: You carry it around and then it nourishes you when you need it.

Charlottesville, Va., May 18/
Los Angeles Times, 5-19:(A)4.

4

When a poem moves you, it moves you in a way that leaves you speechless. Poems, if they're really wonderful poems, have used the best possible words and in the best possible order, and anything you say about them seems like a desecration . . . A good poem is like a bouillon cube. It's concentrated, you carry it around with you, and it nourishes you when you need it.

Interview/Time, 10-18:89.

5

I'm hoping that by the end of my term people will think of a Poet Laureate as someone who's out there with her sleeves rolled up and working, not sitting in an ivory tower looking out at the Potomac [River].

Interview/Time, 10-18:89.

Steve Erickson
Author, Critic

6

I never set out to be a critic. I always wanted to be a novelist. However, I think it behooves a critic to have done something creative and to have been subjected to the judgments of other people—whether the endeavor turns out to be successful or not.

Interview, West Hollywood, Calif./
Publishers Weekly, 3-22:60.

Susan Faludi
Author

7

Having a "career" always sounded to me too much like a way of fitting into the system. Whereas I've always seen writing as my avenue for rattling the system. That's success to me—the degree to which you shake the pillars.

Working Woman, November:52.

Ernest J. Gaines
Author

8

Wallace Stegner once asked me for whom I write, and I told him: no one. He said if he put a

(ERNEST J. GAINES)

gun to me and forced an answer, what would I say. If he did that, I told him, I'd probably say, I write for the black youth of the South, to make them aware of who they are. Who else, he asked. I said the white youth of the South, to make them aware that unless they understand their black neighbors, they cannot understand themselves. But, in fact, I have no intention of addressing any group over another. It's dangerous for writers to think of their audience. I try to write as well as I can; that's tough enough.

Interview, Chattanooga, Tenn./
Publishers Weekly, 5-24:64.

Merrill Joan Gerber
Author

1

[On the wide range of styles and media she has written in]: I've been criticized for spreading myself too thin . . . But you can't say everything you know in everything you write. If you want to write about the Jewish experience in the New World, then you write a novel. If you want to write in a lighter vein and make money, then you write for *Redbook* [magazine]. If you want to write about an art fair, then you write for the local newspaper. If you have three children you need to put through school, then you write young-adult books.

Interview, Sierra Madre, Calif./
Publishers Weekly, 11-8:54.

Kaye Gibbons
Author

2

As a writer, it's my job to come up with 300 pages or so every two years. Each time I begin, I know it's going to happen, but I'm scared it won't. It's working with that element of fear that keeps a book going.

Interview/
Publishers Weekly, 2-8:61.

John Grisham
Author

3

[On writing]: You have to start with an opening so gripping that the reader becomes involved. In

the middle of the book, you must sustain the narrative tension, keep things stirred up. The end should be so compelling that people will stay up all night to finish the book. You must have those three elements: how it starts, the end, and what happens in the middle.

Interview, Oxford, Miss./
Writers Digest, July:34.

David Halberstam
Author

4

[On life in the U.S. 60 years from now, in 2053]: As the literacy rate declines in this country, more and more people are writing books. Are we approaching the moment where more people will write books than will be able to read them?

Interview/
U.S. News & World Report,
10-25:72.

Pete Hamill
Author, Journalist

5

I think that writers have to read differently from other people. They're reading as predators. They're reading to consume this thing. People always mistake that and say, "Well, he's influenced by this guy." Everybody is influenced by everything they ever read. If I had to type my influences down, you would have a 45-page list of names. I think that's true of any writer.

Interview/
Writer's Digest, September:47.

Kathryn Harrison
Author

6

If you're not aware of the sheer volume of books coming out, you have no idea beforehand that it's not even 15 minutes of fame; it's more like 15 nanoseconds of attention that your work will get in the marketplace.

Interview/
Publishers Weekly, 3-1:34.

Barbara Kingsolver
Author

1

Fiction creates empathy, and empathy is the antidote to meanness of spirit. Non-fiction can tell you about the plight of working people, of single mothers; but in a novel you become the character, touch what she touches, struggle with her self-doubt. Then, when you go back to your own life, something inside you has maybe shifted a little.

The Writer, December:3.

Robert K. Massie
Historian, Biographer

2

History consists of an extraordinarily fascinating series of stories. Any historian can manage to give us the significance of the event. But to recreate the flavor, color, immediacy and suspense that the events actually had, it is necessary to work very hard to write well. History is yesterday's news. But when we write about history, it should create all the emotions in the reader that it actually created in the people who were involved. The historian should attempt to make the reader feel the same emotions that the people who participated felt. That's what I try to do.

Interview/
Writer's Digest, February:35.

Michael Mewshaw
Author, Journalist

3

I'm often asked where I get my ideas. I respond that books and articles aren't made out of ideas, they're made out of words. The primary criterion for being a book sports-writer is the same one as for being any kind of writer: to be good with language, to know how to use words, to have the diction and syntax that allow you to convey to a reader the felt reality of the event itself.

Interview,
New York, N.Y./
Publishers Weekly, 4-12:43.

Susan Mitchell
Poet;
Professor of creative writing,
Florida Atlantic University

4

[On her winning the Kingsley Tufts Poetry Award]: I think the message these awards are sending our very materialistic society is that poetry has value. Very often my most gifted student has a father who is horrified because this young person is going to turn away from business, from all those roads which seem more certain.

April 26/
The Washington Post, 4-27:(B)3.

R. K. Narayan
Indian author

5

Sometimes my readers are so enthusiastic, but what they get out of my novels I cannot understand. It is agony for me to read my own novels because I want to change them, and it makes me very discouraged. My business is writing: There is a compulsion to write. But I cannot evaluate what I do; that would be unseemly.

World Press Review, October:49.

Marge Piercy
Poet

6

One of the things you learn as a poet is to pay attention. It's the quality of attention you pay . . . Attention is love. That's a concept that interests me—that blessing things is a way of paying attention to them. It is a way of forcing yourself to experience freshly.

Interview, Cape Cod, Mass./
The Christian Science Monitor,
3-3:16.

Anna Quindlen
Journalist, Author

7

When you're a newspaper reporter who writes a novel, you experience complete liberation. I find fiction liberating precisely because it isn't

(ANNA QUINDLEN)

fact. Reporting on a story, there's always the anecdote you didn't get, the quote that you know would have been there if you had more time to dig for it. In fiction, you don't have to give up. But if you're liberated by the form, you're imprisoned by the characters. You find that out the first time you try to make them say or do something they wouldn't really say or do. You accrue four or five details about a character; she won't say or do certain things. As you add details and events, dialogue, your options get narrower and narrower. One thing is that the person you built becomes her own person. Then you have to report it. What this person will say and do is from his or her perspective, not the writer's. You wind up knowing very little about what to do next, and you have limited options, coming to the reality of these characters.

Interview/
Writer's Digest, March:36.

Anne Rice
Author

1

The well-made novel of small ideas and small emotions is scary to me. When critics look back to the 20th century, they will look to the more eccentric novels. If you talk to people about what they love, it's not always the well-made novel of ideas. People are hungry for an eccentric voice.

Interview, New Orleans, La./
"W" magazine, September:70.

Adrienne Rich
Poet

2

[As a poet,] you have to have will to persevere. You do have to have *will* to not give up the first time someone sends your poetry back, or the first time you stand on a street corner trying to hand out flyers, and people are tearing them up and stamping them into the mud. You *have* to persevere. And you also have to be willing to be alone or very few in number for a while, in order to generate anything. I'm convinced of that, even though I feel that there are so many people out

there who hunger for the kinds of connection that poetry makes.

Interview, New York, N.Y./
Publishers Weekly, 11-29:44.

3

"Is this what *I* want to say, or is this what Poetry, with a capital 'p,' has taught me is what should be said?"—I think that is an important kind of interior question for young poets, and for all poets, to keep asking. Tradition is important, but the voices of tradition can, in your head, become other people's voices that you're using instead of your own.

Interview, New York, N.Y./
Publishers Weekly, 11-29:45.

Philip Roth
Author

4

There are still Jewish readers who take strong exception to my fiction and to anything I write, but, by and large, it has diminished. Largely, the reaction against me was from a generation 25 or 30 years older than I was . . . Among subsequent generations there are people who have been offended, but the numbers are not the same. People who are born or come of age after you've made your reputation as a writer sort of accept you in a different way. The others were people who were trying to stop me at the start or to define me at the start so that it was clear what I was. These battles between readers and writers tend to come at the beginning of careers.

Interview/
The New York Times, 3-9:(B)2.

5

I don't think there's a decline of the novel so much as the decline of the readership. There's been a drastic decline, even a disappearance, of a serious readership. By readers, I don't mean people who pick up a book once in a while. By readers, I mean people who when they are at work think that "after dinner tonight and after the kids are in bed, I'm going to read for two hours." That's what I mean. Number two, these people

(PHILIP ROTH)

do it three or four nights a week for 2½, three hours; and while they do it they don't watch television or answer the phone. So if that's what readers are, how many of them are there? We are down to a gulag archipelago of readers. Of the sort of readers I've described, there are 176 of them in Nashville, 432 in Atlanta, 4,011 in Chicago, 3,017 in Los Angeles and 7,000 in New York. It adds up to 60,000 people. I assure you there are no more. We would be foolish to add a zero. Maybe there are 120,000. But that's it, and that is bizarre.

Interview/
The Washington Post, 3-15:(D)2.

Richard Russo
Author

1

Place is inseparable from character. If I try to write books about people before I have a pretty good sense of the places, that's an indication that I don't know the characters as well as I need to. And it's crucial to have a sense of place as process . . . Many of the contemporary writers I like also have that feeling of the ways in which places and people interact.

Interview, Portland, Maine/
Publishers Weekly, 6-7:43.

Charlie Smith
Author, Poet

2

Poetry has its rules, and they must be followed, and they're not the same as fiction. There are things I can do in one that I can't do in the other, but that's like saying there are some things you can do with a hat that you can't do with shoes! That's true, but it's not a problem: There's a use for hats and a use for shoes. At a very early age, I tried on the hat of poetry and the shoes of fiction, and I like them both.

Interview,
New York, N.Y./
Publishers Weekly, 5-3:280.

Amy Tan
Author

3

[When writing for children,] I became much more critical of myself as a storyteller. The most important thing I discovered from a child's point of view was things have relationships; things are connected in both an emotionally associative way and a linear way. Therefore, a story must go in direct line from beginning to end; it cannot afford to get sidetracked by long, descriptive passages. That's a discipline I learned that's good for me as a writer in any form.

The Writer, February:5.

Rose Tremain
British author

4

I like to write in an unplanned kind of way, a risky way; and teaching creative writing has made me analyze everything I do. I used to say that, for me, writing a novel was like getting on a train, having some concept of where the train was bound for, but not knowing how I was going to get there, who was going to get on the train, where it was going to stop. I probably didn't have as much control of the material as I should have. I think the process of analyzing other people's writing has taught me to control my own material and to justify to myself what a new character is supposed to be doing. I think *now* the right balance has been struck—between the kind of writer I was and the kind of writer my teaching has helped me become.

Interview, London, England/
Publishers Weekly, 4-5:51.

Diana Trilling
Writer, Critic

5

One of the things that interests me is how *political* much reviewing is. Magazines and newspapers define themselves, after all, by their point of view, and they don't want the reviews they publish to go against their position. But the poor people who read the reviews don't know what's behind them—what friendships and enmities inspire them.

Interview, New York, N.Y./
Publishers Weekly, 11-1:54.

Joanna Trollope
British author

1

[On her books' appeal to the middle class]: I think we've lacked the traditional novel, which does reflect how people are living. [People] were desperate for something that mirrored their own lives and preoccupations . . . If it weren't for the middle class, all these intellectual writers and theatre directors would have nobody to read their books or watch their plays.

World Press Review, November:30.

Mona Van Duyn
Poet Laureate
of the United States

2

Poets can only praise the world outside themselves. [That world presents people] to hate or love or respond to, and the world of nature that gives us other beasts and shapes and colors. The most a poet can do is strengthen that wonderful emotion, empathy.

Interview, Washington, D.C./
The Washington Post, 1-5:(C)3.

Paul Watkins
Author

3

Ideas keep cropping up in my head. I wish there were three of me because I want to write all of them at the same time. I know that I can't— and in a way that's reassuring—because I know by my calculation that for the next seven years I have stuff to write. But at the same time, I'm so impatient to get all of this done, the writing becomes almost a hindrance—I can't get it out fast enough!

Interview/
Publishers Weekly, 1-4:56.

Eudora Welty
Author

4

A character couldn't exist if you [the writer] didn't project yourself into it, imagine what their life was like. Otherwise, the character would just be a stick, or a paper doll. Putting yourself under the skin of your subject is a process that goes on all the time in the arts. It's what an actress does on the stage . . . [But as a writer,] you have no right to participate in your own story—that would be devastating. It would be like a magician puncturing the balloon. You don't belong in the story; it's in your mind, but you don't have a role in the story.

Interview, Jackson, Miss./
American Way, 12-1:129.

Alec Wilkinson
Author;
Staff writer,
"The New Yorker" magazine

5

There isn't any category into which I easily fit. The conventional category I suppose I fall into is literary journalist, or writer of literary non-fiction. But it would be easier if there were designations as there are in painting for figurative and abstract. I think of myself as a figurative writer. I describe the world as it appears to me. When you get writers whose personality intersects with the content of their work, you get a kind of writing that is factually based, but is dependent on the character, the nature, the ethics of the writer. John McPhee, Joseph Mitchell [are representative] of a kind of writing that seems diminished by having the title "non-fiction" applied to it. It is not non-anything. These people are working by observing the world, assembling information and writing in a particular form that has a resonance that many works of fiction don't have.

Interview, New York, N.Y./
Publishers Weekly, 2-1:68.

Charles Wright
Professor of English,
University of Virginia;
Winner,
1993 Ruth Lilly Poetry Prize

6

[On poetry]: I think it's great being a practitioner of an art that's always in the process of disappearing but never will. There's something inside of us, some black hole, that always has to have a poem. So people will keep writing, even if there is no $75,000 prize, even if it's only five dollars.

May 4/The Washington Post, 5-5:(B)10.

Medicine and Health

Henry J. Aaron
Economist, Brookings Institution

1

If we want to slow the growth in [health-care] spending over the long haul, we will have to ration [care]. But whether we want to slow the growth remains to be seen, because the choices rationing impose upon us are not any that we would wish to make.

U.S. News & World Report,
6-7:56.

Robert Allnutt
Executive vice president,
Pharmaceutical Manufacturers
Association

2

[On a study which says the pharmaceutical industry makes "excess profits" and charges too-high prices for drugs]: High financial returns are necessary to induce companies to invest in researching new chemical entities. The study comes to inaccurate conclusions that simply do not pertain to the marketplace or industry today . . . The price increases in the industry are the lowest in the last 15 years. In the last 12 months it was 5.1 percent. That is very different from what was going on in the 1970s and 1980s.

News conference, Feb. 25/
The New York Times, 2-26:(C)2.

Drew E. Altman
President,
Henry J. Kaiser Family Foundation

3

[On whether President Clinton should include benefits for abortion in his health-care reform program]: He campaigned as a pro-choice candidate. Because of his commitment to choice [on abortion] and to the full range of services in a basic benefits package, you can't design a package without it. The danger is that this one issue will create enough heat to cause real problems for the overall plan, which is hardly

going to be for want of controversy to begin with. But I really think he has no choice.

Los Angeles Times, 4-14:(A)11.

George J. Annas
Director, law,
medicine and ethics program,
Schools of Medicine
and Public Health,
Boston (Mass.) University

4

I think the right-to-die movement in this country is a direct reaction to the fear people have that if they enter the hospital gravely ill, they will lose control over what happens to them, and will not be given enough medication to take away their pain. Both of these fears are absolutely based in reality, but it's a horrible alternative to say that because these things are true I have to stay home and kill myself.

Ladies' Home Journal, April:48.

Robert Berenson
Member,
White House Task Force
on National Health Care Reform

5

[Supporting an idea to have medical malpractice suits filed, not against the specific doctor involved, but against the insurance company or health maintenance organization that employs the doctor]: We would move to a single-defendant as opposed to the current system, where we have multiple defendants, all sort of pointing the finger at each other. This structural change anticipates where the health system is going anyway. Health care is no longer a case of a single practitioner and a patient. For virtually any service, you're going to have integrated teams of professionals working together. In 10 or 15 years, the whole system is going to be this way. We want to juice the system a little bit and move it faster.

May 20/
The New York Times, 5-21:(A)10.

Virginia Trotter Betts
President,
American Nurses Association

1

The high cost of physician-centered, hospital-oriented, acute care can be greatly reduced through a new emphasis on primary care delivered in community-based settings that are accessible to everyone. By community settings, we mean delivery of an array of health services in schools, work sites, day-care centers and community clinics, as well as home-based care, thus limiting the utilization of specialists, hospitals and expensive technology. If we facilitate primary health-care delivery, which includes prevention, early diagnosis, uncomplicated illness treatment, and self-care and wellness education, we can reduce our overall health-care costs while significantly improving our personal and national health at the same time.

At meeting of White House Task Force
on National Health Care Reform,
Washington, D.C., March 29/
The New York Times, 3-30:(A)10.

2

In the area of primary care, we [nurses] are substitutable for physicians. Research shows that nurse practitioners, nurse midwives and nurse clinical specialists can substitute with lower cost and higher quality . . . Doctors say they are in favor of reform, but, really, to restructure the health-care system to allow non-physician providers to do more doesn't seem to be what they favor . . . They have a monopoly. They're trying to maintain it. And because physicians have a legal monopoly on always being the first person you see, they're always going to get the first dollar in the health-care system, and costs are not necessarily going to come down.

Interview/USA Today, 6-16:(A)11.

Robert J. Blendon
Professor of health policy,
School of Public Health,
Harvard University

3

There is a major difference between what the public sees as the problems of health care and what the experts believe. The public complains about being billed $5 for an aspirin; experts think we use too many aspirin.

Los Angeles Times, 2-22:(A)12.

4

[On the prospect of government health-care reforms]: The biggest thing on the minds of doctors is the loss of their autonomy. They feel incredibly hassled. They feel that their [professional] lives are more restrained. Even if they are doing fine economically, they feel the reasons they went into medicine—their independent judgment-making—is being constrained, and that it is going to get worse.

Los Angeles Times, 3-23:(A)16.

5

[Saying some Americans are concerned that President Clinton's health-care reform plan will result in a lowering of the quality of care]: People are afraid they are going to have to wait too long, that the doctor or nurse won't have enough time with them, that there will be some important medical technology or drug that will help their problem, and they will be denied it because of cost.

Los Angeles Times, 9-21:(A)16.

Thomas J. Bliley, Jr.
United States Representative,
R-Virginia

6

[Arguing against allowing into the U.S. immigrants with HIV, the AIDS virus]: Because HIV is always fatal, the public-health consequences of allowing HIV individuals to immigrate is of the highest order. We have never before permitted immigration of those who were infected in the middle of an epidemic. We should not start now.

3-12:(A)8.

David W. Blois
Executive director
of U.S. regulatory affairs,
Merck Research Laboratories

7

We are seeing the evolution of health-care issues into the health economics side. We will

(DAVID W. BLOIS)

continue to perform the classic trials [of new drugs] for Food And Drug Administration approval; that won't change. What will change is that we will be performing other tests to deal with such issues as quality of life and cost effectiveness.

Los Angeles Times, 6-10:(D)11.

Barry Bosworth
Economist,
Brookings Institution

1

[Criticizing the Clinton Administration for considering price controls on the health-care industry]: I can't believe they are going to do it. I can't believe they are that stupid. The health-care industry is the best example of an industry where price controls won't work.

Los Angeles Times, 4-1:(A)27.

Lonnie R. Bristow
Chairman,
American Medical Association

2

[On President Clinton's health-care reform plan]: The President has offered the country a prescription for what ails our health-care system. While we agree with his general diagnosis, we disagree with some of his treatment decisions. He's prescribing some pretty stiff, new and untried medicine. We are worried that no one really knows what the side effects are going to be.

Before AMA's lobbyists,
Washington, D.C., Sept. 29/
The New York Times, 9-30:(A)1.

Samuel Broder
Director,
National Cancer Institute
of the United States

3

I believe that the NIH as a whole has within its structure the capacity to do the task of preventing and curing AIDS. NIH may have to reinvent itself to complete the job, but that can be done.

The Washington Post,
1-9:(A)2.

Stuart Butler
Director of domestic policy,
Heritage Foundation

4

[On the possibility of new taxes to pay for the Clinton Administration's health-care reform plans]: Ordinary Americans are insured and satisfied with medical services even if they are worried about costs. And the more you talk about taxes, the more people are going to start to wonder whether it's worth it or not.

The Washington Post, 5-3:(A)8.

Carroll A. Campbell, Jr.
Governor of South Carolina (R)

5

[Criticizing President Clinton's health-care reform plan]: It's clear to me that we can't rely on heavy-handed government regulation and bureaucracies to lead the charge toward reform. The 238-page Administration draft is a giant social experiment devised by theorists who have never met a payroll.

Broadcast address to the nation,
Washington, D.C., Sept. 22/
Los Angeles Times, 9-23:(A)14.

William I. Campbell
President,
Philip Morris U.S.A.

6

To my knowledge, it's not been proven that cigarette smoking causes cancer . . . I base that on the fact that traditionally, there is, you know, in scientific terms, there are hurdles related to causation, and at this time . . . they have not been able to reproduce cancer in animals from cigarette smoking.

Lawyer-obtained testimony for a court case/
The New York Times, 12-6:(C)1.

Sharon F. Canner
Official, National Association
of Manufacturers

7

[On corporate America's views on reforming the U.S. health-care system]: It's a mixed re-

(SHARON F. CANNER)

sponse from business because of the diversity of companies: big versus small, older workforce versus younger, service versus manufacturer, union versus non-union. And there's also different company cultures. These factors interact to produce very different agendas.

The Washington Post, 4-13:(D)1.

Arthur L. Caplan
Director,
Center for Biomedical Ethics,
University of Minnesota

1

I honestly believe that home testing [by individuals using new self-use kits of various kinds] is going to revolutionize diagnostic medicine. I think that all factors, including cost, consumer demand, efficiency and speed—meaning not having to wait three days for test results—point in the direction of the laboratory coming into the living room.

Los Angeles Times, 3-3:(A)11.

2

[On the use of animals in medical research]: When we make animals suffer for no good reason, it is unethical. But people who say they don't know what to do when faced with using a pig's heart to save a baby's life have got their moral compass out of kilter.

Ladies' Home Journal, April:57.

3

[On the danger in testing new drugs on human beings]: You're never sure what's going to happen with your first human subjects. Over the years, people have tended to mash together research and therapy; when average people hear the term "clinical trial," they think, "latest, state-of-the-art therapy." The reality is that "clinical trial" should mean: "Possible dangerous substance. Beware. Could be fatal."

Los Angeles Times, 8-25:(A)16.

Benjamin S. Carson
Chief of pediatric neurosurgery,
Johns Hopkins Hospital,
Baltimore, Md.

4

My philosophy is to look at a patient and ask, "What is the worst that could happen if we do something?" It's usually that the patient ends up seriously debilitated, or dead. Then I ask, "What is the worst that could happen if we do nothing?" And it's usually the same thing. So with that as a background, I figure it's always worth trying to do something, if there's any chance at all that doing something might end up helping.

Interview, Baltimore, Md./
The New York Times, 6-8:(B)7.

Jimmy Carter
Former President
of the United States

5

[The U.S.] is a third-world country as far as the attention we give our own children. We have a much higher [disease-] immunization rate in Bangladesh than we do in Atlanta. And this means that in this whole country among African-Americans, we have an infant-mortality rate of 18 per 1,000 babies born. There are a lot of Third World countries that have lower infant-mortality rates than we do among our African-American neighbors.

News conference, Atlanta, Ga.,
March 12/The New York Times, 3-13:8.

Dick Cheney
Secretary of Defense
of the United States

6

[Criticizing President Clinton's health-care reform plan]: Clinton has seriously recommended that we ought to fix problems in the health-care system by taking one seventh of the economy and turning it on its head and creating a huge government-imposed set of regulations. What we've seen so far are all the warm, feel-good statements. We don't know what it will cost; we haven't seen any legislation. So far, it's all been hype.

Interview/
U.S. News & World Report, 10-25:40.

Bill Clinton
President of the United States

1

[Announcing his Task Force on Health Reform, to be chaired by his wife, Hillary]: This is going to be an unprecedented effort. There is an overwhelming knowledge that we have to move and move now [on health-care reform]. We've talked about it long enough. The time has come to act. And I have chosen the course that I think is most likely to lead to action that will improve the lives of millions of Americans.

Washington, D.C., Jan. 25/
Los Angeles Times, 1-26:(A)1.

2

Our nation is the only industrialized nation in the world that does not guarantee childhood vaccination for all children. It ought to be like clean water and clean air. It ought to be a part of the fabric of our life.

Washington, D.C., Feb. 12/
Los Angeles Times, 2-13:(A)1.

3

All our efforts to strengthen the economy will fail—let me say this again; I feel so strongly about this—all of our efforts to strengthen the economy will fail unless we also take this year—not next year, not five years from now, but this year—bold steps to reform our health-care system.

State of the Union address,
Washington, D.C., Feb. 17/
The Washington Post, 2-19:(A)18.

4

I will present a [health-care] plan which would provide the American people the opportunity to have the security of health-care coverage by the end of my first term. Whether or not that plan will pass the Congress in the form I will propose, that's a matter of conjecture; but I think we've got an excellent chance of passing it. In terms of how it will be paid for, let me say that no decision has been made on that. All the surveys show lopsided majorities of the American people are willing to pay *somewhat* more, a little more, if they were guaranteed the security of health coverage when they change jobs, when someone in their family's been sick, when other things happen, when their company can no longer afford it under present circumstances. The key financial conflict in the health-care issue is this: We've got to give the American people the right to know they're going to be covered with health insurance, that they're not going to have their costs going up two or three times the rate of inflation, they're not going to lose the right to pick their doctor. And we know that if we do it in any one of three or four ways, it will save literally hundreds of billions of dollars between now and the end of the decade—of tax money and, more importantly, of private money. Massive amounts of money will be saved, so the question is, how much do you have to raise now in order to save all that money later?

News conference,
Washington, D.C., March 23/
The New York Times, 3-24:(A)6.

5

[Criticizing Republicans who are filibustering against his jobs bill, which also includes funds for child immunizations]: These people, most of them, have been here the last 12 years while we have run immunization into the ground, while we've developed the third-worst rate in the hemisphere. And they've always got some excuse, some of them, for not doing anything. Now, what are we going to do about those children? That ought to be the question of the week. When I go out there on the [White House] lawn, and I think about those kids picking up Easter eggs, I want to be able to think about them all being immunized, and all those children coming along behind them being immunized.

To reporters,
Washington, D.C., April 12/
The New York Times, 4-13:(A)10.

6

[On his yet-to-be-announced health-care reform plan]: I think that most people believe that this plan will be much tougher on small busi-

(BILL CLINTON)

nesses than I believe it will be . . . There is no perfect solution, but I assure you that we're all going to be better off if we enter into an honest debate and we try to work through this and we try to resolve it. The worst thing we can do is to leave it alone. We've got to do something to bring [health] costs within inflation, or it's going to break the country. Costs are going up like crazy . . . I think all employees should make some contribution to their health care . . . because, if they don't, they may get to thinking it's free, and over-utilization is one of the problems. I mean, everybody should pay something in accordance with their ability to pay, [including all businesses].

Before National Federation
of Independent Business,
Washington, D.C., June 29/
Los Angeles Times, 6-30:(A)19.

1

[On health-care reform]: I think there has to be some responsibility in this system for everyone. There are a lot of people today that get a free ride out of the present system who can afford to pay something. I think there should be individual responsibility. I think every American should know that health care is not something paid for by the tooth fairy, that there is no free ride; that people should understand that this system costs a lot of money—it should cost a lot of money [because] it ought to be the world's best. But we should all be acutely aware of the cost each of us impose on it. But I also believe that in order to make individual responsibility meaningful, and in order to control the costs of this system, there has to be some means of achieving universal coverage. If you don't achieve universal coverage, in my judgment, you will not be able to control the costs adequately.

Before National Governors' Association,
Tulsa, Okla., Aug. 16/
The New York Times, 8-17:(A)8.

2

[Saying his soon-to-be-announced health-reform plan would cut down on red tape and paperwork for medical providers]: Instead of all this paper and all these medical forms assuring that the rules are followed and people get healthy, we're stuck in a system where we're ruled by the forms and have less time to make children and adults healthy . . . When doctors and nurses are forced to write out the same information six different times in seven different ways just to satisfy some distant company or agency, it wastes their time and patients' money and, in the end, undermines the integrity of a system that leaves you spending more and caring for fewer people.

Washington, D.C., Sept. 17/
The New York Times, 9-18:6.

3

Despite the dedication of literally millions of talented health-care professionals, our health care [in the U.S.] is too uncertain and too expensive, too bureaucratic and too wasteful. It has too much fraud and too much greed. At long last, after decades of false starts, we must make this our most urgent priority: giving every American health security—health care that can never be taken away, health care that is always there . . . Now, we all know what's right. We're blessed with the best health-care professionals on Earth, the finest health-care institutions, the best medical research, the most sophisticated technology . . . But we also know that we can no longer afford to continue to ignore what is wrong. Millions of Americans are just a pink slip away from losing their health insurance, and one serious illness away from losing all their savings. Millions more are locked into the jobs they have now just because they or someone in their family has once been sick and they have what is called a pre-existing condition. And on any given day, over 37 million Americans, most of them working people and their little children, have no health insurance at all. And in spite of all this, our medical bills are growing at over twice the rate of inflation, and the United States spends over a third more of its income on health care than any other nation on Earth; and the gap is growing, causing many of our companies in global competition severe disadvantage. There is no excuse for this kind of system. We know other people have done better. We know people in our own

(BILL CLINTON)

country are doing better. We have no excuse. My fellow Americans, we must fix this system, and it has to begin with Congressional action.

*Broadcast address to the nation
before a joint session of Congress,
Washington, D.C., Sept. 22/
Los Angeles Times, 9-23:(A)8.*

1

Under our [reform] plan, every American would receive a health-care security card that will guarantee a comprehensive package of benefits over the course of an entire lifetime, roughly comparable to the benefit package offered by most Fortune 500 companies. This health-care security card will offer this package of benefits in a way that can never be taken away. So let us agree on this: Whatever else we disagree on, before this Congress finishes its work next year, you will pass and I will sign legislation to guarantee this security to every citizen of this country. With this card, if you lose your job or you switch jobs, you're covered. If you leave your job to start a small business, you're covered. If you're an early retiree, you're covered. If someone in your family has unfortunately had an illness that qualifies as a pre-existing condition, you're still covered. If you get sick or a member of your family gets sick, even if it's a life-threatening illness, you're covered. And if the insurance company tries to drop you for any reason, you'll still be covered because that will be illegal.

*Broadcast address to the nation
before a joint session of Congress,
Washington, D.C., Sept. 22/
Los Angeles Times, 9-23:(A)8.*

2

[On his health-care reform plan]: This program, for the first time, would provide a broad range of preventive services, including regular check-ups and well-baby visits. Now, it's just common sense. We know—any family doctor will tell you—that people will stay healthier and long-term cost to the health system will be lower if we have comprehensive preventive services.

You know how all of our mothers told us that an ounce of prevention was worth a pound of cure? Our mothers were right. And it's a lesson—like so many lessons from our mothers—that we have waited too long to live by. It is time to start doing it.

*Broadcast address to the nation
before a joint session of Congress,
Washington, D.C., Sept. 22/
Los Angeles Times, 9-23:(A)8.*

3

Today we have more than 1,500 [health-care] insurers with hundreds and hundreds of different forms. No other nation has a system like this. These forms are time-consuming for health-care providers, they're expensive for health-care consumers, they're exasperating for anyone who's ever tried to sit down around a table and wade through them and figure them out. The medical-care industry is literally drowning in paperwork. In recent years the number of administrators in our hospitals has grown by four times the rate that the number of doctors has grown. A hospital ought to be a house of healing, not a monument to paperwork and bureaucracy.

*Broadcast address to the nation
before a joint session of Congress,
Washington, D.C., Sept. 22/
Los Angeles Times, 9-23:(A)8.*

4

[On his health-care reform plan]: Unless everybody is covered—and this is a very important thing—unless everybody is covered, we will never be able to fully put the brakes on health-care inflation. Why is that? Because when people don't have any health insurance, they still get health care. But they get it when it's too late, when it's too expensive—often from the most expensive place of all, the emergency room. Usually by the time they show up, their illnesses are more severe, and their mortality rates are much higher in our hospitals than those who have insurance. So they cost us more. And what else happens? Since they get the care but do not pay, who does pay? All the rest of us. We pay in higher

(BILL CLINTON)

hospital bills and higher insurance premiums. This cost-shifting is a major problem.

Broadcast address to the nation before a joint session of Congress, Washington, D.C., Sept. 22/ Los Angeles Times, 9-23:(A)8.

1

[On his health-care reform plan]: Most of the money would come, under my way of thinking, as it does today, from premiums paid by employers and individuals. That's the way it happens today. But under this health-care security plan, every employer and every individual will be asked to contribute something to health care. This concept was first conveyed to the Congress about 20 years ago by President [Richard] Nixon. And a lot of people agree with the concept of shared responsibility between employers and employees, and that the best thing to do is to ask every employer and every employee to share that. The Chamber of Commerce has said that, and they're not in the business of hurting small business. The American Medical Association has said that. Some call it an employer mandate, but I think it's the fairest way to achieve responsibility in the health-care system. And it's the easiest for ordinary Americans to understand because it builds on what we already have and what already works for so many Americans.

Broadcast address to the nation before a joint session of Congress, Washington, D.C., Sept. 22/ Los Angeles Times, 9-23:(A)9.

2

[On his health-care reform plan]: All of us have to prepare to face the consequences if the cost savings [envisioned by his plan] don't materialize. Then we're going to have to slow down the benefits or raise more money.

At "town hall" meeting, Tampa, Fla., Sept. 23/ Los Angeles Times, 9-24:(A)20.

3

[On his health-care reform plan]: We're [government] not going to run the health-care system. In fact, we're going to have more competition. The system we [now] have is the most inefficient, the most expensive in the advanced world . . . [But] government occasionally does do something right in health care. I think the Medicare program is generally conceded to be fairly well run and some of its cost-control programs have worked quite well. They would have worked better had they been part of an overall managed-competition plan. Government is capable of fixing financing mechanisms and administratively simplifying things.

Interview/ U.S. News & World Report, 9-27:52.

4

[On his health-care reform plan]: [There must be] a comprehensive package of health-care benefits that are always there and that can never be taken away. That is the bill I want to sign; that is my bottom line. I will not support or sign a bill that does not meet that criteria . . . None of us could devise a system more complex, more burdensome, more administratively costly than the one we have now [in the U.S.]. Let us all judge ourselves against, after all, what it is we are attempting to change.

Presenting his reform plan to Congress, Washington, D.C., Oct. 27/ Los Angeles Times, 10-28:(A)1.

5

[On his health-care reform plan]: We could have had a bipartisan solution [to the Federal budget problem] lickety-split, giving the American people a plan that would have reduced the deficit and increased investment . . . if we were not choking on a health-care system that is not working. Let us measure ourselves against the present system and the cost of doing nothing. Let us honestly compare our ideas with one another and ask who wins, who loses and how much does it cost.

Presenting his reform plan to Congress, Washington, D.C., Oct. 27/ The Washington Post, 10-28:(A)19.

(BILL CLINTON)

1

[On AIDS]: In a funny way, this whole disease is bringing out the best and the worst in America, isn't it? I mean, it's exposing some of our prejudice in ways that are self-defeating, since every family and every child is now at risk. And yet it's also showing us the courage, the self-determination, the incredible capacity of the American people to give and to love. We see our legendary refusal to adopt organized and disciplined solutions to big social problems, and yet we also see . . . a remarkable willingness on the part of people who can make a difference to try to do more . . . For nearly every American with eyes and ears open, the face of AIDS is no longer the face of a stranger. Millions and millions of us have now stood at the bedside of a dying friend and grieved. Millions and millions of us now know people who have had AIDS and who have died of it who are both gay and heterosexual—both. Millions and millions of us are now forced to admit that this is a problem which has diminished the life of every American.

At Georgetown Medical Center, Washington, D.C.,
Dec. 1/The New York Times, 12-2:(A)12.

2

We've increased the research funding for AIDS by over 20 percent, and we increased funding in the Ryan White Health Care Act for care by 66 percent. And I want to remind you that this was at a time when overall domestic spending was held absolutely flat, and when over 350 items in the Federal budget this year are smaller than they were last year. Where there was an absolute cut, we got substantial increases [in AIDS research funding].

At Georgetown Medical Center,
Washington, D.C., Dec. 1/
The New York Times, 12-2:(A)12.

Hillary Rodham Clinton
Wife of President
of the United States Bill Clinton;
Chairman, White House Task Force
on National Health Care Reform

3

If we do nothing [to overhaul the U.S. health-care system], if we just say to ourselves, "This is

such a complicated problem, we really don't think we will ever come up with a comprehensive solution to solve all of the aspects of it," then here is what we can look forward to: Experts estimate that the annual cost of health care for an American family will more than double by the end of the decade . . . If we do not deal with the cost of health care from a Federal and state and from a local budget, we will bankrupt cities and counties and states.

At health-care conference,
University of Nebraska,
Lincoln, April 16/
The New York Times, 4-17:8.

4

What we're trying to do [in health-care reform] is to free up people in health care to once again take care of patients and not fill out forms and not be second-guessed by bureaucrats and trying to strip away a lot of paperwork and the red tape that really does stand in the way of people actually coming together as human beings around these really profound and difficult issues of life and death.

Interview, Washington, D.C./
U.S. News & World Report,
5-3:43.

5

We believe, based on everything we know, that for the vast majority of businesses health-care reform will be a net winner. Their costs will stabilize and go down. [Also,] for many small businesses, the same will be true because we intend to move to incorporate workers' compensation and auto insurance in health-care coverage and comprehensive health-care reform.

Before Business Council,
Williamsburg, Va., May 7/
The New York Times, 5-8:7.

6

[On her vision for reform in the U.S. health-care system]: If you change jobs or if you lose your job, you will still be insured. If you are an older American and need help with prescription drugs and a start on long-term care, particularly in your home, you will be insured. If you are a physician or a nurse or a pharmacist or a dentist, you will no longer spend 20 to 40 percent of your time and income filling out countless meaningless forms.

At University of Pennsylvania commencement,
May 17/
The New York Times, 5-18:(A)10.

1

Security is what this health-care debate is all about. Can your family find peace of mind? Can you or your child get the quality of care when you need it most? That's what we have to be focusing on every single day. Talk to your friends and neighbors about what you see every day in terms of price-gouging, cost-shifting, unconscionable profiteering. Explain how you see the system that is being gamed and ripped-off because it has no real discipline, no budget, no controls. Part of the reason we are in this spiraling cost explosion . . . is because too many people have made too much money off of eliminating opportunities for caring for people instead of expanding those.

Before Service Employees
International Union, May 26/
Los Angeles Times, 5-27:(A)18.

2

One of the sad and perhaps unfair tasks that we confront in the health-care reform debate is that most Americans believe there is a very simple answer: "Don't charge as much for what you do." That, to them, is the answer. All the rest of the issues that we have looked at and worried about in the last five months pale in significance against the overwhelming public perception that the real problem is that doctors charge too much, hospitals charge too much, insurance companies charge too much, everybody charges too much, so we should just cut everybody's prices and everything will be fine.

At Johns Hopkins University,
June 10/
Los Angeles Times, 6-11:(A)15.

We need to start with a fundamental commitment to making the practice of medicine again a viable, honored link in our effort to promote the common good. We cannot create the atmosphere of trust, respect and professionalism that you [physicians] deserve to have, and many of you in this room remember from early years, without changing . . . the way the entire system works . . . I can understand how many of you must feel when, instead of being trusted for your expertise, you're expected [under "managed care"] to call an 800-number and get approval for even basic medical procedures from a total stranger. It remains a mystery to me how a person sitting at a computer in some air-conditioned office a thousand miles away could make a judgment about what should or shouldn't happen at a patient's bedside in Illinois or Georgia or California.

Before American Medical Association,
Chicago, Ill., June 13/
The Washington Post, 6-14:(A)6.

4

[On the Clinton Administration's health-care reform plan]: I think what is non-negotiable is a fair and responsible way of funding the system. We think the employer-employee contribution is the best way of doing that, but if there is a better way out there to get it done . . . We have designed this so that there are movable pieces.

To reporters, Washington, D.C./
The New York Times, 9-28:(A)10.

5

[Supporting President Clinton's health-care reform plan]: [The] assumption about government being less efficient than the private sector is not true in the health-care system as it's currently structured . . . The heavy administrative percentages that you will find in the private-sector insurance market is due to a very clear decision, which is, the more money we can spend making sure we don't insure people who might cost us money, the more money we will make . . . And in order to choose among everyone sitting in this room—who is and who is not a good risk—

(HILLARY RODHAM CLINTON)

that takes a lot of time and a lot of manpower, a lot of personnel cost. And so I think that, if you look at the way the current private sector operates, you will find an enormous amount of inefficiency . . . Many of our industries have had to become more efficient in the last 20 years because of external competition. We are now producing high-quality cars in our country that are very productive and are really giving a good run for the money against the competitors. But it took outside competition to come in and do that. We have to create a competitive marketplace. We do not currently have one [in health care].

*Before Senate Labor and
Human Resources Committee,
Washington, D.C., Sept. 29/
The Washington Post, 9-30:(A)6.*

1

[Criticizing the health-insurance industry]: They have the gall to run TV ads that there is a better way [than the Clinton Administration's health-care reform plan], the very industry that brought us to the brink of bankruptcy because of the way that they have financed health care . . . It is time for . . . every American to stand up and say to the insurance industry, "Enough is enough. We want our health-care system back" . . . [The insurance companies] like what is happening today. They like being able to exclude people from coverage because the more they can exclude, the more money they can make. It is time that we stood up and said, "We are tired of insurance companies running our health-care system."

*Before American Academy of Pediatrics,
Washington, D.C., Nov. 1/
The New York Times, 11-2:(A)1;
The Washington Post, 11-2:(A)1.*

2

[On those who are criticizing President Clinton's health-care reform plan]: I have no doubt that the forces of the status quo will dig in their heels and do everything they can, while praising the potential of reform, to try to under-

mine it ever being enacted. If the forces arrayed against reform want a real battle in which their self-interest is exposed and their real agenda is made public, they will get it, because I think there is a lot at stake, and we're going to make sure that people are as informed as possible.

*To journalists,
Washington, D.C., Nov. 8/
The New York Times, 11-9:(A)7.*

3

[Saying the Clinton Administration's health-care reform plan provides choice for the individual]: It is your choice, and every year you choose which health plan [offered] you will be part of. The Federal government . . . does not run the health plan. The Federal government does not tell the doctors what to charge. The Federal government does not determine what choice you make. And in the President's plan, the [health] alliances that will be created in every state will serve that function, and they won't be governmental.

*At conference sponsored by "The Boston Globe,"
Boston, Mass., Dec. 7/
The New York Times, 12-8:(A)13.*

Theodore Cooper
Chairman, Upjohn Company

4

I hope in all the debate [about high pharmaceutical prices] we don't lose the idea of the purpose of the system. If all the rhetoric is on saving money, it would be wrong. The focus ought to be on saving lives.

*Interview, Kalamazoo, Mich./
Los Angeles Times, 4-12:(D)4.*

Martin A. Corry
*Director of Federal affairs,
American Association
of Retired Persons*

5

[On the possibility that Medicare may be incorporated in the Clinton Administration's plans for reform of the U.S. health-care system]:

(MARTIN A. CORRY)

Whenever you talk about changes in Medicare, it makes people nervous . . . Dropping Medicare into an untested new system, based on an unproved theory about how to deliver health care, would be very controversial. Before we do that, we ought to make sure the new system works.

The New York Times, 5-11:(A)1.

Bill Cox
Chief lobbyist,
Catholic Health Association

1

[Criticizing Clinton Administration plans to include public funding for abortions in its health-care reform proposals]: Abortion is an issue that runs so deeply in American society, on both sides, that it, in and of itself, could be the issue that stops health reform in its tracks.

The Washington Post, 5-19:(A)9.

Mario M. Cuomo
Governor of New York (D)

2

[Saying President Clinton must increase Medicaid money to states such as New York if his health-care reform plan is to succeed]: He says he wants a historic reform of the health-care system. But if it institutionalizes this inequity [in Medicaid payments to states that have large numbers of poor people and generous benefits] in a system of universal [health-care] coverage, he would be contradicting himself . . . President Clinton and [his wife] Hillary deserve immense credit for having advanced this [health-care reform] issue. We approve of their objectives. But we don't accept every jot and tittle of their proposal. We certainly don't accept the provisions as to Medicaid, which would perpetuate intolerable and historic inequity against our state.

Interview/
The New York Times,
12-2:(A)9.

Ronald David
Lecturer,
Kennedy School of Government,
Harvard University

3

Originally, infant-mortality statistics were intended to give an index of the health of the community and the health of child-bearing women. But we wrongly interpreted that data in the light of the current medical paradigm, which regards pregnancy as a pathological condition requiring medical intervention. Thus, infant-mortality rates came to be an index of deviant maternal behavior—such as teenage pregnancies—or lack of access to medical prenatal care. The entire focus shifted away from the community and onto the individual. The problem now has been re-defined as one of providing more medical care, and of making women responsible for pregnancy outcomes. Maternal and child health policy is typically concerned with the health of women only for the time that they are potential fetal vessels.

Interview/
The Wall Street Journal,
3-15:(A)12.

Maurice De Wachter
Director,
Institute for Bioethics
(Netherlands)

4

[On the trend in many countries toward legalized euthanasia]: It may be inevitable, but I am troubled by the creation of a legal structure where social control seeps away and the doctors are given too much freedom. [There are cases where the law] accepts "mental suffering" as a valid reason to terminate life, and I'm afraid it will make it only more difficult to draw the line.

The Washington Post, 10-29:(A)32.

John D. Dingell
United States Representative,
D-Michigan

5

[On health-care reform]: I quit talking about the humanitarian concern, because nobody

(JOHN D. DINGELL)

much seems to give a damn about that. I talk now about the economic consequences. General Motors spends $1,086 per car [for health benefits for its workers]. The auto companies are going broke on health care, and every other industry is having similar problems . . . I'm not going to deceive myself and I'm not going to deceive anybody else to think that any other system than single-payer is ultimately going to resolve the nation's problems. Every country's tried it, and they all keep coming to the same conclusion—single payer.

Los Angeles Times, 3-24:(E)2.

Robert J. Dole
United States Senator,
R-Kansas

1

[Criticizing First Lady Hillary Rodham Clinton for her recent verbal attack on the health-insurance industry]: [She is] creating an "enemies list" . . . We just cannot say we will just make the insurance companies villains or the pharmaceutical companies villains or the physicians or the dentists or the hospital administrators or the nurses or whoever it may be, and try to divide everybody, divide and conquer.

Nov. 3/
The New York Times. 11-4:(A)14.

R. Gordon Douglas, Jr.
President, vaccine division,
Merck & Company

2

[Criticizing a proposal that the government buy up all childhood vaccines at a discount and distribute them free to doctors and clinics so that all children could receive them free]: We think our vaccines are reasonably priced [as it is]. We already give a 50 percent discount to the Federal government and the states, which accounts for 55 percent of all sales of our measles, mumps and rebulla vaccines. That is enough to cover all poor people in this country with free vaccine purchased by taxpayers. When there is so much trouble with the Federal budget deficit, why should the government buy vaccine for the 45 percent of the population who can afford it?

Interview,
Washington, D.C., March 1/
The New York Times, 3-2:(A)9.

Robert Dresing
President,
Cystic Fibrosis Foundation

3

When my own son Rob was diagnosed with CF at 18 months, the life expectancy for someone with this disease was then six years. He is 26 today. The only reason he has survived is the fact that we have developed drugs over the last 20 years to control lung infections . . . Without the investment of the drug industry, my child, and others, would not be alive today. Our fear is that, as we strive to control health-care costs, some will make the drug industry into an easy target. By using the drug industry as a scapegoat, we will be shooting ourselves in the foot—stifling the very innovation and development of new products so critical to the health of many Americans.

Before House Subcommittee on
Health and the Environment,
Washington, D.C., Feb. 22/
The Wall Street Journal,
3-9:(A)16.

Arthur L. Eberly
President,
Florida Medical Association

4

[On Clinton Administration plans for reform of the health-care system]: I feel the Administration so far is just giving us a dog-and-pony show. The idea that they are listening to people is nonsense. They've already decided what they want to do, and that is to single out the doctors as the bad guys. I don't make anything like the $191,000 that is supposed to be average for doctors. I've been doing it for 30 years, and I'm only making $130,000 or $140,000 a year. I'm tired of picking up the newspaper and finding us the bad guys.

The New York Times,
3-22:(A)9.

Joycelyn Elders
Surgeon General-designate
of the United States

1

[Saying each community must adopt its own solutions on controversial public-health issues, rather than relying on the Federal government]: I do not believe that we can dictate from above. It's like dancing with a bear. You can't stop dancing when you're tired and sit down. You have to wait until the bear gets tired and then sit down.

At Senate Labor and Human Resources Committee
hearing on her nomination,
Washington, D.C., July 23/
The Washington Post, 7-24:(A)8.

2

[On her support for distributing condoms to students at schools]: We all want abstinence. And if I knew how to get abstinence I would do whatever it takes to do that. [But as a mother,] given a choice between hearing my daughter say "I'm pregnant" or "I used a condom," most mothers would get up in the middle of the night and buy them herself.

At Senate Labor and Human Resources Committee
hearing on her nomination,
Washington, D.C., July 23/
The New York Times, 7-24:6.

Stephen Elmont
Vice president,
National Restaurant Association

3

Our industry is consumed and concerned about health-care reform. For the past few years, restaurateurs have struggled with staggering inflation and health-care premium costs, with cancellations, with denials of coverage, and now with the frightening prospect of [government] mandates. We are not engaged in hyperbole when we say that mandated employer-provided [medical] coverage or higher payroll taxes to pay for health benefits would literally sound the death knell for many restaurants and discourage other restaurants from ever opening . . . We believe the most essential element in health-care reform is cost containment. We adamantly oppose

employer mandates, price controls and global budgets. Instead, we support many of the concepts upon which build the strengths of our free-enterprise free-market system.

At meeting of White House Task Force
on National Health Care Reform,
Washington, D.C., March 29/
The New York Times, 3-30:(A)10.

4

[Criticizing Clinton Administration proposals to require all companies to pay for health insurance for their workers]: For large companies, this is a non-issue, because they are already providing insurance. But for small business, it's a huge issue—not because we don't want to do it, but because it's unbelievably expensive . . . Workers' compensation costs are already out of control. We pay through the teeth in payroll taxes. The Administration has just added a parental-leave requirement, and they're talking about raising the minimum wage. To say we're going to pull out the stops over health insurance is an understatement.

The New York Times, 5-3:(C)3.

Alain C. Enthoven
Professor,
Stanford University
Business School

5

We [in the U.S.] have an extremely wasteful and inefficient [health-care] system that has been bathed in cost-increasing incentives for over 50 years. We badly need a radically more efficient system. That will mean closing hospitals and putting surgeons out of work.

The New York Times, 5-1:7.

6

[On the high cost of health care in California]: California's an attractive place to live, so doctors move here, and the seven major medical schools are turning out doctors who want to stay here. So there is a lot of doctoring being done by a lot of doctors, and that's expensive. Supply has a way of creating its own demand.

Los Angeles Times, 5-5:(D)5.

Jack Faris
President,
National Federation
of Independent Business

1

[Criticizing President Clinton's health-care reform plan, which calls for businesses to pay for 80 percent of their employees' insurance premiums]: We checked the Constitution, and we don't see where it gives you the right to universal health insurance. The Constitution says we have the right to life, liberty and the pursuit of happiness. That's what small business is about. Well, [this health-care plan] is reducing our pursuit of happiness. Every time we turn around, someone in the Federal government is telling us we have to pay more. We want health-care reform, but we want to make sure that the medicine given to the patient doesn't kill the patient.

The New York Times, 9-17:(A)1.

Thomas S. Foley
United States Representative,
D-Washington;
Speaker of the House

2

[President Clinton's health-care reform plan] in the short term, will cost more money because you are bringing back universal coverage that is not cheap. In the long range, it will save money because we will have cost controls that will be a more-rational way to provide services.

Interview/
The Christian Science Monitor,
4-29:3.

Palma Formica
Physician; Trustee,
American Medical Association

3

[On suggestions that nurses be allowed to perform some primary-care services now provided only by doctors]: Nurses simply cannot replace doctors. They are like apples and oranges.

U.S. News & World Report,
12-20:12.

Kristine Gebbie
Director,
National AIDS Program Office
of the United States

4

I've been very supportive of the needle-exchange programs [to provide clean needles to illegal-drug users] in Washington state, because they're part of a spectrum of services. But I'm very leery of sounding like I think anyone should be able to buy a box of syringes and stand at a street corner handing them out. The real issue is how we're going to get more substance abusers into treatment. We've focused enormous attention on arresting drug dealers, but we haven't looked at breaking the addictions that keep demand alive.

Interview/Newsweek, 8-9:62.

5

[Just talking about sex] in terms of don'ts and diseases [is not working. The U.S. needs to see sexuality as] an essentially important and pleasurable thing. [Until it does,] we will continue to be a repressed, Victorian society that misrepresents information, denies sexuality early, denies homosexual sexuality, particularly in teens, and leaves people abandoned with no place to go. I can help just a little bit in my job, standing on the White House lawn talking about sex with no lightning bolts falling on my head.

At conference on teenage pregnancy,
Oct. 20/
The Washington Post, 10-22:(A)21.

Newt Gingrich
United States Representative,
R-Georgia

6

[Criticizing President Clinton's health-care reform plan]: No Administration I know has a bigger gap between the salesperson [Clinton] and the car [the plan]. When you actually see the car, it turns out to be a Yugo. When you listen to the speech, it's a Rolls Royce.

USA Today, 10-29:(A)13.

7

[Criticizing President Clinton's health-care reform plan]: One of the mistakes we've [opponents of the plan] made in the last three months is not to go to the core of the debate [and show the public that Clinton's plan is designed] not for good health care . . . but to seize control of the health system and centralize power in Washington.

Before Empower America,
Washington, D.C., Dec. 14/
The Washington Post, 12-15:(A)11.

Janlori Goldman
Director, Project on
Privacy and Technology,
American Civil Liberties Union

1

[On privacy concerns about a proposed national health-care data bank, which would contain computerized records of people's medical conditions and histories]: Most Americans are shocked to learn that Federal law better protects the records that show that they've rented *Basic Instinct* [at the video store] than those that show their illnesses and treatments. Any health-care plan that bears the government's stamp must therefore go the extra mile to convince individuals that their privacy is protected . . . While a hospital storage room full of paper files may raise some very serious worries, the threat to privacy is at least limited to those who are physically there and can get into the room. With remote access from around the country and around the world, electronic data interchange might make possible multiple invasions at the same time by people scattered across the globe.

Los Angeles Times, 8-24:(A)5.

Frederick K. Goodwin
Director, National Institute
of Mental Health
of the United States

2

[On coverage for mental-health treatment under President Clinton's health-care reform plan]: It's clear that classical psychoanalysis, which is four to five times a week for a four- to five-year duration, will not be covered. It won't

be covered because there is no real evidence that it works.

Time, 11-29:47.

Al Gore
Vice President
of the United States

3

The days when one association [the AMA], no matter how prestigious, can dominate the health-reform debate are over. And they should be . . . We are going to ask you [doctors] to help us control skyrocketing health-care costs. In return, we are going to work very hard to reform the malpractice laws and cut the bureaucracy and the paperwork which makes it difficult for you to be care-givers.

Before American Medical Association,
Washington, D.C., March 24/
USA Today, 3-25:(A)7.

4

The days of business as usual [in health-care financing] are over. We are determined to bring this country sweeping and comprehensive health-care reform. [And] everyone who has been making lots of money off health care in the last 10 years will need to sacrifice in order to make the system work.

At meeting of White House Task Force
on National Health Care Reform,
Washington, D.C., March 29/
The New York Times, 3-30:(A)10.

5

Health-care reform, first and foremost, means giving the American people the freedom from fear. If our task is complex, our goals are simple. We must guarantee health security for every American.

At meeting of White House Task Force
on National Health Care Reform,
Washington, D.C., March 29/
The Washington Post, 4-6:(Health)8.

6

We will offer a comprehensive health-care reform plan that preserves the free-market incen-

(AL GORE)

tives essential to continued American leadership in biotechnology. It is the biotechnology industry that holds the greatest promise for finding effective treatment and cures for the world's most dreaded diseases.

To biotechnology executives,
San Francisco, Calif., June 21/
The New York Times, 6-22:(C)15.

1

[On the Clinton Administration's health-care reform plan]: The numbers in our plan have been submitted to rigorous examination and cross-checking by all of the experts in the various government agencies. They also have been submitted to analysis by private actuaries and accounting experts, companies around the nation. And they stand up very well.

Interview, Sept. 23/
Los Angeles Times, 9-24:(A)21.

Tipper Gore
Wife of Vice President
of the United States Al Gore;
Adviser on mental health
to White House Task Force
on National Health Care Reform

2

[Saying health insurance should cover mental-health disorders as much as it does physical disorders]: Why should a woman with diabetes who needs insulin have it covered by insurance, whereas a woman with manic-depressive illness who needs lithium not be covered in the same way when both diseases can be managed and controlled? What we are arguing for is parity with physical illness. It's a question of fairness . . . I think it's very important that people who need some kind of mental-health help get it. They wouldn't sit in bed with a 104-degree fever and not get treated They should think about mental-health disorders in the same way.

Interview,
Washington, D.C., March 10/
Los Angeles Times, 3-11:(A)1,14.

Phil Gramm
United States Senator,
R-Texas

3

[Criticizing President Clinton's health-care reform plan]: It's frightening. The President may have achieved in one bill something that could finally bankrupt the government and destroy the greatest medical-care system in the history of the world. We're back to the old game of promising stuff we cannot deliver.

USA Today, 9-13:(A)2.

Jonathan Gruber
Medical economist,
Massachusetts Institute
of Technology

4

Government should not be saying what prices [for prescription drugs] are right or wrong and requiring certain behavior [by drug companies]. Rather, it should be helping to make information available to people. Right now, we know more about the apples we eat than the drugs we use.

Time, 3-8:55.

Edmund F. Haislmaier
Policy analyst,
Heritage Foundation

5

[Criticizing the Clinton Administration for considering price controls on the health-care industry]: Almost by definition, if you believe price controls work, you are not an economist. If Clinton's advisers decide to do this, it will show that they've learned nothing from history.

Los Angeles Times, 4-1:(A)27.

Bernadine P. Healy
Director,
National Institutes of Health
of the United States

6

For far too long, research on women's health has been neglected. Men were the normative standard for medical research and treatment.

(BERNADINE P. HEALY)

The corollary for this, of course, is that men's hormones set the standard for us all.

News conference,
Bethesda, Md., March 30/
The New York Times, 3-31:(A)9.

Cathy Hurwit
Health specialist,
Citizen Action

1

[On the high- and low-level insurance plans being proposed in President Clinton's health-reform program]: The question is, is your access to those benefits going to be equal? I think that's the weakness of the President's plan. It's hard to believe the high- and low-cost plans are going to have the same supply of doctors, hospital beds and resources in general.

Los Angeles Times,
9-27:(A)6.

Michael M. E. Johns
Dean,
Johns Hopkins University
School of Medicine

2

[Criticizing President Clinton's health-care reform plan for giving the government the power to determine how many doctors will be trained as general practitioners and how many as specialists in each field of medicine]: Primary [general] care has been under-valued and under-rewarded. We need more primary-care physicians. [But under the President's plan,] the process will be manipulated by political whim, rather than guided by what we need. I don't like the government doing this. Government officials are subject to political pressure. Members of Congress might want [training] "slots" in their hometown. If the Secretary [of HHS] comes from North Dakota, he might allocate more slots there.

The New York Times,
9-15:(A)14.

Gwendylon Johnson
Member,
board of directors,
American Nurses Association

3

Overall, nurses have been delivering primary health care since 1966 as independent practitioners in rural and indigent communities, where physicians do not want to practice. And in every study that has ever been conducted on this subject, the nurse practitioners have delivered care as competently as the physicians and for less money.

Los Angeles Times, 6-28:(A)12.

Lloyd Johnston
Principal investigator
for a University of Michigan
study on student drug use

4

[On his study showing increases in drug use by 8th-grade students]: We may now be in danger of losing some of that hard-won ground as a new, more naive generation of youngsters enters adolescence and as society eases up on its many communications to young people of all ages about drugs . . . The drug-abuse issue has pretty much "fallen off the screen" in this country, both figuratively and literally. Ever since the buildup to the [Persian] Gulf war [of 1991], political leaders and the press talk about it less, television networks have backed off on their prime-time placement of anti-drug ads and, in general, national attention has moved away from the issue.

April 13/
Los Angeles Times, 4-14:(A)11.

Nancy M. Kane
Professor,
School of Public Health,
Harvard University

5

I am . . . astounded by the sense of outrage I hear from hospital administrators of the most powerful institutions at the mere suggestion of an outside, public appraisal of their financial performance. This sense that [hospitals] should not

(NANCY M. KANE)

be held publicly accountable for their use of huge financial resources, made larger still by tax subsidies and exemptions, creates a climate that permits abuse of the public trust.

Before House Subcommittee
on Oversight and Investigations,
Washington, D.C., March 31/
The Washington Post, 4-1:(B)13.

Rhoda Karpatkin
Executive director,
Consumers Union
of the United States

1

The consumer interest is going eyeball-to-eyeball with the [health-] insurance companies' interests, with the hospitals' interests, with the doctors' interests and with the pharmaceutical companies' interests. These are very big interests; they command enormous numbers of people and millions of dollars, and for them it's a life-or-death struggle. There are precious few consumer resources arrayed on the other side. That's why it's very important for us to stay focused on this.

Lear's, April:28.

John Kerry
United States Senator,
D-Massachusetts

2

[If President Clinton] won't seriously fund [drug-abuse] treatment because of budget constraints, he should invoke the national emergency provision that would allow us to fund what's needed off-budget. It's simply unacceptable—and counter-productive—to plead poverty on this. Doing it only halfway won't get the job done, and it will erode support for what we actually do.

Time, 12-20:35.

David A. Kessler
Commissioner,
Food and Drug Administration
of the United States

3

[Urging physicians and others to report to the FDA about adverse reactions and other bad effects patients experience with drugs and other medical products]: What this is about is trying to change the culture of medicine so that reporting products that cause harm becomes a part of it. Right now, the average physician doesn't even know there's a system in place for reporting. This has to change. [Doctors, dentists, nurses and others are] the first to know when a drug or medical device does not perform as it should. The sooner they report it . . . the faster the agency can . . . take corrective action.

Interview,
Washington, D.C., June 1/
Los Angeles Times, 6-2:(A)11.

4

When consumers see a health claim for a dietary supplement, they assume it will provide the benefit it touts. In fact, the marketplace is awash in unsubstantiated claims . . . These claims appear in current catalogues, brochures and other advertising materials, or, in some cases, on the product label. They are also being made by some salespeople at health-food stores; 93 percent of the health-food stores, when we asked, recommended dietary supplements for cancer, to fight infection and to treat high blood pressure.

Before House Health and Environment Subcommittee,
Washington, D.C., July 29/
Los Angeles Times, 7-30:(A)24.

5

[On the formation of the Task Force on AIDS Drug Development, made up of government, pharmaceutical and AIDS-community representatives]: We have never done anything like this before. We will have the government and the [drug] industry and the AIDS community all sitting down together to develop strategy on AIDS-drug development, collaboratively for the first time. We will discuss what drugs to look for, how to find them, what are the best leads now, and are we pursuing them as best we can.

Washington, D.C.,
Nov. 30/
The New York Times, 12-1:(A)10.

Jack Kevorkian
Pathologist

1

[On the controversy about his helping patients commit suicide]: It's tough on me [to assist in suicides]. You've got to steel yourself. Every doctor does. If a doctor didn't do that, he couldn't function. Medicine is a real tragic profession in most cases. You steel yourself and you cannot empathize too much, although I do. Several times, tears have come into my eyes. These are not happy moments. The ending of a human life can never be a good moment . . . I have never cared about anything but the welfare of the patient in front of me. I don't care about the law. I don't care about injunctions. I don't care about legislators.

Interview, Southfield, Mich./
Newsweek, 3-8:48.

2

[On his being charged under Michigan's new law against assisting suicides, which he readily admits doing for terminally ill people]: I will continue helping suffering patients no matter what. I welcome going on trial. It isn't Kevorkian on trial. It isn't assisted suicide on trial. You know what's on trial? It's your civilization and society.

News conference, Aug. 17/
The New York Times, 8-18:(A)7.

Bruce King
Governor of New Mexico (D)

3

Health-care reform will help small business as much as anybody and more than most. Right now, who pays the highest insurance premiums? Small business. Who stands to lose their coverage if one worker gets seriously sick? Small business. Who gets red-lined just because of the business they're in? The restaurant, the hairdresser, the sheet-metal shop, the rancher.

Interview/USA Today, 8-16:(A)2.

Connie Mack
United States Senator,
R-Florida

4

[On President Clinton's health-care reform plan]: The President's plan will force too many Americans to change their health-care coverage. It will give a faceless government bureaucracy more control over your health care. It could even prevent your own doctor from treating you. That's wrong.

Broadcast address to the nation,
Washington, D.C., Sept. 22/
Los Angeles Times, 9-23:(A)14.

Ira C. Magaziner
Manager,
White House Task Force
on National Health Care Reform

5

[On the Clinton Administration's plans for health-care reform]: It would be a birthright of all people to have the guaranteed-benefits package. Every American is going to receive a "health security" card. And regardless of what happens to them—if they lose their jobs, change jobs, get sick or whatever—they're going to be able to get that nationally guaranteed benefits package.

Interview/
U.S. News & World Report,
4-12:26.

6

Often our friends in the media focus their whole attention on health-care reform as if "what specific piece of money might have to be raised next year to help us insure the uninsured" is the most important thing in health care. We know better. We know that what is really going to matter to the American people five years from now, 10 years from now, is not what amount of money was raised initially to get over the hump of getting the uninsured insured. What's really going to matter is, "What happens when I go to my doctor? What happens when I get ill? How does my insurance coverage look? Does it really protect me or not?"

Speech/
The New York Times, 5-3:(A)8.

7

[On President Clinton's health-care reform plan]: What we're doing is, we've taken our best stab. We've got a model that basically shows the interaction of different numbers. They support our particular policies. If you disagree with the policies, disagree with the politics, that's the discussion we need to have . . . The question then gets put on the table: Okay, you think you are slowing the rate of growth [of Medicare and Medicaid] too much and that that's going to have a negative effect on the health-care system? Well, we can discuss that. Do you think the Medicare savings are politically unrealistic? $124-billion? Should it be $100-billion? We can discuss that. Do you get less deficit reduction? You can do that. Do you want to phase in long-term care one year slower? We can look at that.

The New York Times, 9-28:(A)10.

Martha McSteen
President,
National Committee
to Preserve Social Security
and Medicare

1

[Expressing concern that President Clinton's forthcoming health-care reform plan will be partially funded by caps on Medicare spending]: The bottom line is what the whole program will cost seniors. We're having difficulty measuring the value of these new benefits when compared to huge new cuts in Medicare and higher premiums, co-payments and deductibles. Seniors are very concerned that they are going to be asked to foot more than their fair share of the bill, given the recent budget agreement which led to higher taxes on Social Security benefits and $56-billion in cuts in Medicare funding.

Los Angeles Times, 9-10:(A)22.

Mark Mellman
Democratic Party
public-opinion analyst

2

[On President Clinton's pending health-care reform plan]: There's a deep schizophrenia in the American public about this issue. Most people are very satisfied with their own care, but they understand the system is a mess. They have growing reservations about what the President is preparing. In the absence of solid information, they are filling in the blanks with their fears rather than their hopes.

Newsweek, 9-13:37.

Richard E. Merritt
Director,
Intergovernmental Health
Policy Project,
George Washington University

3

[On states that are developing their own health-care reform plans and what they should do pending President Clinton's reform plans on the Federal level]: We get calls from the states all the time, wondering what to do. We advise them not to hold back now. First, there is no guarantee anything will happen at the Federal level. The states have been fooled by [Federal] promises of health-care reform before, and they have a healthy sense of skepticism. Second, they don't have the luxury of being able to wait around. Medicaid benefits are bankrupting them, and they have to balance their budgets.

The Washington Post, 11-26:(A)29.

Michael H. Merson
Director,
Global Program on AIDS,
World Health Organization

4

[Expressing concern about a possible AIDS epidemic in central and eastern Europe]: The risk factors are there, and they're there in a big way. We need to mount our control measures now, before the situation gets out of control . . . One of the great mistakes these countries can make is to do what countries like India and Thailand and Myanmar did, which was to say: "AIDS is an African disease. We don't have homosexuality here; we don't have prostitution; we don't have intravenous drug use. It's not going to happen here. We're not going to worry about it." The real question is whether the countries of central and eastern Europe will rise to the occasion, despite all their other problems, and con-

401

front this. What we have learned from other parts of the world is that action has come too late and too little.

To reporters,
Berlin, Germany, April 7/
The New York Times, 4-8:(A)2.

1

It's best to be frank. There have been disappointments in [the development of new drugs against AIDS]. And we cannot report the big breakthroughs on preventive vaccines for which the world is waiting. We must accept that our scientific advances today are coming in small steps, not leaps and bounds . . . At times, our progress seems desperately slow.

At Ninth International Conference on AIDS,
Berlin, Germany, June 11/
Los Angeles Times, 6-12:(A)4.

Morgan Meyer
Physician;
Former president,
Illinois Medical Society

2

[Criticizing President Clinton's health-care reform plan]: There will be hospitals closing, people out of work, and we're going to be expected to make all health-care decisions according to imposed guidelines. The benefits of this plan are vastly overrated, and the savings they anticipate in Medicare are illusory.

Time, 10-11:28.

Robert H. Michel
United States Representative,
R-Illinois

3

[On his and other critics' differences with President Clinton's health-care reform plan]: [The debate will be] about the role of government in our society, the threat of further expanding bureaucracies, the time-honored nature of the doctor-patient relationship, taxes, fees, mandates and about whether our health-care system

is essentially to retain the private-sector character that has made it great or whether we will embark on an uncharted course of government-run medicine.

Oct. 27/
The Washington Post, 10-28:(A)19.

Kate Michelman
Executive director,
National Abortion Rights
Action League

4

If [President Clinton's] health-care reform plan is to meet the health needs of women, it can't do anything less than include a full range of reproductive health services, including abortion. Reproductive health care includes abortion but is not limited to abortion. It includes prenatal care, contraceptive care, basic gynecological care, even family planning, education and services. And we have to understand abortion not as a political issue but as a health issue for women.

Interview/
USA Today, 10-7:(A)15.

Leonard Minsky
Co-founder,
Coalition for Universities
in the Public Interest

5

[Criticizing the granting to drug companies of exclusive licenses for new drugs developed through Federally funded university research]: The exclusive license is the fulcrum allowing corporations to make excessive profits above and beyond the profits that can be made in a competitive situation. Granting corporations tax breaks for funding their own research, and monopoly control of a product developed with Federal research dollars, is corporate welfare. These are public handouts designed to make U.S. companies competitive, but they're counter-competitive devices that reinforce the disability they're designed to cure. We are subsidizing an inefficient system.

The Atlantic, March:44.

Jerry Mitchell
Vice chairman,
Upjohn Company;
President, Upjohn Laboratories

1

Everyone wants to point fingers at the pharmaceutical industry [for its high drug prices] . . . We're an easy target. But this industry invests at a rate that's three times greater than the average of the rest of American industry. So you've got to get a return that's greater than the rest.

Interview, Kalamazoo, Mich./
Los Angeles Times, 4-12:(D)4.

Daniel Patrick Moynihan
United States Senator,
D-New York

2

[On President Clinton's health-care reform plan]: If 40 percent of [currently] insured Americans are going to pay more, we're going to have to persuade some of those that they're going to get more and others that, on balance, it's their civic duty. We're not always very good at that. But if we're not very good at it, that means no [to the plan].

At Senate Finance Committee hearing,
Washington, D.C., Oct. 28/
The Washington Post, 10-29:(A)1.

Alan R. Nelson
Executive vice president,
American Society
of Internal Medicine

3

There's no denying that internists want fair play, less red tape and greater autonomy in their practice. [But] we have learned the hard way how Washington works. Policy-makers said Medicare payment reform would mean more appropriate pay for primary-care services and less hassles; but the opposite has been true. Why would [we] believe that a system of global budgets and price controls would mean fair play and less micro-management?

Los Angeles Times, 3-23:(A)16.

Don Nickels
United States Senator,
R-Oklahoma

4

[Approving of the Senate's vote to maintain a U.S. ban on immigrants with HIV, the AIDS virus]: This is a serious health issue. Lifting the ban would have contributed to the spread of a deadly disease which has already infected a million Americans. It would also cost hundreds of millions of dollars at a time when we are already struggling to contain health-care costs.

Feb. 18/
Los Angeles Times, 2-19:(A)16.

Jonathan Peck
Official,
Institute for Alternative Futures

5

[Saying advancements in technology may bring doctors back to making "house calls" through electronic communications between home and office]: One hundred years ago, a general practitioner could see three or four patients a day in his buggy. Then patients started coming to his office and he could see 30 or 40 in a day. [With modern technology,] we could have 24-hour monitoring and access via television to a tremendous amount of knowledge. Doctors could make house calls electronically. The ability to do more and spend less will be enormous.

Newsweek, 10-4:66.

Ross Perot
Industrialist;
1992 independent
Presidential candidate

6

[On President Clinton's health-care reform plan]: You tell the people during the [1992 election] campaign that you will revolutionize health care and save tens of billions of dollars a year, net, after adding 30 million people to insurance rolls. I said, "That's a tightwire walk without a tightwire. You can't do it." Now, every time he talks, the cost goes up. The first trial balloon is $30-billion, then comes $60 [-billion], then,

(ROSS PEROT)

$90 [billion], then it's $100 [-billion] to $150-billion. We should try pilot programs to make sure it works. We can stand a small catastrophe. We do not need a nationwide health-care catastrophe.

Interview, Dallas, Texas/
U.S. News & World Report,
5-17:43.

1

[On President Clinton's health-care reform plan]: You and I might like a trip to the stars, but if we can't pay for it, it's just talk, right? That's going to be the big gorilla on this one: How do you pay for it? There is no free lunch, and there's no free health care. For all I know, we may say this is a good plan. But then if we can't pay for it, we'll have to focus on that. We'll have to figure what we can afford and develop a plan that's limited by what we can afford to do, not what we'd like to do.

USA Today, 10-11:(A)2.

Lisa J. Raines
Vice president,
Genzyme Corporation

2

We are deeply disappointed that, after dozens of meetings, members of the [Clinton] Administration still do not understand that Federal review of new-drug prices would have a devastating impact on the biotechnology industry. It's tantamount to price control. We have found that Congress has a deeper understanding of this issue.

Oct. 27/
The New York Times, 10-28:(A)10.

Stephen A. Ralph
Executive vice president,
Huntington Memorial Hospital,
Pasadena, Calif.

3

The economic incentives have changed for hospitals; no longer does more mean better. Hospitals have done a poor job of understanding

our costs. Now we must, or we will go out of business.

The New York Times, 9-29:(A)10.

William K. Reilly
Administrator,
Environmental Protection Agency
of the United States

4

Environmental tobacco smoke, secondhand smoke, involuntary smoking, passive smoking—whatever you want to call it—has now been shown conclusively to increase the risk of lung cancer in healthy non-smokers. Taken together, the total weight of evidence is conclusive that environmental tobacco smoke increases the risk of lung cancer in non-smokers.

News conference,
Washington, D.C., Jan. 7/
The New York Times, 1-8:(A)9.

Uwe E. Reinhardt
Professor of political economy,
Princeton University

5

Health care accounts for a huge chunk of the growth in gross domestic product registered since the early 1980s. In Federal and state government budgets, health care probably displaces investment in education, roads and transportation systems that would be more beneficial for the economy. But we don't really know whether health spending in the private sector displaces the kind of investments that would cause higher economic growth.

The New York Times, 1-5:(A)7.

Robert D. Reischauer
Director,
Congressional Budget Office

6

[On health-care reform]: We are going to have to see a lot of specialists in America transform themselves into retirees or general practitioners.

(ROBERT D. REISCHAUER)

We have somewhere between 60 percent-70 percent of our medical professionals in specialties, 30 percent-40 percent in general practice. Every other country in the world, those percentages are reversed. So it is clear we have many more anesthesiologists, radiologists, surgeons, urologists, whatever, than the least-cost mix of resources. You will see a lot more services being provided by nurse practitioners, by other kinds of technical-support staffs. And for all of this to occur to get the full benefits out of a system, it takes time.

Interview/USA Today, 4-6:(A)11.

1

[On health-care costs in the U.S.]: We have basically no brakes on our system. People ration or determine what they purchase in our society in two different ways. One is individually. You have a budget constraint and you earn a certain amount and you have to decide. And those are personal decisions. Most of what happens in our society happens that way. You also have societal budget constraints. Defense: We decide we're going to spend $268-billion on defense and Congress votes on it, and that's the amount. Health care is controlled by neither of these. The health-care system that we have has no constraints on it because nobody realizes how it's all being paid for. Most Americans don't think they are. And so there's sort of no reason for you to be concerned.

Interview/USA Today, 4-6:(A)11.

Arnold S. Relman
Former editor,
"The New England Journal
of Medicine"

2

The best way to control [health-care] costs and preserve quality is to have the physicians do it. The whole health-care system is built on the behavior of doctors, and that behavior is greatly influenced by the way health is organized.

The New York Times, 3-18:(A)10.

3

[Saying the question of "doctor choice" in health-care reform is overblown]: I think we have to disabuse the average American of the idea that you can't get good care unless you have a large menu of doctors out there, look at their qualifications and pick one. That's not what most people do anyway.

The New York Times, 5-1:7.

Janet A. Rodgers
President,
American Association
of Colleges of Nursing

4

Men and women entering nursing are drawn to the security and career flexibility of being involved in the largest health profession at a time when Americans' demand for health care is exploding. Still, though indeed welcome, current enrollments [in nursing schools] lag behind the levels needed to alleviate the current nursing shortage that is expected to continue into the 21st century . . . The time has never been more critical for increased Federal, state and private partnerships to ensure the nation with sufficient personnel to meet the needs of our increasingly nursing-dominant health-care system.

The Washington Post, 10-29:(B)5.

Charlie Rose
United States Representative,
D-North Carolina

5

[On a big increase in the cigarette tax that the Clinton Administration may propose]: In the past, the [Ronald] Reagan and [George] Bush Administrations were pretty reasonable about taxing tobacco. But I think all of us who represent tobacco [-producing] states knew that the growing concern about smoking and health was going to someday lead to this type of attitude and reaction in the White House. This talk of $2 a pack [in Federal taxes] is scaring us to death, and that's putting it mildly.

The New York Times, 3-22:(A)8.

John Rother
*Director of legislation
and public policy,
American Association
of Retired Persons*

1

Any [health-care] reform will create millions of winners and millions of losers. Health care is the most emotional and personal of all public-policy issues.

Time, 1-18:24.

2

[On President Clinton's forthcoming health-care reform plan]: It's probably not possible to do health reform without getting everyone upset . . . The one big difference [between health reform and economic reform] is the economic plan didn't affect ordinary people that much. The health-care plan will affect every—underline "every"—American. It's going to take a much more sustained and intensive effort [to win public approval].

USA Today, 3-30:(A)2.

3

[On President Clinton's forthcoming health-care reform plan]: We can't afford to have health-care reform be characterized as just another tax bill, and we certainly can't afford to have it mired in more, partisan posturing. [But] what started out, really, in the State of the Union speech as a high moral call for shared sacrifice, in the end degenerated into horse trading and typical special-interest tactics. We can't do health reform that way. We have to see a greater leadership and a greater public will to stand against all the exceptions and loopholes that will inevitably threaten the comprehensiveness of the health-care effort.

The New York Times, 8-9:(A)8.

4

If we're talking about Medicare cuts alone as a way of financing [President Clinton's] health reform, we would fight that with all our strength—we've gone as far as we can go down that road.

The key question is whether there is effective cost containment on the private side to match the savings on the Medicare side. If just Medicare is controlled, our answer is "no way."

Los Angeles Times, 9-10:(A)22.

Michael Roush
*Chief U.S. Senate lobbyist,
National Federation
of Small Businesses*

5

[Arguing against possible Clinton Administration Federal mandates on small businesses requiring them to pay most of their employees' health-insurance premiums]: The cost of health insurance is the Number 1 problem for small businesses. They want the system changed. The status quo is not acceptable, but mandates are off the table. It's very intensely felt. They'll take almost anything other than mandates.

*The Christian Science Monitor,
8-19:2.*

Beverly Rubik
*Biophysicist; Director,
Center for Frontier Sciences,
Temple University*

6

[On research which shows a connection between mind and body in the healing process]: Patients will have to become active participants in their healing, instead of passive bystanders. In the current system, patients surrender control . . . They take their bodies to the doctor the way they take their car to a mechanic. But that really disempowers the mind-body relationship . . . Many doctors like to maintain control. If they feel they're not in control of a patient's disease, they may feel left out. But that's a very artificial system. I hope [to be able to] open up physicians to seeing that they're not in control; the best ones already know this, deep down.

Interview/USA Today, 10-26:(D)4.

Ronald J. Saldarini
*President,
Lederle-Praxis Biologicals*

7

[On the prospect that the government may become the dispenser of vaccines for children

(RONALD J. SALDARINI)

and thus force a lowering of the price of the vaccines]: If I can't be sure that the purchaser will allow me to price my product in a way consistent with recovery of my investment and the years I put into the effort of developing a vaccine, I may be unwilling to consider further development of vaccines.

April 1/
The New York Times, 4-2:(A)12.

Jon S. Saxe
President,
Synergen Corporation

1

Before we ever heard of [President-elect] Bill Clinton [and his criticism of high health-care costs], before he was a Presidential candidate, I believed that in the '90s, just as sure as you had to prove safety and efficacy [of medications], you also would have to convince people that you are delivering economic value, and that even goes for life-saving therapies.

The New York Times, 1-18:(A)1.

Raymond Scaletter
Chairman, board of trustees,
American Medical Association

2

As the patients' advocate, we [the AMA] know that far too many of our patients have no health-insurance coverage. The hassles of providing care and the burden of paperwork and bureaucratic second-guessing frustrates physicians as well as our patients. And the costs of health care are rising too quickly for our patients and the good of the nation. We have not, do not and will not defend the status quo . . . Contrary to perceptions, this nation does have experience in both health-system reform and controlling costs. One lesson to be gained from experience is that true effective cost control has never been achieved in this or any other economy through arbitrary caps on spending or price controls. They did not work in the 1970s, only delaying natural price increases and impeding supply of necessary goods and services. They also will not

work in health care. Price controls, or global budgets, mean arbitrary decisions that will, without basis, limit our ability to deliver needed medical care to our patients. We have suggested a better way, a partnership between government, physicians, employers and others. By working together to isolate the costly failures in the health-care system, true budget predictability can be brought to this nation's health-care costs without limiting patients' access to medical care.

At meeting of White House Task Force
on National Health Care Reform,
Washington, D.C., March 29/
The New York Times, 3-30:(A)10.

Donna E. Shalala
Secretary of Health
and Human Services
of the United States

3

How would we pay for the new [health-care] system? . . . Whatever the framework is, it has to be a combination of reorganizing existing expenditures, whether they be in the private or public sector. Some arrangements for people to make a contribution themselves and for their businesses to make a contribution. There may be an identification of some new taxes. We've talked a lot about "sin" taxes. Certainly, we're looking at a VAT. But all of this would be phased in, and what we first must do is have the mechanisms in place to slow down existing spending and have incentives for running the system more efficiently. There clearly is waste in the system. There clearly is fraud and abuse in the system.

Interview, April 13/
USA Today, 4-14:(A)13.

4

We are committed to containing runaway [health-care] costs while expanding coverage and providing security to families and businesses— not next year or the year after, but right now. And we are committed to doing that by working with a private system as opposed to substituting a public system [of health insurance] . . . [Rising health-care costs are] a one-way ticket to bankruptcy [for small-business owners]. These

(DONNA E. SHALALA)

galloping costs translate into lower wages and reduced benefits for employees, higher prices for consumers and, in the long run, weakened American companies and a higher [Federal budget] deficit. Runaway costs will ruin our economy and will wreck our national future. We have to do better.

At U.S. Chamber of Commerce,
Washington, D.C./
Nation's Business, May:13.

1

[Saying even illegal aliens will be able to receive preventive and emergency care under U.S. President Clinton's soon-to-be-announced health-care plan]: We have got to provide prevention for everybody that's here. One person getting a disease who is an undocumented alien risks all of our health . . . What the President has talked about is American citizens getting health-care cards. But we have indicated that we will continue to have a public health system and no one will be turned away for health care. So there will be a system in place that covers everyone that is in the United States.

To reporters,
San Diego, Calif., July 27/
Los Angeles Times, 7-28:(A)11.

Ben Shwachman
President, Los Angeles County
Medical Association

2

[On the trend toward networks of doctors and hospitals as a way of controlling costs]: You can't just hang up a shingle, open the door and get patients any more. You have to get contracts, and contracts go through huge conglomerates formed by hospitals, physicians or insurance companies. This trend has created a class of millionaire entrepreneur-physicians who own and operate the networks . . . The patients are moved around like cattle [even though they may receive good care].

The New York Times, 8-21:7.

Steven Sieverts
Vice president
of health-care finance,
Blue Cross/Blue Shield
of the National Capital Area

3

No one has put together a system that we think can adequately measure a physician's quality of care. We can differentiate between the acceptable and the unacceptable. But there are no tools available that can differentiate between good and excellent doctors.

U.S. News & World Report,
4-19:48.

Henry E. Simmons
President,
National Leadership Coalition
for Health Care Reform

4

[On the opposition from small businesses to a Clinton Administration health-care reform plan that may require them to pay for medical insurance for their employees]: If small business got off its knee-jerk opposition to a mandate and analyzed these proposals, they'd say it is extremely fair. It would control their costs and enable them to do something most of them are already doing—providing health coverage—without having their health costs double every six years.

The New York Times, 5-3:(C)3.

Steven Simmons
Spokesman, People for the
Ethical Treatment of Animals

5

[On the use of animals in medical research]: While government turns a blind eye to the intense suffering and scientific fraud that occur in laboratories, animals die because of their inability to fight back. The actions of those brave enough to expose cruelty may seem extreme, but allowing atrocities to go unchecked is a more frightening prospect.

Ladies' Home Journal, April:57.

Jonathan Slater
Child psychiatrist,
pediatric cardiac
transplantation team,
Columbia-Presbyterian Medical
Center's Babies Hospital,
New York, N.Y.

1

[On parents who agree to donate organs from their brain-dead children]: How do you have the presence of mind in this situation to think about donating organs? I think the people who do it are just extraordinary. Donating doesn't lessen their pain, but it can give them a tremendous sense of continuity—that the loss has not been for naught—and that can be very helpful.

The New York Times, 5-11:(B)5.

Howard Spiro
Professor of medicine,
Yale University Medical School

2

Technology has vastly improved the world since my graduation in 1947, but it has made medicine more visual, focusing on disease— what the doctor can find, rather than on illness— what the patient can tell. The first ultrasounds and CT scans of the 1970s seem laughably imprecise now, like the late-night weather maps on TV. But their views of internal anatomy completely changed how we physicians regard our patients or, to be more precise, their organs. The images—the icons, really—of technology have let the eye dominate definitions of disease; the ear has subsided into silence . . . The Golden Age [of medicine] is yet to come—and will always be just ahead, thanks to science and technology. On the personal level, however, matters have worsened. Technology has widened the gap between patient and physician, has made many doctors feel like mere conduits of power, no longer healing agents but simply purveyors of pills or wielders of scalpels; rulers out of disease, anyway. Team medicine has diffused personal responsibility and lessened the importance of personal virtue or character in our hospitals.

At Yale University Medical School commencement,
May 24/
The Wall Street Journal,
5-26:(A)16.

James H. Stacey
Spokesman,
American Medical Association

3

[On the trend toward self-testing by individuals using at-home kits of various kinds]: We aren't opposed to home tests, especially the [blood glucose] kinds associated with diabetes monitoring. But physicians feel strongly that they treat patients—they don't treat test results. It's very important for the doctors to get to know the patient. A test should only be used as an auxiliary in diagnostic procedures.

Los Angeles Times, 3-3:(A)11.

Fortney H. "Pete" Stark
United States Representative,
D-California

4

[Criticizing the idea of "managed competition," which is an underpinning of President Clinton's evolving health-care reform plan]: What I have trouble with is a program that suggests to me that we can save money, broaden access and provide better medical care—and I can't figure out what it costs, what hurts, what do we change. It's something akin to [evangelist] Pat Robertson: If we just pray the right prayer to the right God, all our cares will go away . . . There are 900 billion real dollars being spent on medical care in the United States, and there are at least 40 million real Americans who don't have access to that system in a reasonable way . . . And I can tell you it's probably going to cost $50-billion a year to provide for them.

News conference,
Washington, D.C., March 5/
Los Angeles Times, 3-6:(A)20.

5

[On Germany's health-care system]: The system has elements of what we should have here [in the U.S.]. The fascinating thing is that [in Germany] no one questions it. It isn't, "Why should we be paying for those who can't afford health care?" . . . It is accepted by everybody. With a public who believes that, and accepts that as a way of life, they are 90 percent there.

USA Today, 3-18:(A)9.

(FORTNEY H. "PETE" STARK)

1

[There] is some dream of people who say competition and free enterprise can do better than any government can do [in providing health insurance for the country]. That's not true. [The government] can run circles around an Aetna or Pru [Prudential insurance companies] and the rest of them.

May 13/
The Washington Post, 5-14:(A)18.

George Stephanopoulos
Senior Adviser
to President of the United States
Bill Clinton

2

[On selling President Clinton's health-care reform plan to the people]: First and foremost will be the theme of "security." That is the emotional core of this plan. It speaks to people's deepest fears. The idea is that no matter what happens to you—if you lose your job, if your wife loses her job, if you switch jobs, or if your company goes under—your health care will be nationally guaranteed.

Sept. 19/
The New York Times, 9-20:(A)9.

Frank Sulloway
Visiting scholar
of science history,
Massachusetts Institute
of Technology

3

Psychoanalysis is built on quicksand. It's like a 10-story hotel sinking into an unsound foundation. And the analysts are in this building. You tell them it's sinking, and they say, "It's okay; we're on the 10th floor."

Time, 11-29:51.

James S. Todd
Executive vice president,
American Medical Association

4

Any reform of the health-care system will fail without the support of the medical profession.

The New York Times, 3-5:(A)8.

5

[Nurses] make the claim that they can do 80 percent of what a primary-care physician can do—and cheaper—and I would agree with them. But, prospectively, can they tell the 20 percent from the 80 percent? And do patients want to risk going to someone who is not trained to look at the fine nuances of disease processes and physiology? [And] if the nurses suddenly become primary-care providers, who's going to take care of patients in hospitals?

Los Angeles Times, 6-28:(A)12.

6

[On President Clinton's just-delivered address to Congress and the nation on his health-care reform plan]: Tonight belongs to the President. He made the case for change in a very, very emotional, highly dedicated fashion and we compliment him for it. [But] tomorrow, when the sun comes up, we're going to have to roll up our sleeves and see what it takes to get it done. We're going to have to address the reality of how we pay for it . . . What the checks and balances are going to be . . . One of the most significant things the President said tonight was that everyone was going to have to participate—and it's a wake-up call to every family and organization to bear their fair share.

Sept. 22/
Los Angeles Times, 9-23:(A)12.

Bernard Tresnowski
President,
Blue Cross/Blue Shield Association

7

[Supporting changes in the tax code to give incentives to people covered by company-provided health plans to seek lower-cost plans]: The most powerful incentive is the tax code. We've been through five decades of teaching the individual that health care is a free good. If you're going to change that, you're going to have to go where the rubber meets the road. I can't think of anything better than changing the tax code.

The Washington Post, 1-7:(A)18.

Paul E. Tsongas
Former United States Senator,
D-Massachusetts

1

If you set up a [health-care] system . . . where doctors feel they're imposed upon, particularly because they've not been included in negotiations, you then have thousands upon thousands of physicians who have no self-interest in the system working. And that's like having termites in your system.

USA Today, 4-15:(A)4.

2

[On the Canadian vs. the U.S. health-insurance system]: My concern about [the Canadian single-payer system] is that Canadians buy insurance for access to American hospitals. I don't know anybody in the United States who buys insurance to access into the Canadian health system. So I think you can acknowledge the value of the Canadian system, but also understand that it works, in part, because people can come here [to the U.S.] for procedures they'd be on a waiting list for, or [that] are simply not available, in Canada.

Interview/USA Today, 7-22:(A)9.

P. Roy Vagelos
Chairman,
Merck & Company
(pharmaceuticals)

3

[On the high cost of prescription drugs]: We have the highest risks of any industry I know. We are betting on things that may or may not mature and become available to the public in 10 or 15 years. That has to be rewarded.

The New York Times, 3-16:(C)2.

George Voinovich
Governor of Ohio (R)

4

Almost by default, health-care reform has been at the top of my agenda as, each year, increasing amounts of general revenue dollars are being diverted to our public health-care pro-grams, like Medicaid, and away from areas like education and economic development . . . Piecemeal efforts . . . are doomed to failure. The goal of health-care reform should be to provide access to cost-effective, quality health care for all Americans. Short of that, we're just tinkering around the margins.

Interview/USA Today, 8-16:(A)2.

Henry A. Waxman
United States Representative,
D-California

5

[On a study that says drug companies charge too-high prices for their products]:Competition simply does not work in the market for prescription drugs. That is why prescription drugs are no longer affordable in this country. [The study] tells us where to look for cuts: the excess profits which appear to be as high as $2-billion per year; the $10-billion per year spent on wasteful and detrimental advertising and promotion; the billions of dollars spent on research and development for drugs that offer no therapeutic gain.

News conference, Feb. 25/
The New York Times, 2-26:(C)2.

6

[On the Clinton Administration's proposal for "managed competition" as a way of reforming the health-care system]: I don't know if managed competition will live up to all the expectations, but it does seem to me to make some sense to give people as much choice as possible, to let consumers have more of a role in what kind of health-care system they may want to be part of.

Los Angeles Times, 5-6:(A)5.

7

[Criticizing the part of President Clinton's health-care reform plan that limits the subsidies for retirees, small businesses and poor people]: It's a real serious problem, a serious flaw in the Administration's proposal. It undermines the credibility of the Administration promise of universal coverage—health-care security that will

WHAT THEY SAID IN 1993

always be there—because it won't be there if they run out of money.

Oct. 27/
Los Angeles Times, 10-28:(A)22.

Burton Weisbrod
Professor of economics,
Northwestern University

1

There is no reason to believe that health care expenditures as a percent of GDP would be very much higher today than 25 years ago if technology had not changed. Technology is what is driving up expenses rather than [society] just paying more for the same old things.

U.S. News & World Report,
6-7:56.

Robert J. White
Professor of surgery,
Case Western Reserve University
Medical School

2

The history of medicine in the 20th century is heavily based on animal research, and there is no doubt in my mind that the future of medicine, including finding a vaccine for AIDS, will continue to rely heavily on experiments involving animals.

Ladies' Home Journal, April:57.

Patti Wilcox
Co-director,
Breast Surveillance Service,
Johns Hopkins Hospital,
Baltimore, Md.

3

Essentially, the message is that your chances of getting breast cancer increase as you don't die from other things [as you get older]. The important thing for women to remember is that the odds of not getting breast cancer are always greater than those of getting it. The really key number is that for every 100 women who get breast cancer, 70 have no risk factors. I don't think we can underestimate the fact that breast cancer is sneaky as hell. While I don't think there's been an understatement of the problem, there may be an overstatement of who is at risk.

The Washington Post, 1-5:(Health)12.

Ron Wyden
United States Representative,
D-Oregon

4

I firmly believe that any good national health bill has to contain the key features of the Oregon plan—specifically, universal coverage, preventive health care, cost containment through managed care, extensive use of non-physician providers, and an emphasis on what's medically effective for our citizens.

The Washington Post, 3-20:(A)10.

Ruth Yoshpe
Health economist,
American Psychiatric Association

5

[On the increasing competition to psychiatrists from psychologists and sociologists]: Psychiatrists are experiencing a shift in the very nature of what they do. At a time when we are actually arriving at the greatest understanding of the mind and body connection, there are market forces that are working to separate that connection . . . This is like telling Freud he can't probe into the subconscious, that he can only prescribe medicine.

Los Angeles Times, 6-18:(D)1.

The Performing Arts

BROADCASTING

William Abbott
Director,
Foundation to Improve Television

1

[Calling for curbs on violence in TV programming]: We must be aware of First Amendment issues. But that should be the beginning of the discussion, not the end. We are already protecting our children [from obscenity and pornography]. All we are asking is that we extend that protection into the home . . . Violence has been proven to harm children.

The Christian Science Monitor,
8-10:13.

William J. Bennett
Former Secretary of Education
of the United States

2

[On TV programming, especially that aimed at children]: It's a disaster. The claim made for television since the 1940s has been that it would make kids smarter. It's not only not made them smarter, it's contributed to their dumbing-down. I don't think PBS has done a very good job at all. We'll see [about its plans to expand children's programming]. But I am doubtful, because what is likely to pass muster will be what I call "values-lite."

The Washington Post, 12-8:(A)10.

Joanna Bistany
Vice president,
ABC News

3

Entertainment [TV] shows usually have a finite life span and, with some exceptions, they tend to be either hits, or they're canceled. [But] what we've learned with [TV] newsmagazines is that they take time to build and grow. It's pos-

sible that this trend [of more TV newsmagazine shows] will peak. But if the talent, format and stories are right, a newsmagazine can renew itself because reality is compelling and, at least in theory, you can never run out of stories.

Los Angeles Times, 1-7:(F)3.

Steven Bochco
Producer

4

[On the controversy about his forthcoming TV series *NYPD Blue,* which goes beyond normal network standards for violence, language and nudity]: People have told me my timing is all wrong [considering Congressional hearings being held about TV program content], but when is the timing ever right for doing something that's never been done before? . . . I don't think I'm all that dangerous. The last time I looked, this was still America and I had a right to ply my trade, and other people have a right to scream and yell about it. In the final analysis, it's the audience who decides whether to get behind this or not. I believe in this work, and I'm happy to let this work speak for itself.

Interview, Los Angeles, Calif./
The Washington Post, 6-15:(B)8.

5

[Defending the use of raw language, nudity and other grittness in his TV programs such as *NYPD Blue*]: I felt for a long time that part of why we're losing the medium of network television is that we're not keeping pace with the sensibilities of the culture. Ten years ago, 12 years ago, free network TV was the only game in town. If you wanted to see a movie or go to the theatre or see a sporting event, or whatever, you had to leave your home. Now everything is on your TV [via cable and satellite]. Everything. And in that

(STEVEN BOCHCO)

context, free television is dying . . . It's dying in part because of the restrictions placed on serious storytelling by the networks. When we're viewed side by side with all those movies that are available to you on your TV set, we can't compete . . . I want to be able to say, "Folks, in a changing world, in a changing environment where I am in direct competition with every R-rated movie that was in the theatre six months ago"—all you have to do is click your channel over one notch and there it is—"let me at least compete to a tiny degree in terms of what I can say and show," so that we can get an audience for this thing.

Interview, New York, N.Y./
Lear's, November:16.

Beth Bressan
Vice president,
CBS Broadcast Group

1

[On calls for restrictions on violence in TV programming]: The decision-making process is subjective and, in a free, democratic society, needs to remain so. The process is also a creative one. To be too mechanistic in our approach will only inhibit creativity and stop diverse programming . . . Right now, there are not very many cable [-TV] entities out there using any standards or guidelines. When there are so many cable outlets out there saying, in effect, "Come watch us because we do not self-regulate," how much of the television landscape is really going to change? It's very unfair to say the [broadcast TV] networks should do more [to curb violent programming] when [those] networks are the only ones who have done anything to date.

Los Angeles Times, 7-18:(Calendar)76.

Kent Conrad
United States Senator,
D-North Dakota

2

There is too much murder, too much mayhem, too much violence and too many glamorous, glorified views of violence on American televi-

sion. The time for studies is over. The time for debate is over. It is time to act.

News conference,
Washington, D.C., Dec. 15/
Los Angeles Times, 12-16:(A)35.

Dewey Cornell
Clinical psychologist,
University of Virginia

3

[On violence in TV programming]: We have created a culture that increasingly accepts and glamourizes violence. I don't care what the network executives say. [Violence in TV and the media] does desensitize you.

Time, 8-23:32.

Norman Corwin
Former playwright
and radio writer

4

My first love is radio. It makes a collaborator of the listener—through his imagination and because nothing is literal. The ear, after all, is the poet of the senses. It can perceive the most abstract and universal of the arts, music, and it can make the word sovereign. Sometimes, you know, a word is worth a thousand pictures.

Interview/
Los Angeles Times, 12-2:(F)12.

Bill Cosby
Actor, Comedian

5

[On how to improve the quality of TV programs]: Someone at the very top has to say, "Okay, enough of this. I'm going to hire a couple of great psychologists to look over these scripts and then try to lift the consciousness of these writers." The message should be: change, or get out. I'm not talking about political correctness. I'm talking about quality. When you looked at a Dick Van Dyke or a Mary Tyler Moore show, you saw truly believable characters. You saw that somebody was *thinking*. Today's writers look on TV as just a joke machine.

Interview/Newsweek, 12-6:60.

Christopher Crowe
Producer

1

[On calls for reducing violence in TV programming, such as in his program *The Untouchables*]: If I'm forced to make changes, I will. One has to stay alive, after all. [But] there are certain milieus which by their very nature are violent. If you are to depict those events, then you have to depict violence. If you tell that kind of story without violence, then you're not being honest, and you're telling a tale that is being directed by external pressures.

Los Angeles Times, 7-31:(F)1.

Maire Messenger Davies
*Associate professor
of broadcasting,
Boston (Mass.) University*

2

Television and movies need to help us protect our children. TV is a teacher, like families and schools. But TV and movies never show the outcome or consequences of violence, how awful it is to lose someone in a shooting. Nobody on TV mourns them.

*The Christian Science Monitor,
10-22:2.*

Ervin S. Duggan
*Commissioner,
Federal Communications Commission;
President-designate,
Public Broadcasting Service*

3

[On competition to standard broadcasting from services delivered by cable and satellite]: There is a myth in the air that the broadcasting delivery system is doomed. [But] nobody dies. You change and adapt. Hollywood was supposed to die when television was invented—and [today] the movie companies are making more money than ever before . . . Radio was supposed to die when television came about; [but] what we found out is that it adapted to a new kind of medium. It has been forced to change; it has not become extinct. So it's silly to think the broadcasting delivery system, which efficiently

serves everybody simultaneously, will become irrelevant.

*Interview,
Washington, D.C., Dec. 1/
Los Angeles Times, 12-2:(F)9.*

Reuven Frank
Former president, NBC News

4

[On the proliferation of TV newsmagazine programs]: They're becoming indistinguishable. They compete with each other and with the tabloid shows. They don't have much style, and they don't deal with anything very big. It's peeping-Tom journalism—all these stories about people's intimate problems, sexual and psychological. It's like [tabloid-show hosts] Oprah [Winfrey] and Geraldo [Rivera] with better production values. You don't see an attempt to deal with the big problems that are facing the society.

Los Angeles Times, 8-11:(F)8.

Larry Gelbart
*Stage, screen and television
writer*

5

It's not that [TV has] gotten worse—it is what it's always been: pockets of quality and the rest is shameless. But TV today has a vocabulary of about seven words: "rape," "murder," "Amy" and "Joey," and three others. But truly I don't watch it. That's not a put-down; it's just that after so many years, the shows don't surprise me anymore and I can't really watch without rewriting what I'm hearing.

*Interview, Beverly Hills, Calif./
The Washington Post, 3-20:(D)9.*

Todd Gitlin
*Professor of sociology,
University of California,
Berkeley*

6

[On U.S. TV 60 years from now, in 2053]: Alongside the mainstream media, there will be plenty of niche broadcasts for those who can

(TODD GITLIN)

afford them. So while it will probably be possible for some Americans to receive broadcasts in 100 languages, to the poor it will continue to be said, "Let them eat game shows."

Interview/
U.S. News & World Report,
10-25:72.

Al Gore
Vice President
of the United States

1

The [Clinton] Administration will support removal, over time, under appropriate conditions, of judicial and legislative restrictions on all types of telecommunications companies: cable, telephone, utilities, TV and satellite. We will do it by avoiding both extremes: regulation for regulation's sake and the blind adherence to the dead hand of a free-market economist.

Before National Press Club,
Washington, D.C., Dec. 21/
The Christian Science Monitor,
12-23:9.

David Grant
Executive vice president
for business operations,
Fox Broadcasting Company

2

[On calls for restrictions on violence in TV programming]: What happens to kids when they watch violent programs? Is there a difference between "action" and "violence"? Is the impact on people the same when a robot blows up as when a person is shot? I want to know these things. Violence in dramatic works has been around forever. What we need to do is meld our responsibility with our sense of dramatic creation, and not go nuts one way or another.

Los Angeles Times, 7-18:(Calendar)76.

Don Hewitt
Executive producer,
"60 Minutes," CBS-TV

3

[On the quality of TV newsmagazine programs]: If the networks think there aren't enough first-rate entertainment producers in Hollywood to fill up their prime-time schedules with worthwhile programming, what makes them think there are enough first-rate newsmagazine producers who can do that? . . . What it adds up to in many cases is less about reporting news to America than it is about giving notice to Hollywood that "anything you can do, we [in the news division] can do cheaper [financially]."

Lecture at Museum
of Television and Radio,
New York, N.Y./
Los Angeles Times, 8-11:(F)9.

Andrew Heyward
Executive producer,
"48 Hours," CBS-TV

4

When the [TV] networks began putting on a number of new newsmagazines several years ago, the economics of the shows was a key force in their gaining slots in the prime-time schedules. The conventional wisdom was that, in a time slot where the network was likely to be second or third to the competition, a newsmagazine [with half the budget of an entertainment program] was attractive programming. What's interesting about the current TV season is that not only are these shows financially attractive to the networks, they're among the highest-rated shows in prime-time.

Los Angeles Times, 1-7:(F)3.

Leonard Hill
Producer

5

[On threats by some in government to regulate TV programs to control their violent content]: The campaign is under-informed and nearly hysterical, and people have sponsored it without watching network television . . . It is the new political correctness of Washington to bash network television as if it were the cause of violence in society.

The Washington Post,
10-29:(B)4.

Carol Nagy Jacklin
Dean,
division of social science
and communication,
University of Southern California

1

The [U.S.] Surgeon General's reports for years have said that violence on television is related to violence in children. It's so upsetting that, on the one hand, we seem to deplore this violence but, on the other, we are not stopping it in the ways that we know it needs to be stopped.

Newsweek, 8-2:48.

William Kilpatrick
Professor of education,
Boston (Mass.) College

2

[On TV]: It's already done a great deal of damage, in my estimation. The thing about television is that, unlike the schools, the television set is omnipresent. It's like Big Brother in *1984*—you just can't get away from it. And because of its pervasiveness, it shapes the way we think and alters the way we perceive reality . . . [Parents] certainly can't wait for the entertainment industry to reform itself. That could happen over time with enough pressure, but in the meantime you've got to worry about your own children. That means turning the television set off, going to the library, bringing back some books, and instituting the practice of family reading. That means parents choose the models and morals that come into the home, rather than some distant scriptwriter.

Interview/Christianity Today, 10-4:70.

Marvin Kitman
Television critic,
"New York Newsday"

3

The truly diabolical effect of television is that it makes you forget. What has happened through television is that we have a cassette in our brains, and all this information is pouring in. We're sitting there gobbling it up, and then we take the cassette out and put it away, because our attention span lasts only half an hour. This is the great

Orwellian thing that's happened. The only history we have is television reruns now; our idea of scholarship is the study of television reruns. Everybody is an expert. There are people out there who know all the episodes of *The Honeymooners* and can recite them line by line. But when it comes to the other things, they have no memory. Ancient history to Americans is Elvis [Presley]. That's when it began, and that's as far back as they can go.

Interview, New York, N.Y./
Lear's, September:24.

Jay Leno
Host,
"The Tonight Show," NBC-TV

4

I kind of laugh because people tell me, "You're too nice [to host a TV talk show]. You're going to get screwed." And I say, "Well, I'm here, aren't I?" I mean, I'm hosting *The Tonight Show*. How much bigger can you get? I held on to the job. We're the Number 1 talk show. We have the highest demographics in our time period, blah, blah, blah. So what's wrong with being nice?

Interview, Burbank, Calif./
Los Angeles Times, 5-24:(F)12.

John Malone
Chief executive officer,
Tele-Communications, Inc.

5

We anticipate cable [TV's] next generation of residential equipment will be the most powerful computing device in the average home, by far. It will make possible new forms of distance education; high-resolution TV displays; videophone; high-speed computer networking; interactive armchair shopping; an enormous range of sports, news and entertainment choices; and, eventually, movies on demand and other programming. It will give consumers more choice in their television service. And it will change the very definition of television. The new technology will give families control over their television rather than the other way around.

Interview/
U.S. News & World Report, 5-3:63.

Edward J. Markey
United States Representative,
D-Massachusetts

1

Televised violence is ubiquitous and insidious. Even the most conscientious parents are often powerless to monitor their children's viewing all week long, leaving them susceptible to the excessive level of "murder and mayhem" that comes over the air and through the cable.

News conference,
Washington, D.C., Aug. 5/
Los Angeles Times, 8-6:(D)5.

Leslie Moonves
President, Lorimar Television

2

[On criticism that there is too much violence in TV programming]: I'd love to do another [family-oriented series like] *I'll Fly Away,* but the corporate bosses won't let me [because of the low audience ratings]. When you get burned with quality programming you get gun-shy—you feel you need to stick to the shows that make money. You know what the problem is? Network change. Somebody like [the late head of CBS] Bill Paley used to say that he didn't care if he got a 12 share [a low rating], because there was a public trust and social responsibility to put on an *I'll Fly Away.* GE buys a network [NBC], and you've got a different agenda. Network presidents don't keep their jobs based on the number of Emmy awards. Let's face it: There is more sensation and violence because it works. The movie of the week has become the killer-of-the-week story. Do we have a responsibility to our public? Of course. [But] I honestly don't know what to do about it.

Interview/Mother Jones, July-Aug.:19.

Robert Peck
Legislative counsel,
American Civil Liberties Union

3

[Criticizing proposed government action to curb gratuitous violence in TV programming]: The idea of government officials combing television programs [to determine] when violence is gratuitous or not has all the elements of low comedy. To me, there's no way that a law is going to come up with a definition of gratuitous dramatized violence that will satisfy the Constitution's requirement that laws be specific.

Los Angeles Times, 12-16:(A)35.

Christopher Plummer
Actor

4

Young actors sadly don't get enough theatre training as did the actors of my day, simply because television has swallowed everything. The kids want to immediately become TV stars. I don't blame them. It doesn't mean they don't have talent. [But] their friends get on a [TV] show and become big names, and the others say, "Why should I have to go through all this nonsense of training?"

Interview/
The Christian Science Monitor,
10-8:12.

Alvin F. Poussaint
Associate professor of psychiatry,
Harvard University
Medical School

5

People are now watching television 20 to 30 hours a week on average. High doses of violence, high doses of sexual innuendo. All kinds of information. Before TV, the family was confined to the surrounding community. Parents didn't have to expose their children to certain things. Today, mom is watching the soaps and her three-year-old is seeing people simulating intercourse. Anything children watch on TV exposes them to views and behaviors that may make them less accepting of their parents' point of view. Sitcomes, movies and commercials all argue that materialism is good, that buying a pair of sneakers will make you feel worthwhile. So the media are competing with the parents for the minds of the children.

Interview,
New York, N.Y./
Lear's, February:14.

Michael Pressman
Producer

1

[Criticizing calls for government regulation of violence in TV programming]: I think there is a genuine concern about rising violence in society. The fact that children are exposed to a lot of violence on the screen and television is one of the concerns being expressed. I believe, however, that you can't create legislation about this, because it is censorship. To make legislation is, in essence, to put the judgment in the hands of the government.

Los Angeles Times, 12-26:(Calendar)4.

James H. Quello
Commissioner,
Federal Communications Commission

2

[Saying traditional broadcast TV will survive even in the era of cable and other video technologies]: The era of 40 percent profit margins may be over, but there will always be reasonably profitable local TV stations providing essential free, local TV. I disagree with those who claim TV-station broadcasting has a questionable future. People watch TV programs and stations, not delivery systems. Broadcasters have the most experience and an entrenched position in developing and procuring attractive TV programming to serve local tastes and needs.

At Entertainment Business Conference
sponsored by "Variety" and Wertheim Schroder,
New York, N.Y., March 23/
Daily Variety, 3-24:14.

Dan Rather
Anchorman, CBS News; Host,
"48 Hours," CBS-TV

3

[On TV newsmagazine programs]: There is fierce competition among newsmagazines, and that can create pressure to go for the [lowest] common denominator. But I think the record shows that *60 Minutes* has succeeded with serious stories and serious standards. We certainly have to be concerned with ratings on *48*

Hours, and we've been told it was suicidal to do stories on the economy or Israelis and Palestinians. But we did those stories. If viewers think you're offering something of quality overall, you don't have to win the ratings every week to survive.

Los Angeles Times, 8-11:(F)9.

Janet Reno
Attorney General
of the United States

4

[On the TV industry's attempts to police itself in reducing gratuitous violence in its programs]: I believe these are positive steps. They are, however, extremely small steps—in fact, itty-bitty steps . . . There are many things the television industry can do . . . My instincts militate against government involvement in this area. But I also believe that television violence and the development of our youth . . . go to the heart of our society's values . . . Parents can bring economic pressure to bear on companies who sponsor violent programming. A national campaign would let advertisers and programmers know that Americans are willing to show their frustration with television violence with their wallets as well as their remote controls.

Before Senate Commerce Committee,
Washington, D.C., Oct. 20/
Los Angeles Times, 10-21:(A)22.

5

The regulation [by government of TV] violence is Constitutionally permissible . . . [But what] I am asking today is that the entertainment industry—and that includes the movies, the broadcasting networks, cable TV and the independents—acknowledge their role and their responsibilities, and pledge to work with us to use every tool they have to address the problem. And more than pledging, start doing something about it now.

Before Senate Commerce Committee,
Washington, D.C., Oct. 20/
The Washington Post, 10-21:(A)1.

Lucie Salhany
Chairman,
Fox Broadcasting Company

1

[On calls for a "V-chip," a device parents could use to make a TV set inoperable when there are programs broadcast that they don't want their children to watch because of violent content]: The very idea of the V-chip scares me [because of the potential for cutting out other types of programming as well] . . . have we so abrogated our responsibility as parents to talk about things like violence on television with our children that we have to ask technology to stand in for us? Let's keep freedom of choice and responsibility for our children in the homes.

Before Television Critics Association,
Los Angeles, Calif./
Daily Variety, 7-12:12.

Charles E. Schumer
United States Representative,
D-New York

2

[On violence in TV programming]: I'm trying to make it a health issue. I think we're at the stage cigarettes were 30 years ago—before the Surgeon General issued his [anti-smoking] study, but when there were private studies that started to show quite conclusively that smoking was bad for you.

Los Angeles Times, 7-18:(Calendar)3.

Paul Simon
United States Senator,
D-Illinois

3

[Criticizing gratuitous violence in TV programming]: I hope that [we will] create a general atmosphere that recognizes, on the part of all the people who have such influence on the public, that there is a responsibility to move away from the pattern of violence that we have . . . I don't want to get into the delicate First Amendment area. Ideally, we can solve the problem without the heavy hand of government, without setting a precedent which we may regret later . . . TV news portrays violence but does not glamorize it,

but entertainment shows do just that. That is where the problem is, and that is the pattern we must move away from.

Interview/
The Christian Science Monitor,
5-4:12.

4

[Saying the TV industry should monitor its programming to cut down on violent content]: The industry needs encouragement to a higher sense of responsibility and good taste. Without some type of monitoring, the lure of profits will entice those less responsible to abuse their privilege. Either you [in the industry] will initiate the effort for such a monitoring office, or those outside the industry will do it. I started in this effort as a somewhat lonely voice in Congress, but I now find many of my colleagues want to go much further than is healthy for a free society. My request . . . is not an assault on the First Amendment, but if within the industry you do not exercise self-restraint, neither will many of those who are concerned. The surest solution is governmental intervention, but it is also the most dangerous.

At entertainment industry conference,
Beverly Hills, Calif., Aug. 2/
The Washington Post, 8-3:(E)1.

5

[On excessive violence in TV programming]: No major public-health problem has been so studiously ignored by the TV industry as this one . . . [Evidence linking TV violence to street violence is] solid and unquestioned by any serious scholar. [But the entertainment industry] still [does] not acknowledge a tie-in . . . Too many people in the TV industry say, "Why don't you do something about poverty?" or "Why don't you do something about guns?" But they sound too much like the National Rifle Association leaders who blame everyone else for the cause of crime. Television moguls who worship the dollar more than responsibility to society invite legislative solutions.

Before National Press Club,
Washington, D.C., Sept. 16/
Daily Variety, 9-17:3,36.

(PAUL SIMON)

1

[Criticizing gratuitous violence in TV programming]: Broadcasting blames cable, which blames the movies. Executives say they use what producers give them; producers blame the screenwriters; and the screenwriters say they script what they have been instructed to write. And then they all point the finger at others.

Before National Press Club,
Washington, D.C./
Los Angeles Times, 12-26:(Calendar)3.

Aaron Spelling
Producer

2

I love television because it's a producer's medium. You can follow your instincts and make it happen on the television screen. You don't have to be rich to watch television. It reaches everyone. You do a show and 30 million people can see it in one evening. With syndication, you can reach a billion people. Entertainment isn't a dirty word. Television has to appeal to the heart.

Daily Variety, 4-28:5.

Keith Spicer
Chairman,
Canadian Radio
and Television Commission

3

[Saying there is too much violence on U.S. TV]: We're doing our damndest to avoid laws and regulations, because that is an extreme solution no one feels comfortable about. What we have been doing for the last seven months is to try to find a civilized balance between creative freedom and responsibility to children. This is not a freedom-of-speech issue. It's a child-protection issue.

Los Angeles Times, 2-1:(F)10.

Victor Strasburger
Authority on television
and health,
University of New Mexico
Medical School

4

Television is certainly a health risk [for children]. We can't say every child who watches television five hours a day will be obese. But we know television represents the single biggest influence on kids that we can change easily.

Los Angeles Times, 3-10:(E)1.

Howard Stringer
President,
CBS Broadcast Group

5

[Criticizing gratuitous violence in TV programming]: At CBS, we are going to become much tougher on violence in our [program] lineup this fall. It is the chill of violence that worries me, not so much the physical action. It is the callousness involved and the role we have in shaping the attitudes of young people to their victims. Gratuitous violence has to be erased from the network. We must admit our responsibility.

At conference sponsored by
Wertheim Schroder and "Variety,"
New York, N.Y./
The Christian Science Monitor,
5-4:12.

6

[On his skepticism about labeling or eliminating violence in TV programming, as some have called for]: We don't want to turn the vast wasteland into the dull wasteland. When anyone starts talking about the next step [in cutting down on violence], I start to get nervous. It is the nature of [the] violence [in TV programming] and the absence of consequences that we are concerned about. We have, in effect, depersonalized violence. There is no grief, no remorse, no feelings. That's the kind that sends a message to children that it's okay.

News conference,
Washington, D.C., June 30/
The Washington Post, 7-1:(A)9.

7

The great thing about cable [TV] is that they've figured out a way to get the American people to pay for [broadcast-] network reruns. I admire their ingenuity, but we still have a government regulating broadcasting at a time when

(HOWARD STRINGER)

cable is operating as a vertically integrated monopoly. The digital TV, interactive TV and other technology that's being discussed is expensive to consumers. We stand in danger of creating an information underclass in this society. I believe there is a real value to television-that-is-available-to-everyone.

Interview, New York, N.Y./
Los Angeles Times, 12-19:(Calendar)89.

Elizabeth Thoman
Founder,
Center for Media and Values

1

We are humans; we have a brain, and TV doesn't. But TV is so powerful and gets you, because it's visual. So one of the first things you have to teach children is that not everything on TV is right or necessarily true and that you're smarter than TV—and that if it doesn't make sense, trust yourself.

Interview/
Los Angeles Times, 3-13:(F)15.

Laurence A. Tisch
Chairman, CBS, Inc.

2

In 1992, free television made some tentative headway in the area of regulatory reform. Deregulation of broadcasting is absolutely necessary for the long-term vitality of free television, particularly with the advent of 500-channel systems operated by well-endowed cable and telephone companies.

At CBS annual meeting,
New York, N.Y./
Daily Variety, 5-13:4.

Ted Turner
Chairman,
Turner Broadcasting System

3

[Saying TV executives are responsible for much of the violence in society because of the violent content of many of the programs they

broadcast]: [They] are guilty of murder, as far as I can see. They all are. Me, too . . . [If broadcasters don't adopt a ratings system to warn parents of TV violence content, then Congress should] ram it down their throats . . . [If TV becomes less violent, then it] will be more Pollyanna than it was before. But what's wrong with more shows like [the family-oriented] *Cosby Show*?

Before House Telecommunications
Subcommittee, Washington, D.C., June 25/
Daily Variety 6-28:1,11.

Jack Valenti
President,
Motion Picture Association
of America

4

[Saying criticism of gratuitous violence in TV programming should not lead to censorship]: I am an implacable foe of censorship by any group, self-appointed or elected or otherwise. We must not tell creative people how to tell their stories. [The creative process] is so fragile, so easily shattered. I would try to direct a creative person to soften a violent scene and still get the same kind of impact.

The Christian Science Monitor,
5-4:12.

5

[On the idea that there is a connection between violence in TV programming and violence in society]: Long before there was an electronic box in millions of American homes, there was violence . . . I refuse to believe all the cruelties visited upon this society are caused by television.

The Christian Science Monitor,
6-10:1.

6

[Criticizing calls for imposed limits on violence in TV programming]: Congress and the TV industry should authorize someone, a dispassionate researcher, to certify and measure all the research that has been done to date—because it

(JACK VALENTI)

doesn't prove anything [about TV violence being harmful to society] . . . Nobody is going to force a creative person to limit violence. We're going to do it inside our own house.

Interview, July 29/
Los Angeles Times, 7-30:(D)5.

Peter Weir
Australian
motion-picture director

1

Not having television was very important for me as far as developing my own creative sensibility. TV didn't come to Australia until 1956 when I was 12, so those early formative years were spent with books and idle hours. A child needs to be bored for the imagination to develop, and I spent long afternoons in the yard with sticks and a patch of dirt.

Interview/
Los Angeles Times, 10-17:(Calendar)26.

Jacqueline Weiss
Project executive,
Public Broadcasting Service

2

There is no question that television teaches. The question is what it teaches. It can abuse . . . And it can be a constructive, powerful research tool.

The Washington Post, 12-8:(A)1.

Dick Wolf
Producer

3

[Arguing against restrictions on violence in TV programming]: I do not dispute that violent programming or movies may trigger a response in a very small proportion of the population that is mentally disturbed. But at the same time, those people can apparently be triggered by other stimuli. I don't know that society has a responsibility to protect itself from that tiny minority.

USA Today, 7-1:(A)2.

4

[On threats by some in government to regulate TV programs to control their violent content]: The potential exists for these shows, the highest level of television, the dramas, to be destroyed by this legislation because ad agencies are sheep. They will avoid [placing advertising on programs with violent-content] warning labels like the plague. I would hate to live in a television environment where there was no *Hill Street [Blues]*, no *Picket Fences*, no *Law and Order*, no *NYPD Blue*.

The Washington Post, 10-29:(B)4.

Jeff Zucker
Producer, NBC News

5

[On TV newsmagazine programs]: Newsmagazines are the TV dramas of the 1990s. At a time when the entertainment divisions [of the networks] are having difficulty creating successful fictional dramas, viewers are tuning in to see dramatic stories of real-life people on newsmagazines.

Los Angeles Times, 8-11:(F)1.

MOTION PICTURES

Robert Altman
Director

1

The people who get into this business are fast-buck operators, carnival people, always have been. They don't try to make good movies now; they're trying to make [economically] successful movies. The marketing people run it now. You don't really see too many smart people running the studios, running the video companies. They're all making big money, but they're not looking for, they don't have a vested interest in, the shelf life of a movie. There's no overview. No one says, "Forty years from now, who's going to want to see this?" No visionaries.

Interview, Los Angeles, Calif./
The New York Times, 7-29:(B)6.

2

Writers, actors and directors in this quasi-art business start off very sincere. But eventually they get corrupted—I should say *we* get corrupted. If the merchants that market them could just order this stuff up without having to deal with artists, they'd do it. I think that was pretty much what the Japanese had in mind when they started to buy [U.S.] studios.

Interview, Connecticut/
Newsweek, 8-23:52.

3

[On his films]: I don't kid myself. I don't think any of these films mean diddly-squat. I think it's all worthless. I think ultimately if it all disappeared like that, it would mean nothing to everybody but me. A film is like a sandcastle. You go down there and get six friends and build a little sandcastle on the beach. You work your ass off and you finish it. You come up here and sit and have a beer and you look at it. Then the tide comes in and takes it away. And pretty soon it's just as smooth as sand out there. Then, everybody goes home a little disappointed—no, not disappointed, but they're saying, "Well, want to meet next week and do another one?" And someone says, "Yeah, I'm going to come back, but I'm not going to do the [sandcastle's] windows this time. I want to do the moat!"

Interview, Malibu, Calif./
Vanity Fair, October:180.

Peter Bart
Editorial director,
"Variety" and "Daily Variety";
Former motion-picture producer

4

[As a producer,] you have the dubious pleasure of going to the set of a movie that's way behind schedule, going into the Winnebago [trailer] with the director and saying something loving like, "Listen, you [expletive], if you lose one day, you're out of here" . . . Stars and directors and producers: They live by intimidation. It is the only tactic in life they understand.

Interview/
The Washington Post, 4-26:(D)1.

Andrew Bergman
Director

5

Someone once said that a good director is like the host of a good party, and to some extent that's true. Some people think you operate best through fear, but I've never found that to be true in my life. If people are relaxed, they take risks. That's how I got Marlon Brando on ice skates [in a film], which is no easy thing.

Interview, New York, N.Y./
The New York Times, 8-30:(B)3.

Leon Brittan
Commissioner for Competition
of the European Community

1

[Objecting to U.S. demands for fewer restrictions on American movies and other entertainment products in the European market as part of a GATT agreement]: What we are prepared to do on the audio-visual question is balanced and reasonable. The United States already has 80 percent of the European movie market, and that market is growing. This is not an American industry fighting for survival. The European Community wants to have the capacity to support its own culture, and that seems to me to be reasonable.

Brussels, Belgium, Dec. 13/
The New York Times, 12-14:(C)6.

Michael Caine
Actor

2

A lot of British pictures are polemics or too precious for words. The social ramifications always have to come into it. You come up with a movie idea that has murder, detectives and so on, and they ask, "What about the police brutality, the corruption? How are you showing what it's like in England?" I don't want to do films like that. To people who say, "Let's make a movie about the homeless," I say, "Make *Terminator 2* and use the profits to build homes for them."

People, 7-26:158.

Andrew Davis
Director

3

Action films only work if you care about the people [in them]. The action part is the easiest—anyone can run and jump and blow things up. The hard part is weaving in a story with people who are believable, people who seem real . . . [Action films are] not taken very seriously by critics, who often look down on action films. But [such films are] certainly taken seriously at the box office. Action films can be serious. And they work if you inject elements of intelligence, humor and real

acting, if you genuinely care about the people in them.

Interview/
The New York Times, 7-6:(B)1,2.

Catherine Deneuve
Actress

4

The cinema is unfair to actors. Why are there actors in some parts who are very good actors but you don't give a damn if they're there or not? I saw [the film] *Basic Instinct*—which is really not my kind of film—and I think that if [actress] Sharon Stone hadn't been in the film, I would have got bored. To watch the development of Sharon Stone over two hours on the screen—that's entirely satisfying.

Interview, Paris, France/
"Interview" magazine, January:54.

5

Physical beauty is the foundation of cinema. Actors have a problem accepting this idea . . . Women should disappear from the screen between 45 and 60, when they can play older parts . . . The older men get, the more they need and want younger women. Perhaps we need young directors. They won't be so anxious about the sight of an aging woman.

Interview, New York, N.Y./
Lear's, February:66,93.

Michael Douglas
Actor

6

This concern of making pictures that are morally and socially responsible so that they mirror all the right values—that I don't quite understand. Films have to have some sense of reality, too. Yes, you feel responsible for what you do, but it's also my responsibility to make two hours of entertainment. And if I'm able to leave people with some morsel, some grain of thought, then so much the better.

Interview, New York, N.Y./
The New York Times, 3-11:(B)8.

425

Clint Eastwood
Actor, Director

1

Hollywood pays too much attention to home runs [hugely successful hit films]. Singles and doubles can win the game when longevity is the goal. Besides, if all I ever did was hit one home run, the only thing I'd be now is a celebrity has-been.

Time, 4-5:56.

2

Making a film takes on a life of its own. You guide that life along like a platoon leader, getting everybody kind of enthused to charge the hill.

Time, 4-5:56.

Federico Fellini
Director

3

[On directing]: I found this precious thing. I could be a painter *and* a sculptor. An admiral. The fountain out of the water. As a director, I *was* everything I talked about.

Interview, Rome, Italy/
People, 1-18:90.

Richard Fleischer
Director

4

I'd love to make pictures [again], sure. But I haven't found anything I like, and I'm not getting the offers anymore. I'm not as young as I used to be. Not that I'm incapable of making pictures, but I think other people think that I am . . . There's an age line. After you cross that age line you can't do anything: You can't walk, you can't direct, you can't hold a megaphone, yell at actors.

Interview, Los Angeles, Calif./
Los Angeles Times, 7-24:(F)9.

Vittorio Gassman
Actor

5

[An actor is someone] half-way between a priest and a whore. More of a whore in the movies, closer to holiness on the stage.

Interview/Approach, February:30.

Larry Gelbart
Stage, screen
and television writer

6

The arrogance [of Hollywood]—that we have the answer to everything; that because we can dramatize every issue, we're in touch with those issues. But hard copy is not hard experience.

Interview, Beverly Hills, Calif./
The Washington Post, 3-20:(D)9.

Bo Goldman
Screenwriter

7

[On screenwriting]: It's a painful profession, with all this tension. And if you're lucky enough to get recognition and be good at it, then this tension gets tighter and tighter between you and the studio and the director. You're fighting for your work all the time. That's the pain. The pain comes from that tension. And they hold all the cards. And to them it's shoes. They're selling shoes . . . It's such a tricky thing, being a screenwriter, a strange combination of talents. You have to have the instincts to want to express yourself like any writer, but at the same time you have to have a very powerful collaborative instinct.

Interview, Los Angeles, Calif./
The New York Times, 2-25:(B)3.

Peter Guber
Chairman,
Sony Pictures Entertainment

8

No matter how grand our quest to become global entertainment giants, or pioneers of revolutionary technologies, we cannot forget [it is] the story that lies at the core of every successful form of entertainment. As we expand into new territories, markets and technologies around the globe, we cannot afford to lose contact with the audiences that are the heart and soul of our business. It is the story that they are interested in— not the distributor or the budget. When you're done with all the fancy venues, with the great production value of a film, with the wonderful cast, with the wardrobe, with the music, with the sets, with the budget, what's up on the screen is the story, the central focus of the entertainment business.

At Entertainment Business Conference sponsored by "Variety" and Wertheim Schroder, New York, N.Y., March 23/ Daily Variety, 3-24:14.

Pete Hamill
Author, Journalist

1

I find scriptwriting [for films] the least satisfying of any form because of the process of writing screenplays. You don't have any control over it. You write it and, with very few exceptions, the writer has no control over what's done to the screenplay. Most of the things I've worked on, I've taken my name off. Scriptwriting is obviously fairly lucrative or nobody would do it. But the creative process is not really in your hands.

Interview/ Writer's Digest, September:47.

Molly Haskell
Film critic

2

[Saying good women's roles are rare in films today]: Men are now playing *all* the roles. They get the macho roles *and* the sweet-sensitive roles, and they play the sexual pinups, too. The best woman's role of 1992 was in *The Crying Game,* and *that* was played by a man.

Time, 4-5:58.

Hal Holbrook
Actor

3

The motion-picture business has become, like everything else, a panderer to the lowest common denominator instead of the highest . . . There are some glorious exceptions but they are so very slim. Everybody's out for the fast whore buck. No one is trying to elevate taste. People in charge are trying to play down to basic primitive instincts instead of trying to bring people up. But

what's the sense of even talking about it? I mean, there's no money in raising people up. There's no money in doing *King Lear,* or in projects like that. *There's no money it it!* That's the whole watchword, the saintly phrase of our society. There's no money in it! That's the criterion upon which our society finally has come to rest.

Interview, San Diego, Calif./ Los Angeles Times, 7-4:(Calendar)70.

Bob Hope
Entertainer

4

[A director once] told me that everything you do in movies is through your eyes and you can't perform in movies like you do on the stage. The best advice I ever got. You perform with your eyes. Of course, they had to pull me down after a couple of movies because I was throwing my eyes all over the studio. I learned.

Interview/ The New York Times, 5-3:(B)4.

Anthony Hopkins
Actor

5

I was frustrated as a kid, born in Wales; my father was a baker. I was hopeless at school. Then came a moment when I met an actor in south Wales who happened to be Richard Burton, and I said I wanted to be like him. I think a lot of people in this profession are damaged goods.

Interview, Los Angeles, Calif./ Los Angeles Times, 10-31:(Calendar)28.

6

I suppose my purpose in life is to communicate to people, through a cinema screen or from a stage. I'm not equipped any other way, since I'm not a speaker, a writer, a painter, a musician, or a businessman. My task or objective is to communicate the human condition. That sounds terribly grand, but my parts . . . seem involved with conveying some form of love, even if it's repressed or hidden. Love exists, but it's locked up. And then it's revealed, and then in the next

(ANTHONY HOPKINS)

role, maybe it's locked up again. But we always know that it is there.

Interview, New York, N.Y./
The Christian Science Monitor,
12-8:16.

James Ivory
Director

1

Film-making isn't like being a painter, writer, sculptor or composer. It's more like architecture. You can design a beautiful building, but you have to rely on a lot of people to help put it together. Film-making is a collaborative art. You have to enjoy yourself, make the films you believe in, and hope the audience agrees with you. I may have all kinds of unrealized dreams, but certainly no regrets, because I have always made my own choices and followed my own dreams.

Daily Variety, 11-2:5.

Philip Kaufman
Director

2

We've lost the great [film] writing of the '40s, and Hollywood's become disdainful of the audience. You end up with fascism if you only appeal to the basest instincts. I much prefer to live in a world of romance than of boredom and dissatisfaction. But then I guess some people like a McDonald's dinner. I really prefer Chez Panisse.

Interview, San Francisco, Calif./
"W" magazine, 7-19:30.

Harvey Keitel
Actor

3

The independent film [as opposed to films made by the major studios] movement is growing because of the power of the stories that are being told and the way they're being told, with passion and spirit and sacrifice. You look at the people running the [major] studios and you can only ask:

What are their values? What do they want? What do they aspire to? I don't know. Are they making films that deal with the conflict we all face in our lives? No! I think audiences are saying, "Enough already."

Interview, Santa Monica, Calif./
The New York Times, 3-29:(B)1.

Arnold Kopelson
Producer

4

[Saying he's a producer who gets actively involved in the making of the film]: If a director won't let me in, there's no way he or she will be in. I'm not about to give birth to a project and hand it over to someone who won't listen to me. I've been on the set of just about every film I've produced since *Platoon*. You can't make movies from far away.

Interview, Beverly Hills, Calif./
Los Angeles Times, 7-8:(F)11.

Irving Lazar
Literary and film agent

5

The [current] Hollywood community is a lower-middle-class community whose people never have been anywhere, whose people don't know anything about art or books or culture. What does Tom Cruise know? Or Tom Hanks? Or Julia Roberts? They don't know a thing. They've never been any place. They've got a lot of money. That's all. You think [today's] producers or executives are any different? Of course not. It's not like [old-timers] Charlie Feldman, who traveled all over the the world, or David Selznick, who was a great gambler who wanted to live, or Leland Hayward, who had great taste, living on one coast with Katharine Hepburn and the other coast with Ginger Rogers; that takes a little bit of doing. [In the old days,] the people who ran the studios were there for 30 years and they were going to be there for another 30 years. Now you don't know who the hell you're dealing with. The agents [are] the same thing. They're young, ambitious Sammy Glicks. No background. Could they handle Noel Coward? Hemingway?

Interview, Beverly Hills, Calif./
The New York Times, 3-29:(B)4.

Jack Lemmon
Actor

1

In order to be an artist, period, I think—not just an actor—you have to be ultra-sensitive to be good, have a sensitivity and an intelligence beyond the norm. And to me—this is "Lemmon's Theory"—intelligence and sensitivity are interlocked to a great extent. The *talent* comes in only in the final stage—of showing an audience, through your acting ability, something that you have found out about human behavior and this character. That's an intellectual process of hide and seek. Good actors have this sensitivity and this awareness, beyond the norm, of human behavior—or the *ability* to use it. And yet, they've got to have skin like a rhinoceros because of this constant rejection.

Interview/
Film Comment, March-April:22.

Sophia Loren
Actress

2

I put into acting whatever are the experiences of my life. If you want to become a good actress, you have to experience many things and become very mature and understanding—you have to analyze feelings, whatever you feel inside. Then, when you're ready for it, you have to be able to deliver a page of life.

Interview, Geneva, Switzerland/
"Interview" magazine, October:93.

Jeff Maguire
Screenwriter

3

[On his first successful screenplay for the film *In the Line of Fire*]: People keep telling me that I don't seem as excited as I should be. Well, I worked so hard, and over so many years, not to get depressed when things were really bad, I try not to get too elated now . . . If I was 25, it would go to my head, or up my nose with drugs. But I've been here [in Hollywood] a long time. I've seen people come and go. I've seen people who think they're on top of the world only to have it pulled out from under them a second later.

Interview, Los Angeles, Calif./
The New York Times, 7-20:(B)1,2.

Louis Malle
Director

4

[On filming erotic love scenes]: We're always trying not to shoot like 25 takes because you just can't do that so many times in a row. It's not just a question of whether they [the actors] like each other or love each other. It's completely different from life. On the screen it either happens or it doesn't happen. It's like electricity: The current goes through or not.

Interview, Los Angeles, Calif./
USA Today, 1-5:(D)5.

Marcello Mastroianni
Actor

5

An actor in the beginning—as a young man, as a boy—is trying to express himself. He lacks courage, so he assumes the skin of another. An actor is like a canvas without paint: He needs the colors of somebody else. Ah, acting . . . It's exhibitionism. An actor is like a child: He wants everybody to be interested in him. A child is accustomed to be loved and not to have to give back. If you want to be loved, really loved, don't ask an actor!

Interview, West Hollywood, Calif./
Los Angeles Times, 3-23:(F)1.

Michael Medved
Film critic;
Co-host, "Sneak Previews," PBS-TV

6

To me, the most damaging message that Hollywood sends is a message of pessimism: that the future is going to be worse than the present; that there's nothing you can do; that we live in a nightmare world; that we cannot avoid being assaulted by decay, violence and every kind of cruelty. This is in jarring contrast with what most people experience in their own families . . . The Associated Press media general poll found that 80 percent of Americans think there is too much bad language in films; 82 percent, too much violence, 72 percent, too much sex. I can think of almost no other issue that gets that kind of unanimity from the American people . . . I'm opposed to censor-

(MICHAEL MEDVED)

ship. I don't want to cut off anybody's right to self-expression. But I do want to encourage corporate responsibility . . . What a company chooses to produce has nothing to do with the First Amendment. Every year the Writers Guild of America has 27,000 scripts registered with it. Of those, fewer than 600 are produced. What about those 26,400 screen writers whose scripts don't get produced? Are their First Amendment rights violated? Are they being censored? Of course not! All I'm saying is that, when you're deciding what you're going to make, that you introduce into the equation some consideration of its effect on the society we live in.

Interview/
Christianity Today, 3-8:23,25.

Ismael Merchant
Producer

1

Being an independent film-maker gives you the freedom to do the things you most want to do. It can be an esoteric subject, an actor you wish to present in some new way, or a writer you believe in. There is the fascination of always learning and discovering something new. My advice to young film-makers is to trust your dreams, and follow your ideals. Be passionate. Hunt for it. There will be obstacles, but never get discouraged. Persist. I rarely shy away from anything.

Daily Variety, 11-2:5.

Helen Mirren
British actress

2

[On directors]: They've got to be good crafts-men—and often they're not, which is really diffi-cult to deal with. Directors always used to be like the police to me—the enemy, the people to tell me what to do when I didn't want to do it. But I've lived with one [her husband] for a while now, and I guess I can put myself more in their position. [But] you shouldn't be too sympathetic to them.

Interview, London, England/
"Interview" magazine, January:111.

Jeanne Moreau
Actress

3

The important thing [for an actor] is not to be successful all the time. You have to have failure, too. Life is like a piece of land, and you have a certain amount of time to discover it. Some [of my] films were better than others, but the impor-tant thing was to have done all of them.

Interview, Paris, France/
The Washington Post, 12-25:(B)2.

Mike Nichols
Director

4

[On his recent critical and box-office disap-pointments]: When somebody talented starts, it startles everybody and expectations get higher and higher as they go along. It gets harder: It gets harder to find material; it gets harder to surprise people; it gets harder to fulfill expectations and keep going and renew yourself. And, finally, it gets hard because you don't get credit for still doing it. I've directed movies for 30 years. There are a lot of people who started when I did who aren't doing it anymore. Sure, you're hoping for some astonishing piece of movie material that knocks everybody out. That doesn't happen.

Interview, Culver City, Calif./
The New York Times, 3-15:(B)2.

Michael Ovitz
Chairman,
Creative Artists Agency

5

This industry invented conflicts of interest. In what other business would you have a lawyer who represents the chairman of a major film studio, and also represents an important actor, be the guy who makes the deal between the actor and the studio chief? Hollywood is a small, familial place. Everyone does business with everybody else. The same complications occur in investment banking. But just as they build a Chinese wall to separate the parts of their com-panies that have competing or conflicting inter-ests, we have built a Chinese wall at [his agency]. It's all about ethics and how you do business.

Interview/Time, 4-19:56.

Wolfgang Petersen
Director

1

I've always aspired to work in the manner of [the late director] David Lean, who had a great talent for combining the excitement of a large-scale visual experience, with very concentrated, intimate character studies. I'm not interested in wall-to-wall action; I want to be touched and moved. But that doesn't mean the characters have to sit in the kitchen all the time and talk. This is, after all, a visual medium.

Interview, Culver City, Calif./
Los Angeles Times, 7-4:(Calendar)66.

Christopher Plummer
Actor

2

I'm a little bit snobbish about my critics; I like them to be top critics, because so many today are not trained or they move down from the sports pages. The ones who genuinely love theatre and films, and love being critics, are not out to destroy, or just be funny, or mock at the expense of someone. They give a tough assessment, and I'll listen to it.

Interview/
The Christian Science Monitor,
10-8:12.

Sydney Pollack
Director

3

I find directing enormously difficult. It's very demanding. It provokes all kinds of anxieties. You doubt yourself all the time and worry like hell. I don't know why anybody'd want to do it, or if the kids in film school know what they're letting themselves in for. That's why I've enjoyed the bit of acting I've done.

Interview/
Los Angeles Times, 6-27:(Calendar)5.

Ivan Reitman
Producer, Director

4

All of my films have been socially relevant to some degree, but I try not to make it too obvious.

I like cynical comedies, but that's not what I do. I'm personally an optimist . . . I think my optimism comes across in the pure entertainment value of my films. The audience is never bored, and they have a good time. There are very few people making grand-scale entertainment who are proud of it.

Interview, Universal City, Calif./
"W" magazine, 5-10:14.

Alan Rudolph
Director

5

The mechanics of making a film are so overwhelming, if you care about every facet of it, that the style or the approach is something that I try not to think about too much. Usually big ideas happen early, and if the film is really something that generates and evolves in its dimension as it goes along . . . I was walking down the street yesterday and I got 15 ideas for this next film. That usually tells me that the subject or source of the subject is big.

Interview/Film Comment, May-June:60.

Susan Sarandon
Actress

6

I had never thought of film-making as necessarily an art or creative. I was always very selfishly looking at it as something that forced me—a very boring, kind of lazy person—to really see and really hear. Because that's all that acting's about: listening, reacting, you're in your space, hopefully with some interesting part of your personality. And trying not to take anything for granted. Acting forced me to live life in a clearer, ultimately more compassionate way—to be present in my life. What I try to do is go toward that which scares me, knowing that if I'm frightened, I'll have to think on my feet and figure something out. So, in other words, I can construct my life in such a way by choosing things that will hopefully keep me fresh and not turn me into a caricature.

Interview/
Film Comment, March-April:46.

431

John Sayles
Director, Screenwriter

1

Every time out, people like your movie or they don't like your movie. It makes a lot of money or it doesn't. I don't take any of that personally. For me, it's such a triumph just to get a movie financed and made, that the very existence of these movies is success enough.

Interview/People, 3-8:90.

Joel Schumacher
Director

2

Film-making is like mountain climbing. No matter how many times you've climbed, you can still fall off. Even if you've climbed Everest seven times, the eighth time can be your last.

Interview, Burbank, Calif./
The New York Times, 3-3:(B)1.

Arnold Schwarzenegger
Actor

3

[The movie business] isn't a competition, but the mass media makes it out to be one. I make movies that people want to see . . . What does it matter if you win two Oscars but nobody goes to your film?

Mexico City, Mexico/
Los Angeles Times, 8-6:(F)2.

Valda Setterfield
Dancer, Actress

4

In dancing, I believe that just doing the steps is enough, but I'm not sure that in acting just saying the words is enough, and I'm surprised to find myself saying that. Stanislavsky said that acting is about action. Having to find a reason for those actions is a fascinating thing that stretches the imagination, that encourages all my thinking faculties to determine what those things are, so that I can give clarity to the role.

Interview/
Dance Magazine, February:54.

Ron Silver
Actor;
President, Actors' Equity

5

To be really good at [acting] requires a lot of energy and concentration and skill. And I approached it like I approach everything else: "Okay, who are the great teachers, what are the great things to read about? Let me do the research on this so I know what I'm talking about." I didn't realize what I realize now: Acting is not about knowing all this stuff; it's about character. I know people, I compete with people who are not as well educated as I am who are better actors than I will ever be. There's a certain intelligence that actors require that I don't fully possess.

Interview, New York, N.Y./
The New York Times, 12-29:(B)2.

Alberto Sordi
Italian actor

6

[The camera is] like a microscope, looking inside you. With a lot of actors, the camera understands that they are not really feeling anything; they are just waiting to say their lines. If you really feel it, your eyes and your face will express it. You don't have to say it.

Interview, New York, N.Y./
The New York Times, 3-11:(B)3.

Steven Spielberg
Director

7

[On his latest film, *Schindler's List,* a story of the Nazi era, which is a departure from his usual immensely popular entertainment films]: I've always been the victim of my own success. I have so many years of sort of the Good Housekeeping Seal of Approval stamped on my forehead. I sort of wear that the way the Jews wore the star, you know, and I'm proud of it; the Jews were proud to wear the star as well. But it's been detrimental in many ways—simply getting taken seriously, or getting people to imagine that I might be able to tell a story that didn't fall prey to the tricks of the trade and the tools of the trade that I've been able to use to make for myself a career. When people

(STEVEN SPIELBERG)

first heard I was tackling the [Nazi] subject, even friends of mine were skeptical.

Interview, Washington, D.C.,/
The Washington Post, 12-15:(B)1.

Sylvester Stallone
Actor

1

Violence [in films] is supposed to be "out" and family entertainment is supposed to be "in." Well, I'm in the R-rated business. R is reality. The Earth is not a family-oriented spot.

Interview, Cannes, France/
Los Angeles Times, 5-21:(D)4.

Brian Stonehill
Director,
media-studies program,
Pomona (Calif.) College

2

[On the technical wizardry in many of today's movies]: What gets lost is the ability of our new technology to give us insight into how we think and feel, or how we can care more about each other. Rather, it's getting much easier to tell ourselves ghost, dragon and dinosaur stories that have nothing to do with how we are, and everything to do with what we would like to think about . . . less to do with exploring and more to do with escaping.

The Christian Science Monitor,
9-23:11.

Emma Thompson
British actress

3

Acting is the ultimate luxury. This is one of the luckiest things you could possibly be doing. "Hard" is going down a bloody coal mine or living in Somalia or in a war zone. That's hard.

Time, 3-29:54.

4

I love to work with people *again,* because for me when you go onto a set it's about creating a

family. Because if you know everyone very well, they sort of become invisible. If you're working with someone you don't know very well, you feel as if you're being watched and then you start to "perform," and the camera sees you "performing" instead of acting.

Interview, Los Angeles, Calif./
Los Angeles Times, 10-31:(Calendar)22.

Daniel Toscan de Plantier
President, Unifrance
(French film industry association)

5

[Criticizing U.S. domination of the film scene in Europe]: There is a sudden realization in Europe now that a country or continent with a strong movie and broadcasting industry will be strong in the next century, and those without these industries will be weak.

The New York Times, 12-22:(B)1.

Liv Ullmann
Actress

6

[On whether she has been impatient with some of her directors]: Oh, sure. You feel you've developed a few things you believe in. Sometimes you get irritated at having to listen, especially to men, while they do their homework in front of you. The best thing I came away with was the memory of bad directors. I loved the cast and wanted them to do their thing, but to trust me to tell them, "Don't forget to shut your mouth and keep your stomach in." Good actors need good blocking. You can't just tell them to wander back and forth. I did a play called *Ghosts* on Broadway. The director had us all improvise and saved himself the trouble of doing any work.

Interview, New York, N.Y./
Films in Review, June:174.

Jack Valenti
President,
Motion Picture Association
of America

7

[Saying that of the 431 films released in 1991, only 36 earned $20-million or more for their producers/distributors]: There is an inescapable melancholy about those numbers. They tell us we work in an industry built on hazard. The odds for cinema success are ambiguous, imprecise and often perilous . . . As an industry, we must beckon so beguilingly to our audience that they will come. This, in my judgment, is a mingling of inventive marketing and first-class entertaining films.

At National Association of Theatre Owners/
ShoWest convention,
Las Vegas, Nev., March 9/
Daily Variety, 3-10:4.

Christopher Walken
Actor

1

The last thing good actors talk about is acting. They talk about the great restaurants they went to, the girls they just met. Actors share an unspoken language. They may be going after different angles, but they're focused on the same thing, which is making the scene work. There are different kinds of energies. My energy is a kind of implosion. I think I've always been that way—it's one of my qualities. The point is that someone with the capacity for implosion also has the capacity to explode . . . What you are as an actor is a reflection of what you are in real life and, in a way, everything you do in your life is information for your acting.

Interview, New York, N.Y./
"Interview" magazine, July:72.

Peter Weir
Australian director

2

Many creative people—and this is particularly true of writers—struggle to resolve key episodes from their childhood through their work, but I've never approached film-making that way. My childhood was fairly idyllic. Moreover, I've sort of blocked out all my memories prior to the age of 20. Instead of investigating my past, I experience the making of a film as a journey that puts the past behind me. The great thing about film-making is that each film is a new experience that you live through in real time. Unlike the reflective life of a writer, you move at a great rate when you make a film because there's a clock ticking, and there's no time for speculation until it's over.

Interview/
Los Angeles Times, 10-17:(Calendar)26.

Billy Wilder
Director, Screenwriter

3

I went through a lot of decades when power went from studios to producers to directors, and now it's in the lap of agents and actors. It's all packaging. The agent says, "You want Paul Newman for your film?" He must make it opposite, whoever, Susan Sarandon. And it must be this supporting actor, this cameraman—other people he [the agent] represents. You have to have the whole package. Studio writers used to write two or three pictures a year; a studio would have 50 directors under contract. A script would be there for, say, Clark Gable or Spencer Tracy, and the studio would say, "Go on, take him." There weren't all these big sessions with CAA [a large agency] that go on for months. You were living *movies,* not percentages of gross.

Interview/
Los Angeles Times, 6-27:(Calendar)54.

Debra Winger
Actress

4

The camera is open. Many people are not. A director can spend a whole day setting up a shot, getting the angles just right, the lighting perfect; but visually, if the actor isn't open, it's a dead end. It's got nothing to do with physical beauty, either. You can shoot identical twins; if one is open and one is closed, the open twin will resonate on film and the closed one won't . . . It's not something you can necessarily learn in the process of becoming a successful actor. A few people may be born with it, but usually it's something that's revealed to you in the course of your growth, your spiritual growth. When you finally shake loose from your normal perspectives, when you jar yourself free from preconceptions and stop making judgments, you momentarily lose your self-consciousness. That's when duality shat-

(DEBRA WINGER)

ters and you open up. To the world, to the camera. The more luggage you bring with you into a role, the less room there is for your character there. We're all so cloaked in unfounded opinions and unexamined information, it's a wonder we register on film at all. Absolute, non-judgmental attentiveness is what unlocks the spirit and allows it to be seen.

Interview/Esquire, February:74.

Stephen Woolley
British producer

1

[On British films]: You don't really have film-makers in the [United] States today who can supply what we can supply, which is films that have strong literary or theatrical roots. These roots, which are so much a part of British culture generally, have actually been endemic in our movies since we've been making films. It's just that Americans are now craving [these qualities] because their films have become so disappointing at that level; they don't have any real substance. So when you do get a film with a certain degree of unpredictability, intellectual content, slower pace, and character development—our funny little odd creatures—you kind of feel like it's a treat.

Interview,
London, England/
The Christian Science Monitor,
3-26:12.

MUSIC

Daniel Barenboim
Conductor

1

Wagner is essential for a conductor. Few things are. Mozart is—for any musician. I'm not distinguishing between opera and the symphonic music. Mozart is essential for one's own education, as hygienic treatment. Everything is transparent. Every fault shows. Wagner is essential from the point of view of size, for building a musical structure over a huge span. Even the Bruckner Eighth is short after Act I of *Parsifal*. But it's not just a question of staying power. Wagner is essential for the art of transition, for a continuous ebb and flow. And all the different means of expression are stretched to the limit.
Interview, Bayreuth, Germany/
Opera News, 3-27:24.

Marc Belfort
Director, International Opera Studio
(Switzerland)

2

[An opera] singer has to have a "gymnastic" intelligence—a feeling for the way his or her body responds as a singing instrument. This is a profession in which to be even mediocre you have to be sensational. I don't think of myself as a star-maker. Whether or not a person is going to be a star interests me not at all. So many good singers are needed, over and above the handful of so-called stars, that you can have an enormously active and satisfying career, contributing a great deal to the opera world, without being encumbered by this idea.
Interview/Opera News, May:28.

Luciano Berio
Italian opera composer

3

[Criticizing the state of opera administration in Italy]: There is total corruption, political corrup-

tion. Except for a few theatres—such as Florence, Bologna and naturally La Scala—nothing works. And there are too many of them; at least half [the theatres] should be closed down.
Broadcast interview/
The New York Times, 5-3:(B)1.

Alfred Brendel
Pianist

4

[On his recording the same compositions several times during his career]: Masterpieces always present something new. They're like powerhouses of energy that regenerate the energy of the player. In trying to do better, to improve, you keep in touch with yourself. I don't believe in starting a piece, playing it, recording it and discarding it. For me, the procedure is to find the right works with which one can live a lifetime.
Interview, London, England/
Los Angeles Times, 4-11:(Calendar)8.

Anthony Burgess
Composer, Author

5

I was brought up as a musician, and my ambition was always to be a great composer, not a writer. Obviously, music is trying to say something, but what it is we don't know. I'm still striving hard to find out. Music is obviously desperately important, or we wouldn't have so much of it. I think some of the magic that applies to music probably also applies to language. There's a mystery going on in the human mouth and in the human ear that we'll never, never understand.
Interview/
U.S. News & World Report,
10-18:73.

Alain Carignon
Minister of Communications
of France

1

[On a proposal in the French Parliament that requires 40 percent of all songs played on French radio to be of French origin]: A 40 percent quota seems to me to be reasonable. How could anyone find the idea that two songs out of five should be French excessive? Without such measures, our culture will be homogenized.

The New York Times, 12-22:(B)1.

Dick Clark
Entertainment producer

2

[On the lyrics of today's music, which some find objectionable]: The parents who are objecting . . . are the ones who loved the early rock that *their* parents criticized. The music is more graphic today because the world is full of bloodshed, pain, violence and anger.

Interview, Burbank, Calif./
USA Today, 1-22:(D)8.

Bill Clinton
President of the United States

3

Jazz is really America's classical music. Like our country itself and especially like the people who created it, jazz is a music born of struggle but played in celebration.

At White House concert celebrating
the 40th anniversary of the
Newport Jazz Festival,
Washington, D.C., June 18/
Daily Variety, 6-21:10.

Phyllis Curtin
Dean emeritus,
School for the Arts,
Boston (Mass.) University;
Former opera singer

4

[On today's opera singers]: We are very much given nowadays to going on feeling and impulse—a singularly self-centered way of

approaching [an operatic] role. The primary director is the composer in the score, not your own personality. People come from the theatre to inform the opera world, but if you don't come from the music, you are not going to find a complete operatic performance.

Interview/Opera News, 1-30:14.

Lorenzo Ferrero
Artistic director,
Verona (Italy) opera company

5

A relatively small town like Verona has a big [opera] theatre, with up to 1,500 employees in the summer. That makes it a big political fact. The workers of the theatre are too well paid and work too little. This is the reason the theatres cost so much and produce so little. If we go on this way, the theatres will exist only to pay salaries and not to make opera.

The New York Times, 5-3:(B)4.

John Eliot Gardiner
Opera director

6

There's nothing wrong with the 20th-century practice of dividing the responsibility between a musical director, a stage director and a designer, so long as the collaboration is mutually sympathetic to the basic aesthetic approach. What I disagree with is the rather decadent idea held by many impresarios that creatively interesting things must as a rule be born of conflict between the collaborators.

Interview, Stuttgart, Germany/
Opera News, 1-2:20.

David Geffen
Record producer

7

I think music becomes a more important part of people's lives with each generation. With Walkman and other portable carriers of music, it's underscoring everybody's life for a larger portion of the day. It's underscoring their lives on the streets, in their cars, when they're jogging, when they're walking, when they're screwing, and so I

(DAVID GEFFEN)

would say that the prognosis for the music business is very good.

Los Angeles Times, 3-7:(Calendar)86.

Boris Goldovsky
*Former opera director
and impresario*
1

Touring [in the days before TV] was good for the singers, and it was good for the country. Audiences could hear opera on the radio or listen to it on recordings, but they didn't have the chance to hear live performances by good, well-trained singers. For us, opera was not a staged concert performance. The idea that singers can act as well as sing became an established principle. Not everyone can do it equally well, but the public now comes to the opera *expecting* that they will do it well.

*Interview, Brookline, Mass./
Opera News, 1-30:16.*

Emmylou Harris
Country-music singer
2

One of the criticisms country [-music] radio has with me [is] they say I'm stuck in a rut. Well, I happen to like this rut, if that's what you call it. To me, life is about searching, and music should reflect that search. That's one of the reasons music means so much to us. Whether you are listening to Billie Holliday or Loretta Lynn, Hank Williams or Bob Dylan, the best artists are trying to articulate the things we all feel inside.

*Interview/
Los Angeles Times, 10-17:(Calendar)76.*

Milt Hinton
Jazz musician
3

Music is an auditory art. We go by *sound*. Not who your daddy was. Not your ethnicity. B-flat is the same in Japan as it is here [in the U.S.]. We can't speak the same language, but we can *play* together.

*Interview/
Down Beat, December:33.*

Christopher Hogwood
Conductor
4

[Saying audiences should be reacquainted with the works of Mozart and other works of the classical musical heritage]: This is not just an American problem. Certainly there is more music education in Europe, but it is still inadequate. And I don't see that politicizing these words addresses the problem, either. Certainly national differences count for something; certainly something like *Carmen* is going to "cut" a little differently in France than it will in Germany. But I don't believe that Salzburg "owns" Mozart any more than America does simply because the man was Austrian. These works are available to any civilized human being.

*Interview/
The Washington Post,
6-26:(B)6.*

Billy Joel
Musician
5

When I look at great works of art or listen to inspired music, I sense intimate portraits of the specific times in which they were created. And they have lasted because someone, somewhere, felt compelled to create it, and someone else understood what they were trying to do. Why do we still respond when we hear the opening notes of Beethoven's *Fifth Symphony*—DA DA DA DA? Or Gershwin's *Rhapsody in Blue*? Or Little Richard's *Tutti Fruitti*? Because when we hear it we realize that we are still bound by a common emotion to those who came before us. Like family, we are irrevocably tied to each other because that same emotion exists today . . . If you make this music for the human needs you have within yourself, then you do it for all humans who need the same things. Ultimately, you enrich humanity with the profound expression of these feelings.

*At Berklee College
of Music commencement/
The Christian Science Monitor,
6-15:16.*

Christopher Keene
General director,
New York City Opera

1

As a musician, I favor giving operas in the language in which they were composed. As a theatre person, I consider opera in the vernacular the more trenchant and viable art. No matter how well they're coached, singers just aren't as expressive in a second or third language. When I conduct opera in English, I hear complaints after the first act that the orchestra is much too loud. That doesn't happen so much otherwise. And when opera is given in English, people pay less attention to the display of costumes, or to vocal beauty.

Opera News, November:18.

Sharon Pratt Kelly
Mayor of Washington, D.C.

2

Music is one of the few products that America has and the whole world buys.

At University of the District of Columbia,
Aug. 23/
The Washington Post, 8-26:(DC)3.

Robert Lepage
Stage director

3

I've always envied opera directors because there's a lot of latitude in opera work. The fact that people are singing emotions and actions has a very strong theatricality, which gives you a lot of space that you don't have in the spoken theatre. In theatre, more and more these days, we seem stuck with naturalism. Especially in America, directors are always trying to make things look real. But in opera there's room to be both more expressionistic and more impressionistic.

Interview/Opera News, 1-30:18.

Ramsey Lewis
Jazz musician

4

[On his advice to aspiring musicians]: Get a formal education. Included in that formal educa-

tion should be general knowledge. There are other things besides music, because life consists of other things. If you get a general education specializing in music, it gives you the opportunity to not only be a performer but also a teacher, a composer. There might be eight or nine different ways to earn money in the music industry if you have the knowledge from a practical education. I seem to be doing eight or nine myself right now.

Interview/Down Beat, July:23.

Joe Lovano
Jazz musician

5

To be an honest musician, you play from your history. As your experiences grow, the music comes out. All my favorite players developed like that. Of course, we play from the history of the music around us, too. But *your* history, what *you* experience, is what really comes out if you can get deep inside yourself, the music and the personalities of the people you play with, and not just treat your instrument like a technical thing.

Interview/Down Beat, March:17.

Christa Ludwig
Opera singer

6

After you learn a role, there is a very important time when you speak with the stage director about a character. [Opera] singers are not like movie actors. They are not chosen for what they look like but for their voices. I could not play a demonic Carmen, because I don't look like a demonic Carmen. The stage director has to work with a singer to make the character fit.

Interview/Opera News, 3-13:24.

Branford Marsalis
Jazz musician;
Orchestra director,
"The Tonight Show," NBC-TV

7

The thing that's always excited me about jazz is, you're dealing with real music in the present tense. Very few [jazz musicians] play it like that, to be honest with you. Very few people improvise

(BRANFORD MARSALIS)

in the present tense. They basically play what they've learned or what they know. And when the music is in the present tense, people have problems with it. They don't get it. Because when we play it and it's working, ideas are just bouncing around all over the place.

Interview, Burbank, Calif./
Down Beat, July:20.

Wynton Marsalis
Jazz musician

1

What a kid learns from playing jazz is how to express his individuality without stepping on somebody else's. The first thing I tell kids is, "Play anything you want, but make it sound like you." The next step is learning to control that self-expression. Don't just blurt something out; adapt it to what the other guy is doing. Being a good neighbor, that's what jazz is about. Jazz is democracy in action.

Interview/Life, August:62.

Terry McEwen
Former general director,
San Francisco Opera

2

Opera is not really a living art form. To say that opera houses should not be museums is hypocrisy, because they *are* in a sense museums. The product they are exposing is a historical product, by and large. The contemporary percentage in any repertory is very small, even in the most adventurous houses. To say it's a living art form—well, it may be alive, but barely. We should face that truth and live with the consequences. It's a wonderful repertory, and there are lots of wonderful things to be discovered and done again. But there has to be depth, a profound attitude toward it, which is disappearing because of the speed with which life moves in our time. Everything is limited by financial and time considerations. Depth, whether in artist development or the conceptual side of a production, is often missing.

Interview/Opera News, August:28.

Jean-Pierre Ozannat
Director general,
Europe 1 (French radio station)

3

[Criticizing a proposed French law requiring 40 percent of all songs played on French radio to be of French origin]: This law is absurd, and I reject the idea of quotas. The real problem in France is not distribution, but production. Instead of applying quotas, we should encourage the production of good music. A radio station has to play what people like.

The New York Times, 12-22:(B)1.

Sonny Rollins
Jazz musician

4

Black artists [used to be] seen primarily as entertainers. You couldn't just be a musician; there had to be dancing, comedy or some other entertainment element when a black person was performing. When [musician] Charlie Parker got up on stage, though, he wouldn't smile and he wouldn't be jiving around; he'd be very serious about what he was playing. He made it clear that be-bop was an intellectually advanced music, that it was a music of freedom, of breaking with the past. Before long, we were all standing very still on stage because we wanted to be like [him].

Interview, New York, N.Y./
The Washington Post, 3-5:(Weekend)12.

Linda Ronstadt
Singer

5

The purpose of music is to help you identify your feelings, and if I am singing something, then I'm usually identifying with my feelings. But it doesn't necessarily mean it is something that I experienced. Something people might see as my personal love story might be something I notice someone else going through.

Interview, San Francisco, Calif./
Los Angeles Times, 12-5:(Calendar)67.

David Sanborn
Jazz musician

6

I can give you . . . reasons why I wouldn't consider myself a jazz musician, like I don't really

(DAVID SANBORN)

have a command of the vocabulary that comes out of the tradition. But actually, I don't know why anybody would want to call themselves *anything*. The implication is exclusionary. I'm a jazz musician—so that means I'm *not* a rock & roll musician, not a rhythm & blues musician? If somebody describes themselves as a jazz musician—I'm interested in what that means to other people and why somebody *would* describe themselves as a jazz musician.

Interview, New York, N.Y./
Down Beat, February:17.

Paul Simon
Singer, Composer

1

For the last 10 years, I've thought it was worth it to try and get really interesting language into a song without it becoming an art song and turning everybody off. That always seemed to me one of the big failings of rock and roll—the language never gets anywhere. You've got artists now who've grown up playing rock and roll; they're sophisticated, mature in their life. But in their music they're not using language. There's no reason rock and roll can't have sophisticated words.

Interview, New York, N.Y./
Life, November:92.

Joe Smith
President, Capital-EMI Music

2

[On his imminent retirement from his present job]: The nature of this [recording] business began to change a number of years ago, when it became very big money and major corporations moved in . . . And to the extent that it's become a bigger business, it's become necessary to put people in charge who are more business-oriented than those of us who were very music-oriented. We're very much like other businesses now . . . Fifteen years ago we might have blithely gone ahead and done what we thought was right musically. Today, there are bound to be some business considerations applied, and to an extent

that hurts music because you don't know what you're missing.

Interview/
Los Angeles Times, 3-13:(F)1.

Georg Solti
Music director laureate,
Chicago Symphony Orchestra

3

I think what is most essential for a recording conductor is a critical sense. You have no time to hear a tape twice, because during the [recording] sessions they will play it for you only once, and that's it. In that time, you must make up your mind very quickly what is *wrong*—not what is good but what is bad in terms of balance, tempo, distortion, dynamics. This is probably my best side as a musician, that I have a very acute critical sense.

Interview, Chicago, Ill./
The Christian Science Monitor,
12-3:14.

Pete Townshend
Rock musician

4

[On the success of his rock musical *Tommy* on Broadway]: There's a hunger in the rock audience. When you're my age and you want to go to a concert, you think very hard about whether it will be a relaxing experience or a disturbing one. So you tend to go to the movies, to restaurants [instead]. You don't go and watch rock-'n'-roll shows. A lot of people are looking for a doorway into the [legitimate] theatre.

Time, 7-12:55.

Dawn Upshaw
Opera singer and recitalist

5

Just this past season I've become preoccupied with the stodginess that I feel has overtaken the song recital, and I'm trying to break loose. I feel it's too formal and conservative. All season I've been talking through my programs. This has broken a certain barrier between me and the audience, which has been great. Suddenly I feel that they're thinking, "She's relaxed—we can relax." And you get more active listening and more for involvement. I also get tired of recitalists coming on- and offstage all the time, standing by the piano, waiting for the pianist to get ready. I wish the whole thing could have more of a living-room, chamber-music type of feeling. And I'd like to change the attire a bit. Sometimes I enjoy wearing fancy gowns, but I often think the formality of a floor-length gown doesn't help the problem of stiffness. I've never been crazy about the idea of treating the artist like some kind of deity. It plays dirty tricks with people's minds, and it hurts the music. All this is bad news, and unfortunately in the opera world, we've been behaving this way for quite a while.

Interview/Opera News, 1-16:22.

Benita Valente
Opera singer

1

To me it's still fascinating that I can stand up and sing. I've done it so many years and learned a lot about it, but I'll never learn all there is to know, because it's too elusive. I used to go to [cellist Pablo] Casals' master classes at Marlboro and think, "My God, if I could just make a sound like that!" When he drew a bow across the string, it was like a whole world opened up. But he had the same piece of wood and the same piece of horsehair as everyone else—why was his sound so different? Well, it was the experience of this man, combined with the kind of pressure he'd put on the bow, combined with what he felt about the music. It was the magic combination we're all looking for that hits you right in the gut. If we keep stirring around, we're liable to hit on it once every hundred thousand notes. That's really what keeps me going.

Interview, Philadelphia, Pa./
Opera News, June:20.

John Vickers
Opera singer

2

One of the great tragedies of our time in music is that young people are trying to force success rather than concentrating on learning their trade. There are kids today who step onto the Met [-ropolitan Opera] stage who know one or two operas and nothing of the art song, and certainly nothing of oratorio. I knew more oratorio than opera when I started my career, and I still think there is no substitute for repertoire. I mean, if I know *Don Carlo* and *Aida* and *Forza del Destino,* these add something to my Wagner, and the other way around, too, I'm not saying we were totally right. I'm just saying the emphasis is different. I challenge any young singer to sing Pergolesi's "O cessate di piagarmi." If you really can sing that song, you know a hell of a lot about *how* to sing.

Interview, Bermuda/Opera News, 4-10:15.

Udo Zimmermann
Composer, Conductor; Intendant,
Leipzig Opera (Germany)

3

In Germany, the attitude of opera administrators tends to be, "I have the money—now what am I going to do with it?" When the question should be, "I want to make art—now how will I finance it?" To define ourselves by what we have, rather than by who we are, would be the end of civilization. But that's also bureaucracy . . . Only artists can save opera from the bureaucrats.

Opera News, August:25.

THE STAGE

JoAnne Akalaitis
Former artistic director,
New York Public Theatre

1

A play like *Woyzeck* is a world-class masterpiece, and we [at the Public Theatre] proved there's a strong audience for such serious theatre. [But] there were people on the board who said to me, "You have to do more happy plays or musicals." [The success of *A Chorus Line* was] in some ways the biggest liability in the American theatre. These boards began to think that you could figure out a strategy to win the Broadway lottery, and then you have all this money and you could do all this other "serious" stuff. That kind of thinking is a disaster.

Newsweek, 3-29:63.

Jane Alexander
Actress; Chairman,
National Endowment for the Arts
of the United States

2

I don't know anybody, anybody who takes more rejection than an actor. From trying to get the job to then being subjected to merciless criticism in the press and constantly being subjected, if you are onstage every night, to audience approval or disapproval. I am an old hand at this. I am a little like those clowns that have a weight at the bottom and you knock them down and they pop right up again.

Interview, Washington, D.C./
The Washington Post, 10-14:(C)10.

Bibi Andersson
Swedish actress

3

Being onstage is a heightened life experience . . . Onstage you have to concentrate, you have to be there, have to live the situation. You have an identification with the role but also a total awareness of what you're doing. Suddenly, it's a very nice feeling: tense and energetic. So I understand that acting is like a life essence, very important for some people, and very scary if you don't reach it. And every once in a while it comes to you as a gift.

Interview, Los Angeles, Calif./
Los Angeles Times, 7-24:(F)7.

Kay Cummings
Director, dance department,
Tisch School of the Arts,
New York University

4

Because dance is hard to define in the same way as the other fine arts, it has a harder time being accepted [at the college level]. It is because it is physical, because the time demands are so unique, because it demands working in a studio with enormous discipline, trying to find a deeper way every single day, not being able to hide, or cheat, or sit in the back and not raise your hand.

Panel discussion/
Dance Magazine, September:47.

Merce Cunningham
Choreographer

5

I have, for lack of any other word, a passion for movement. And it isn't limited to a particular kind of movement, although it might seem so to many people. Very often, while teaching, I see something the dancers are doing that I am not familiar with, so then I try to remember it and employ it. If you have never seen a tree before, you don't have to be told about it. You go, and there it is; it's a new experience. For me, it's always better to come up on something I don't know, not having been told how to react.

Interview, New York, N.Y./
"Interview" magazine, March:54.

443

Rosemary Dunleavy
Ballet mistress,
New York City Ballet

1

Music is the key [to dance]. It's the music that gives me the memory of the steps. When I hear the music, I see the ballet and I feel the ballet. That's how it works for me. It's the music and its rhythms that make me remember the steps.

Interview/Dance Magazine, May:34.

Larry Gelbart
Stage, screen
and television writer

2

My last theatre experience [*City of Angels*] was a dream, just heaven. But everywhere else [on Broadway] is horrendous. Sure, the writer has the freedom, but he is not as well off financially. And producing has changed. You have to be careful where you tread. People who are not really producers are now—well, the kindest word you can use is "players"—and they have a great deal to say about whether you live or die. So, while I hope to do more in the theatre, the bloom is off that somewhat.

Interview, Beverly Hills, Calif./
The Washington Post, 3-20:(D)9.

Hal Holbrook
Actor

3

The wonderful thing about the theatre that I've experienced is that outside of New York in the past 30 years theatre has developed a wonderful edge. The thing we dreamed of when we were young, where every city had its repertory company, is happening. Now we have regional theatres. And, by God, a lot of it is damn good. Look, you can criticize productions at Seattle Rep, here at [San Diego's] Old Globe, La Jolla, Hartford, Dallas, L.A.'s Taper, but they are there. They're there!

Interview,
San Diego, Calif./
Los Angeles Times, 7-4:(Calendar)70.

Anthony Hopkins
Actor

4

I've never felt at home in the British theatre. I'm just tempermentally unsuited to it all . . . The routine of it all. Getting into the theatre. Getting your dressing-room key from the front desk. Sitting down. The dresser coming in with your clothes. All that sweaty misery . . . In the theatre, people talk, talk, talk until the cows come home about journeys of discovery and about what Hazlitt thought of a line of Shakespeare. I can't stand it. I mean, I *hate* it.

Interview/Lear's, December:89.

Jay Leno
Comedian; Host,
"The Tonight Show," NBC-TV

5

As far as I'm concerned, there's nothing better than being on the road [as a comedian] . . . For me, the best gigs are one-nighters. Being in the road company of a play—say, doing *Godspell* for eight weeks in Cincinnati—would drive me batty. I would rather do a one-nighter than be anywhere for three or four days. You rack up the points and you move on to the next place. If there's a fire, an earthquake, you're out of there, you're on to the next place. Riots in Los Angeles? You're in Detroit. Something happening in Detroit? You're in Cincinnati. That's the great thing about show business. When you finish shaking that hand and saying hello, you don't have to come back a month later and reshake it because you said hello wrong. I mean, it's over, it's gone, you've made the sale, you move on.

Interview/
Cosmopolitan, December:76.

Natalia Makarova
Actress; Former ballerina

6

It was very hard to take up this business of acting. On the other hand, I've always been an artist. I mean, I've not been a computer engineer or an electronics engineer. I come to the stage already equipped. I know the theatre. I know the public. I know how to create an atmosphere, both

(NATALIA MAKAROVA)

spiritually and physically. People say I have a sense of timing, but this also comes from my past life in dance—it comes from my response to music. In fact, what I miss most about acting is the music. It's music that drove me in ballet. You know, even if you feel an emptiness inside, the music will drive you in the right direction. In acting, you don't have music, so you have to create your own inner music.

Interview/
Dance Magazine, January:50.

Des McAnuff
Artistic director,
La Jolla (Calif.) Playhouse

1

Theatre might only reach a relatively few . . . people, but it can affect those people in a really meaningful way. I know it's true of me. I'm a real film lover, but I have a harder time remembering films than I do theatre experiences. I think it's the human connection when you're in a room with live people. They're real; they're actually living their lives before you. Even though with film there's a high degree of verisimilitude, it's not real, it's an illusion. I think we make a different kind of emotional investment in it.

Interview, Beverly Hills, Calif./
Los Angeles Times, 7-18:(Calendar)80.

Arthur Miller
Playwright

2

Stage plays today have been influenced by the movies, in which a character needs no past. [They] want forward motion and action. I think that's why we come back to the great plays again and again, like Chekhov and Shakespeare, because the characters have something in them.

The Writer, April:4.

Charles Moulton
Choreographer

3

I think that one of the main issues of my work is entertainment. My father was a vaudevillian and

my grandfather was a vaudevillian and I grew up in musical theatre. I am interested in structure and in larger issues, but I'm also constantly interested in giving people a way into something. I feel that a lot of work takes itself too seriously. So I always try to have a sense of humor about what I'm doing as a [so-called] "serious post-modern artist."

Interview/
Los Angeles Times, 7-18:(Calendar)4.

Christopher Plummer
Actor

4

The truth is that New York doesn't mean as much as it used to in theatre. The most important thing is that more and more small towns have their own theatres, which is strangely like Europe many years ago. What we need is to have young people go back to the theatres for training, you know what training is. New York has become a kind of personal-appearance town, a hot-ticket town instead of a place where every top writer from all over the world was represented in one season. It used to be more exciting than London.

Interview/
The Christian Science Monitor, 10-8:12.

Tony Randall
Actor;
Founder and artistic director,
National Actors Theater

5

We don't have enough classical theatre [in the U.S.]. I'm obviously trying to do something about that. But the fact is that every state in the Union should have a state theatre devoted to the classics. So that everybody, especially kids, can see the great plays . . . We don't have an enormous pool of actors well-schooled in the classics. If you were to ask every American who was the best Oedipus he ever saw, well, probably 99.999 percent have never seen one. That's criminal. Everyone should have seen the Greek classics. They're the origin of our theatre. They don't even teach that in schools. They teach Shakespeare, so you'll hate him forever.

Interview, New York, N.Y./
The Christian Science Monitor,
2-25:12.

445

Paul Rudnick
Author, Playwright

1

With [writing] plays you only have to fill the center of the page. Novels take a tremendous amount of typing.

Interview/Newsweek, 2-8:64.

Antoinette Sibley
President, Royal Academy
of Dancing (Britain);
Former prima ballerina,
Royal Ballet (Britain)

2

I think the RAD provides a wonderful starting point for children. The technique is sound. We're not asking people to push their legs up for the sake of ever-higher extensions or do extraordinary things. It's simple, pure. You start knowing true line and the correct way to hold yourself; that's your basis. We are very particular to stress that with our teachers. Dance, after all, is handing down, and it must be handed down the right way. I think if young children start off with our program and go right through the system, they can't go wrong. You can embellish all you like—later.

Interview,
New York, N.Y./
Dance Magazine, January:47.

Philosophy

Maya Angelou
Author, Poet

1

I think creativity is like electricity; we don't understand electricity at all. We've harnessed about one-millionth of one percent of it. Electricity makes no demands. It says, "I'm here. If you want to use me constructively, here I am. If destructively, that's up to you." I think creativity is like that.

Interview/
The Christian Science Monitor,
10-20:16.

Christiaan Barnard
Former heart-transplant
surgeon

2

The heart has mystical importance for humans, because it's the seat of emotions. That's why I became famous. I was never the best surgeon. I was just lucky enough to be the first to do a heart.

World Press Review, May:27.

Steven C. Beering
President, Purdue University

3

We can't teach you vision at a university, but we can help you learn to open your minds, and that is why I have no worries about the future of this country or this world. The purpose of this education was not just to prepare you for a career or to transmit a body of knowledge. It was to unleash your creative powers . . . None of the obstacles to progress that history has placed before the human race has been a match for the inquisitive, open and educated mind. It is the greatest power on earth.

At Purdue University commencement/
The Christian Science Monitor,
6-15:17.

Daniel J. Boorstin
Historian;
Librarian-emeritus
of Congress
of the United States

4

All peoples want to create. Everybody wants, from childhood on, to make things, put things together—and tear them down, too, I suppose—but certainly to make something. But that yen to "make" in Western civilization somehow has been focused on the making of the new—originality or making something from nothing. The Eastern cultures have produced wonderful things, but the premium in their cultures is not on originality, on the new. That's an opportunity, but there's a price, too, in the Western way, because it leads people to value the new for its newness and not for what it has made of experience.

Interview/
Humanities, Jan.-Feb.:5.

Tom Brokaw
Anchorman, NBC News

5

[Addressing university graduates]: You may think of [your degree] as a ticket to the good life. But why not consider it a ticket as well to join the revolution of democracy. You may say, "But democracy is already here. I have what the others want." True. And you also have certain assumptions, and you are not alone. Among them: There will be more of everything—more affluence, more freedom, more rights because it's our due, somehow. This expectation is not confined to your generation. As a society, we have come to believe, all of us, that what we do have is maintenance-free. It is not. It requires vigilance and nourishment. That is your responsibility—and it is mine. It is the obligation of all, but it is especially the responsibility of the educated.

At University of Virginia commencement/
The Christian Science Monitor,
6-15:16.

447

Helen Gurley Brown
Editor-in-chief,
"Cosmopolitan" magazine

1

[On aging]: There are always things in your life that you have a little guilt about, and you try to get them fixed up. But *age* . . . To have to be guilty because you plopped down on this Earth at a particular time—that's not fair. It's just pussyfooting and ridiculous to not give your real age. It's nothing to be ashamed of. You couldn't help it, so don't apologize for it.

Interview/
The Washington Post, 3-19:(F)5.

Zbigniew Brzezinski
Counsellor,
Center for Strategic
and International Studies;
Former Assistant
to the President of the United States
(Jimmy Carter)
for National Security Affairs

2

If you don't have criteria based on some absolutes, either ethical, moral or religious, you're not able to make choices. And if you're not able to make choices, then exponential growth in ability to do things becomes a dynamic that's out of control.

Interview, Washington, D.C./
The Christian Science Monitor,
4-29:14.

Kim Campbell
Minister of Defense
of Canada

3

I don't like to get into this thing where if women ruled the world, there would be more truth, beauty and justice.

Los Angeles Times, 3-2:(H)1.

Warren Christopher
Secretary of State
of the United States

4

Governments have a responsibility to preserve civil order. But even in times of intense political struggle, the imperative of civil order must be reconciled with free expression. Even when battling the forces of reaction, true democrats have nothing to fear from a free press.

At Academy of National Economy,
Moscow, Russia/
The Christian Science Monitor,
10-25:3.

Dick Clark
Entertainment producer

5

[On the keys to success]: Bulldog determination, hard work and a combination of good luck and reasonable intelligence can take you a long way.

Interview, Burbank, Calif./
USA Today, 1-22:(D)8.

Bill Clinton
President of the United States

6

We must be concerned over every retreat from democracy [in the world], but not every growing pain within democracy. Let me remind you of our own early history. It was marked by a revision of our governing charter and fist fights in Congress.

Before American Society of Newspaper Editors,
Annapolis, Md., April 1/
The New York Times, 4-2:(A)6.

7

Knowledge divorced from values can only serve to deepen the human nightmare, [and] a head without a heart is not humanity.

At dedication of Holocaust Memorial Museum,
Washington, D.C., April 22/
The New York Times, 4-23:(A)1.

Hillary Rodham Clinton
Wife of President
of United States
Bill Clinton

8

When does life start? When does life end? Who makes those decisions? How do we dare impinge upon these . . . delicate, difficult questions? Yet every day, in hospitals, homes and hospices . . . people are struggling with those very profound issues. These aren't issues we have guide books about . . . We have to summon up what we believe is morally and ethically and spiritually correct and do the best we can with God's guidance.

At University of Texas,
Austin, April 6/
USA Today, 4-7:(A)2.

1

The '80s were about acquiring—acquiring wealth, power, prestige. I know. I acquired more wealth, power and prestige than most. But you can acquire all you want and still feel empty. What power wouldn't I trade for a little more time with my family? What price wouldn't I pay for an evening with friends? It took a deathly [family] illness to put me eye-to-eye with that truth, but it is a truth that the country, caught up in its ruthless ambitions and moral decay, can learn on my dime.

The Washington Post, 5-6:(D)2.

2

How do we strike the right balance between individual rights and responsibility? How do we create a new spirit of community given all the problems that we are so aware of? Regrettably, the balance between the individual and the community, between rights and responsibilities, has been thrown out of kilter over the last years. Throughout the 1980s, we did hear too much about individual gain and the ethos of selfishness and greed. We did not hear enough about how to be a good member of a community, to defend the common good and to repair the social contract. And we also found that while prosperity does not trickle down from the most powerful to the rest of us, all too often indifference and even intolerance do.

At University of Pennsylvania commencement,
May 17/
The New York Times, 5-18:(A)10.

3

Excellence is not just a word, it is a benchmark . . . And when I talk about excellence, let me just expand for a moment on what I mean. To me, excellence is not found in any single moment in our lives. It is not about those who shine always in the sun, or those who fail to succeed in the darkness of human error or mistake. It is not about who is up or down today or this week. It is about who we are, what we believe in, what we do with every day of our lives. And for me, it is always telling . . . as to how someone deals with adversity and challenge.

At University of Michigan commencement/
The Christian Science Monitor,
6-15:16.

Robert Conquest
Senior research fellow,
Hoover Institution,
Stanford University;
Former British diplomat

4

Nationalism versus democracy—these are not, in fact, contradictories. France has always been nationalistic and often been very democratic. I don't think these contradict each other in essence. They do beyond a certain point. If you get the perverse nationalism and the Nazi ideological nationalism, or the super tribal-murder nationalism—what's now going on in the Balkans—yes, of course these are incompatible with democracy. But I don't think that it's a true statement of most of Eastern Europe and even of Russia as yet. It's true that they haven't yet got democracy and they haven't yet got what to my mind is more important than formal democracy, the rule of law. After all, how democratic was England in the 1800s? It was democratic in one sense: It was consensual, it was civic. But only a tenth of the population, if that, had the vote. The rule of law they did have. In England even today you don't hear the expression, "We're a democracy," in pubs. You hear the expression, "It's a free country, isn't it?" And I think freedom, political freedom, is more important and more basic than democracy.

Interview/Humanities, May-June:13.

Katie Couric
Co-host,
"Today" show, NBC-TV

1

My job gives me access to some of the most successful people in the world . . . I've found that there's one common denominator among successful people. They all love their jobs. The dictionary definition of work includes "toil," "drudgery" and "travail." Those should be antonyms, not synonyms. Ideally, work should feel like play. If you love what you're doing, the devotion will follow. And so will success. Getting a hold of the brass ring isn't very fulfilling if you don't enjoy riding the merry-go-round.

At Villanova (Pa.) University commencement/
The Christian Science Monitor,
6-15:16.

Jim Courier
Tennis player

2

Tennis is a matter of winning or losing matches. Life, the longer you're around, is a matter of losing close ones, of struggling through relationships. I've found out that life can make me way more miserable than tennis possibly could.

The New York Times,
3-15:(B)10.

Elizabeth Hanford Dole
President,
American Red Cross;
Former Secretary of Labor
of the United States

3

Some women . . . believe that concepts such as power and ambition are inconsistent with the mission of guiding their steps and their conscience. Over the years, though, women have come to realize that power is a positive force if it's used for positive purposes.

Interview,
Washington, D.C./
The Christian Science Monitor,
8-17:14.

Amitai Etzioni
Sociologist,
George Washington University

4

Because of society's shift from "me-ism" to "we-ism," volunteerism is likely to grow. We have seen what the world is like when everybody tries to push their own self-interest, and we realize that is not a livable world.

U.S. News & World Report,
10-4:114.

Robert Frank
Professor of economics,
ethics and public policy,
Cornell University

5

People don't get born into this world knowing what the rules [of ethics] are. It's very important to teach them, and I think that's been part of the problem—that we haven't been teaching people the rules anywhere near the same degree as we used to . . . Emotions, such as sympathy and guilt, are what support honest behavior. People whose oral sentiments steer them straight are different in a variety of subtle and observable ways.

The Christian Science Monitor,
1-14:4.

Betty Friedan
Author;
Women's rights advocate

6

Age is the unmapped period of life. It's the time to do things not risked before. It's the unknown adventure . . . It's very encouraging to me that the baby-boom generation is thinking ahead. Everyone their age has been too youth-oriented for too long. Now I hope they're beginning to realize that some of the best years are ahead, years when they can truly come into their own. Wouldn't that be wonderful if a whole generation could say "Yes" to time!

Interview,
Sag Harbor, N.Y./
Good Housekeeping, October:60,61.

Howard Gardner
Professor of education,
Graduate School of Education,
Harvard University

1

I think there are certain people who from a very early age seem to be in touch with the world of human beings and the world of objects in the way that the rest of us are not. They have a sixth sense of where things are coming from and where they are going, and they often project this sixth sense . . . They can take on quite important roles as leaders and inspirers. If you'd asked me 10 years ago, I would have said that's just interpersonal intelligence: Some people understand other people better and can work with them. I'm no longer persuaded that that's the case. I think some people really are tuned into an aspect of the world—the human world and the non-human world—that others of us aren't.

Interview, Boston, Mass./
The Christian Science Monitor,
3-29:11.

David Geffen
Motion-picture
and record producer

2

[On his involvement in the fight against AIDS]: One thing [AIDS] does is make you realize the future is an illusion. All you have is right now. And you aren't alive five years from now; you aren't alive 10 years from now; you aren't alive 30 years from now. You're just alive today. And to start living your life for the future is dumb. There is no future.

Los Angeles Times, 3-7:(Calendar)80.

Mel Gibson
Actor

3

I refuse to worry about the future. When I was a little kid, one of the most surprising things my father told me—and it has really worked for me—was that it is a sin to worry too much. I've always remembered that. I don't seek too much out of life, and since I have no expectations, I can't be disappointed.

Interview/
Good Housekeeping, January:40.

Sheldon Hackney
President,
University of Pennsylvania;
Chairman-designate,
National Endowment
for the Humanities
of the United States

4

Every human experience is enhanced by higher levels of knowledge. When I listen to a piece of music, I may like it and think it beautiful, but the person who knows the historical context of its composition understands what the composer was trying to accomplish technically and can compare the composition and the performance to others [and] will get infinitely more out of the experience than I will. That is why I enjoy talking about common experiences with people who will see it through a lens different from mine.

At Senate Committee hearing
on his nomination,
Washington, D.C., June 25/
Humanities, Sept.-Oct:5.

Vaclav Havel
President of the Czech Republic

5

I have often compared the condition of our society, of all societies that have rid themselves of Communism, to the post-penitentiary condition of someone released from prison. Something I have experienced a number of times myself . . . A person who was accustomed for many years to living under rigorous rules that prevented him from making his own decisions suffers from a kind of shock, which manifests itself in many ways. It is a sudden change, which brings new freedom and responsibilities, and many find it difficult to cope with them. They find themselves in a state of uncertainty, in which they tend to look for pseudo-certainties. One of those might be submerging themselves in a crowd, a community, and defining themselves in contrast to other communities.

Interview,
Prague, Czech Republic/
The New York Times, 12-10:(A)4.

Immanuel Jakobovits
Former Chief Rabbi
of the British Commonwealth

1

You will never be able to eliminate very basic differences of cultures and histories. This is the stuff of human progress. It's not differences that cause conflict, it's the intolerance of differences.

U.S. News & World Report,
6-14:61.

John Paul II
Pope

2

In developed countries, a serious moral crisis is already affecting the lives of many young people, leaving them adrift, often without hope, and conditioned to look only for instant gratification. Only by instilling a high moral vision can a society insure that its young people are given the possibility to mature as free and intelligent human beings, endowed with a robust sense of responsibility to the common good, capable of working with others to create a community and a nation with a strong moral fiber . . . To educate without a value system based on truth is to abandon young people to moral confusion, personal insecurity and every manipulation. No country, not even the most powerful, can endure if it deprives its own children of this essential good.

Speech on arrival in Denver, Colo.,
Aug. 12/
The New York Times, 8-13:(A)10.

3

The value of democracy, understood as participative management of the state through specific organs of representation and control in the service of the common good [rests in] a democracy which, above and beyond its rules, has in the first place a soul made up of the fundamental values without which it easily turns into open or thinly disguised totalitarianism.

At University of Riga, Latvia,
Sept. 9/
Los Angeles Times, 9-10:(A)8.

Michael Josephson
President,
Josephson Institute of Ethics

4

[On ethics]: Prudence says it's the *smart* thing to do—you know, good ethics make good business. Virtue says it's the *right* thing to do. I argue that what we need today is not more self-interest ethics, but more virtue ethics.

The Christian Science Monitor,
1-14:4.

Garrison Keillor
Author

5

I don't believe in amusement or entertainment that much. We're surrounded by entertainment, inundated by it. Anybody could, if they wished, sit down in a dark room and have access to a hundred channels of television. And some day soon, I'm sure, thousands, endless channels, and through computers, infinite other sources of amusement. But none of this exactly advances us toward what we want, which is to be ourselves and to feel brave, competent and funny and handsome and beloved.

Interview/
U.S. News & World Report,
11-15:77.

Lee Kuan Yew
Former Prime Minister
of Singapore

6

[Saying foreign cultures should not destroy a country's own culture, through advertising and other media]: Up to a point, you can block or limit cultural exchange . . . You should not abandon your basic pattern of culture, because there is a real danger of deculturalization, of losing your own basic values, without absorbing the essence of the other culture. Culture does not consist of only customs, forms, external manifestations. There's an inner spirit to it, which holds a set of values into a coherent whole . . . Ideas, values of right and wrong, behavior within the family, behavior to friends, behavior to authority—they were not taught in school. They

(LEE KUAN YEW)

sprang from the home. Before you destroy that by showing [for example] how Americans live—what they do with their governments, how they fix each other up or help each other—a little thought may show it's not helpful to destroy what is basically good and will help people retain their dignity and integrity.

Interview/
The Christian Science Monitor,
12-8:13.

John Major
Prime Minister
of the United Kingdom

1

Very often decisions which are right are unpopular. It does not make them less right.

Los Angeles Times, 9-11:(A)6.

Bill Moyers
Broadcast journalist

2

Although I'm 59, I sometimes have the instincts of an 18-year-old. But then my body says, "Wait a minute, not so fast." Erik Erikson once said that in our 20s, we should discover what we want to be; in our 30s, learn how to do it; and in our 40s and 50s, do it well. As I approach my 60s, I have to think about how time takes its toll and requires its changes. The prospect of getting very old does not appeal to me. I fear being very old, crippled, speechless. I fear being dependent. I'll do everything I can to avoid those. But nature still has the last word.

Interview/
Modern Maturity, Oct.-Nov.:71.

Oliver L. North
Lieutenant Colonel,
United States Marine Corps (Ret.);
Political commentator

3

What we need as a nation is to find men and women who understand that we're not here on this Earth to endure the future. We're here

to change it. We don't have a "new world order." It's a "new world disorder." It's not the Ten Suggestions we live by. It's the Ten Commandments.

Speech/
The New York Times, 3-2:(A)6.

Alan Page
Justice, Supreme Court
of Minnesota;
Former football player,
Minnesota "Vikings"
and Chicago "Bears"

4

[On his becoming the first black to serve on the Minnesota Supreme Court, after having had a successful football career]: Success comes with hard work; it comes with preparation. And when you do prepare, then you can achieve your hopes and dreams. That's something that I think all children need to see—to see that things just don't "happen." My having been elected [to the Court] was not a matter of luck.

Jan. 4/USA Today, 1-5:(C)13.

Neil Postman
Chairman, department of
culture and communications,
New York University

5

[On life sixty years from now, in 2053]: Public life will have disappeared because we did not see, in time to reverse the process, that our dazzling technologies were privatizing almost all social activities. It became first possible, then necessary, to vote at home, shop at home, listen to music at home, see movies at home. We replaced our libraries with interactive videotext, which even encouraged individuals to change the ending of stories if they didn't like them, so that there no longer existed a common literature. We replaced schools with home computers and television. We replaced meeting friends with the video telephone and electronic mail. We replaced visits to faraway places with virtual reality. We became afraid of real people and eventually forgot how to behave in public places,

(NEIL POSTMAN)

which had become occupied almost entirely by criminals. The rest of us had no need to be with each other.

Interview/
U.S. News & World Report,
10-25:78.

Judith Rodin
Provost, Yale University

1

My bottom-line concern is that we don't tolerate diversity well in this society. There's one "right" way to be, and people who aren't that way are deviant. My goal, whether I'm working on a committee on minorities at Yale or writing a book about body image, is to persuade people that it's diversity we're aiming at. Because if we have just one image of what's perfect, we'll moralize it and decide that anything that deviates is less good, less deserving, less adequate.

Working Woman, March:63.

Susan Sarandon
Actress

2

I really think people divide in two classes: people who want to know and people who don't want to know. We're in a culture where we're told not to know. Everything tells you don't ask questions. Every moment that you live, you're preparing for death in a way, so that right there is creative. You create this entire life, you buy property, you have children—things that would seem to suggest some kind of permanence and control over your life—and in fact, you have absolutely none. I guess because death is so frightening—it certainly is for me—you do spend a lot of your time allowing yourself to be lulled into some kind of complacency. And if you try to stay awake, that is a lifetime experience—to stay awake, and see things and not take things for granted.

Interview/
Film Comment, March-April:52.

Peter Sellars
Artistic director,
Los Angeles (Calif.) Festival

3

I need work that reflects that something is *in motion*. It could break the stalemate of society and permit society to be in motion once again. It moves beyond the dead-end thinking of the '80s, and into a notion of the '90s, the current flux we are in, politically and in all areas of the world. [Find that] moment of beauty. If you don't have that little moment, then take my advice and do what countless others have done before you: *Go and get it*. Live a little. Try *life*.

Los Angeles, Calif./
Los Angeles Times, 4-18:(Calendar)3.

George Soros
Investor, Philanthropist

4

Part of what I learned was the futility of making money for money's sake. Wealth can be a dead weight.

Time, 5-31:55.

Gay Talese
Author

5

[On life 60 years from now, in 2053]: I hope there will be a rebellion against the demons of correctness and we'll once again extol the virtue of individualism. Maybe, everything we now see as proper and correct will be seen, instead, as a representation of a false attitude and a limit to possibilities.

Interview/
U.S. News & World Report,
10-25:72.

Randall L. Tobias
Vice chairman,
American Telephone
& Telegraph Company

6

It has long been recognized that the pen is mightier than the sword. The modern version of that is: The fax machine is mightier than the rifle.

(RANDALL L. TOBIAS)

It is impossible for a society that has more open telecommunications to continue to be repressive.

The New York Times, 5-7:(A)1.

Cornel West
Professor of religion
and director of
Afro-American studies program,
Princeton University

1

To be a philosopher in a society that understands itself to be democratic puts a special kind of burden on [you], because . . . you want to hold that society to its own self-understanding, its own ideals. The real benchmark of democratic ideals is the notion that ordinary people ought to live lives of decency and dignity. So you're forever examining the various ways in which ordinary people are, or are not, living lives of decency and dignity—which leads you to the question of whether ordinary people's voices are actually being heard in decision-making processes in institutions that guide and regulate their lives. So as a philosopher, you're involved in a quest for wisdom, you're grappling with the question "How to live?"—which is that three-word question each and every one of us have to ask as we move from womb to tomb.

Interview, Los Angeles, Calif./
Los Angeles Times, 5-9:(M)3.

Religion

Roberto Blancarte
President,
Center for Religious Studies
(Mexico)

1

There was [a] general perception that Catholicism was *the* religion of Mexico. [But it is] a country where there are now more than 400 recognized churches with equal legal status. There's a new awareness of plurality in the country. That means the Catholic Church no longer has an exclusive relationship with the government [of Mexico]. It's a good relationship but one that's more clearly relative. And the relationship between the government and other churches is more open and direct now.

The Christian Science Monitor,
8-11:4.

Robert Boston
Official,
Americans United for Separation
of Church and State

2

Everybody likes the idea that churches are ministering to the poor, [and] everybody wants a church to go to on Sunday . . . but no one wants one in their neighborhood. Churches are not perceived as good neighbors the way they once were.

The Washington Post, 10-21:(A)1.

Jack Brooks
United States Representative,
D-Texas

3

[Criticizing a 1990 Supreme Court ruling that put restrictions on many religious practices]: The Supreme Court's decision three years ago transformed a most-hallowed liberty into a mundane concept with little more status than a fishing license, thus subjecting religious freedom to the whims of government officials.

The Christian Science Monitor,
5-17:1.

Joan B. Campbell
General secretary,
National Council
of Churches

4

[Arguing against stereotyping Muslims as terrorists because of the Islamic affiliation of many who have been involved in terrorism]: We don't deny there are extremists. There are extremists of many different faiths, including Christians. But we must be clear that the problem is the extremism, not the faith group.

The New York Times, 3-13:8.

Benjamin F. Chavis, Jr.
Vice president,
National Council
of Churches

5

I think those extreme forces on the religious right are going to find themselves irrelevant. It's not because anyone is shutting the door in their face, but because their ideology increasingly does not apply to the American condition.

Los Angeles Times, 2-2:(A)15.

Bill Clinton
President of the United States

6

[Disagreeing with the idea that separation of church and state should mean that public officials should not express their religious feelings]: The fact that we have freedom of religion doesn't mean that those of us who have faith shouldn't frankly admit that we are animated by that faith, that we try to live by it—and that it does affect what we feel, what we think and what we do. It is hard to take a totally secular approach to the [problems facing the country].

At White House prayer breakfast,
Washington, D.C., Aug. 30/
Los Angeles Times,
8-31:(A)9.

Charles Colson
Columnist;
Former Special Counsel
to the President
of the United States
(Richard M. Nixon)

1

Religion is the only way to reach into the darkest corners of every community, into the darkest corners of every mind. Religion provides a moral impulse to do good . . . Religion also provides the power to *be* good . . . I sense some of you are squirming, and I know what many people think: "Christians just want to cram their religious values down reluctant throats." But that is not my intention. I want simply to argue that Christians bring something important to our culture, something that cannot be easily replaced. I want to argue that they deserve an honored place at the table, that in a free, pluralistic society, we can contend in the public square for the truths we cherish without "imposing" them on anyone. The great paradox of our age is this: In the interest of tolerance, we are aggressively seeking to scrub religious values, and even reminders of our religious heritage, out of our public life. Yet it is that religious heritage that is essential for the recovery of character.

At National Press Club,
Washington, D.C., March 11/
Christianity Today, 8-16:32.

Louis Farrakhan
Spiritual leader,
Nation of Islam
in the United States

2

[On his criticism of Jews]: Look at me like a Jewish mother who may spank her child not because she hates the child. She wants the child to take a correct course. If I have spoken words that hurt, the question comes right down to this: Did he speak the truth? . . . [When] I said that Israel has not had any peace in 40 years, and she cannot have any peace because there can be no peace structured on lying, thievery and injustice and using God's name as a shield for your dirty religion, I never mentioned Judaism nor did I ever have Judaism in mind. But I can under-

stand, based upon the words and the context, that it could be deduced that I was condemning Judaism. That I will accept, and that is my mistake. I don't call it an error, because an error is an intentional affront. I was speaking of the action of Israel toward the Palestinians.

Interview/Newsweek, 6-28:31.

Peter J. Gomes
Professor of Christian morals,
Harvard University

3

[On religion sixty years from now, in 2053]: Now that Christianity has survived modernity, what will it become? Denominationalism, as we know it, will cease to exist. Religious loyalty and identity will depend not so much upon the label or even the institutional style or inheritance but more upon the capacity of the faith to help people come to terms with the meaning and end of one's life.

Interview/
U.S. News & World Report,
10-25:80.

Billy Graham
Evangelist

4

[On the separation of church and state in the U.S.]: We've leaned too far. The Founding Fathers meant that there should be no state church, but we've separated the state from all religion . . . It's ironic that we're not allowed to talk about God and the Bible in our schools, and in Russia they're begging for it.

Interview/
U.S. News & World Report,
5-3:72.

5

[The late] Chancellor Konrad Adenauer of West Germany asked me once if I believed in the Resurrection of Jesus Christ. I said, "Yes, I do." He said, "So do I. And if Jesus Christ was not raised from the dead, there's no hope for the human race." I hold the same view. Christianity wouldn't be Christianity without it.

Interview/Time, 11-15:74.

Irving Greenberg
Rabbi; President,
National Jewish Center
for Learning and Leadership

1

[I] believe that choice [about Jewishness] should play a greater role in our religion. But having thought about it for 10 years, I think the movement toward pure choice is excessive. Life is more subtle than that. There remains an element of election, which birth represents; an element of the given, which the body represents. The Jewish response is that we are not pure birth or tribe, but we are not pure choice, either. Biology does speak. This does greater justice to the embodied situation.

The New York Times,
8-7:6.

Yvonne Haddad
Professor
of Islamic history,
University of Massachusetts,
Amherst

2

[On the Islamic religion]: The word Islam comes from the three-letter root word in Arabic, "slm," which stands for peace. And, in a sense, Islam is the religion of peace. That's just the way the Koran talks about it—the religion of peace. When you become a Muslim, you become at peace with God. And that's what Islam means, to surrender to God, to stop fighting God. To be at peace with Him, to have a relationship of peace. People should know that Islam, in a sense, urges people to worship the same God that Christianity and Judaism do. That we share not only the same God, but the same perception about accountability in this life. The accountability at the end of time on Earth. And also for the way we live our lives. It also calls for brotherhood and understanding, and it's very hard to teach that because most people have a prejudiced idea about what it is at the moment [because of a public perception of Muslims being linked to terrorism].

Interview/
USA Today,
3-10:(A)11.

Amanda Hiley
Administrator,
Southern Baptist Women
in Ministry

3

Women are not seeking ordination simply to be defiant. They pay a heavy price for ordination, the personal ridicule they have to put up with. They have to be very serious about their call to the ministry in this environment to accept ordination.

The Washington Post, 5-8:(G)11.

David Allan Hubbard
President,
Fuller Theological Seminary,
Pasadena, Calif.

4

We [religious seminaries] have to discern the ways secular thinking is making inroads in the church. That means we have to be more effective and actively counter-culture than we have been. The entertainment and information media are much more pagan than Christian. We have to know how to survive in the midst of that and not capitulate. And we have to know how to prepare others to deal with it. We need to help students minister in a society whose value system is being eroded and whose very pluralism and diversity makes it harder for us to think in terms of theological absolutes. In the whole mood of political correctness—which has some positive sides—we have to offer *theological* correctness that recognizes diversity yet makes concern about diversity subservient to the unity of the church and the kingdom.

Interview/
Christianity Today, 5-17:46.

John Jamnicky
Chaplain, O'Hare Airport,
Chicago, Ill.;
Former president,
International Association
of Civil Aviation Chaplains

5

[On his airport chapel]: I have walked by the chapel on numerous occasions and there will be a

(JOHN JAMNICKY)

Muslim on the prayer rug up in front, praying, a Catholic on a kneeler, praying, and a Jew on the side, in prayer, all exactly at the same time and in the same place. It's beautiful that we can all be here together praying to God in different languages, and with different prayers, and in different postures, but all with the same basic kind of faith, love and respect.

Interview/
The Christian Science Monitor,
12-2:20.

John Paul II
Pope

1

The only struggle which religions can justify, the only struggle worthy of man, is the moral struggle against man's own disordered passions, against every kind of selfishness, against attempts to oppress others, against every type of hatred and violence.

Mass, Khartoum, Sudan, Feb. 10/
The New York Times, 2-12:(A)7.

John F. Kinney
Roman Catholic Bishop
of Bismarck, N.D.

2

[On the committee he will head that will investigate and try to prevent sexual abuse of minors by priests]: I want to make sure that all of us bishops understand the depth and seriousness, the pain and the agony of this problem, and why it strikes at the very heart of the Church's trust level and credibility. [The process may] involve uncomfortable listening, nationally as well as back home. It might be messy listening, but that might well be necessary if we are to lance the boil.

At National Conference
of Catholic Bishops meeting,
New Orleans, La., June 17/
The New York Times,
6-18:(A)1.

Hans Kung
Swiss theologian

3

I am convinced that a man can live a moral life without religion, as the lives of people, now alive or in the past, demonstrate concretely. The right to religious freedom also means the right to live without religion.

World Press Review, November:30.

Barbara Labuda
Member of Polish Sejm
(Parliament)

4

The strong participation of the church [in Polish politics] is dangerous both for the state and the church [because] the center of real power is transferred from the bodies that are controlled by the people to another body that can't be controlled.

The Christian Science Monitor,
5-26:9.

Roger Mahony
Roman Catholic Archbishop
of Los Angeles, Calif.

5

The crucial issue that we are having to look at in terms of ordination of women as priests is this: Has the church received the authority from Christ to make that kind of dramatic change? Not, "Is it a good idea?" It has nothing to do with the value of women—that isn't the issue. The question that we're having to wrestle with is: Has Christ given the church the authority to make that kind of change? And so far, the response and reflection in prayer is no. That isn't a question of whether we should or shouldn't; it is that we don't have the authority to do it.

Interview, Los Angeles, Calif./
Los Angeles Times, 12-26:(M)3.

6

[On celibacy in the clergy]: We have to look at what are the core faith dimensions of our Catholic tradition, what is changeable and negotiable, and what is not. Certainly, celibacy is not

(ROGER MAHONY)

the lifelong tradition of the church at all. In fact, just the opposite. Not only in the first 12 centuries did we have married clergy, the whole Eastern Catholic church has had married clergy down to the present time. So the discipline of celibacy is not something that has to be retained at all.

Interview, Los Angeles, Calif./
Los Angeles Times, 12-26:(M)3.

Pamela Maraldo
President,
Planned Parenthood Federation
of America

1

Surveys have been done that show that most Catholics in America are pro-choice on abortion and believe in contraception. The Catholic Church is also a social institution run by men, and they take positions they think are beneficial to its own non-religious self-interest. From my perspective, the church hasn't kept up with the times.

Interview, New York, N.Y./
The Washington Post, 3-2:(E)3.

Martin E. Marty
Professor of church history,
University of Chicago
Divinity School

2

No God or religion or spirituality, no issue of truth or beauty or goodness, no faith or hope or love, no justice or mercy; only winning and losing in the churching game matters [to many religionists today].

Time, 4-5:48.

3

[Criticizing attempts to increase church membership by changing church doctrine to fit what people want]: To give the whole store away to match what this year's market says the unchurched want is to have the people who know least about faith determine most about its expression.

Newsweek, 8-9:48.

Michael Medved
Film critic;
Co-host, "Sneak Previews," PBS-TV

4

All the surveys show that most Americans pray every week; 45 percent go to church or synagogue every week. This is never reflected in motion pictures or on TV. Only characters from the past are allowed to be identified with regular religious practices—like the minister in *A River Runs Through It,* which is set in the 1920s, and so he's allowed to go to church. Anyone in the 1980s—forget it. If a character goes to church, chances are he's a crook or crazy—like Robert De Niro in *Cape Fear,* who has a gigantic cross tattooed on his back. Just before he goes to rape Jessica Lange, he says, "Are you ready to be born again?" No other group in America could be traduced with such breathtaking impunity.

Interview/
Christianity Today, 3-8:24.

Jurgen Moltmann
Professor of theology,
University of Tubingen
(Germany)

5

[On ancient and classical Christian creeds and writings]: The confessions of faith should lead to actual faith. They are not abstract formulas that we recite in worship services but nobody actually thinks about. According to my Reformed understanding of creedal confession, the creeds are a manual for faith today. Therefore, we should rewrite these creeds and confessions, without neglecting the tradition behind them.

Interview/
Christianity Today, 1-11:33.

Ralph Reed
Director, Christian Coalition

6

[On his forceful drive for the political revival of the Christian right]: I am in the political arena and my job is to win. If you are a middle linebacker for the Chicago *Bears* and you are an agnostic, and if you are a middle linebacker for the Chicago *Bears* and you are a Christian, your

(RALPH REED)

job is the same. If a running back comes over the middle, you lay him on the ground.

Washington, D.C./
The Washington Post, 9-10:(A)4.

James Richardson
Sociologist of religion,
University of Nevada, Reno

1

[On the recent siege and violence at a religious-cult compound in Waco, Texas]: We forget that 99 percent of minority religious groups are benign and peaceful and just want to be left alone. When they abide by the law, they have this right, and the focus of the Waco tragedy should not lead to more harassment of the 99 percent. Regrettably, however, Waco may be just the excuse some [people] are looking for to exercise more control over minority religious groups.

The New York Times, 4-24:8.

Helmut Schmidt
Principal editor,
"Die Zeit" (Germany);
Former Chancellor
of West Germany

2

In Western democracies there is hardly any understanding of Islam and its historical development . . . Late in my life, I learned the immense scientific and cultural achievements of Islam. For the Western world, it's important to learn to understand Islam, to learn to discuss with Muslims more than oil.

At symposium on Islam/
Los Angeles Times, 4-6:(H)6.

John Stott
British evangelist

3

The post-war resurgence of evangelicalism in Britain has been remarkable. When I was

ordained in 1945, evangelicals in the Church of England were a tiny, despised minority. I've seen us grow in numbers, in scholarship, in cohesion and in influence. Today, what worries me more than anything else is—as somebody else has said—that evangelicals are less a party than a coalition. I've been concerned for and committed to the unity of the evangelical movement all my life. But now I see it breaking up or in danger of breaking up.

Interview/
Christianity Today, 2-8:38.

Elie Wiesel
Author;
Winner, 1986 Nobel Peace Prize

4

[On the fact that there are no monuments to Jews who saved Jews during the Nazi era]: It's a very poignant question. I think we should do something. It's absolutely necessary to recognize them for the heroes they are. These were men and women who not only overcame their fear, but their prudence, their caution, and risked their lives in order to save others. That should not diminish the respect and admiration I have for the non-Jewish rescuers—because in their case, it was not expected.

The Washington Post, 4-17:(G)10.

D. Newell Williams
Church historian,
Christian Theological Seminary,
Indianapolis, Ind.

5

The denominations no longer offer a distinctive Christian standard for judging statements about God or moral action. Many people now see no reason to be Christian. The mainline churches are just plain boring, but the Gospel is not boring.

Newsweek, 8-9:47.

Science and Technology

Robert E. Allen
Chairman,
American Telephone
& Telegraph Company

1

Before this decade is out, business people will take it for granted that they have a choice of communicating electronically with handwriting, data, images or video as easily and as often as they do with voice today. Every day, multimedia communication will take no more effort than making a phone call. Office and mobile communications systems will respond to voice commands, whether to send a jotted memo, research a customer's questions or set up a business lunch. Many of us will become accustomed to seeing the people we're talking with, even on conference calls. During the call, we'll be able to read documents quickly, call upon experts or access remote systems to run an analysis . . . The most urgent role for government is to clear the way—to provide the incentives and opportunities—for industry to create a fully competitive information infrastructure.

Interview/
U.S. News & World Report,
5-3:63.

Robert Birgeneau
Dean,
School of Science,
Massachusetts Institute
of Technology

2

[On foreign students studying science at U.S. colleges]: The input from foreign students is absolutely necessary if the United States wants to stay at the forefront technologically. We simply don't have enough outstanding American citizens who want to pursue careers in science and engineering.

U.S. News & World Report,
3-22:75.

Jack Brooks
United States Representative,
D-Texas

3

[Supporting U.S. development of a space station]: History has shown that the great nations have been those that had a spark of risk-taking, of adventure, of being willing to operate at the frontiers of knowledge and exploration.

Washington, D.C., June 23/
The New York Times,
6-24:(A)9.

George E. Brown, Jr.
United States Representative,
D-California

4

[Without a space station,] eight [space shuttle] launches a year would go down to three or four a year. The cost of a launch would run up into billions and the shuttle itself would become a very attractive target for budget cutting. If you are willing to shoot down a $2-billion-a-year space station, what would you do with a shuttle costing more and more, and going without a real mission?

Los Angeles Times,
5-20:(A)18.

5

[On the House's decision to stop funding the superconducting super-collider project]: It is obviously energetic budget-cutting. But you are threatening the economic development of the country in a very broad sense. You have a majority [in Congress] who weren't even around when this project was started. It is a high-priority target for them. A project that takes this long may no longer be viable in a Congress that has no collective memory. The space station will be their target to kill next year.

Los Angeles Times,
10-21:(A)27.

Nolan Bushnell
Chairman, Octus, Inc.;
Inventor of the first video game

1

[On computers sixty years from now, in 2053]: Computers will be around in greater numbers than ever, but they'll be hidden. Walk into a store, pick up what you want and leave. A scanner will identify you, record your purchases and bill your credit card. People who fear computers will have less to fear; operations and programming will be transparent.

Interview/
U.S. News & World Report,
10-25:78.

Bill Clinton
President of the United States

2

[Supporting a U.S. space-station program, but one that is less costly than before]: We need to stay first in science and technology, we need to stay first in space. I think it would be a mistake to scrap all the work we've done . . . There is no doubt that we are facing difficult budget decisions. However, we cannot retreat from our obligations to invest in our future . . . [The space-station project] will yield benefits in medical research, aerospace and other critical technology areas. [It is] a mode of peaceful international cooperation.

News conference,
Washington, D.C., June 17/
Los Angeles Times, 6-18:(A)1.

3

At a time when our long-term economic strength depends on our technological leadership and our ability to reduce the [Federal budget] deficit, we must invest in technology but invest wisely, making the best possible use of every dollar.

News conference,
Washington, D.C., June 17/
The New York Times,
6-18:(A)8.

Vic Fazio
United States Representative,
D-California

4

[Supporting U.S. funding of the superconducting super-collider project]: This is the most important scientific project of our lifetimes. It is far more important for us economically to be exploring the innermost corners of matter than to be visiting the far reaches of space.

Before the House, Washington, D.C./
Los Angeles Times, 6-25:(A)23.

John Frazee
President, Sprint Corporation

5

[Saying land lines will remain the heart of the telephone system]: There are literally billions of dollars being spent on the deployment of fiber-optic [land-line technology]. While wireless is a tremendous addition to the world's portfolio of technologies for telecommunications, it is just that. No one technology is going to dominate. Cellular has a lot of capacity, but it doesn't have the capacity that's going to be required for video in the house or large volumes of data from the business or the house . . . The real wild card . . . is regulation. Right now, you have heavy [government] regulation of the telephone companies and less regulation of other technologies. We want fair competition.

The Christian Science Monitor,
4-15:9.

Bill Gates
Chairman, Microsoft Corporation

6

Today, a lot of electronic devices perform a few specialized functions. But imagine a single wallet-size device from which you could activate all of your other devices—your tablet-size or desktop personal computer, appliances in your house, whatever large-screen display you have in your home. I envision a wallet that allows interchange and communications between all these other devices . . . I think government should be careful, however, not to assume that we understand how the industries around this digital convergence will take shape. It is way too early to assume a static set of assumptions about what will happen and draw up a regulatory model or start thinking about what needs to be restricted, or even facilitated. This could have the impact of freezing the right technology, or facilitating what turns out to be the wrong technology, or discouraging entry by a particular industry that might have something to contribute.

Interview/
U.S. News & World Report,
5-3:62.

John Glenn
United States Senator,
D-Ohio; Former astronaut

1

[Supporting a proposed joint U.S.-Russian space station]: The quest for knowledge, the curiosity about the unknown almost always seems to pay off in the future beyond anything we anticipate.

Los Angeles Times, 9-22:(A)20.

Daniel S. Goldin
Administrator,
National Aeronautics
and Space Administration
of the United States

2

The Cold War is over, and NASA cannot survive as a relic of bygone days. I personally am tired of Apollo [spacecraft] stories . . . It's time we started writing history, and not reading it.

Before American Astronautical Society,
Arlington, Va., March 10/
The Washington Post, 3-11:(A)11.

3

Ending our [U.S.] commitment to space would be a catastrophe. I believe that space is going to play a significant role in the future of this country, and that this [Clinton] Administration recognizes that. A nation that is not a space-faring nation is a nation that will be in trouble in the next

couple of decades . . . This nation critically needs space for its ecological infrastructure, its technological infrastructure and its communications infrastructure. You can't just turn a switch off for five or 10 years and say that we'll come back to it when we're ready.

The Washington Post, 4-16:(F)3.

4

NASA is in chaos [because of continuous budget cutting by Congress]. We can't develop a strategic plan . . . Give us a stable budget. Every three or four months we are adjusting our budget. We can't perform . . . We must stand by our people. We must stand by the merits of this program. We can't expect the same performance if we keep making cuts. It's that simple.

Before Senate Science,
Technology and Space Subcommittee,
Washington, D.C.,Nov. 16/
The Washington Post, 11-17:(A)24.

Al Gore
Vice President
of the United States

5

[On the importance of government help to high-tech industries]: One hundred dollars' worth of computer chips will have more leverage over the future of business and industry than $100 worth of potato chips. The knowledge gained in manufacturing the computer chips will provide an advantage in manufacturing the next generation of computer chips and an advantage in understanding all of the machines in which the computer chips are used.

Interview/
U.S. News & World Report,
3-8:30.

6

The object [in developing new communications technology] is not simply to create a zillion-channel cable-TV capacity. It is to empower the American people with interactive, multiway networks that allow the emergence of all these new services and products that we can't yet

(AL GORE)

imagine. In a real sense, the printing press made possible the modern nation-state and representative democracy by giving citizens of a large geographic area enough civic knowledge to participate in decision-making. If the printing press did that, then how much richer in spirit can our country be if our people are empowered with the knowledge that these high-capacity computer networks can distribute? It's a very exciting prospect.

Interview/
U.S. News & World Report,
12-6:62.

Mae Jemison
American astronaut

1

You know what I took with me when I went up [in space]? An Alvin Ailey American Dance Theatre poster, an Alpha Kappa Alpha banner, a flag that had flown over the Organization of African Unity, and proclamations from Chicago's DuSable Museum of African-American History and the Chicago public-school system. I wanted everyone to know that space belongs to all of us. There is science in dance, and art in science. It belongs to everyone. I'm not the first or the only African-American woman who had the skills and the talent to become an astronaut. I had the opportunity. All people have produced scientists and astronauts.

Interview/Essence, April:60.

Joan Johnson-Freese
Space analyst, Air War College,
Maxwell Air Force Base,
Alabama

2

[On the apparent failure of the billion-dollar Mars Observer mission, which has brought into question the practicality of high-cost, complex space projects]: I think it all goes back to the idea that this is how the NASA bureaucracy is geared—you do big things, you have big spectaculars. Who pays any attention to the little-package deals? Nobody. You go for flybys of

Saturn, you go for a Mars Observer, things that will get media attention. Unfortunately, that sometimes backfires when the engineering glitch occurs. And this is what you get.

The Washington Post, 8-26:(A)16.

Makoto Kuroda
Managing director,
Mitsubishi Corporation (Japan)

3

[Supporting U.S. President Clinton's plan for the government to financially support American high-technology industry]: We need a strong America. It's good for Japan and good for the world. We are not afraid of fair competition . . . Now Americans are clearly saying, "We are in support of investing in technology for the sake of the economy and the world." We say, "Okay, come on. That's what we've [Japan] been doing for 20 years."

Los Angeles Times, 2-25:(D)1.

Donald N. Langenberg
Chancellor,
University of Maryland

4

[On the House's decision to stop funding the superconducting super-collider project]: I do have to ask what really are our chances of getting foreign countries intimately involved with a project that our Congress can unceremoniously dump with no notice. The U.S. is not a reliable partner in either multinational or other cooperative large projects. We sucker [Texas] into spending large amounts of their resources [for the collider] and then right in the middle we turn it into a political football and kick it away. The U.S. government is an inconsistent lover, to use a Shakespearean term.

Los Angeles Times, 10-21:(A)27.

John M. Logsdon
Director, Space Policy Institute,
George Washington University

5

Sadly, what is really dead is space as something special—as something that embodies American

(JOHN M. LOGSDON)

values and self-image. I think we're back to an Eisenhower space policy: We'll do space when it has tangible benefits for the country . . . But we are no longer going to invest for preeminence. We clearly are not going to seek space leadership for its own sake.

Los Angeles Times, 4-15:(D)1.

1

[Supporting U.S.-Russian cooperation in space science]: Cooperation is a win-win opportunity. Space exploration only makes sense if it's done on a cooperative basis . . . Human spaceflight has always been driven by [the inefficiency of] national rivalry. It's taken 30 years to dissipate that, and now it's gone.

Time, 4-19:51.

Alex Michalos
Social scientist,
University of Guelph (Canada)

2

In science, as in everything else, people should treat every pronouncement of human beings as fallible in the first place, and tentative in the second place.

Los Angeles Times, 4-24:(A)21.

Lewis J. Perelman
Senior researcher,
Discovery Institute

3

One of today's fundamental technological developments is the creation of intelligence built into our machines and networks. By intelligence, I mean the ability of these machines to filter the huge ocean of available data and to present it in a way that makes sense to the human mind. In this respect, the possibility to "visualize" information and to create virtual realities is of crucial importance. That's what makes me believe that we are not going to face an information glut but that we are, instead, entering into the Age of Knowledge.

Interview/
The Christian Science Monitor,
9-22:9.

John Pike
Space analyst,
Federation of American Scientists

4

[Criticizing plans to cut back on development of a U.S. space station]: If we do not have a permanently occupied, American space station by the end of the decade . . . it's going to be the end of the [manned] space program. We hoped we were sailing with Christopher Columbus, opening a new frontier in space; but there is a danger we may be sailing with Leif Ericson, defeated by the frontier.

Los Angeles Times, 5-20:(A)1.

Paula Raymond
Associate professor of sociology,
Wellesley (Mass.) College

5

We are looking at why there are so few women in the sciences and particularly why this is continuing in the 1990s at a time when more and more occupations are requiring technical literacy. One of the key findings is that mother's encouragement is as important as father's encouragement. Having the support of one is good. Having both is better.

The Christian Science Monitor,
12-13:15.

Axel Roth
Deputy Director
of Space Station Work,
Marshall Space Flight Center,
National Aeronautics
and Space Administration
of the United States

6

[Criticizing plans to cut back on U.S. development of a space station]: There is no way I can envision that we will go forward in space without a space station. I am convinced that whether this space station is killed or not, there will be a space station one day, larger than [the Russian] MIR or Skylab. We're going to have one. It's just a matter of whether we get it now or get it later. And it's going to cost a whole lot more later.

Los Angeles Times, 5-20:(A)19.

Beverly Rubik
Biophysicist; Director,
Center for Frontier Science,
Temple University

1

Science has become a very closed-minded, dogmatic establishment that rejects any challenges to the status quo and rejects novel discoveries that are paradigm-shaking. There's a code of behavior in the scientific community that almost prohibits people from looking too far from the mainstream. If they do, they suffer extraordinary obstacles—they can't publish in peer-reviewed journals, funding is reduced or eliminated, they're ostracized. They're regarded as kooks, and they may even lose their jobs if they're not tenured.

Interview/USA Today, 10-26:(D)4.

F. James Rutherford
Director, Project 2061,
American Association
for the Advancement of Science

2

Today's over-stuffed [school science] curriculum places too much emphasis on memorizing countless formulas and generalizations, which severely hinders students' abilities to learn and understand material. By teaching less material—but teaching it better—and making the connection to arts, humanities and vocational subjects, students will learn more and have a better understanding of [science] facts and concepts.

The Christian Science Monitor,
10-26:13.

William C. Snoddy
Deputy Director
of Program Development,
Marshall Space Flight Center,
National Aeronautics
and Space Administration
of the United States

3

[Supporting the manned space program]: When you go out to the Space Camp here [in Huntsville, Ala.] and talk to the kids, they're not training to . . . send out robots and take measurements. They want to do it themselves . . . It's the challenge that it offers youth. It's the audacity of some of the things that NASA has done. I think you lose all that without having humans in space.

Huntsville, Ala./
Los Angeles Times, 5-20:(A)19.

Edward Teller
Nuclear physicist;
Senior fellow,
Hoover Institution,
Stanford University

4

We [in the U.S.] have succeeded in keeping [scientific] secrets from our people but failed to keep secrets from our competitors. Long-term secrecy in the scientific field is a real mistake. From every point of view, we would be better off opening up, and persuading other countries to open up.

Los Angeles Times, 7-13:(A)12.

James D. Watson
Biologist; Winner,
1962 Nobel Prize
in Physiology and Medicine

5

[On whether he worries that genetic engineering will be misused]: Life is filled with blanking out negative things. When we drive a car, we don't think that some idiot out there on the road is going to end our life. No, I don't worry about things like: "We're going to have some evil dictator who'll change everyone's genes so we're all subservient to him." The most serious issue is that the data will be used only by a small segment of the population. To me, the ethical dilemma is how to get genetic diagnosis widespread and make it cheap.

At Sidwell Friends School,
Washington, D.C., March 9/
The New York Times,
3-10:(A)11.

467

William G. Wells, Jr.
Professor of management science,
George Washington University

1

[Supporting a proposal for Federal-state cooperation in science and technology policy]: States and local governments have much more intimate relationships with their local industries than is possible or even appropriate for the Federal government, and states are far more capable of reaching small enterprises. And states can benefit from a Federal partnership because they often lack adequate resources and sufficient access to technical information and assistance.

Los Angeles Times, 1-6:(A)9.

Laurel L. Wilkening
Provost,
University of Washington

2

The belief that space is the next frontier and that America will follow its manifest destiny and lead mankind into space is over. We are still the leader because it just so happens our competitors are in worse shape than we are . . . No space-faring country seems able to do what it takes to keep people in space in a value-enhancing way.

Los Angeles Times,
4-15:(D)4.

Sports

Ernie Harwell
Baseball broadcaster,
Detroit "Tigers"

1

One of the things that amazes me is that at the ballparks there are so many people who aren't watching the game. They're picnicking or they're out at the concession stands, and it doesn't bother them that they missed a few outs. Which points up to me that baseball's sort of a leisurely game . . . It's a little more cerebral, maybe, than basketball or football.

Interview/
The Christian Science Monitor,
10-8:14.

2

When you're broadcasting on the radio, your real job is to react pretty much like a player does to each pitch, except you react with your tongue and hopefully with your brain, whereas a player reacts with his glove or his bat . . . It's sort of a game within a game.

Interview/
The Christian Science Monitor,
10-8:14.

Clifford Alexander
Consultant to Major League Baseball
on minority hiring;
Former Chairman,
Equal Employment
Opportunity Commission
of the United States

3

Our goal in baseball is that in all [management] positions, minorities and women should be considered. We've gotten baseball beyond the point of "no qualified this, no qualified that." That sort of nonsense doesn't come up anymore. As for on-the-field positions, some baseball people felt you had to be in the Hall of Fame to get them. That silliness is through, too. It's worked out of the system. There are 28 teams.

Some are not doing the job at all, but the overall picture is improving. It needs to improve more, and it's an ongoing process.

The Washington Post, 7-12:(C)8.

Felipe Alou
Baseball manager,
Montreal "Expos"

4

It was not until I managed my first game that I realized the responsibility that goes with being a [black] manager. As a minority, I have to be a good example. Those of us [minority managers] who are in eminence now have to show people that we are capable of controlling a game, handling players and the media, and can have a [good] relationship with the fans and the city in which we manage. If we don't manage well or mix well with the fans, the next minority guy isn't going to have much of a chance.

Interview/Ebony, May:112.

Sparky Anderson
Baseball manager,
Detroit "Tigers"

5

I don't think you manage [a team] today unless you truly respect the players. I respect players on all teams . . . It looks easy and wonderful [to be a player], but they're away from their families all the time, traveling, and taking abuse from the fans. They're put on a pedestal and expected to be like God, and they're not. They're human beings who make mistakes like everybody else. I really respect how they go about their work.

USA Today, 4-5:(F)3.

6

I think that my whole secret as a manager has been I was never afraid to lose my job. I tell other managers, "Don't even think about what's going on upstairs [with the owner]." You can't stop them if they want to fire you. Just do the best job you can. If you're a manager, there's no disgrace to being fired. Managers are fired all the time. But it is a disgrace to sell your honor.

Interview/
The New York Times, 6-29:(B)10.

Al Arbour
Hockey coach,
New York "Islanders"

1

With the change in society, you naturally have a different brand of [hockey] player today. You used to tell a player something, and he would do it with no questions asked because he was scared to death of losing his job. The players run the game now, and money has made the game a business. Now, when a coach tells a player to do something, [the player] wants to know why.

Los Angeles Times, 1-10:(C)7.

Larry Baer
Executive vice president,
San Francisco "Giants"
baseball team

2

[On his team's scheduling more day games at home]: It was a little risky because there was a conventional wisdom that in today's busy world nobody has time to take off in their work schedule to go to a baseball game. [But] we found that people like to unbusy themselves to go to a day baseball game. A lot of people said, "This reminds me of going to games as a kid" . . . I think there's a backlash that everything is scheduled at night to meet television schedules. With all that, people think there's something refreshing about a lazy afternoon in August and taking your kid who is out of school and sitting in the sun. As far as baseball is a part of nostalgia, that's how it used to be.

The New York Times, 8-21:29.

Dusty Baker
Baseball manager,
San Francisco "Giants"

3

[Players] know who's the manager. They know who's the boss. They know I'm the boss.

They know when I'm joking and when I'm serious. I operate on stern discipline and understanding. I don't tolerate a lack of effort. I still realize how hard the game is. It's *hard*. Some of these guys make it look easy, but it never really is.

USA Today, 9-10:(C)2.

Charles Barkley
Basketball player,
Philadelphia "76ers"

4

I'm not paid to be a role model [for fans]. I'm paid to wreak havoc on the basketball court.

Newsweek, 6-28:56.

Bill Bartholomay
Chairman, Atlanta "Braves"
baseball team

5

[On his heading the search committee for a new baseball commissioner]: My dedication, and I think the committee feels the same way, will be to get it as right as we can . . . This can't be a stepping-stone [for the new commissioner] or anything else; it's dedication time. We have to get things done with not too much learning-curve time. I feel we need someone who can take us through to the next century, and stay with it. It doesn't have to be a [NFL Commissioner] Pete Rozelle for 33 years, or whatever, but somebody who can address the problems and challenges we have and take us for a good long run.

USA Today, 2-15:(C)12.

Gary Bettman
Commissioner,
National Hockey League

6

I think there is a perception that [hockey] needs to be improved from a public-relations standpoint and a marketing standpoint. Some of the criticism and negativism has been overblown. We've got a great product that is underappreciated . . . We're going to have to improve the way we are perceived, the way we are followed, the way we look. We can be worthy of attention.

To reporters,
New York, N.Y., Feb. 1/
The New York Times, 2-2:(B)12.

(GARY BETTMAN)

1

[On the NHL's new team alignment and playoff system]: A lot has been written over time that suggests either [hockey] has gotten stale or is redundant because you play [division foes] so many times in the regular season and then see the same teams in the playoffs. This [new system] is an opportunity to have more teams involved in the hunt, an opportunity for fans to have more teams brought into a building and brought back on TV, and to stimulate more interest for a longer time.

March 31/
The Washington Post, 4-1:(B)6.

Wade Boggs
Baseball player,
New York "Yankees"

2

[In batting,] luck is everything. If you're not lucky, you don't find that little hole or that bad hop or the ball doesn't get in the alley or something. You've done your part if you put on a good swing and hit the ball hard. Then luck has to ride with the ball after that.

USA Today, 6-23:(C)2.

3

Winning brings a lot out in people. When you win, you reach down and get a little extra. That was brought out in spring training when we had a 20-12 record. It built confidence in guys. If we had had a bad spring, gotten off to a bad start and been buried in the doldrums in fourth or fifth place, then you could say we don't have the talent. But we've been winning all year. Circumstances bring out the best in an individual. The circumstances were we were in a pennant race all year and it brought out the best in guys.

Interview, Sept. 22/
The New York Times, 9-23:(B)9.

Jim Bunning
United States Representative,
R-Kentucky;
Former major-league baseball pitcher

4

[Calling for an end to baseball's antitrust exemption]: Seventy years is a long time for a bad law to be on the books—a law that was not enacted by Congress but rather by a mistake in the courts . . . As it stands, 28 [team] owners totally control the destiny of the sport and the lives of those it affects, like so many Roman gods sitting comfortably on their thrones.

At House Economic and
Commercial Law Subcommittee hearing,
Washington, D.C., March 31/
The Washington Post, 4-1:(B)10.

George W. Bush
Owner, Texas "Rangers"
baseball team

5

[Criticizing the new three-division set-up in each baseball league to take effect in 1994]: I don't like it. I don't like this one bit. I made my arguments [to the other owners] and went down in flames. This is an exercise in folly, but I will go down defending principle and hope history judges me correct. I represent the silent voices of baseball's purists.

USA Today, 9-10:(C)4.

Brett Butler
Baseball player,
Los Angeles "Dodgers"

6

Usually, the winter goes just about right and I'm ready for spring training when it opens; but this year I was biting at the bit a month before. There's a number of factors for that. I think one is how poorly we played last season and wanting to get here to prove a point. And the other is just the love for the game. When you are at home for a couple of months, you get to be with your family and you enjoy that; but that boy inside the ballplayer just wants to play.

Interview, Vero Beach, Fla./
Los Angeles Times, 3-1:(C)9.

7

We [the team] have great days and bad days. There are players who want to play and players who don't. There are some players who get upset when we lose, and other players who couldn't

(BRETT BUTLER)

care less. There are some who have given up on the season, and others who won't give up until we are mathematically eliminated. This is common for a losing team, but not a winning team. A winning team is all on the same page, pulling on the same side of the rope.

Los Angeles, Calif., Aug. 11/
Los Angeles Times, 8-12:(C)6.

Lou Campanelli
Basketball coach,
University of California,
Berkeley

1

[Saying college freshmen should be ineligible for the basketball team]: If we really want to put academics first, we have to let freshmen spend their first year without pressure and free to study. I think it would be all right to let them practice three days a week to keep their game sharp, but I have seen the pressure [freshmen players are] under and I think it is harmful . . . [But] the media is looking for a Messiah. It is looking for a new Michael Jordan or [Larry] Bird or Magic [Johnson]. It just never lets up.

Los Angeles Times, 1-6:(C)2.

2

[On his being fired as coach because of his post-game locker-room tirades against his players]: What you say in a locker room should be between the coach and the players. No one else's business. I may have used some curse words. [But] from George Raveling to Bobby Knight to Dean Smith, there's not a coach in the country who doesn't.

Feb. 12/
The New York Times, 2-15:(B)5.

Jose Canseco
Baseball player,
Texas "Rangers"

3

[On his years of playing with the Oakland *Athletics*]: There's just so much tension, so much

pressure, so much emphasis on winning, winning, winning with the *A's* at no matter the cost or how they use people. And if they don't win, they blame it on one individual, as they did me after the 1990 World Series. That's the most absurd, immature, self-righteous thing I've ever heard. One player doesn't win or lose a World Series by himself. But instead of being classy about it and saying we lost as a team, they laid it on me. Talk about not protecting your players and not being committed to them!

Interview, Port Charlotte, Fla./
Los Angeles Times, 3-11:(C)8.

Harry Caray
Baseball broadcaster,
Chicago "Cubs"

4

All I read about is how the [audience] ratings for baseball have gone down. Well, did it ever occur to anyone that announcers broadcasting statistics is not what the people want? The fans want opinion. They want announcers who aren't afraid to criticize the players, managers and management. The networks have conformist announcers because they want to keep their jobs. But reading off statistics is no way to keep viewers.

Washington, D.C., May 17/
USA Today, 5-18:(C)3.

John Chaney
Basketball coach,
Temple University

5

I respect [college] coaches who raise kids [their players] the right way, who won't allow their kids to go out looking for a fight, taunting, gyrating. Taunting and gyrating? I don't like coaches who allow that. I might be an ass myself, but my players are not permitted. They represent so much more than just basketball. If I ever saw one of my kids doing that, I'd take him out. I have some bad kids sometimes, some stinkers like anybody else. But the guy who's a stinker won't be around long. I'm concerned with the larger issue of how coaches raise their players to play this game . . . Coaches—we don't teach

(JOHN CHANEY)

any damn classes. All we've got to do is develop character. You've got 11, 12, 13 kids harnessed and you cannot control the taunting? That, to me, is inexcusable. Many of us in this business are following some other kind of music. To have discipline and direction for our kids . . . We are the last chance at it. Character is the thing they better have.

Interview,
Seattle, Wash., March 28/
The Washington Post, 3-29:(C)9.

Penny Chenery
Former owner of Secretariat,
the horse that won
the Triple Crown in 1973

1

There has to be something colorful or attractive about [a race] horse itself to capture attention. A, its performance. B, something about the horse that lets you dream. Racing is about dreams, and you have to [have] an appropriate hero. Secretariat was that kind of hero.

Los Angeles Times, 5-2:(C)1.

Ralph Cindrich
Sports agent;
Former player,
National Football League

2

Relatively few pro athletes are ready when their careers end, educationally, psychologically or, sometimes, financially. Even when they say they are, they aren't. These are guys who think they're invincible. They've always made the cut and beat the odds, and believe they can continue to do so. In football, we're talking about people who've been to college, but often they still don't understand how different from sports the "real world" is. There are no crowds cheering or people telling them how wonderful they are, and few clear-cut results like they got in their games. And the transition is so fast—almost overnight—that it can be, literally, stunning.

Interview/
The Wall Street Journal,
7-16:(A)7.

Jim Courier
Tennis player

3

[On his being a tennis star]: The less you think about it, the more fun it is. Once you cross the line and have gotten somewhere in this profession, and probably any profession, you don't want to lose it . . . [But] it's very, very dangerous to have your self-worth riding on your results as an athlete. All the cliches are true.

The New York Times, 3-15:(B)10.

Chuck Daley
Basketball coach,
New Jersey "Nets"

4

[On coaching]: You have to know something about these [professional basketball] players. Sometime back in the seventh or the eighth grade, they were called out of line and designated as special. Why? Because they were a little better at basketball than the next kid. They started getting special treatment. And it has never changed. All they have ever known is special treatment. You cannot try to be a parent. You cannot be too demanding. At this level, there has got to be constant give-and-take. You take the assets you have and put them in a system that works, offensively and defensively. And if you're lucky, if you can sell them on all that, sometimes you can build something *together* that lasts.

Interview/Esquire, January:36.

Al Davis
Owner,
Los Angeles "Raiders"
football team

5

I derived my interest in football from baseball. It wasn't the great players that inspired me, although I admired them. It was the great organization of the *Yankees.* They represented certain things to me—fear, intimidation, power. Big people. The home run. It looked like they always got great players from other teams who could finish with the *Yankees* and be great. Then along came Branch Rickey in the early 1940s

473

(AL DAVIS)

with the *Dodgers*. And they developed a way of playing baseball with an emphasis on speed, teaching fundamentals and a willingness to take chances. I thought Rickey was a pioneer. I used to think that I could take these two organizations, combine their qualities and put them into one.

Interview, El Segundo, Calif., Jan. 26/
Los Angeles Times, 1-27:(C)6.

Michael Douglas
Actor

1

I'm a big sports fanatic. I love sports largely because you don't know how things are going to end. You might guess the ending of a movie, but with sports you never know. And I also really admire the performance level of athletes. It's pure performance. No retakes.

Interview, New York, N.Y./
The New York Times, 3-11:(B)8.

Joe Duff
Head baseball coach,
United States Naval Academy

2

Fundamentals are lacking in all [college] sports now, not only baseball but basketball and football. Everybody today is a star, and it's very difficult to teach them. Some of it is concentration and some of it is lack of self-discipline. Baseball is a game of concentration. You may stand in right field for five innings with nothing to do, but you'd better be ready when something comes your way.

Interview, Annapolis, Md./
The Washington Post, 5-14:(F)5.

Dick Edell
Lacrosse coach,
University of Maryland

3

[On lacrosse]: The game combines so many of the best aspects of other sports and eliminates some of the bad ones. It has the speed of hockey,

but without the fighting. It has the teamwork of soccer, but with more scoring. People are drawn to the continuous action, to the speed of the game and to the physical contact. It has a little of everything and yet there's no need for a 300-pound lineman or a seven-foot center. There are no physical prejudices.

The Washington Post, 5-28:(C)7.

Larry Ellis
President,
USA Track & Field

4

[Saying track-and-field meets are becoming too long]: We have to make an attractive package for the audience. The increase in the length of the meets is killing the sport. I don't want to sit down for 10 hours. That's the same problem baseball is having. The game is long and boring.

At USA Track & Field meeting,
Eugene, Ore., June 18/
The New York Times, 6-19:33.

Donald Fehr
Executive director,
Major League (baseball)
Players Association

5

[On athletes as role models]: Anybody who is in the public eye is foolish if he doesn't recognize that he or she is paid attention to by other people and by kids if you're in sports or entertainment. At the same time, we all have to recognize that some people are well-suited for that role and others aren't. Some of the players are parents with kids and know their way around; but some of them are 19 and 20 years old and are no more than recent kids themselves.

The New York Times, 7-23:(B)10.

6

[Criticizing proposals for an expanded playoff system in baseball]: The players do not believe it is a good idea to conduct an additional round of playoffs within the traditional two-league, four-division structure, with the eight playoff teams being the first- and second-place finishers in the

(DONALD FEHR)

existing four divisions. Simply put, the obvious damage that format would do to the nature of the divisional championship races makes this approach untenable. The players do not want to play for second place or home-field advantage. The integrity of the division races would be compromised.

News conference,
New York, N.Y., Aug. 23/
Los Angeles Times, 8-24:(C)5.

Joe Gibbs
Football coach,
Washington "Redskins"

1

[On arguments and differences of opinion between coaches and players]: The way I see it, is that's part of football . . . There are going to be arguments and differences of opinion. A football team is like your family, and it's silly to think there wouldn't be disagreements . . . Now, the important thing is how you handle it . . . I don't lose my temper much in a time like that. Those things end up being discussed in one-on-one meetings. I've had hundreds of those. There's always something going on inside a team. Someone always has something on their mind, and I like to get to it right away. I don't like to give things time to get worse.

The Washington Post, 1-5:(E)4.

Ira Glasser
Executive director,
American Civil Liberties Union

2

[On what he would do if he were Commissioner of Baseball]: The first thing I'd want to do is convince the [team] owners that they are a single employer, an economic entity, all dependent on each other. Their product is exciting competition. Next, what I call "the fiction of loyalty" must be returned to the game. Players have to be loyal to their clubs and clubs have to be loyal to their fans and fans have to be loyal to their players. We can't go choosing sides every year. There has to be continuity. Long-term con-

tracts. No jumping around from team to team. The worst traits of the owners have been transferred to the players, and the fans are losing interest. And let's not forget this is a kids' game. How do we make sure the kids are awake for the World Series? How do we keep the playoffs without allowing them to cheapen the long season?

Interview, New York, N.Y./
The New York Times, 5-28:(B)13.

Bob Graham
United States Senator,
D-Florida

3

[Questioning the advisibility of continuing baseball's antitrust exemption]: When the Baltimore *Orioles* are sold for $173-million, how can baseball's owners continue to call their business a game? Baseball has become an enormous commercial enterprise and should be treated that way.

Aug. 5/
USA Today, 8-6:(C)3.

Charles Grantham
Executive director,
National Basketball
Players Association

4

[Criticizing the salary caps in the NBA]: The value of the clubs has gone up from $15-20-million in 1983 to over $100-million today. We're glad the owners are worth so much. But we say don't throw us a salary cap while your values are escalating.

The New York Times, 1-8:(B)9.

Stephen D. Greenberg
Deputy Commissioner
of Baseball

5

[Criticizing the possible revocation by Congress of baseball's antitrust exemption]: Right now we have a convergence of forces and factors [in baseball] that are unfortunately negative. For that reason alone, baseball needs to take this issue seriously . . . Lifting the exemption would

(STEPHEN D. GREENBERG)

make it much easier for financially troubled teams or not-so-troubled teams to shop around and find better deals in communities and pack up in the middle of the night [and move their franchises to new cities] . . . [Also,] over 170 communities around the country enjoy minor-league baseball. Tinkering [with the antitrust exemption] would almost certainly mean the elimination of a great number of [those] teams.

Interview/
The Washington Post, 1-4:(D)2.

Marvin Hagler
Former boxer

1

I would like to see these guys [veteran boxers] like [George] Foreman, [Thomas] Hearns and [Roberto] Duran retire. Don't make boxing look bad. It's a great sport and they were great champions. [But] when you lose, you're always a bum.

USA Today, 1-15:(C)6.

Jim Haney
Executive director,
National Association
of Basketball Coaches

2

[Criticizing the mid-season firings of college coaches]: Coaches are hired and fired all the time. We have to accept that fact. But at the same time, we have concern about in-season firings because it is inconsistent, in our view, with what intercollegiate athletics is all about.

The Christian Science Monitor,
2-23:13.

Thomas K. Hearn, Jr.
President,
Wake Forest University

3

[On the suggestion by NCAA director Richard Schultz that a college football playoff game could raise new revenue]: He's been saying publicly and privately he thinks this is an idea whose time

will come. Whether that time is now, I don't think any of us are prepared to say. But on the face of it, it will be a problem for those of us in trying to suggest that cost containment and not revenue enhancement is the inevitable wave of the future. We are concerned about the continued expansion of season lengths and playing seasons . . . That's the whole history of athletics for the last quarter century: Every time there's another problem, find some more money and throw some more money at it. But many institutions—certainly many [college] presidents—are of the opinion that we've about played that string out.

Dallas, Texas, Jan. 13/
The New York Times, 1-14:(B)7.

Calvin Hill
Vice president,
Baltimore "Orioles"
baseball team

4

My own feeling is that baseball is probably doing better [in the hiring of minorities in management] than football and not as good as the NBA. I look at the [Washington football] *Redskins,* for example, and they've got four black employees, total—[assistant general manager] Bobby Mitchell, a trainer and two assistant coaches. What would happen if [civil-rights leader] Jesse Jackson would try to boycott the *Redskins*? People would tell him to go to hell. In baseball, clearly it's not where it ought to be, but it's getting better. And to tell you the truth, if I was rating the problems affecting blacks in this country today, blacks in sports management would be 20th on a list of things we should concern ourselves with. It's extremely important, but it's not pivotal.

The Washington Post, 7-12:(C)8.

Bob Huggins
Basketball coach,
University of Cincinnati (Ohio)

5

We try to play hard and make things happen with our defense. You can't control your shooting, but you can play aggressive defense. More games are won with good defense than with good offense.

The Washington Post, 3-24:(D)4.

Jesse L. Jackson
Civil-rights leader

1

[Advocating some kind of payment to college athletes whose sports bring revenue to the school]: I believe you must figure out a way to pay people who work. The student-athlete works for coaches; coaches work for the universities. Now they have it down to a maximum of 20 hours a week you are allowed to spend on your sport. Even with that, a lot of these athletes work more hours than professors.

Grapevine, Texas, Jan. 12/
The New York Times, 1-13:(B)11.

2

[Calling for more hiring of minorities in all areas of sports, not just players]: We've succeeded in playing sports because it's a free market. The rules are public and clear: You knock somebody down for the ten-count, you hit a ball over the fence—everyone knows what that means. In the closed market off the field, where subjective decisions are made, we've hardly made an inch of progress in 50 years.

USA Today, 2-26:(C)2.

3

[Saying black athletes should put pressure on management to place more blacks in coaching and front-office positions]: The players must match dignity with dollars. They must show courage beyond the lines of protection and regulation . . . The present-day athletes, the prime beneficiaries of our struggle, must not be silent, not be naive about the great issues of our day. Even the best of them at the high noon of their careers must know that sundown is coming.

At meeting of Rainbow Coalition
for Fairness in Athletics,
Washington, D.C., Feb. 26/
The Washington Post, 2-27:(G)7.

4

[Criticizing baseball's new plan to expand the involvement of minorities at various levels of the sport]: [The plan is] disappointing and inadequate to the size and nature of the problem . . . [It] sets forth a series of good principles and good intentions to be implemented individually and voluntarily, but contains no overall or team-by-team plan to correct the situation, sets forth no specific goals, and has no time frame to accomplish the general goals. There is no directive or incentive involved to implement an affirmative-action plan, and [baseball] will impose no sanctions on any team that fails to implement the good intentions and principles.

March 29/
Los Angeles Times, 3-30:(C)4.

Reggie Jackson
Former baseball player,
New York "Yankees"
and Oakland "Athletics"

5

We're just caretakers, links in the chain of baseball tradition. So, if your name is [team owners] Peter O'Malley or George Steinbrenner or Ted Turner, or if [you're a player and] your name is Kirby, Roger, Barry or Cal, if the game is lost to the economic forces that drive it, then we've lost the uniqueness of the game. Let's remember the people who paved the way and be mindful of the game's vulnerability. We need to humanize it, not exploit it to a point where future generations won't be able to afford the bill when it comes due.

Speech upon induction into
Baseball Hall of Fame,
Cooperstown, N.Y., Aug. 1/
Los Angeles Times, 8-2:(C)1.

Michael Jordan
Basketball player,
Chicago "Bulls"

6

[Announcing his retirement at age 30]: It's not because I don't love the game. I love basketball. I just feel that . . . I've reached the pinnacle of my career [and] I don't have anything else for myself to prove . . . The word "retire" means you can do anything you want, from this day on. So, if I desire to come back and play again, maybe that's what I want to do. Maybe that's the chal-

(MICHAEL JORDAN)

lenge that I may need someday down the road. I'm not going to close that door. I don't believe in "never."

U.S. News & World Report,
10-18:20.

Bob Knight
Basketball coach,
Indiana University

1

[Saying basketball is different from what it used to be]: The [45-second shot] clock has taken something away from me. The three-point shot has taken something away from me. I'm not as good a coach as I was before the clock and the three-point shot. When we got ahead before the clock, we didn't lose . . . It was more of a coaches' game then than it is now. What we have now is a fans' thing, and I'm not saying that is good or bad.

Interview, Bloomington, Ind./
The Christian Science Monitor,
3-12:14.

2

I'll see a kid play and I say to myself, "That kid can't play for me." Well, that simply means one thing—the kid can't play for me . . . That doesn't mean that he's a bad player or that he's a bad kid. He may be a hell of a player and he may be the best kid possible, but he has a way of playing or an approach to playing that isn't going to fit into what I want to do. Then, I also have to think to myself that it isn't just that that kid can't play for me, but from that kid's standpoint, I'm not the coach for him.

To reporters,
St. Louis, Mo., March 26/
The Washington Post, 3-27:(D)6.

3

A team has got to have quickness; it's got to have a strength; it's got to be able to shoot the ball. Now, the better they are at any one of these, or all of them, the better the team it can be. Then, the next most important ingredient is some kind

of depth. Once a team brings any or all of those four ingredients to the floor, then it has to be put together. And that's where coaching comes into play . . . There are a lot of teams that have the basketball ingredients, but just never get put together properly.

To reporters,
St. Louis, Mo., March 26/
The Washington Post, 3-29:(C)8.

Mitch Kupchak
Assistant general manager,
Los Angeles "Lakers"
basketball team

4

[On "sleepers," basketball players with talent who have not been discovered by major teams]: I think it's possible to find a sleeper at large that the public hasn't heard of. But I don't think it's possible to find somebody that NBA scouts haven't heard of. Scouting now is so comprehensive that there's not a name that slips by that we or other teams don't know of. Now, we might be wrong on how we project that guy or what ultimately happens with that guy, but there's not a Scottie Pippin playing in some small town that nobody knows about. There are no hidden players that nobody knows about. Everybody knows about all the players. Only the opinions are going to be different.

Interview/
Los Angeles Times, 6-29:(C)3.

Tom Lantos
United States Representative,
D-California

5

[Arguing against allowing China to host the 2000 Olympic Games because of human-rights violations there]: The notion that it doesn't make any difference whether the Olympics are held in a country where there are no human-rights violations or in a country where human-rights violations are the norm—a country where people are killed, arrested, beaten daily for political reasons—is outrageous. There is no aspect of society that is free [of a discussion] of human rights.

July 1/
The Washington Post, 7-2:(A)15.

Richard Lapchick
Director,
Center for Sports and Society
1

There's a perception in the black community that there are fewer opportunities in baseball. Black kids aren't playing. Urban areas are restricted by poor facilities and lack of funds, [so] kids are playing basketball. And the lack of blacks playing [baseball] has had an impact on the number of black fans.

The Washington Post, 7-12:(C)8.

Eric Lindros
Hockey player,
Philadelphia "Flyers"
2

[On the roughness of play in hockey]: I get a charge out of pounding a guy. All the guys do. Hey, if you can't get a goal, get a hit. You can always hit somebody out there.

USA Today, 1-6:(C)11.

Ricky Mahorn
Former basketball player,
Detroit "Pistons"
3

If I were NBA Commissioner and [a player] threw a punch, it'd be an automatic five-game suspension the first time. Next time you throw a punch, you miss 10 games. And so on. See how quickly guys stop fighting then . . . I'm telling you, nobody can understand the magnitude when it comes to taking money and food from your family. No matter how much you make, if the fine is stiff enough and the suspension long enough, you will get a whole different respect for what you have to do on the court and how to act like a professional . . . If you know you'll have to give a big chunk of [your salary] back, you're just going to play basketball, and play it the way it's supposed to be played.

USA Today, 4-13:(C)8.

Seamus Malin
American soccer commentator
4

In soccer, we see clever players improvising situations in which they can use their individual

strengths against a perceived weakness in a particular defender, like, for example, a speedy winger against a fullback. I hope American spectators will eventually see a midfield struggle as something interesting, and no longer need to focus on the only thing they can [now] understand—the score sheet.

Interview, Harvard University/
The Christian Science Monitor, 11-19:14.

Alan May
Hockey player,
Washington "Capitals"
5

As the [hockey] season progresses, you always get more emotion, because the games mean more. But this season it's been far more noticeable, because guys weren't sure how to cope with the new rules on fighting. I think a lot of guys forgot they could hit, because they were scared of getting penalties. But I never felt that, just because of the new rules, you had to quit playing aggressively. Before, when you'd hit a guy, he'd take exception to it. You can't retaliate that much now. You have to play smart. When somebody takes a shot at you, you have to turn away and get even with a solid hit later. If you throw a punch or swing your stick, you'll get hit with big penalties.

The Washington Post, 1-7:(D)3.

Tim McCarver
Baseball analyst, CBS-TV
6

Many of [baseball's] problems have been overblown by the media. That causes [team] owners to over-react, to say "oh, my God, there's something wrong with the game." It's fashionable, for instance, to say games are too long, but you don't hear fans say "that was a great game but it took too long."

USA Today, 4-5:(F)3.

Jerry McMorris
Owner,
Colorado "Rockies"
baseball team
7

Expansion [of major-league baseball to Mexico] would help fix a lot of problems. That would include scheduling and satisfy communities that sincerely want baseball and, I would suspect, deserve baseball. I like the concept of us playing in Canada, the United States and Mexico. I'm one of the new owners—one of the younger owners—and this probably breaks from tradition, but I think that's a unique opportunity for us.

USA Today, 7-2:(C)3.

Howard M. Metzenbaum
United States Senator,
D-Ohio

1

[Calling for the lifting of baseball's antitrust exemption]: Giving baseball owners a free rein to decide what's in the best interest of the game is like giving the members of OPEC free rein to set world energy policy.

News conference, March 4/
The Washington Post, 3-5:(F)5.

Terry Murray
Hockey coach,
Washington "Capitals"

2

Why can't hockey coaches be in the job as long as NFL coaches? Why can't this happen? Basketball and football coaches are sometimes around 15 or 20 years. We're very quick to pull the trigger [on coaches] in the NHL, it seems. You have 20 people in front of you. All are young guys compared to other sports and you've got to get them all on page one. It takes time.

The Washington Post, 1-6:(B)4.

Martina Navratilova
Tennis player

3

I know some of my self-worth comes from tennis, and it's hard to think of doing something else where you know you'll never be the best. Tennis players are rare creatures: Where else in

the world can you know that you're the best? The definitiveness of it is the beauty of it.

News conference announcing her
retirement after next year,
New York, N.Y., Sept. 29/
The New York Times, 9-30:(B)6.

Don Nehlen
Football coach,
West Virginia University

4

[Player] weight is the most overrated commodity in football. Freshmen constantly come in here and think bigger is better, but it's not . . . They can't run, they can't move, and fatigue makes a coward out of them.

USA Today, 8-24:(C)8.

Terry Nelson
Football player,
University of Cincinnati

5

[Saying college players should be paid]: College players are glorified slaves. The NCAA is nothing more than a system of institutional slavery. It's a disgrace the way athletes are used. It's sick. I'm going to try and do something about it . . . There's all this money going around, and the players don't get any of it. If players don't win, coaches get fired, true. But if we do win, coaches get bigger contracts and get richer, while players get nothing. I think it's up to the players to change things.

Interview,
East Rutherford, N.J., March 25/
The New York Times, 3-26:(B)13.

Ernie Nestor
Basketball coach,
George Mason University

6

[College basketball] has become a more unforgiving business in recent years. I think some of it has drifted down from the NBA. The external influences on kids are far greater than 10 years ago. A lot of kids find it difficult to translate individual achievement into team basketball. I think

(ERNIE NESTOR)

the ultimate was in 1991, when both Duke and North Carolina went to the Final Four and each team lost two kids because they didn't play enough.

Interview/
The Washington Post, 3-2:(C)3.

1

[On his being forced to resign as coach]: You know on the front end that this is part of the business. It's become a more unfortunate business in recent years and the external influences on the kids [players] are far greater than 10 years ago. It's more difficult to translate individual achievement into team basketball. This is a job of highs and lows, with not a lot in the middle. You're judged on success, and we haven't had a lot the last two years.

Richmond, Va., March 8/
The Washington Post, 3-9:(E)4.

Johnny Oates
Baseball manager,
Baltimore "Orioles"

2

People like to tell you they can leave the game at the ballpark. I try to do that, but I can't. I try to hide it. Everybody around me will think I'm not thinking about baseball; except my family—they know when something is bothering me. My wife says she knows the minute I come out of the clubhouse [after a game] what the night will be like. She doesn't even have to say, "Hello, how are you doing?" She just looks at me, and she knows.

Bradenton, Fla., March 5/
The Washington Post, 3-6:(G)2.

Susan O'Malley
President,
Washington "Bullets"
basketball team

3

[On her team's raising the price of admission tickets]: We still are in the bottom half of ticket

prices in the league. Prices don't correlate to wins. If that was true, the [Chicago] *Bulls* would charge $1,000 a seat. Running a franchise in Washington costs the same as running a franchise in Los Angeles or Chicago, because of things like the [player salary] cap.

May 4/
The Washington Post, 5-5:(D)1.

4

[On running a team]: I like the measurability of it all: Is the arena empty or full? Is my team winning or losing? That, and that moment before the game starts and everyone is standing and I know I'm responsible for them being there. It sounds corny, but it's true—that's "success" to me.

Working Woman, November:55.

Bill Parcells
Football coach,
New England "Patriots"

5

[On his team's new uniforms]: I don't have any expertise in uniforms. I think all uniforms look nice if you've got good players in them.

Los Angeles Times, 4-17:(C)2.

Jim Quinn
Lawyer,
National Football League
Players Association

6

[On the new free-agency system for NFL players]: [Now, no team] is going to be able to sit back and say they made a bad draft pick and are going to be lousy again. There's a major plus in the excitement generated by the prospect of free agency . . . Free agency will make teams treat players with dignity. And the ones that are tyrannical will be without players.

Jan. 6/USA Today, 1-7:(C)3.

Joe Restic
Football coach,
Harvard University

7

[College] football is not a religion. It's just a game. It has a place in our society, no question,

481

(JOE RESTIC)

and the benefits are great—if it's approached in the right way . . . The game is really an instrument that should be used in a very positive, constructive way. [Student-players who] stay the course will come out of here stronger, better, more ethical, because we play by the rules.

Interview, Harvard University/
The Christian Science Monitor,
11-5:14.

Pat Riley
Basketball coach,
New York "Knicks"

1

When I was coaching the [Los Angeles] *Lakers* . . . the [Boston] *Celtics* would beat us and we'd pat them on the back and say, "Great game, great series." That's BS. You can't win worrying about whether people like you. You just can't.

Interview/
Los Angeles Times, 4-1:(C)2.

Billy Ripken
Baseball player,
Texas "Rangers"

2

Errors are part of the game, but [baseball founder] Abner Doubleday was a jerk for inventing them.

Los Angeles Times, 3-26:(C)2.

Garry Roberts
Vice dean,
Tulane University Law School

3

[University athletic] coaches are motivated by values that are inconsistent with those of a university. They have to be. Because we've created this monster where we have to win to get the revenues. We're running an enterprise that, on the marketing and sales side, is a big-time professional sport; but on the labor side, it's purely amateur. All this talk of reform [in college athletics] is nothing more than putting a pretty face on an ugly structure.

March 18/USA Today, 3-19:(C)6.

John Robinson
Football coach,
University of
Southern California

4

Times have changed. Football has not changed. It does not change. It evolves some, certainly, but the premises of football—it's a physical game . . . If you entertain any chance to win, you must play the game physically—that has not changed. It will never change.

News conference,
University of Southern California, Jan. 3/
Los Angeles Times, 1-4:(C)6.

Buck Rodgers
Baseball manager,
California "Angels"

5

I've got far less patience with talented players who malinger. To me the stomach [a player's guts and heart] is far more important than the arms and legs. Give me an average player with a good stomach and I'll take him over a guy with super ability in most instances. When we scout, we're tool people—strong arms, legs, power. [But] the more you manage, you realize it's not the tools that beat you. It's the guy who's not afraid to be up there when the game's on the line.

Interview,
Tempe, Ariz./
USA Today, 3-8:(C)4.

6

We've got a screwed-up [financial] system [in baseball] right now. It's tough to differentiate right from wrong. We're rewarding guys for hitting .220. I mean, we offered a three-year contract to Dick Schofield for $6.5-million. And he's dumber than we are. He turned it down. It's like we're trying to out-dumb each other. They asked me, "What would you do about Schofield?" I said, "I'd release the guy. If you can't find a guy who can hit .220, there's something wrong with this game."

Los Angeles Times,
3-10:(C)10.

Dan Rooney
Owner,
Pittsburgh "Steelers"
football team

1

[On the new free-agency system for NFL players]: I think it's changed the culture and changed the atmosphere, and I think people [in management] are very fearful of that. But free agency is a reality . . . I think there will be different operations for different teams. Everybody will not do it the same way . . . It will be a process of learning about it and putting it into effect how it will work for you. I feel we can compete and we'll be all right, providing two things: One is the revenue-sharing [among NFL teams] and that we move forward in other ideas of revenue-sharing, and also that we continue to get support from the football fans.

Jan. 7/
The Washington Post, 1-8:(D)9.

Nolan Ryan
Baseball pitcher,
Texas "Rangers"

2

Baseball and pitching has always been a serious thing with me. I've never taken winning for granted. I know you have to work at this game even in the off-season, and I've been willing to do that. I always wanted the ball [wanted to pitch], regardless of the team in the other dugout. I always wanted to go out there every three or four days and pitch. I think when a pitcher doesn't feel that way, he ought to quit.

Interview/
The Christian Science Monitor,
10-1:14.

Juan Antonio Samaranch
President,
International Olympic Committee

3

In Olympic sports, there is no prize money, and we will keep this tradition. Athletes can be helped [financially] by their [home] federations or national Olympic committees or sponsors. But I think it is most important for athletes taking part in the Olympic Games and world championships not to run for a money prize, but only for the honor and to get one of the medals.

To reporters,
New York, N.Y., Feb. 9/
The Washington Post, 2-10:(F)2.

Bud Selig
Owner,
Milwaukee "Brewers"
baseball team;
Chairman,
baseball's Executive Council

4

[Arguing against lifting baseball's antitrust exemption]: If you look at history, the antitrust exemption protects the public . . . What does it do for you if you take away the exemption? The fact of the matter is, when all is said and done, the antitrust exemption has been a protection for the fans and baseball hasn't abused it.

News conference,
Phoenix, Ariz., March 4/
The New York Times, 3-5:(B)9.

5

[On changes being contemplated in baseball's league and division lineup]: Some people say we never move, we never change, but then when we do, they say we're tampering with the game. Look, we're in a very competitive business, and we're trying to look at every phase. No industry should stand pat without considering its options.

Phoenix, Ariz., March 4/
Los Angeles Times, 3-5:(C)4.

6

[On baseball's new plan to expand the involvement of minorities at various levels of the sport]: Baseball has made great progress in minority hiring over the last six years. This program is broader and more diverse than anything we've tried before, and will ensure, through the minority vending components, that more jobs, and therefore more money, is generated for minority-group members.

March 29/
Los Angeles Times, 3-30:(C)4.

John Shaw
Executive vice president,
Los Angeles "Rams"
football team;
Member,
National Football League
Management Council

1

The quality of the game is [our] big issue. And the quality of the teams improves if [every player] signs before training camp. Holdouts hurt every team that has them. That's why you must have a [free-agent] signing period every year—to get the [disruptions] out of the way.

Los Angeles Times, 1-6:(C)5.

2

[On the salary cap expected to affect NFL players next season]: In looking at the cap, you have to stay focused on the big picture rather than taking a microscopic glance at one particular player. What we are saying to the players now is that we are partners in this business, and for this business to succeed we have to do it together as a partnership. We are saying to the players, as our partners we are giving you 62 to 65 percent of our defined gross revenue. If our business has some unhealthy years, then you players, as our partners, have to share in the downside of those years. You still get the same percentage, but you share in a lesser portion of defined gross income. As this business expands and matures, then as our partner you will get more as the gross increases. Taking less money is a difficult concept for some to understand, but as in any partnership, when you're not doing well, all the partners have to take less.

Los Angeles Times, 9-14:(C)4.

Don Shula
Football coach,
Miami "Dolphins"

3

My coaching philosophy is that it's my responsibility to get the most of of the talent I have to work with . . . What you have to do is determine what their talent is, and then give them all of the weapons that you can so you can get the most out of them.

USA Today, 10-29:(C)7.

David Simmons
Athletic director,
Howard University

4

[On his university's women's basketball coach being paid less than the men's basketball coach]: Our men's basketball team generates $400,000 in revenue. Our women's basketball team loses $100,000 to $150,000 a year. Part of the revenue from the men's team pays for some of the losses of the women's team. I certainly understand what the law is, but we as an athletic community are headed toward real problems if we don't take into account revenue-generating sports.

The Washington Post, 6-26:(G)3.

Jackie Slater
Football player,
Los Angeles "Rams"

5

[On pay cuts and salary caps and job losses expected to affect NFL players next season]: There are a lot of people who are in for a rude awakening. You will no longer have the middle-of-the-road guy, the solid, stable backup who has been paid good money to do what he does. That job is going to be eliminated. Guys that have the ambition of playing a long time and who have set economic goals are going to become disenchanted when they realize their dream is unattainable because of what the union has done with the collective-bargaining agreement. There are going to be cuts in pay, and there are going to be lots of young guys making little or no money. Everybody is looking at last year and thinking they are getting ready to break the bank. They are totally ignoring that little bitty thing—the salary cap.

Los Angeles Times, 9-14:(C)1.

Hollis Stacy
Golfer

6

Most PGA tour players don't have a clue about what's fantasy and what's reality because most of them have never read a newspaper. They think real life is playing golf all day on perfect golf

(HOLLIS STACY)

courses for millions of dollars. Real life is poor people who can't afford to eat.

Newsweek, 9-20:17.

George Steinbrenner
Owner,
New York "Yankees"
baseball team

1

I've seen a lot of great athletes. I've learned in my lifetime to know who the guys are who can deliver. [Reggie Jackson is] near the top of the hit parade of guys in baseball, or any sport, who can deliver. He belongs in the Hall of Fame. He can live up to his reputation under pressure, and that's a pretty tremendous way to judge a performer.

USA Today, 1-5:(C)10.

2

I now understand the difference between a human error and a mental error [on the part of players]. When people are being paid $2-million or $3-million a year to play baseball, there shouldn't be mental errors. Human errors are different. When a ground ball bounces off a guy's glove, or something, that happens. I've become far more tolerant of that.

Interview, Tampa, Fla./
USA Today, 9-23:(C)2.

David Stern
Commissioner,
National Basketball Association

3

[On basketball]: If you come to our games, it's going to be only about two hours and 12 minutes, and you're going to get closer to the players than in any other sport . . . Sports really is the international language, and we think basketball is up there at the top of that list in terms of dialect . . . Our sport has federations and leagues in every country. We are tapping into a reservoir of extraordinary support.

USA Today, 6-18:(A)1,2.

Paul Tagliabue
Commissioner,
National Football League

4

[On the new free-agency system for NFL players]: There'll be some surprises, some stumbles, I'm sure, in terms of how people adjust to the new system. But hopefully we can still end up with a very high quality product. And, of course, as the system kicks in over time, there will be a salary cap. That's both an important fact from the standpoint of financial stability for the League and the players, because it links the player's interests to the League's interests, the team's interest. But it's also an important factor because no club will have any greater resources than any other club, and no club will be able to stockpile players unfairly.

Jan. 6/USA Today, 1-7:(C)3.

Lee Trevino
Golfer

5

I'm a golfaholic, no question about that. Counseling wouldn't help me. They'd have to put me in prison, and then I'd talk the warden into building a hole or two and teach him how to play.

Los Angeles Times, 6-17:(C)2.

Al Unser, Jr.
Auto-racing driver

6

[On the Indianapolis 500 race]: Winning Indy never goes away the way it does when you win other races. When I win at Long beach, even when I win as many times as I have [four in a row from 1988-1991], it's forgotten by the next race. When you win Indy, it's never forgotten.

Interview, Indianapolis, Ind./
Los Angeles Times, 5-26:(C)4.

Gene Upshaw
Executive director,
National Football League
Players Association

7

[On the new agreement permitting free agency for NFL players]: We finally got it over the goal

485

(GENE UPSHAW)

line . . . If we didn't do it now, it never would have been done. We'd always be second-class citizens. Now the players are partners with the owners; we have a vested interest in the game. We'll be rowing down the river together now.

Jan. 6/
The Washington Post, 1-7:(D)8.

Fay Vincent
Former Commissioner of Baseball

1

I've had time to study the history of the [Baseball] Commissionership. [Kenesaw M.] Landis had broad powers, so maybe they didn't want [Happy] Chandler to have so much. When Ford Frick became Commissioner, they took away the "best-interests-of-the-game" clause, and when he retired, he made a very eloquent speech for them to put it back. There is an ebb and flow to baseball . . . I don't think people should worry about baseball. It has its ups and downs, its ebbs and flows, but it will be around. It is the perfectly designed game.

Interview, Sutton Courtenay, England/
Los Angeles Times, 6-23:(B)8.

2

[On suggestions that he was "soft on labor" when he was Commissioner]: Being soft on labor doesn't go over. It's like being soft on Communism in the 1950s. I think I was right that there must be a partnership, a compromise [by the owners and] the players. If the Palestinians and the Israelies can get together in the [White House] Rose Garden, certainly you would think that these people [in baseball] can get together.

Broadcast interview/
Pre-game show, CBS-TV, 9-18.

LeRoy Walker
President,
United States Olympic Committee

3

[Arguing against the U.S. taking the position that China not be allowed to host the 2000 Olympic Games because of human-rights violations there]: We certainly aren't at odds over the principle of human rights . . . [But] we think that with the interference of power politics—which affected us in 1980 and '84, and that we were very glad not to affect us in Barcelona in 1993—there could be a domino effect on this all the way down to the athletes. To make an official, formal position of this government is quite contrary to the wishes of the IOC and also to the wishes expressed after 1980, when we said we would take power politics out of the Olympic Games.

Interview,
Washington, D.C., July 1/
The Washington Post, 7-2:(A)15.

Duane Ward
Baseball pitcher
and player representative,
Toronto "Blue Jays"

4

Right now, baseball is good. But we [players and owners] can't keep knocking each other. When fans read about us bashing ownership and ownership bashing us, nobody gets interested. We've got to get baseball back on track to being the national pastime for the fans.

USA Today, 4-2:(C)7.

Paul Weiler
Professor,
Harvard University Law School

5

There is absolutely no case for baseball having [the antitrust exemption it has enjoyed for 70 years]. That is the easy point. The hard point, and one that Congress hasn't realized, is that applying antitrust to sports is difficult.

The Washington Post, 1-4:(D)2.

Bob Whitsitt
President,
Seattle "SuperSonics"
basketball team

6

[When drafting basketball players,] you can measure certain things physically, but you can't

(BOB WHITSITT)

totally measure the ability to read situations and read plays. You can't exactly read how they're going to fit in with your situation and play with your players. You can't read how they're going to get along in your locker room. You can't absolutely tell what happens after you give them millions of dollars before they go to work, and you can't tell how they're going to respond to media hype and fan pressure. It's not an exact science, because you're dealing with people.

Interview/
Los Angeles Times, 6-29:(C)3.

Monty Williams
Basketball player,
University of Notre Dame

1

[On players, like himself, with heart or other health problems]: All athletes have that thing where they think they're invincible. I think I have that, too. I don't think you can be a great athlete unless you have that little aura of arrogance about where you can do anything. But you also have to have that aura of reality in your life, too. You have to understand that anything can happen to anybody at any time. The risk factor goes both ways. I could go out and get hurt or something like that, or I could play and not be hurt. It's a fifty-fifty chance.

Interview/
The Washington Post, 8-6:(B)6.

Pat Williams
President,
Orlando "Magic"
basketball team

2

[In drafting basketball players,] we're dealing with unknowns. You can measure skill, but you can't measure what's inside a kid. You can't measure his heart, his desire and his thinking process. That's the thing you will never know until you get a kid. You don't know how badly he wants it and how much he's going to work and how much he wants to improve.

Interview/
Los Angeles Times, 6-29:(C)3.

Ron Wilson
Hockey coach,
"Mighty Ducks"
of Anaheim

3

[Player] fighting is part of [hockey]. I feel in 10 years that fighting will be eliminated in the NHL. In the meantime, if fighting is part of the game, you've got to have people to go out there and stand up for their teammates. I'm not particularly in favor of fighting for fighting's sake, but if a team is getting carried away, you have to have people to respond.

News conference,
Anaheim, Calif., June 30/
Los Angeles Times, 7-1:(C)7.

Dave Winfield
Baseball player,
Minnesota "Twins"

4

Athletes are a key role model for many people, and they can and should be; but in an ideal situation they should not be the primary. The parent should be first, the teacher should be second and then maybe the athletes or other non family members. You can fit a lot of people in that last category. Unfortunately, in this day and age, it doesn't necessarily work like that. So athletes do impact and influence a lot of people, whether the athlete wants to or not.

The New York Times, 7-23:(B)10.

John Wooden
Former basketball coach,
University of California,
Los Angeles

5

[Saying he is against foul language being used by college basketball coaches]: I think the coaches teaching youngsters in high school and college today should be required to practice a certain decorum . . . They're in a leadership role, and I think our youngsters need models more than they need criticism. There have been some very successful coaches that have been very profane . . . I don't blame them. I blame the people that hired them . . . If you used profanity in [my] practice, you were off the floor for a day.

USA Today, 4-13:(C)12.

Index to Speakers

A

Index to Subjects

A

Abbas, Abu, 251:1
Abortion—*see* Women
Absolutes, 448:2
Achievement, 33:2
Acquired immune deficiency syndrome (AIDS)—
see Medicine
Acting/actors:
  about action, 432:4
  age aspect, 425:5
  assuming skin of another, 429:5
  character, acting is about, 432:5
  a child, 429:5
  classics, schooled in the, 445:5
  communication with people, 427:6
  corrupted, 424:2
  courage aspect, 429:5
  critics/criticism, 431:2, 443:2
  damaged goods, actors as, 427:5
  dance aspect, 432:4, 444:6
  directing compared with, 431:3
  directors, relationship with, 426:4, 433:6
  energy, 434:1
  exhibitionism, 429:5
  experiences, use of, 429:2
  the eyes, 427:4
  feeling aspect, 432:6
  fright aspect, 431:6
  getting under skin of character, 380:4
  has-been, 426:1
  identification with role, 443:3
  intelligence aspect, 429:1, 432:5
  intimidation aspect, 424:4
  life essence, 443:3
  listening/reacting aspect, 431:6
  love scenes, 429:4
  loved, need to be, 429:5
  luxury, the ultimate, 433:3
  open, being, 434:4
  opera aspect, 438:1, 439:6
  page of life, delivering, 429:2
  "performing" aspect, 433:4
  physical beauty, 425:5, 434:4
  power in the business, 434:3
  priest/whore aspect, 426:5
  reacting—*see* listening, *this secction*
  reflection of real life, 434:1
  rejection, 429:1, 443:2

Acting/actors *(continued)*
  roles/parts, 425:4
  sensitivity, 429:1
  stage/theatre, 418:4, 426:5, 433:6, 443:2,
    443:3, 444:4, 444:6, 445:4
  stars, 424:4
  success/failure, 430:3
  talent, 429:1
  talk among actors, 434:1
  teachers—*see* training, *this section*
  television, 418:4
  training/teachers, 418:4, 432:5, 445:4
  women, 425:5, 427:2
Adenauer, Konrad, 457;5
Advertising—*see* Commerce
Aerospace industry, 98:2, 99:5
Aetna (insurance co.), 410:1
Afghanistan, 273:3
Africa, pp. 240-252
  AIDS aspect, 401:4
  economy, 251:2
  education, 140:3
  foreign negotiations, 229:5
  relations with:
    Cuba, 264:5
    U.S., 242:3, 251;2
  See also specific African countries
America/U.S., pp. 33-37
  achievement principle, 33:2
  becoming, in act of, 36:5
  best days ahead, 36:5
  change aspect, 34:1, 34:3
  community, sense of/sharing, 35:1, 35:6
  cultural issues, 33:1
  diversity, 35:2, 43:2
  dream, American, 34:2, 202:5
  egalitarianism, 33:2
  families, 33:1, 35:1, 36:3
  immigration, 35:3, 35:4
    See also Foreign affairs
  individualism, 35:1
  national-service plan, 34:2, 34:4, 35:6
  optimism, 34:5
  political correctness, 33:2
  problems, 33:1, 33:3, 33:4
  prosperity/wealth, 36:4
  quality of life, 201:6

Many references to Bill Clinton are not listed in this index due to the numerous routine mentions of his name throughout the book. Only references that are specifically about him, personally or professionally, are listed here.